# IMAGE RESTORATION – RECENT ADVANCES AND APPLICATIONS

Edited by **Aymeric Histace**

**Image Restoration – Recent Advances and Applications**
Edited by Aymeric Histace

**Published by InTech**
Janeza Trdine 9, 51000 Rijeka, Croatia



**Publishing Process Manager** Marija Radja

**Technical Editor** Teodora Smiljanic

**Cover Designer** InTech Design Team

Additional hard copies can be obtained from orders@intechopen.com

Image Restoration – Recent Advances and Applications, Edited by Aymeric Histace
p. cm.
ISBN 978-953-51-0388-2

For EU product safety concerns:
IN TECH d.o.o., Prolaz Marije Krucifikse Kozulić 3, 51000 Rijeka, Croatia,
info@intechopen.com or visit our website at intechopen.com.

# Meet the editor

Dr Aymeric Histace was born in 1977 in Lyon, France. He received the Master degree in Signals/Images for Computer Aided Diagnosis in 2001 (University of Angers, France). He received, in 2004, the Ph.D degree in signal and image processing at the Laboratoire d'Ingénierie des Systèmes Automatisés (LISA), University d'Angers, France. He is since 2006, an associate professor in signal and image processing with application to life sciences (mainly Computer Aided Diagnosis) at the University of Cergy-Pontoise, Cergy, France with ETIS laboratory (UMR CNRS 8051).

# Contents

# Preface

This book represents a sample of recent contributions of researchers all around the world in the field of image restoration.

The book consists of 15 chapters organized in three main sections (Theory, Applications, Interdisciplinarity). Topics cover some different aspects of the theory of image restoration. But this book is also an occasion to highlight some new topics of research related to the emergence of some original imaging devices (see "Applications" Section). From this arise some real challenging problems related to image reconstruction/restoration that open the way to some new fundamental scientific questions closely related with the world we interact with.

An effort has been made by each author to give a large access to their work: Image restoration is not only a problem that interests specialists but also other researchers from different areas (like Robotic, AI, etc.) who can find some inspiration in the proposed Chapters (let have a look to Chapter 15 for instance!)

This book is certainly a small sample of the research activity going on around the globe as you read it, but it surely covers a good deal of what has been done in the field recently, and as such it works as a valuable source for researchers interested in the involved subjects.

Special thanks to all authors who have interested a great deal of time to write such interesting chapters and who have accepted to share their work.

**Aymeric Histace**
University of Cergy-Pontoise, Cergy,
France

# Part 1

## Theory and Scientific Advances

1

# Space-Variant Image Restoration with Running Sinusoidal Transforms

Vitaly Kober
*Computer Science Department, CICESE, Mexico*

## 1. Introduction

Various restoration methods (linear, nonlinear, iterative, noniterative, deterministic, stochastic, etc.) optimized with respect to different criteria have been introduced (Bertero & Boccacci, 1998; Biemond et al., 1990; Kundur, & Hatzinakos, 1996; Banham & Katsaggelos, 1997; Jain, 1989; Bovik, 2005; Gonzalez & Woods, 2008). These techniques may be broadly divided in two classes: (i) fundamental algorithms and (ii) specialized algorithms. One of the most popular fundamental techniques is a linear minimum mean square error (LMMSE) method. It finds the linear estimate of the ideal image for which the mean square error between the estimate and the ideal image is minimum. The linear operator acting on the observed image to determine the estimate is obtained on the basis of a priori second-order statistical information about the image and noise processes. In the case of stationary processes and space-invariant blurs, the LMMSE estimator takes the form of the Wiener filter (Jain, 1989). The Kalman filter determines the causal LMMSE estimate recursively. Specialized algorithms can be viewed as extensions of the fundamental algorithms to specific restoration problems. It is based on a state-space representation of the imaging system, and image data are used to define the state vectors. Specialized algorithms can be viewed as extensions of the fundamental algorithms to specific restoration problems. In this paper we deal with restoration of images degraded by space-variant blurs. Basically, all fundamental algorithms apply to the restoration of images degraded by space-variant blurs. However, because Fourier transforms cannot be utilized when the blur is space-variant, space-domain implementations of these algorithms may be computationally formidable due to large matrix operations. Several specialized methods were developed to attack the space-variant restoration problem. The first class referred to as sectioning is based on assumption that the blur is approximately space-invariant within local regions of the image. Therefore, the entire image can be restored by applying well-known space-invariant techniques to the local image regions. A drawback of sectioning methods is the generation of artifacts at the region boundaries. The second class is based on a coordinate transformation (Sawchuk, 1974), which is applied to the observed image so that the blur in the transformed coordinates becomes space-invariant. Therefore, the transformed image can be restored by a space-invariant filter and then transformed back to obtain the final restored image. However, the statistical properties of the image and noise processes are affected by the coordinate transformation. In particular, the stationarity in the original spatial coordinates is not preserved in the transform coordinate system.

In this chapter, we carry out the space-variant restoration using running discrete sinusoidal transform coefficients. The running transform is based on the concept of short-time signal processing (Oppenheim & Shafer 1989). A short-time orthogonal transform of a signal $x_k$ is defined as

$$X_s^k = \sum_{n=-\infty}^{\infty} x_{k+n} w_n \psi(n,s), \tag{1}$$

where $w_n$ is a window sequence, $\psi(n,s)$ represents the basis functions of an orthogonal transform. We use one-dimensional notation for simplicity. Equation (1) can be interpreted as the orthogonal transform of $x_{k+n}$ as viewed through the window $w_n$. $X_s^k$ displays the orthogonal transform characteristics of the signal around time $k$. Note that while increased window length and resolution are typically beneficial in the spectral analysis of stationary data, for time-varying data it is preferable to keep the window length sufficiently short so that the signal is approximately stationary over the window duration. Assume that the window has finite length around $n$=0, and it is unity for all $n \in [-N_1, N_2]$. Here $N_1$ and $N_2$ are integer values. This leads to signal processing in a running window (Vitkus & Yaroslavsky, 1987; Yaroslavsky & Eden, 1996). In other words, local filters in the domain of an orthogonal transform at each position of a moving window modify the orthogonal transform coefficients of a signal to obtain only an estimate of the pixel $x_k$ of the window. The choice of orthogonal transform for running signal processing depends on many factors.

We carry out the space-variant restoration using running discrete transform coefficients. The discrete cosine transforms (DCT) and discrete sine transforms (DST) are widely used. This is because the DCT and DST perform close to the optimum Karhunen-Loeve transform (KLT) for the first-order Markov stationary data (Jain, 1989). For signals with the correlation coefficient near to unity, the DCT provides a better approximation of the KLT than the DST. On the other hand, the DST is closer to the KLT, when the correlation coefficient lies in the interval (-0.5, 0.5). Since the KLT is constructed from the eigenvectors of the covariance matrix of data, there are neither single unique transform for all random processes nor fast algorithms. Unlike the KLT, the DCT and DST are not data dependent, and many fast algorithms were proposed. To provide image processing in real time, fast recursive algorithms for computing the running sinusoidal transforms are utilized (Kober, 2004, 2007). We introduce local adaptive restoration of nonuniform degraded images using several running sinusoidal transforms. Computer simulation results using a real image are provided and compared with those of common restoration techniques.

## 2. Fast algorithms of running discrete sinusoidal transforms

The discrete cosine and sine transforms are widely used in signal processing applications. Recently, forward and inverse algorithms for fast computing of various DCTs ({DCT-I, DCT-II, DCT-III, DCT-IV) and DSTs (DST-I, DST-II, DST-III, DST-IV) were proposed (Kober, 2004).

## 2.1 Discrete sinusoidal transforms

First, we recall the definitions for various discrete sinusoidal transforms. Notation {.} denotes a matrix, the order of which is represented by a subscript. For clarity, the normalization factor $\sqrt{2/N}$ for all forward transforms is neglected until the inverse transforms. The kernel of the orthogonal DCT-I for the order $N$+1 is defined as

$$DCT-I_{N+1} = \left\{ k_s k_n \cos\left( \pi \frac{ns}{N} \right) \right\}, \tag{2}$$

where $n$, $s$=0,..., N; $k_{m\ (m=n\ or\ m=s)} = \begin{cases} 1/\sqrt{2} & if\ m=0\ or\ m=N, \\ 1 & otherwise. \end{cases}$

The kernels of the DCT-II, DCT-III, and DCT-IV for the order $N$ are given as

$$DCT-II_N = \left\{ k_s \cos\left( \pi \frac{s(n+1/2)}{N} \right) \right\}, \tag{3}$$

$$DCT-III_N = \left\{ k_n \cos\left( \pi \frac{n(s+1/2)}{N} \right) \right\}, \tag{4}$$

$$DCT-IV_N = \left\{ \cos\left( \pi \frac{(n+1/2)(s+1/2)}{N} \right) \right\}, \tag{5}$$

where $n$, $s$=0, 1,..., $N$-1. The kernel of the DST-I for the order $N$-1 is defined as

$$DST-I_{N-1} = \left\{ \sin\left( \pi \frac{ns}{N} \right) \right\}, \tag{6}$$

where n, s=1, 2,..., N-1. The kernels of the DST-II, DST-III, and DST-IV for the order N are given as follows:

$$DST-II_N = \left\{ k_s \sin\left( \pi \frac{s(n-1/2)}{N} \right) \right\}, \tag{7}$$

$$DST-III_N = \left\{ k_n \sin\left( \pi \frac{n(s-1/2)}{N} \right) \right\}, \tag{8}$$

$$DST-IV_N = \left\{ \sin\left( \pi \frac{(n-1/2)(s-1/2)}{N} \right) \right\}, \tag{9}$$

where $n$, $s$=1, 2,..., $N$.

### 2.2 Fast forward algorithms for computing running discrete sinusoidal transforms

The fast forward algorithms are based on recursive relationships between three subsequent local running spectra. These algorithms for running DCTs (SDCTs) and running DSTs (SDSTs) are based on the second-order recursive equations summarized in Table I.

| N | Transforms | Recursive equations |
|---|---|---|
| 1 | SDCT-I | $X_s^{k+1} = \left(2X_s^k - \left(x_{k-N_1} + (-1)^s x_{k+N_2}\right)\right)\cos\left(\frac{\pi s}{N}\right) - X_s^{k-1} + \left(x_{k-N_1-1} + (-1)^s x_{k+N_2+1}\right)$ |
| 2 | SDCT-II | $X_s^{k+1} = 2X_s^k \cos\left(\frac{\pi s}{N}\right) - X_s^{k-1} + \cos\left(\frac{\pi s}{2N}\right)\left(x_{k-N_1-1} - x_{k-N_1} + (-1)^s\left(x_{k+N_2+1} - x_{k+N_2}\right)\right)$ |
| 3 | SDCT-III | $X_s^{k+1} = \left(2X_s^k - x_{k-N_1}\right)\cos\left(\frac{\pi(s+1/2)}{N}\right) - X_s^{k-1} + x_{k-N_1-1} + (-1)^s x_{k+N_2+1} \sin\left(\frac{\pi(s+1/2)}{N}\right)$ |
| 4 | SDCT-IV | $X_s^{k+1} = 2X_s^k \cos\left(\frac{\pi(s+1/2)}{N}\right) - X_s^{k-1} + \left(x_{k-N_1-1} - x_{k-N_1}\right) \mathrm{x} \cos\left(\frac{\pi(s+1/2)}{2N}\right) + (-1)^s\left(x_{k+N_2} + x_{k+N_2+1}\right)\sin\left(\frac{\pi(s+1/2)}{2N}\right)$ |
| 5 | SDST-I | $X_s^{k+1} = 2X_s^k \cos\left(\frac{\pi s}{N}\right) - X_s^{k-1} + \left(x_{k-N_1-1} - (-1)^s x_{k+N_2+1}\right)\sin\left(\frac{\pi s}{N}\right)$ |
| 6 | SDST-II | $X_s^{k+1} = 2X_s^k \cos\left(\frac{\pi s}{N}\right) - X_s^{k-1} + \left(x_{k-N_1-1} + x_{k-N_1} - (-1)^s\left(x_{k+N_2+1} + x_{k+N_2}\right)\right)\sin\left(\frac{\pi s}{2N}\right)$ |
| 7 | SDST-III | $X_s^{k+1} = 2X_s^k \cos\left(\frac{\pi(s-1/2)}{N}\right) - X_s^{k-1} - (-1)^s x_{k+N_2+1} + x_{k-N_1-1} \sin\left(\frac{\pi(s-1/2)}{N}\right) + (-1)^s x_{k+N_2} \cos\left(\frac{\pi(s-1/2)}{N}\right)$ |
| 8 | SDST-IV | $X_s^{k+1} = 2X_s^k \cos\left(\frac{\pi(s-1/2)}{N}\right) - X_s^{k-1} + \left(x_{k-N_1-1} + x_{k-N_1}\right) \mathrm{x} \sin\left(\frac{\pi(s-1/2)}{2N}\right) + (-1)^s\left(x_{k+N_2} - x_{k+N_2+1}\right)\cos\left(\frac{\pi(s-1/2)}{2N}\right)$ |

Table 1. Recursive equations for the computation of forward running sinusoidal transforms.

The number of arithmetic operations required for computing the running discrete cosine transforms at a given window position is evaluated as follows. The SDCT-I for the order $N$+1 with $N=N_1+N_2$ requires $N$-1 multiplication operations and 4($N$+2) addition operations. The SDCT-II for the order $N$ with $N= N_1+ N_2+1$ requires 2($N$-1) multiplication operations and 2$N$+5 addition operations. A fast algorithm for the SDCT-III for the order $N$ with $N=N_1+ N_2+1$ is based on the recursive equation given in line 3 of Table 1. Next it is useful to represent the equation as

$$X_s^{k+1} = \left(X_s^k + \tilde{X}_s^k\right)\cos\left(\frac{\pi(s+1/2)}{N}\right) - \tilde{X}_s^{k-1} + (-1)^s x_{k+N_2+1}\sin\left(\frac{\pi(s+1/2)}{N}\right), \tag{10}$$

where the array $\left\{\tilde{X}_s^k = X_s^k - x_{k-N_1}; s=0,1,...N-1\right\}$ is stored in a memory buffer of $N$ elements. From the property of symmetry of the sine function, $\sin\left(\pi(s+1/2)/N\right) = \sin\left(\pi(N-s-1/2)/N\right), s=0,1,...[N/2]$ (here [x/y] is the integer quotient) and Eq. (10), the number of operations required to compute the DSCT-III can be evaluated as [3/2$N$] multiplication operations and 4$N$ addition operations. An additional memory buffer of $N$ elements is also required. Finally, the SDCT-IV for the order $N$ with $N=N_1+ N_2+1$ requires 3$N$ multiplication operations and 3$N$+2 addition operations.

The number of arithmetic operations required for computing the running discrete sine transforms at a given window position can be evaluated as follows. The SDST-I for the order $N$-1 with $N=N_1+ N_2+1$ requires 2($N$-1) multiplication operations and 2$N$ addition operations. However, if $N$ is even, $f(s) = \left(x_{k-N_1-1} - (-1)^s x_{k+N_2+1}\right)\sin(\pi s/N)$ in line 5 of Table I is symmetric on the interval [1, $N$-1]; that is, $f(s)=f(N-s)$, $s$=1,..$N$/2-1. Therefore, only $N$/2-1 multiplication operations are required to compute this term. The total number of multiplications is reduced to 3$N$/2-2. The SDST-II for the order $N$ with $N=N_1+ N_2+1$ requires 2($N$-1) multiplication operations and 2$N$+5 addition operations. Taking into account the property of symmetry of the sine and cosine functions, the SDST-III for the order $N$ with $N=N_1+ N_2+1$ requires 2$N$ multiplications and 4$N$ addition operations. However, if $N$ is even, the sum $g(s) = x_{k-N_1-1}\sin\left(\pi(s-1/2)/N\right) + (-1)^s x_{k+N_2}\cos\left(\pi(s-1/2)/N\right)$ in line 7 of Table I is symmetric on the interval [1, $N$]; that is, $g(s)=g(N-s+1)$, $s$=1,..$N$/2. Therefore, only $N$/2 addition operations are required to compute the sum. If $N$ is odd, the sum $p(s) = x_{k-N_1-1}\sin\left(\pi(s-1/2)/N\right) - (-1)^s x_{k+N_2+1}$ in line 7 of Table I is symmetric on the interval [1, $N$]; that is, $p(s)=p(N-s+1)$, $s$=1,..[$N$/2]. Hence, [$N$/2] addition operations are required to compute this sum. So, the total number of additions can be reduced to [7$N$/2]. Finally, the SDST-IV for the order $N$ with $N=N_1+ N_2+1$ requires 3$N$ multiplication operations and 3$N$+2 addition operations. The length of a moving window for the proposed algorithms may be an arbitrary integer.

### 2.3 Fast inverse algorithms for running signal processing with sinusoidal transforms

The inverse discrete cosine and sine transforms for signal processing in a running window are performed for computing only the pixel $x_k$ of the window. The running signal processing can be performed with the use of the SDCT and SDST algorithms.

The inverse algorithms for the running DCTs can be written as follows.

IDCT-I:

$$x_k = \frac{1}{N}\left(2\sum_{s=1}^{N-1} X_s^k \cos\left(\pi\frac{N_1 s}{N}\right) + X_0^k + (-1)^{N_1} X_N^k\right), \tag{11}$$

where $N=N_1+N_2$. If $x_k$ is the central pixel of the window; that is, $N_1=N_2$ then the inverse transform is simplified to

$$x_k = \frac{1}{N}\left(2\sum_{s=1}^{N_1-1} (-1)^s X_{2s}^k + X_0^k + (-1)^{N_1} X_N^k\right). \tag{12}$$

Therefore, in the computation only the spectral coefficients with even indices are involved. The number of required operations of multiplication and addition becomes one and $N_1+1$, respectively.

IDCT-II:

$$x_k = \frac{1}{N}\left(2\sum_{s=1}^{N-1} X_s^k \cos\left(\pi\frac{(N_1+1/2)s}{N}\right) + X_0^k\right), \tag{13}$$

where $N=N_1+N_2+1$. If $x_k$ is the central pixel of the window, that is, $N_1=N_2$ then the inverse transform is given by

$$x_k = \frac{1}{N}\left(2\sum_{s=1}^{N_1} (-1)^s X_{2s}^k + X_0^k\right). \tag{14}$$

We see that in the computation only the spectral coefficients with even indices are involved. The computation requires one multiplication operation and $N_1+1$ addition operations.

IDCT-III:

$$x_k = \frac{2}{N}\sum_{s=0}^{N-1} X_s^k \cos\left(\pi\frac{N_1(s+1/2)}{N}\right), \tag{15}$$

where $N=N_1+N_2+1$. If $x_k$ is the central pixel of the window, that is, $N_1=N_2$ then the inverse transform is

$$x_k = \frac{2}{N}\left(\sum_{s=0}^{N_1-1}\left(X_s^k + (-1)^{N_1} X_{N-s-1}^k\right)\cos\left(\pi\frac{N_1(s+1/2)}{N}\right) + (-1)^{[N_1/2]} X_{N_1}^k \frac{\left(1+(-1)^{N_1}\right)\left(1+(-1)^{N-1}\right)}{4}\right). \tag{16}$$

If $N_1$ is even, then the computation requires $N_1+1$ multiplication operations and $2N_1$ addition operations. Otherwise, the complexity is reduced to $N_1$ multiplication operations and $2N_1 - 1$ addition operations.

IDCT-IV:

$$x_k = \frac{2}{N}\sum_{s=0}^{N-1} X_s^k \cos\left(\pi \frac{(N_1+1/2)(s+1/2)}{N}\right), \tag{17}$$

where $N=N_1+N_2+1$. If $x_k$ is the central pixel of the window, that is, $N_1=N_2$ then the inverse transform is given by

$$x_k = \frac{\sqrt{2}}{N}\left(\sum_{s=1}^{N_1}(-1)^s\left(X_{2s}^k + X_{2s-1}^k\right) + X_0^k\right). \tag{18}$$

One multiplication operation and $N$-1 addition operations are required to perform this computation.

The inverse algorithms for the running DSTs are given as follows.

IDST-I:

$$x_k = \frac{2}{N}\sum_{s=1}^{N-1} X_s^k \sin\left(\pi \frac{(N_1+1)s}{N}\right), \tag{19}$$

where $N=N_1+N_2+2$. If $x_k$ is the central pixel of the window; that is, $N_1=N_2$ then the inverse transform is simplified to

$$x_k = \frac{2}{N}\sum_{s=0}^{N_1}(-1)^s X_{2s+1}^k . \tag{20}$$

Therefore, in the computation only the spectral coefficients with odd indices are involved. The complexity is one multiplication operation and $N_1$ addition operations.

IDST-II:

$$x_k = \frac{1}{N}\left(2\sum_{s=1}^{N-1} X_s^k \sin\left(\pi \frac{(N_1+1/2)s}{N}\right) + (-1)^{N_1} X_N^k\right), \tag{21}$$

where $N=N_1+N_2+1$. If $x_k$ is the central pixel of the window; that is, $N_1=N_2$ then the inverse transform is given by

$$x_k = \frac{1}{N}\left(2\sum_{s=0}^{N_1-1}(-1)^s X_{2s+1}^k + (-1)^{N_1} X_N^k\right). \tag{22}$$

In the computation only the spectral coefficients with odd indices are involved. The computational complexity is one multiplication operation and $N_1$+1 addition operations.

IDST-III:

$$x_k = \frac{2}{N}\sum_{s=1}^{N} X_s^k \sin\left(\pi \frac{(N_1+1)(s-1/2)}{N}\right), \tag{23}$$

where $N=N_1+N_2+1$. If $x_k$ is the central pixel of the window; that is, $N_1=N_2$ then we can rewrite

$$x_k = \frac{2}{N}\left(\sum_{s=1}^{N_1}\left(X_s^k + (-1)^{N_1} X_{N-s+1}^k\right)\sin\left(\pi\frac{(N_1+1)(s-1/2)}{N}\right) + (-1)^{[N_1/2]} X_{N_1+1}^k \frac{\left(1+(-1)^{N_1}\right)\left(1+(-1)^{N-1}\right)}{4}\right). \quad (24)$$

If $N_1$ is even, then the computation requires $N_1+1$ multiplication operations and $2N_1$ addition operations. Otherwise, the complexity is reduced to $N_1$ multiplication operations and $2N_1 - 1$ addition operations.

IDST-IV:

$$x_k = \frac{2}{N}\sum_{s=1}^{N} X_s^k \sin\left(\pi\frac{(N_1+1/2)(s-1/2)}{N}\right), \quad (25)$$

where $=N_1+N_2+1$. If $x_k$ is the central pixel of the window; that is, $N_1=N_2$, then the inverse transform is given by

$$x_k = \frac{\sqrt{2}}{N}\left(\sum_{s=1}^{N_1}(-1)^{s-1}\left(X_{2s}^k + X_{2s-1}^k\right) + (-1)^{N_1} X_N^k\right). \quad (26)$$

The complexity is one multiplication operation and $N$-1 addition operations.

## 3. Local image restoration with running transforms

First we define a local criterion of the performance of filters for image processing and then derive optimal local adaptive filters with respect to the criterion. One the most used criterion in signal processing is the minimum mean-square error (MSE). Since the processing is carried out in a moving window, then for each position of a moving window an estimate of the central element of the window is computed. Suppose that the signal to be processed is approximately stationary within the window. The signal may be distorted by sensor's noise.

Let us consider a generalized linear filtering of a fragment of the input one-dimensional signal (for instance for a fixed position of the moving window). Let $a=[a_k]$ be undistorted real signal, $x=[x_k]$ be observed signal, $k=1,\ldots, N$, $N$ be the size of the fragment, U be the matrix of the discrete sinusoidal transform, $E\{.\}$ be the expected value, superscript T denotes the transpose. Let $\bar{a} = Hx$ be a linear estimate of the undistorted signal, which minimizes the MSE averaged over the window

$$MMSE = E\left\{(a-\bar{a})^T (a-\bar{a})\right\}/N. \quad (27)$$

The optimal filter for this problem is the Wiener filter (Jain, 1989):

$$H = E\left\{a x^T\right\}\left[E\left\{x x^T\right\}\right]^{-1}. \quad (28)$$

Let us consider the known model of a linear degradation:

$$x_k = \sum_n w_{k,n} a_n + v_k , \tag{29}$$

where $W=[w_{k,n}]$ is a distortion matrix, $v=[v_k]$ is additive noise with zero mean, $k,n=1,\ldots N$, $N$ is the size of fragment. The equation can be rewritten as

$$\mathrm{x} = \mathrm{Wa} + \mathrm{v} , \tag{30}$$

and the optimal filter is given by

$$\mathrm{H} = \mathrm{K}_{aa}\mathrm{W}^T\left[\mathrm{WK}_{aa}\mathrm{W}^T + \mathrm{K}_{vv}\right]^{-1} , \tag{31}$$

where $\mathrm{K}_{aa} = E\left\{\mathrm{aa}^T\right\}$, $\mathrm{K}_{vv} = E\left\{\mathbf{vv}^T\right\}$, $E\left\{\mathrm{a}\mathbf{v}^T\right\} = 0$ are the covariance matrices. It is assumed that the input signal and noise are uncorrelated.

The obtained optimal filter is based on an assumption that an input signal within the window is stationary. The result of filtering is the restored window signal. This corresponds to signal processing in nonoverlapping fragments. The computational complexity of the processing is $O(N^2)$. However, if the matrix of the optimal filter is diagonal, the complexity is reduced to $O(N)$. Such filter is referred as a scalar filter. Actually, any linear filtering can be performed with a scalar filter using corresponding unitary transforms. Now suppose that the signal is processed in a moving window in the domain of a running discrete sinusoidal transform. For each position of the window an estimate of the central pixel should be computed. Using the equations for inverse sinusoidal transforms presented in the previous section, the point-wise MSE (PMSE) for reconstruction of the central element of the window can be written as follows:

$$PMSE(k) = E\left\{\left[a(k) - \bar{a}(k)\right]^2\right\} = E\left\{\left[\sum_{l=1}^{N} \alpha(l)\left(A(l) - \bar{A}(l)\right)\right]^2\right\} , \tag{32}$$

where $\bar{\mathrm{A}} = \left[\bar{A}(l) = H(l)X(l)\right]$ is a vector of signal estimate in the domain of a sinusoidal transform, $\mathrm{H}_U = \left[H(l)\right]$ is a diagonal matrix of the scalar filter, $\boldsymbol{\alpha} = \left[\alpha(l)\right]$ is a diagonal matrix of the size $N\mathrm{x}N$ of the coefficients of an inverse sinusoidal transform (see Eqs. (12), (14), (16), (18), (20), (22), (24), and (26)). Minimizing Eq. (32), we obtain

$$\mathrm{H}_U = [\mathrm{P}_{xx}]^{-1}\mathrm{P}_{ax}\mathrm{I}_\alpha , \tag{33}$$

where $\mathrm{I}_\alpha = diag\left[\bar{\delta}(\alpha(1)), \bar{\delta}(\alpha(2)), \ldots, \bar{\delta}(\alpha(N))\right]$ is a diagonal matrix of the size $N\mathrm{x}N$, $\bar{\delta}(x) = 1$ if $x \neq 0$, else $0$, $\mathrm{P}_{ax} = \left[E\{A(l)X(k)\}\right]$, $\mathrm{P}_{xx} = \left[E\{X(l)X(k)\}\right]$. Note that matrix $\boldsymbol{\alpha} = \left[\alpha(l)\right]$ is sparse; the number of its non-zero entries is approximately twice less than the size of the window signal. Therefore, the computational complexity of the scalar filters in Eq. (33) and signal processing can be significantly reduced comparing to the complexity for the filter in Eq. (31). For the model of signal distortion in Eq. (30) the filter matrix is given as

$$H_U = \left[ U\left( WK_{aa} W^T + K_{vv} \right) U^T \right]^{-1} UK_{aa} W^T U^T I_\alpha . \tag{34}$$

If the matrices $U\left(WK_{aa} W^T + K_{vv}\right)U^T$ and $UK_{aa} W^T U^T$ in Eq. (34) are close to diagonal, the matrix of the scalar filter in (34) is close to diagonal, and the filter can be written as

$$H(l) \approx \frac{P_1(l)}{P_2(l) + P_{vv}(l)}, \tag{35}$$

where $P_1(l),\ P_2(l),\ P_{nn}(l)$ are diagonal elements of the following matrices $UK_{aa} W^T U^T I_\alpha,\ UWK_{aa} W^T U^T,\ UK_{vv} U^T$, *l=1,...* $N$.

For a real symmetric matrix of the covariance function, say $K$, there exists a unitary matrix $U$ such that $UKU^T$ is a diagonal matrix. Actually, it is the KLT. It was shown (Jain, 1989) that some discrete sinusoidal transforms perform close to the optimum KLT for the first-order Markov stationary data under specific conditions. In our case, the covariance matrices $K_{aa} W^T U^T$ and $WK_{aa} W^T$ are not symmetric. Therefore, under different conditions of degradation different discrete sinusoidal transforms can better diagonalize these matrices. For instance, if a signal has a high correlation coefficient and a smoothed version of the signal is corrupted by additive, weakly-correlated noise, then the matrix $U\left(WK_{aa} W^T + K_{vv}\right)U^T$ is close to diagonal. Figure 1 shows the covariance matrix of the smoothed and noisy signal having the correlation coefficient of 0.95 as well as the discrete cosine transform of the covariance matrix. The linear convolution between a signal $x$ and the matrix $K_{aa} W^T$ in the domain of the running DCT-II can be well approximated by a diagonal matrix $diag\left(UK_{aa} W^T U^T I_\alpha\right)X$. Therefore, the matrix of the scalar filter in Eq. (34) will be close to diagonal.

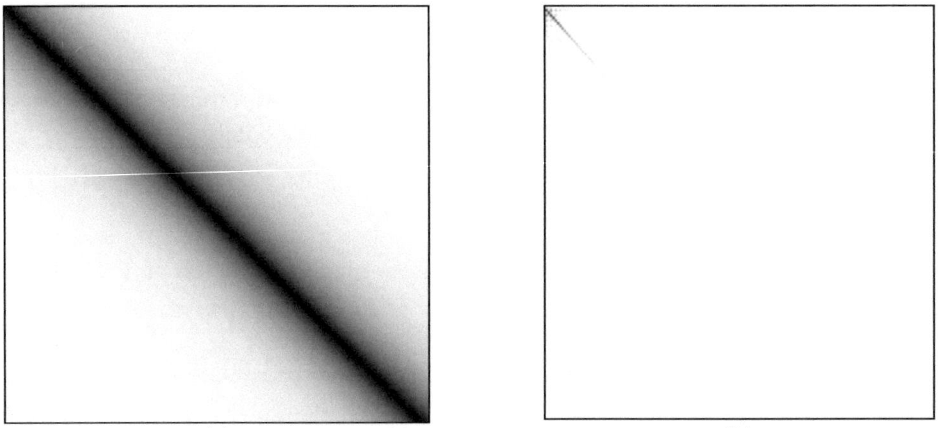

(a) (b)

Fig. 1. (a) Covariance matrix of a noisy signal, (b) DCT-II of the covariance matrix.

For the design of local adaptive filters in the domain of running sinusoidal transforms the covariance matrices and power spectra of fragments of a signal are required. Since they are often unknown, in practice, these matrices can be estimated from observed signals (Yaroslavsky & Eden, 1996).

## 4. Computer simulation results

The objective of this section is to develop a technique for local adaptive restoration of images degraded by nonuniform motion blur. Assume that the blur is owing to horizontal relative motion between the camera and the image, and it is approximately space-invariant within local regions of the image. It is known that point spread functions for motion and focus blurs do have zeros in the frequency domain, and they can be uniquely identified by the location of these zero crossings (Biemond et al., 1990). We assume also that the observation noise is a zero-mean, white Gaussian process that is uncorrelated to the image signal. In this case, the noise field is completely characterized by its variance, which is commonly estimated by the sample variance computed over a low-contrast local region of the observed image. To guarantee statistically correct results, 30 statistical trials of each experiment for different realizations of the random noise process were performed. The MSE criterion is used for comparing the quality of restoration. Additionally, a subjective visual criterion is used. In our computer simulation, the MSE is given by

$$MSE(a,\bar{a}) = \frac{\sum_{i}^{N}\left[a(i)-\bar{a}(i)\right]^2}{N}, \tag{36}$$

where $\{a(i), i=1,..N\}$ is the original image, and $\{\bar{a}(i), i=1,..N\}$ is the restored image. The subjective visual criterion is defined as an enhanced difference between original and restored images. A pixel is displayed as gray if there is no error between the original image and the restored image. For maximum error, the pixel is displayed either black or white (with intensity values of 0 and 1, respectively). First, with the help of computer simulation we answer to the question: how to choose the best running discrete sinusoidal transform for local image restoration?

### 4.1 Choice of discrete sinusoidal transform for local image restoration

The objective of this section is to test the performance of the scalar filter (see Eq. (34)) designed with different running sinusoidal transforms for local image restoration while the statistics of the degraded image are varied. In our experiments we used realizations of a wide-sense colored stationary process, which is completely defined by the second-order statistics. The zero-mean process has the bi-exponential covariance function with varying correlation coefficient $\rho$.

The generated synthetic image is degraded by running 1D horizontal averaging of 5 pixels, and then a white Gaussian noise with a given standard deviation $\sigma_n$ is added. The size of images is 1024x1024. The quality of restoration is measured in terms of the MSE. The size of moving window for local image restoration is 15x15. The best running discrete sinusoidal transform a function of the model parameters ($\sigma_n$ and $\rho$) is presented in Table 2. So, in similar degradation circumstances and image model, local adaptive restoration yields the best results if the three sinusoidal transforms depending on local statistics of the processed image are used. The decision rule for choosing the best sinusoidal transform at each position of the moving window is given in Table 2. Next, we carry out adaptive local restoration with real images.

| $\sigma_n$ | 0.05 | 0.1 | 0.2 | 0.25 |
|---|---|---|---|---|
| $\rho = 0.95$ | SDCT-II | SDCT-II | SDCT-II | SDCT-II |
| $\rho = 0.9$ | SDCT-II | SDCT-II | SDCT-II | SDCT-II |
| $\rho = 0.8$ | SDCT-II | SDCT-II | SDCT-II | SDCT-II |
| $\rho = 0.7$ | SDCT-II | SDCT-II | SDCT-II | SDCT-II |
| $\rho = 0.6$ | SDCT-II | SDCT-II | SDCT-II | SDCT-II |
| $\rho = 0.5$ | SDST-I | SDCT-II | SDCT-II | SDCT-II |
| $\rho = 0.3$ | SDST-I | SDST-I | SDST-I | SDST-I |
| $\rho = 0$ | SDST-I | SDST-I | SDST-I | SDST-I |
| $\rho = -0.3$ | SDST-I | SDST-I | SDST-I | SDST-I |
| $\rho = -0.5$ | SDST-II | SDST-II | SDST-II | SDST-II |
| $\rho = -0.7$ | SDST-II | SDST-II | SDST-II | SDST-II |
| $\rho = -0.8$ | SDST-II | SDST-II | SDST-II | SDST-II |
| $\rho = -0.9$ | SDST-II | SDST-II | SDST-II | SDST-II |

Table 2. Best local restoration with running discrete sinusoidal transforms versus the model parameters.

### 4.2 Local adaptive restoration of real degraded image

A real test aerial image is shown in Fig. 2(a). The size of image is 512x512, each pixel has 256 levels of quantization. The signal range is [0, 1]. The image quadrants are degraded by running 1D horizontal averaging with the following sizes of the moving window: 5, 6, 4, and 3 pixels (for quadrants from left to right, from top to bottom). The image is also corrupted by a zero-mean additive white Gaussian noise. The degraded image with the noise standard deviation of 0.05 is shown in Fig. 2(b).

In our tests the window length of 15x15 pixels is used, it is determined by the minimal size of details to be preserved after filtering. Since there exists difference in spectral distributions of the image signal and wide-band noise, the power spectrum of noise can be easily measured from the experimental covariance matrix. We carried out three parallel processing of the degraded image with the use of SDCT-II, SDST-I, and SDST-II transforms. At each position of the moving window the local correlation coefficient is estimated from the restored images. On the base of the correlation value and the standard deviation of noise, the resultant image is formed from the outputs obtained with either SDCT-II or SDST-I, or SDST-II according to Table 2.

(a) (b)

Fig. 2. (a) Test image, (b) space-variant degraded test image.

The results of image restoration by the global parametric Wiener filtering (Jain, 1989) and the proposed method are shown in Figs. 3(a) and 3(b), respectively. Figs. 3(c) and 3(d) show differences between the original image and images restored by global Wiener algorithm and by the proposed algorithm, respectively.

We also performed local image restoration using only the SDCT. As expected, the result of restoration is slightly worse than that of adaptive local restoration. We see that the proposed algorithm is capable to perform a good space-variant image restoration and noise suppression. Finally, we investigate the robustness of the tested restoration techniques to additive noise. The performance of the global parametric Wiener filtering and the local adaptive filtering is shown in Fig. 4.

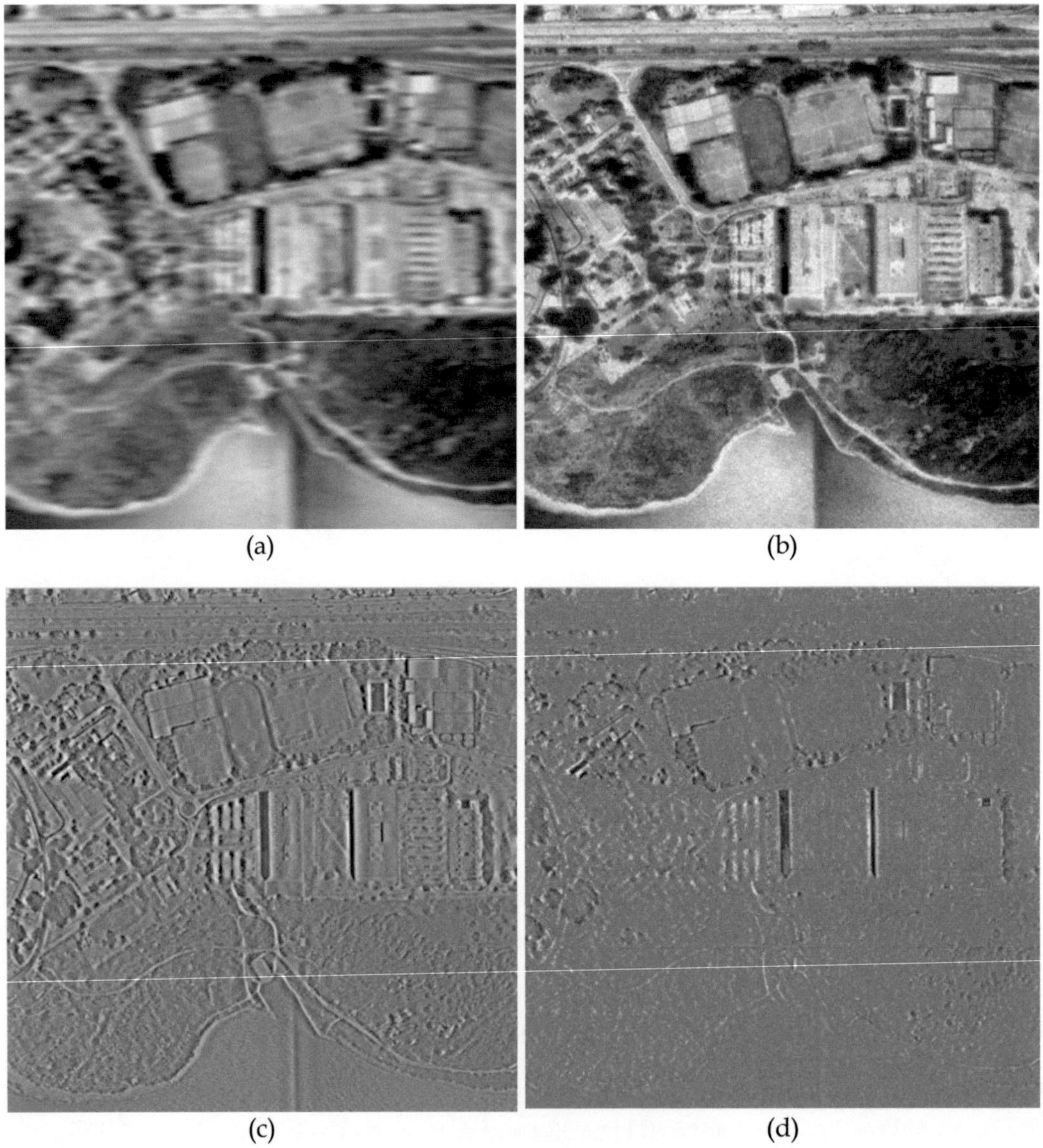

Fig. 3. (a) Global Wiener restoration, (b) local adaptive restoration in domain of running transforms, (c) difference between the original image and restored image by Wiener filtering, (d) difference between the original image and restored image by proposed algorithm.

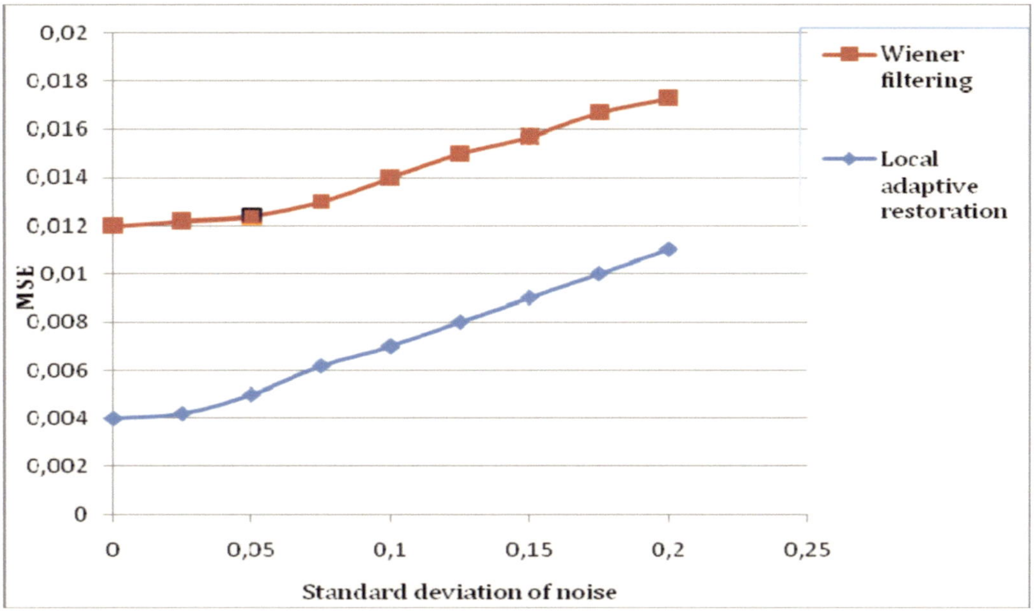


Fig. 4. Performance of restoration algorithms in terms of MSE versus standard deviation of additive noise.

## 4. Conclusion

In this chapter we treated the problem of local adaptive technique for space-variant restoring linearly degraded and noisy images. The minimum MSE estimator in the domain of running discrete sinusoidal transforms was derived. To provide image processing at high rate, fast recursive algorithms for computing the running sinusoidal transforms were utilized. Extensive testing using various parameters of degradations (nonuniform motion blurring and corruption by noise) has shown that the original image can be well restored by proper choice of the parameters of the proposed adaptive local restoration algorithm.

## 5. References

Banham, M. & Katsaggelos, A. (1997). Digital image restoration. *IEEE Signal Processing Magazine,* Vol. 14, No.2, (March 1997), pp. 24-41, ISSN 1053-5888

Bertero, M. & Boccacci, P. (1998). *Introduction to inverse problems in imaging,* Institute of Physics Publishing, ISBN 0-7503-0435-9, Bristol, UK

Biemond, J., Lagendijk, R.L. & Mersereau, R.M. (1990). Iterative methods for image deblurring. *Proc. IEEE. Vol. 78,* No. 5, (May 1990) (856-883), ISSN 0018-9219

Bovik, A. (2005). *Handbook of image and video processing* (2nd ed.), Academic Press, ISBN 0-12-119792-1, NJ, USA

González, R. & Woods, R. (2008). *Digital image processing* (3rd ed.), Prentice Hall, ISBN 0-13-1687288, NJ, USA

Jain, A.K. (1989). *Fundamentals of digital image processing*, Prentice Hall, ISBN 0-13-332578-4, NY, USA

Kober, V. (2004). Fast algorithms for the computation of running discrete sinusoidal transforms. *IEEE Trans. on Signal Process.* Vol. 52, No 6, (June 2004), pp. 1704-1710, ISSN 1053-587X

Kober, V. (2007). Fast algorithms for the computation of running discrete Hartley transforms. *IEEE Trans. on Signal Process.* Vol. 55, No 6, (June 2007), pp. 2937-2944, ISSN 1053-587X

Kober, V. & Ovseevich, I.A. (2008). Image restoration with running sinusoidal transforms. *Pattern Recognition and Image Analysis* Vol. 18, No. 4, (December 2008), pp. 650-654, ISSN 1054-6618

Kundur, D. & Hatzinakos, D. (1996). Blind image deconvolution. *IEEE Signal Processing Magazine,* Vol. 13, No. 3, (May 1996), pp. 73-76, ISSN 1053-5888

Oppenheim, A.V. & Shafer, R.W. (1989). *Discrete-time signal processing*, Prentice Hall, ISBN 0-13-216292-X, NJ, USA

Sawchuk, A.A. (1974). Space-variant image restoration by coordinate transformations. *J. Opt. Soc. Am.* Vol. 64, No. 2, (February 1974), pp. 138—144, ISSN 1084-7529

Vitkus, R.Y. & Yaroslavsky, L.P. (1987). Recursive algorithms for local adaptive linear filtration. in: *Mathematical Research.*, Academy Verlag, pp. 34-39, Berlin, Germany

Yaroslavsky, L. P. & Eden, M. (1996). *Fundamentals of digital optics,* Birkhauser, ISBN 3-7643-3833-9, Boston, USA

# 2

# Statistical-Based Approaches for Noise Removal

State Luminița[1], Cătălina-Lucia Cocianu[1] and Vlamos Panayiotis[2]
[1]*University of Pitești*
[2]*Academy of Economic Studies*
[3]*Ionian University*
[1,2]*Romania*
[3]*Greece*

## 1. Introduction

Image restoration methods are used to improve the appearance of an image by the application of a restoration process based on a mathematical model to explain the way the image was distorted by noise. Examples of types of degradation include blurring caused by motion or atmospheric disturbance, geometric distortion caused by imperfect lenses, superimposed interference patterns caused by mechanical systems, and noise induced by electronic sources.

Usually, it is assumed that the degradation model is either known or can be estimated from data. The general idea is to model the degradation process and then apply the inverse process to restore the original image. In cases when the available knowledge does not allow to adopt a reasonable model for the degradation mechanism it becomes necessary to extract information about the noise directed by data and then to use this information for restoration purposes. The knowledge about the particular generation process of the image is application specific. For example, it proves helpful to know how a specific lens distorts an image or how mechanical vibration from a satellite affects an image. This information can be gathered from the analysis of the image acquisition process and by applying image analysis techniques to samples of degraded images.

The restoration can be viewed as a process that attempts to reconstruct or recover a degraded image using some available knowledge about the degradation mechanism. Typically, the noise can be modeled with either a Gaussian, uniform or salt and pepper distribution. The restoration techniques are usually oriented toward modeling the type of degradation in order to infer the inverse process for recovering the given image. This approach usually involves the option for a criterion to numerically evaluate the quality of the resulted image and consequently the restoration process can be expressed in terms of an optimization problem.

The special filtering techniques of mean type prove particularly useful in reducing the normal/uniform noise component when the mean parameter is close to 0. In other words, the effects determined by the application of mean filters are merely the decrease of the local variance corresponding to each processed window, and consequently to inhibit the variance component of the noise. The AMVR algorithm (Adaptive Mean Variance Removal) allows the removal of the normal/uniform noise whatever the mean of the noise is (Cocianu, State, & Vlamos, 2002). Similar to MMSE (Minimum Mean Square Error) filtering technique (Umbaugh, 1998) the application of the AMVR algorithm requires that the noise parameters and some additional features are known.

The multiresolution support set is a data structure suitable for developing noise removal algorithms. (Bacchelli & Papi, 2006; Balster et al., 2003). The multiresolution algorithms perform the restoration tasks by combining, at each resolution level, according to a certain rule, the pixels of a binary support image. Some others use a selective wavelet shrinkage algorithm for digital image denoising aiming to improve the performance. For instance Balster (Balster, Zheng & Ewing, 2003) proposes an attempt of this sort together with a computation scheme, the denoising methodology incorporated in this algorithm involving a two-threshold validation process for real time selection of wavelet coefficients.

A new solution of the denoising problem based on the description length of the noiseless data in the subspace of the basis is proposed in (Beheshti & Dahleh, 2003), where the desired description length is estimated for each subspace and the selection of the subspace corresponding to the minimum length is suggested.

In (Bacchelli & Papi, 2006), a method for removing Gaussian noise from digital images based on the combination of the wavelet packet transform and the PCA is proposed. The method leads to tailored filters by applying the Karhunen-Loeve transform in the wavelet packet domain and acts with a suitable shrinkage function on these new coefficients, allowing the noise removal without blurring the edges and other important characteristics of the images.

Wavelet thresholding methods modifying the noisy coefficients were proposed by several authors (Buades, Coll & Morel, 2005; Stark, Murtagh & Bijaoui, 1995). The attempts are based on the idea that images are represented by large wavelet coefficients that have to be preserved whereas the noise is distributed across the set of small coefficients that have to be canceled. Since the edges lead to a considerable amount of wavelet coefficients of lower values than the threshold, the cancellation of these wavelet coefficients may cause small oscillations near the edges resulting spurious wavelets in the restored image.

## 2. Mathematics behind the noise removal and image restoration algorithms

### 2.1 Principal Component Analysis (PCA) and Independent Component Analysis (ICA)

We assume that the signal is represented by a n-dimensional real-valued random vector X of 0 mean and covariance matrix Σ. The principal directions of the repartition of X are the directions corresponding to the maximum variability, where the variability is expressed in terms of the variance.

Definition. The vector $\Psi_1 \in R^n$ is the first principal direction if $\|\Psi_1\| = 1$ and $\operatorname{var}\left(\Psi_1^T X\right) = \sup_{\substack{\Phi \in R^n \\ \|\Phi\|=1}} \operatorname{var}\left(\Phi^T X\right)$.

The value $\Psi_1^T X$ is referred as the first principal component of X.

Now, recursively, for any k, $2 \le k \le n$, if we denote by $L^{\perp}(\Psi_1,...,\Psi_{k-1})$ the linear subspace orthogonal on the linear subspace generated by the first (k-1) directions, $\Psi_k \in R^n$ is the k-th principal direction if $\|\Psi_k\| = 1$ and $\text{var}(\Psi_k^T X) = \sup_{\substack{\Phi \in L^{\perp}(\Psi_1,...,\Psi_{k-1}) \\ \|\Phi\|=1}} \text{var}(\Phi^T X)$.

The value $\Psi_k^T X$ is referred as the k-th principal component of the signal X.

Note that the principal directions $\Psi_1,...,\Psi_n$ of any signal are an orthogonal basis of $R^n$, and $Y = \Psi^T X$ is the signal representation in terms of the principal directions, where $\Psi = [\Psi_1,...,\Psi_n]$. Obviously, $\Psi\Psi^T = \Psi^T\Psi = I_n$, $E(Y) = 0$ and $Cov(Y,Y^T) = \Psi^T \Sigma \Psi$. Consequently, if $\Psi_1,...,\Psi_n$ are unit eigen vectors of Σ, then $Cov(Y,Y^T) = \Lambda = diag(\lambda_1,...,\lambda_n)$, where $\lambda_1,...,\lambda_n$ are the eigen values of Σ, that is the linear transform of matrix $\Psi^T$ de-correlates the components of X. In the particular case of Gaussian signals, X~$N(0,\Sigma)$, the components of Y are also normal distributed, $Y_i \sim N(0,\lambda_i)$, $1 \le i \le n$.

The fundamental result is given by the celebrated Karhunen-Loeve theorem:

Theorem. Let X be a n-dimensional real-valued random vector such that $E(X) = 0$ and $Cov(X,X^T) = \Sigma$. If we denote by $\lambda_1 \ge \lambda_2 \ge ... \ge \lambda_n$ the eigen values of Σ, then, for any k, $1 \le k \le n$, the k-th principal direction is an eigen vector of Σ associated to $\lambda_k$.

A series of approaches are based on the assumption that the signal results as a mixture of a finite number of hidden independent sources and noise. This sort of attempts are usually referred as techniques of Independent Component Analysis type. The simplest model is the linear one, given by X=AS+$\eta$, where A is an unknown matrix (mixing matrix), S is the n-dimensional random vector whose components are independent and $\eta = (\eta_1,\eta_2,...,\eta_n)^T$ is a random vector representing the noise. The problem is to recover the hidden sources being given the signal X without knowing the mixing matrix A.

For simplicity sake, the noise model is of Gaussian type, that is $\eta \sim N(0,\Sigma_\eta)$. Then, if we denote $V = AS$, then, for any vector $w \in R^n$, $w^T X = w^T V + w^T \eta$. Consequently, the non-Gaussianity of $w^T V$ can be maximized on the basis of $w^T X$ if we use an expression that vanishes the component $w^T \eta$.

The kurtosis (the fourth-order cumulant) corresponding to a real-valued random variable Y is defined as $kurt(Y) = E(Y^4) - 3(E(Y^2))^2$. In case Y is normally distributed, we get $kurt(Y) = 0$. Since $\eta \sim N(0,\Sigma_\eta)$, for any $w \in R^n$, $w^T\eta \sim N(0, w^T \Sigma_\eta w)$, that is $kurt(w^T\eta) = 0$.

The non-Gaussianity can be also measured using the Shannon neg-entropy (mutual information). Being given the computational difficulty of evaluating the exact expression of neg-entropy, usually an approximation of it is used instead, for instance the approximation proposed in (Hyvarinen, Karhunen & Oja, 2001), $J_G(w^T V) = [E(G(w^T V)) - E(G(\nu))]^2$, where G is a non-polynomial function and $\nu \sim N(0,1)$.

Usually the maximization of non-Gaussianity is performed on the pre-processed signal version $\tilde{X}$, applied in order to whiten the original clean signal. In case of the additive noise superposition model, $X = X_0 + \eta$, where $X_0$ is the original clean signal (unknown) and

$\eta \sim N(0,\Sigma_\eta)$. In case $X_0$ and $\eta$ are independent and $Cov(\eta,\eta^T)=\Sigma_\eta$ is known, we get $Cov(X_0,X_0^T)=\Sigma-\Sigma_\eta$, where $Cov(X,X^T)=\Sigma$ and the covariance matrix $\Sigma$ corresponding to the observed signal X is assumed to be estimated from data. Then $\tilde{X}=(\Sigma-\Sigma_\eta)^{-\frac{1}{2}}X=(\Sigma-\Sigma_\eta)^{-\frac{1}{2}}X_0+(\Sigma-\Sigma_\eta)^{-\frac{1}{2}}\eta=(\Sigma-\Sigma_\eta)^{-\frac{1}{2}}X_0+\tilde{\eta}$, where $(\Sigma-\Sigma_\eta)^{-\frac{1}{2}}X_0$ and $\tilde{\eta}$ are independent and the covariance matrix of $(\Sigma-\Sigma_\eta)^{-\frac{1}{2}}X_0$ is the unit matrix $I_n$ .If $X_0$ results by the linear transform of matrix A applied to the sources S, $X_0=AS$, then $\tilde{X}=BS+\tilde{\eta}$, where $B=(\Sigma-\Sigma_\eta)^{-\frac{1}{2}}A$. Consequently, the sources S are determined by maximizing the non-Gaussianity of $\tilde{X}=BS+\tilde{\eta}$. Usually, for simplicity sake, the matrix B is assumed to be orthogonal.

### 2.2 The use of concepts and tools of multiresolution analysis for noise removal and image restoration purposes

The multiresolution based algorithms perform the restoration tasks by combining, at each resolution level, according to a certain rule, the pixels of a binary support image. The values of the support image pixels are either 1 or 0 depending on their significance degree. At each resolution level, the contiguous areas of the support image corresponding to 1-value pixels are taken as possible objects of the image. The multiresolution support is the set of all support images and it can be computed using the statistically significant wavelet coefficients.

Let $j$ be a certain multiresolution level. Then, for each pixel $(x,y)$ of the input image $I$, the multiresolution support at the level $j$ is $M(I;j,x,y)=1 \Leftrightarrow I$ contains significant information at the level $j$ about the pixel $(x,y)$.

If we denote by $\psi$ be the mother wavelet function, then the generic evaluation of the multiresolution support set results by computing the wavelet transform of the input image using $\psi$ followed by the computation of $M(I;j,x,y)$ on the basis of the statistically significant wavelet coefficients for each resolution level $j$ and for each pixel $(x,y)$.

The computation of the wavelet transform of an one dimensional signal can be performed using the algorithm "À Trous" (Stark, Murtagh & Bijaoui, 1995). The algorithm can be extended to perform this computation in case of two-dimensional signals as, for instance, image signals

Using the resolution levels $1,2,...,p$, where $p$ is a selected level, the "À Trous" algorithm computes the wavelet coefficients according to the following scheme (Stark, Murtagh & Bijaoui, 1995).

Input: The sampled signal $\{c_0(k)\}$

For $j$=0,1,…,$p$ do

**Step 1.** $j$=$j$+1; compute, $c_j(k)=\sum_l h(l)c_{j-1}(k+2^{j-1}l)$.

**Step 2.** Step 2. Compute $\omega_j(k)=c_{j-1}(k)-c_j(k)$

End-for

Output: The set $\{\omega_j(k), c_p\}_{j=1,\ldots,p}$.

Note that the computation of $c_j(k)$ carried out in Step 1 imposes that either the periodicity condition $c_j(k+N) = c_j(k)$ or the continuity property $c_j(k+N) = c_j(N)$ holds.

Since the representation of the original sampled signal is $c_0(k) = c_p(k) + \sum_{j=1}^{p} \omega_j(k)$, in case of images, the values of $c_0$ are computed for each pixel (*x*,*y*) as $c_0(x,y) = c_p(x,y) + \sum_{j=1}^{p} \omega_j(x,y)$.

If the input image *I* encodes a noise component $\eta$, then the wavelet coefficients also encode some information about $\eta$. A label procedure is applied to each $\omega_j(x,y)$ in order to remove the noise component from the wavelet coefficients computed for *I*. In case for each pixel (*x*,*y*) of *I*, the distribution of the coefficients is available, the significance level corresponding to each component $\omega_j(x,y)$ can be established using a statistical test. We say that *I* is local constant at the resolution level *j* in case the amount of noise in *I* at this resolution level can be neglected. Let $\mathrm{H}_0$ be the hypothesis $\mathrm{H}_0$ : *I* is local constant at the resolution level *j*. In case there is significant amount of noise in *I* at the resolution level *j*, we get that the alternative hypothesis $\neg\, \mathrm{H}_0 : \omega_j(x,y) \sim N(0,\sigma_j^2)$. In order to define the critical region *W* of the statistical test we proceed as follows. Let $0 < \varepsilon < 1$ be the *a priori* selected significance level and let $z_\varepsilon$ be such that when $\neg\, \mathrm{H}_0$ is true,

$$1 - \varepsilon = \mathrm{Prob}\left(\left|\omega_j(x,y)\right| < z_\varepsilon\right) = \frac{1}{\sqrt{2\pi}\sigma_j} \int_{-z_\varepsilon}^{z_\varepsilon} \exp\left\{-\frac{t^2}{2\sigma_j^{\,2}}\right\} dt \tag{1}$$

In other words, the probability of rejecting $\neg\, \mathrm{H}_0$ (hence accept $\mathrm{H}_0$) when $\neg\, \mathrm{H}_0$ is true is $\varepsilon$ and consequently, the critical region is $W = [-z_\varepsilon, z_\varepsilon]$. Accordingly, the significance level of the wavelet coefficients is given by the rule: $\omega_j(x,y)$ is a significant coefficient if and only if $\omega_j(x,y) \notin W$.

Usually, $z_\varepsilon$ is taken as $k\sigma_j$, where *k* is a selected constant $k \approx 3$, because

$$\begin{aligned} P\left(\left|\omega_j(x,y)\right| > k\sigma_j\right) &= P\left(\omega_j(x,y) > k\sigma_j\right) + P\left(\omega_j(x,y) < -k\sigma_j\right) = \\ &= 2P\left(\omega_j(x,y) > k\sigma_j\right) = 2\left(1 - P\left(\omega_j(x,y) \le k\sigma_j\right)\right) \end{aligned}$$

$$z_{k\sigma_j} < \varepsilon \Rightarrow P\left(\left|\omega_j(x,y)\right| > k\sigma_j\right) \ge 2(1-\varepsilon)$$

Using the significance level, we set to 1 the statistically significant coefficient and respectively we set to 0 the non-significant ones. The restored image $\tilde{I}$ is,

$$\tilde{I}(x,y) = c_p(x,y) + \sum_{j=1}^{p} g\left(\sigma_j, \omega_j(x,y)\right)\omega_j(x,y), \tag{2}$$

where *g* is defined by

$$g\left(\sigma_j,\omega_j(x,y)\right)=\begin{cases}1, & \left|\omega_j(x,y)\right|\geq k\sigma_j\\ 0, & \left|\omega_j(x,y)\right|<k\sigma_j\end{cases}.$$

### 2.3 Information-based approaches in image restoration

The basics of the informational-based method for image restoration purposes are given by the following theoretical results (State, Cocianu & Vlamos, 2001).

Lemma 1 Let $X$ be a continuous $n$-dimensional random vector and $A\in M_n(R)$ a non-singular matrix, $Y=AX$. Then, $H(X)=H(Y)-\ln|A|$, where

$$H(X)=-\int_{R^n} f(x)\ln f(x)dx$$

is the differential entropy (Shannon), and $f$ is the density function of $X$ .

Lemma 2 Let $X$ be a continuous $n$-dimensional normally distributed random vector, $X\sim N(0,\Sigma)$ and let $q$ be a natural number, $1\leq q$<n. If $X=\begin{pmatrix}X^{(1)}\\ X^{(2)}\end{pmatrix}$ where $X^{(1)}$ is $q$-dimensional, then, for any $x^{(2)}\in$ Rn-q, $H\left(X^{(1)}\middle|X^{(2)}=x^{(2)}\right)=H\left(X^{(1)}-E\left(X^{(1)}\middle|X^{(2)}=x^{(2)}\right)\right)$, where

$$E\left(X^{(1)}\middle|X^{(2)}=x^{(2)}\right)$$

is the regression function of $X^{(1)}$ on $X^{(2)}=x^{(2)}$, and $H\left(X^{(1)}\middle|X^{(2)}=x^{(2)}\right)$ is the conditional entropy of $X^{(1)}$ on $X^{(2)}=x^{(2)}$.

Since $H\left(X^{(1)}\middle|X^{(2)}=x^{(2)}\right)$ represents a measure of the amount of incertitude still remaining with respect to $X^{(1)}$ when $X^{(2)}$ is known, we get that the whole information carried by $X^{(2)}$ with respect to $X^{(1)}$ is concentrated on $E\left(X^{(1)}\middle|X^{(2)}=x^{(2)}\right)$.

If we denote $\Sigma_{11}=\mathrm{cov}\left(X^{(1)},X^{(1)T}\right)$, $\Sigma_{22}=\mathrm{cov}\left(X^{(2)},X^{(2)T}\right)$, $\Sigma_{12}=\mathrm{cov}\left(X^{(1)},X^{(2)T}\right)$, we get $E\left(X^{(1)}\middle|X^{(2)}=x^{(2)}\right)=\Sigma_{12}\Sigma_{22}^{-1}x^{(2)}$ and $Y^{(1)}\sim N(0,\Sigma_{11.2})$,

where $Y^{(1)}=X^{(1)}-\Sigma_{12}\Sigma_{22}^{-1}x^{(2)}=X^{(1)}-E\left(X^{(1)}\middle|X^{(2)}=x^{(2)}\right)$, and $\Sigma_{11.2}=\Sigma_{11}-\Sigma_{12}\Sigma_{22}^{-1}\left(\Sigma_{12}\right)^T$

Consequently $H\left(X^{(1)}-E\left(X^{(1)}\middle|X^{(2)}=x^{(2)}\right)\right)=H\left(X^{(1)}\middle|X^{(2)}=x^{(2)}\right)=\frac{q}{2}\ln 2\pi e+\frac{1}{2}\ln\left|\Sigma_{11.2}\right|$ .

### 2.4 The image restoration method based on scatter matrices and on bounds on the probability of error

In statistical discriminant analysis, within-class, between-class and mixture scatter matrices are used to formulate criteria of class separability.

In case we need to discriminate between $m$ classes $H_i, i=\overline{1,m}$ and $\left\{X_1^{(i)},\dots,X_N^{(i)}\right\}$ are examples of patterns coming respectively from these classes, the within -class scatter matrix shows the scatter of samples around their class expected vectors and it is typically given by the expression $S_w = \sum_{i=1}^{m} \xi_i \sum_{k=1}^{N} \left(X_k^{(i)} - \hat{\mu}_i\right)\left(X_k^{(i)} - \hat{\mu}_i\right)^T$, where $\hat{\mu}_i$ is the prototype of $H_i$ and $\xi_i$ is the *a priori* probability of $H_i, i = \overline{1,m}$.

Very often, the *a priori* probabilities are taken $\xi_i = \frac{1}{m}$ and each prototype is computed as the weighted mean of the patterns belonging to the respective class.

The between-class scatter matrix is the scatter of the expected vectors around the mixture mean as $S_b = \sum_{i=1}^{m} \xi_i \sum_{k=1}^{N} (\hat{\mu}_i - \mu_0)(\hat{\mu}_i - \mu_0)^T$ where $\mu_0$ represents the expected vector of the mixture distribution; usually $\mu_0$ is taken as $\mu_0 = \sum_{i=1}^{m} \xi_i \hat{\mu}_i$.

The mixture scatter matrix is the covariance matrix of all samples regardless of their class assignments and it is defined by $S_m = S_w + S_b$. Note that all these scatter matrices are invariant under coordinate shifts.

In order to formulate criteria for class separability, these matrices should be converted into a number. This number should be larger when the between-class scatter is larger or the within-class scatter is smaller. Typical criteria are $J_1 = tr\left(S_2^{-1} S_1\right)$, $J_2 = \ln\left|S_2^{-1} S_1\right|$, where $(S_1, S_2) \in \{(S_b, S_w), (S_b, S_m), (S_w, S_m), (S_m, S_w)\}$ and their values can be taken as measures of overall class separability. Obviously, both criteria are invariant under linear non-singular transforms and they are currently used for feature extraction purposes [8]. When the linear feature extraction problem is solved on the base of either $J_1$ or $J_2$, their values are taken as numerical indicators of the loss of information implied by the reduction of dimensionality and implicitly deteriorating class separability. Consequently, the best linear feature extraction is formulated as the optimization problem $\arg\left(\inf_{A \in R^{n*m}} \left|J_k(m,A) - J_k\right|\right)$ where m stands for the desired number of features, $J_k(m,A)$ is the value of the criterion $J_k, k = 1,2$ in the transformed m-dimensional space of $Y = A^T X$, where A is a $n*m$ matrix.

If the pattern classes are represented by the noisy image $X^{(\eta)}$ and the filtered image $F\left(X^{(\eta)}\right)$ respectively, the value of each of the criteria $J_k, k = 1,2$ is a measure of overall class separability as well as well as a measure of the amount of information discriminating between these classes. In other words, $J_k, k = 1,2$ can be taken as measuring the effects of the noise removing filter expressing a measure of the quantity of information lost due to the use of the particular filter.

Lemma 3. For any m, $1 \le m \le n$,

$\arg\left(\inf_{A \in R^{n*m}} \left|J_k(m,A) - J_k\right|\right) = \left\{A\Psi \middle| A = (\Phi_1, \Phi_2, ..., \Phi_m), \Psi \in R^{m*m}, |\Psi| \neq 0\right\}$, where $\Phi_1, ..., \Phi_m$ are unit eigenvectors corresponding to the m largest eigenvalues of $S_2^{-1} S_1$ (Cocianu, State & Vlamos, 2004).

The probability of error is the most effective measure of a classification decision rule usefulness, but its evaluation involves integrations on complicated regions in high dimensional spaces. When a closed-form expression for the error probability can not be obtained, we may seek either for approximate expressions, or upper/lower bounds for the error probability.

Assume that the design of the Bayes classifier is intended to discriminate between two pattern classes and the available information is represented by mean vectors $\mu_i$, $i=1,2$ and the covariance matrices $\Sigma_i$, $i=1,2$ corresponding to the repartitions of the classes respectively. The Chernoff upper bounds of the Bayesian error (Fukunaga, 1990) are given by $\varepsilon_s = \xi_1^s \xi_2^{1-s} \int (f_1(x))^s (f_2(x))^{1-s} dx$ , $s \in [0,1]$ , where $\xi = (\xi_1, \xi_2)$ is the *a priori* distribution and $f_i$ is the density function corresponding to the $i-th$ class, $i=1,2$. When both density functions are normal, $f_i \sim N(\mu_i, \Sigma_i)$ $i=1,2$, the integration can be carried out to obtain a closed-form expression for $\varepsilon_s$, that is $\int (f_1(x))^s (f_2(x))^{1-s} dx = \exp(-\mu(s))$ where

$$\mu(s) = \frac{s(1-s)}{2}(\mu_2-\mu_1)^T (s\Sigma_1 + (1-s)\Sigma_2)^{-1}(\mu_2-\mu_1) + \frac{1}{2}\ln\frac{|s\Sigma_1+(1-s)\Sigma_2|}{|\Sigma_1|^s|\Sigma_2|^{1-s}} \tag{3}$$

The upper bound $\mu\left(\frac{1}{2}\right) = \frac{1}{8}(\mu_2-\mu_1)^T \left(\frac{\Sigma_1+\Sigma_2}{2}\right)^{-1}(\mu_2-\mu_1) + \frac{1}{2}\ln\frac{\left|\frac{\Sigma_1+\Sigma_2}{2}\right|}{\sqrt{|\Sigma_1||\Sigma_2|}}$ is called the Bhattacharyya distance and it is frequently used as a measure of the separability between two repartitions. Using straightforward computations, the Bhattacharyya distance can be written as,

$$\mu\left(\frac{1}{2}\right) = \frac{1}{8}tr\left\{\bar{\Sigma}^{-1}(\mu_2-\mu_1)(\mu_2-\mu_1)^T\right\} + \frac{1}{4}\ln\left|2I_n + \Sigma_1\Sigma_2^{-1} + \Sigma_2\Sigma_1^{-1}\right| - \frac{n}{4}\ln 2 \tag{4}$$

where

$$\bar{\Sigma} = \frac{\Sigma_1+\Sigma_2}{2}$$

Note that one of the first two terms in (4) vanishes, when $\mu_1=\mu_2$, $\Sigma_1=\Sigma_2$ respectively, that is the first term expresses the class separability due to the mean-difference while the second one gives the class separability due to the covariance difference.

The Bhattacharyya distance can be used as criterion function as well to express the quality of a linear feature extractor of matrix $A \in R^{nxm}$.

When $\Sigma_1=\Sigma_2=\Sigma$, $J=\mu\left(\frac{1}{2}\right)=\frac{1}{8}tr\left\{\bar{\Sigma}^{-1}(\mu_2-\mu_1)(\mu_2-\mu_1)^T\right\}$ therefore $J$ is a particular case of the criterion $J_1$ for $S_2=\Sigma$ and $S_1=S_b=(\mu_2-\mu_1)(\mu_2-\mu_1)^T$. Consequently the whole information about the class separability is contained by an unique feature $\Phi_1 = \frac{\Sigma^{-1}(\mu_2-\mu_1)}{\left\|\Sigma^{-1}(\mu_2-\mu_1)\right\|}$. When $\mu_1=\mu_2$ and $\Sigma_1 \neq \Sigma_2$,

$$J=\frac{1}{4}\ln\left|2I_n+\Sigma_2^{-1}\Sigma_1+\Sigma_1^{-1}\Sigma_2\right|-\frac{n}{4}\ln 2=\frac{1}{4}\sum_{j=1}^{n}\left(2+\lambda_j+\frac{1}{\lambda_j}\right)-\frac{n}{4}\ln 2 \tag{5}$$

where $\lambda_j, j=1,n$ are the eigenvalues of $\Sigma_1^{-1}\Sigma_2$.

If the linear feature extractor is defined by the matrix $A\in R^{nxm}$, then the value of the Bhattacharyya distance in the transformed space $Y=A^TX$ is given by,

$$J\ (m,A)=\frac{1}{4}\ln\left|2I_m+\left(A^T\Sigma_2A\right)^{-1}\left(A^T\Sigma_1A\right)+\left(A^T\Sigma_1A\right)^{-1}\left(A^T\Sigma_2A\right)\right|-\frac{m}{4}\ln 2\,. \tag{6}$$

The critical points of $J\ (m,A)$ are the solutions of the equation $\frac{\partial J(m,A)}{\partial A}=0$ that is,

$$B\left\{\Sigma_2A\Sigma_2^{-1}(m)\Sigma_1(m)\Sigma_2^{-1}(m)-\Sigma_1A\Sigma_2^{-1}(m)\right\}+B\left\{\Sigma_1A\Sigma_2^{-1}(m)\Sigma_2(m)\Sigma_1^{-1}(m)-\Sigma_2A\Sigma_1^{-1}(m)\right\}=0 \tag{7}$$

where

$$\Sigma_i(m)=A^T\Sigma_iA\,,i=1,2 \text{ and } B=\left[\left(A^T\Sigma_1A\right)^{-1}\left(A^T\Sigma_2A\right)+\left(A^T\Sigma_2A\right)^{-1}\left(A^T\Sigma_1A\right)+2I_m\right]^{-1}.$$

Suboptimal solutions can be identified as the solutions of the system

$$\begin{cases}\Sigma_2A\Sigma_2^{-1}(m)\Sigma_1(m)\Sigma_2^{-1}(m)-\Sigma_1A\Sigma_2^{-1}(m)=0\\ \Sigma_1A\Sigma_1^{-1}(m)\Sigma_2(m)\Sigma_1^{-1}(m)-\Sigma_2A\Sigma_1^{-1}(m)=0\end{cases} \tag{8}$$

or equivalently, $\Sigma_2^{-1}\Sigma_1A=A\Sigma_2^{-1}(m)\Sigma_1(m)$.

Obviously the criterion function $J$ is invariant with respect to non-singular transforms and, using standard arguments, one can prove that $\Phi^{(m)}=(\Phi_1,...,\Phi_m)$ can be taken as the suboptimal linear feature extractor where $\Phi_i, i=1,m$ are unit eigenvectors corresponding to the eigenvalues $\lambda_{,1}...,\lambda_m$ of $\Sigma_2^{-1}\Sigma_1$ such that $\lambda_1+\frac{1}{\lambda_1}\geq...\geq\lambda_m+\frac{1}{\lambda_m}\geq...\geq\lambda_n+\frac{1}{\lambda_n}$.

But, in case of image restoration problem, each of the assumptions $\mu_1=\mu_2$, $\Sigma_1=\Sigma_2$ is unrealistic, therefore, we are forced to accept the hypothesis that $\mu_1\neq\mu_2$ and $\Sigma_1\neq\Sigma_2$. Since there is no known procedure available to optimize the criterion $J$ when $\Sigma_1\neq\Sigma_2$ and $\mu_1\neq\mu_2$, a series of attempts to find suboptimal feature extractors have been proposed instead (Fukunaga, 1990)

## 3. Noise removal algorithms

### 3.1 Minimum mean-square error filtering (MMSE), and the adaptive mean-variance removal algorithm (AMVR)

The minimum mean-square error filter (MMSE) is an adaptive filter in the sense that its basic behavior changes as the image is processed. Therefore an adaptive filter could process differently on different segments of an image. The particular MMSE filter may act as a mean filter on some windows of the image and as a median filter on other windows of the image. The MMSE filter allows the removal of the normal/uniform additive noise and its computation is carried out as

$$\overline{X}(l,c) = Y(l,c) - \frac{\sigma^2}{\sigma_{l,c}^2}\left[Y(l,c) - \mu_{l,c}\right],$$

for $t \le l \le R-t, t \le c \le C-t$, where Y is a $R \times C$ noisy image, $W_{l,c}$ is the $n \times n$ window centered in (l,c), where $n = 2t+1, t \le l \le R-t, t \le c \le C-t$, $\sigma^2$ is the noise variance, $\sigma_{l,c}^2$ is the local variance (in the window $W_{l,c}$), and $\mu_{l,c}^2$ is the local mean (average in the window $W_{l,c}$).

Note that since the background region of the image is an area of fairly constant value in the original uncorrupted image, the noise variance is almost equal to the local variance, and consequently the MMSE performs as a mean filter. In image areas where the local variances are much larger than the noise variance, the filter computes a value close to the pixel value corresponding to the unfiltered image data. The magnitude of the original and local means respectively used to modify the initial image are weighted by $\frac{\sigma^2}{\sigma_{l,c}^2}$, the ratio of noise to local variance. As the value of the ratio increases, implying primarily noise in the window, the filter returns primarily the value of the local average. As this ratio decreases, implying high local detail, the filter returns more of the original unfiltered image. Consequently, the MMSE filter adapts itself to the local image properties, preserving image details while removing noise.(Umbaugh,1998).

The special filtering techniques of mean type prove particularly useful in reducing the normal/uniform noise component when the mean parameter is close to 0. In other words, the effects determined by the application of mean filters are merely the decrease of each processed window local variance and consequently the removal of the variance component of the noise.

The AMVR algorithm allows to remove the normal/uniform noise whatever the mean of the noise is. Similar to MMSE filtering technique in application of the AMVR algorithm, the noise parameters and features are known. Basically, the AMVR algorithm works in two stages, namely the removal of the mean component of the noise (Step 1 and Step 2), and the decrease of the variance of the noise using the adaptive filter MMSE. The description of the AMVR algorithm is (Cocianu, State & Vlamos, 2002) is,

Input The image Y of dimensions $R \times C$, representing a normal/uniform disturbed version of the initial image X, $Y(l,c) = X(l,c) + \eta_{l,c}^0$, $1 \le l \le R, 1 \le c \le C$, where $\eta_{l,c}^0$ is a sample of the random variable $\eta_{l,c}$ distributed either $N\left(\mu_{l,c}, \sigma_{l,c}^2\right)$ or $U\left(\mu_{l,c}, \sigma_{l,c}^2\right)$.

**Step 1.** Generate the sample of images $\{X_1, X_2, \ldots, X_n\}$, by subtracting the noise $\eta_{l,c}$ from the processed image Y, where $X_i(l,c) = Y(l,c) - \eta_{l,c}^i$, $1 \le l \le L, 1 \le c \le C$ and $\eta_{l,c}^i$ is a sample of the random variable $\eta_{l,c}$.

**Step 2.** Compute $\overline{X}$, the sample mean estimate of the initial image X, by averaging the pixel values, $\overline{X}(l,c) = \frac{1}{n}\sum_{i=1}^{n} X_i(l,c)$, $1 \le l \le R, 1 \le c \le C$.

**Step 3.** Compute the estimate $\hat{X}$ of X using the adaptive filter MMSE, $\hat{X} = MMSE\left(\overline{X}\right)$.

Output The image $\hat{X}$.

### 3.2 Information-based algorithms for noise removal

Let us consider the following information transmission/processing system. The signal $X$ representing a certain image is transmitted through a channel and its noise-corrupted version $X^{(\eta)}$ is received. Next, a noise-removing binomial filter is applied to the output $X^{(\eta)}$ resulting $F\left(X^{(\eta)}\right)$. Finally, the signal $F\left(X^{(\eta)}\right)$ is submitted to a restoration process producing $\overline{X}$, an approximation of the initial signal $X$. In our attempt (Cocianu, State & Vlamos, 2004) we assumed that there is no available information about the initial signal $X$, therefore the restoration process should be based exclusively on $X^{(\eta)}$ and $F\left(X^{(\eta)}\right)$. We assume that the message $X$ is transmitted $N$ times and we denote by $X_1^{(2)},...,X_N^{(2)}$ the resulted outputs and by $X_1^{(1)},...,X_N^{(1)}$ their corresponding filtered versions.

If we denote the given image by $X$, then we model $\left\{X_1^{(2)},...,X_N^{(2)}\right\}$ as a Bernoullian sample of the random $r\times c$-dimensional vector $X^{(\eta)} = X+\eta$ where $\eta \sim N(\mu,\Sigma)$ and $\left\{X_1^{(1)},...,X_N^{(1)}\right\}$ is a sample of the filtered random vector $F\left(X^{(\eta)}\right)$. Obviously, $X^{(\eta)}$ and $F\left(X^{(\eta)}\right)$ are normally distributed. Let us denote $\mu^{(1)} = E\left(F\left(X^{(\eta)}\right)\right)$, $\mu^{(2)} = E\left(X^{(\eta)}\right)$ and let $\Sigma_{11}$, $\Sigma_{22}$ be their covariance matrices. We consider the working assumption that the $2\times$ $r\times c$-dimensional vector $\left(X^{(\eta)},F\left(X^{(\eta)}\right)\right)$ is also normally distributed, therefore the conditional distribution of $F\left(X^{(\eta)}\right)$ on $X^{(\eta)}$ is $N\left(\mu^{(1)}+\Sigma_{12}\Sigma_{22}^{-1}\left(X^{(\eta)}-\mu^{(2)}\right),\Sigma_{11.2}\right)$, where

$$E\left(F\left(X^{(\eta)}\right)\middle|X^{(\eta)}\right) = \mu^{(1)}+\Sigma_{12}\Sigma_{22}^{-1}\left(X^{(\eta)}-\mu^{(2)}\right) \tag{9}$$

is the regression function of $F\left(X^{(\eta)}\right)$ on $X^{(\eta)}$,

and $\Sigma_{12} = \operatorname{cov}\left(F\left(X^{(\eta)}\right),X^{(\eta)}\right)$ $\Sigma_{11.2} = \Sigma_{11} - \Sigma_{12}\Sigma_{22}^{-1}\left(\Sigma_{12}\right)^T$ (see § 2.3).

It is well known (Anderson, 1958) that $F\left(X^{(\eta)}\right)-E\left(F\left(X^{(\eta)}\right)\middle|X^{(\eta)}\right)$ minimizes the variance and maximizes the correlation between $F\left(X^{(\eta)}\right)$ and $X^{(\eta)}$ in the class of linear functions of $X^{(\eta)}$. Moreover, $E\left(F\left(X^{(\eta)}\right)\middle|X^{(\eta)}\right)$ is $X^{(\eta)}$-measurable and, since $F\left(X^{(\eta)}\right)-E\left(F\left(X^{(\eta)}\right)\middle|X^{(\eta)}\right)$ and $X^{(\eta)}$ are independent, the whole information carried by $X^{(\eta)}$ with respect to $F\left(X^{(\eta)}\right)$ is contained by $E\left(F\left(X^{(\eta)}\right)\middle|X^{(\eta)}\right)$.

As a particular case , using the conclusions established by the lemmas 1 and 2 (§ 2.3), we can conclude that $H\left(F\left(X^{(\eta)}\right)-E\left(F\left(X^{(\eta)}\right)\middle|X^{(\eta)}\right)\right) = H\left(F\left(X^{(\eta)}\right)\middle|X^{(\eta)}\right)$ and $E\left(F\left(X^{(\eta)}\right)\middle|X^{(\eta)}\right)$ contains the whole information existing in $X^{(\eta)}$ with respect to $F\left(X^{(\eta)}\right)$ a part of it being responsible for the initial existing noise $\eta$ and another component being responsible for the quality degradation.

According to our regression-based algorithm, the rows of the restored image $\overline{X}$ are computed sequentially on the basis of the samples $\left\{X_1^{(2)},...,X_N^{(2)}\right\}$ and $\left\{X_1^{(1)},...,X_N^{(1)}\right\}$ representing the available information about $X^{(\eta)}$ and $F\left(X^{(\eta)}\right)$

If we denote by $X_k^{(p)}(i)$ the i-th row of $X_k^{(p)}$, $p=1,2, 1\le k\le N$, then the mean vectors $\mu^{(p)}$ are estimated by the corresponding sample means $\hat{\mu}^{(p)}=\left(\hat{\mu}^{(p)}(1),...,\hat{\mu}^{(p)}(r)\right)$, where $\hat{\mu}^{(p)}(i)=\frac{1}{N}\sum_{k=1}^{N}X_k^{(p)}(i), 1\le i\le r$ and the covariance matrices $\Sigma_{ts}(i), t,s=1,2$ are estimated respectively by their sample covariance matrices counterparts, $\hat{\Sigma}_{ts}(i)=\frac{1}{N-1}\sum_{k=1}^{N}\left(X_k^{(t)}(i)-\hat{\mu}^{(t)}(i)\right)\left(X_k^{(s)}(i)-\hat{\mu}^{(s)}(i)\right)^T$. Frequently enough it happens that the matrices $\hat{\Sigma}_{tt}(i), t=1,2$ are ill conditioned, therefore in our method the Penrose pseudoinverse $\left(\hat{\Sigma}_{tt}(i)\right)^+$ is used instead of $\left(\hat{\Sigma}_{tt}(i)\right)^{-1}$.

Since the aim is to restore as much as possible the initial image X, we have to find out ways to improve the quality of $F\left(X^{(\eta)}\right)$ in the same time preventing the introduction additional noise.

Obviously,

$$\mu^{(1)}=E(F(X+\eta))=F(X+E(\eta))=F(X)+F(E(\eta))=F(X)+E(\eta) \tag{10}$$

$$\mu^{(2)}=E(X+\eta)=X+E(\eta) \tag{11}$$

hence $\mu^{(1)}-\mu^{(2)}=F(X)-X$ and $X^{(\eta)}-\mu^{(1)}=X-F(X)+\eta-E(\eta)$. In other words, $\mu^{(1)}-\mu^{(2)}$ can be viewed as measuring the effects of the noise $\eta$ as well as the quality degradation while the term $X^{(\eta)}-\mu^{(1)}$ retains more information about the quality of image and less information about $\eta$ (Cocianu, State & Vlamos, 2004). This argument entails the heuristic used by our method (Step 4), the restored image being obtained by applying a threshold filter to $\mu^{(1)}$ and adding the correction term $\rho\Sigma_{12}\Sigma_{22}^{-1}\left(\mu^{(2)}-\mu^{(1)}\right)$, $\overline{X}=T\left(\hat{\mu}^{(1)}(i)\right)+\rho\Sigma_{12}\Sigma_{22}^{-1}\left(\mu^{(2)}-\mu^{(1)}\right)$.

The heuristic regression -based algorithm (HRBA) for image restoration (Cocianu, State & Vlamos, 2004)

Input: The sample $\left\{X_1^{(2)},...,X_N^{(2)}\right\}$ of noise corrupted versions of the $r\times c-$dimensional image X

**Step 1.** Compute the sample $\left\{X_1^{(1)},...,X_N^{(1)}\right\}$ by applying the binomial filter of mask

$M_t = \frac{1}{12+t}\begin{bmatrix} 1 & 2 & 1 \\ 2 & t & 2 \\ 1 & 2 & 1 \end{bmatrix}$, $t \geq 4$ to each component of $\left\{X_1^{(2)},...,X_N^{(2)}\right\}$,

$X_i^{(1)} = F\left(X_i^{(2)}\right), 1 \leq i \leq N$.

**Step 2.** For each row $1 \leq i \leq r$, compute $\hat{\mu}^{(p)}(i) = \frac{1}{N}\sum_{k=1}^{N} X_k^{(p)}(i), 1 \leq i \leq r, p = 1,2$,

$\hat{\Sigma}_{ts}(i) = \frac{1}{N-1}\sum_{k=1}^{N}\left(X_k^{(t)}(i) - \hat{\mu}^{(t)}(i)\right)\left(X_k^{(s)}(i) - \hat{\mu}^{(s)}(i)\right)^T, t,s = 1,2$.

**Step 3.** For each row $1 \leq i \leq r$, compute $T\left(\hat{\mu}^{(1)}(i)\right)$ by applying a threshold filter to $\hat{\mu}^{(1)}(i)$.

**Step 4.** Compute the rows $\overline{X}(i)$ of the restored image $\overline{X}$, $\overline{X}(i) = T\left(\hat{\mu}^{(1)}(i)\right) + \rho\hat{\Sigma}_{12}(i)\left(\hat{\Sigma}_{22}(i)\right)^{+}\left(\hat{\mu}^{(2)}(i) - \hat{\mu}^{(1)}(i)\right)$, where $\rho$ is a noise-preventing constant conveniently determined to prevent the restoration of the initial noise. By experimental arguments, the recommended range of $\rho$ is $[1.5, 5.5]$.

Note that since the regression function can be written as,

$$E\left(F\left(X^{(\eta)}\right)\middle|X^{(\eta)}\right) = \mu^{(1)} + \Sigma_{12}\Sigma_{22}^{-1}\left(X^{(\eta)} - \mu^{(2)}\right) = \Sigma_{12}\Sigma_{22}^{-1}\left(X^{(\eta)} - \mu^{(1)}\right) + \mu^{(1)} - \Sigma_{12}\Sigma_{22}^{-1}\left(\mu^{(2)} - \mu^{(1)}\right) \quad (12)$$

the correction term used at Step 4 is precisely the sample mean estimation of the $E\left(\Sigma_{12}\Sigma_{22}^{-1}\left(X^{(\eta)} - \mu^{(1)}\right)\right)$.

The idea of our attempt is to use the most informative features discriminating between $X^{(\eta)}$ and $F\left(X^{(\eta)}\right)$ for getting correction terms in restoring the filtered images $F\left(X^{(\eta)}\right)$. The attempt is justified by the argument that besides information about the removed noise, the most informative features discriminating between $X^{(\eta)}$ and $F\left(X^{(\eta)}\right)$ would contain appropriate information allowing quality improvement of the image $F\left(X^{(\eta)}\right)$ (Cocianu, State & Vlamos, 2004). Let $\left\{X_1^{(2)},...,X_N^{(2)}\right\}$ be the sample of noise corrupted versions of the $r \times c-$ dimensional image X and $\left\{X_1^{(1)},...,X_N^{(1)}\right\}$ their filtered versions, $X_i^{(1)} = F\left(X_i^{(2)}\right), 1 \leq i \leq N$. We assume $\xi_1 = \xi_2 = 0.5$, therefore the scatter matrices become $S_w = \hat{\Sigma}_1 + \hat{\Sigma}_2$, $S_b = \left(\hat{\mu}^{(1)} - \hat{\mu}^{(2)}\right)\left(\hat{\mu}^{(1)} - \hat{\mu}^{(2)}\right)^T$ and $S_m = S_w + S_b$ where

$$\hat{\mu}^{(i)} = \frac{1}{N}\sum_{k=1}^{N} X_k^{(i)}, \quad \hat{\Sigma}_i = \frac{1}{N-1}\sum_{k=1}^{N}\left(X_k^{(i)} - \hat{\mu}^{(i)}\right)\left(X_k^{(i)} - \hat{\mu}^{(i)}\right)^T, \quad i = 1,2$$

Since $rank(S_b) = 1$, we get $rank\left(S_w^{-1}S_b\right) = 1$, that is when $S_2 = S_w$ and $S_1 = S_b$ ,the matrix $S_2^{-1}S_1$ has an unique positive eigenvalue, one of its unit eigenvectors being given by

$$\Phi_1 = \frac{S_w^{-1}\left(\mu^{(1)} - \mu^{(2)}\right)}{\left\|S_w^{-1}\left(\mu^{(1)} - \mu^{(2)}\right)\right\|}.$$

The heuristic scatter matrices-based algorithms (HSBA) for image restoration (Cocianu, State & Vlamos, 2004)

The idea of our attempt is to use the most informative features discriminating between $X^{(\eta)}$ and $F\left(X^{(\eta)}\right)$ for getting correction terms in restoring the filtered images $F\left(X^{(\eta)}\right)$ The attempt is justified by the argument that besides information about the removed noise, the most informative features discriminating between $X^{(\eta)}$ and $F\left(X^{(\eta)}\right)$ would contain appropriate information allowing quality improvement of the image $F\left(X^{(\eta)}\right)$ (Cocianu, State & Vlamos, 2004). Let $\left\{X_1^{(2)},...,X_N^{(2)}\right\}$ be the sample of noise corrupted versions of the $r \times c$ – dimensional image X and $\left\{X_1^{(1)},...,X_N^{(1)}\right\}$ their filtered versions, $X_i^{(1)} = F\left(X_i^{(2)}\right), 1 \le i \le N$. We assume $\xi_1 = \xi_2 = 0.5$ ,therefore the scatter matrices are

$$S_w = \hat{\Sigma}_1 + \hat{\Sigma}_2,\ S_b = \left(\hat{\mu}^{(1)} - \hat{\mu}^{(2)}\right)\left(\hat{\mu}^{(1)} - \hat{\mu}^{(2)}\right)^T \text{ and } S_m = S_w + S_b$$

where

$$\hat{\mu}^{(i)} = \frac{1}{N}\sum_{k=1}^{N} X_k^{(i)},\ \hat{\Sigma}_i = \frac{1}{N-1}\sum_{k=1}^{N}\left(X_k^{(i)} - \hat{\mu}^{(i)}\right)\left(X_k^{(i)} - \hat{\mu}^{(i)}\right)^T,\ i = 1,2.$$

Since $rank(S_b) = 1$, we get $rank\left(S_w^{-1}S_b\right) = 1$, that is when $S_2 = S_w$ and $S_1 = S_b$ ,the matrix $S_2^{-1}S_1$ has an unique positive eigenvalue, its unit eigenvector being given by

$$\Phi_1 = \frac{S_w^{-1}\left(\mu^{(1)} - \mu^{(2)}\right)}{\left\|S_w^{-1}\left(\mu^{(1)} - \mu^{(2)}\right)\right\|}$$

a. The variant of the HSBA when $S_2 = S_w$ and $S_1 = S_b$ (Cocianu, State & Vlamos, 2004)

Input : The sample $\left\{X_1^{(2)},...,X_N^{(2)}\right\}$ of noise corrupted versions of the $r \times c$ -dimensional image X

**Step 1.** Compute the sample $\left\{X_1^{(1)},...,X_N^{(1)}\right\}$ by applying the binomial filter as in Step 1 of HRBA.

**Step 2.** For each row $1 \le i \le r$, do Step 3 until Step 7

**Step 3.** Compute $\hat{\mu}^{(p)}(i) = \frac{1}{N}\sum_{k=1}^{N} X_k^{(p)}(i),\ \hat{\Sigma}_p(i) = \frac{1}{N-1}\sum_{k=1}^{N}\left(X_k^{(p)}(i) - \hat{\mu}^{(p)}(i)\right)\left(X_k^{(p)}(i) - \hat{\mu}^{(p)}(i)\right)^T$, $p = 1,2$

**Step 4.** Compute $S_b(i)=\left(\hat{\mu}^{(1)}(i)-\hat{\mu}^{(2)}(i)\right)\left(\hat{\mu}^{(1)}(i)-\hat{\mu}^{(2)}(i)\right)^T$ and the Penrose pseudoinverse $S_w^+(i)$ of the matrix $S_w(i)=\hat{\hat{\Sigma}}_1(i)+\hat{\Sigma}_2(i)$

**Step 5.** Compute the optimal linear feature extractor $\Phi_1(i)=\dfrac{S_w^{-1}\left(\mu^{(1)}(i)-\mu^{(2)}(i)\right)}{\left\|S_w^{-1}\left(\mu^{(1)}(i)-\mu^{(2)}(i)\right)\right\|}$ containing the information about class separability between $\left\{X_1^{(2)}(i),...,X_N^{(2)}(i)\right\}$ and $\left\{X_1^{(1)}(i),...,X_N^{(1)}(i)\right\}$ expressed in terms of the criterion function $J_1$ (see §2.4)

**Step 6.** Compute $T\left(\hat{\mu}^{(1)}(i)\right)$ by applying a threshold filter to $\hat{\mu}^{(1)}(i)$ and the correction term $Y(i)=\Phi_1^T\ \hat{\mu}^{(1)}(i)$

**Step 7.** Compute the row $\overline{X}(i)$ of the restored image $\overline{X}$ by correcting the filtered image $T\left(\hat{\mu}^{(1)}(i)\right)$ using the most informative feature, $\overline{X}(i)=T\left(\hat{\mu}^{(1)}(i)\right)+\sigma Y(i)\Phi_1$ ,where $\sigma$ is a noise-preventing constant conveniently determined to prevent the restoration of the initial noise, $0<\sigma<1$.

Note that at Step 4, the computation of $S_w^+(i)$ is carried out instead of $S_w^{-1}(i)$, this modification being needed because the matrix $S_w(i)$ could happen to be ill-conditioned.

b. The variant of the HSBA when $S_2=S_m$ and $S_1=S_w$ (Cocianu, State & Vlamos, 2004)

Let $\Lambda=diag(\lambda_1,...,\lambda_n)$ be the eigenvalue matrix of $S_m$ and $\Phi$ the matrix having as columns the corresponding unit eigenvectors. According to the algorithm of simultaneous diagonalization (Duda & Hart, 1973), the optimal linear feature extractor is given by $A=\Phi\Lambda^{-\frac{1}{2}}\Psi$ where $\Psi$ is an orthogonal matrix whose columns are unit eigenvectors of $K=\left(\Phi\Lambda^{-\frac{1}{2}}\right)^T S_w\Phi\Lambda^{-\frac{1}{2}}$. The most informative features about the separability of the classes represented by the samples $\left\{X_1^{(2)},...,X_N^{(2)}\right\}$ and $\left\{X_1^{(1)},...,X_N^{(1)}\right\}$ are the entries of $Y=A^+\ \hat{\mu}^{(1)}$, therefore the restoration can be performed by adding the correction term $\sigma AY$ to $T\left(\hat{\mu}^{(1)}(i)\right)$ the filtered prototype of $\left\{X_1^{(1)},...,X_N^{(1)}\right\}$.

The number of significant features is either pre-established or dynamically determined by the magnitude of the eigenvalues of $S_2^{-1}S_1$.

The variant of HSBA when $S_2=S_m$ and $S_1=S_w$ can be described as follows.

Input : The sample $\left\{X_1^{(2)},...,X_N^{(2)}\right\}$ of noise corrupted versions of the $r\times c$ -dimensional image X

**Step 1.** Compute the sample $\left\{X_1^{(1)},...,X_N^{(1)}\right\}$ as described in Step 1 of the variant (a) of the HSBA

**Step 2.** For each row $1 \le i \le r$, do Step 3 until Step 8

**Step 3.** Compute $\hat{\mu}^{(p)}(i) = \frac{1}{N}\sum_{k=1}^{N} X_k^{(p)}(i)$, $\hat{\Sigma}_p(i) = \frac{1}{N-1}\sum_{k=1}^{N}\left(X_k^{(p)}(i) - \hat{\mu}^{(p)}(i)\right)\left(X_k^{(p)}(i) - \hat{\mu}^{(p)}(i)\right)^T$, $p = 1,2$

**Step 4.** Compute $S_w(i) = \hat{\hat{\Sigma}}_1(i) + \hat{\Sigma}_2(i)$ and $S_m(i) = S_w(i) + \left(\hat{\mu}^{(1)}(i) - \hat{\mu}^{(2)}(i)\right)\left(\hat{\mu}^{(1)}(i) - \hat{\mu}^{(2)}(i)\right)^T$

**Step 5.** Compute the eigenvalues $\left(\lambda_1(i),...,\lambda_n(i)\right)$ and the corresponding unit eigenvectors $\left(\Phi_1(i),...,\Phi_n(i)\right)$ of $S_m(i)$. Select the largest $t$ eigenvalues and let $\Lambda_t(i) = diag\left(\lambda_1(i),...,\lambda_t(i)\right)$, $\varphi^{(t)}(i) = \left(\Phi_1(i),...,\Phi_t(i)\right)$

$$K(i) = \left(\Phi^{(t)}(i)\Lambda_t^{-\frac{1}{2}}(i)\right)^T S_w \left(\Phi^{(t)}(i)\Lambda_t^{-\frac{1}{2}}(i)\right).$$

**Step 6.** Compute $\Psi(i)$ a matrix whose columns are unit eigenvectors of $K(i)$. The most informative feature vectors responsible for the class separability between $\left\{X_1^{(2)}(i),...,X_N^{(2)}(i)\right\}$ and $\left\{X_1^{(1)}(i),...,X_N^{(1)}(i)\right\}$ are the columns of

$$A(i) = \Phi^{(t)}(i)\Lambda_t^{-\frac{1}{2}}(i)\Psi(i).$$

**Step 7.** Compute $T\left(\hat{\mu}^{(1)}(i)\right)$ by applying a threshold filter to $\hat{\mu}^{(1)}(i)$ and the correction term

$$Y(i) = A^+(i)\, T\left(\hat{\mu}^{(1)}(i)\right)$$

**Step 8.** Compute the row $\overline{X}(i)$ of the restored image $\overline{X}$ by correcting the filtered image $T\left(\hat{\mu}^{(1)}(i)\right)$ using the information contained by the selected features, $\overline{X}(i) = T\left(\hat{\mu}^{(1)}(i)\right) + \sigma A(i) Y(i)$, where $\sigma$ is a noise-preventing constant conveniently determined to prevent the restoration of the initial noise, $0 < \sigma < 1$.

c. The variant of the HSBA when $S_2 = S_w$ and $S_1 = S_m$ (Cocianu, State & Vlamos, 2004)

In case we take $S_2 = S_w$ and $S_1 = S_m$ we obtain a variant of the HSBA similar to the variant (b). In our approach, for each row $1 \le i \le r$ of the processed images, the most informative features used in getting the correction term are determined using the matrix $M(i)$ whose columns are eigenvectors of $S_w^+ S_m$ such that $M(i)M^T(i) = S_w^+(i)$.

Our image restoration algorithm based on the Bhattacharyya distance can be described as follows.

The HBA for image restoration (Cocianu, State & Vlamos, 2004)

Input : The sample $\left\{X_1^{(2)},...,X_N^{(2)}\right\}$ of noise corrupted versions of the $r \times c$-dimensional image $X$ and the number $k$ of desired features.

**Step 1.** Compute the sample $\left\{X_1^{(1)},...,X_N^{(1)}\right\}$ as described in Step 1 of the variant (a) of the HSBA

**Step 2.** For each row $1 \le i \le r$, do Step 3 until Step 8

**Step 3.** Compute

$$\hat{\mu}^{(p)}(i)=\frac{1}{N}\sum_{k=1}^{N}X_k^{(p)}(i)\,,\ \hat{\Sigma}_p(i)=\frac{1}{N-1}\sum_{k=1}^{N}\left(X_k^{(p)}(i)-\hat{\mu}^{(p)}(i)\right)\left(X_k^{(p)}(i)-\hat{\mu}^{(p)}(i)\right)^T,\ p=1,2$$

**Step 4.** Compute

$$\mu\left(\frac{1}{2},i\right)=\frac{1}{8}\left(\hat{\mu}^{(2)}(i)-\hat{\mu}^{(1)}(i)\right)^T\left(\frac{\hat{\Sigma}_1(i)+\hat{\Sigma}_2(i)}{2}\right)^{-1}\left(\hat{\mu}^{(2)}(i)-\hat{\mu}^{(1)}(i)\right)+\frac{1}{2}\ln\frac{\left|\frac{\hat{\Sigma}_1(i)+\hat{\Sigma}_2(i)}{2}\right|}{\sqrt{\left|\hat{\Sigma}_1(i)\right|\left|\hat{\Sigma}_2(i)\right|}}$$

**Step 5.** Compute the eigenvalues $(\lambda_1,\dots,\lambda_c)$ of the matrix $\hat{\Sigma}_2^{-1}(i)\hat{\Sigma}_1(i)$ and a matrix $A(i)$ whose columns $\Phi_i$ are eigenvectors of $\hat{\Sigma}_2^{-1}(i)\hat{\Sigma}_1(i)$ such that $A(i)A^T(i)=\hat{\Sigma}_2^{-1}(i)$, $i=1,c$.

**Step 6.** Arrange the eigenvalues such that for any $1\le s<j\le c$ ,

$$\frac{\left[\Phi_s^T\left(\hat{\mu}^{(2)}(i)-\hat{\mu}^{(1)}(i)\right)\right]^2}{1+\lambda_s}+\ln\left(2+\lambda_s+\frac{1}{\lambda_s}\right)\ge\frac{\left[\Phi_j^T\left(\hat{\mu}^{(2)}(i)-\hat{\mu}^{(1)}(i)\right)\right]^2}{1+\lambda_j}+\ln\left(2+\lambda_j+\frac{1}{\lambda_j}\right)$$

and select the feature matrix $M(i)=(\Phi_1,\dots,\Phi_k)^T$.

**Step 7.** Compute $T\left(\hat{\mu}^{(1)}(i)\right)$ by applying a threshold filter to $\hat{\mu}^{(1)}(i)$ and the correction term $Y(i)=M^T(i)\ T\left(\hat{\mu}^{(1)}(i)\right)$

**Step 8.** Compute the row $\overline{X}(i)$ of the restored image $\overline{X}$ by correcting the filtered image $T\left(\hat{\mu}^{(1)}(i)\right)$ using the information contained by the selected features, $\overline{X}(i)=T\left(\hat{\mu}^{(1)}(i)\right)+\sigma M(i)Y(i)$

where $\sigma$ is a noise-preventing constant conveniently determined to prevent the restoration of the initial noise, $0<\sigma<1$.

### 3.3 Wavelet-based denoising

The multiresolution support provides a suitable framework for noise filtering and image restoration by noise removal. Briefly, the idea is to determine a set of statistically significant wavelet coefficients from which the multiresolution support is extracted, that is the procedure is mainly based on an underlying statistical image model governing the whole process. The multiresolution support is the basis of subsequent filtering process.

We extend the MNR algorithm to the algorithm GMNR to allow the noise removal in more general cases when the noise mean can be any real number, and compare the performances of the resulted method against the most frequently used restoration algorithms (MMSE and AMVR). Briefly, the MNR algorithm is described as follows (Stark, Murtagh & Bijaoui, 1995). The parameter k used in Step 2 controls the width of the confidence interval, its value being set to a value around 3.

Input: The image $X_0$, the number of resolution levels p and the heuristic threshold k.

**Step 1.** Compute the sequence of image variants $\{X_j\}_{j=1,p}$ using a discrete low-pass filter h and get the wavelet coefficients by applying the "À Trous" algorithm

$$X_j(r,c)=\sum_l\sum_k h(l,k)X_{j-1}\left(r+2^{j-1}l,c+2^{j-1}k\right),\ \omega_j(r,c)=X_{j-1}(r,c)-X_j(r,c),$$

**Step 2.** Select the significant coefficients where $\omega_j(r,c)$ is taken as being significant if $\left|\omega_j(r,c)\right|\geq k\sigma_j$, for $j=1,\ldots,p$

**Step 3.** Use the filter g defined by $g\left(\sigma_j,\omega_j(r,c)\right)=\begin{cases}1, \left|\omega_j(r,c)\right|\geq k\sigma_j\\ 0, \left|\omega_j(r,c)\right|< k\sigma_j\end{cases}$ to compute the restored image, $\tilde{X}(r,c)=X_p(r,c)+\sum_{j=1}^{p}g\left(\sigma_j,\omega_j(r,c)\right)\omega_j(r,c)$,

Output The restored image $\tilde{X}$.

In the following, the algorithm GMNR is an extension of the MNR algorithm aiming to get the multiresolution support set in case of arbitrary noise mean, and to use this support set for noise removal purposes (Cocianu, State, Stefanescu, Vlamos, 2004). Let us denote by X the original "clean" image, and $\eta\sim N\left(m,\sigma^2\right)$ be the additively superimposed noise, that is the image to be processed is $Y=X+\eta$. Using the two-dimensional filter $\phi$, the sampled variants of X, Y and $\eta$ result by convoluting them with $\phi$ respectively,

$$c_0(x,y)=\left\langle Y(l,c),\phi(x-l,y-c)\right\rangle,\ I_0(x,y)=\left\langle X(l,c),\phi(x-l,y-c)\right\rangle,$$

$$E_0(x,y)=\left\langle \eta(l,c),\phi(x-l,y-c)\right\rangle, c_0=I_0+E_0.$$

The wavelet coefficients of $c_0$ computed by the algorithm "À Trous" are,

$$\omega_j^{c_0}(x,y)=\ \omega_j^{I_0}(x,y)+\omega_j^{E_0}(x,y), \text{ where } \frac{1}{2}\psi\left(\frac{x}{2}\right)=\varphi(x)-\frac{1}{2}\varphi\left(\frac{x}{2}\right).$$

For any pixel $(x,y)$, we get $c_p(x,y)=I_p(x,y)+E_p(x,y)$, where p stands for the number of the resolution levels, and the image $c_0$ is

$$c_0(x,y)=\ I_p(x,y)+E_p(x,y)+\sum_{j=1}^{p}\omega_j^{I_0}(x,y)+\sum_{j=1}^{p}\omega_j^{E_0}(x,y) \tag{13}$$

The noise mean can be inhibited by applying the following "white-wall" type technique.

**Step 1.** Get the set of images $E^{(i)}$, $1\leq i\leq n$, by additively superimposing noise $N\left(m,\sigma^2\right)$ on a "white wall" image.

**Step 2.** Compute $c_j$, $E_j^{(i)}$, and the coefficients $\omega_j^{c_0}$, $\omega_j^{E^{(i)}}$, $1\leq i\leq n$, $1\leq j\leq p$, by applying the "À Trous" algorithm.

**Step 3.** Get the image $\tilde{I}$ by averaging the resulted versions,

$$\tilde{I}(x,y)=\frac{1}{n}\sum_{i=1}^{n}\left[c_p(x,y)-E_p^{(i)}(x,y)+\sum_{j=1}^{p}\left(\omega_j^{c_0}(x,y)-\omega_j^{E^{(i)}}(x,y)\right)\right].$$

**Step 4.** Compute an approximation of the original image $I_0$ using the multiresolution filtering based on the statistically significant wavelet coefficients.

Note that $\tilde{I}$ computed at Step 3 is $\tilde{I}=I_0+E'$, where $E' \sim N\left(m',\sigma'^2\right)$, $m'\approx 0$ and $E\left(\sigma'^2\right)\approx\sigma^2$.

### 3.4 A combined noise removal method based on PCA and shrinkage functions

In the following, the data $\mathbf{X}$ is a collection of image representations modeled as a sample $\mathbf{X}_0$ coming from a multivariate wide sense stationary stochastic process of mean $\boldsymbol{\mu}$ and covariance matrix $\boldsymbol{\Sigma}$, each instance being affected by additively superimposed random noise. In general, the parameters $\boldsymbol{\mu}$ and $\boldsymbol{\Sigma}$ can not be assumed as been known and they are estimated from data. The most frequently used model for the noise component $\boldsymbol{\eta}$ is also a wide sense multivariate stationary stochastic process of Gaussian type. Denoting by n the dimensionality of the image representations, the simplest noise model is the "white" model, that is $\boldsymbol{\eta}=\left(\boldsymbol{\eta}_t,t\in[0,\infty)\right)$, where for any t≥0, $\boldsymbol{\eta}_t \sim N\left(\mathbf{0},\sigma^2\mathbf{I}_n\right)$. Consequently, the mathematical model for the noisy image versions is, $\mathbf{X}=\mathbf{X}_0+\boldsymbol{\eta}$.

The aim is to process the data $\mathbf{X}$ using estimates of $\boldsymbol{\mu}$, $\boldsymbol{\Sigma}$ and $\sigma^2$ to derive accurate approximations of $\mathbf{X}_0$.

The data are preprocessed to get normalized and centered representations. The preprocessing step is needed to enable the hypotheses that $0<\sigma^2<1$. If $\mathbf{Y}=\mathbf{X}_0-\boldsymbol{\mu}+\boldsymbol{\eta}$, then $\operatorname{Cov}\left(\mathbf{Y},\mathbf{Y}^T\right)=\boldsymbol{\Sigma}+\sigma^2\mathbf{I}_n$. Let $\theta_1\ge\theta_2\ge...\ge\theta_n$ be the eigen values of $\boldsymbol{\Sigma}$, $\boldsymbol{\Phi}=(\boldsymbol{\Phi}_1,\boldsymbol{\Phi}_2,...,\boldsymbol{\Phi}_n)$ an orthogonal matrix whose columns are unit eigen vectors of $\boldsymbol{\Sigma}$, and $\boldsymbol{\Lambda}=\operatorname{diag}(\lambda_1,\lambda_2,...,\lambda_n)$ the diagonal matrix whose entries are $\lambda_i=1+\frac{\sigma^2}{\theta_i}$.

We apply the linear transform of matrix $\mathbf{A}^T=\boldsymbol{\Lambda}^{-\frac{1}{2}}\boldsymbol{\Phi}^T$ to Y and get the representation $\mathbf{Z}=\mathbf{A}^T\mathbf{Y}=\mathbf{A}^T(\mathbf{X}_0-\boldsymbol{\mu})+\mathbf{A}^T\boldsymbol{\eta}$. Using the assumptions concerning the noise, $\mathbf{A}^T\boldsymbol{\eta}\sim N\left(\mathbf{0},\sigma^2\boldsymbol{\Lambda}^{-1}\right)$ and consequently, the components of $\mathbf{A}^T\boldsymbol{\eta}$ are independent, each component being of Gaussian type.

By applying the shrinkage function $g(y)=\operatorname{sign}(y)\max\left(0,|y|-\sqrt{2}\frac{\sigma^2}{\lambda_i}\right)$ to $\mathbf{Z}$ (Hyvarinen, 2001), we get the estimate $\tilde{\mathbf{Z}}_0$ of $\mathbf{Z}_0=\mathbf{A}^T(\mathbf{X}_0-\boldsymbol{\mu})$. Finally, using the equation $AA^T=\Sigma^{-1}$, we get the estimate $\hat{\mathbf{X}}_0=\boldsymbol{\mu}+\boldsymbol{\Sigma}\mathbf{A}\tilde{\mathbf{Z}}_0$ of $X_0$.

In the following, we combine the above described estimation process with a compression/decompression scheme, in order to remove the noise in a feature space of less dimensionality. For given $m, 1\le m\le n$, we denote by $\boldsymbol{\Phi}^m=(\boldsymbol{\Phi}_1,\boldsymbol{\Phi}_2,...,\boldsymbol{\Phi}_m)$ and $\boldsymbol{\Lambda}_m=\operatorname{diag}(\lambda_1,\lambda_2,...,\lambda_m)$ the matrix having as columns the first m columns of $\Phi$ and the diagonal matrix having as entries the first m entries of $\lambda$ respectively.

The noise removal process in the m-dimensional feature space applied to $F=\left(\mathbf{\Lambda}_m\right)^{-\frac{1}{2}}\left(\mathbf{\Phi}^m\right)^T\mathbf{Y}$ produces the cleaned version $F_0$, and consequently the estimate of $\mathbf{X}_0$ results by decompressing

$$F_0,\ \hat{\mathbf{X}}_0=\left(\left(\mathbf{\Lambda}_m\right)^{-\frac{1}{2}}\left(\mathbf{\Phi}^m\right)^T\right)^{+}F_0 .$$

The model-free version of CSPCA is a learning from data method that computes estimates of the first and second order statistics on the basis of a series of n-dimensional noisy images $\mathbf{X}_1,\mathbf{X}_2,...,\mathbf{X}_N,...$ (State, Cocianu, Sararu, Vlamos, 2009). Also, the estimates of the eigen values and eigen vectors of the sample covariance matrix are obtained using first order approximations derived in terms of perturbation theory. The first and second order statistics are computed in a classical way, that is

$$\boldsymbol{\mu}_N=\frac{1}{N}\sum_{i=1}^{N}\mathbf{X}_i \text{ and } \mathbf{\Sigma}_N=\frac{1}{N-1}\sum_{i=1}^{N}\left(\mathbf{X}_i-\boldsymbol{\mu}_N\right)\left(\mathbf{X}_i-\boldsymbol{\mu}_N\right)^T .$$

Using staightforward computation, the following recursive equations can be derived

$$\boldsymbol{\mu}_{N+1}=\frac{N}{N+1}\boldsymbol{\mu}_N+\frac{1}{N+1}\mathbf{X}_{N+1},\ \mathbf{\Sigma}_{N+1}=\mathbf{\Sigma}_N-\frac{1}{N}\mathbf{\Sigma}_N+\frac{1}{N+1}\left(\mathbf{X}_{N+1}-\boldsymbol{\mu}_N\right)\left(\mathbf{X}_{N+1}-\boldsymbol{\mu}_N\right)^T .$$

Denoting by $\Delta\mathbf{\Sigma}_N=\mathbf{\Sigma}_{N+1}-\mathbf{\Sigma}_N$, in case the eigen values of $\mathbf{\Sigma}_N$ are pairwise distinct, using arguments of perturbation theory type, the recursive equations for the eigen values and eigen vectors can be also derived (State, Cocianu, Vlamos, Stefanescu, 2006)

$$\lambda_i^{N+1}=\lambda_i^N+\left(\boldsymbol{\psi}_i^N\right)^T\Delta\mathbf{\Sigma}_N\boldsymbol{\psi}_i^N,\ \boldsymbol{\psi}_i^{N+1}=\boldsymbol{\psi}_i^N+\sum_{\substack{j=1\\ j\neq i}}^{n}\frac{\left(\boldsymbol{\psi}_N^j\right)^T\Delta\mathbf{\Sigma}_N\boldsymbol{\psi}_i^N}{\lambda_i^N-\lambda_j^N}\boldsymbol{\psi}_j^N .$$

Assume that the information is represented by $\boldsymbol{\mu}_N, \mathbf{\Sigma}_N, \mathbf{\Lambda}_N, \mathbf{\Phi}_N$, and a new noisy image $X_{N+1}$ is presented as input. Then the cleaned version $\hat{\mathbf{X}}_{N+1}$ of $X_{N+1}$ is computed and supplied as output followed by the updating $\boldsymbol{\mu}_{N+1}, \mathbf{\Sigma}_{N+1}, \mathbf{\Lambda}_{N+1}, \mathbf{\Phi}_{N+1}$. The updated values of these parameters are fed into the restoration module and they will be used for the next test.

The restoring algorithm can be described as follows. Assuming that $\mathbf{X}_1,\mathbf{X}_2,...,\mathbf{X}_{N_0}$ is the initial collection of noisy images, we evaluate $\boldsymbol{\mu}_{N_0}, \mathbf{\Sigma}_{N_0}, \mathbf{\Lambda}_{N_0}, \mathbf{\Phi}_{N_0}$. On the basis of these information, a number of M noisy images $\mathbf{X}_{N_0+1},...,\mathbf{X}_{N_0+M}$ are next processed according to the following scheme.

$k\leftarrow 1$

While $(k\le M)$

Get $\mathbf{X}_{N_0+k}$

Compute $\boldsymbol{\mu}_{N_0+k}, \mathbf{\Sigma}_{N_0+k}, \mathbf{\Lambda}_{N_0+k}, \mathbf{\Phi}_{N_0+k}$ (M1)

Compute $\hat{\mathbf{X}}_{N_0+k}$ (M2)

Output $\hat{\mathbf{X}}_{N_0+k}$

$k = k+1$

Endwhile

The computations carried out in the module M1 involve the stored parameters $\boldsymbol{\mu}_{N_0+k-1}, \boldsymbol{\Sigma}_{N_0+k-1}, \boldsymbol{\Lambda}_{N_0+k-1}, \boldsymbol{\Phi}_{N_0+k-1}$ and the noisy current image $\mathbf{X}_{N_0+k}$ to update the new values of the parameters $\boldsymbol{\mu}_{N_0+k}, \boldsymbol{\Sigma}_{N_0+k}, \boldsymbol{\Lambda}_{N_0+k}, \boldsymbol{\Phi}_{N_0+k}$. The new values of the parameters are fed into the module M2 and they are used to clean the input. The computation of the new values of the parameters is performed as,

$$\boldsymbol{\mu}_{N_0+k} = \frac{N_0+k-1}{N_0+k}\boldsymbol{\mu}_{N_0+k-1} + \frac{1}{N_0+k}\mathbf{X}_{N_0+k}$$

$$\boldsymbol{\Sigma}_{N_0+k} = \boldsymbol{\Sigma}_{N_0+k-1} - \frac{1}{N_0+k-1}\boldsymbol{\Sigma}_{N_0+k-1} + \frac{1}{N_0+k}\left(\mathbf{X}_{N_0+k} - \boldsymbol{\mu}_{N_0+k-1}\right)\left(\mathbf{X}_{N_0+k} - \boldsymbol{\mu}_{N_0+k-1}\right)^T$$

$$\lambda_i^{N_0+k} = \lambda_i^{N_0+k-1} + \left(\boldsymbol{\psi}_i^{N_0+k-1}\right)^T \Delta\boldsymbol{\Sigma}_{N_0+k-1}\boldsymbol{\psi}_i^{N_0+k-1}$$

$$\boldsymbol{\psi}_i^{N_0+k} = \boldsymbol{\psi}_i^{N_0+k-1} + \sum_{\substack{j=1 \\ j\neq i}}^{n} \frac{\left(\boldsymbol{\psi}_j^{N_0+k-1}\right)^T \Delta\boldsymbol{\Sigma}_{N_0+k-1}\boldsymbol{\psi}_i^{N_0+k-1}}{\lambda_i^{N_0+k-1} - \lambda_j^{N_0+k-1}}\boldsymbol{\psi}_j^{N_0+k-1}$$

$$\boldsymbol{\Lambda}_{N_0+k} = diag\left\{\lambda_1^{N_0+k},...,\lambda_n^{N_0+k}\right\}$$

$$\boldsymbol{\Phi}_{N_0+k} = \left(\boldsymbol{\psi}_1^{N_0+k},...,\boldsymbol{\psi}_n^{N_0+k}\right)$$

The cleaned version $\hat{\mathbf{X}}_{N_0+k}$ of each input $\mathbf{X}_{N_0+k}$ is obtained by applying the previously described shrinkage technique, as follows.

$$\mathbf{Y}_{N_0+k} = \mathbf{X}_{N_0+k} - \boldsymbol{\mu}_{N_0+k}$$

$$\mathbf{A}_{N_0+k} = \boldsymbol{\Phi}_{N_0+k}\left(\boldsymbol{\Lambda}_{N_0+k}\right)^{-\frac{1}{2}}$$

$$\mathbf{Z}_{N_0+k} = \left(\mathbf{A}_{N_0+k}\right)^T \mathbf{Y}_{N_0+k}$$

Compute $\tilde{\mathbf{Z}}_{N_0+k}$ by applying the shrinkage function to $\mathbf{Z}_{N_0+k}$.

$$\hat{\mathbf{X}}_{N_0+k} = \boldsymbol{\mu}_{N_0+k} + \boldsymbol{\Sigma}_{N_0+k}\mathbf{A}_{N_0+k}\tilde{\mathbf{Z}}_{N_0+k}$$

Let us assume that the L gray levels of the initial image X are affected by noise of Gaussian type $\eta \sim N(0,\Sigma)$, and denote by $\Phi$ an orthogonal $n \times n$ matrix whose columns are unit eigen vectors of $\Sigma$, where n is the dimension of the input space. If $\Sigma$ is known, the matrix $\Phi$ can be computed by classical techniques, respectively in cases when $\Sigma$ is not known, the columns of $\Phi$ can be learned adaptively by PCA networks (Rosca, State, Cocianu, 2008).

We denote by Y the resulted image, $Y = X + \eta$. The images are represented by RxC matrices, they are processed by blocks of size $R \times C_1$, $C = pC_1, 2 \le p < C$. In the preprocessing step, using the matrix $\Phi$, the noise is removed by applying the MNR algorithm to the de-correlated blocks of $Y' = \Phi^T Y$.

The restoration process of the image Y using the learned features is performed as follows (State, Cocianu, 2007)

**Step 1.** Compute the image Y′ on the basis of the initial image by de-correlating the noise component $Y'_{i,j} = \Phi^T Y_{i,j} = \Phi^T X_{i,j} + \eta'$, $1 \le i \le R$, $1 \le j \le C_1$, where $\Phi$ is a matrix of unit eigen vectors of the noise covariance matrix. Then $\eta' = \Phi^T \eta \sim N(0,\Lambda)$ because $\Phi^T \Sigma \Phi = \Lambda = diag\{\lambda_1, \lambda_2, ..., \lambda_n\}$, where $\{\lambda_1, \lambda_2, ..., \lambda_n\}$ are the eigen values of $\Sigma$.

**Step 2.** Remove the noise $\eta'$ from the image Y′ using its multirezolution support. The image Y″ results by labeling each wavelet coefficient of each pixel.

$$Y''_{i,j} = MNR\left(Y'_{i,j}\right) \cong \Phi^T X_{i,j},\ \forall i = 1,...,R,\ j = 1,...,C_1,$$

**Step 3.** Compute an approximation $\tilde{X} \approx X$ of the initial image X by applying the linear transform of matrix $\Phi$ to Y″, $\tilde{X}_{i,j} = \Phi Y''_{i,j} \cong \Phi\Phi^T X_{i,j} = X_{i,j}$, $\forall i = 1,...,R$, $j = 1,...,C_1$

## 4. Conclusions and experimental comparative analysis on the performances of some noise removal and restoration algorithms

In order to evaluate the performance of the proposed noise removal algorithms, a series of experiments were performed on different 256 gray level images. We compare the performance of our algorithm NFPCA against MMSE, AMVR, and GMNR. The implementation of the GMNR algorithm used the masks

$$h_1 = \begin{pmatrix} \frac{1}{256} & \frac{1}{64} & \frac{3}{128} & \frac{1}{64} & \frac{1}{256} \\ \frac{1}{64} & \frac{1}{16} & \frac{3}{32} & \frac{1}{16} & \frac{1}{64} \\ \frac{3}{128} & \frac{3}{32} & \frac{9}{64} & \frac{3}{32} & \frac{3}{128} \\ \frac{1}{64} & \frac{1}{16} & \frac{3}{32} & \frac{1}{16} & \frac{1}{64} \\ \frac{1}{256} & \frac{1}{64} & \frac{3}{128} & \frac{1}{64} & \frac{1}{256} \end{pmatrix} \text{ and } h_2 = \begin{pmatrix} \frac{1}{20} & \frac{1}{10} & \frac{1}{20} \\ \frac{1}{10} & \frac{2}{5} & \frac{1}{10} \\ \frac{1}{20} & \frac{1}{10} & \frac{1}{20} \end{pmatrix}.$$

Some of the conclusions experimentally derived concerning the comparative analysis of the restoration algorithms presented in the paper against some similar techniques are presented in Table 1, and Table 2. The aims of the comparative analysis were to establish quantitative indicators to express both the quality and efficiency of each algorithm. The values of the variances in modeling the noise in images processed by the NFPCA represent the maximum of the variances per pixel resulted from the decorrelation process. We denote by U(a,b) the uniform distribution on the interval [a,b] and by $N(\mu,\sigma^2)$ the Gaussian distribution of mean $\mu$ and variance $\sigma^2$.

It seems that the AMVR algorithm proves better performances from the point of view of mean error per pixel in case of uniform distributed noise as well as in case of Gaussian type noise. Also, it seems that at least for 0-mean Gaussian distributed noise, the mask $h_2$ provides less mean error per pixel when the restoration is performed by the MNR algorithm.

Several tests were performed to investigate the potential of the proposed CSPCA. The tests were performed on data represented by linearized monochrome images decomposed in blocks of size 8x8. The preprocessing step was included in order to get normalized, centered representations. Most of the tests were performed on samples of volume 20, the images of each sample sharing the same statistical properties. The proposed method proved good performance for cleaning noisy images keeping the computational complexity at a reasonable level. An example of noisy image and its cleaned version respectively are presented in Figure 1.

| *Restoration algorithm* | *Type of noise* | *Mean error/pixel* |
|---|---|---|
| MMSE | U(30,80) | 52.08 |
| AMVR | | 10.94 |
| MMSE | U(40,70) | 50.58 |
| AMVR | | 8,07 |
| MMSE | N(40,200) | 37.51 |
| AMVR | | 11.54 |
| GMNR | | 14.65 |
| NFPCA | | 12.65 |
| MMSE | N(50,100) | 46.58 |
| AMVR | | 9.39 |
| GMNR | | 12.23 |
| NFPCA | | 10.67 |

Table 1. Comparative analysis on the performance of the proposed algorithms

| *Restoration algorithm* | *Type of noise* | *Mean error/pixel* |
|---|---|---|
| MNR $(h_1)$ | N(0,100) | 11.6 |
| MNR $(h_2)$ | | 9.53 |
| MNR $(h_1)$ | N(0,200) | 14.16 |
| MNR $(h_2)$ | | 11.74 |

Table 2. Comparative analysis on MNR

The tests performed on new sample of images pointed out good generalization capacities and robustness of CSPCA. The computational complexity of CSPCA method is less than the complexity of the ICA code shrinkage method.

A synthesis of the comparative analysis on the quality and efficiency corresponding to the restoration algorithms presented in section 3.2 is supplied in Table 3.

So far, the tests were performed on monochrome images only. Some efforts that are still in progress aim to adapt and extend the proposed methodology to colored images. Although the extension is not straightforward and some major modifications have to be done, the already obtained results encourage the hopes that efficient variants of these algorithms can be obtained for noise removal in case of colored images too.

The tests on the proposed algorithms were performed on images of size 256x256 pixels, by splitting the images in blocks of smaller size, depending on the particular algorithm. For instance, in case of algorithms MNR and GMNR, the images are processed pixel by pixel, and the computation of the wavelet coefficients by the "A Trous" algorithm is carried out using 3x3 and 5x5 masks. The tests performed on NFPCA, CSPCA, and the model free version of CSPCA processed blocks of 8x8 pixels.

| *Restoration algorithm* | *Mean error/pixel* Noise distributed N(30,150) | *Mean error/pixel* Noise distributed N(50,200) |
|---|---|---|
| Mean | 9.422317 | 12.346784 |
| HRBA | 9.333114 | 11.747860 |
| HSBA | 9.022712 | 11.500245 |
| HBA | 9.370968 | 11.484837 |

Table 3. Comparative analysis on the performance of the proposed algorithms

The initial noisy image

The cleaned version of the initial image

Fig. 1. The performance of model-free version of CSPCA

The comparison of the proposed algorithm NFPCA and the currently used approaches MMSE and AMVR points out better results of NFPCA in terms of the mean error per pixel. Some of the conclusions are summarized in Table 1 and Table 2, where the noise was modeled using the uniform and normal distributions. As it is shown in Table 1, in case of the AMVR algorithm the mean error per pixel is slightly less than in case of using NFPCA, but the AMVR algorithm induces some blur effect in the image while the use of the NFPCA seems to assure reasonable small errors without inducing any annoying side effects.

The tests performed on new sample of images pointed out good generalization capacities and robustness of CSPCA. The computational complexity of CSPCA method is less than the complexity of the ICA code shrinkage method. The authors aim to extend the work from both, methodological and practical points of view. From methodological point of view, some refinements of the proposed procedures and their performances are going to be evaluated on standard large size image databases are in progress. From practical point of view, the procedures are going to be extended in solving specifics GIS tasks.

So far, the tests were performed on monochrome images only. Some efforts that are still in progress aim to adapt and extend the proposed methodology to colored images. Although the extension is not straightforward and some major modifications have to be done, the already obtained results encourage the hopes that efficient variants of these algorithms can be obtained for noise removal in case of colored images too.

The tests on the proposed algorithms were performed on images of size 256x256 pixels, by splitting the images in blocks of smaller size, depending on the particular algorithm. For instance, in case of the algorithms MNR and GMNR, the images are processed pixel by pixel, and the computation of the wavelet coefficients by the "A Trous" algorithm is carried out using 3x3 and 5x5 masks. The tests performed on NFPCA, CSPCA, and the model free version of CSPCA processed blocks of 8x8 pixels.

## 5. References


Anderson, T.W. (1958) An Introduction to Multivariate Statistical Analysis, John Wiley &Sons

Bacchelli, S., Papi S. (2006). Image denoising using principal component analysis in the wavelet domain. Journal of Computational and Applied Mathematics, *Volume 189, Issues 1-2*, 1 May 2006, 606-62

Balster, E. J., Zheng, Y. F., Ewing, R. L. (2003). Fast, Feature-Based Wavelet Shrinkage Algorithm for Image Denoising. In: International Conference on Integration of Knowledge IntensiveMulti-Agent Systems. KIMAS '03: Modeling, Exploration, and Engineering Held in Cambridge, MA on 30 September-October 4

Beheshti, S. and Dahleh, M.A. , (2003 ) *A new information-theoretic approach to signal denoising and best basis selection In:* IEEE Trans. On *Signal Processing*, Volume: 53, Issue:10,Part 1, 2003: 3613- 3624

Buades, A., Coll, B., and Morel, J.-M., (2005) *A non-local algorithm for image denoising, In:*IEEE Computer Society Conference on Computer Vision and Pattern Recognition. CVPR 2005. Volume 2, Issue , 20-25 June 2005 Page(s): 60 - 65 vol. 2

Chatterjee, C., Roychowdhury, V.P., Chong, E.K.P. (1998). On Relative Convergence Properties of Principal Component Analysis Algorithms. In: IEEE Transaction on Neural Networks, vol.9,no.2

Chellappa, R. , Jinchi, H. (1985). A nonrecursive Filter for Edge Preserving Image Restoration In: Proc. Intl.Conf.on Acoustic, Speech and Signal Processing, Tampa 1985

Cocianu, C., State, L., Stefanescu, V., Vlamos, P. (2004) On the Efficiency of a Certain Class of Noise Removal Algorithms in Solving Image Processing Tasks. In: Proceedings of the ICINCO 2004, Setubal, Portugal

Cocianu, C., State, L., Vlamos, P. (2002). On a Certain Class of Algorithms for Noise Removal in Image Processing:A Comparative Study, In: Proceedings of the Third IEEE Conference on Information Technology ITCC-2002, Las Vegas, Nevada, USA, April 8-10, 2002

Cocianu, C., State, L., Vlamos, P. (2007). Principal Axes - Based Classification with Application in Gaussian Distributed Sample Recognition. Economic Computation and Economic Cybernetics Studies and Research, Vol. 41, No 1-2/2007, 159-166

Deng, G., Tay, D., Marusic, S. (2007). *A signal denoising algorithm based on overcomplete wavelet representations and Gaussian models.* Signal Processing *Volume 87, Issue 5 (May 2007),* 866-876

Diamantaras, K.I., Kung, S.Y. (1996). Principal Component Neural Networks: theory and applications,. John Wiley &Sons

Duda, R.O., Hart,P.E. Pattern Classification and Scene Analysis,Wiley&Sons, 1973

Fukunaga K., Introduction to Statistical Pattern Recognition, Academic Press,Inc. 1990

Gonzales, R., Woods, R. (2002) Digital Image Processing, Prentice Hall

Haykin, S. (1999) Neural Networks A Comprehensive Foundation, Prentice Hall, Inc.

Hyvarinen, A., Hoyer, P., Oja, P. (1999). Image Denoising by Sparse Code Shrinkage, *www.cis.hut.fi/projects/ica,*

Hyvarinen, A., Karhunen, J., Oja,E. (2001) Independent Component Analysis, John Wiley &Sons

J. Karhunen, E. Oja. (1982). New Methods for Stochastic Approximations of Truncated Karhunen-Loeve Expansions, In: Proceedings 6$^{th}$ International Conference on Pattern Recognition, Springer Verlag

Jain, A. K., Kasturi, R., Schnuck, B. G. (1995) Machine Vision, McGraw Hill

Pitas, I. (1993). Digital Image Processing Algorithms, Prentice Hall

Rioul, O., Vetterli, M. (1991). Wavelets and signal processing. IEEE Signal Processing Mag. 8(4), 14-38

Rosca, I., State, L., Cocianu, C. (2008) Learning Schemes in Using PCA Neural Networks for Image Restoration Purposes. WSEAS Transactions on Information Science and Applications, Vol. 5, July 2008, 1149-1159,

Sanger, T.D. (1989). An Optimality Principle for Unsupervised Learning, Advances in Neural Information Systems, ed. D.S. Touretzky, Morgan Kaufmann

Sonka, M., Hlavac, V. (1997). Image Processing, Analyses and Machine Vision, Chapman & Hall Computing

Stark, J.L., Murtagh, F., Bijaoui, A. (1995). Multiresolution Support Applied to Image Filtering and Restoration, Technical Report

State L, Cocianu C, Panayiotis V., Attempts in Using Statistical Tools for Image Restoration Purposes, The Proceedings of SCI2001, Orlando, USA, July 22-25, 2001

State, L, Cocianu, C, Vlamos, P. (2008). A New Unsupervized Learning Scheme to Classify Data of Relative Small Volume. Economic Computation and Economic Cybernetics Studies and Research, 2008, 109-120

State, L, Cocianu, C, Vlamos, P., Stefanescu, V. (2006) PCA-Based Data Mining Probabilistic and Fuzzy Approaches with Applications in Pattern Recognition.In: Proceedings of ICSOFT 2006

State, L., Cocianu, C., Săraru, C., Vlamos, P. (2009) New Approaches in Image Compression and Noise Removal, Proceedings of the First International Conference on Advances in Satellite and Space Communications, SPACOMM 2009, IEEE Computer Society Press, 2009

State, L., Cocianu, C., Vlamos, P. (2007) The Use of Features Extracted from Noisy Samples for Iimage Restoration Purposes, Informatica Economică, Nr. 41/2007

State, L., Cocianu, C., Vlamos, P., Stefanescu, V.(2005) Noise Removal Algorithm Based on Code Shrinkage Technique, Proceedings of the 9th World Multiconference on Systemics, Cybernetics and Informatics (WMSCI 2005), Orlando, USA

Umbaugh, S. (1998). Computer Vision and Image Processing, Prentice Hall

# 3

# Entropic Image Restoration as a Dynamic System with Entropy Operator

Yuri S. Popkov
*Institute for Systems Analysis*
*Russia*

## 1. Introduction

Entropy and the classical variational principle of the statistical physics are the effective tools for modeling and solving a lot of applied problems. There are many definitions of "entropy" functions. The book by Kapur (1989) contains some of them. The classical definition of the *physical* entropy was introduced by L.Boltzmann Boltzmann (1871) and was developed for Fermi- and Einstein-statistics Landau & Livshitz (1964). Notion of entropy was introduced for para-statistics that have position between Fermi- and Einstein-statistics (Ohnuki & Kamefuchi (1982), Dorofeev et al. (2008)).

Variation principle of entropy maximization turned out very useful for information theory, the base of which connected with Shannon (Shannon (1948), Kullback & Leibler (1951)). This direction is developed in the book Popkov (1995), where introduced generalized information entropies by Fermi-Dirac and Bose-Einstein (entropy with parameters). Entropy maximization are applied to image reconstruction from projections Byrne (1993). A large number of applications of the entropy maximization principle is contained in Fang et al. (1997), Maslov (2003).

In these papers the entropy conditional maximization problems with linear constraints equalities were considered only. However there are many problems of entropy maximization with feasible set that is described by a system of inequalities and not only a linear one.

In this paper we design the models of the entropy image reconstruction from projections (EIRP) as the entropy linear (ELP) and quadratic maximization problems (EQP), where the feasible sets are described by the system of the equalities and inequalities of appropriate types (linear and quadratic one).

The regular procedure for design of multiplicative algorithms with $p$-active variables with respect to dual variables and to mixed (dual and primal) variables proposed for the problem solving. The choice of the active variables is implemented by feedback control with respect to the current state of the iterative process.

The problem of reconstruction of images of the objects distorted by noises and hidden from direct observation arises in the different fields. One of the trends in the solution of the problem is based on the tomographic investigation of an object, i.e., the construction of its layer-by-layer projections. The projections can be formed as external irradiation sources(X-ray, ultrasonic sources) and internal ones (positron emission) as also with the aid of their combination (nuclear magnetic resonance) (Herman (1980), Dhawan (2003)). In Popkov (1997) is shown that a distribution of the absobed photons in slab maximizes the generalized entropy by Fermi-Dirac under the set of projections. A generalization consists in the inclusion of an additional parameters in entropy function, through which it is possible to take into account prior information on the object.

Our contribution to the theory and applications of the EIRP consists in three parts.

*The first contribution* is the general entropy models in the terms of entropy linear programming (ELP) or entropy quadratic programming (EQP) that underlie in the *static* procedures of computer tomography. At the beginning of the static procedure, it is occured an accumulation of a complete set of the projections by means of the external irradiation of the object. Then it is solved the ELP or EQP. As a result, for the prescribed prior image, we obtain an entropy-optimal restored image, which we will be called a *posterior image*.

It calls for a rather high irradiation intensity so as to afford a sufficient noise immunity of a reconstructed image. However, for some classes of tomographic investigations a high irradiation intensity is extremely undesirable.

Multiplicative procedures represent to the ELP and EQP solving. Apparently, the first general approach for synthesis of such procedures was proposed in (Dubov et al. (1983)). Simple multiplicative algorithm was applied to minimization of strictly convex functions on nonnegative orthant. Later, the multiplicative algorithms with respect to dual variables are used for solving conditional minimization and mathematical programming problems (Aliev et al. (1985), Popkov (1988), Popkov (1995a)). Also, the multiplicative algorithms are used for solving nonlinear equations (Popkov (1996)). The multiplicative procedures for finding nonnegative solutions of the minimization problems over nonnegative optant were proposed again in the paper (Iusem et al. (1996)).

Some types of the multiplicative algorithms are derived from approach based on the Bregman function and generalized projections with Shannon's entropy. In this case we obtain so-called *row-action algorithms*, iterations of which have a multiplicative form. The algorithms of this type was developed and modified (Herman (1982), Censor (1981), Censor (1987), Byrne (1996), Censor & Zenios (1997)).

It is necessary to note that in the most cited works the multiplicative algorithms are applied to the problems of entropy maximization with linear constraints equalities. We consider the ELP problem, where a feasible set is described by the system of the linear equalities and inequalities. The regular procedure for design of multiplicative algorithms with *p-active* variables is proposed for solving of this problem. On the basis of the procedure above we sinthesize the algorithms with respect to dual variables and to mixed (dual and primal) variables simultaneously. The choice of the active variables is implemented by feedback control with respect to the current state of the iterative process. Convergence study of the multiplicative algorithms is based on the continuous analogues of the algorithms and equivalence of the iterative sequences generated by the dual and mixed type algorithms. (Popkov (2006)).

*Our second contribution* is connected with a *basically another approach* to the EIRP. It is a *dynamic* procedure consisting in the sequential refinement in time of the image synthesized. The suggested procedures do not require a high irradiation intensity and display a high noise stability.

On the each step $t$ of the dynamic procedure *t-posterior image* is build up as a solution of the ELP or EQP, using the current *t-prior image* and the current projection. The $(t-s),(t-s+1),\ldots,$ *t-posterior images* take part in formation of *(t+1)-prior image*. So the dynamic procedures are procedures with feedback.

The dynamic procedures are closed in the sense that at each stage for the current *t-prior image* and the *t-projection*, the entropy-optimal *t-posterior image* is built up, by which the *(t+1)-prior image* is corrected.

We consider a diverse structures of the dynamic procedures with feedback and investigate their properties. The example of application of these procedures is presented.

It is shown that the proposed dynamic procedures of the EIRP represent the dynamic systems with entropy operator (DSEO). And *our third contribution* is an elements of the *qualitative analysis of the DSEO*. We consider the properties of the entropy operator (boundedness, Lipschitz constant).

## 2. Mathematical model of the static EIRP procedure

Consider a common diagram of monochrome tomographic investigation (fig. 1), where external beams of photons $\mathbb{S}$ irradiate the flat object in the direction $AB$. The object is monochromatic, and is described by the two-dimensional function of optical density $\psi(x,y)$ in the system of Cartesian coordinates. Positive values of the density function are limited:

$$0 < a \leq \psi(x,y) \leq b < 1. \tag{2.1}$$

The intensity of irradiation (projection) $w$ at the point $B$ of the detector $\mathbb{D}$ (fig. 1) is related by the Radon transformation:

$$w(B) = \exp\left(-\int_{l\in AB} \psi(x,y)dl\right), \tag{2.2}$$

where the integration is realized along straight $AB$.

It is common to manipulate the digital representation of the density function $\psi(l,s)$, $(l=\overline{1,L},\ s=\overline{1,S})$. Introduce $i=S(l-1)+s$, $i=\overline{1,m}$, $m=LS$, and martix $\Psi=[\psi(l,s)|\, l=\overline{1,L},\ s=\overline{1,S}]$ as a vector $\bar{\psi}=\{\psi_1,\ldots,\psi_m\}$.

The tomographic procedure form some feasible sets for the vector $\bar{\psi}$:

$$\mathcal{L} = \{\bar{\psi} : \mathbf{L}(\bar{\psi}) \leq \mathbf{g}\}, \tag{2.3}$$

where $\mathbf{L}(\bar{\psi})$ is the $h$-vector function, and $\mathbf{g}$ is the $h$-vector. We consider the quadratic approximation of the function $L$:

$$\mathbf{L}(\bar{\psi}) = L\,\bar{\psi} + \mathbf{Q}(\bar{\psi}), \tag{2.4}$$

where $L$ is the $(h\times m)$-matrix with nonnegative elements $l_{ki}\geq 0$; $\mathbf{Q}(\bar{\psi})$ is the $h$-vector of the quadratic forms:

$$\mathbf{Q}(\bar{\psi}) = \bar{\psi}'\, Q^k\, \bar{\psi}, \tag{2.5}$$

where $Q^k$ is the symmetric $(m\times m)$-matrix with elements $q^k_{ij}\geq 0$.

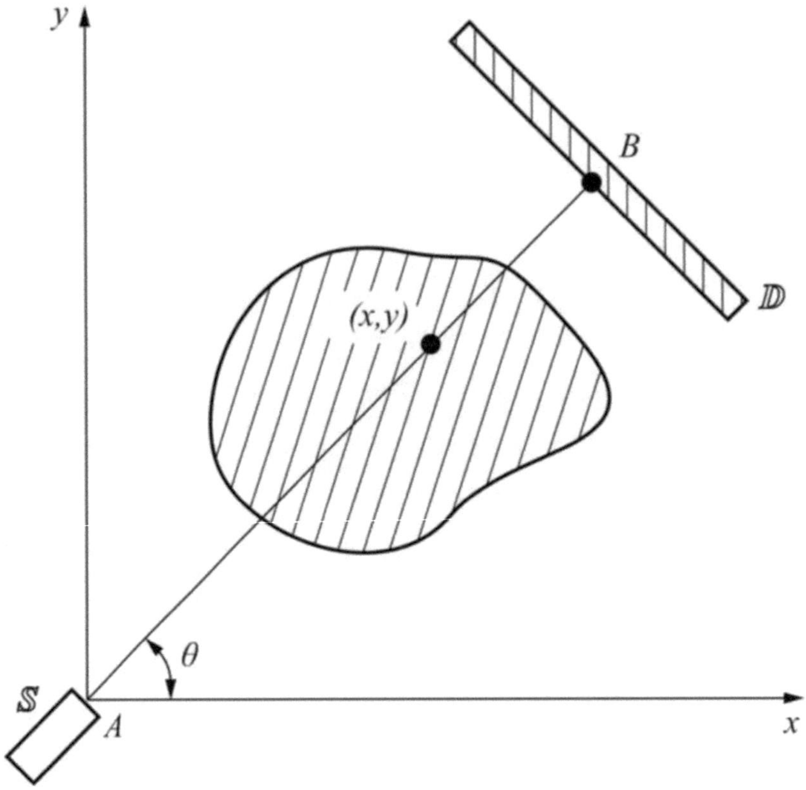


Fig. 1. Tomography scheme

Now it is returned to the projection function (2.2), and we use its quadratic approximation:

$$\mathbf{w}(B) \simeq T\,\bar{\psi} + \mathbf{F}(\bar{\psi}) = \mathbf{u}, \tag{2.6}$$

where: $\mathbf{w}(B) = \{w(B_1), \ldots, w(B_n)\}$, $T$ is the $(n \times m)$-matrix with elements $t_{ki} \geq 0$; $\mathbf{F}(\bar{\psi})$ is the $n$-vector function with components $F^r\bar{\psi}) = \bar{\psi}'\,F^r\,\bar{\psi}$, where $F^r$ is the symmetric $(m \times m)$-matrix with elements $f^r_{ij} \geq 0$.

Any tomographic investigation occurs in the presence of noises. So the $n$-projections vector $\mathbf{u}$ is a random vector with independent components $u_n$, $n = \overline{1,m}$, $\mathcal{M}\,\mathbf{u} = \mathbf{u}^0 \geq 0, \mathcal{M}\,(\mathbf{u} - \mathbf{u}^0)^2 = \text{diag}\,[\sigma^2]$, where $\mathbf{u}^0$ is the ideal projections vector (without noise), and $\sigma^2$ is the dispersion of the noise. It is assumed that the dispersions of the noise components are equal.

Thus, the feasible set $\mathcal{D}(\bar{\psi})$ is described the following expressions:

- the projections are

$$T\bar{\psi} + \mathbf{F}(\bar{\psi}) = \mathbf{u}, \tag{2.7}$$

- the possible set of the density vectors is

$$L\,\bar{\psi} + \mathbf{Q}(\bar{\psi}) \leq \mathbf{g}. \tag{2.8}$$

The class $\mathcal{P}$ of the density vectors is characterized by the following inequalities:

$$\mathbf{0} < \mathbf{a} \leq \bar{\psi} \leq \mathbf{b} < \mathbf{1}. \tag{2.9}$$

It is assumed that among dimensions of the density vectors ($m$), the projection vectors ($n$), and the possible set ($h$) the following inequality exists:

$$m > n + h. \tag{2.10}$$

It is assumed that the feasible set is nonempty for the class (2.9), and there exists a set of the density vectors $\bar{\psi}$ (2.9), that belong to the feasible set $\mathcal{D}$ (2.7, 2.8).

We will use the variation principle of the EIRP Popkov (1997), according to which the realizable density vector (function) $\bar{\psi}$ maximizes the entropy (the generalized information entropy by Fermi-Dirac):

$$H(\bar{\psi} \,|\, \mathbf{a}, \mathbf{b}, \mathbf{E}) = -[\bar{\psi} - \mathbf{a}]' \ln \frac{\bar{\psi} - \mathbf{a}}{\mathbf{E}} - [\mathbf{b} - \bar{\psi}]' \ln[\mathbf{b} - \bar{\psi}], \tag{2.11}$$

where:

- $\mathbf{E} = \{E_1, \ldots, E_m\}$ is the $m$-vector characterizing the prior image (prior probabilities of photon absorption in the object);

- $\ln[(\bar{\psi} - \mathbf{a}) \,/\, \mathbf{E}]$ is the vector with components $\ln[(\psi_i - a_i) \,/\, E_i]$;

- $\ln[\mathbf{b} - \bar{\psi}]$ is the vector with components $\ln(b_i - \psi_i)$.

If there is information about more or less "grey" object then we can use the next entropy function (the generalized information entropy by Boltzmann):

$$H(\bar{\psi} \,|\, \mathbf{E}) = -\bar{\psi}' \ln \frac{\bar{\psi}}{e\mathbf{E}}, \tag{2.12}$$

where $e = 2{,}73$.

Thus, the problem of the EIRP can be formulated in the next form:

$$H(\bar{\psi} \,|\, \mathbf{a}, \mathbf{b}, \mathbf{E}) \Rightarrow \max_{\bar{\psi}}, \qquad \bar{\psi} \in \mathcal{D}(\bar{\psi}) \bigcap \mathcal{P}, \tag{2.13}$$

where the feasible set $\mathcal{D}(\bar{\psi})$ is described by the expressions (2.7 - 2.8) and the class $\mathcal{P}$ is described by the inequalities (2.9). This problem is related to the EQP or the ELP depend on the feasible set construction.

## 3. Statements and algorithms for the ELP and the EQP

Transform the problem (2.13) to the general form, for that introduce the following designations:

$$\begin{aligned} \mathbf{x} &= \bar{\psi} - \mathbf{a}, \quad \tilde{\mathbf{b}} = \mathbf{b} - \mathbf{a}, \\ \tilde{\mathbf{g}} &= \mathbf{g} - \{\mathbf{a}'\, Q^k\, \mathbf{a},\, k = \overline{1,h}\} - L\mathbf{a}, \\ \tilde{\mathbf{u}} &= \mathbf{u} - \{\mathbf{a}'\, F^r\, \mathbf{a},\, r = \overline{1,n}\} - T\mathbf{a}. \end{aligned} \tag{3.1}$$

Then the problem (2.13) takes a form:

$$H(\mathbf{x}, \tilde{\mathbf{b}}, \mathbf{E}) = -\mathbf{x}' \ln \frac{\mathbf{x}}{\mathbf{E}} - [\tilde{\mathbf{b}} - \mathbf{x}]' \ln[\tilde{\mathbf{b}} - \mathbf{x}] \Rightarrow \max, \tag{3.2}$$

under the following constraints:

- the projections

$$\tilde{T}\mathbf{x} + \{\mathbf{x}' F^r \mathbf{x}, r = \overline{1,n}\} = \tilde{\mathbf{u}}, \tag{3.3}$$

- the possible set

$$\tilde{L}\mathbf{x} + \{\mathbf{x}' Q^k \mathbf{x}, k = \overline{1,h}\} \leq \tilde{\mathbf{g}}, \tag{3.4}$$

where

$$\begin{aligned} \tilde{T} &= T + A_F,, \qquad A_F = 2[\mathbf{a}' F^r, r = \overline{1,n}], \\ \tilde{L} &= L + A_Q, \qquad A_Q = 2[\mathbf{a}' Q^k, k = \overline{1,h}] \end{aligned} \tag{3.5}$$

Remark that the constraints (2.9) are absent in the problem (3.2, 3.4), as they are included to the goal function.

### 3.1 The ELP problem

**1. Optimality conditions.** The feasible set in the ELP problem is described by the next expressions:

$$T\mathbf{x} = \hat{\mathbf{u}}, \qquad L\mathbf{x} \leq \hat{\mathbf{g}}, \tag{3.6}$$

where

$$\hat{\mathbf{u}} = \mathbf{u} - T\mathbf{a}, \qquad \hat{\mathbf{g}} = \mathbf{g} - L\mathbf{a}. \tag{3.7}$$

Consider the Lagrange function for the ELP (3.2, 3.6):

$$\mathrm{L}(\mathbf{x}, \bar{\lambda}, \bar{\mu}) = H(\mathbf{x}, \tilde{\mathbf{b}}, \mathbf{E}) + [\hat{\mathbf{u}} - T\mathbf{x}]' \bar{\lambda} + [\hat{\mathbf{g}} - L\mathbf{x}]' \bar{\mu}, \tag{3.8}$$

where $\bar{\lambda}, \bar{\mu}$ are the Lagrange multipliers for constraints-equalities and -inequalities (3.6) correspondingly. Assume that the Slater conditions are valid, i.e., there exists a vector $\mathbf{x}^0$ such that $L\mathbf{x}^0 < \hat{\mathbf{g}},\ T\mathbf{x}^0 = \hat{\mathbf{u}}$.

According to Polyak (1987) the following expressions give the necessary and sufficient conditions optimality of the triple $(\mathbf{x}, \bar{\lambda}, \bar{\mu})$ for the problem (3.2 - 3.5):

$$\nabla_{\mathbf{x}}\mathrm{L} = 0, \quad \nabla_{\bar{\lambda}}\mathrm{L} = 0, \quad \nabla_{\bar{\mu}}\mathrm{L} \geq 0, \tag{3.9}$$

$$\bar{\mu} \otimes \nabla_{\mu}\mathrm{L} = 0, \qquad \bar{\mu} \geq 0, \tag{3.10}$$

where $\otimes$ designates a coordinate-wise multiplication.

The following designations are used in these expressions:

$$\nabla_{\mathbf{x}}\mathrm{L} = \frac{\partial H}{\partial \mathbf{x}} - T' \bar{\lambda} - L' \bar{\mu}, \tag{3.11}$$

$$\nabla_{\bar{\lambda}}\mathrm{L} = \hat{\mathbf{u}} - T\mathbf{x}, \tag{3.12}$$

$$\nabla_{\bar{\mu}}\mathrm{L} = \hat{\mathbf{g}} - L\mathbf{x}, \tag{3.13}$$

(3.14)

From the optimality conditions (3.9) we have:

$$
\begin{aligned}
&x_i(\mathbf{z},\bar{\mu}) = y_i(\mathbf{z})\, d_i(\bar{\mu}),\\
&y_i(\mathbf{z}) = \tilde{b}_i \left[1 + \frac{1}{E_i}\prod_{j=1}^{n} z_j^{t_{ji}}\right]^{-1},\\
&d_i(\bar{\mu}) = \tilde{b}_i \left[1 + \frac{1}{E_i}\exp\left(\sum_{k=1}^{h}\mu_k l_{ki}\right)\right]^{-1},\\
&\tilde{b}_i = \sqrt{b_i}, \qquad i = \overline{1,m}.
\end{aligned}
\tag{3.15}
$$

The Lagrange multipliers $\bar{\mu}$ and the exponential Lagrange multipliers $\mathbf{z} = \exp(\bar{\lambda})$ are defined by the next equations and inequalities:

$$
\begin{aligned}
&\Theta_j(\mathbf{z},\bar{\mu}) = \frac{1}{u_j}\sum_{i=1}^{m} t_{ji} y_i(\mathbf{z}) d_i(\bar{\mu}) = 1, \qquad j = \overline{1,n},\\
&\Gamma_k(\mathbf{z},\bar{\mu}) = g_k - \sum_{i=1}^{m} l_{ki} y_i(\mathbf{z}) d_i(\bar{\mu}) \geq 0,\\
&\mu_k \Gamma_k(\mathbf{z},\bar{\mu}) = 0, \quad \mu_k \geq 0, \qquad k = \overline{1,h}.
\end{aligned}
\tag{3.16}
$$

**2. Multiplicative algorithms with $(p+q)$-active variables** An active variables are vary at the $s$th iteration, and the remaining variables are not vary. We will consider multiplicative algorithms with respect to dual variables $(\mathbf{z},\, \bar{\mu})$ for solution of the system (3.16). At the each step of iteration it will be used $p$ components of the vector $\mathbf{z}$, and $q$ components of the vector $\bar{\mu}$. The number of the active variables is valid to the next relation:

$$
p + q \leq n + h. \tag{3.17}
$$

The multiplicative algorithms with $p$+$q$-active variables can be represented in the following form:

(a)*initial step*

$$
\mathbf{z}^0 \geq 0, \qquad \bar{\mu}^0 \geq 0;
$$

(b)*iterative step*

$$
\begin{aligned}
z^{s+1}_{j_1(s)} &= z^{s}_{j_1(s)} \Theta^{\gamma}_{j_1(s)}(\mathbf{z}^s,\, \bar{\mu}^s),\\
\cdots & \quad \cdots \quad \cdots \quad \cdots,\\
z^{s+1}_{j_p(s)} &= z^{s}_{j_p(s)} \Theta^{\gamma}_{j_p(s)}(\mathbf{z}^s,\, \bar{\mu}^s),\\
z^{s+1}_{j} &= z^{s}_{j}, \quad j = \overline{1,n},\ j \neq j_1(s),\ldots,j_p(s);
\end{aligned}
\tag{3.18}
$$

$$
\begin{aligned}
\mu^{s+1}_{t_1(s)} &= \mu^{s}_{t_1(s)}[1 - \alpha\Gamma_{t_1(s)}(\mathbf{z}^s,\, \bar{\mu}^s),\\
\cdots & \quad \cdots \quad \cdots \quad \cdots,\\
\mu^{s+1}_{t_q(s)} &= \mu^{s}_{t_q(s)}[1 - \alpha\Gamma_{t_q(s)}(\mathbf{z}^s,\, \bar{\mu}^s),\\
\mu^{s+1}_{t} &= \mu^{s}_{t}, \quad t = \overline{1,h},\ t \neq t_1(s),\ldots,t_q(s);
\end{aligned}
\tag{3.19}
$$

The parameters $\gamma, \alpha$ are the step coefficients. In Popkov (2006) the multiplicative algorithms in respect to the mixed type (prime and dual variables) are introduced, and the method of the convergence of these algorithms are proposed.

### 3.2 The EQL problem

**1. Optimality condition.** Consider the EQL problem (3.2 - 3.5), and introduce the Lagrange function:

$$\begin{aligned} \mathrm{L}(\mathbf{x}, \bar{\lambda}, \bar{\mu}) &= H(\mathbf{x}, \tilde{\mathbf{b}}, \mathbf{E}) + \bar{\lambda}'[\,\tilde{\mathbf{u}} - \tilde{T}\mathbf{x} - \{\mathbf{x}'\, F^r\,\mathbf{x},\, r = \overline{1,n}\}] + \\ &+ \bar{\mu}'[\,\tilde{\mathbf{g}} - \tilde{L}\mathbf{x} - \{\mathbf{x}'\, Q^k\,\mathbf{x},\, k = \overline{1,h}\}\,]. \end{aligned} \tag{3.20}$$

According to the optimality conditions (3.9, 3.10) we have:

$$\begin{aligned} &\nabla_{\mathbf{x}}\mathrm{L} = \frac{\partial H}{\partial \mathbf{x}} - [\,T + \Phi(\mathbf{x})\,]'\bar{\lambda} - [\,L + \Pi(\mathbf{x})\,]'\bar{\mu} = 0, \\ &\nabla_{\bar{\lambda}}\mathrm{L} = \tilde{\mathbf{u}} - T\mathbf{x} - \{\mathbf{x}'\, F^r\,\mathbf{x},\, r = \overline{1,n}\}, \\ &\nabla_{\bar{\mu}}\mathrm{L} = \tilde{\mathbf{g}} - L\mathbf{x} - \{\mathbf{x}'\, Q^k\,\mathbf{x},\, k = \overline{1,n}\} \geq 0, \\ &\bar{\mu} \otimes \nabla_{\bar{\mu}}\mathrm{L} = 0, \qquad \mathbf{x} \geq 0,\ \bar{\mu} \geq 0, \end{aligned} \tag{3.21}$$

where

$$\Phi(\mathbf{x}) = [\varphi_{ri}(\mathbf{x}) \,|\, r = \overline{1,n},\, i = \overline{1,m}], \qquad \varphi_{ri}(\mathbf{x}) = 2\sum_{j=1}^{m} x_j f_{ij}^r,$$

$$\Pi(\mathbf{x}) = [\pi_{ki}(\mathbf{x}) \,|\, k = \overline{1,h},\, i = \overline{1,m}], \qquad \pi_{kj}(\mathbf{x}) = 2\sum_{j=1}^{m} x_j q_{ij}^k.$$

Transform these equations and inequalities to the conventional form in which all variables are nonnegative one:

$$\begin{aligned} &\frac{A_j(\mathbf{x}, \mathbf{z}, \bar{\mu})\, E_j}{x_j[1 + A_j(\mathbf{x}, \mathbf{z}, \bar{\mu})\, E_j]} = \mathcal{A}_j(\mathbf{x}, \mathbf{z}, \bar{\mu}) = 1, \qquad j = \overline{1,m}, \\ &\frac{1}{\tilde{u}_r}\left(\sum_{i=1}^{m} \tilde{t}_{ri} x_i + \sum_{i,l=1}^{m} x_i\, x_l\, f_{il}^r\right) = \mathcal{B}_r(\mathbf{x}) = 1, \qquad r = \overline{1,n}, \\ &\frac{\mu_k}{\tilde{g}_k}\left(\sum_{i=1}^{m} \tilde{l}_{ki} x_i + \sum_{i,l=1}^{m} x_i\, x_l\, q_{il}^k\right) = \mathcal{C}_k(\mathbf{x}) = 0, \qquad k = \overline{1,h}, \\ &\mathbf{x} \geq 0, \quad \mathbf{z} = \exp(-\bar{\lambda}) \geq 0, \quad \bar{\mu} \geq 0, \end{aligned} \tag{3.22}$$

where

$$\begin{aligned} A_j(\mathbf{x}, \mathbf{z}, \bar{\mu}) &= \prod_{r=1}^{n} z_r^{\tilde{t}_{rj}} \prod_{p=1}^{n} z_r^{\varphi_{rj}(\mathbf{x})} \times \\ &\times \exp\left(-\sum_{k=1}^{h} \mu_k \tilde{l}_{kj}\right) \exp\left(-\sum_{k=1}^{h} \mu_k \sum_{l=1}^{m} x_l q_{jl}^k\right). \end{aligned} \tag{3.23}$$

**2. Multiplicative algorithms of the mixed type with $(p{+}q{+}w)$-active variables.** We use $p$ active prime $\mathbf{x}$ variables, $q$ active dual variables $\mathbf{z}$ for the constraints-equalities, and $w$ active dual $\bar{\mu}$ variables for the the constraints-inequalities. The algorithm takes a form:

(a)*initial step*

$$\mathbf{x}^0 \geq 0, \quad \mathbf{z}^0 \geq 0, \qquad \bar{\mu}^0 \geq 0;$$

(b)*iterative step*

$$\begin{aligned} x_{j_1(s)}^{s+1} &= x_{j_1(s)}^{s} \mathcal{A}_{j_1(s)}^{\beta}(\mathbf{x}^s, \mathbf{z}^s, \bar{\mu}^s), \\ \cdots & \quad \cdots \quad \cdots \quad \cdots, \\ x_{j_p(s)}^{s+1} &= x_{j_p(s)}^{s} \mathcal{A}_{j_p(s)}^{\beta}(\mathbf{x}^s, \mathbf{z}^s, \bar{\mu}^s), \\ x_j^{s+1} &= x_j^s, \quad j = \overline{1,m}, \ j \neq j_1(s), \dots, j_p(s); \end{aligned} \tag{3.24}$$

$$\begin{aligned} z_{t_1(s)}^{s+1} &= z_{t_1(s)}^{s} \mathcal{B}_{t_1}^{\gamma}(\mathbf{x}^s), \\ \cdots & \quad \cdots \quad \cdots \quad \cdots, \\ z_{t_q(s)}^{s+1} &= z_{t_q(s)}^{s} \mathcal{B}_{t_q}^{\gamma}(\mathbf{x})^s, \\ z_t^{s+1} &= z_t^s, \quad t = \overline{1,n}, \ t \neq t_1(s), \dots, t_q(s); \end{aligned} \tag{3.25}$$

$$\begin{aligned} \mu_{k_1(s)}^{s+1} &= \mu_{k_1(s)}^{s} [1 - \alpha \mathcal{C}_{k_1}(\mathbf{x}^s)], \\ \cdots & \quad \cdots \quad \cdots \quad \cdots, \\ \mu_{k_w(s)}^{s+1} &= \mu_{k_w(s)}^{s} [1 - \alpha \mathcal{C}_{k_w}(\mathbf{x}^s)], \\ \mu_k^{s+1} &= \mu_k^s, \quad k = \overline{1,h}, \ k \neq k_1(s), \dots, k_w(s); \end{aligned} \tag{3.26}$$

The parameters $\beta, \gamma, \alpha$ are the step coefficients.

**3. Active variables.** To choice active variables we use feedback control with respect to the residuals on the each step of iteration. Consider the choosing rule of the active variables for the ELP problem (3.2, 3.3, 3.4). Introduce the residuals

$$\begin{aligned} \vartheta_i(\mathbf{z}^s, \bar{\mu}^s) &= |1 - \Theta_i(\mathbf{z}^s, \bar{\mu}^s)|, \qquad i = \overline{1,n}; \\ \varepsilon_k(\mathbf{z}^s, \bar{\mu}^s) &= \mu_k \Gamma_k(\mathbf{z}^s, \bar{\mu}^s), \qquad k = \overline{1,h}. \end{aligned} \tag{3.27}$$

One of the possible rules is a choice with respect the maximum residual. In this case it is necessary to select $p$ maximum residual $\vartheta_{i_1}, \dots, \vartheta_{i_p}$ and $q$ maximum residual $\varepsilon_{k_1}, \dots, \varepsilon_{k_q}$ for the each iterative step $s$. The numbers $i_1, \dots, i_p$ and $k_1, \dots, k_q$ belong to the intervals $[1, n]$ and $[1, h]$ respectively.

Consider the step $s$ and find the maximal residual $\vartheta_{i_1}(\mathbf{z}^s, \bar{\mu}^s)$ among $\vartheta_1(\mathbf{z}^s, \bar{\mu}^s), \dots, \vartheta_n(\mathbf{z}^s, \bar{\mu}^s)$. Exclude the residual $\vartheta_{i_1}(\mathbf{z}^s, \bar{\mu}^s)$ from the set $\vartheta_1(\mathbf{z}^s, \bar{\mu}^s)$, $\dots, \vartheta_n(\mathbf{z}^s, \bar{\mu}^s)$, and find the maximal residual $\vartheta_{i_2}(\mathbf{z}^s, \bar{\mu}^s)$ among $\vartheta_1(\mathbf{z}^s, \bar{\mu}^s), \dots,$ $\vartheta_{i_1-1}(\mathbf{z}^s, \bar{\mu}^s), \vartheta_{i_1+1}(\mathbf{z}^s, \bar{\mu}^s)\vartheta_n(\mathbf{z}^s, \bar{\mu}^s)$, and etc., until all $p$ maximal residuals will be found. Selection of the maximal residuals $\varepsilon_{k_1}(\mathbf{z}^s, \bar{\mu}^s), \dots, \varepsilon_{k_q}(\mathbf{z}^s, \bar{\mu}^s)$ is implemented similary.

Now we represent the formalized procedure of selection. Introduce the following designations:

$$\frac{n}{p} = I + \delta, \qquad I = \left[\frac{n}{p}\right], \quad 0 \le \delta \le p-1;$$

$$\frac{h}{q} = J + \omega, \qquad J = \left[\frac{h}{q}\right], \quad 0 \le \omega \le q-1. \tag{3.28}$$

$$\varrho = s\,(\mathrm{mod}\,(I+1)), \qquad \kappa = s\,(\mathrm{mod}\,(J+1)). \tag{3.29}$$

Consider the index sets:

$$N = \{1,\ldots,n\} \qquad N_r(s) = \{i_1(s),\ldots,i_r(s)\};$$

$$K = \{1,\ldots,h\} \qquad K_v(s) = \{k_1(s),\ldots,k_v(s)\}, \tag{3.30}$$

where

$$r = \begin{cases} [1,p], & \text{if } \varrho < I; \\ [1,\delta], & \text{if } \varrho = I;, \\ 0, & \text{if } \delta = 0 \end{cases} \qquad v = \begin{cases} [1,q], & \text{if } \kappa < J; \\ [1,\omega] & \text{if } \kappa = J; \\ 0, & \text{if } \omega = 0. \end{cases} \tag{3.31}$$

Introduce the following sets:

$$P_{r-1}(s) = \left[\bigcup_{l=1}^{\varrho} N_p(s-l)\right] \bigcup N_{r-1}(s), \qquad G_{r-1} = N \setminus P_{r-1}(s).$$

$$Q_{v-1}(s) = \left[\bigcup_{l=1}^{\kappa} K_v(s-l)\right] \bigcup K_{v-1}(s), \qquad R_{v-1} = K \setminus Q_{v-1}(s). \tag{3.32}$$

The numbers $r$ and $v$ are determined by the equalities (3.31), and

$$N_0(s) = K_0(s) = P_0(s) = G_0(s) = Q_0(s) = R_0(s) = \varnothing, \quad \text{for all } s.$$

Now we define the rule of the $(p+q)$-maximal residual in the following form:

$$i_j(s) = \arg \max_{[i \in G_{j-1}(s)]} \vartheta_i(\mathbf{z}^s, \bar{\mu}^s),$$

$$k_l(s) = \arg \max_{[k \in R_{l-1}(s)]} \varepsilon_k(\mathbf{z}^s, \bar{\mu}^s). \tag{3.33}$$

According to this rule we have the chain of inequalities:

$$\vartheta_{i_p}(\mathbf{z}^s, \bar{\mu}^s) < \vartheta_{i_{p-1}}(\mathbf{z}^s, \bar{\mu}^s) < \cdots < \vartheta_{i_1}(\mathbf{z}^s, \bar{\mu}^s),$$

$$\varepsilon_{k_q}(\mathbf{z}^s, \bar{\mu}^s) < \varepsilon_{k_{q-1}}(\mathbf{z}^s, \bar{\mu}^s) < \cdots < \varepsilon_{k_1}(\mathbf{z}^s, \bar{\mu}^s). \tag{3.34}$$

We can see that all dual variables are sequentially transformed to active ones during $I+J+2$ iterations It is repeated with a period of $I+J+2$.

## 4. Dynamic EIRP procedure with feedback

The basic idea of the dynamic procedure lies in the sequential (stage by stage) obtaining of the projections and the solution of the sequence of the appropriate ELP or EQP. The feasible sets in these problems consist on two subsets. One of them describes the class of the possible density functions (2.7), and it is not depends from irradiation of the object. The other subset depends on the measured projections (2.8).

On the stage $t$ we have the *t-prior* image $\mathbf{E}^t$, the projection's vector $\mathbf{u}^t$, measured with noise $\bar{\xi}$. The problem (2.7 - 2.9, 2.13) is solved and we have *t-posteriori image*

$$\bar{\psi}^t_*(\mathbf{E}^t|\mathbf{u}^t) = \arg\max_{\bar{\psi}} \left\{ H(\bar{\psi}, \mathbf{E}^t) | \bar{\psi}^t \in \mathcal{D}(\mathbf{u}^t) \right\}. \tag{4.1}$$

On the next $(t+1)$*-stage* the prior image $\mathbf{E}^{(t+1)}$ is formed on the basis of $t, (t-1), \ldots, (t-s)$-posterior images $\bar{\psi}^{(t,*)}, \bar{\psi}^{((t-1),*)}, \ldots, \bar{\psi}^{((t-s),*)}$. Each of posterior images are reconstructed by the rule (4.1).

In the general case the procedure holds

$$\mathbf{E}^{(t+1)} = \tilde{\mathcal{L}}(\mathbf{E}^t, \bar{\psi}^{(t,*)}, \ldots, \bar{\psi}^{((t-s),*)}), \tag{4.2}$$

where $\mathcal{L}$ is the feedback operator, which characterizes the transformation of the *t-prior* image, and $t, (t-1), \ldots, (t-s)$*-posterior* images to the $(t+1)$*-prior* image.

Represent the operator $\tilde{\mathcal{L}}$ in the following form:

$$\tilde{\mathcal{L}}(\mathbf{E}^t, \bar{\psi}^{(t,*)}, \ldots, \bar{\psi}^{((t-s),*)}) = \mathbf{E}^t + \epsilon\, \mathcal{L}(\mathbf{E}^t, \bar{\psi}^{(t,*)}, \ldots, \bar{\psi}^{((t-s),*)}), \tag{4.3}$$

where $\epsilon$ is a small positive real number.

Then the dynamic EIRP procedure (the discrete procedure) takes a form:

$$\mathbf{E}^{(t+1)} = \mathbf{E}^t + \epsilon\, \mathcal{L}(\mathbf{E}^t, \bar{\psi}^{(t,*)}, \ldots, \bar{\psi}^{((t-s),*)}). \tag{4.4}$$

Now let the variable $t$ is continuous one. Then under $\epsilon \to 0$ we will have the continuous dynamic EIRP that is described be the differential equation:

$$\frac{d\mathbf{E}(t)}{dt} = \mathcal{L}(\mathbf{E}^t, \bar{\psi}^{(t,*)}, \ldots, \bar{\psi}^{((t-s),*)}). \tag{4.5}$$

The $t, (t-1), \ldots, (t-s)$*-posterior* images are defined by the ELP or EQP problems, which represent the appropriate *entropy operators* (4.1). So the dynamic EIRP procedure (4.1, 4.2, (4.4)) represents the discrete dynamic system with entropy operator (the discrete DSEO) and its the continuous analog (4.5) represents the continuous dynamic system with entropy operator (the continuous DSEO). Some general properties of the DSEO will be described in the next section.

### 4.1 Structures of the dynamic EIRP procedures

Let us consider some partial cases. One of them relates to the examination of a Markov version of the procedure when the information only on the $t$-posterior image is used to shape up $\mathbf{E}^{(t+1)}$:

$$\mathbf{E}^{(t+1)} = \mathcal{L}(\mathbf{E}^t, \bar{\psi}^{t,*}). \tag{4.6}$$

In the second case, information collections at $t, t-1, \ldots, t-s$ stages are used for the estimation of the current mean $\bar{\psi}^t$ of the posterior image:

$$E^{(t+1)} = \mathcal{L}(E^t, \bar{\bar{\psi}}^t). \tag{4.7}$$

Finally, in the third case, information collections at $t, t-1, \ldots, t-s$ stages are used for the estimation of the current mean $\bar{\bar{\psi}}^t$ and dispersion $\mathbf{d}^t$ of the posterior image:

$$\mathbf{E}^{(t+1)} = \mathcal{L}(\mathbf{E}^t, \bar{\bar{\psi}}^t, \mathbf{d}^t). \tag{4.8}$$

We will introduce the following types of the dynamic procedures of the EIRP:

- the identical feedback ($I - feedback$)

$$\mathbf{E}^{(t+1)} = \arg\max_{\psi^t} H(\bar{\psi}^t)|\mathbf{E}^t) \mid \bar{\psi}^t \in \mathcal{D}(\mathbf{u}^t); \tag{4.9}$$

- the feedback with respect to the current mean of image ($CM - feedback$)

$$\begin{aligned} \mathbf{E}^{(t+1)} &= \mathbf{E}^t + \alpha(\mathbf{E}^t - \bar{\bar{\psi}}^t), \\ \bar{\bar{\psi}}^{(t+1)} &= \bar{\bar{\psi}}^t + \frac{1}{t+1}\left(\psi^{(t,*)} - \bar{\bar{\psi}}^t\right); \\ \bar{\psi}^{(t,*)} &= \arg\max_{\psi}\{H(\bar{\psi}^t, \mathbf{E}^t)|\bar{\psi}^t \in \mathcal{D}(\mathbf{u}^t)\}; \end{aligned} \tag{4.10}$$

$$\tag{4.11}$$

- the feedback with respect to the current mean and dispersion of image ($CMD - feedback$)

$$\mathbf{E}^{(t+1)} = \mathbf{E}^t + \alpha(\mathbf{d}^t)(\mathbf{E}^t - \bar{\bar{\psi}}^t), \tag{4.12}$$

$$\bar{\bar{\psi}}^{(t+1)} = \bar{\bar{\psi}}^t + \frac{1}{t+1}\left(\bar{\psi}^{(t,*)} - \bar{\bar{\psi}}^t\right), \tag{4.13}$$

$$\begin{aligned} \mathbf{d}^{(t+1)} &= \mathbf{d}^t + \frac{1}{t+1}\left(\mathbf{d}^t + [\bar{\psi}^{(t,*)} - \bar{\bar{\psi}}^t]^2\right), \\ \bar{\psi}^{(t,*)} &= \arg\max_{\psi}\{H(\bar{\psi}, \mathbf{E}^t) \mid \bar{\psi}^t \in \mathcal{D}(u^t)\}. \end{aligned} \tag{4.14}$$

## 4.2 Investigation of the dynamic EIRP procedure with *I*-feedback

Consider the problem (2.13) in which the feasible set is the polyhedron, $\mathbf{a} = \mathbf{0}, \mathbf{b} = \mathbf{1}$, and the constraints to the possible density functions (2.7) are absent. In this case $t$-posterior density function hold:

$$\psi_i^{t,*} = \frac{E_i^t}{E_i^t + \prod_{j=1}^n [z_j^t]^{t_{ji}}}, \qquad i = \overline{1,m}. \tag{4.15}$$

The exponential Lagrange multipliers $z_1, \ldots, z_n$ are defined from the following equations:

$$\Phi_j(\mathbf{z}^t) = \sum_{i=1}^m \frac{t_{ji} E_i^t}{E_i^t + \prod_{j=1}^n [z_j^t]^{t_{ji}}} = u_j, \qquad j = \overline{1,n}. \tag{4.16}$$

According to the definition of the *I*-feedback procedure we have:

$$E_i^{t+1} = \Psi_i(\mathbf{E}^t) = \frac{E_i^t}{E_i^t + \varphi_i[\mathbf{z}^t(\mathbf{E}^t)]}, \qquad i = \overline{1,m}, \tag{4.17}$$

where

$$\varphi_i[\mathbf{z}^t(\mathbf{E}^t)] = \prod_{j=1}^{n}[z_j^t]^{t_{ji}} \geq 0. \tag{4.18}$$

The iterative process (4.17) can be considered as the method of the simple iteration applying to the eguations:

$$E_i = \frac{E_i}{E_i + \varphi_i[\mathbf{z}(\mathbf{E})]}, \qquad i = \overline{1,m}. \tag{4.19}$$

**Theorem 1.***Let* $\varphi_i[\mathbf{z}(\mathbf{E})] \leq 1$ *for all* $i = \overline{1,m}, \mathbf{z} \geq \mathbf{0}, \mathbf{0} \leq \mathbf{E} \leq \mathbf{1}$.

*Then the system of equations (4.19) has the unique solution* $\mathbf{E}^*$.

**Proof.** Consider the auxiliary equation:

$$x = \Psi(x) = \frac{x}{x+a}, \quad x \geq 0.$$

We can see that the function $\Psi(x)$ is strictly monotone increasing ($\Psi'(x) > 0$ for all $x > 0$ and $\Psi(\infty) = 0$), and is strictly convex ($\Psi''(x) < 0, \quad x > 0$ and $\Psi''(\infty) = 0$).

If $\Psi'(0) = 1/a \geq 1, \ (a \leq 1)$, then the auxiliary equation has the unique solution, and the method of the simple iteration is converged to this solution.

Now it is necessary to find a conditions when $\varphi_i[\mathbf{z}(\mathbf{E})] \leq 1$. The sufficient conditions for it is formed by the following theorem.

**Theorem 2.** *Let the matrix T in (2.7) has the complete rank n, and the following conditions be valid*:

$$\max_{j\in[1,n]}\left(\sum_{i=1}^{m} t_{ji}\right) - u_{max} > 0, \qquad u_{max} = \max_{j\in[1,n]} u_j; \tag{4.20}$$

$$\min_{j\in[1,n]}\left(\sum_{i=1}^{m} t_{ji}\left(\frac{E_i^t}{E_i^t+1}\right)\right) - u_{min} < 0, \qquad u_{min} = \min_{j\in[1,n]} u_j. \tag{4.21}$$

*Then* $\varphi_i[\mathbf{z}(\mathbf{E})] \leq 1$ *for all* $i = \overline{1,m}$.

**Proof.** Consider the Jacobian of the vector-function $\bar{\Phi}(\mathbf{z}^t)$. Its elements take a form:

$$\frac{\partial \Phi_j(\mathbf{z}^t)}{\partial z_k} = -\frac{1}{z_k}\sum_{i=1}^{m}\frac{t_{ji}\,t_{ki}\,E_i^t\,\varphi_i(\mathbf{z}^t)}{[E_i^t + \varphi_i(\mathbf{z}^t)]^2} \leq 0, \qquad (j,k) = \overline{1,n}.$$

The equality to zero is reached when $\mathbf{z} \to \infty$. So, the functions $\Phi_1, \ldots, \Phi_n$ are strictly monotone decreasing.

Therefore, under the theorem's conditions, the solution of the equations (4.16) $z_j^* \in [0,1], \ j = \overline{1,n}$, and the functions $0 < \phi_j(\mathbf{z}(\mathbf{E})) \leq 1$.

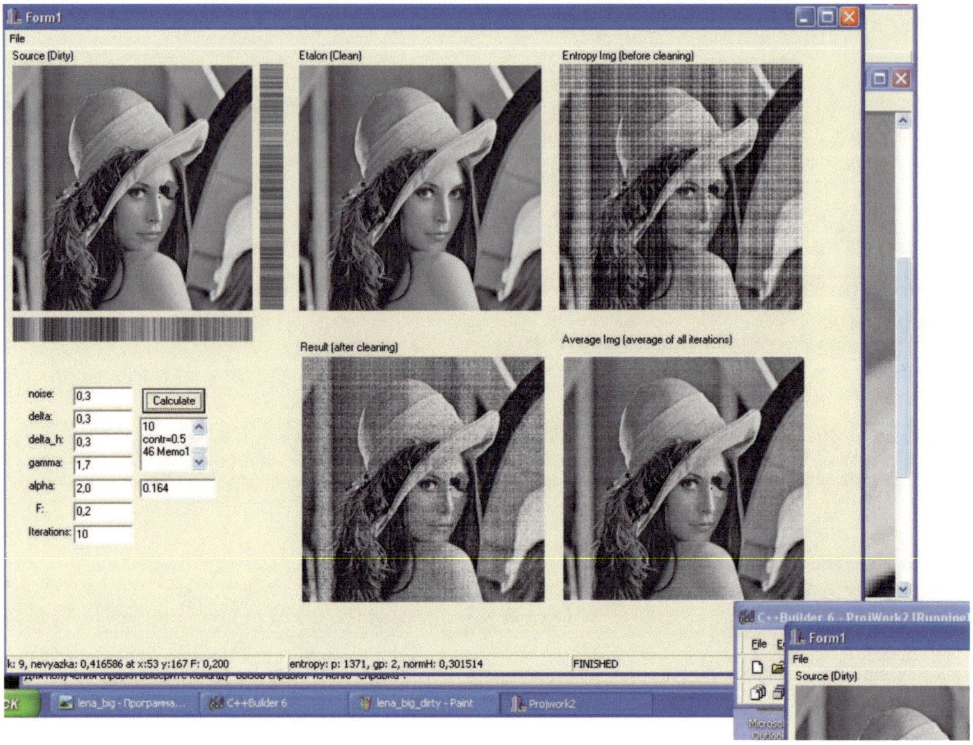


Fig. 2. Test image 1

#### 4.3 Computer experiment

Consider the dynamic EIRP when the tomographic device gives the orthogonal linear projections with the matrix

$$T = \begin{pmatrix} 1 & \cdots & 1 & \cdots & 0 & \cdots & 0 \\ \cdots & \cdots & \cdots & \cdots & \cdots & \cdots & \cdots \\ 0 & \cdots & 0 & \cdots & 1 & \cdots & 1 \\ 1 & \cdots & 0 & \cdots & 1 & \cdots & \cdots \\ \cdots & \cdots & \cdots & \cdots & \cdots & \cdots & \cdots \\ 0 & \cdots & 1 & \cdots & 0 & \cdots & 1 \end{pmatrix} \quad (4.22)$$

As a test image, use is made of the LENA test (IEEE Image Processing), on which the spot is placed (fig. 2, the left upper window).

To the right and below window, the projections with noise are shown. In the example, the noise/signal ratio amounted to 0.3.

It is necessary to restored *the LENA with the spot* having the noisy projections. We use "the pure LENA", which is shown in the second upper window, as the 0-*prior image* $E^0 = \{E_1^0, \ldots, E_m^0\}$.

This problem of the EIRP is described by the ELP with the constrains-equalities. The multiplicative algorithms with 1-active dual variable (3.18) is used for solution of the problem.

Fig. 3. Test image 2

The modification of the dynamic procedure with *I- feedback* involved the following. At each stage $t$ we shaped up the auxiliary vector

$$\tilde{\psi}_i^{(t,*)} = \begin{cases} \psi_i^{(t,*)}, & \text{if } |E_i^t - \psi_i^{(t,*)}| \geq \delta, \\ E_i^t, & \text{if } |E_i^t - \psi_i^{(t,*)}| < \delta \end{cases}, \tag{4.23}$$

$$i = \overline{1,m}. \tag{4.24}$$

In parallel, the current mean of the components of the vector $\tilde{\psi}^{t,*}$ are calculated:

$$\bar{\tilde{\psi}}_i^{(t+1)} = \bar{\tilde{\psi}}_i^t + \frac{1}{t+1}(\tilde{\psi}_i^{t,*} - \bar{\tilde{\psi}}^t). \tag{4.25}$$

The modified dynamic procedure takes the form:

$$E_i^{t+1} = \bar{\tilde{\psi}}_i^{(t+1)}, \qquad i = \overline{1,m}. \tag{4.26}$$

In fig. 2, in the right upper window, the result of the EIRP with the static procedure is shown. In the middle lower window, fig. 2 shows results of the EIRP by the dynamic procedure with *I -feedback*, and in the right lower window results of the modified dynamic procedure is shown. The quality of the right image is obvious.

The test image 2 is shown in the fig. 3.

## 5. Dynamic systems with entropy operator (DSEO)

We can see that dynamic procedures of the image restoration from projections represent a dynamic discrete system with the particular type of the entropy operator with the generalized entropy Fermi-Dirac (3.2), and the feasible set that is described by the inequality and the equality (3.4).

In general case the class of the continuous DSEO is described by the following differential equations:

$$\frac{d\mathbf{u}(t)}{dt} = \mathcal{U}\left(\mathbf{u}(t), \mathbf{v}(t), \mathbf{y}[t, \mathbf{u}(t), \mathbf{v}(t)]\right), \qquad \mathbf{u}(0) = \mathbf{u}^0. \tag{5.1}$$

$$\frac{d\mathbf{v}(t)}{dt} = \mathcal{V}\left(\mathbf{u}(t), \mathbf{v}(t), \mathbf{y}[t, \mathbf{u}(t), \mathbf{v}(t)]\right), \qquad \mathbf{v}(0) = \mathbf{v}^0. \tag{5.2}$$

with the entropy operator:

$$\mathbf{y}[t, \mathbf{u}(t), \mathbf{v}(t)] = \arg\max_{\mathbf{y}} \{H(t, \mathbf{y}, \mathbf{u}(t)) \,|\, \mathbf{y} \in \mathcal{D}[t, \mathbf{v}(t)]\}, \tag{5.3}$$

where: $H(t, \mathbf{y} \,|\, \mathbf{u})$ is an entropy function with the $H$-parameters $\mathbf{u}$; the vectors $(\mathbf{y}, \mathbf{u}) \in R^n$, $\mathbf{v} \in R^m$ , and $\mathcal{D}(t, \mathbf{v})$ is a feasible set depended from the $\mathcal{D}$-parameters $\mathbf{v}$.

In these equations $\mathcal{U}$ is the $n$-vector-function, and $\mathcal{V}$ is the $m$-vector-function.

### 5.1 Classification of the DSEO

Some physical analogues we will use for construction of the classificatory graph. In particular, from the equations (5.1, 5.2) it is seen the rates of parameters is proportional to the flows. The entropy function is a probability characteristics of a stochastic process. So the $H$-parameters are the parameters of this process.

We will use the following classificatory indicators:

- $(\mathbb{A})$, types of the state coordinates ($\langle H\rangle$-coordinates $\mathbf{u}$, $\langle D\rangle$-coordinates $\mathbf{v}$, $\langle HD\rangle$-coordinates $\mathbf{u}, \mathbf{v}$);
- $(\mathbb{B})$, flows ($\langle Add\rangle$ - an additive flow, $\langle Mlt\rangle$ - a multiplicative flow);
- $(\mathbb{C})$, entropy functions ($\langle F\rangle$-Fermi-, $\langle E\rangle$-Einstein-, $\langle B\rangle$-Boltzmann-entropy functions);
- $(\mathbb{D})$, models of the feasible sets ($\langle Eq\rangle$-equalities, $\langle Ieq\rangle$-inequalities, $\langle Mx\rangle$-mixed);
- $(\mathbb{F})$, types of the feasible sets ($\langle Plh\rangle$- polyhedron, $\langle Cnv\rangle$-convex, $\langle nCnv\rangle$-non-convex).

The classificatory graph is shown in the fig. 4.

At the beginning we consider some properties of the entropy operator, notably, the $\langle HD, B, Eq, Plh\rangle$-entropy operator that is included to the $\langle HD\rangle$-DSEO:

$$\mathbf{y}[\mathbf{u}, \mathbf{v}] = \arg\max \left\{H_B[\mathbf{y}, \mathbf{u}] \,|\, \mathbf{y} \in \tilde{\mathcal{D}}[\mathbf{v}]\right\}, \tag{5.4}$$

where Boltzmann-entropy function is

$$H(\mathbf{y} \,|\, \mathbf{u}) = -\left(\mathbf{y}' \ln \frac{\mathbf{y}}{e\mathbf{u}}\right), \quad \mathbf{y} \in R^m_+, \tag{5.5}$$

and the feasible set is

$$\tilde{\mathcal{D}}[\mathbf{v}] = \{\mathbf{y} : \tilde{T}\mathbf{y} = \mathbf{v},\ \mathbf{y} \geq \mathbf{0}\}. \tag{5.6}$$

In these expressions the vector $\ln \frac{\mathbf{y}}{e\mathbf{u}} = \{\ln \frac{y_1}{eu_1}, \ldots, \ln \frac{y_m}{eu_m}\}$, and the vectors

$$\mathbf{u} \in U^m_+(\mathbf{u}^-, \mathbf{u}^+) \subset R^m_+, \quad \mathbf{v} \in V^n_+(\mathbf{v}^-, \mathbf{v}^+) \subset R^n_+, \qquad n < m, \tag{5.7}$$

and

$$\begin{aligned} U^m_+(\mathbf{u}^-, \mathbf{u}^+) &= \{\mathbf{u} : \mathbf{0} < \mathbf{u}^- \leq \mathbf{u} \leq \mathbf{u}^+ \leq \mathbf{1}\}, \\ V^n_+(\mathbf{v}^-, \mathbf{v}^+) &= \{\mathbf{v} : \mathbf{0} < \mathbf{v}^- \leq \mathbf{v} \leq \mathbf{v}^+\}. \end{aligned} \tag{5.8}$$

The $(n \times m)$-matrix $\tilde{T} = [\tilde{t}_{ki} \geq 0]$ has a full rank equal $n$.

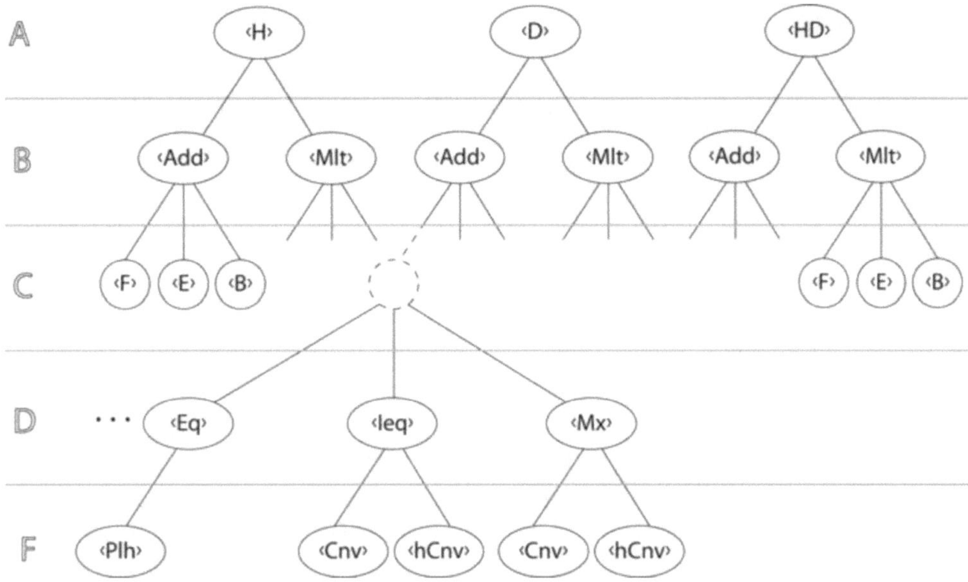


Fig. 4. Classificatory graph

### 5.2 Estimation of the local Lipschitz-constants for the $\langle HD, B, Eq, Plh\rangle$-entropy operator.

The $\langle HD, B, Eq, Plh\rangle$-entropy operator describes the mapping of the sets $U_+^m(\mathbf{u}^-, \mathbf{u}^+)$ and $V_+^n(\mathbf{v}^-, \mathbf{v}^+)$ into the set $\mathcal{Y} \subset R_+^m$ of the operator's values. We will characterize this mapping by two local Lipschitz-constants - $L_U$ and $L_V$, i.e.

$$\|\mathbf{y}[\mathbf{u}^{(1)}, \mathbf{v}^{(1)}] - \mathbf{y}[\mathbf{u}^{(2)}, \mathbf{v}^{(2)}]\| \leq L_U \, \|\mathbf{u}^{(1)} - \mathbf{u}^{(2)}\| + L_V \, \|\mathbf{v}^{(1)} - \mathbf{v}^{(2)}\|. \qquad (5.9)$$

We will use the upper estimations of local Lipschitz-constant:

$$L_U \leq \max_{U_+^m} \|Y_U\|, \qquad L_V = \max_{V_+^n} \|Y_V\|, \qquad (5.10)$$

where $Y_U$ and $Y_V$ are the $U$-Jacobian and the $V$-Jacobian of the operator $\mathbf{y}[\mathbf{u}, \mathbf{v}]$ respectively.

Evaluate *the normalized entropy operator* in the following form:

$$\mathbf{x}(\mathbf{u}, \mathbf{v}) = \arg\max \left( H[\mathbf{x}, \mathbf{u}] \mid T\mathbf{x} = \mathbf{v}, \ \mathbf{x} \geq \mathbf{0} \right), \qquad (5.11)$$

where

$$H(\mathbf{x} \mid \mathbf{u}) = -\left( \mathbf{x}' \ln \frac{\mathbf{x}}{e\mathbf{u}} \right). \qquad (5.12)$$

$$t_i = \sum_{k=1}^{n} \tilde{t}_{ki}, \ \ t_{ki} = \frac{\tilde{t}_{ki}}{t_i}, \ \ i = \overline{1, m}. \qquad (5.13)$$

The matrix $T$ in (5.11) has a full rank $n$ and the normalized elements, i.e. $\sum_{k=1}^{n} t_{ki} = 1$ for all $i = \overline{1, m}$. Also it is assumed that the condition of the dominating diagonal is valid for the quadratic matrix $T\,T'$, i.e. the following inequalities take a form:

$$\sum_{i=1}^{m} \left( t_{ki}^2 - \sum_{j \neq k}^{n} t_{ki} t_{ji} \right) \geq \varrho > 0, \qquad k = \overline{1, n}. \qquad (5.14)$$

The feasible set $\mathcal{D} = \{\mathbf{x} : T\mathbf{x} = \mathbf{v}, \mathbf{x} \geq \mathbf{0}\}$ is not empty, notable, there exists some subset of the nonnegative vectors $\mathbf{x} \in \mathcal{D}$.

Designate the Lipschitz-constant for the normalized operator (5.11) as $\tilde{L}_U$ and $\tilde{L}_V$ respectively, i.e.

$$\|\mathbf{x}[\mathbf{u}^{(1)}, \mathbf{v}^{(1)}] - \mathbf{x}[\mathbf{u}^{(2)}, \mathbf{v}^{(2)}]\| \leq \tilde{L}_U \|\mathbf{u}^{(1)} - \mathbf{u}^{(2)}\| + \tilde{L}_V \|\mathbf{v}^{(1)} - \mathbf{v}^{(2)}\|. \tag{5.15}$$

We will use the upper estimations of local Lipschitz-constant:

$$\tilde{L}_U \leq \max_{U_+^m} \|X_U\|, \qquad \tilde{L}_V = \max_{V_+^n} \|X_V\|, \tag{5.16}$$

where $X_U$ and $X_V$ are the $U$-Jacobian and the $V$-Jacobian of the operator $\mathbf{x}[\mathbf{u}, \mathbf{v}]$ respectively.

According to (5.13), the following relation between the operators $\mathbf{y}(\mathbf{u}, \mathbf{v})$ (5.4) and $\mathbf{x}(\mathbf{u}, \mathbf{v})$ (5.11) exists:

$$\mathbf{y}(\mathbf{u}, \mathbf{v}) = \mathbf{t}^{-1} \otimes \mathbf{x}(\mathbf{u}, \mathbf{v}), \tag{5.17}$$

where the vector $\mathbf{t}^{-1} = \{t_1^{-1}, \ldots, t_m^{-1}\}$, where the components $t_i$ are defined by the equalities (5.13), and $\otimes$ implies the coordinate-wise multiplication of the vectors.

Thus we have the following equalities:

$$L_U = \|\mathbf{t}^{-1}\| \tilde{L}_U, \qquad L_V = \|\mathbf{t}^{-1}\| \tilde{L}_V, \tag{5.18}$$

Thus, we will calculate the local Lipschitz-constants estimations for the normalized entropy operator (5.11, 5.12) and then apply the formulas (5.17, 5.18).

The normalized entropy operator $\mathbf{x}(\mathbf{u}, \mathbf{v})$ can be represented by the form:

$$x_i(\mathbf{u}, \mathbf{v}) = u_i \exp\left( -\sum_{j=1}^{n} \lambda_j(\mathbf{u}, \mathbf{v})\, t_{ji} \right), \qquad i = \overline{1, m}, \tag{5.19}$$

where the Lagrange multipliers $\lambda_j(\mathbf{u}, \mathbf{v})$, $(j = \overline{1, n})$ as the implicit functions from $\mathbf{u}, \mathbf{v}$ define by the equations:

$$\Phi_k[\mathbf{u}, \lambda(\mathbf{u}, \mathbf{v})] = \sum_{i=1}^{m} u_i t_{ki} \exp\left( -\sum_{j=1}^{n} \lambda_j(\mathbf{u}, \mathbf{v})\, t_{ji} \right) = v_k, \quad k = \overline{1, n}. \tag{5.20}$$

**1. Estimations of the norm's matrix $X_U$.** The $(m \times m)$-matrix $X_U$ takes a form:

$$X_U = \left[ \frac{\partial x_i}{\partial u_j}, \; (i, j) = \overline{1, m} \right],$$

We will use Euclidean vector norm ($\|\mathbf{y}\|_2$), with which two matrix norm are consisted (see Voevodin (1984)):

- the spectral norm

$$\|A\|_2 = \sqrt{\sigma_{max}},$$

where $\sigma_{max}$ is the maximal eigenvalue of the matrix $A$;

- and the Euclidean norm

$$\|A\|_E = \sqrt{\sum_{i,j} |a_{ij}|^2}.$$

It is known that

$$\|A\|_2 \leq \|A\|_E$$

It is assumed that $\|X_U\| = \|X_U\|_2$. We have from (5.19) the following equality:

$$X_U = X_{\mathbf{u}} + X_\lambda \Lambda_U, \tag{5.21}$$

where the $(m \times m)$-matrix

$$X_{\mathbf{u}} = \text{diag}\,[\frac{x_i}{u_i} \mid i = \overline{1,m}]; \tag{5.22}$$

the $(m \times n)$-matrix

$$X_\lambda = -\mathbf{x} \otimes T'; \tag{5.23}$$

and the $n \times m$-matrix

$$\Lambda_U = \left[\frac{\partial \lambda_j}{\partial u_i},\, j = \overline{1,n},\, i = \overline{1,m}\right] \tag{5.24}$$

In these expressions $\otimes$ is coordinate-wise multiplication of the vector's components to the rows of the matrix.

According to (5.21) and the relation between the spectral norm and the Euclidean norm, we have:

$$\|X_U\|_2 \leq \|X_{\mathbf{u}}\|_E + \|X_\lambda\|_E \, \|\Lambda_U\|_E, \tag{5.25}$$

where

$$\|X_{\mathbf{u}}\|_E \leq \sqrt{m}\, \frac{x^{max}}{u^-_{min}}, \tag{5.26}$$

$$x^{max} = \max_{(i,\mathbf{u},\mathbf{v})} x_i(\mathbf{u},\mathbf{v}),\; u^-_{min} = \min_i u^-_i. \tag{5.27}$$

$$\|X_\lambda\|_E \leq x^{max} \|T\|_E = x^{max} \sqrt{\sum_{i=1,j=1}^{m,n} t^2_{ij}}. \tag{5.28}$$

Now consider the equations (5.20), and differentiate the left and right sides of these equations by $\mathbf{u}$. We obtain the following matrix equation:

$$\Phi_\lambda \Lambda_U = -\Phi_{\mathbf{u}}, \tag{5.29}$$

From this implies that

$$\Lambda_U = \left[\frac{\partial \lambda_k}{\partial u_i} \mid k = \overline{1,n},\, i = \overline{1,m}\right] = -\Phi_\lambda^{-1} \Phi_{\mathbf{u}}. \tag{5.30}$$

Here the $(n \times n)$-matrix $\Phi_\lambda$ has elements

$$\phi^\lambda_{ks} = -\sum_{i=1}^{m} u_i t_{ki} t_{js} \exp\left(-\sum_{j=1}^{n} \lambda_j(\mathbf{u},\mathbf{v}) t_{ji}\right), \qquad (k,s) = \overline{1,n}; \tag{5.31}$$

and the $(n \times m)$-matrix $\Phi_{\mathbf{u}}$ has elements

$$\phi^{\mathbf{u}}_{ki} = t_{ki} \exp\left( - \sum_{j=1}^{n} \lambda_j(\mathbf{u}, \mathbf{v}) t_{ji} \right), \qquad k = \overline{1, n},\ i = \overline{1, m}. \tag{5.32}$$

According to (5.30) we have

$$\|\Lambda_U\|_2 \leq \|\Phi_\lambda^{-1}\|_2 \frac{x^{max}}{u^-_{min}} \sqrt{\sum_{j=1,i=1}^{n,m} t^2_{ji}}. \tag{5.33}$$

Thus the norm's estimation of the matrix $X_U$ takes a form:

$$\|X_U\|_2 \leq \frac{x^{max}}{u^-_{min}} \left( \sqrt{m} + x^{max} \|\Phi_\lambda^{-1}\|_2 \sum_{i=1,j=1}^{m,n} t^2_{ij} \right). \tag{5.34}$$

**2. Estimations of the norm's matrix** $X_V$**.**The $(m \times n)$-matrix $X_V$ takes a form

$$X_V = \left[ \frac{\partial x_i}{\partial v_k},\ i = \overline{1, m},\ k = \overline{1, n} \right].$$

It is assumed that $\|X_V\| = \|X_V\|_2$. We have from (5.19) the following equality:

$$X_U = X_\lambda \Lambda_V, \tag{5.35}$$

where the $(m \times n)$-matrix

$$X_\lambda = -\mathbf{x} \otimes T'; \tag{5.36}$$

and the $n \times n$-matrix

$$\Lambda_V = \left[ \frac{\partial \lambda_k}{\partial v_j},\ (k, j) = \overline{1, n} \right]. \tag{5.37}$$

According to (5.36) and the relation between the spectral norm and the Euclidean norm, we have:

$$\|X_V\|_2 \leq \|X_\lambda\|_E \|\Lambda_V\|_E, \tag{5.38}$$

where

$$\|X_\lambda\|_E \leq x^{max} \|T\|_E = x^{max} \sqrt{\sum_{i=1,j=1}^{m,n} t^2_{ij}}. \tag{5.39}$$

Now consider the equations (5.20), and differentiate the left and right sides of these equations by $\mathbf{v}$. We obtain the following matrix equation:

$$\Phi_\lambda \Lambda_V = I. \tag{5.40}$$

From this implies that

$$\Lambda_U = \Phi_\lambda^{-1}. \tag{5.41}$$

Here the $(n \times n)$-matrix $\Phi_\lambda$ is defined by (5.31). According to (5.41) we have

$$\|\Lambda_V\|_2 \leq \|\Phi_\lambda^{-1}\|_2. \tag{5.42}$$

Thus the norm's estimation of the matrix $X_V$ takes a form:

$$\|X_V\|_2 \leq \|\Phi_\lambda^{-1}\|_2 \, x^{max} \sqrt{\sum_{i=1,j=1}^{m,n} t_{ij}^2}. \tag{5.43}$$

So, we can see that it is necessary to construct the norm's estimation for the matrix $\Phi_\lambda^{-1}$, as well as for the norm's estimation of the matrix $X_U$ .

**3. Estimation of the spectral norm of the matrix $\Phi_\lambda^{-1}$.** The matrix $\Phi_\lambda$ (5.31) is symmetric and strictly negative defined for all $\lambda$. Therefore, it has $n$ real, various, and negative eigenvalues (see Wilkinson (1970)). We will order them in the following way:

$$\mu_1 = \mu_{min} < \mu_2 < \cdots < \mu_n = \mu_{max} < 0, \qquad |\mu_{max}| > M. \tag{5.44}$$

The spectral norm of an inverse matrix is equal to the inverse value of the *modulus* of the maximum eigenvalue $\mu_{max}$ of the initial matrix, i.e.

$$\|\Phi_\lambda^{-1}\| \leq M^{-1}. \tag{5.45}$$

To definite the value $M$ we resort to the Gershgorin theorem (see Wilkinson (1970)). According to the theorem any eigenvalue of a symmetric strictly negative definite matrix lies at least in one of the intervals with center $-c_k(\lambda)$ and the width $2\,\rho_k(\lambda)$:

$$-g_k^+(\lambda) = -c_k(\lambda) - \rho_k(\lambda) \leq \mu \leq -c_k(\lambda) + \rho_k(\lambda) = -g_k^-(\lambda), \qquad k = \overline{1,n}, \tag{5.46}$$

where according to (5.19)

$$\begin{aligned} g_k^+(\lambda) &= \sum_{i=1}^{m} x_i \left( t_{ki}^2 + \sum_{j\neq k}^{n} t_{ki} t_{ji} \right), \\ g_k^-(\lambda) &= \sum_{i=1}^{m} x_i \left( t_{ki}^2 - \sum_{j\neq k}^{n} t_{ki} t_{ji} \right), \end{aligned} \tag{5.47}$$

From the conditions (5.46) it follows that

$$|\mu_{max}| \in [\min_{k,\lambda} g_k^-(\lambda)\,,\, \max_{k,\lambda} g_k^+(\lambda)]. \tag{5.48}$$

We can apply the lower estimation for the left side of this interval using (5.14):

$$\min_{k,\lambda} g_k^-(\lambda) \geq M = \varrho\, x^{min}, \tag{5.49}$$

where

$$x^{min} = \min_{(i,\mathbf{u},\mathbf{v})} x_i(\mathbf{u},\mathbf{v}). \tag{5.50}$$

Thus, in a view of (5.28), we have

$$\|\Phi_\lambda^{-1}\|_2 \leq (\varrho\, x_{min})^{-1}. \tag{5.51}$$

**4. Estimation of the local Lipschitz-constants.** According to (5.34) and (5.51), the estimation of the local $U$-Lipshitz-constant for the normalized entropy operator (5.19) takes a form:

$$\tilde{L}_U \le \frac{x^{max}}{u^{-}_{min}} \left( \sqrt{m} + \frac{x^{max}}{\varrho x^{min}} \sum_{i=1,j=1}^{m,n} t_{ij}^2 \right). \tag{5.52}$$

The estimation (5.43) of the local $V$-Lipschitz-constant for the normalized entropy operator (5.19) takes a form:

$$\tilde{L}_V \le \frac{x^{max}}{x^{min}\,\varrho} \sqrt{\sum_{i=1,j=1}^{m,n} t_{ij}^2}. \tag{5.53}$$

Using the links (5.18) between the normalized entropy operator (5.19) and the entropy operator (5.4) we will have:

$$L_U \le \sqrt{\sum_{i=1}^{m} \left( \sum_{k=1}^{n} t_{ki} \right)^2} \frac{x^{max}}{u^{-}_{min}} \left( \sqrt{m} + \frac{x^{max}}{\varrho x^{min}} \sum_{i=1,j=1}^{m,n} t_{ij}^2 \right),$$

$$L_V \le \sqrt{\sum_{i=1}^{m} \left( \sum_{k=1}^{n} t_{ki} \right)^2} \frac{x^{max}}{(x^{min}\,\varrho)} \sqrt{\sum_{i=1,j=1}^{m,n} t_{ij}^2}. \tag{5.54}$$

### 5.3 Boundedness of the normalized entropy operator

Let us consider the normalized entropy operator (5.11, 5.19, 5.20), the parameters of which $\mathbf{u} \in U_{+}^{m}(\mathbf{u}^{-}, \mathbf{u}^{+})$ and $, \mathbf{v} \in V_{+}^{n}(\mathbf{v}^{-}, \mathbf{v}^{+})$.

Rewrite the equations (5.19, 5.20) in respect to the exponential Lagrange multipliers $z_j = \exp(-\lambda_j)$:

$$x_i(\mathbf{z}, \mathbf{u}) = u_i \prod_{j=1}^{n} z_j^{t_{ji}}, \qquad \overline{1, m}, \tag{5.55}$$

$$\Psi_k[\mathbf{z}, \mathbf{u}] = \sum_{i=1}^{m} t_{ki}\, u_i \prod_{j=1}^{n} z_j^{t_{ji}} = v_k, \qquad \mathbf{z} \ge 0, \quad k = \overline{1, n}. \tag{5.56}$$

It is known some properties of the operator (5.55, 5.56) are defined by the Jacobians of the functions $\mathbf{x}(\mathbf{z}, \mathbf{u})$ and $\Phi(\mathbf{z}, \mathbf{u})$ in respect to the variables $\mathbf{z}, \mathbf{u}$.

Consider the function $\mathbf{x}(\mathbf{z}, \mathbf{u})$. We have the Jacobians:

- $G_{\mathbf{z}}$ with the elements

$$g_{ik}^{\mathbf{z}} = u_i t_{ki} \frac{1}{z_k} \prod_{j=1}^{n} z_j^{t_{ji}} \ge 0, \qquad i = \overline{1, m},\ k = \overline{1, n}; \tag{5.57}$$

and

- $G_{\mathbf{u}}$ with the elements

$$g_{is}^{\mathbf{u}} = \prod_{j=1}^{n} z_j^{t_{ji}} \ge 0, \qquad (i, s) = \overline{1, m} \tag{5.58}$$

We can see that the elements of these Jacobians are nonnegative for all $\mathbf{z} \geq \mathbf{0}$ and $\mathbf{u} \in U_{+}^{m}(\mathbf{u}^{-},\mathbf{u}^{+})$, where $\mathbf{u}^{-} > \mathbf{0}$, $\mathbf{u}^{+} \leq \mathbf{1}$. Thus the functions $\mathbf{x}(\mathbf{z},\mathbf{u})$ increase in a monotone way on these sets.

Now consider the function $\Psi(\mathbf{z},\mathbf{u})$ and its the Jacobians:

- $P_{\mathbf{z}}$ with the elements

$$p_{kl}^{\mathbf{z}} = \sum_{i=1}^{m} u_i t_{ki} \frac{1}{z_l} \prod_{j=1}^{n} z_j^{t_{ji}} \geq 0, \qquad (k,l) = \overline{1,n}; \tag{5.59}$$

and

- $P_{\mathbf{u}}$ with the elements

$$p_{ks}^{\mathbf{u}} = t_{ks} \prod_{j=1}^{n} z_j^{t_{js}} \geq 0, \qquad k = \overline{1,n}, \; s = \overline{1,m}. \tag{5.60}$$

The elements of the matrix $P_{\mathbf{z}}$ and $P_{\mathbf{u}}$ are nonnegative. Thus, the function $\Psi(\mathbf{z},\mathbf{u})$ increase in a monotone way on the sets $\mathbf{z} \geq \mathbf{0}$ and $\mathbf{u} \in U_{+}^{m}(\mathbf{u}^{-},\mathbf{u}^{+})$.

According to (5.55) the function $\mathbf{x}(\mathbf{z},\mathbf{u})$ is analytical one. The system of the equations define the unique differentiable implicit function $\mathbf{z}(\mathbf{u},\mathbf{v})$ on the sets $U_{+}^{m}(\mathbf{u}^{-},\mathbf{u}^{+})$ and $V_{+}^{n}(\mathbf{v}^{-},\mathbf{v}^{+})$ (see theorem 5, pp. 91-92; theorems 1, 2, pp. 95-96, Popkov (1995)).

**1. Estimation of the minimum value of the normalized $\langle HD, B, Eq, Plh\rangle$-entropy operator.** The solution of the problem can be represented by the following theorem.

**Theorem 2.** *Let the matrix $T$ (5.11) has a full rank and $\mathbf{u} \in U_{+}^{m}(\mathbf{u}^{-},\mathbf{u}^{+})$.*

*Then $x^{min} = \min_i x_i(\mathbf{u}^{-}, z^{min})$, where:*

$$z^{min} = \min_j \tilde{z}_j, \qquad j = \overline{1,n},$$

*and $\tilde{z}_1, \ldots, \tilde{z}_n$ are the components of the solution of the equation*

$$\Psi(\mathbf{z},\mathbf{u}^{-}) = \mathbf{v}^{-},$$

*and the vectors $\mathbf{u}^{-}$, $\mathbf{v}^{-}$ have enough small components.*

*Proof.* According to (5.55) $\mathbf{x}(\mathbf{z},\mathbf{0}) = 0$ and $\mathbf{x}(z_1,\ldots,z_{i-1},0,z_{i+1},\ldots,z_n;\, \mathbf{u}) = 0$. As the function (5.55) increases in a monotone way and analytical one, then $x^{min} = \min_i x_i(\mathbf{u}^{-}, z^{min})$ for enough small components $\mathbf{u}^{-}$.

Consider the equations (5.56). We have $\Psi(\mathbf{z},\mathbf{0}), = \Psi(z_1,\ldots,z_{i-1},0,z_{i+1},\ldots,z_n;$ $\mathbf{u}) = \mathbf{0}$. As the function $\Psi(\mathbf{z},\mathbf{u})$ increase in a monotone way and analytical one, then the proposition of the theorem is valid.

**2. Estimation of the maximum value of the normalized $\langle HD, B, Eq, Plh\rangle$-entropy operator.** This problem is more complicated then the previous one. So, at the beginning we describe the general procedure of the estimation forming.

On the first step we reduce the equations (5.56) to the equations with a monotone operator, which also depends on the variable $\mathbf{z}$ and parameters $\mathbf{u}, \mathbf{v}$.

On the second step we define the variable $\mathbf{z}^0 < \mathbf{z}_{min}$, where the vector $\mathbf{z}_{min}$ has the components $z^{min}$ (theorem 2). The vector $\mathbf{z}^0 = \{z^0, \dots, z^0\}$ such that the values of the monotone operator at the point $\mathbf{z}^0$ is more or equal to $\mathbf{z}^0$.

On the third, we define the vector $\mathbf{z}_{max} = \{z^{max}, \dots, z^{max}\}$ such that the monotone operator is less then $\mathbf{z}_{max}$. For determination of the $\mathbf{z}_{max}$ we use the majorant of the monotone operator.

Consider each of the steps in detail.

*2.1. Transformation of the equations (5.56).* Introduce the monotone increasing operator $A(\mathbf{z}, \mathbf{u}, \mathbf{v})$ with the components:

$$A_k(\mathbf{z}, \mathbf{u}, \mathbf{v}) = \frac{z_k}{v_k} \Psi_k[\mathbf{z}, \mathbf{u}], \qquad k = \overline{1, n}. \tag{5.61}$$

Represent the equations (5.56) in the form:

$$A(\mathbf{z}, \mathbf{u}, \mathbf{v}) = \mathbf{z}. \tag{5.62}$$

This equation has the unique zero-solution $\mathbf{z}^*[\mathbf{u}, \mathbf{v}] \equiv \mathbf{0}$ and the unique nonnegative solution $\mathbf{z}^*[\mathbf{u}, \mathbf{v}] \geq \mathbf{0}$. Also recall that the elements of the matrix $T$ and of the vector $\mathbf{v}$ in (5.39) are nonnegative.

2.2. *Choice* $z^0$. According to the theorem 2 $\tilde{\mathbf{z}}$ is the solution of the equation (5.62) for $\mathbf{u}^-$, $\mathbf{v}^-$. So,

$$\frac{\partial}{\partial z_j} A_k(\mathbf{z}, \mathbf{u}^-, \mathbf{v}^-) \mid_{\tilde{\mathbf{z}}} < 1,$$

It is follows that there exists the vector

$$\mathbf{z}^0 = \tilde{\mathbf{z}} - \varepsilon, \tag{5.63}$$

where $\varepsilon$ is a vector with small components $\varepsilon_k > 0$, such that in the $\varepsilon$-neighborhood $\tilde{\mathbf{z}}$ is valid the following inequality:

$$A(\mathbf{z}^0, \mathbf{u}^-, \mathbf{v}^- - \varepsilon) > \mathbf{z}^0. \tag{5.64}$$

2.3. *Choice* $z^{max}$. Exact value of $z^{max}$ is defined by the solution of the global optimization problem Strongin & Sergeev (2000):

$$z^{max} = \arg \max_{\mathbf{u} \in U^m_+, \mathbf{v} \in V^n_+, j \in [1,n]} z^*_j(\mathbf{u}, \mathbf{v}),$$

where $\mathbf{z}^*(\mathbf{u}, \mathbf{v})$ is a solution of the equation:

$$\Psi(\mathbf{z}, \mathbf{u}) = \mathbf{v}.$$

However this problem is very complicated. So we will calculate an upper estimation of the value $z^{max}$.

Let us assume that we can find the vector $\hat{\mathbf{z}}$ such that

$$A(\hat{\mathbf{z}}, \mathbf{u}, \mathbf{v}) \leq \hat{\mathbf{z}}.$$

Choice $z^{max}$ is equal to $\max_j \hat{z}_j$. Then the nonzero-solution $\mathbf{z}^*$ of the equation (5.62) will belong to the following vector interval (see Krasnoselskii et al. (1969)):

$$\mathbf{z}_{min} \leq \mathbf{z}^* \leq \mathbf{z}_{max}, \tag{5.65}$$

where the vector $\mathbf{z}_{max}$ has the components $z^{max}$.

For realization of the this way it is necessary to construct the *majorant* of the operator (5.61, 5.62). We use the following inequality Bellman (1961):

$$\prod_{j=1}^{n} h_j^{\alpha_j} \leq \sum_{j=1}^{n} \alpha_j h_j, \qquad (\alpha_j, h_j) \geq 0, \quad \sum_{j=1}^{n} \alpha_j = 1. \tag{5.66}$$

Then for the operator (5.62) the following estimate is valid:

$$A(\mathbf{z}, \mathbf{u}, \mathbf{v}) \leq \mathbf{v}^{-1} \otimes C\, \mathbf{z}, \tag{5.67}$$

where the matrix C has the elements

$$c_{kj} = \max_{\mathbf{u}} \sum_{i=1}^{m} u_i t_{ki}\, t_{ji} = \sum_{i=1}^{m} t_{ki}\, t_{ji}, \quad (k, j) = \overline{1, n}. \tag{5.68}$$

It is follows from (5.68) that the matrix $C$ takes a form:

$$C = T\,T', \tag{5.69}$$

Thus, we can consider in the capacity of $\hat{\mathbf{z}}$ the nonnegative solution of the equation:

$$C\mathbf{z} = \mathbf{v}, \qquad \mathbf{z} \geq \mathbf{0}. \tag{5.70}$$

The general solution of the equation (5.70) can be represented in the following form:

$$\hat{z}_k(\mathbf{v}) = \frac{\det C^k}{\det C} \geq 0, \qquad k = \overline{1, n}, \tag{5.71}$$

where

$$\det C \neq 0, \tag{5.72}$$

as the matrix $T$ has the full rank, and

$$\det\, C^k = \sum_{j=1}^{n} a_{kj} v_j, \qquad k = \overline{1, n}, \tag{5.73}$$

where

$$a_{kj} = (-1)^{(k+j)} M_{kj}, \tag{5.74}$$

and $M_{kj}$ is the $(k, j)$-minor of the matrix $C$.

Introduce the following polyhedral sets:

$$W_+ = \left\{ \mathbf{v} : \sum_{j=1}^{n} a_{kj} v_j \geq 0, \quad k = \overline{1, n} \right\},$$

$$W_- = \left\{ \mathbf{v} : \sum_{j=1}^{n} a_{kj} v_j < 0, \quad k = \overline{1, n} \right\}. \tag{5.75}$$

and the set

$$Q = \begin{cases} V_+^n \bigcap W_+, & \text{if } \det C \geq 0, \\ V_+^n \bigcap W_-, & \text{if } \det C < 0. \end{cases} \tag{5.76}$$

From this definition it follows that the set $Q$ is the set of the vectors $\mathbf{v}$ for which the equation (5.70) has the nonnegative solutions. Therefore

$$z^{max} = \max_j \max_{\mathbf{v} \in Q} \hat{z}_j(\mathbf{v}). \tag{5.77}$$

Thus we proved the following **theorem 3**: *Let the matrix T (5.11) has a full rank and* $\mathbf{v} \in Q$ *(5.76). Then* $x^{max} = \max_i x_i(\mathbf{1}, z^{max})$, *where:*

$$z^{max} = \max_j \max_{\mathbf{v} \in Q} \hat{z}_j(\mathbf{v}),$$

*and* $\hat{z}_j(\mathbf{v})$ *are the solution of the linear equation*

$$(T' \, T)\mathbf{z} = \mathbf{v}.$$

## 6. Conclusions

Many applied problems can be formulated as the ELP or EQP, models of which it is proposed in the paper. The multiplicative algorithms with $p$-active variables and feedback are the effective methods of their solution. The dynamic procedure of the image restoration from projections (IRP) increase appreciably the quality of the restored image in the presence of noise in the measurements. It is represented a classification of the dynamic procedures and it is investigated a stability of the procedure with $I$-feedback. Also it is shown that in general case the dynamic procedure of the IRP is the dynamic system with entropy operator (EO). The analytical- numerical methods investigation the problem of the EO-boundedness and calculation of the Lipschitz constant for EO are proposed.

## 7. References

Aliev, A.S.; Dubov, Yu.A.; Izmailov, R.N.; Popkov, Yu.S. (1985). Convergence multiplicative algorithms for solving of convex programming problem, in: *Dynamics of Nonhomogeneous Systems, Proceedings of VNIISI*, pp. 59-67, Nauka, Moscow (in Russian).

Boltzmann, L. (1871). *On the link between the second beginning of mechanical calorie theory and probability theory in theorems of thermal equilibrium*, in: *Classics of Science*, Nauka, Moscow.

Beckenbach, E.F. & Bellman, R. (1961). *Inequlities*, Springer-Verlag, Berlin.

Byrne, C.L. (1993). Iterative Image Reconstruction Algorithm Based on Cross-Entropy Minimization. *IEEE Trans. Img. Proc.*, Vol. 2, No. 1, pp. 96-103.

Byrne, C. (1996). Block-iterative methods for image reconstruction from projections. *IEEE Trans. Image Processing*, Vol. 8, pp. 275-291.

Censor Y. (1981). Row-Action Methods for Huge and Sparse Systems and Their Application. *SIAM Review*, Vol. 23, No. 4, pp. 444-464.

Censor, Y. & Segman, J. (1987). On block-iterative entropy maximization. *J. Inform. Optim. Sci.*, Vol. 8, pp. 275-291.

Censor, Y. & Zenios, S.A. (1997). *Parallel Optimization: Theory, Algorithms and Applications*, Oxford University Press, New York.

Dorofeev, D.G.; Zon, B.A.; Popkov, Yu.S. (2008). Probabilistic Characteristics of Paramacrosystems. *Automation and Remote Control*, Vol. 69, No. 2, pp. 223-232.

Dhawan, A.P. (2003). *Medical Image Analysis*. John Wiley and Sons, New York.

Dubov, Yu.A.; Imelbaev, Sh.S.; Popkov, Yu.S. (1983). Multiplicative schemes for iterative optimization algorithms, *Soviet Math. Dokl.*, Vol. 22, No. 2, pp. 524-526.

Fang, S-C.; Rajasekera, J.R.; Tsao, H.S.J. (1997). *Entropy Optimization and Mathematical Programming*, Kluwer Academic Publisher, Dordrecht.

Herman, G.T. (1980). *Image reconstruction from projections: the fundamentals of computerized tomography*, Academic Press, New York.

Herman, G.T. (1982). Mathematical optimization versus practical performance: a case study based on the maximum entropy criterion in image reconstruction. *Mathematical Programming Study*, Vol. 20, pp. 96-112.

Iusem, A.N.; Svaiter, B.F.; Teboulle, M. (1996). Multiplicative Interior Gradient Methods for Minimization over the Nonnegative Orthant. *SIAM J. Control and Optimization*, Vol. 34, No. 1, pp. 319-446.

Kapur, J.N. (1989). *Maximum Entropy Models in Science and Engneering*, John Willey and Sons, New York.

Krasnosel'skii, M.A.; Rutitcki, Ja.B.; Stecenko, V.Ja.; Vainikko, G.M.; Zabreiko, P.P. (1969). *Approximate Solutions of Operator Equations*, Nauka, Moscow.

Kullback, S. & Leibler, R.A. (1951). On Information and Sufficiency. *Annals of Mathematical Statistics*, Vol. 22(1), pp. 79-86.

Landau, L.D. & Livshitz, E.M. (1964). *Statistical Physiscs*, Nauka, Moscow.

Maslov, V.P. & Cherny, A.S. (2003). About Entropy Minimization and Maximization in the Different disciplines. *Theory of Probabilities and thier Applications*, Vol. 48, No. 3, pp. 466-486.

Ohnuki, Y. & Kamefuchi, S. (1982). *Quantum Field and Parastatistics*, University of Tokyo Press, Berlin, Heidelberg, New York.

Polyak, B.T. (1987). *Introduction to Optimization*, Optimization Software, New York.

Popkov, Yu.S. (1988). A Multiplicative Algorithm for Fermi — Models of Macrosystems. *Automation and Remote Control*, Vol. 49, No. 7, Part 1, pp. 320-927.

Popkov, Y.S. (1995). *Macrosystems Theory and Applications. Lecture Notes in Control and Information Sciences 203*, Springer, London.

Popkov, Yu.S. (1995). Multiplicative algorithms for finding nonnegative solutions of convex programming problems. *Control and Cybernetics*, Vol. 24, No. 2, pp. 155-169.

Popkov, Yu.S. (1996). Multiplicative algorithms for determining positive solutions of nonlinear equations. *J. of Computational and Applied Math.*, Vol. 69, pp. 27-37.

Popkov, Yu.S. (1997). Variation Principle of Image Reconstruction from Projections. *Automation and Remote control*, No. 12, pp. 131-139.

Popkov, Y.S. (2006). New class of multiplicative algorithms for solving of entropy-linear programs. *European Journal of Operation Research*, Vol. 174, pp. 1368-1379.

Shannon, C.E. (1948). Mathematical Theory of Communication. *Bell System Technical Journal*, Vol. 27(1):379-423, pp. 623-656.

Strongin, R.G. & Sergeev, Y.D. (2000). *Global Optimization with Non-convex Constraints*, Kluwer Acad. Press.

Voevodin, V.V. & Kuznetsov, Yu.A. (1984). *Matrix and calculations*, p. 318, Nauka, Moscow (in Russian).

Wilkinson, J.H. (1970). *The Algebraic Eigenvalue Problem*, p. 564, Clarendon Press, Oxford.

# 4

# Surface Topography and Texture Restoration from Sectional Optical Imaging by Focus Analysis

Mathieu Fernandes, Yann Gavet and Jean-Charles Pinoli
*École Nationale Supérieure des Mines de Saint-Étienne, CIS/LPMG-CNRS*
*France*

## 1. Introduction

Observing through any optical imaging device with traditional lens system is often "stained" by restricted depth-of-field. Such a simplified optical imaging system consisting of a convex lens (objective), a spherical diaphragm and a sensor plane (image plane) is depicted in Fig. 1. Let $(O, \vec{x}, \vec{y}, \vec{z})$ denote a Cartesian coordinate system: $O$ is the optical center and the $z$-axis is along the optical axis. Imaging with this optical system effectively presents a common characteristic: the limited depth-of-field $\delta z$ around its so-called object focal plane[1]:

$$\delta z = \frac{n_i \lambda}{\mathrm{NA}^2}, \tag{1}$$

moreover when the numerical aperture NA becomes larger:

$$\mathrm{NA} = n_i \sin(\alpha), \tag{2}$$

where $\lambda$ is the wavelength of illumination, $n_i$ is the refractive index of the medium in front of the objective and $\alpha$ is the angular semi-aperture of the diaphragm (Born & Wolf, 1991; Horn, 2001). Consider a scene surface, either opaque and observed in reflected light or sufficiently transparent and observed in transmitted light, whose profile covers more than this attainable depth-of-field (then described as "thick"). Thus, only portions of the observed surface that lie within the depth-of-field appear in-focus and sharp on the acquired image, whereas the remaining out-of-focus parts are blurred[2] by the point spread function (PSF) of the system (Born & Wolf, 1991; Horn, 2001). The PSF results from the contribution of many blur factors, such as the defocusing, the optical diffraction and aberrations and the sampling, principally. Many theoretical models of PSF have been proposed, with

[1] A Gaussian convex lens of focal length $f$ theoretically focuses on a fixed image plane at $z_i$ only the light rays arising from a single object plane at $z_o$, the so-called object focal plane, obeying the Snell's formula: $1/z_i - 1/z_o = 1/f$ for the same medium refractive indexes in both front and back of the lens.

[2] By regarding the illumination as incoherent, blurring can be modelled by a 2-D shift-variant linear convolution of the "ideal" sharp image of the object with the point spread function (*i.e.* with the response of the system to a purely impulsive point object that notably varies with the distance of defocus for $x, y$-shifting).

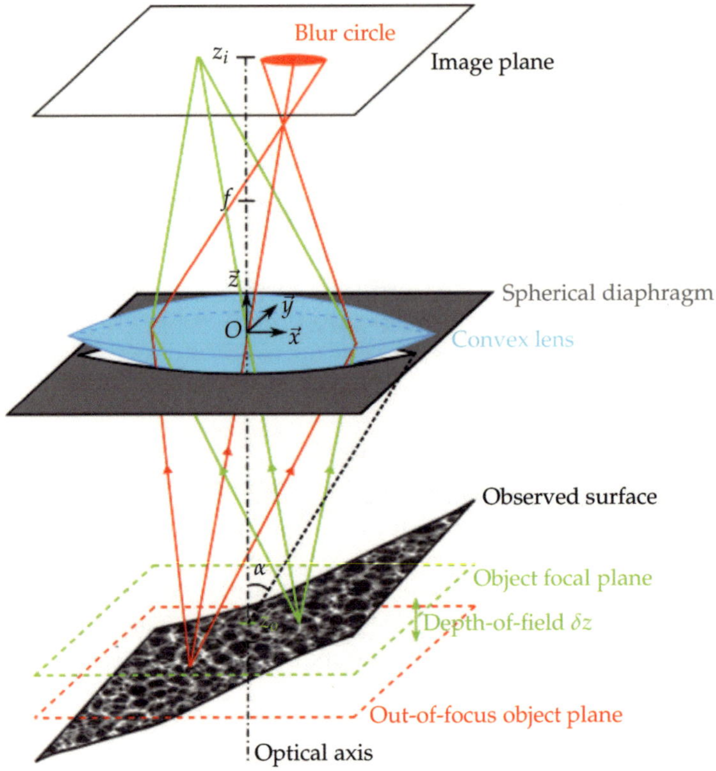


Fig. 1. Illustration of the basic image formation geometry. The green light rays radiated by an in-focus point of the observed surface are well refracted by the convex lens onto the sensor plane contrary to red light rays arising from an out-of-focus point, which converge forward and whose energies are distributed over the "blur circle" patch.

accuracies that depend on considered factors and used approximations[3] (Mahajan, 1998; 2001). Introduced by Pentland, a 2-D Gaussian function is often suggested as a PSF model with a widening standard deviation as the distance of defocus increases (Pentland, 1987). Ultimately, the PSF always behaves as a low-pass filter, whose cut-off spatial frequency falls when the degree of defocus raises. In order to fully observe such a "thick" scene surface, a common way then consists in scanning it with the object focal plane of the optical system, more formally by acquiring a large sequence of 2-D images by optical sectioning (Agard, 1984). The final sequence of 2-D images is thus collected by gradually moving the object focal plane along the $z$-direction throughout the surface. Each 2-D optical section joins out-of-focus blurred and in-focus sharp portions, respectively related to parts of the object surface outside and inside the depth-of-field. Less damaged by the low-pass PSF, the latter exhibit much more of high-spatial frequency components corresponding to surface textural details. From such an image sequence, this chapter then focuses on image restoration of both topographical and textural information of the observed surface through the common concepts of Shape-From-Focus (or Depth-From-focus) and Extended Depth-of-Field. Importantly, both

[3] According to geometrical optics, a first-order approximation of the defocusing PSF consists in a homogeneous patch, the so-called blur circle in the case of a spherical diaphragm whose radius increases with the distance of defocus.

concepts require an original sequence with image sections spatially registered, principally by considering magnification variations due to changes in focus setting through the perspective projection of most optical imaging system[4] (as in Fig. 1) (Willson & Shafer, 1991). These magnification changes can be corrected using optical approaches, such as zoom adjustments based on system calibration (Willson, 1994), or computational techniques, commonly referred to as image warping (Darrell & Wohn, 1988). Notice that acquiring the image sequence by displacing either the scene or the imaging system along the $z$-direction with respect to a fixed focus setting ensures at least a constant magnification $\gamma$ for all successive object focal planes, but not for the out-of-focus object planes that always suffer different magnifications than the focal ones (Nayar & Nakagawa, 1994). Otherwise, an all-over constant magnification can be reached through orthographic projection of telecentric optics (Watanabe & Nayar, 1997).

After briefly describing both Shape-From-Focus (SFF) and Extended Depth-of-Field (EDF) concepts in section 2, their linchpin step consisting in a focus measurement will be particularly studied, reviewed and finally "morphed" in section 3. Indeed, this work especially strives to make changes to classical state-of-the-art focus measurements through different strategies into new evolved approaches that are custom-made to cope with frequently encountered issues, such as ill-illuminated/poor textured or noisy/disturbed acquisitions. An ill-illuminated/poor textured observed surface effectively exhibits few focus cues (high-spatial frequency components) on which the restoration process is based. On the contrary, noisy/disturbed data introducing during the acquisitions produce "false focus cues" that misleads the restoration process. Such issues thus require rather opposite focus measurement behaviours: a high sensitivity to focus cues and a strong robustness to noise, respectively. Thereafter, several tests will be conducted, illustrated and discussed in section 4 on both simulated data and real acquisitions from different application fields (metallography, granulometry, ophthalmology) in conventional optical microscopy. Through such optical imaging system, the inherent use of large magnifications $\gamma \sim$ NA significantly limits the offered depth-of-field and the performed projection tends towards an orthographic behaviour (and therefore an all-over constant magnification) since the working distance WD $= |z_o|$ is much larger than the profile thickness of the observed surface (Horn, 2001). Finally, the new introduced approaches (2-D LIP-based focus measurements and 3-D statistical focus measurements) will be compared to classical state-of-the-art ones and will clearly show their efficiency in presence of aforementioned acquisition issues.

## 2. Surface topography and texture restoration

The Shape-From-Focus (SFF) concept exploits the limited depth-of-field to infer the topography of the observed surface by maximizing a focus measurement throughout the $z$-direction of the image sequence. Likewise, the Extended depth-of-field (EDF) concept conversely tries to overcome the depth-of-field limitation by joining through a focus measurement the most in-focus information from the image sequence into a single image: the so-called "texture image". Both complementary approaches work similarly and foremost rely upon an essential preliminary focus measurement that mainly interests this work and will be more closely studied in the next section 3. They are graphically summarized in Fig. 2 and

[4] Since the intersections of the so-called principal rays (the ones passing undeflected through the center of the lens $O$) with the sensor plane vary with the position of this latter, the image magnification changes with defocus.

will be further described below. Notice that a 3-D reconstruction of the surface can finally be obtained by mapping the texture image onto the topography, as illustrated in Fig. 3. Before going on, let us introduce some notations. Let $\mathcal{I}(x,y,z)$ denotes the sequence of images acquired by optical sectioning, defined on the spatial support $\mathbb{D} = \mathbb{D}_x \times \mathbb{D}_y \times \mathbb{D}_z \subset \mathbb{R}^3$ and valued into a positive real range $[0, M)$ of intensity values. Applying a focus measurement function (FM) on $\mathcal{I}(x,y,z)$ yields a 3-D focus degree measure $\mathcal{F}(x,y,z)$ as follows:

$$\begin{aligned} \mathcal{F}: \quad & \mathbb{D} \rightarrow \mathbb{R}^+ \\ & (x,y,z) \mapsto \mathrm{FM}(\mathcal{I}(x,y,z)), \end{aligned} \tag{3}$$

wherein the profile at location $(x,y)$ along the $z$-direction is designated as $\mathcal{F}|_{x,y} : \mathbb{D}_z \rightarrow \mathbb{R}^+$.

### 2.1 Topographical information: Shape-From-Focus (SFF)

The $z$-coordinates (referred to as depths) of the voxels that exhibit the largest degrees of focus infer the topography (or the so-called depth map) $\mathcal{D}$ of the observed surface from its image sequence $\mathcal{I}(x,y,z)$ as follows:

$$\begin{aligned} \mathcal{D}: \mathbb{D}_x \times \mathbb{D}_y & \rightarrow \mathbb{D}_z \\ (x,y) & \mapsto \underset{z \in \mathbb{D}_z}{\operatorname{argmax}} \mathcal{F}|_{x,y}(z). \end{aligned} \tag{4}$$

Because of the significant thickness $\delta z$ of the depth-of-field, the recovered topography $\mathcal{D}$ shows inherent "staircase" effects and an interpolation approach must then be embedded in this basic process of reconstruction. Introduced by Nayar and Nakagawa, the traditional one consists in fitting a Gaussian distribution, whose mean finally constitutes the interpolated depth value, to the three degrees of focus lying on the largest mode (Nayar & Nakagawa, 1994). Similarly, a quadratic (or even more) polynomial model can be fitted, sometimes regarding more than three degrees of focus (Niederöst et al., 2003; Subbarao & Choi, 1995). A subsequent approach (referred to as Focused Image Surface) locally tries to refine the initial recovered topography $\mathcal{D}$ by optimizing both position and orientation of 2-D planar (then curved) windows throughout the 3-D measure $\mathcal{F}$ so as to maximize the covered degrees of focus (Ahmad & Choi, 2005; Asif & Choi, 2001; Subbarao & Choi, 1995; Yun & Choi, 1999). Finally, the topography is often smoothed through average, median or recently bilateral filters (Helmli & Scherer, 2001; Khan et al., 2010; Mahmood et al., 2008; Niederöst et al., 2003). Interpolation techniques lying beyond the scope of this paper, only the traditional one will be used herein, sometimes finalised by a median filter.

### 2.2 Textural information: Extended Depth-of-Field (EDF)

Throughout the image sequence $\mathcal{I}(x,y,z)$, the texture image $\mathcal{T}$ of the observed surface is restored by joining the intensity voxels with the largest degrees of focus:

$$\begin{aligned} \mathcal{T}: \mathbb{D}_x \times \mathbb{D}_y & \rightarrow [0, M) \\ (x,y) & \mapsto \mathcal{I}(x,y, \underset{z \in \mathbb{D}_z}{\operatorname{argmax}} \mathcal{F}|_{x,y}(z)). \end{aligned} \tag{5}$$

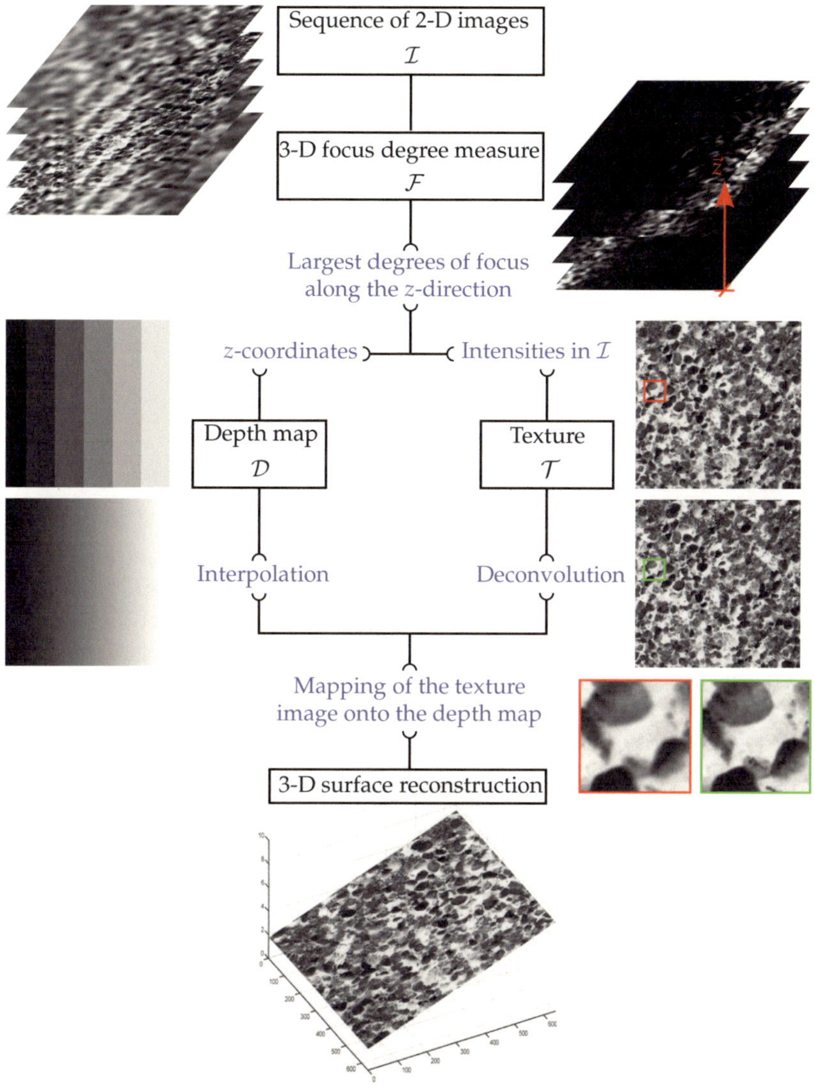


Fig. 2. Basic illustrated diagram representing both complementary Shape-From-Focus (left) and Extended Depth-of-Field (right) concepts.

When the optical sectioning step is larger than the depth-of-field $\delta z$, some regions of the observed surface may never appear in-focus throughout the image sequence and therefore on the restored texture image. Pradeed and Ragajolan then proposed to perform a non-stationary Wiener filter to locally deconvolve the texture image $\mathcal{T}$ (Pradeep & Rajagopalan, 2007). Note that no deconvolution process will be used herein.

## 3. Focus measurements

Let us now focus on the essential step of focus measurement, firstly through a literature review that will yield the retention of some classical and recent methods making a representative

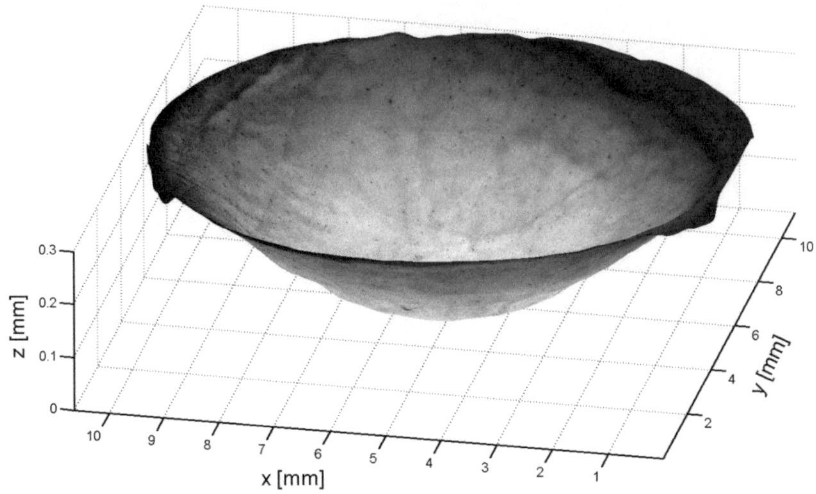


Fig. 3. 3-D reconstruction of a human corneal graft by the **2-D SML$_\triangle$** LIP-based focus measurement from a sequence of 32 image sections acquired in conventional optical microscopy by steps of 9.33 $\mu$m through a $\times$ 4 / 0.1 NA objective in air immersion. Each image section composed of 1932 $\times$ 2029 pixels representing 10.62 $\times$ 11.11 mm is an undersampled version of a registered mosaic of 5 $\times$ 7 image acquisitions.

sample group from a strategic as well as chronological point of view. Some of them will then be developed into novel evolved approaches designated as 2-D LIP-based focus measurements and 3-D statistical focus measurements.

### 3.1 State-of-the-art focus measurements

In view of the fact that the PSF of defocus acts as a low-pass filter, focus measurements thus try to locally emphasize and quantify high-spatial frequency components of the original image sequence $\mathcal{I}$. They can be classified according to the dimensionality of the adopted strategy to do that.

#### 3.1.1 One-dimensional (point-based) approaches

From the early 1980s, some methods using maximum or minimum selection rules throughout single-voxel stacks along the $z$-direction of the image sequence are first proposed $\mathcal{I}$ (Pieper & Korpel, 1983; Sugimoto & Ichioka, 1985), therefore not offering a large robustness.

#### 3.1.2 Two-dimensional approaches

For the last 40 years, a lot of more reliable focus measurements independently acting (in 2-D) on each image section of the sequence $\mathcal{I}$ then arose, categorized below as either neighborhood-based or multiresolution-based methods.

3.1.2.1 Neighborhood-based methods

Neighborhood-based focus measurements work over local sectional fixed-size windows, described herein by the size value $r$ corresponding to an operating window of $(2r + 1) \times$

$(2r+1)$ pixels. Given this local behaviour, a certain depth regularity of the observed surface is implicitly assumed. On the one hand, the considered neighborhood has to be as small as possible to guarantee an approximately constant depth within itself and therefore to avoid too much "smoothing" the restoration process around sharp depth slopes and even depth discontinuities (Malik & Choi, 2007). On the other hand, it has to be as large as possible both to always capture focus cues (*i.e.* high-spatial frequency components) within wide homogeneous textural contents of the surface and to average out noise. Consequently, the selection of the optimal window size $r$ appears as a trade-off. These approaches classically include two successive steps aiming to emphasize and quantify focus cues, respectively. The second one is simply an energy measurement that is commonly the sum over the considered neighborhoods of the absolute values resulting from the first one, therefore improving the robustness to noise and/or to wide textural contents of the measurement. The first step differs in the specialized literature. Most are based on high-pass filtering (norms of derivatives), such as Laplacian energy (Subbarao et al., 1993), sum-modified-Laplacian (Nayar & Nakagawa, 1994), Brenner (Brenner et al., 1976) or Tenenbaum (Krotkov, 1987) gradients, among others... Others, usually more robust to noise, use statistical tools in the considered neighborhoods, such as (normalized) variance (Groen et al., 1985; Sugimoto & Ichioka, 1985), autocorrelation (Vollath, 1987), sum of eigenvalues (Wee & Paramesran, 2007) or various moments (Yap & Raveendran, 2004; Zhang et al., 2000). Remark that some of them directly combine the two aforementioned steps, *e.g.* the variance in the neighborhoods. The last ones work in different frequency domains through discrete cosine (Kristan et al., 2006) or Fourier (Boddeke et al., 1994; Malik & Choi, 2008) transforms. The latter exploit more robust band-pass filters but lack sensitivity in return. At first, note that neighborhood-based focus measurements was often employed to computationally autofocus imaging system.

Throughout these state-of-the-art section, some fundamental and recent methods will be retained; their designations, details and references will be summarized as follows:

**2-D VAR** VARiance in a 2-D window (Groen et al., 1985; Sugimoto & Ichioka, 1985).

**2-D TEN** Sum over a 2-D window of the squared $L^2$-norms of the first derivatives approximated by the horizontal and vertical Sobel operators (TENengrad) (Krotkov, 1987).

**2-D SML** Sum over a 2-D window of the $L^1$-norms of the second derivatives approximated by the Laplacian operator (Sum-Modified-Laplacian) (Nayar & Nakagawa, 1994).

**2-D OPT** Sum over a 2-D window of the absolute values of the real part responses in the spatial domain to an "OPTical" band-pass filter applied in the Fourier domain and based on bipolar incoherent image processing (Malik & Choi, 2008).

3.1.2.2 Multiresolution-based methods

Other 2-D approaches rely on some form of multiresolution analysis: *e.g.* Laplacian (Burt & Adelson, 1983), ratio-of-low-pass (Toet, 1989), gradient (Burt & Kolczynski, 1993) and steerable pyramids (Liu et al., 2001), and wavelet (Forster et al., 2004; Pajares & de la Cruz, 2004; Valdecasas et al., 2001), shapelet (Meneses et al., 2008) and curvelet (Minhas et al., 2011) transforms, in order to perform high-pass filtering at different resolution level. Contrary to afore-described neighborhood-based methods, these ones thus avoid the choice of a fixed-size filter. They are regularly introduced in the practical context of image fusion that consists in combining information from some (generally between 2 and 5) multi-focus or multimodal images of the same scene into a single composite representation. An overview of multiresolution-based schemes for image fusion can be found in (Zhang & Blum, 1999). First, each image section of the original sequence is decomposed into a collection of sub-images at different scales, called a pyramid structure, through alternate combination of convolution and sub-sampling. Different types of details (focus cues) are thus put forward at different levels in the associated pyramid structure. Note that the original image section can be reconstructed by the reverse procedure. A (pixel-based, window-based or region-based (Piella, 2003)) salience measurement (absolute value, sum or variance of absolute values) then tries to quantify focus cues throughout every pyramid structures. The depth map is thus inferred from the largest salience measures. Besides, a composite pyramid structure is constructed by combining coefficients of the original pyramid structures in function of their exhibited salience measures (choose-max or weighted average). Next, a (window-based or region-based) consistency verification is performed on the composite pyramid structure (and on the recovered depth map) so as to check that best salience measures come from the same original image sections, which is equivalent to a smoothing post-processing step. Once the composite pyramid structure is fused, the final texture image is lastly restored by reverse decomposition.

**2-D DWT** Use of the Discrete Wavelet Transform (DWT) based on complex Daubechies wavelets as multiresolution analysis, of the largest absolute value of the wavelet coefficients in the subbands (up to 10 levels) as (pixel-based) salience measurement and of both spatial (window of size $r = 1$) and typical subband consistency checks on the wavelet coefficients. (Forster et al., 2004).

By independently working on each individual image section of the sequence $\mathcal{I}$, these 2-D methods are inevitably misled by a rather isolated sectional noisy/disturbance data that appears sharpest, in theory contrary to the following 3-D approaches.

### 3.1.3 Three-dimensional approaches

Recently, a 3-D focus measurement has been introduced by Mahmood & Choi (2008) takes fully advantage of the three spatial dimensions of the original image sequence $\mathcal{I}$. It is locally based on a Principal Component Analysis (PCA) within a stack of collected sectional neighborhoods along the $z$-direction. Consequently, it simultaneously exploits all focus cues along the axial (or cross-sectional) $z$-direction in order to estimate sectional degrees of focus. Contrary to 1-D/2-D ones, this novel 3-D strategy would allow to improve the robustness. However, it actually appears ineffective due to a severe loss of sensitivity. Indeed, it finally uses the largest principal component to discriminate in-focus information, which represents the global content of the data. Hence, the authors combine it with various previous transforms, such as discrete wavelet (Mahmood, Shim & Choi, 2009) or cosine (Mahmood et al., 2008) transforms, and lately kernel function (Khan et al., 2010). Alternatively, they perform pre- or post-processings through bilateral filtering (Mahmood, Khan & Choi, 2009) or kernel regression (Mahmood & Choi, 2010), respectively.

**3-D DCT-PCA** Discrete cosine transformation (DCT) over sectional 2-D/3-D windows and discrimination of all axially-collected sectional AC[5] data by the first feature of a Principal Component Analysis (PCA) (Mahmood et al., 2008).

[5] By analogy with an electrical signal, the alternating components of the discrete cosine transform.

### 3.2 Two-dimensional LIP-based focus measurements

This first work aims at improving sensitivity to focus cues of usual measurements in order to well operate in difficult regions of the observed surface, such as its ill-illuminated/poor textured parts. Let us start with a brief introduction of the Logarithmic Image Processing (LIP) framework.

#### 3.2.1 Logarithmic image processing (LIP) framework

An original mathematical framework, the LIP model, has been introduced in the middle of the 1980s for the processing of intensity images valued in a bounded range (Jourlin & Pinoli, 1987; 1988; 2001). This model is mathematically well defined as well as physically consistent. The reader can refer to Pinoli (1997a;b) for a complete mathematical theory and many physical and/or psychophysical connections and justifications about the LIP framework.

3.2.1.1 Mathematical fundamentals

In the LIP model, the intensity of an image is completely represented by its associated gray tone function $f$. Such a function is defined on the spatial suppport $\mathbb{D}$ and valued in the real number range interval $[0, M)$, called the gray tone range. Thereafter, this class of gray tone functions, extended to the real number interval $(-\infty, M)$ and structured with the after-specified vector addition $\triangle\!\!\!\!\!+$, scalar multiplication $\triangle\!\!\!\!\!\times$ and scalar subtraction $\triangle\!\!\!\!\!-$ defines a real vector space denoted $S$:

$$
\begin{aligned}
&\forall f, g \in S \quad f \triangle\!\!\!\!\!+ g = f + g - \tfrac{fg}{M}, \\
&\forall f \in S, \forall a \in \mathbb{R} \quad a \triangle\!\!\!\!\!\times f = M - M\left(1 - \tfrac{f}{M}\right)^{a}, \\
&\forall f, g \in S \quad f \triangle\!\!\!\!\!- g = M\tfrac{f-g}{M-g}.
\end{aligned} \tag{6}
$$

This gray tone vector space $S$ is algebraically and topologically isomorphic to the classical vector space defined on the spatial support $\mathbb{D}$ with values in the real number set $\mathbb{R}$ through the mapping $\varphi$ (called the isomorphic transformation) defined as:

$$
\forall f \in S \quad \varphi(f) = -M \ln\left(1 - \frac{f}{M}\right), \tag{7}
$$

which is the isomorphic transform of the gray tone $f$. The inverse isomorphic transformation $\varphi^{-1}$ is then defined as:

$$
f = \varphi^{-1}(\varphi(f)) = M\left(1 - \exp\left(-\frac{\varphi(f)}{M}\right)\right). \tag{8}
$$

In addition to abstract linear algebra, this class of (extended) gray tone functions is an ordered real vector space with the classical order relation $\geq$ (Pinoli, 1997a).

3.2.1.2 Physical connections

The LIP framework has been proved to be consistent with the transmittance image formation model (Jourlin & Pinoli, 1988), the multiplicative reflectance and transmittance

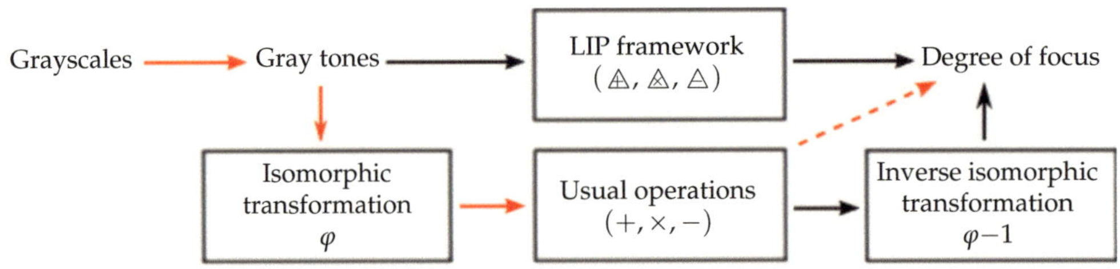


Fig. 4. Basic diagram representing both theoritical and practical (in red) computation of the LIP-based focus measurements.

image formation models (Pinoli, 1997a) and with several laws and characteristics of human brightness perception (Pinoli, 1997b). In the LIP approach, the gray tone range is inverted contrary to the classical grayscale convention. The relationship between a gray tone function $f(x,y)$ and its corresponding classical grayscale function, denoted $\bar{f}(x,y)$, is given by:

$$f(x,y) = M - \bar{f}(x,y)\,. \tag{9}$$

Indeed, the limits of the gray tone range $[0, M)$ are anticlassically defined: 0 designates the total whiteness, while the real number $M$ represents the absolute blackness. This scale inversion has been justified on mathematical reasons (Pinoli, 1997a), and physical (in the setting of transmitted light imaging processes) (Jourlin & Pinoli, 1988; 2001) and psychophysical grounds (Pinoli, 1997b).

### 3.2.2 Two-dimensional LIP-based focus measurements

LIP-based focus measurements simply consist in reinterpretations of classical ones using the LIP fremawork (*i.e.* by popularizing, from usual operations $+, \times, -$ to respective LIP ones $\triangle\!\!\!\!+, \triangle\!\!\!\!\times, \triangle\!\!\!\!-$ (Eq. 6)). For the sake of convenience, we only consider the three more widely used 2-D focus measurements: **2-D VAR**, **2-D TEN** and **2-D SML**. Among all retained methods, other 2-D ones work through various frequency transforms that make their reinterpretations less obvious and the selected 3-D strategy strongly damages the sensitivity. These reinterpretations, denoted **2-D VAR**$_\triangle$, **2-D TEN**$_\triangle$ and **2-D SML**$_\triangle$, can be clearly simplified through the use of the LIP fundamental isomorphic $\varphi$ (see Fig. 4). Nevertheless, they involve a practical subtlety to succeed from a computional point of view. Indeed, LIP-based focus measurements imply some costly operations (typically such as raising to the square) that are not enough distinguishable in the digitized case. The machine precision does not enable to well discriminate such arithmetics, notably in terms of the classical order relation $\geq$ for maximizing the resulted degrees of focus. In view of the strictly increasing behaviour of the inverse isomorphic transformation $\varphi^{-1}$ (Eq. 8), the LIP-based focus measurements can thus be computationally reduced to the computation of the respective classical ones (with usual operations $+, \times, -$) on isomorphic transform $\varphi$ of the gray tone function (see Fig. 4).

In the context of human brightness perception, a gray tone function $f(x,y)$ corresponds to an incident light intensity function $F(x,y)$ by the following relationship:

$$f(x,y) = M\left(1 - \frac{F(x,y)}{F_{\max}}\right), \tag{10}$$

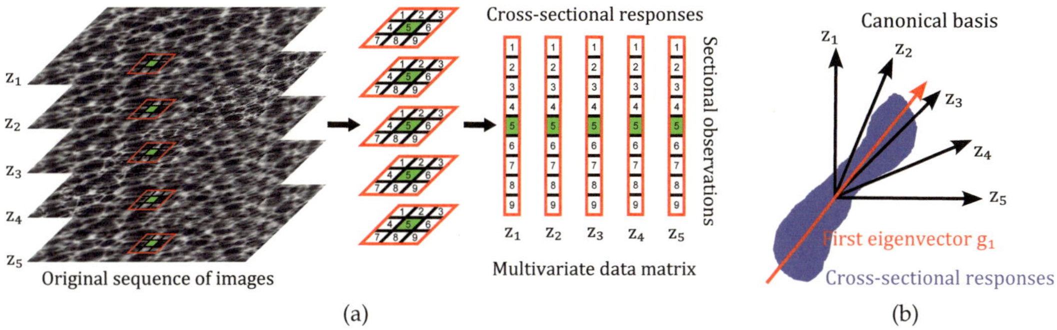


Fig. 5. Illustrations for the **3-D EIG** and **3-D N-EIG** statistical focus measurements: (a) creation of the multivariate data matrix $X$, (b) canonical basis vs. eigenbasis.

where $F_{\text{max}}$ is the saturating light intensity level ("glare limit") (Pinoli, 1997b). First, Weber described the human visual detection between two light intensity values $F$ and $G$ with a "just noticeable difference". The LIP subtraction $f \triangle g$ is consistent with Weber's law (Pinoli, 1997b). In fact, the LIP model defines specific operations acting directly on the physical light intensity function (stimulus) through the gray tone function notion. A few years after Weber, Fechner established logarithmic relationship between the light intensity $F$ (stimulus) and the subjectively perceived brightness $B$ (light intensity sensation). It has been shown in Pinoli (1997b) that $B$ is an affine map of the isomorphic transform $\varphi(f)$ of the gray tone $f$. Consequently, the fundamental isomorphism $\varphi$ (Eq. 7) of the LIP model should enable to deal with brightness (via the usual operations). About human brightness perception, the aforegiven practical limitation accordingly results in revisited measurements attempting to estimate degree of focus in terms of brightness (intensity sensation from physical light stimuli). Further details about these 2-D LIP-based focus measurements can be found in Fernandes et al. (2011a).

### 3.3 Three-dimensional statistical focus measurements

This second work conversely aims at creating novel 3-D focus measurements offering a large robustness to noise, while preserving a sufficient sensitivity to focus cues (contrary to the **3-D DCT-PCA** method), in order to well operate through noisy/disturbed acquisitions. In spite of a similar basic tool, the after-described multivariate statistical analyses are totally different than the state-of-the-art **3-D DCT-PCA** method. Moreover, they do not require any previous transformations or processings.

From a stack of single-voxels along the $z$-direction of the original sequence $\mathcal{I}(x,y,z)$ of $n$ image sections, 2-D sectional windows of $m$ pixels are considered and a multivariate $m$-by-$n$ data matrix $X$ is formed as shown in Fig. 5(a). The rows of this data matrix $X$ referred to as the cross-sectional responses are constituted by the same components of all considered sectional windows. Let $(e_i)_{i\in[1,n]}$ denotes the canonical basis of these cross-sectional responses, whose each canonical vector $e_i$ thus abstracts a different depth $z_i$ throughout the image sequence. Alternatively, each of the columns referred to as the sectional observations fully corresponds to a different original window at depth $z$. Note that the variability in variance of these sectional observations along the $z$-direction matches with the degree of focus, which is the concept of the traditional **2-D VAR** focus measurement. Each sectional observation is centered, and normalized or not by their means (that will finally yield a couple of different focus measurements denoted **3-D EIG** and **3-D NEIG**, respectively). The normalization enables to locally compensate for differences in intensity means between the image sections of the sequence. The covariance matrix $C_X$ of the sectional observations of $X$ is then calculated as follows:

$$C_X = \frac{1}{m-1} \, {}^t XX, \tag{11}$$

where $^t$ denotes the transpose operation. Afterwards, $C_X$ is diagonalized such as:

$$C_X G = \Lambda G, \tag{12}$$

in order to obtain both its eigenvalues $(\lambda_i)_{i\in[1,n]}$ in increasing order and its eigenvectors $(g_i)_{i\in[1,n]}$, diagonal components and columns of the matrixes $\Lambda$ and $G$ respectively. The eigenvectors form a novel orthornormal basis (EIGenbasis) for the cross-sectional responses of $X$. Each of them is associated with a particular eigenvalue that reveals its captured amount of variance among the total one $\sum_{i\in[1,n]} \lambda_i$ exhibited by the sectional observations of $X$. During the decomposition process of the covariance matrix $C_X$, the first eigenvector $g_1$ accounts for as much of this total variance as possible and the next ones then maximize the remaining total variance, in order and subject to the orthogonality condition. Furthermore, less influential noisy information is, to the greatest extent possible, pushed into least dominant (last) eigenvectors, whereas one of interest remains within the first eigenvectors. Finally, the degree of focus at the depth $z_i$ (with $i \in [1, n]$) is the norm of the orthogonal projection of the first eigenvector $g_1$ onto the corresponding canonical vector $e_i$, that is simply equal to the absolute value of the $i^{th}$ component of $g_1$. In the simple schematic example of Fig. 5(b), the largest degree of focus is clearly assigned to the depth $z$ of index 3 that maximizes the orthogonal projection norm of the first eigenvector $g_1$. Obviously, several first eigenvectors can be considered, *e.g.* the first $K$ eigenvectors, hence the sum of their orthogonal projection norms respectively weighted by their eigenvalues is regarded. The **3-D EIG** and **3-D NEIG** focus analyses then become less robust to noise but relatively gain sensitivity to focus cues. Further details about these 3-D statistical focus measurements can be found in Fernandes et al. (2011b; n.d.).

## 4. Results

Both retained state-of-the-art and novel developed focus measurements will now be illustrated, tested and compared through various simulation and real experiments.

### 4.1 Performance comparison in simulation

A first serie of experiments using simulated data is conducted in order to dispose of ground truths for carrying out quantitative assessments of the results produced by all aforementioned methods.

#### 4.1.1 Simulation process & performance assessment

By first mapping an arbitrary texture onto a simulated depth map (that constitutes the ground truth), an artificial 3-D surface is constructed. This virtual surface is then discretized along the

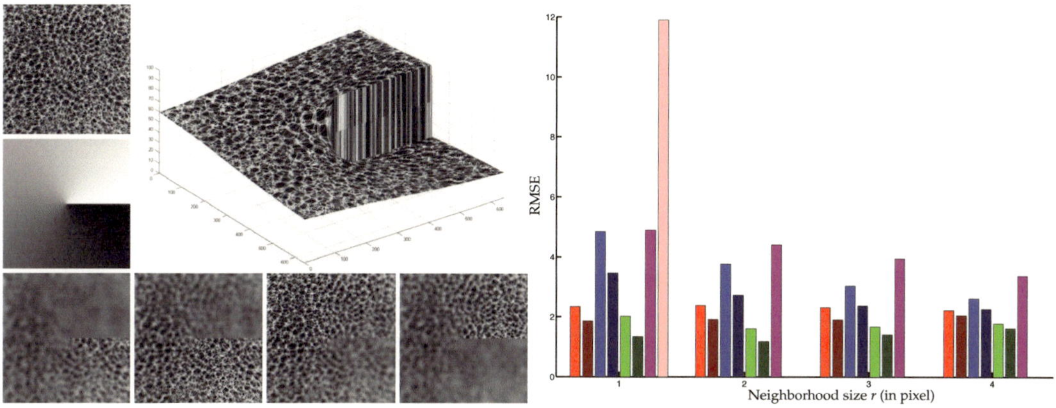


(a) (b)

Fig. 6. (a) Generation of a simulated sequence of images: Brodatz texture D111 (Brodatz, 1966) and artificial depth map (upper left), 3-D synthetic surface (upper right) and four individual image sections (sections 1, 11, 20 and 30 respectively) of the simulated sequence (lower). (b) Performances (RMSE) of the studied 2-D focus measurements for the simulated data in (a) as a function of the size $r$ of the used neighborhood. Graph key: ■ **2-D VAR** ■ **2-D VAR$_\triangle$** ■ **2-D TEN** ■ **2-D TEN$_\triangle$** ■ **2-D SML** ■ **2-D SML$_\triangle$** ■ **2-D OPT** ■ **2-D DWT**. Note that the multiresolution-based **2-D DWT** method is put into the $r = 1$ bin, as the size of the window used for the spatial consistency check. The 2-D psychophysical LIP-based focus measurements undoubtedly make fewer errors of restoration than their respective traditional ones as well as the other state-of-the-art 2-D approaches.

$z$-direction by constant steps as successive locations of the object focal plane. Afterwards, a sequence is collected by making an image for each of these locations through the 2-D shift-variant linear convolution of the "ideal" image of the surface (*i.e.* the texture image) with a modelled PSF function of the distance of defocus (*i.e.* the distance between the considered location and the depth map). The 2-D PSF is approximated by a 2-D Gaussian function (Pentland, 1987) normalized to account for an uniform illumination (*e.g.* a Köhler illumination) (Forster et al., 2004), whose standard deviation is proportional to the distance of defocus. Two different simulated image sequences are generated with various textural and topographical properties: a first exhibiting some discontinuities to assess accuracy and sensitivity of the studied focus measurements (Fig. 6(a)), and a second one imaging a smoother surface but with additive Gaussian or impulse noises to theoretically test their robustness (Fig. 7(a)). Finally, performances are measured in terms of the root-mean-square-error (RMSE) metric with respect to the ground truth (Gonzalez & Woods, 2008).

### 4.1.2 Results & discussion

The first simulated experiment in Fig. 6 puts most sensitive studied 2-D focus measurements to the test, as a function of the used neighborhood size $r$. It notably aims at evaluating the 2-D psychophysical LIP-based focus measurements (**2-D VAR$_\triangle$**, **2-D TEN$_\triangle$** and **2-D SML$_\triangle$**) versus their respective traditional ones (**2-D VAR**, **2-D TEN** and **2-D SML**). The LIP-based reinterpretations clearly outperform their traditional ones (for any of the intances of $r$). They are more sensivite, that is to say they offer a better capacity to distinguish focus cues of

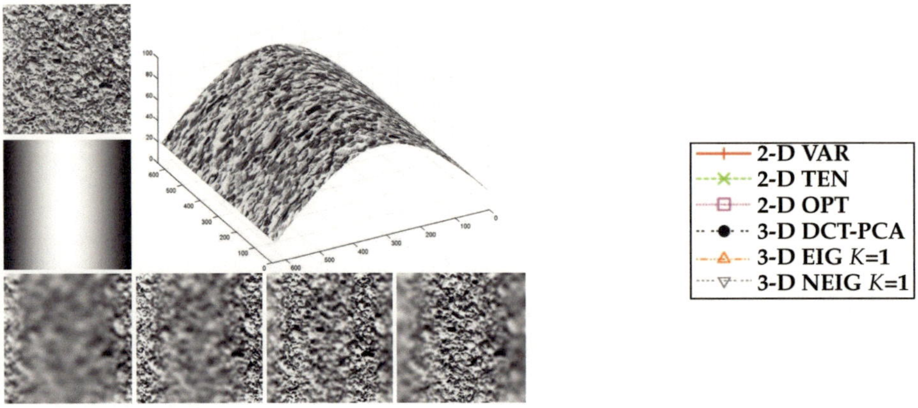


(a)

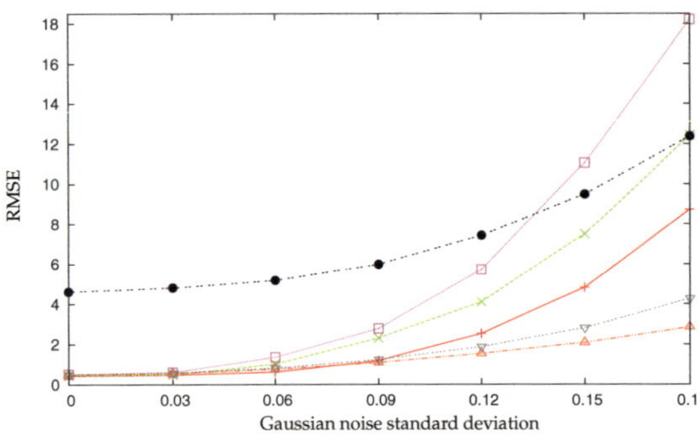


(b) Gaussian noise

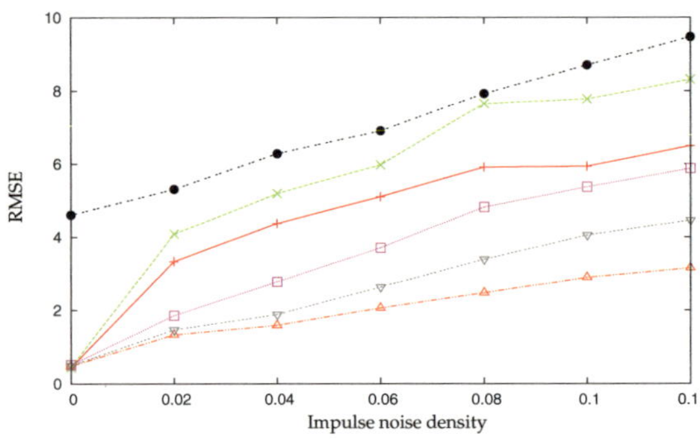


(c) Impulsive noise

Fig. 7. (a) Generation of a simulated sequence of images: Brodatz texture D5 (Brodatz, 1966) and artificial depth map (upper left), 3-D synthetic surface (upper right) and four individual image sections (sections 1, 11, 20 and 30 respectively) of the simulated sequence (lower). (b-c) Performances (RMSE) of the most robust studied focus measurements for the simulated data in (a) under various noisy conditions ($r = 8$ pixels). The proposed 3-D statistical analyses **3-D EIG** and **3-D NEIG** with $K$ set to 1 make fewer errors of restoration in presence of artificial impulsive or Gaussian noises.

poor contrasted/textured or ill-illuminated regions, but at the expense of a sligh loss of robustess. Notice that the improvements are even more obvious for smaller neighborhood sizes. This enables to employ smaller operating windows that smooth less the restoration process, most notably around sharp depth slopes or even discontinuities of the observed surface. Incidentally, LIP-based focus measurements also make fewer restoration errors than the other 2-D retained methods. On account of its multiresolution analysis, the **2-D DWT** approach avoids operating over fixed-size windows, but does not guarantee stability in return. As for the **2-D OPT** focus measurement, its band-pass filter designed for offering robustess inevitably damages the sensitivity, a bit like 3-D approaches that favour robustness to sensitivity.

In Fig. 7, the second simulated test studies most robust aforementioned focus measurements under various artificial noisy conditions. In view of the fact that the synthetic depth map

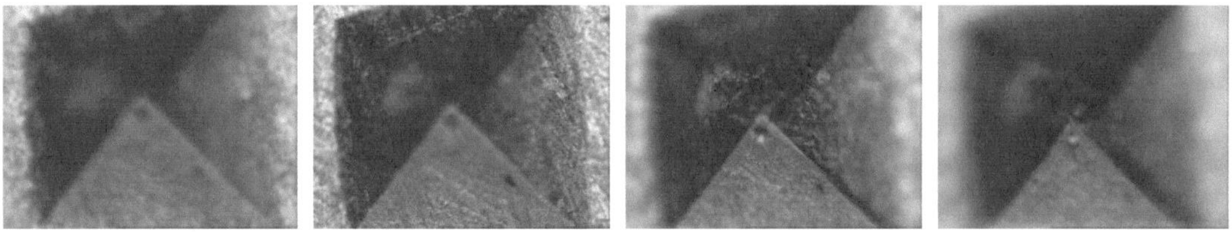

(a) Section 1 (b) Section 14 (c) Section 28 (d) Section 42

Fig. 8. Some individual 2-D image sections among the 42 constituting the image sequence of the grain of sand. This sequence was imaged in steps of 3.2 $\mu$m through a reflected white-light microscope equipped with a $\times$ 20 / 0.46 NA objective in air immersion. Each image section is 766 $\times$ 573 pixels, representating 635 $\times$ 475 $\mu$m.

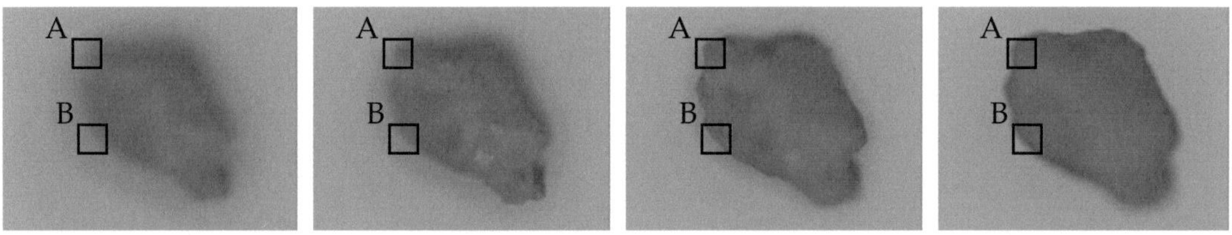


(a) Section 1 (b) Section 17 (c) Section 34 (d) Section 50

Fig. 9. Some individual 2-D image sections among the 50 constituting the image sequence of the Vickers hardness test. This sequence was imaged in steps of 9 $\mu$m through a reflected white-light microscope equipped with a $\times$ 10 / 0.3 NA objective in air immersion. Each image section is 766 $\times$ 573 pixels, representating 1262 $\times$ 944 $\mu$m. The marked regions A and B will be used as sites for comparing the different restored textures.

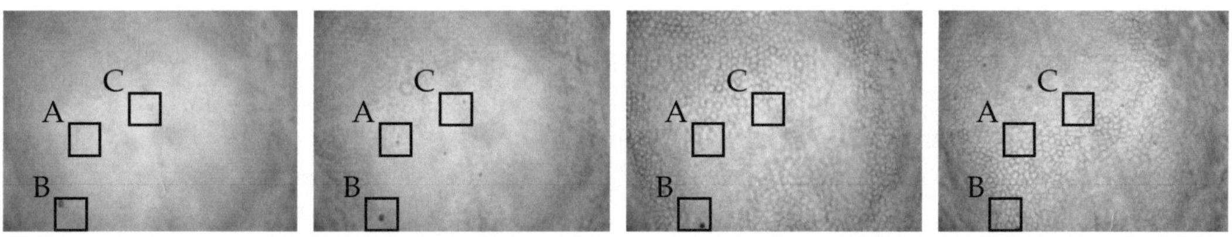


(a) Section 1 (b) Section 10 (c) Section 20 (d) Section 30

Fig. 10. Some individual 2-D image sections among the 40 constituting the image sequence of the human *ex-vivo* corneal endothelium. This sequence was imaged in steps of 4.5 $\mu$m through a transmitted white-light microscope equipped with a $\times$ 10 / 0.25 NA objective in air immersion. Each image section is 1040 $\times$ 772 pixels, representating 718 $\times$ 533 $\mu$m. Note that both bottom left corner and right edge regions never appear in-focus throughout the sequence. The marked regions A, B and C will be used as sites for comparing the different restored textures. Some cell fragments present in the immersion biochemical solution are clearly visible on (a) and (b) as small dark spots, *e.g.* throughout the region B. Futhermore, some contrast reversals emerge: the endothelial cell borders, which are normally darker than the cell bodies, look brighter for a specific range of distances of defocus.

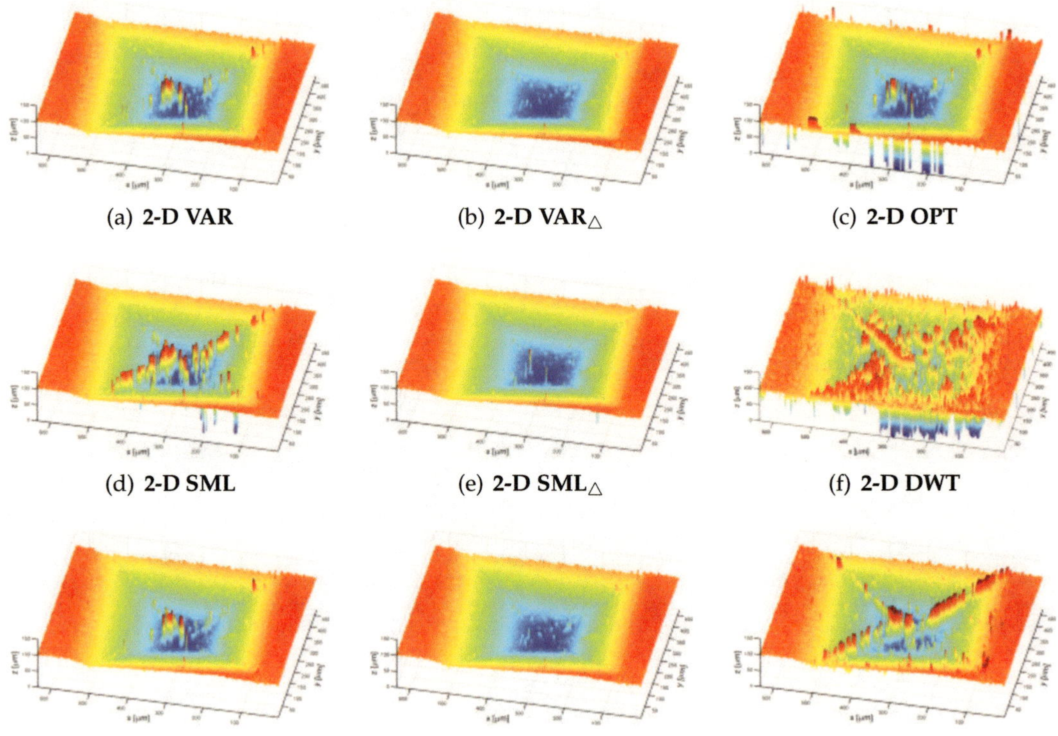

(a) **2-D VAR** (b) **2-D VAR**$_\triangle$ (c) **2-D OPT**

(d) **2-D SML** (e) **2-D SML**$_\triangle$ (f) **2-D DWT**

(g) **3-D EIG** $K$**=1** (h) **3-D NEIG** $K$**=1** (i) **3-D DCT-PCA**

Fig. 11. Reconstructed depth maps for the image sequence of the Vickers hardness test presented in Fig. 8 ($r = 3$ pixels) after a median filtering ($r = 2$ pixels). The color $z$-scale is: 0 • • 30 • • 60 • • 90 • • 120 $\mu m$ •. The depth maps recovered by our proposed methods (b),(e), (g) and (h) more reveal the pyramid-shaped structure of the sample.

exhibits neither sharp depth slopes nor discontinuities, we opt for a rather large neighborhood size $r$ ($r = 8$ pixels), moreover necessary to average out noise. In presence of noise, the proposed **3-D EIG** and **3-D NEIG** methods with $K$ set to 1 clearly outperform the state-of-the-art other ones. The adopted 3-D statistical strategies make possible a better discrimination of focus cues "drowned" in noise. Notice that the **3-D EIG** version offers a more robust behaviour than the normalized **3-D NEIG** one. As for the other 3-D focus measurement (**3-D DCT-PCA**), it shows the weakest performances by lack of sensitivity, the previous transformation being not sufficient to improve it.

### 4.2 Results on experimental data

We now illustrate the potential of the suggested focus measurements on real image sequence acquisitions.

#### 4.2.1 Experimental setup

The real test dataset is made up of three image sequences exclusively acquired in conventional optical microscopy by gradually shifting the samples along the optical axis direction with a

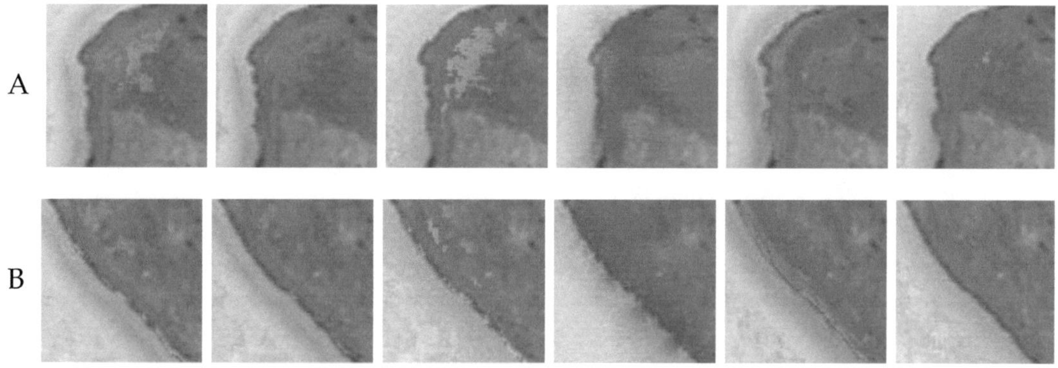


(a) **2-D TEN** (b) **2-D TEN$_\triangle$** (c) **2-D OPT** (d) **2-D DWT** (e) **3-D DCT-PCA** (f) **3-D NEIG $K$=1**

Fig. 12. Details of the restored textures in the regions A and B for the image sequence of the grain of sand presented in Fig. 9 ($r = 4$ pixels). In the details (b) and (f) resulting from our suggested methods, there are less bright artefacts and the grain borders appear darker and sharper.

motorized stage, but through different configurations (using reflected or transmitted light) and magnifications. Related to various application fields, three samples with varying textural and topographical properties are regarded so as to rigorously test both selected and proposed methods. The first two ones are a Vickers hardness test[6] performed on a polished aluminium plate surface and a grain of sand; their reflected white-light acquisitions are illustrated and described in Fig. 8 and Fig. 9, respectively. These real image sequences exhibit some difficult regions: *e.g.* around the sharp borders of the sand grain and at the bottom of the Vickers pyramid-shaped indentation, thus requiring a good sensitivity from the focus measurements. Moreover, they are necessarly degraded by some noisy data introduced by the imaging system during the acquisition, but in much lesser extent than the third one. This latter, illustrated and described in Fig. 10, images using transmitted white-light an human *ex-vivo* corneal endothelium[7] folded after storage of the graft in a specific preservation medium (Pels & Schuchard, 1983). Effectively, it appears very disturbed by intense contrast reversals and some cell fragments present in the graft immersion solution. For these real image sequences, the assessment will be only qualitative, *i.e.* by visually examining and comparing the restored depth maps and/or textures; these latter will be highlighted in some crucial regions for a better visibility.

#### 4.2.2 Results & discussion

The topography of the Vickers hardness test reconstructed by the major part of the aforementioned focus measurements are shown in Fig. 11. Those related to proposed methods clearly exhibit less artefacts (*e.g.* wrong sharp peaks), notably at the bottom and the edges of

[6] The test of Vickers consists in examining the deformation of a material from a standard pyramid-shaped diamond indenter to deduce a measure of hardness (Tabor, 2000).

[7] The endothelium is the innermost layer of the cornea and is constituted of a monolayer and hexagonal mosaic of cells. Given that those non-regenerative cells make keeping the cornea clear, the estimation of its cell density is essential in the corneal transplant process (Thuret et al., 2004; 2003).

(a) (b)

Fig. 13. 3-D surface reconstructions (a) of the grain of sand using the **3-D NEIG** method and (b) of the Vickers hardness test using the **2-D VAR**$_{\triangle}$ method.

the pyramid-shaped indentation. Compared to classical **2-D VAR** and **2-D SML** methods, the respective psyschophysical LIP-based reinterpretations (**2-D VAR**$_{\triangle}$ and **2-D SML**$_{\triangle}$) are able to deal with more difficult regions, such as poorly textured and/or ill-illuminated ones. Moreover, they offer a relative robustness to noise sufficient for most real usual cases. In same cases, the more sensitive normalized **3-D NEIG** method with $K$ set to 1 will be preferred to **3-D EIG** $K$**=1** one, except for much noisier acquisitions as encountered in the last example below. The normalization effectively provides some accuracy and stability to the analysis, up to a certain degree of noise in the image sequence. A 3-D reconstruction of the Vickers hardness test is shown in Fig. 13(a).

Concerning the grain of sand, the textures resulting from a more restricted set of aforementioned focus measurements are highlighted and compared in Fig. 12. First, the light-gray stains around the grain corner of the region A that designate false textural restorations are much less frequent with our suggested **2-D TEN**$_{\triangle}$ and, even more so, **3-D NEIG** $K$**=1** methods. Second, the inspection of the grain borders within B clearly reveals marked improvements with the same **2-D TEN**$_{\triangle}$ and **3-D NEIG** $K$**=1** methods. As previously, there are less bright artefacts in and around the borders, which moreover appear much darker and sharper. As previously, a 3-D reconstruction of the grain of sand is shown in Fig. 13(b), in which a binary mask is used so as to exclude the background from the reconstruction process (Niederöst et al., 2003).

In Fig. 14, we compare both depth map and texture obtained with the most robust studied focus measurements from the noisy and disturbed image sequence of the corneal endothelium. Contrary to above real examples, a larger neighborhood size ($r = 10$ pixels) is used, because of both wider textural content and noisier aspect of the image sequence. Moreover, this is here non-prejudicial in view of the complete absence of discontinuities and sharp slopes. First, the depth map recovered by the proposed **3-D EIG** $K$**=1** method clearly exhibits less artefacts, anatomically impossible as the endothelial surface is necessarily continuous. Indeed, it distinctly contains less underestimated (over-red) and overestimated (blue) regions caused by cell fragments and contrast reversals, respectively. As for the restored textures, their inspection corroborates the above appreciation (moreover knowing that each of them is intimately related to its respective depth map). The texture tagged with **3-D EIG** $K$**=1**

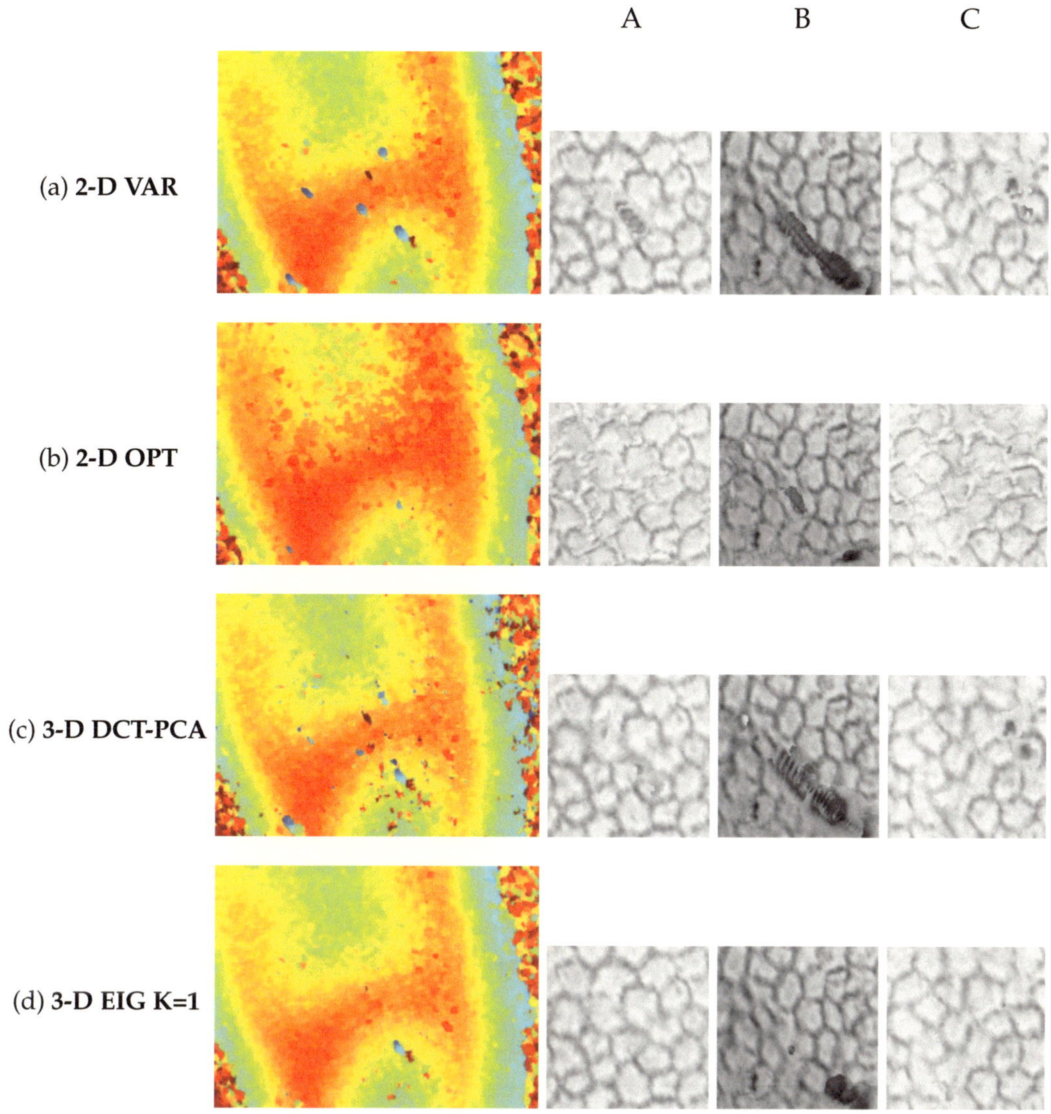


Fig. 14. Reconstructed depth maps (left) and details of the restored textures in the regions A, B and C (right) for the image sequence of the human *ex-vivo* corneal endothelium presented in Fig. 10 ($r = 10$ pixels). The color $z$-scale is: **0** • • 29.25 • • 58.5 • • 87.75 • • 117 • • 146.25 • • 175.5 $\mu$m. The **3-D EIG K=1** depth map in (d) distincly contains fewer blue spots and over-red regions respectively caused by moving cell fragments and cell border contrast reversals, moreover attested by the details of its respective texture in (d) that noticeably exhibit less artefacts attributed to both disturbances.

is not too much damaged by disturbances, like dark steaks and bright cell borders due to moving cell fragments and contrast reversals, respectively.

## 5. Conclusions

This chapter has focused on image restoration of both topographical and textural information of an observed surface from a registered image sequence acquired by optical sectioning through the common concepts of Shape-From-Focus (SFF) and Extended Depth-of-Field (EDF). More particularly, the essential step of these complementary processes of restoration: the focus measurement, has been examined. After a brief specialized review, we have introduced novel evolved focus measurements that push the limits of state-of-the-art ones in terms of sensitivity and robustness, in order to cope with various frequently encountered acquisition issues.

On the one hand, reinterpretations with the LIP framework (**2-D VAR**$_{\triangle}$, **2-D TEN**$_{\triangle}$ and **2-D SML**$_{\triangle}$) of three traditional 2-D focus measurements (**2-D VAR, 2-D TEN** and **2-D SML**) have been suggested. From a computational point of view, they involve some subtleties to succeed that, about human brightness perception, accordingly result in revisited focus measurements attempting to work in terms of brightness (intensity sensation from physical light stimuli). Firstly designed to deal with difficult ill-illuminated and poor textured parts of the obserbed surface, the strategy of using the LIP model effectively confers higher sensitivity to focus cues, at the expense of a slight loss of noise robustness that nevertheless remains sufficient in most usual cases. On the other hand, novel 3-D statistical focus measurements (**3-D EIG** and **3-D NEIG**) have been developed in order to conversely handle noisy and disturbed acquisitions. Contrary to 2-D sectional way adopted by the major part of the current methods, a 3-D strategy is originally achieved throughout the image sequence via multivariate statistical analyses within local stacks of collected 2-D sectional windows along the axial direction, thereby offering a strong robustness to noise while preserving a sufficient sensitivity (contrary to the state-of-the-art **3-D DCT-PCA** one). The efficiency of all proposed focus measurements have been clearly demonstrated on simulated data and real experimental acquisitions.

The concept of reinterpreting traditional focus measurements through the LIP framework is obviously restricted to neither image processing frameworks nor to specific focus measurements. While the studied focus measurements are illustrated in the context of conventional optical microscopy, they are also applicable to the wider range of imaging systems offering a limited depth-of-field, provided the acquired image sequence is previously registered. Morever, they can be used for all application issues requiring focus degree information (obviously after considering the focus measurement strategy and dimensionality), such as autofocusing. Finally, we believe that the use of adaptive windows instead of fixed-size ones for measuring degrees of focus could improve the restoration process, with a view to always capturing focus cues (whatever the textural content of the observed surface) while reducing the inherent smoothing effect (around sharp depth slopes and discontinuities of the observed surface).

## 6. Acknowledgments

The authors would like to thank the different partners from the University Hospital Center of Saint-Etienne, and from the LPMG and PECM CNRS Units in France who have kindly supplied the different original images studied in this chapter.

## 7. References


Agard, D. A. (1984). Optical sectioning microscopy: Cellular architecture in three dimensions, *Annual Review of Biophysics and Bioengineering* 13: 191–219.

Ahmad, M. B. & Choi, T. S. (2005). A heuristic approach for finding best focused shape, *IEEE Transactions on Circuits and Systems for Video Technology* 15(4): 566–574.

Asif, M. & Choi, T. S. (2001). Shape from focus using multilayer feedforward neural networks, *IEEE Transactions on Image Processing* 10(11): 1670–1675.

Boddeke, F. R., Van Vliet, L. J., Netten, H. & Young, I. T. (1994). Autofocusing in microscopy based on the otf and sampling, *Bioimaging* 2(4): 193–203.

Born, M. & Wolf, E. (1991). *Principles of Optics - Electromagnetic Theory of Propagation Interference and Diffraction of Light*, 6th (corrected) edn, Pergamon Press, New York, USA.

Brenner, J. F., Dew, B. S., Horton, J. B., King, T., Neurath, P. W. & Selles, W. D. (1976). Automated microscope for cytologic research: Preliminary evaluation, *Journal of Histochemistry & Cytochemistry* 24(1): 100–111.

Brodatz, P. (1966). *Textures: A Photographic Album for Artists and Designers*, Dover Publications, New York, USA.

Burt, P. & Adelson, E. (1983). The laplacian pyramid as a compact image code, *IEEE Transactions on Communications* 31: 532–540.

Burt, P. J. & Kolczynski, R. J. (1993). Enhanced image capture through fusion, *Proceedings of the IEEE International Conference on Computer Vision*, Berlin, Germany, pp. 173–182.

Darrell, T. & Wohn, K. (1988). Pyramid based depth from focus, *Proceedings of the IEEE Conference on Computer Vision and Pattern Recognition*, Ann Arbor, MI , USA, pp. 504–509.

Fernandes, M., Gavet, Y. & Pinoli, J.-C. (2011a). Improving focus measurements using logarithmic image processing, *Journal of Microscopy* 242(3): 228–241.

Fernandes, M., Gavet, Y. & Pinoli, J.-C. (2011b). Robust shape-from-focus by 3-D multivariate statistical analyses, *Proceedings of the IEEE International Conference on Image Processing*, Brussels, Belgium, pp. 2113–2116.

Fernandes, M., Gavet, Y. & Pinoli, J.-C. (n.d.). Robust 3-D reconstruction of surfaces from image focus by local cross-sectional multivariate statistical analyses: application to human ex-vivo corneal endotheliums, Submitted.

Forster, B., Van De Ville, D., Berent, J., Sage, D. & Unser, M. (2004). Complex wavelets for extended depth-of-field: A new method for the fusion of multichannel microscopy images, *Microscopy Research and Technique* 65(1-2): 33–42.

Gonzalez, R. C. & Woods, R. E. (2008). *Digital Image Processing*, 3rd edn, Prentice-Hall, Inc., Upper Saddle River, NJ, USA.

Groen, F. C. A., Young, I. T. & Ligthart, G. (1985). A comparison of different focus functions for use in autofocus algorithms, *Cytometry* 6(2): 81–91.

Helmli, F. S. & Scherer, S. (2001). Adaptive shape from focus with an error estimation in light microscopy, *Proceedings of the IEEE International Symposium on Image and Signal Processing and Analysis*, Pula , Croatia, pp. 188–193.

Horn, B. K. P. (2001). *Robot Vision*, 13th edn, The MIT Press, Cambridge, MA, USA.

Jourlin, M. & Pinoli, J.-C. (1987). Logarithmic image processing, *Acta Stereologica* 6: 651–656.

Jourlin, M. & Pinoli, J.-C. (1988). A model for logarithmic image processing, *Journal of Microscopy* 149: 21–35.

Jourlin, M. & Pinoli, J. C. (2001). Logarithmic image processing - the mathematical and physical framework for the representation and processing of transmitted images, *Advances in Imaging and Electron Physics* 115: 129–196.

Khan, A., Mahmood, M. T. & Choi, T. S. (2010). A nonlinear transform based three-dimensional shape recovery from image focus, *International Journal of Pattern Recognition and Artificial Intelligence* 24(5): 719–736.

Kristan, M., Perš, J., Perše, M. & Kovačič, S. (2006). A bayes-spectral-entropy-based measure of camera focus using a discrete cosine transform, *Pattern Recognition Letters* 27(13): 1431–1439.

Krotkov, E. (1987). Focusing, *International Journal of Computer Vision* 1(3): 223–237.

Liu, Z., Tsukada, K., Hanasaki, K., Ho, Y. K. & Dai, Y. P. (2001). Image fusion by using steerable pyramid, *Pattern Recognition Letters* 22(9): 929–939.

Mahajan, V. N. (1998). *Optical Imaging and Aberrations Part I: Ray Geometrical Optics*, SPIE Press, Bellingham, Washington, USA.

Mahajan, V. N. (2001). *Optical Imaging and Aberrations Part II: Wave Diffraction Optics*, SPIE Press, Bellingham, Washington, USA.

Mahmood, M. T. & Choi, T. S. (2008). A feature analysis approach to estimate 3D shape from image focus, *Proceedings of the IEEE International Conference on Image Processing*, Vol. 1–5, San Diego, CA , USA, pp. 3216–3219.

Mahmood, M. T. & Choi, T. S. (2010). 3D shape recovery from image focus using kernel regression in eigenspace, *Image and Vision Computing* 28(4): 634–643.

Mahmood, M. T., Choi, W. J. & Choi, T. S. (2008). PCA-based method for 3D shape recovery of microscopic objects from image focus using discrete cosine transform, *Microscopy Research and Technique* 71(12): 897–907.

Mahmood, M. T., Khan, A. & Choi, T. S. (2009). Shape from focus based on bilateral filtering and principal component analysis, *Applications of Soft Computing: From Theory to Praxis* 58: 453–462.

Mahmood, M. T., Shim, S. O. & Choi, T. S. (2009). Shape from focus using principal component analysis in discrete wavelet transform, *Optical Engineering* 48(5): 057203.

Malik, A. S. & Choi, T. S. (2007). Consideration of illumination effects and optimization of window size for accurate calculation of depth map for 3D shape recovery, *Pattern Recognition* 40(1): 154–170.

Malik, A. S. & Choi, T. S. (2008). A novel algorithm for estimation of depth map using image focus for 3D shape recovery in the presence of noise, *Pattern Recognition* 41(7): 2200–2225.

Meneses, J., Suarez, M. A., Braga, J. & Gharbi, T. (2008). Extended depth of field using shapelet-based image analysis, *Applied Optics* 47(2): 169–178.

Minhas, R., Mohammed, A. A. & Wu, Q. M. J. (2011). Shape from focus using fast discrete curvelet transform, *Pattern Recognition* 44(4): 839–853.

Nayar, S. K. & Nakagawa, Y. (1994). Shape from focus, *IEEE Transactions on Pattern Analysis and Machine Intelligence* 16(8): 824–831.

Niederöst, M., Niederöst, J. & Ščučka, J. (2003). Automatic 3D reconstruction and visualization of microscopic objects from a monoscopic multifocus image sequence, *International Archives of the Photogrammetry, Remote Sensing and Spatial Information Sciences*, Vol. XXXIV-5/W10.

Pajares, G. & de la Cruz, J. M. (2004). A wavelet-based image fusion tutorial, *Pattern Recognition* 37(9): 1855–1872.

Pels, E. & Schuchard, Y. (1983). Organ-culture preservation of human corneas, *Documenta Ophthalmologica* 56(1-2): 147–153.

Pentland, A. P. (1987). A new sense for depth of field, *IEEE Transactions on Pattern Analysis and Machine Intelligence* 9(4): 523–531.

Piella, G. (2003). A general framework for multiresolution image fusion: From pixels to regions, *Information Fusion* 4(4): 259–280.

Pieper, R. J. & Korpel, A. (1983). Image processing for extended depth of field, *Applied Optics* 22(10): 1449–1453.

Pinoli, J.-C. (1997a). A general comparative study of the multiplicative homomorphic, log-ratio and logarithmic image processing approaches, *Signal Processing* 58(1): 11–45.

Pinoli, J.-C. (1997b). The logarithmic image processing model: Connections with human brightness perception and contrast estimators, *Journal of Mathematical Imaging and Vision* 7(4): 341–358.

Pradeep, K. S. & Rajagopalan, A. N. (2007). Improving shape from focus using defocus cue, *IEEE Transactions on Image Processing* 16(7): 1920–1925.

Subbarao, M. & Choi, T. (1995). Accurate recovery of three-dimensional shape from image focus, *IEEE Transactions on Pattern Analysis and Machine Intelligence* 17(3): 266–274.

Subbarao, M., Choi, T. & Nikzad, A. (1993). Focusing techniques, *Optical Engineering* 32(11): 2824–2836.

Sugimoto, S. A. & Ichioka, Y. (1985). Digital composition of images with increased depth of focus considering depth information, *Applied Optics* 24(14): 2076–2080.

Tabor, D. (2000). *The Hardness of Metals*, Oxford University Press, Oxford, UK.

Thuret, G., Manissolle, C., Acquart, S., Garraud, O., Campos-Guyotat, L., Maugery, J. & Gain, P. (2004). Urgent need for normalization of corneal graft quality controls in french eye banks, *Transplantation* 78(9): 1299–1302.

Thuret, G., Manissolle, C., Acquart, S., Le Petit, J. C., Maugery, J., Campos-Guyotat, L., Doughty, M. J. & Gain, P. (2003). Is manual counting of corneal endothelial cell density in eye banks still acceptable? The French experience, *British Journal of Ophthalmology* 87(12): 1481–1486.

Toet, A. (1989). Image fusion by a ratio of low-pass pyramid, *Pattern Recognition Letters* 9(4): 245–253.

Valdecasas, A. G., Marshall, D., Becerra, J. M. & Terrero, J. J. (2001). On the extended depth of focus algorithms for bright field microscopy, *Micron* 32(6): 559–569.

Vollath, D. (1987). Automatic focusing by correlative methods, *Journal of Microscopy* 147: 279–288.

Watanabe, M. & Nayar, S. K. (1997). Telecentric optics for focus analysis, *IEEE Transactions on Pattern Analysis and Machine Intelligence* 19(12): 1360–1365.

Wee, C. Y. & Paramesran, R. (2007). Measure of image sharpness using eigenvalues, *Information Sciences* 177(12): 2533–2552.

Willson, R. G. (1994). Modeling and calibration of automated zoom lenses, *Technical Report CMU-RI-TR-94-03*, The Robotics Institute, Carnegie Mellon University, Pittsburgh, PA, USA.

Willson, R. G. & Shafer, S. A. (1991). Dynamic lens compensation for active color imaging and constant magnification focusing, *Technical Report CMU-RI-TR-91-26*, The Robotics Institute, Carnegie Mellon University, Pittsburgh, PA, USA.

Yap, P. T. & Raveendran, P. (2004). Image focus measure based on chebyshev moments, *IEE Proceedings - Vision Image and Signal Processing* 151(2): 128–136.

Yun, J. & Choi, T. S. (1999). Accurate 3-D shape recovery using curved window focus measure, *Proceedings of the IEEE International Conference on Image Processing*, Vol. 3, Kobe , Japan, pp. 910–914.

Zhang, Y., Zhang, Y. & Wen, C. Y. (2000). A new focus measure method using moments, *Image and Vision Computing* 18(12): 959–965.

Zhang, Z. & Blum, R. S. (1999). A categorization of multiscale-decomposition-based image fusion schemes with a performance study for a digital camera application, *Proceedings of the IEEE* 87(8): 1315–1326.

# 5

# Image Restoration via Topological Derivative

Ignacio Larrabide[1,2] and Raúl A. Feijóo[2]
[1]*Center for Computational Imaging and Simulation Technologies in Biomedicine (CISTIB), Networking Research Center on Bioengineering, Biomaterials and Nanomedicine (CIBER-BBN), Universitat Pompeu Fabra, Barcelona*
[2]*National Laboratory for Scientific Computation (LNCC), National Institute of Science and Technology in Medicine Assisted by Scientific Computing (INCT-MACC), Petrópolis, RJ*
[1]*Spain*
[2]*Brazil*

## 1. Introduction

The problem of image restoration has deserved considerable attention in resent years. For the visual analysis of images, clarity and visibility of details are important factors, but for advanced processing, a high signal-to-noise ratio (SNR) is essential, as further processing steps (such as segmentation and classification) are sensitive to noise. Though the years, different techniques have been studied to improve the SNR or a degraded image. Techniques based on post-processing have the advantage of not affecting the acquisition process (Gonzalez & Woods (2001); Jain (1989); Weickert (1995)). More recently, the work of Tschumperle (2006) has explored the more extensive use of curve-preserving PDE's for restoration of images. The calculation of mean intensities over neighboring pixels, equivalent to isotropic diffusion, considerably increases the SNR, but degrades the quality of image features (edges, lines and dots). This effect can be reduced with non-linear filters. The median filter has the characteristic of maintaining these features, but details are lost, degrading the image resolution. Perhaps the most popular technique introduced in the last couple of years is anisotropic diffusion, initially proposed by Perona and Malik (Black et al. (1998); Perona & Malik (1990)).

This problem has motivated interdisciplinary research and the use of techniques actually born in other areas, as is the case of the Topological Derivative (TD). The TD has been originally conceived for the study of topology optimization and property identification problems. Since 1994 different works proposed this new paradigm for the study of such problems. The pioneer works of Eschenauer in 1994 (Eschenauer et al. (1994)) and Schumacher in 1995 (Schumacher (1995)) introduced a way to obtain the optimal shape and topology using Topological Sensitivity Analysis. In summary, this new concept called asymptotical topological expansion is posed as follows. Let $\mathcal{J}(\Omega) = \mathcal{F}(u(\Omega))$ be an arbitrary cost function that measures the "quality" associated to a given topology characterized by the state function $u(\Omega)$, which is restricted to be the solution of a variational equation defined in $\Omega$. Given a sufficiently small positive number $\epsilon$, a positive function $f(\epsilon)$ that goes to zero with $\epsilon$, we call

$\Omega_\epsilon$ the perturbed domain after the inclusion at $\widehat{\mathbf{x}}$ of a hole of infinitesimal size governed by $\epsilon$. Therefore, the asymptotical topological expansion

$$\mathcal{J}(\Omega_\epsilon) = \mathcal{J}(\Omega) + f(\epsilon)D_T(\widehat{\mathbf{x}}) + \mathcal{O}(f(\epsilon)) \tag{1}$$

provides an estimate of the cost function value in the perturbed domain for a sufficiently small $\epsilon$, where $D_T$ is known as the TD. The Topological Derivative can then be defined as (Novotny (2003))

*A scalar function, defined in $\Omega$, indicating in each point $\widehat{\mathbf{x}} \in \Omega$ the sensitivity of a cost function when a hole of infinitesimal size $\epsilon$ is introduced at that point.*

### 1.1 Motivation for the use of Topological Derivative in image restoration

In 2005 appeared the first papers using the TD in image processing: restoration by Belaid et al. (2007) and Larrabide *et al.* (Larrabide, Novotny, Feijóo & Taroco (2005; 2006)), where the objective was to recover an image that suffered some kind of degradation; segmentation by Larrabide *et al.* (Larrabide, Feijóo, Novotny, Taroco & Masmoudi (2005); Larrabide, Feijóo, Taroco & Novotny (2006)) and Hintermüler (2005), in medical images where the interest is in the identification of different organs for posterior reconstruction; and image classification by Auroux et al. (2006). He & Osher (2006) established a relation between the TD and other techniques broadly used in image processing as is the case of level sets. A remarkable feature of the TD is that it allows to compute the variation of a cost function with respect to a parameter that changes non-smoothly (e.g., characteristic function of the domain, material properties or non-continuous change of the forces acting on the problem). This derivative can be used to identify, according to some criterion, the characteristic function of an optimal domain, the material properties and their distribution in a given domain, or even the forces acting on a given domain and how they are distributed. This problem appears frequently in the context of image processing. As examples we can mention identification of edges, identification of objects, object tracking, decomposition of texture and geometry and reconstruction from projections, where the use of the TD appears as a natural way to solve these problems.

Regarding image restoration, the stationary heat equation has been used for this purpose (Kornprobst et al. (1997)). In this approach, the diffusion coefficient is usually given by

$$c(|\nabla u|) = \frac{\phi'(|\nabla u|)}{|\nabla u|} .$$

The problem consists in determining the function $\phi$ that allowed to remove noise preserving edges in the image. One property that characterized restoration methods based on non-linear isotropic diffusion was removing noise along the edges in the image. This unwanted property of non-linear diffusion, but still isotropic, was partially reduced when a non-linear anisotropic diffusion tensor was introduced (Frangakis & Hegerl (2001)). In this case, a diffusivity tensor $\mathbf{c}(|\nabla u|)$ was constructed from two eigenvectors and eigenvalues of tensor $J = \nabla u \otimes \nabla u$. Still, as diffusion across edges is not completely stopped, heuristic criterion must be introduced to avoid the loss of image details.

Stoping the diffusion in the direction orthogonal to the intensity iso-lines of $u$ is somehow equivalent to introducing a crack in the same direction. In this way, the use of the TD in image restoration appears naturally as it allows to analyze abrupt variations in the material properties. For instance, the TD can be used to determine the diffusion tensor, which in the following we recall as $K$. To formalize this, we consider the image characterized by its intensity $u_0 \in L^2(\Omega)$ defined in a limited open domain $\Omega \in \mathbb{R}^2$ (the extension to $\mathbb{R}^3$ is straightforward). For each restored image, characterized by the intensity $u \in H^1(\Omega)$, we can associate the cost function

$$\mathcal{J}(u) = \int_\Omega \nabla u \cdot \nabla u \, d\Omega \,,$$

measuring the "quality" of the restoration given by the solution of the following variational problem: Determine $u \in H^1(\Omega)$ such that

$$\int_\Omega k \nabla u \cdot \nabla \eta \, d\Omega + \int_\Omega (u - u_0)\eta \, d\Omega = 0 \quad \forall \eta \in H^1(\Omega) \,.$$

Different methods exist to remove noise and enhance edges of a degraded image. We can distinguish two types: based on the solution of a stationary problem and based on the solution of an evolutionary problem. Both types of methods are based on the application of non-linear/anisotropic diffusion on the image. In both cases, the diffusion coefficient or tensor is computed as a function of the local image gradient. This coefficient takes small values for high gradients (edges) thus stoping diffusion, and higher values when the gradient is small (homogeneous regions) promoting a higher diffusion. Both methods have two parameters. The stationary method has a parameter determining which gradients will be considered as edges and which ones not, and a second one characterizing the intensity of the diffusion to be applied. In the case of evolutionary methods, the first parameter is in some way similar to the one used by the stationary method to determine the threshold for gradients that are considered edges, and the number of iterations. For both methods, the parameter determining the gradient threshold can be estimated. But this does not happen for the other parameters, which need to be set depending on the noise type and intensity. In both cases, the the selection of this parameter will determine the quality of the result.

## 2. Topological Derivative

Topological sensitivity analysis allows to characterize the sensitivity of a problem when the domain $\Omega$ where the problem is defined is perturbed in some way. This perturbation can be a:

- change in topology: the domain $\Omega$ is perturbed introducing a hole of an arbitrary shape $\omega_\epsilon$ at the point $\hat{\mathbf{x}} \in \Omega$, and the TD provides the sensitivity of a cost function when $\epsilon \to 0$ (see Eq. (1)).
- change in material properties: a perturbation in the material properties at point $\hat{\mathbf{x}} \in \Omega$ of an arbitrary shape $\omega_\epsilon$ is introduced and the TD provides the sensitivity of the cost function when $\epsilon \to 0$ (see Eq. (1)). By "material properties" is meant the coefficients that define the variational problem associated to the problem.
- change in the forces/sources acting on $\Omega$: similar to the previous case, but perturbing the forces/sources.

In the following, and for the sake of simplicity, only the first case will be considered, namely the perturbation of the domain by the introduction of a hole. The extension to the other two cases is straightforward.

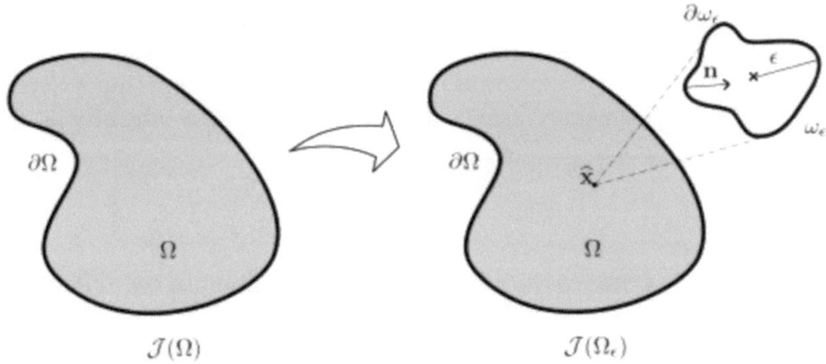


Fig. 1. Topological derivative - Change in topology

### 2.1 Topological shape sensitivity analysis

Let a problem be defined in $\Omega$ where the quality/performance is characterized by a cost function $\mathcal{J}(\Omega) = \mathcal{F}(\Omega, u(\Omega))$ where $\Omega \subset \mathbb{R}^n, n = 2, 3$, is a regular domain of open boundary $\partial\Omega$ with exterior normal $\mathbf{n}$. With the notation $(\Omega, u(\Omega))$ we empathize that $\mathcal{F}$ depends on $\Omega$ explicitly and implicitly through $u(\Omega)$, solution of the variational equation (state equation), that can be written in the abstract form as: determine $u \in \mathcal{U} = \mathcal{U}(\Omega)$ such that

$$a(u, \eta) = l(\eta) \quad \forall \eta \in \mathcal{V}, \tag{2}$$

where $\mathcal{U}$ characterizes a set (usually a linear manifold of $\mathcal{V}$) of admissible functions defined in $\Omega$ e $\mathcal{V} = \mathcal{V}(\Omega)$ the vector space of admissible variations. Also, $a(.,.) : \mathcal{U} \times \mathcal{V} \mapsto \mathbb{R}$ is a symmetrical bilinear form and $l(.) : \mathcal{V} \mapsto \mathbb{R}$ a linear form. These forms also satisfy the properties of continuity and coercivity to warrant existence and uniqueness of solution $u$.

Let $\omega$ be a open domain arbitrarily shaped and of regular boundary $\partial\omega$ containing the origin. Given $\epsilon > 0$ sufficiently small it can be defined for any point $\mathbf{x} \in \Omega$ the domain $\omega_\epsilon$ given by $\omega_\epsilon = \widehat{\mathbf{x}} + \epsilon\omega$. In this way, the introduction of a hole $\omega_\epsilon$ centered in $\widehat{\mathbf{x}} \in \Omega$ allows to characterize the perturbed domain $\Omega_\epsilon$ (Fig. 1) given by

$$\Omega_\epsilon = \Omega \setminus \overline{\omega_\epsilon}. \tag{3}$$

From Eq. (1), $D_T$ in $\widehat{\mathbf{x}} \in \Omega$ can be defined as

$$D_T(\widehat{\mathbf{x}}) = \lim_{\epsilon \to 0} \frac{\mathcal{J}(\Omega_\epsilon) - \mathcal{J}(\Omega)}{f(\epsilon)} \tag{4}$$

where $f(\epsilon)$ is a positive monotone decreasing function ($f(\epsilon) \to 0$ with $\epsilon \to 0$). Furthermore, $\mathcal{J}(\Omega_\epsilon) = \mathcal{F}(\Omega_\epsilon, u_\epsilon(\Omega_\epsilon))$, being $u_\epsilon$ the solution of the same state equation now defined in the perturbed domain, namely in $\Omega_\epsilon$: Determine $u_\epsilon \in \mathcal{U}_\epsilon = \mathcal{U}(\Omega_\epsilon)$ such that

$$a_{\Omega_\epsilon}(u_\epsilon, \eta) = l_{\Omega_\epsilon}(\eta) \quad \forall \eta \in \mathcal{V}_\epsilon = \mathcal{V}(\Omega_\epsilon). \tag{5}$$

In the work of Novotny et al. (2003) a relation between the TD and classical shape sensitivity analysis (Haug et al. (1986); Murat & Simon (1976)) is established. This result permits to use tools developed in classical sensitivity analysis for the computation of the TD. This new approach can be stated in the form of theorem as:

**Theorem 1.** *Let $f(\epsilon)$ be a function chosen such that $0 < |D_T(\hat{x})| < \infty$, then the limit when $\epsilon \to 0$ appearing in* (4)*, can be written as*

$$D_T(\hat{x}) = \lim_{\epsilon \to 0} \frac{1}{f'(\epsilon)} \left. \frac{d\mathcal{J}(\Omega_\tau)}{d\tau} \right|_{\tau=0} \tag{6}$$

*where* $\dfrac{d\mathcal{J}(\Omega_\tau)}{d\tau}$ *is the classical shape sensitivity.*

**Proof 1.** *The proof of this theorem can be found in the work of Novotny et al. (2003).*

In the previous expression is implicit the domain transformation (deformation) $\chi_\tau : \mathbf{x}_\epsilon \in \Omega_\epsilon \to \mathbf{x}_\tau \in \Omega_\tau$ defined as

$$\mathbf{x}_\tau = \mathbf{x}_\epsilon + \tau \mathbf{v}(\mathbf{x}_\epsilon) \tag{7}$$

where $\mathbf{v}$ is the velocity field characterizing the shape change and $\Omega_\tau|_{\tau=0} = \Omega_\epsilon$. The field $\mathbf{v}$ is characterized by

$$\mathbf{v}(\mathbf{x}) = -\mathbf{n} \; \forall \mathbf{x} \in \partial\omega_\epsilon \text{ e } \mathbf{v}(\mathbf{x}) = 0 \; \forall \mathbf{x} \in \partial\Omega_\epsilon \setminus \partial\omega_\epsilon. \tag{8}$$

For further information on this type of transformation see the work of Haug et al. (1986) and Haug & Céa (1981), Pironneau (1984), Sokolowski & Zolésio (1992) and Zolésio (1981).

From this theorem is naturally deduced the *Topological-Shape Sensitivity Method*, which will be explored in the following. The shape change derivative of the cost function in relation to the parameter $\tau$ can be written as

$$\begin{cases} \textbf{Compute}: \dfrac{d}{d\tau}\mathcal{J}_\tau(u_\tau) \\ \textbf{subject to}: a_\tau(u_\tau, \eta) = l_\tau(\eta) \quad \forall \eta \in \mathcal{V}_\tau. \end{cases} \tag{9}$$

where $a_{\Omega_\tau}(\cdot,\cdot)$ is given by $a_\tau(\cdot,\cdot)$, $l_{\Omega_\tau}(\cdot)$ with $l_\tau(\cdot)$ and where the notation $\mathcal{J}_\tau(u_\tau)$ evidences the dependency of the cost function on $u_\tau$ and on $\Omega_\tau$.

To compute the derivative to change in shape considering the state equation as a restriction, the Lagrangian method is used (i.e., relaxing the restriction by the introduction of a Lagrange multiplier). The Lagrangian of this problem is written as

$$\mathcal{L}_\tau(v,\eta) = \mathcal{J}_\tau(v) + a_\tau(v,\eta) - l_\tau(\eta) \quad \forall \eta \in \mathcal{V}_\tau \text{ e } v \in \mathcal{U}_\tau. \tag{10}$$

We verify, for $v = u_\tau$, that

$$\begin{aligned} \mathcal{L}_\tau(u_\tau,\eta) &= \mathcal{J}_\tau(u_\tau) + \underbrace{a_\tau(u_\tau,\eta) - l_\tau(\eta)}_{=0, \text{ solution of the state equation}} \quad \forall \eta \in \mathcal{V}_\tau \\ &= \mathcal{J}_\tau(u_\tau) \quad \forall \eta \in \mathcal{V}_\tau. \end{aligned} \tag{11}$$

We compute the derivative with respect to $\tau$ in Eq. (10), then

$$\frac{d\mathcal{L}_\tau(v,\eta)}{d\tau} = \frac{\partial \mathcal{L}_\tau}{\partial \tau} + \left\langle \frac{\partial \mathcal{L}_\tau}{\partial v}; \frac{dv}{d\tau} \right\rangle + \left\langle \frac{\partial \mathcal{L}_\tau}{\partial \eta}; \frac{d\eta}{d\tau} \right\rangle. \tag{12}$$

We then work term by term on Eq. (12). Starting by the third term on the right-hand side we have

$$\left\langle \frac{\partial \mathcal{L}_\tau}{\partial \eta}; \frac{d\eta}{d\tau} \right\rangle = a_\tau\left(v, \frac{d\eta}{d\tau}\right) - l_\tau\left(\frac{d\eta}{d\tau}\right) \quad \forall \frac{d\eta}{d\tau} \in \mathcal{V}_\tau \tag{13}$$

Then, for the particular case $v = u_\tau$, Eq. (13) is zero. Considering the second term of Eq. (12), we have

$$\left\langle \frac{\partial \mathcal{L}_\tau}{\partial v}; \frac{dv}{d\tau} \right\rangle = \left\langle \frac{\partial \mathcal{J}_\tau}{\partial v}; \frac{dv}{d\tau} \right\rangle + a_\tau \left( \eta, \frac{dv}{d\tau} \right) \; \forall \frac{dv}{d\tau} \in \mathcal{V}_\tau \tag{14}$$

where the symmetry of $a_\tau(\cdot,\cdot)$ was used. In this expression, $\eta$ can be chosen arbitrarily. In articular, it will be selected $\eta = q_\tau$, being $q_\tau \in \mathcal{V}_\tau$ the solution to the adjoint equation given by

$$\left\langle \frac{\partial \mathcal{J}_\tau}{\partial v}; \frac{dv}{d\tau} \right\rangle \bigg|_{v=u_\tau} + a_\tau \left( q_\tau, \frac{dv}{d\tau} \right) = 0 \; \forall \frac{dv}{d\tau} \in \mathcal{V}_\tau. \tag{15}$$

The previous equation is known as "(variational) adjoint equation", and its solution $q_\tau$ (or $q_\epsilon$ and $q$ if the adjoint equation is defined in the domain $\Omega_\epsilon$ and $\Omega$ respectively) as "adjoint solution". We note that, because of the properties of $a(\cdot,\cdot)$, the adjoint equation is of the same kind as the state equation (Eq. (2), or its counterpart in the perturbed domain Eq. (5)). From the computational point of view, the former means that the same computational system used to compute the solution of the state equation $u$ (or $u_\epsilon$) can be used to compute $q$ (or $q_\epsilon$).

The total derivative with respect to parameter $\tau$ of the Lagrangian is given by

$$\begin{aligned} \frac{d\mathcal{J}(\Omega_\tau)}{d\tau}\bigg|_{\tau=0} &= \frac{\partial \mathcal{L}_\tau(v,\eta)}{\partial \tau}\bigg|_{\substack{v=u_\tau \\ \eta=q_\tau}}\bigg|_{\tau=0} \\ &= \left[ \frac{\partial \mathcal{J}_\tau(v)}{\partial \tau} + \frac{\partial a_\tau(v,\eta)}{\partial \tau} - \frac{\partial l_\tau(\eta)}{\partial \tau} \right]_{\substack{v=u_\tau \\ \eta=q_\tau}}\bigg|_{\tau=0} . \end{aligned} \tag{16}$$

We notice that $u_\tau|_{\tau=0} = u_\epsilon$ and $q_\tau|_{\tau=0} = q_\epsilon$. Therefore, the former expression results in a function of $u_\epsilon$ and $q_\epsilon$ and its derivatives. As we noted before, only the boundary $\partial\omega_\epsilon$ is perturbed by a uniform expansion (Eq. (8)). Then, the derivative to shape change results in an integral only defined on the boundary $\partial\omega_\epsilon$. Therefore, the topological derivative is given by an expression of the form

$$D_T(\widehat{\mathbf{x}}) = -\lim_{\epsilon\to 0} \frac{1}{f'(\epsilon)} \int_{\partial\omega_\epsilon} \mathbf{\Sigma}_\epsilon \mathbf{n} \cdot \mathbf{n} \, d\partial\omega_\epsilon \tag{17}$$

where $\mathbf{\Sigma}_\epsilon$ depends on $u_\epsilon$ and $q_\epsilon$, and it can be interpreted as a generalization of the Eshelby momentum energy tensor proposed by Eshelby (1985). The tensor $\mathbf{\Sigma}_\epsilon$ must be identified for each particular problem, which depends on the cost function adopted and the state equation associated to $u_\epsilon$.

Finally, its necessary to compute the limit when $\epsilon \to 0$ to obtain the $D_T$ expression. For this, it is necessary to study the behavior of solutions $u_\epsilon$ and $q_\epsilon$ when $\epsilon \to 0$. This behavior can be obtained with asymptotical analysis on the neighborhood of the hole. At this point, different alternatives can be used depending on the problem under consideration (boundary conditions, type of perturbation, etc.). In all these cases, asymptotical analysis allows to express $u_\epsilon$ and $q_\epsilon$ as a function of $\epsilon$, $u(\widehat{\mathbf{x}})$, $q(\widehat{\mathbf{x}})$ and there derivatives in $\widehat{\mathbf{x}}$, respectively. Namely, as a function of the solutions of the state and adjoint equation defined in the domain **without** perturbation providing as well the function $f(\epsilon)$. In this way, substituting these equation in Eq. (17) and from the computation of the limit for $\epsilon \to 0$ the final expression of the $D_T$ at point

$\widehat{\mathbf{x}}$ is obtained. As mentioned, this expression will only depend on the values of $u$ and $q$ and its derivatives at point $\widehat{\mathbf{x}}$. The former has consequences from the computational point of view and in fact, once $u$ and $q$ are obtained, **the computation of the TD is just a post processing**.

Then, for a given cost function $\mathcal{F}(\Omega, u(\Omega))$ the *Topological-Shape Sensitivity Method* can be summarized in the following steps:

1. Compute the shape change derivative for the cost function $\mathcal{F}(\Omega_\epsilon, u_\epsilon(\Omega_\epsilon))$, using the Lagrangian method.
2. Identify the Eshelby momentum tensor $\mathbf{\Sigma}_\epsilon$ and write the sensitivity expression as an integral defined on the boundary $\partial\omega_\epsilon$.
3. Do the asymptotical analysis to study the behavior of $u_\epsilon$ and $q_\epsilon$ when $\epsilon \to 0$.
4. From the asymptotical analysis, chose $f(\epsilon)$.
5. Compute the $D_T$ using Eq. (17).

This is a general and systematic way to compute the $D_T$ for an arbitrary cost function. The particular case presented in this chapter is applied to the introduction of a perturbation in the domain $\Omega$ in the shape of a crack, which is then presented as part of an algorithm for the restoration of degraded images.

## 3. Topological Derivative in image restoration

The concept of the TD, allows to quantify the sensitivity of a performance measure of cost function when the problem definition domain is perturbed. Therefore, if the cost function is associated to the noise present in the image, it will be possible to use its TD to develop appropriate image restoration algorithms. In this context, two state equations are studied: the first one based on a stationary problem and the second one on the evolutionary problem. The TD will allow to determine the location and orientation of the cracks that should be introduced in the domain to minimize the cost function. From the point of view of the state equation, the cracks will stop diffusion in the orthogonal direction, only allowing diffusion in the tangent direction. In other words, the TD provides a procedure to compute the diffusion anisotropic tensorial field that will be used to restore the image preserving the image edges.

### 3.1 Continuous approach - $R_{D_T}$-continuous

This approach is based in introducing cracks in an image under the effect of diffusion. These cracks are introduced at specific locations in the image using the information provided by the TD. For a small $\epsilon$, let $\Omega_\epsilon = \Omega \setminus \gamma_\epsilon$ be the domain perturbed by the insertion of a crack $\gamma_\epsilon = \widehat{\mathbf{x}} + \epsilon\gamma$, where $\widehat{\mathbf{x}} \in \Omega$ and $\gamma(\mathbf{m})$ is a straight crack, being $\mathbf{m}$ the normal direction of $\gamma$ (Fig. 2). Let $u_\epsilon$ be the solution of the same variational problem in the perturbed domain $\Omega_\epsilon$ and $\mathcal{J}(u_\epsilon)$ a cost function associated to it. Then, we obtain the following asymptotic topological expansion of $\mathcal{J}_\epsilon(u_\epsilon)$ when $\epsilon \to 0$, i.e.,

$$\mathcal{J}_\epsilon(u_\epsilon) = \mathcal{J}(u) + f(\epsilon) D_T(\widehat{\mathbf{x}}, \mathbf{m}) + \mathcal{O}(f(\epsilon)),$$

where

$$D_T(\widehat{\mathbf{x}}, \mathbf{m}) = M\, \mathbf{m} \cdot \mathbf{m}$$

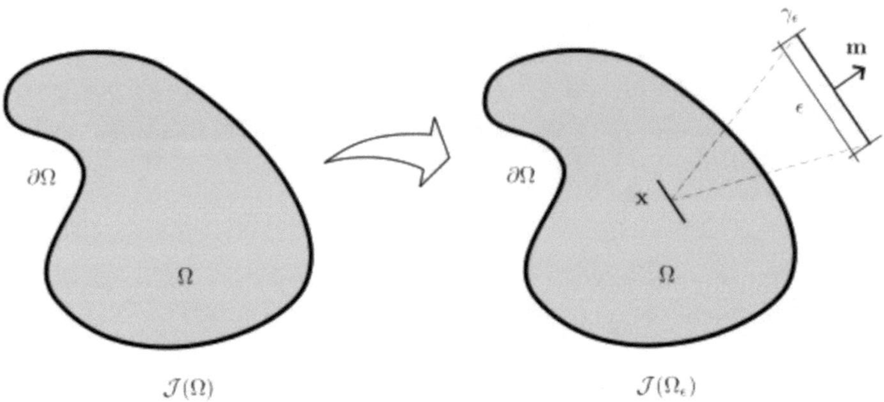


Fig. 2. Topological Derivative concept for cracks.

being $M$ a symmetric tensor given by

$$M = -\Big(\nabla u \otimes \nabla u + k(\nabla u \otimes_s \nabla q)\Big) \, . \tag{18}$$

and $q$ the solution of the adjoint equation

$$\int_{\Omega}(k\nabla q \cdot \nabla \eta \, + \, q\eta) \, d\Omega = - \int_{\Omega} \nabla u \cdot \nabla \eta \, d\Omega \; \forall \, \eta \in \mathcal{V}.$$

For any point $\widehat{\mathbf{x}}$, $D_T(\widehat{\mathbf{x}}, \mathbf{m})$ reaches its minimum when $\mathbf{m}$ is an eigenvector associated to the smallest eigenvalue $\kappa_{min}$ of $M$. Then, it is considered as the optimal direction of the crack $\gamma_\epsilon(\mathbf{m})$ the eigenvector corresponding to the eigenvalue $\kappa_{min}$. This value will be adopted as the TD associated to the creation of a crack at the point $\widehat{\mathbf{x}}$. In Fig. 3 is presented an example for the Lena image (SNR = 26dB).

As mentioned, for any $\widehat{\mathbf{x}}$ , $D_T(\widehat{\mathbf{x}}, \mathbf{m})$ takes the minimal value when $\mathbf{m}$ is the eigenvector associated to the smallest eigenvalue $\kappa_{min}$ of $M$. Then, by considering the orientation of the crack $\gamma_\epsilon(\mathbf{m})$ the eigenvector corresponding to the eigenvalue $\kappa_{min}$. This minimal value will be adopted as the TD associated to the creation of a crack at the point $\widehat{\mathbf{x}}$. The algorithm proposed here consists in computing the TD and introducing small cracks in the locations where the derivative is smaller than a given value $D_{T\,Lim}$. Two algorithms are presented: isotropic and anisotropic.

To solve the numerical problem, the introduction of a small diffusion coefficient (or a conductivity tensor that acts on one direction) is interpreted as the presence of a crack. In the proposed algorithms, the tensor $K(\mathbf{x})$ for the isotropic and anisotropic case are computed as a function of the TD, namely $K = K(\mathbf{x}, D_T)$:

- Isotropic diffusion based on the TD ($R_{D_T}$-Continuous (Iso)):
  - $K(\mathbf{x}) = k_\varepsilon \, I$ if $D_T(\mathbf{x}) \leq D_{T\,Lim}$;
  - $K(\mathbf{x}) = k_0 \, I$ otherwise.
- Anisotropic diffusion based on the TD ($R_{D_T}$-Continuous (Aniso)):
  - $K(\mathbf{x}) = k_\varepsilon(\mathbf{n} \otimes \mathbf{n}) + k_0(\mathbf{t} \otimes \mathbf{t})$ if $D_T(\mathbf{x}) \leq D_{T\,Lim}$;

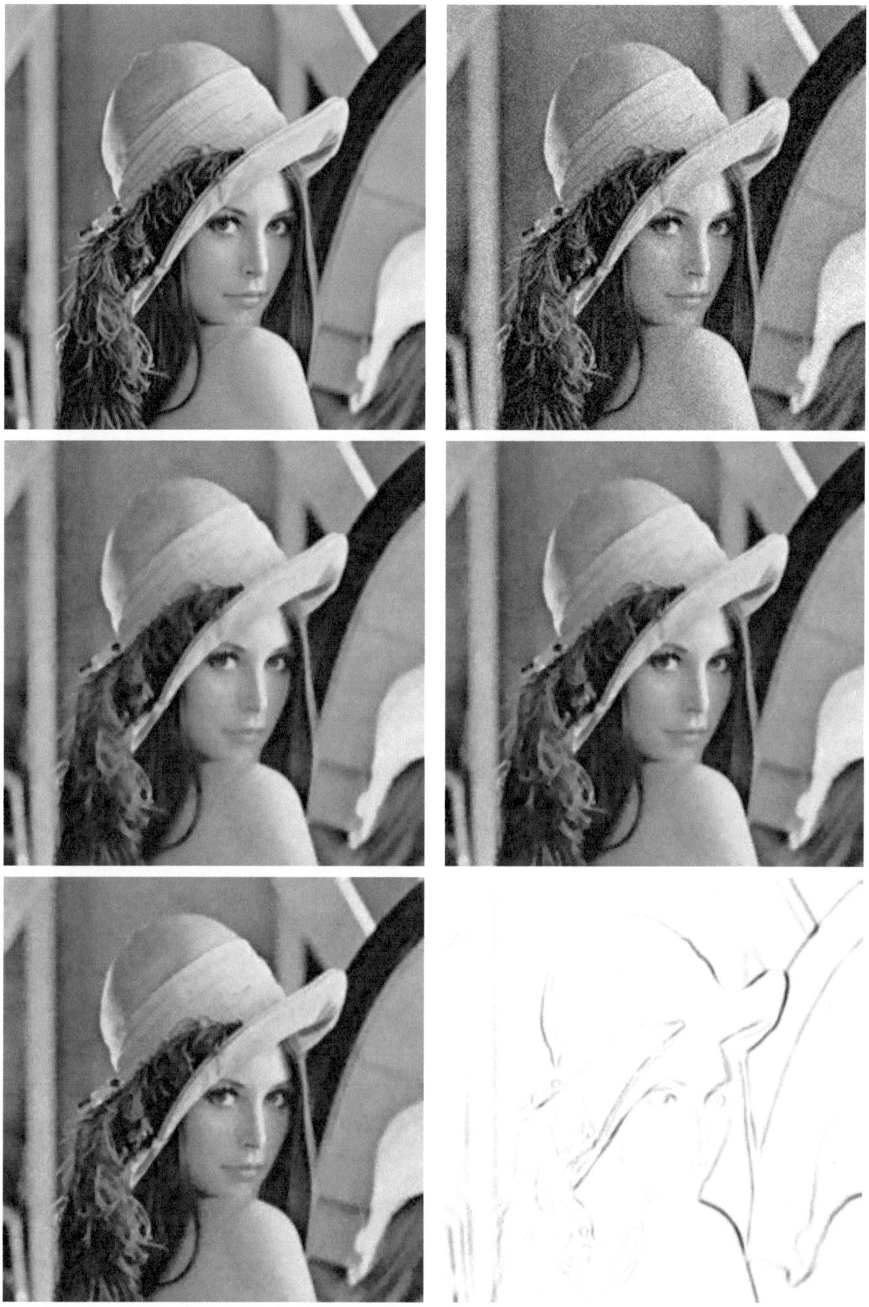

Fig. 3. Image restoration with the continuous TD algorithm $R_{D_T}$-Continuous (Iso) of the Lena image with $k_0 = 2$, upper row: $\alpha = 0.10, 0.20$, lower row: $\alpha = 0.30$ and TD value for each pixel.

– $K(\mathbf{x}) = k_0\, I$ otherwise.

Fig. 4. Image restoration with the continuous TD algorithm $R_{D_T}$-Continuous (Aniso) for the Lena image with $k_0 = 2$, upper row: $\alpha = 0.10, 0.20$, lower row: $\alpha = 0.30$ and TD value for each pixel.

for $k_\epsilon \ll 1$, $k_0$ a positive real number, $\mathbf{n}$ and $\mathbf{t}$ the normal ad tangent directions to the crack, respectively.

With this diffusion tensor the restored image is obtained by solving the following variational problem: Determine $u^* \in H^1(\Omega)$ such that

$$\int_\Omega K \nabla u^* \cdot \nabla \eta \, d\Omega + \int_\Omega (u^* - u_0)\eta \, d\Omega = 0 \quad \forall \eta \in H^1(\Omega) . \tag{19}$$

As the solution $u^*$ of the variational problem given by Eq. (19) cannot be explicitly known in general, its necessary to compute an approximate solution. The Finite Element Method is used for this purpose Hughes (2000). Then, using the simplest finite element given by quadrilateral bilinear element (for the 2 dimensional case) or a trilinear parallelepiped (for the 3 dimensional case) whose nodal points coincide with the centers of the image elements,

(a) Lena image.

(b) Lena image with low contrast.

(c) Topological derivative for the previous images.

Fig. 5. Lena image with different contrast. The second row corresponds to the TD for each image using the same color scale in both cases.

approximate solutions $u^h$ of $u$, $q^h$ of $q$ and $u^{*h}$ of $u^*$ can be easily obtained for any image $u_0 \in L^2(\Omega)$. Using these solution, an approximation by finite elements $M^h$ of the tensor $M$ is given by

$$M^h = -\left(\nabla u^h \otimes \nabla u^h + k(\nabla u^h \otimes_s \nabla q^h)\right) . \tag{20}$$

To find the restored image, three boundary value problems need to be computed. These correspond to the scalar fields of $u^h$ the isotropic problem, $q^h$ the adjoint problem and $u^{*h}$ the problem with the diffusivity tensor $K(\mathbf{x})$ computed using $R_{D_T}$-Continuous (Iso or Aniso).

**Algorithm 1** Image restoration based in the continuous topological derivative - $R_{D_T}$-Continuous

**Require:** Degraded image $u_0 \in L^2(\Omega)$, parameters $D_{TLim}$ e $k_0$.
**Ensure:** Restored image $u^* \in H^1(\Omega)$.
compute $u$ and $q$, solutions of the state and adjoint equation, respectively,
compute the matrix $2 \times 2$ $M$ and its minimal eigenvalue $\kappa_{min}$ for each point in $\Omega$,
find $K$ using $R_{D_T}$-Continuous (Iso or Aniso),
compute $u^*$, a restored image, using $K(\mathbf{x})$ previously obtained.

This algorithm uses one parameter ($D_{TLim}$) to select the elements in the image that will have their coefficients with a modified diffusivity. Then, depending on the TD value of the image being processed, this coefficient will be modified in a different number of points (e.g., two similar images with different contrast will produce a different TD, as it depends on $\nabla u$, see Fig. 5). It is easy to verify that the parameter $D_{TLim}$ must be a value in the interval $[D_{TMIN}, 0)$ (being $D_{TMIN}$ the minimum value of the $D_T$). $D_{TMIN}$ and the distribution of values of the TD in this interval can vary considerably for different images. This will require readjusting this parameter for different images making its estimation more complex.

A different alternative, presented in Larrabide, Feijóo, Novotny & Taroco (2008), is to modify the diffusivity coefficient using a fixed point algorithm. This consists in sorting in growing order the values of the TD and selecting a percentage $\alpha$ of the most negative values and use this value as threshold for the insertion of cracks in the image. We then define the set $\mathcal{M}_\alpha$ as

$$\begin{aligned}\mathcal{M}_\alpha := \{&D_T(s) : D_T(s) < 0 \\ &\text{and } D_T(s) \text{ is in the } \alpha\% \text{ most negative values of the } D_T\}. \end{aligned} \tag{21}$$

For $s$ between one and the number of elements in the image. This alternative provides a better control on the algorithm (Algorithm 2).

**Algorithm 2** Image restoration based on the continuous TD II

**Require:** Degraded image $u_0 \in L^2(\Omega)$, parameters $\alpha$ e $k_0$.
**Ensure:** Restored image $u^* \in H^1(\Omega)$.
compute $u$ and $q$, solutions of the state and adjoint equation, respectively,
compute the matrix $2 \times 2$ $M$ and its minimal eigenvalue $\kappa_{min}$ for each point in $\Omega$,
find $K$ using $R_{D_T}$-Continuous (Iso or Aniso) and Eq. (21),
compute $u^*$, the restored image, using $K(\mathbf{x})$ previously obtained.

### 3.2 Continuous approach results

It can be observed in Fig. 3 the result obtained with Algorithm 2 for $D_T$-Iso using the tensor $K$ for the Lena image degraded wit white Gaussian noise (degraded image is presented in Fig. 3). For all the experiments presented $k_0 = 2$ was used. Visually, we observe that the noise is removed in the 3 cases. The results obtained in the three experiments, namely $\alpha$ = 0.10, 0.20 and 0.30, present considerable improvement in the SNR, going from 26.92 in the degraded image to 29.57, 30.36 and 30.88 in the processed images, respectively. By analyzing in detail these images, we observe that as other non-linear isotropic methods, it has difficulties to remove noise along edges. In Fig. 4 are presented the results corresponding to $K$ computed using $D_T$-Aniso and the same Lena image. The same values of $\alpha$ (namely $\alpha$ = 0.10, 0.20 and

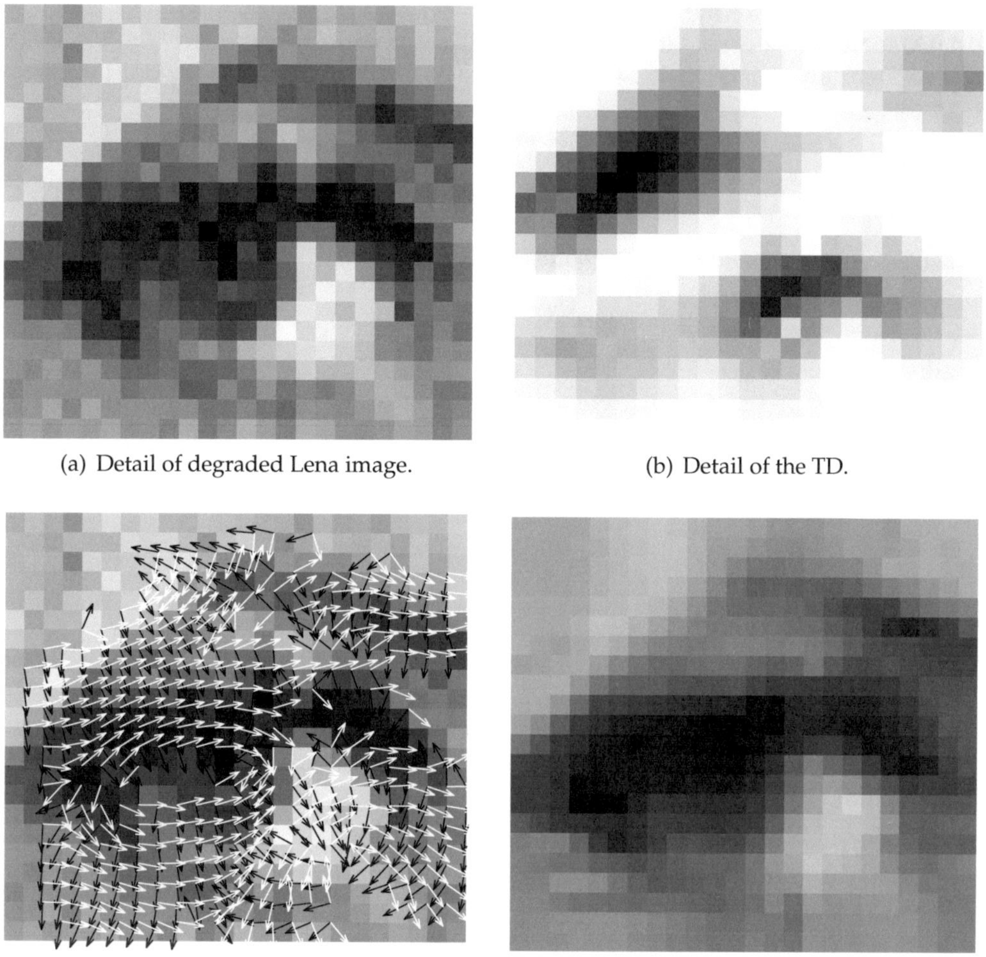

(a) Detail of degraded Lena image.

(b) Detail of the TD.

(c) Detail of the crack normal and tangent directions.

(d) Detail of the restored image.

Fig. 6. Detail of Lena's image topological derivative, crack normal (black) and tangent (white) directions and final result.

0.30) where used. Again, the SNR improves going from 26.92 in the degraded image to 28.47, 28.85 and 29.05 in the processed images, respectively. This time, and even if the SNR of the isotropic case are not reached, the noise along edges is more efficiently removed. Finally, in Fig. 6 is presented a detail of the TD, the vectors normal (in black) and tangent (in white) to the cracks and the restored image.

### 3.3 Discrete approach - $R_{D_T}$-discrete

The discrete approach relies on an auxiliary transient heat equation. In this case, cracks are introduced in the image to stop the diffusion in given points and directions. In this way, the information provided by the TD is used to determine the location of these cracks.

In the discrete approach, the image is characterized by a matrix of pixels with an intensity associated to them. We consider a bi-dimensional image $u$ given by a set of $M \times N$ pixels $s$. In each pixel $s$, the image $u$ intensity will be denoted as $u^s$. Then, the image belongs to the space $\mathcal{U}^d$

$$\mathcal{U}^d := \{u; u^s = \text{ constant in } \omega^s, s = 1 \cdots M \times N\}, \tag{22}$$

with $\overline{\Omega} = \cup_s \overline{\omega}^s$, being $\omega^s$ the domain of $s$. The set of neighbors $n^s$ of pixel $s$ was defined as the four pixels[1]

The cost function adopted by the discrete approach is

$$\mathcal{J}^d(u_t^s) = \sum_s \sum_{p \in n^s} k^{s,p} \widehat{\Delta u}_t^{s,p} \cdot \widehat{\Delta u}_t^{s,p},$$

which can be interpreted as a discrete approximation of the energy norm of the field $u$. In this expression the term $k^{s,p}$ is the diffusion coefficient of pixel $s$ with its neighbor $p$, $n^s = \{n, s, e, w\}$ are the neighbors of pixel $s$ and $\widehat{\Delta u}_t^{s,p}$ is defined as

$$\widehat{\Delta u}_t^{s,p} = u_t^p - u_t^s. \tag{23}$$

In this case, $u_t^s$ is explicitly computed as

$$u_t^s(\mathbf{k}^s) = u_{t-1}^s + \Delta t \sum_{p \in n^s} k^{s,p} \widehat{\Delta u}_{t-1}^{s,p} \tag{24}$$

where the index $t \geq 1$ represents the iteration number, being $u_0^s$ the intensity at pixel $s$, $\mathbf{k}^s = \{k^{s,o}, k^{s,l}, k^{s,n}, k^{s,s}\}$ characterizes the set of coefficients associated to pixel $s$, $\Delta t$ is the artificial step size in time.

As opposed to the continuous case, because $u_t^s$ is an explicit function and given the discrete set $\mathbf{k}^s$, it is possible to compute the exact *total variation* of the cost function for each perturbation in $k^{s,p}$. Also, we call $\mathbf{k}_\epsilon^s$ the perturbed configuration of pixel $s$ diffusivity coefficients. The value of the cost function when the perturbation is introduced is given by

$$\mathcal{J}^d(u_t^s(\mathbf{k}_\epsilon^s)) = \mathcal{J}^d(u_t^s(\mathbf{k}^s)) + D_T(s, \mathbf{k}_\epsilon^s), \tag{25}$$

where $D_T(s, \mathbf{k}_\epsilon^s)$ represents the *total variation* of the cost function due to a perturbation in the diffusivity coefficients of pixel $s$ characterized by the set $\mathbf{k}_\epsilon^s$. Likewise in the continuous case, the introduction of a perturbation to pixel $s$ where $D_T$ is negative, will produce a decrease in the value of the cost function $\mathcal{J}^d$. Using this information we can select the best candidate pixels for perturbations.

We assume $k^{s,p} \in \{k_\varepsilon, k_0\}$, so the set of all possible configurations for $\mathbf{k}^s$ is defined as

$$C(s) := \{\mathbf{k}^s = (k^{s,w}, k^{s,e}, k^{s,n}, k^{s,s}); k^{s,p} \in \{k_\varepsilon, k_0\}, p = \{\text{w,e,n,s}\}\}.$$

We see that 16 possible combinations for $\mathbf{k}^s$ exist (values are $k^{s,p} = k_\varepsilon$ or $k^{s,p} = k_0$, for each neighbor, then $2^4 = 16$ cases are possible). The case $k^{s,w} = k^{s,e} = k^{s,n} = k^{s,s} = k_\varepsilon$ is not taken into account as it does not change the value of the cost function. The 15 remaining combinations are

---

[1] i.e. *north, south, east* e *west* of pixel $s$.

**Algorithm 3** Image restoration based on a discrete version of the TD - $R_{D_T}$-Discrete

**Require:** The 2D image $u_0 \in \mathcal{U}$, a diffusivity coefficient $k_0$ and a parameter $\alpha$.
**Ensure:** The restored image $\overline{u}^s \in \mathcal{U}$.
make t=1; stop = *FALSE*; $\mathbf{k}^s = \mathbf{k}^s_{iso}$, $s = 1..M \times N$
**while** stop = *FALSE* **do**
  **for** each pixel $s$ **do**
    **for** each $\mathbf{k}^s_\epsilon \in \mathcal{C}_\sigma$ **do**
      compute $D_T(s, \mathbf{k}^s_\epsilon)$ following Eq. (27)
    **end for**
  **end for**
  **for** each pixel $s \in \mathcal{M}_\alpha$ **do**
    make $D_T(s) = \min_{\epsilon^*}\{D_T(s, \mathbf{k}^s_\epsilon), \mathbf{k}^s_\epsilon \in \mathcal{C}_\sigma\}$
    make $\mathbf{k}^s = \mathbf{k}^s_{\epsilon^*}$ the diffusivity coefficient associated to $D_T(s)$
  **end for**
  compute $u^s_t(\mathbf{k}^s)$ using Eq. (24).
  **if** $|\mathcal{J}^d_\epsilon u^s_t) - \mathcal{J}^d({}_\epsilon u^s_{t-1})| > tol$ **then**
    $t = t + 1$
  **else**
    $\overline{u}^s = u^s_t, s = 1, \cdots, M \times N$, stop = *TRUE*
  **end if**
**end while**

- no diffusion with one neighbor,
- no diffusion with two neighbors sharing one vertex,
- no diffusion with three neighbors,
- diffuse on x direction,
- diffuse in y direction,
- diffuse in all directions.

The last case corresponds to isotropic diffusion and is defined as $\mathbf{k}^s_{iso} = \{k_0, k_0, k_0, k_0\}$.

To compute the value of $D_T$ for a determined pixel, its necessary to introduce a perturbation. This is done by changing, for one pixel $s$, the set $\mathbf{k}^s$ for $\mathbf{k}^s_\epsilon \in \mathcal{C}_\sigma$. Then, the cost function $\mathcal{J}^d_\epsilon({}_\epsilon u^s_t)$ takes the value

$$\mathcal{J}^d_\epsilon({}_\epsilon u^s_t) = \mathcal{J}^d(u^s_t) - \sum_{p \in n^s} k^{s,p} \widehat{\Delta} u^{s,p}_t \cdot \widehat{\Delta} u^{s,p}_t + \sum_{p \in n^s} k^{s,p}_\epsilon \widehat{\Delta}_\epsilon u^{s,p}_t \cdot \widehat{\Delta}_\epsilon u^{s,p}_t, \tag{26}$$

for $u^s_t = u^s_t(\mathbf{k}^s)$ and ${}_\epsilon u^s_t = u^s_t(\mathbf{k}^s_\epsilon)$ computed using Eq. (24) and $\widehat{\Delta}_\epsilon u^{s,p}_t = u^p_t -_\epsilon u^s_t$, respectively.

For Eqs. (25) and (26) the total variation of the cost function $\mathcal{J}^d$ due to the perturbation $\mathbf{k}^s_\epsilon$ is written as

$$D_T(s, \mathbf{k}^s_\epsilon) = \sum_{p \in n^s} k^{s,p}_\epsilon \widehat{\Delta}_\epsilon u^{s,p}_t \cdot \widehat{\Delta}_\epsilon u^{s,p}_t - \sum_{p \in n^s} k^{s,p} \widehat{\Delta} u^{s,p}_t \cdot \widehat{\Delta} u^{s,p}_t. \tag{27}$$

As in the continuous case, it will be considered a perturbation $\mathbf{k}^s_\epsilon$ that minimizes the value of $D_T(s, \mathbf{k}^s_\epsilon)$. Using this information is proposed the following discrete image restoration algorithm based on the TD 3).

Fig. 7. Image restoration with the $R_{D_T}$-Discrete algorithm of the Lena image. Results correspond to $k_0 = 1$ and $\alpha = 0.05, 0.15$ e $0.25$ respectively.

### 3.4 Discrete approach results

The set $\mathcal{M}_\alpha$ is defined as in Eq. (21). As in the continuous case, the parameter $\alpha$ allows to control the values of the TD that will introduce changes in $\mathbf{k}^s$. In all the cases it was used $\triangle t = \frac{1}{4}$ e $k_0 = 1$, the maximum values that warrant the Courant-Friedrichs-Levy (stability) of the iterative solution algorithm. In Fig. 7 are presented some results obtained with this technique. The three images presented (corresponding to the results for values of $\alpha = 0.05$, $0.15$ e $0.25$ respectively) present a considerable improvement of SNR (going from 26.91 in the degraded image to 28.49, 29.61 and 29.53 in the processed images, respectively).

In Figs. 8 are presented the results after different number of iterations. The edges introduced in the image are highlighted in white. We observe that after some iterations, the image has edges in almost all the edges. In this way, the variation of the cost function is practically null in two consecutive iterations, stopping the algorithm. The number of edges that are added to the image in each iteration is controlled by parameter $\alpha$. In Fig. 9 is presented the detail of a region of the image before and after the processing.

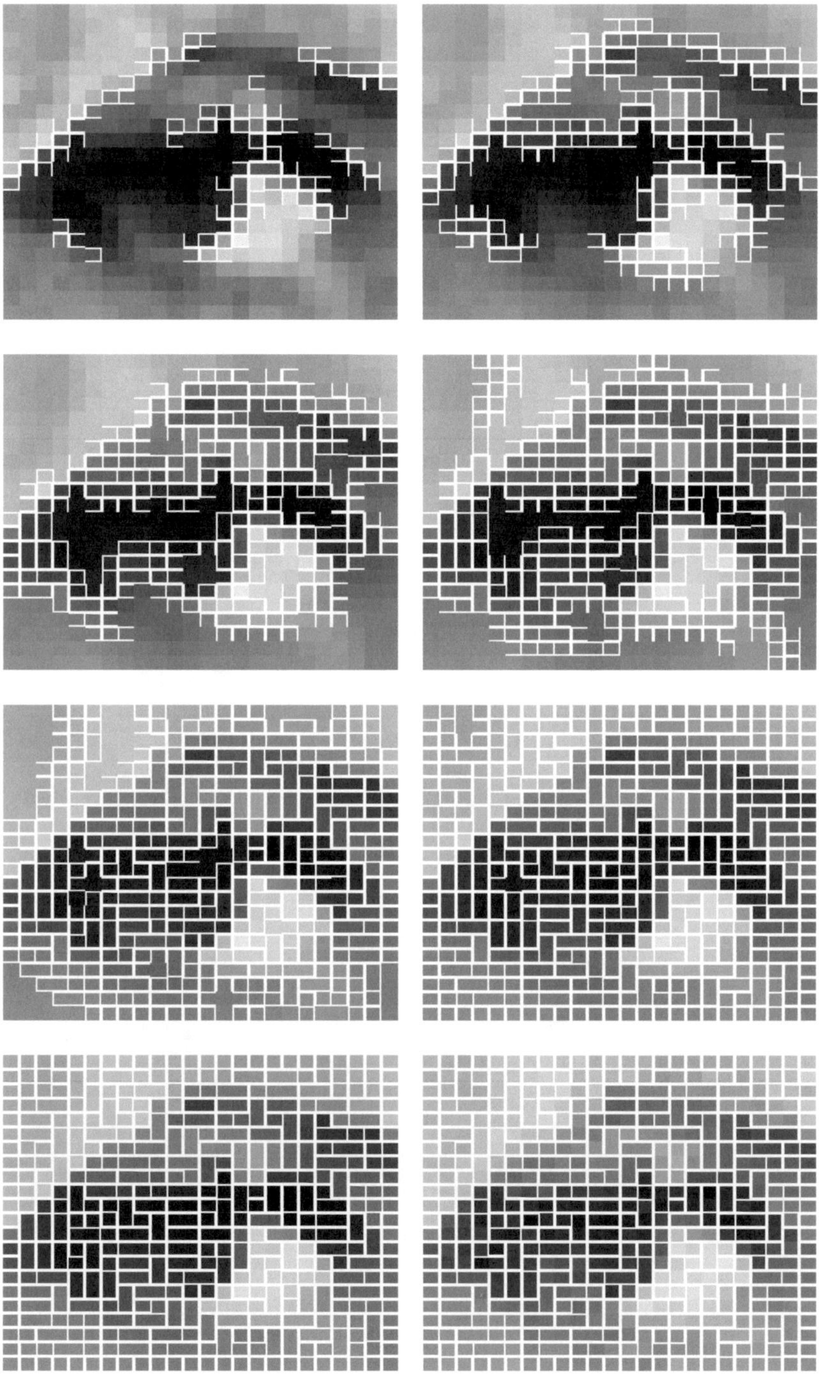

Fig. 8. Detail of the crack configuration introduced to the image during the processing ($k_0 = 1$ and $\alpha = 0.20$).

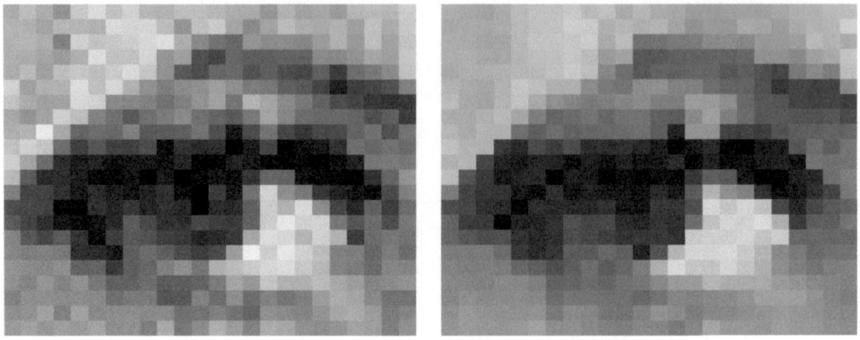

Fig. 9. Detail of Lena image before and after the processing ($k_0 = 1$ and $\alpha = 0.20$).

(a) Perona & Malik (b) Black *et al.* (c) Selective smoothing

(d) Semi-quadratic minimization (e) $R_{D_T}$-Discrete (f) $R_{D_T}$-Continuous

Fig. 10. Results for the Lena image restored using different methods.

## 4. Results

The methods based on the TD have been compared to other methods proposed in the literature

- Evolutionary methods:
  - Perona & Malik (Perona & Malik (1990)),

  - Black. *et al.* (Black et al. (1998)),
  - Selective smoothing (Alvarez et al. (1992)) and
  - Discrete $R_{D_T}$.
- Stationary methods:
  - Semi-quadratic minimization (Kornprobst et al. (1997)),
  - Continuous $R_{D_T}$(Belaid et al. (2007)).

In Fig. 10 are presented results for classical and TD image restoration methods. The processed image corresponds to the artificially degraded image of Lena (see Fig. 3) with uniform noise ($r = 20$), with an approximate SNR of 27 dB. All the classical methods depend on a parameter $\sigma$ with equivalent meaning. This parameter is used to control the diffusion on the edges of the image to preserve relevant characteristics. For the classical methods, $\sigma$ was adjusted using the technique proposed by Black et al. (1998), which allows to estimate the value of $\sigma$ as a function of the gradient of the image processed. In the case of the evolutionary methods, the number of iterations was fixed to 10, 20 and 30. The results for 20 iterations where found to shield the lowest SNR and, thus, these are reported. For the semi-quadratic minimization, the same analysis was performed for parameter $\lambda$ and the best SNR was obtained with $\lambda \approx 10$ in this case.

Parameter selection in the case of TD methods is different. Both, the Discrete and Continuous $R_{D_T}$ methods, depend on parameter $\alpha$ (a real value between 0 and 1), that determines the amount of cracks to be introduced in the image. This parameter determines the quantity (as a %) of the pixels that will be introduced in cracks to stop diffusion. As before, parameter $\alpha$ was analyzed to select the value that provides the best SNR (in the case of Discrete $R_{D_T}$ $\alpha = 0.18$ and for Continuous $R_{D_T}$ $\alpha = 0.80$.

As presented, the proposed restoration methods use information of the cost function sensitivity to a change in the topology. This information is used to find the optimal domain topology that, in the presence of diffusion, will eliminate noise preserving image features. In the continuous case, we observe that this technique eliminates most of the noise but has difficulties to remove noise in regions of elevated gradients. For the Discrete $R_{D_T}$, we observe that the noise is removed from the whole image, even from the edges. This algorithm is also capable of improving the sharpness of the edges, enhancing the image features.

In Table 1 are presented qualitative results for the Lena image. The different columns present the PSNR, SNR, $\mu(e)$ (mean error) and $\overline{\sigma}(e)$ (error standard deviation) between the processed image and the original one (i.e., without degradation). We observe similar results for the different methods, where the best performers were the evolutive method proposed by Black *et al.* with respect to PSNR (30.58dB) and SNR (30.37dB) and the one by Perona & Malik with respect to $\overline{\sigma}(e)$ (6.807). The proposed methods, Discrete $R_{D_T}$ and Continuous $R_{D_T}$, provide results of similar quality to the existing methods.

The proposed methods provide an intuitive tool for image restoration based on the concept of the TD. These methods are intended to modify the topology of the image by inserting cracks in selected location that, in the presence of diffusion, will improve the quality of a degraded image. The diffusion will eliminate noise while preserving edges and details in the image.

| | PSNR (dB) | SNR (dB) | $\mu(e)$ | $\overline{\sigma}(e)$ |
|---|---|---|---|---|
| Degraded image | 26.88 | 26.67 | 0.6005 | 11.535 |
| Perona & Malik | 30.36 | 30.15 | 1.1013 | 6.8077 |
| Black *et al.* | 30.58 | 30.37 | 1.1003 | 7.1221 |
| Selective smoothing | 29.68 | 29.27 | 1.0106 | 8.0220 |
| Semi-quadratic minimization | 30.15 | 30.04 | 1.0968 | 7.3185 |
| Discrete $R_{D_T}$ | 29.98 | 29.73 | 1.1463 | 8.0455 |
| Continuous $R_{D_T}$ | 29.93 | 29.89 | 1.0944 | 8.3446 |

Table 1. Comparison between the proposed and classical image restoration methods.

## 5. Online material

The computational implementation of these methods in Matlab is available online at Matlab Central [2]. A more complete description of the mathematical and numerical methods used in this work can be found in the work of Larrabide (2007).

## 6. Acknowledgements

Ignacio Larrabide was partly supported by the Brazilian agency CNPq (141336/2003-0) and CIBER-BBN, Barcelona, Spain. The authors would also like to acknowledge the contribution of Prof. Andre Novotny in the form of fruitful discussions that helped improving the quality of this work.

## 7. References

Alvarez, L., Guichard, F., Lions, P. & Morel, J. (1992). Axiomatisation et nouveaux operatéurs de la morphologie mathematique, *Comptes Rendus de l'Académie des Sciences* t. 315, Série I: 265–268.

Auroux, D., Masmoudi, M. & Belaid, L. (2006). Image restoration and classification by topological asymptotic expansion, *Variational Formulations in Mechanics: Theory and Applications - CIMNE, Barcelona, Spain 2006 (In press)* .

Belaid, L. J., Jaoua, M., Masmoudi, M. & Siala, L. (2007). Application of the topological gradient to image restoration and edge detection, *To apper on Special Issue on "Shape and Topological Sensitivity Analysis: Theory and Application" of the Engineering Analysis with Boundary Element Journal* .

Black, M. J., Sapiro, G., Marimont, D. H. & Heeger, D. (1998). Robust anisotropic diffusion, *IEEE Transactions on Image Processing* 7(3): 421–423.

Eschenauer, H. A., Kobelev, V. V. & Schumacher, A. (1994). Bubble method for topology and shape optimization of structures, *Structural Optimization* 8: 42–51.

Eshelby, J. D. (1985). The elastic energy-momentum tensor, *J. Elasticity 5* pp. 321–335.

Frangakis, A. S. & Hegerl, R. (2001). Noise reduction in electron tomographic reconstructions using nonlinear anisotropic diffusion, *J. Struct. Biol.* 1(135): 239–250.

Gonzalez, C. R. & Woods, R. E. (2001). *Digital Image Processing - Second Edition*, Prentice Hall.

Haug, E. J. & Céa, J. (1981). Optimization of distributed parameters structures, *Iowa - USA*.

[2] http://www.mathworks.com/matlabcentral/fileexchange/14223-image-restoration-via-topological-derivative

Haug, E. J., Choi, K. K. & Komkov, V. (1986). *Design Sensitivity Analysis of Structural Systems*, Academic Press.

He, L. & Osher, S. (2006). Solving the chan-vese model by multiphase level set algorithm based on the topological derivative, *Technical Report 56*, UCLA - CAM.

Hintermüler, M. (2005). Fast level set based algorithms usind shape and topological sensitivity, *Control and Cybernetics* 34(1): 305–324.

Hughes, T. J. R. (2000). *The Finite Element Method - Linear Static and Dynamic Finite Element Analysis*, Prentice-Hall.

Jain, A. K. (1989). *Fundamentals of Digital Image Processing*, Prentice Hall.

Kornprobst, P., Deriche, R. & Aubert, G. (1997). Nonlinear operators in image restoration, *Proceedings of the International Conference on Computer Vision and Pattern Recognition*, IEEE, Puerto-Rico, pp. 325–331.
URL: *citeseer.ist.psu.edu/kornprobst97nonlinear.html*

Larrabide, I. (2007). *Image processing via topological derivative and its applications to Human Cardiovascular System modelling and simulation*, PhD thesis, Laboratório Nacional de Computação Científica - LNCC/MCT, Petrópolis - Brazil.

Larrabide, I., Feijóo, R. A., Novotny, A. A. & Taroco, E. A. (2008). Topological derivative: A tool for image processing, *Computers & Structures* 86: 1386–1403.

Larrabide, I., Feijóo, R. A., Novotny, A. A., Taroco, E. & Masmoudi, M. (2005). An image segmentation method based on a discrete version of the topological derivative, *World Congress Structural and Multidisciplinary Optimization 6, Rio de Janeiro*, International Society for Structural and Multidisciplinary Optimization.

Larrabide, I., Feijóo, R., Taroco, E. & Novotny, A. (2006). Configurational derivative as a tool for image segmentation, *Proceedings of the ECCM 2006. LNEC - Lisbon, Portugal 5th-9th June*, European Committee of Computational Solid and Structural Mechanics - ECCSM.

Larrabide, I., Novotny, A. A., Feijóo, R. A. & Taroco, E. (2005). A medical image enhancement algorithm based on topological derivative and anisotropic diffusion, *Proceedings of the XXVI Iberian Latin-American Congress on Computational Methods in Engineering - CILAMCE 2005 - Guarapari, Espírito Santo, Brazil.*

Larrabide, I., Novotny, A. A., Feijóo, R. A. & Taroco, E. (2006). Topological derivative as a tool for image processing: Image segmentation, *Technical Report 15/2006*, LNCC - Laboratório Nacional de Computação Científica.

Murat, F. & Simon, J. (1976). *Sur le Contrôle par un Domaine Géométrique*, PhD thesis, Université Pierre et Marie Curie, Paris - France.

Novotny, A. A. (2003). *Análise de Sensibilidade Topológica*, Phd thesis, Laboratorio Nacional de Computação Científica, Petrópolis - RJ - Brazil.

Novotny, A. A., Feijóo, R. A., Taroco, E. & Padra, C. (2003). Topological sensitivity analysis, *Computer Methods in Applied Mechanics and Engineering* 192: 803–829.

Perona, P. & Malik, J. (1990). Scale-space and edge detection using anisotropic diffusion, *IEEE Trans. Pattern Anal. Machine Intell.* 12(7): 629–639.

Pironneau, O. (1984). *Optimal Shape Design for Elliptic Systems*, Springer-Verlag.

Schumacher, A. (1995). *Topologieoptimierung von Bauteilstrukturen unter Verwendung von Lochpositionierungkriterien*, PhD thesis, Universität-Gesamthochschule-Siegen.

Sokolowski, J. & Zolésio, J. P. (1992). *Introduction to Shape Optimization - Shape Sensitivity Analysis*, Springer-Verlag.

Tschumperle, D. (2006). Fast anisotropic smoothing of multi-valued images using curvature-preserving pde's, *International Journal of Computer Vision* 68(1): 65–82.

Weickert, J. (1995). Multiscale texture enhancement, *V. Hlavac, R. Sara (Eds.), Computer analysis of images and patterns, Lecture Notes in Computer Science* 970: 230–237.

Zolésio, J. P. (1981). *The material derivative (or speed) method for shape optimization, in: Optimization of Distributed Parameter Structures*, Vol. II(50), NATO Adv. Study Inst. Ser. E, Appl. Sci., pp. 1089–1151.

# 6

# Regularized Image Restoration

Pradeepa D. Samarasinghe and Rodney A. Kennedy
*Research School of Engineering, College of Engineering and Computer Science, The Australian National University, Canberra, ACT, Australia*

## 1. Introduction

Image restoration or deconvolution of a blurred natural image is a mature research activity with a rich set of available techniques and algorithms, well-summarised in review articles, Banham & Katsaggelos (1997); Kundur & Hatzinakos (1996). Despite this history and volume of work, there is current research activity motivated by the desire to find yet superior methods to restore the ground truth image (GTI). Important performance metrics to assess the efficacy of restoration methods include: restoration accuracy, computational complexity and convergence speed. In this chapter we use these performance metrics in the development of restoration methods of greatest utility for real-world applications where complexity/speed is a major concern and the evaluation of image restoration needs to take into account the highly structured features of natural images and, to a lesser extent, the human visual system.

The scope of this work focusses on non-blind image restoration where the point spread function (PSF) of the blur convolutional kernel is known. Blind deconvolution is, by its nature, a more challenging problem, Haykin (1994); Kundur & Hatzinakos (1996). However with effective and efficient PSF estimation techniques, Fergus et al. (2006); Joshi et al. (2008); Krahmer et al. (2006); Nayar & Ben-Ezra (2004); Oliveira et al. (2007), the research trend has been to handling blind deconvolution in two steps, with PSF estimation as the first step and image estimation as the second step, Levin et al. (2009). This motivates us to focus on efficient algorithms for image restoration where the blur convolutional kernel is known.

In this chapter, we first analyze existing linear deterministic restoration models and develop a class of novel models with better performance. Then using regularization as the basis, we link linear deterministic and stochastic restoration models. By introducing a previously developed novel visual metric to image regularization analysis, we study the purported superior performance of stochastic prior models and demonstrate that those models are not superior to simpler linear deterministic prior models. In addition, we show that the high complexity "derivative likelihood" models under the maximum a posteriori (MAP) framework offer no significant advantage to a properly configured, efficient "normal likelihood" model.

## 2. Quadratic regularization in image restoration

### 2.1 Regularization

Image acquisition being an inverse problem can be modeled by a continuous model in an infinite dimensional space, which is categorized as a (linear) Fredholm integral equation of the first kind, Demoment (1989). In the sense of Hardamard, Hadamard (1952), a solution to a well-posed problem satisfies the conditions of existence, uniqueness and stability. As Fredholm integral equations of the first kind do not meet the criteria for a well-posed problem, image restoration belongs into the general class of problems which are classified as ill-posed problems, Tikhonov & Arsenin (1977). The ill-posed nature of image restoration problem implies that, small bounded perturbations in the data may lead to unbounded deviations in the solution, Phillips (1962).

For images defined on a discrete set, linear algebra can be used to find solutions for ill-posed problems such as image restoration. One of the simplest methods to restore images affected by a linear distortion is the use of the pseudo inverse, Albert (1972), for which the solution fulfils the first two conditions (existence and uniqueness) of Hardamard's well-posed problem, Hadamard (1952), but fails in meeting the stability condition. This motivates or leads to regularization as one of the most widely accepted and used techniques, in which the solution fulfils all three conditions of a well-posed problem. The concept underlying regularization is to find an acceptable solution from imperfect data, for which, the problem should be stated more completely by including some extra or priori information, Miller (1970); Tikhonov & Arsenin (1977).

Regularization approaches to image restoration are classified broadly in two ways: stochastic regularization which uses the knowledge of covariance matrices of the GTI and noise; and deterministic regularization which deems that most natural images are relatively featureless with limited high-frequency activity, Banham & Katsaggelos (1997). While stochastic regularization has been used extensively in the past, with important contributions to the field such as Wiener filter, Wiener (1942), recently, much emphasis has been on the use of derivative filters with deterministic regularization, Fergus et al. (2006); Levin et al. (2007). Thus, our contribution in this chapter relates to deterministic regularization and the term regularization, henceforth, refers to deterministic regularization techniques.

Among many regularization techniques, Tikhonov, Tikhonov & Arsenin (1977) regularization is one of the first and best-known techniques for stabilization. It was proposed in Tikhonov & Arsenin (1977), that the solution for

$$b = \mathcal{K}g + n, \tag{1}$$

where $b$ is the measured data, $g$ is the original data (ground truth), $\mathcal{K}$ is the distortion operator or the transformation and $n$ represents additive random noise, can be achieved by constrained minimization of a functional $\Phi(g)$, which is called the *stabilizing functional*. Under the stabilizing functional approach, the image restoration problem is formulated as determining an estimate $\widehat{g}$ of $g$, which minimizes the functional $\Phi(g)$ under the condition that the estimate $\widehat{g}$ satisfies

$$\|b - \mathcal{K}g\|^2 = \delta, \tag{2}$$

where $\delta$ is a positive constant and $\|\cdot\|$ denotes the Frobenius norm

$$\|A\| = \sqrt{\sum_{i=1}^{m_1}\sum_{j=1}^{m_2} a_{ij}^2} \tag{3}$$

for some matrix $A$ and $a_{ij}$ is the $(i,j)$ entry. The constrained minimization problem in (2) can be solved by the method of Lagrange multipliers, which is to determine $\widehat{g}$, an estimate of ground truth $g$, by minimizing the functional

$$\|b - \mathcal{K}g\|^2 + \lambda\,\Phi(g), \tag{4}$$

where $\lambda > 0$ is the Lagrange multiplier and is often called as the *regularization parameter*. As the regularization parameter, $\lambda$, controls the tradeoff between the solution accuracy $\|b - \mathcal{K}g\|^2$ and its degree of regularity $\Phi(g)$, choosing a proper value for $\lambda$ is important in image restoration.

The first term in (4), named as *data-fidelity term* fits to the data, while *stabilizing functional* incorporates "believed" properties of the GTI. Generally the *data-fidelity term* is a standard fixed choice. In contrast, the richness and variety of image restoration techniques comes down to different choices of the regularization term, reflecting different implicit models. As the choice of the *stabilizing functional* can take a variety of forms, in this chapter, we selected two widely used model classes for our analysis: the fast quadratic stabilizing functionals introduced in section 2.2, and Sparse and Laplacian prior methods in section 3.2. The latter model class can be developed from relating the *stabilizing functional* to the *priori* knowledge using a probabilistic viewpoint and is claimed to have better performance, Levin et al. (2007).

When the stabilizing functional $\Phi(g)$ in (4) belongs to the class of nonnegative quadratic functionals, the minimization problem can be expressed as

$$\widehat{g} = \arg\min_{g}\ \|b - \mathcal{K}g\|^2 + \lambda\,\|\mathcal{D}g\|^2, \tag{5}$$

where $\mathcal{D}$ is a bounded linear operator, Miller (1970) and is often called the *regularization operator* or *stabilizing operator*. It is shown in Hunt (1973), that the minimization problem in (5) can be formulated as a constrained least squares image restoration problem when the solution $g$ satisfies the necessary and sufficient condition of

$$(\mathcal{K}^T\mathcal{K} + \lambda\,\mathcal{D}^T\mathcal{D})g = \mathcal{K}^T b. \tag{6}$$

This leads to the closed form solution for (5) in the form

$$\widehat{g} = \left(\mathcal{K}^T\mathcal{K} + \lambda(\mathcal{D}^T\mathcal{D})\right)^{-1}\mathcal{K}^T b. \tag{7}$$

We extend, in a trivial way, the above formulation by considering $\mathcal{D}$ as the combination of $R$ component regularization operators, in the form of

$$\mathcal{D}g \triangleq \left(\mathcal{D}_1^T, \mathcal{D}_2^T, \ldots, \mathcal{D}_R^T\right)^T g. \tag{8}$$

With the introduction of $R$ Lagrange multipliers, the general form of (5) can be expressed as

$$\widehat{g} = \arg\min_{g}\ \|b - \mathcal{K}g\|^2 + \sum_{r=1}^{R} \lambda_r\|\mathcal{D}_r g\|^2, \tag{9}$$

for which, the closed form solution is given by

$$\widehat{g} = \left(\mathcal{K}\mathcal{K}^T + \sum_{r=1}^{R} \lambda_r(\mathcal{D}_r^T\mathcal{D}_r)\right)^{-1}\mathcal{K}^T b. \tag{10}$$

As the images are of limited support and when the corresponding hypothesis of uniformity on image edges can be made, the matrices $\mathcal{K}$ and $\mathcal{D}$ in (10) have a special structure and are called block circulant matrices, Hunt (1971). As circulant matrices can be diagonalized by the discrete Fourier transform, the minimization in (9) can be solved extremely quickly using the Fourier domain techniques, Hunt (1973).

### 2.2 Regularization operators as components in quadratic stabilizing functionals

The generality of the regularization operator allows the development of a class of linear operators and the minimization in (9) will be the source of many regularizing solutions for (1) depending on the choice of the regularization operator. This choice is usually based on the known details of the image formation process and plays an important role in the regularization.

The simplest regularization operator is when $\mathcal{D}$ is an identity matrix, where $\mathcal{D}g = g$, and the regularized solution for this was referred as *minimum norm restoration*, Hunt & Andrews (1977). In general, $\mathcal{D}$ often takes the form of a sparsifying operator such as a discrete approximation of a derivative operator. Through the experiments in Zhu & Mumford (1997), it was shown that even though the statistics of natural images vary from image to image, the histograms for the response of derivative filters are relatively consistent and scale invariant across the images. Taking these factors into consideration, in this section, we discuss a class of regularization operators based on the partial derivative operators (PDO), which could be used in the quadratic stabilizing functional.

#### 2.2.1 First order partial derivative operator

When first order partial derivative operators (FOPDO) are considered as the regularization operators, $\mathcal{D}g$ in (8) can be expressed as

$$\mathcal{D}g = \begin{pmatrix} \partial_x \\ \partial_y \end{pmatrix} g,$$

where $\partial_x$ and $\partial_y$ are any discrete space, spatially invariant linear operators that emulate first order derivative in $x$ and $y$ directions, respectively, Levin et al. (2007). This type of regularization uses two component regularization operators.

#### 2.2.2 Second order partial derivative operator

Second order partial derivative operators (SOPDO), can be derived mainly in two forms.

1. Isotropic SOPDO – When the regularization operator takes the form

$$\mathcal{D}g = \begin{pmatrix} \partial_{xx} \\ \partial_{yy} \end{pmatrix} g,$$

   it is called the isotropic SOPDO. Though the SOPDO defined above cannot be considered as a true isotropic differential operator, such as the continuous Laplacian operator, it gives the simplest possible isotropic operator with even-order derivatives, Leung & Lu (1995). Similar to FOPDO, $\partial_{xx}$ and $\partial_{yy}$ represent any discrete space, spatially invariant linear operators that emulate second order derivatives.

2. Non-isotropic SOPDO – The non-isotropic SOPDO is formed by

$$\mathcal{D}g = \begin{pmatrix} \partial_{xx} \\ \partial_{xy} \\ \partial_{yy} \end{pmatrix} g.$$

As the edges and lines in images may occur in any direction, when the differential operator is isotropic it would give better results than a non-isotropic differential operator, Leung & Lu (1995).

### 2.2.3 Mixed partial derivative operator

In general, considering only even-order derivatives, the use of directional derivatives in more than one dimensional can be expressed as

$$\mathcal{D}g = (\partial^p_{s_1^p}, \partial^p_{s_2^p}, \ldots, \partial^p_{s_m^p})g. \tag{11}$$

where $p$ is the order of the derivatives, $m$ is the number of dimensions and $s_1$ to $s_m$ represent the direction of the derivatives.

Using the above general model, we introduce a new regularization operator, with different combinations of higher order derivative operators. In this discussion, we limit the use of higher order derivative operators up to the second order, and the new PDO is called first and second order derivative operator (FSOPDO). With FSOPDO, $\mathcal{D}g$ in (11) takes the form

$$\mathcal{D}g = \begin{pmatrix} \partial_{x} \\ \partial_{y} \\ \partial_{xx} \\ \partial_{yy} \end{pmatrix} g.$$

These quadratic regularization functionals are compared in a new perspective with the widely used prior models which are believed to result in better performance in section 3.5.

## 2.3 Non-blind image restoration through SOPDO

### 2.3.1 Noisy image deconvolution

Although most previous image restoration algorithms have considered FOPDO as the regularization model, Levin et al. (2007), we claim that SOPDO has better performance in terms of the difference between the ground truth and the estimated data on images which are susceptible to noise. Here, we deal only with additive Gaussian noise, as it effectively models the noise in many different imaging scenarios. In this section, we study in detail a few simulation results which are used to do comparison evaluations with other existing image restoration techniques.

We take non-isotropic SOPDO as the regularization operator for image restoration through least squares restoration as given in section 2.2. In order to compare the performance of the non-isotropic SOPDO prior model, we take two regularization models, FOPDO and a sparse stabilizing functional defined in Levin et al. (2007). Relating regularization to probability, the stabilizing functional in image restoration is also referred as prior model and

| Smoo-thing weight | Non-isotropic SOPDO | | FOPDO | | Sparse | | |
|---|---|---|---|---|---|---|---|
| | $MSE$ $\times 10^{-4}$ | Time in seconds | $MSE$ $\times 10^{-4}$ | Time in seconds | Itera-tions | $MSE$ $\times 10^{-4}$ | Time in seconds |
| 0.1 | 4.978 | 0.43 | 5.168 | 0.44 | 10 | 8.050 | 27 |
| 0.05 | 4.646 | 0.42 | 4.730 | 0.44 | 10 | 6.899 | 27 |
| | | | | | 50 | 6.153 | 117 |
| | | | | | 100 | 6.128 | 231 |
| 0.01 | 6.043 | 0.42 | 7.561 | 0.44 | 10 | 4.289 | 27 |

Table 1. Comparison of stabilizing functional model.

a detailed discussion of the Bayesian interpretation to regularization, including the Sparse prior model, is covered in section 3.2. The deconvolution with non-isotropic SOPDO and FOPDO regularization lead to closed form solutions with highly efficient computation, while the Sparse prior cannot be minimized in closed form, Levin et al. (2007). In all the simulations discussed in this section we use

$$\lambda_r = \lambda, \quad \forall\, r \in 1 \ldots R, \tag{12}$$

for the quadratic regularization functionals, where the value of $R$ depends on the respective model such as $R = 2$ for FOPDO and $R = 3$ for non-isotropic SOPDO model.

We claim, using non-isotropic SOPDO prior gives better results for images which are susceptible to noise over the FOPDO. When comparing the non-isotropic SOPDO regularization with the Sparse prior, we found that the non-isotropic SOPDO regularization outperforms Sparse prior significantly in speed. These results are shown in Table 1.

For the experiment in Table 1, we added "Gaussian" noise to the original "Picasso" image, Shan et al. (2008) with a standard deviation of 0.0001 (relative to the image value range of 0 to 1). The original colored image was first converted to greyscale with the pixel values resulting in the range from 0 to 1 and the original image was considered to be periodic. The term MSE stands for mean square error and for a two dimensional image, MSE is defined as

$$MSE \triangleq \frac{1}{L_1 L_2} \sum_{\ell_1=1}^{L_1} \sum_{\ell_2=1}^{L_2} \left(g(\ell_1,\ell_2) - \widehat{g}(\ell_1,\ell_2)\right)^2 \tag{13}$$

where $g$ and $\widehat{g}$ represent GTI and the estimated GTI, respectively while $L_1$ and $L_2$ represent the size of the image in $x$ and $y$ directions, respectively. The MSE values in Table 1 are in multiples of $10^{-4}$ while the time is given in seconds. The results show that the non-isotropic SOPDO outperforms FOPDO on MSE and has a significant advantage over Sparse prior on speed performance.

### 2.3.2 Efficiency in deconvolution

As SOPDO can use frequency domain deconvolution techniques, it can be implemented highly efficiently than most of the recent non-blind deblurring techniques. The comparison was done with the Sparse deconvolution algorithm in Levin et al. (2007) named as "Levin Sparse deconvolution" and the non blind deconvolution of, Shan et al. (2008) (distributed online) named as "Shan executable". The results in Table 2 support the claim that

| Restoration Technique | Efficiency in seconds |
|---|---|
| Levin Sparse deconvolution (50 iterations) | 556 |
| Levin Sparse deconvolution (10 iterations) | 124 |
| Shan executable | 39 |
| Non-isotropic SOPDO deconvolution | 2 |

Table 2. Efficiency in non-blind image deconvolution

| Restoration Technique | Image size in pixels | Kernel size in pixels | Efficiency in seconds |
|---|---|---|---|
| Levin Sparse deconv. (50 iterations) | $484 \times 752$ | $19 \times 27$ | 576 |
| | | $99 \times 99$ | 556 |
| | $910 \times 903$ | $99 \times 99$ | 1240 |
| | $1107 \times 1694$ | $99 \times 99$ | 2429 |
| Shan executable | $484 \times 752$ | $19 \times 27$ | 40 |
| | | $99 \times 99$ | 73 |
| | $910 \times 903$ | $99 \times 99$ | 166 |
| | $1107 \times 1694$ | $99 \times 99$ | Error |
| Non-isotropic SOPDO regularization | $484 \times 752$ | $19 \times 27$ | 2.34 |
| | | $99 \times 99$ | 2.44 |
| | $910 \times 903$ | $99 \times 99$ | 5.54 |
| | $1107 \times 1694$ | $99 \times 99$ | 13.17 |

Table 3. Efficiency results on scaling

non-isotropic SOPDO regularization model results in the best speed performance when compared with "Levin Sparse deconvolution" and "Shan executable" methods.

Further, we tested for the robustness of non-isotropic SOPDO regularization by using different sized images with varying sized kernels. The detailed results are shown in Table 3. All the images used for this experiment are color images, having separate *rgb* (red, green, blue) channels. The image and kernel sizes are given in pixels and the efficiency was measured in seconds. The results clearly show the robustness and the efficiency of the non-isotropic SOPDO regularization model with respect to different scales of image and kernel.

### 2.3.3 Performance in deconvolution

Several computational experiments were carried out in order to compare non-isotropic SOPDO regularization with "Levin Sparse deconvolution" and "Shan executable". The performance of these deconvolution techniques on a naturally blurred, highly textured image, given in Shan et al. (2008), are shown in Fig. 1 and Fig. 2. The blur kernel used in this experiment was retrieved through the blind deconvolution package of, Shan et al. (2008) distributed online. Closer visual inspection of the image results show that non-isotropic SOPDO technique best shows the tree branches and leaves while the other techniques have a blurring effect still remaining on the estimated result. This fact is further discussed and evidenced by evaluating the deconvolution in a new perspective in section 3.5.

(a) 27 × 27 Blur Kernel scaled upwards

(b) Blurred Image

Fig. 1. Image results for a highly textured image

## 3. Comparison of sparse prior models to quadratic regularization

### 3.1 Key issues

While the development of regularized solutions for ill-posed problems is widely discussed in the signal processing literature, recently by looking at the ill-posed image restoration problem from a probabilistic view point, some researchers claim that the Sparse prior model, Fergus et al. (2006); Levin et al. (2007) (discussed in more detail below in section 3.2.1) outperforms quadratic regularization models (discussed in section 2.2). The analytical study in this section addresses the following problems:

1. Are sparse prior models superior to quadratic regularization models?
2. What is the source of better performance of sparse prior models?
3. Are fast quadratic regularization models good enough for image restoration?

### 3.2 Regularization – Bayesian interpretation

Inverse problems such as image restoration are seen as probabilistic inference problems, where lack of information is compensated by assumptions. Therefore, it is not surprising, when the nature of the regularization detailed above is taken into consideration, to see that there is a close relationship between regularization and Bayesian estimation. Applying Bayes theorem to the image restoration problem in (1), for a known blur kernel, the posterior distribution can be written as

$$p(g|b) \propto p(b|g)\, p(g), \tag{14}$$

where $p(b|g)$ represents the likelihood and $p(g)$ represents the prior for the ground truth image. The estimation of the GTI based on posterior distribution can be classified in several ways. The minimum mean-square error estimate represents the mean of the posterior density, the MAP estimate stands for the mode of the posterior density while the maximum likelihood

(a) Shan executable

(b) Levin Sparse deconvolution – 10 iterations

(c) Levin Sparse deconvolution – 50 iterations

(d) non-isotropic SOPDO regularization

Fig. 2. Image results for a highly textured image

(ML) estimate may be viewed as a special case of MAP where no prior distribution is used, Hunt (1977).

Under the MAP technique, estimation of the GTI simplifies to

$$\hat{g} = \arg\max_{g} p(g|b). \tag{15}$$

Considering the non-blind image deconvolution process, we convert (15) to an energy minimization problem, where the energy is defined as

$$E(g) \triangleq -\log\left(p(g|b)\right). \tag{16}$$

Different likelihood and prior models on the ground truth have been applied for image restoration in literature. An analysis of existing prior models can be found in Mignotte (2006).

Considering the fact that for a given $g$, the variation in $b$ is due to the noise $n$, Hunt (1977), together with the above definitions, non-blind image restoration problem can be recast as seeking the unknown GTI, $g(i,j)$, that minimizes the functional

$$\|b-\mathcal{K}g\|^2+\sum_{r=1}^{R}\sum_{ij}\lambda_r\,\rho(\mathcal{D}_r g(i,j)), \tag{17}$$

where $\mathcal{D}_r$ is the $r$th of $R$ linear operators, $i$, $j$ are pixel indices, $\lambda_r > 0$ are the regularization parameters, $\|\cdot\|$ stands for the Frobenius norm and $\rho(\cdot)$ is a scalar memoryless nonlinear mapping, generally taking the form

$$\rho(z) \triangleq |z|^{\alpha} \tag{18}$$

for judicious choice of real parameter $\alpha$ (not necessarily integer).

Many techniques belong to this class and differ only in: the set of linear operators $\mathcal{D}_r$, $r = 1,2,\ldots,R$, and the nonlinear mapping $\rho(z)$ (or choice of $\alpha$). Numerous image restoration techniques have been developed under this framework from the early work, Geman & Geman (1984); Greig et al. (1989) to the most recent research, Fergus et al. (2006); Levin et al. (2007; 2009); Shan et al. (2008).

### 3.2.1 Sparse prior model

In recent literature, it is shown that, when derivative filters are applied to natural images, the filter outputs tend to be sparse, Olshausen et al. (1996); Simoncelli (1997). That is, the histogram of the derivative filtered image peaks at zero and falls off much faster than a Gaussian distribution. These heavy tailed natural image priors are used in a number of applications in image processing literature, such as denoising, Roth & Black (2005); Simoncelli (1999), reflection separation, Levin & Weiss (2007); Weiss (2001) and deconvolution, Levin (2007); Shan et al. (2008) in which, they are implemented in various ways such as student-$t$ distributions, Roth & Black (2005) and scale mixtures of Gaussian distributions, Fergus et al. (2006); Portilla et al. (2003).

In Levin et al. (2007), sparsity is incorporated by having $\mathcal{D}_r$ as the derivative filters and $\alpha = 0.8$ in (18) as the prior term, which results in

$$\|b-\mathcal{K}g\|^2+\sum_{r=1}^{R}\sum_{ij}\lambda_r(\mathcal{D}_r g(i,j))^{0.8}. \tag{19}$$

This can be solved in the spatial domain using the Conjugate Gradient algorithm, Barrett et al. (1994).

### 3.2.2 Laplacian prior model

Although not as close as the Sparse prior to the natural image priors, Laplacian prior with $\alpha = 1$ in (18) is expected to result in a less smooth solution than the Gaussian prior. With the Laplacian prior, the optimization becomes

$$\|b-\mathcal{K}g\|^2+\sum_{r=1}^{R}\lambda_r\|\mathcal{D}_r g\|_1. \tag{20}$$

Recently, much attention has been paid in solving $L^1$ norm regularization problems through compressed sensing. in Kim et al. (2007), an efficient method for optimizing a solution to a problem similar to (20) was discussed when $\mathcal{D}_r$ are invertible.

### 3.2.3 Gaussian prior model

When $\alpha = 2$, minimization in (17) is called the Gaussian prior deconvolution in Levin et al. (2007) and is equivalent to the quadratic regularization problem in (9). Thus, in this chapter, we use the terms Gaussian prior and quadratic (specifically isotropic SOPDO) regularization interchangeably.

## 3.3 Image restoration evaluation

### 3.3.1 Visual metric for evaluation

For all the restoration performance analysis and comparisons in this paper, we use a recently developed visual metric called SSIM (Structured SIMilarity) index, Wang et al. (2004), which has not been used for the comparison of prior models in the image restoration literature to date. The approach of SSIM is motivated by the highly structured characteristics of the natural image, where the strong neighborhood dependencies carry important information about the structures of the objects in the visual scene, Wang & Bovik (2009).

Assuming $x$ and $y$ are local image patches representing the same patch in the original and estimated images, the local SSIM index measures the similarities of three elements of the image patches: the similarity $\ell(x,y)$ of the local patch luminances (brightness values), the similarity $c(x,y)$ of the local patch contrasts, and the similarity $s(x,y)$ of the local patch structures. These local similarities are expressed using simple, easily computed statistics, and combined together to form local SSIM, $S(x,y)$, Wang & Bovik (2009).

$$\begin{aligned} S(x,y) &= \ell(x,y) \cdot c(x,y) \cdot s(x,y) \\ &= \left(\frac{2\mu_x\mu_y + C_1}{\mu_x^2 + \mu_y^2 + C_1}\right) \cdot \left(\frac{2\sigma_x\sigma_y + C_2}{\sigma_x^2 + \sigma_y^2 + C_2}\right) \cdot \left(\frac{\sigma_{xy} + C_3}{\sigma_x\sigma_y + C_3}\right), \end{aligned} \tag{21}$$

where $\mu_x$ and $\mu_y$ are the local sample means of $x$ and $y$, respectively, $\sigma_x$ and $\sigma_y$ are the local sample standard deviations of $x$ and $y$, respectively, and $\sigma_{xy}$ is the sample cross correlation of $x$ and $y$ after removing their means. The items $C_1$, $C_2$, and $C_3$ are small positive constants that stabilize each term, so that near zero sample means, variances or correlations do not lead to numerical instability.

Due to the fact that the underlying principle of SSIM is to extract the structural information which complies with the human visual system, SSIM maps are asserted to be a better signal fidelity measurement over MSE, Wang & Bovik (2009). In evaluating images through MSE, all image pixels are treated equally and content dependent variations in image fidelity are not accounted for. The two main indicators in SSIM evaluations, mean SSIM (MSSIM) and SSIM maps have values in the range from 0 to 1, where 1 indicates the best restoration. Although MSSIM and SSIM maps are generally used as visual fidelity metrics, we evaluate image restoration with the histogram of the SSIM map, as it provides an accurate view of the local restoration.

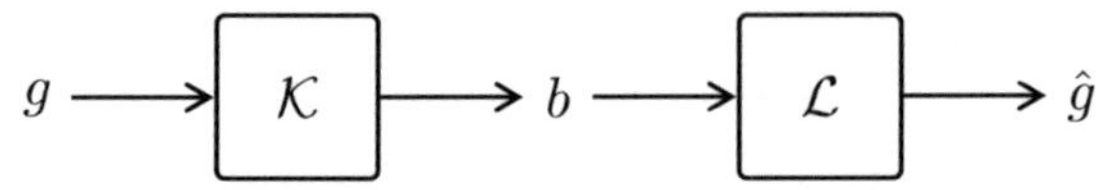


Fig. 3. Image restoration model, where $g$ is the ground truth image, $b$ is the distorted image, $\mathcal{K}$ is the blur operator, $\mathcal{L}$ is the deblur process and $\hat{g}$ is the estimated image.

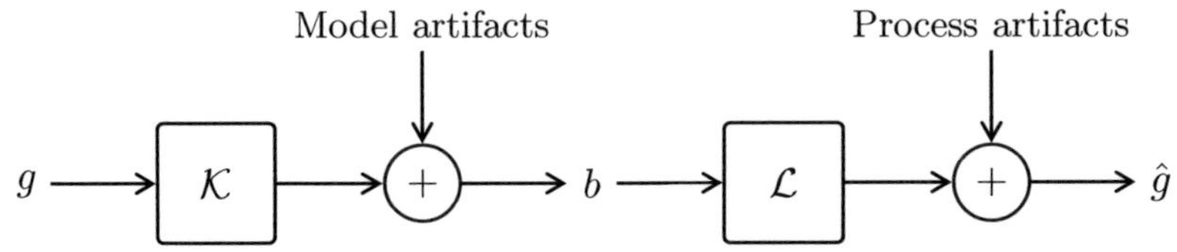


Fig. 4. Simulated image restoration model.

### 3.3.2 Image restoration models

Ignoring the presence of noise in image acquisition represented by (1), general image restoration could be represented by the model shown in Fig. 3, where $\mathcal{L}$ represents the deblur process. The notation in (1) and the representation in Fig. 3 may be an over-simplification. From physical intuition, we could see that even though $g$ is continuous by nature, image recording imposes limitations on the spatial extent of $g$ and $b$, leading to artifacts which impact on the final estimate of image restoration.

As illustrated in Fig. 4, we categorize these spatial artifacts in two ways. The "Model artifacts" are those, which are not present on naturally blurred images, but introduced in blur simulations as a result of sharp intensity transitions at the boundary of a finite image. Generating a blur image from a finite GTI causes unnatural blur distortions in the vicinity of the boundary of the image. Suppression of these "Model artifacts" could be accomplished by preprocessing the observed degraded image with techniques such as truncation and reducing the size of the blurred image. On the other hand, "Process artifacts" come along with the deblur process $\mathcal{L}$ due to finite $b$, which affect the performance of most deconvolution algorithms.

In order to show the effect of "Process artifacts", we restore an image, originally, of size $255 \times 255$ pixels, but truncated in order to remove the "Model artifacts" introduced by a $13 \times 13$ pixels blur kernel, making the final image of size $242 \times 242$. The results of restoration with Sparse, Laplacian and Gaussian priors are shown in Fig. 5. In this experiment, deconvolution with Sparse and Laplacian priors were carried out using iterative re-weighted least squares (IRLS) method, Meer (2004), through the code available online, Levin et al. (2007), while the Gaussian prior is processed with both IRLS and fast Fourier techniques (FFT) separately. In our simulations, we processed IRLS for 150 iterations beyond which there were no further improvements. Analyzing the results of the performance of the Gaussian prior model with the FFT and IRLS techniques, we see that process artifacts are better handled by the IRLS technique than the FFT and this result is justified by the IRLS processing of Sparse and Laplacian prior models.

Both the "Model" and "Process" artifacts discussed above are not part of natural images, but are imposed artificially by the image modeling and processing techniques. Thus we claim that

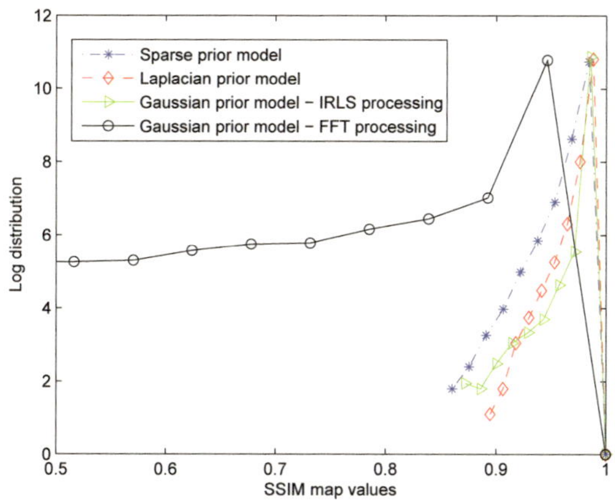


Fig. 5. Image restoration results with prior models.

| Regularization operator | $r$ | $\lambda_r$ |
|---|---|---|
| FOPDO | 1, 2 | $\beta_1$ |
| SOPDO | 3, 4 | $\beta_2$ |
| FSOPDO | 1, 2 | $\beta_1$ |
| | 3, 4 | $\beta_2$ |

Table 4. Choice of regularization parameter ($\lambda$) values for different quadratic regularization operators used in the simulations of Table 5

the evaluation of image restoration should be carried out excluding these artifacts to properly assess the performance of any image restoration method.

### 3.4 Performance of quadratic regularization operators

In order to achieve the objective of studying the performance of different operators in the quadratic regularization as detailed in section 2.2, we carried out some simulations, where we avoided the effect of "Model artifacts" by taking a boundary strip off from the blurred image. In our evaluations, we used FOPDO, SOPDO and FSOPDO models to compare the performance. From this point onwards the term SOPDO refers to isotropic-SOPDO unless stated otherwise.

The simulations, for which the results are demonstrated in Fig. 6, are executed in the same environment as the simulation for Fig. 5, but with quadratic regularization models. We evaluated the performance of the regularization models under varying regularization parameter ($\lambda$) values as discussed in section 2.2. While the choice of parameters representing $\lambda$ for FOPDO, SOPDO and FSOPDO are given in Table 4, the actual values for the respective parameters are given in Table 5.

While the overall SSIM values for few of the simulation results under varying $\lambda$ values are shown in Table 5, the histogram distribution representing the first line of Table 5 is shown in Fig. 7. Overall, by analyzing these results, we claim that, in the presence of "Process artifacts", a better performance could be achieved with FSOPDO over FOPDO and SOPDO

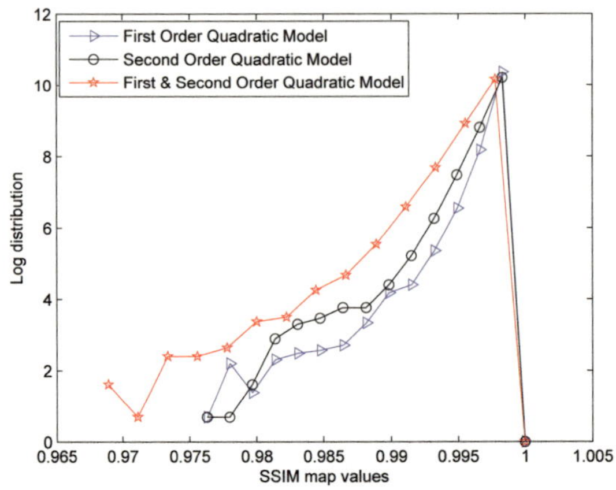


Fig. 6. Image restoration results with quadratic regularization models.

| Regularization parameter | MSSIM values for FOPDO | SOPDO | FSOPDO |
|---|---|---|---|
| $\beta_1 = \beta_2 = 0.001$ | 0.9412 | 0.9597 | 0.9626 |
| $\beta_1 = 0.001, \beta_2 = 0.003$ | 0.9596 | 0.9597 | 0.9657 |
| $\beta_1 = 0.003, \beta_2 = 0.001$ | 0.9412 | 0.9674 | 0.968 |

Table 5. Performance of quadratic regularization operators under varying regularization parameter values

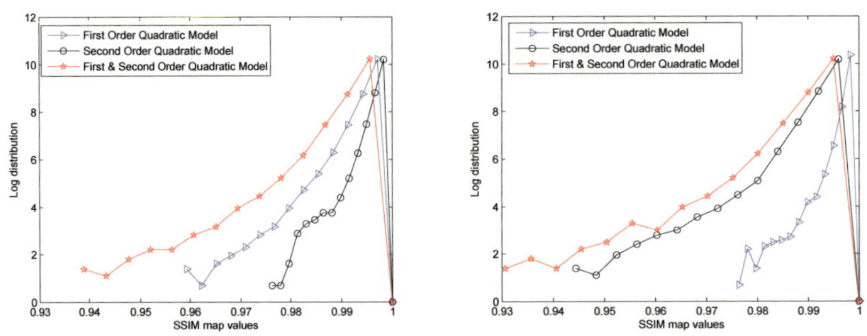


(a) Result for row 2 (b) Result for row 3

Fig. 7. Image restoration results for simulations in Table 5

models. In the next section we compare the performance of these quadratic regularization models by removing the "Process" and "Model" artifacts.

### 3.5 Regularization model performance comparison

As shown earlier in section 2.2, we modeled the regularization of image restoration based on the quadratic regularization terms (sometimes called as the least squares regularization) and in section 3.2, we discussed the existing probabilistic models under a MAP framework.

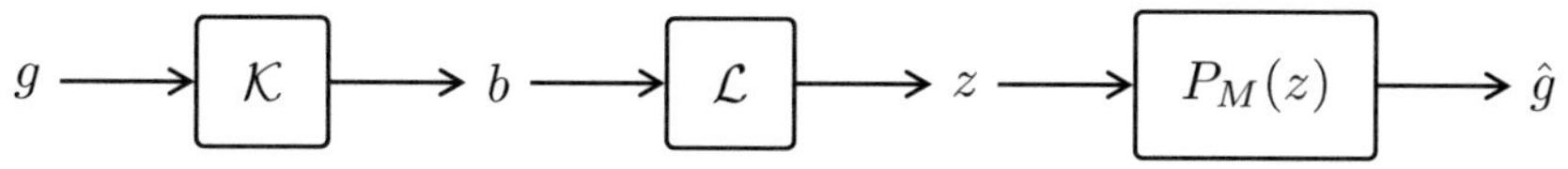


Fig. 8. Image restoration model for a naturally blurred image, where $\mathcal{K}$ is the blur process, $\mathcal{L}$ is the deblur process, $g$, $b$, $z$, $\widehat{g}$ stand for GTI, blur image, deblurred image with artifacts, and the final estimated GTI respectively. The process $P_M(z)$ decouples "Model" and "Process" artifacts from the deblurred image .

These models form a method of regularization in image restoration. This section is devoted for the comparison of these models. The comparison in this section will guide us for making recommendations for the appropriate regularization technique and is discussed at the end of this section.

### 3.5.1 SSIM performance comparison

As the objective of our simulations is to evaluate the contribution of the regularization models towards image restoration, we use the restoration model shown in Fig. 8, where we decouple artifact effects from restoration by projecting the estimated image with

$$P_M(z)(i,j) = \begin{cases} z(i,j), & \text{if } i,j \in M \\ 0, & \text{otherwise} \end{cases} \tag{22}$$

where $M$ is a region without "Model" and "Process" artifacts.

To be consistent with the SSIM map region in Fig. 5, we take a large image of support $1024 \times 1024$ and project the final image to a $242 \times 242$ region within the inner region of the estimated image, which is least affected by the artifacts. The restoration was carried out with FFT processing of the Gaussian prior and IRLS processing of Sparse and Laplacian priors. The comparison of the performance of the priors is shown in Fig. 9. In it we note that Gaussian prior with FFT processing has performed as well as or better to the Sparse and Laplacian prior models.

As the literature claims that iterative algorithms such as conjugate gradient algorithms suppress noise and perform better in noisy blur image restoration, we simulated a noisy blurred restoration under the same conditions given for Fig. 9, but with different regularization parameter values, as more weight should now be given to the prior over data. The noise added was Gaussian with zero mean and 0.01 variance. The optimal results we obtained for varying $\lambda$ are shown in Fig. 10. With these results, we claim that Gaussian prior handles noisy images as better as the Sparse and Laplacian prior models.

Thus, these results pave a new path of thinking and we claim that quadratic regularization with SOPDO model, when appropriately configured and used in a realistic context, free from unnatural artifacts, is comparable to Sparse prior model in terms of image restoration performance under the SSIM criterion.

### 3.5.2 Efficiency comparison

As the optimization problem in least-squares regularization is convex and as the fast Fourier techniques could be applied for the computation, for an image of size $L \times L$ pixels, the restoration through least-squares regulation has a complexity of $O(L \log L)$ operations. In

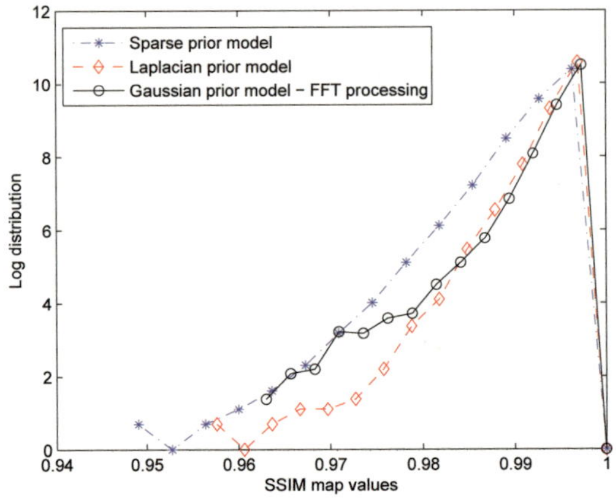


Fig. 9. Image restoration results for the system in Fig. 8 with FFT processing of Gaussian Prior and IRLS processing of Sparse and Laplacian prior models.

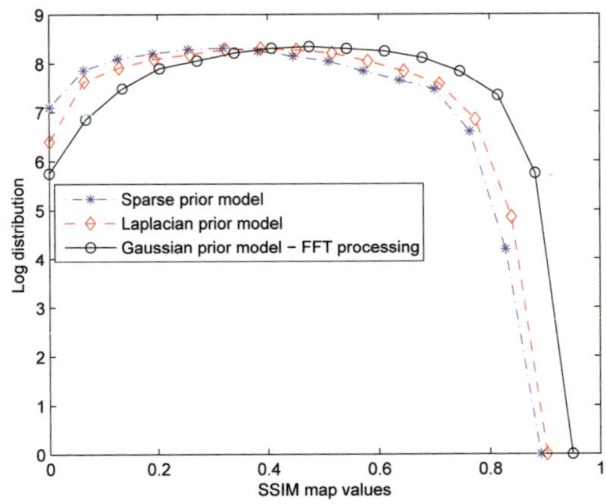


Fig. 10. Image restoration results for a noisy image under the same environment in Fig. 9.

contrast, when a Sparse prior is used, the optimization problem is no longer convex and cannot be minimized in closed form. Using the conjugate gradient method, Barrett et al. (1994), or IRLS method, the optimization can be solved in $O(L\,i_{\max})$ where $i_{\max}$ represent the maximum number of iterations.

A few simulation results on efficiency are shown in Table 6, where all the values are in seconds and represent the time taken for the restoration using each of the respective model. While the quadratic regularization deconvolution was carried out using Fourier domain techniques, the Sparse deconvolution was carried out using the IRLS method. Under the IRLS algorithm, it is experienced that in order to achieve an acceptable result, the number of iterations should be at least 50 and better results could be achieved when the number of iterations are above 100. From the results shown, it is evident that when the size of the image increases, the relative efficiency of the restoration through Sparse prior model becomes extremely low.

| Image size in pixels | Time for Quadratic regularization with FFT | Time for Sparse prior | |
|---|---|---|---|
| | | 50 iterations | 100 iterations |
| grey-scale 255 × 255 | 0.08 | 30 | 60 |
| grey-scale 1024 × 1024 | 1.1 | 303 | 596 |
| colored 484 × 752 | 1.7 | 371 | 730 |
| colored 1107 × 1694 | 9.0 | 2180 | 4292 |

Table 6. Efficiency of regularization operators. The times taken for restoration of grey-scale and colored images are given in seconds for each of the regularization operators.

### 3.5.3 Regularization recommendations

In addition to lower efficiency and not-superior performance, Sparse prior models lack in proper theoretical guidelines for selecting the best regularization parameter. In contrast, the quadratic regularization models can use well-established methods such as L-curve criterion, Hansen (1998) and the Generalized Cross Validation criterion, Hansen (1998) for choosing the value of $\lambda$. Difficulties in selecting the optimal converging point in non-convex minimization techniques such as IRLS also is an issue.

According to the theoretical and experimental details provided above, we propose that if we could decouple image restoration and "Process artifact" handling, then the use of quadratic regularization models will result in more efficient and effective image restoration in comparison to Sparse and Laplacian prior models. The decoupling of image restoration and "Process" artifact handling could be achieved through techniques such as tiling, Liu & Jia (2008), which enables the uses of the efficient least squares regularization.

Thus, coming back to our problem formulation in section 3.1, we claim that:

1. Sparse prior models are not superior to quadratic regularization models in terms of performance in image restoration.
2. In terms of efficiency, Sparse prior models are significantly inferior to quadratic regularization models.
3. The performance through Sparse prior model increases over quadratic regularization models when boundary effects are not addressed and processing artifacts are not compensated for.
4. Quadratic regularization models provide the best image restoration for large images in terms of efficiency and effectiveness while they provide a good enough solution for other images when the boundary artifacts are taken care of.

Analyzing the above items further, if the improvements of the Sparse prior model are in artifact handling, not in image restoration, we can pose the following questions.

"Do more complicated prior models such as Sparse, which are asserted be better matched to natural images, actually help image restoration in terms of restoring natural image features?"

"If those complicated prior models hold no significant advantage, is it worth the effort spend on them compared to simple and efficient prior models which restore closer or better than those prior models?"

## 4. Likelihood model analysis

Different likelihood models in the prior model in (14) have been studied in various ways. The fact that most of these models are not justified with proper theoretical foundations encouraged us to analyze and understand the variations and the validity and accuracy of the (implicit) underlying assumptions, which could explain the different performances.

This investigation guides our development of a new scheme for the multiple image likelihood model described in section 4.1.2. The likelihood model analysis is carried out using this new model and the theoretical analysis is corroborated by the computational experiments detailed in section 4.3.

### 4.1 Likelihood models in image restoration

#### 4.1.1 Likelihood model for a single image

In image restoration literature, the likelihood for a single image is defined by modeling the image noise ($n$) as a set of independently and identically distributed (i.i.d.) random variables following a Gaussian distribution for all pixels, which is given by

$$p(b|g) = \prod_{\ell_1=1}^{L_1} \prod_{\ell_2=1}^{L_2} N(n(\ell_1, \ell_2)|0, \sigma), \tag{23}$$

where $N(\cdot|\mu, \sigma)$ denotes a Gaussian distribution with mean $\mu$ and variance $\sigma^2$, while $L_1$ and $L_2$ represent the image support.

#### 4.1.2 Likelihood model for multiple images

Based on the above likelihood model for a single image, we develop a new model for the likelihood of multiple images as detailed below.

Given a set of $R$ degraded images of a common GTI $g$, the posterior distribution for the GTI can be derived by extending (14), resulting in

$$p(g|b_1, b_2, \ldots, b_R) \propto p(b_1, b_2, \ldots, b_R|g)\, p(g), \tag{24}$$

where, generalizing (1),

$$b_r = \mathcal{K}_r g + n_r, \quad r = 1, 2, 3, \ldots, R \tag{25}$$

and $\mathcal{K}_r$ are operators representing possibly different but known blurs, and $n_r$ are noise images. Under the assumption that $n_p$ is independent of $n_q$ for all $p \neq q$, the likelihood in (24) is

$$p(b_1, b_2, \ldots, b_R|g) = \prod_{r=1}^{R} N(n_r). \tag{26}$$

Thus, for a group of $R$ images satisfying the noise independency condition in (26), the likelihood can be modeled as

$$p(b_1, b_2, \ldots, b_R|g) = \prod_{r=1}^{R} \prod_{\ell_1=1}^{L_1} \prod_{\ell_2=1}^{L_2} N(n_r(\ell_1, \ell_2)|0, \sigma_r), \tag{27}$$

where $\sigma_r$ represent the standard deviation of the Gaussian distribution for $n_r$. This new model for the likelihood of multiple images will be used for the analysis of likelihood models in the next section.

| $r$ | $\partial_r$ | $\partial_r n$ | $\omega(\partial_r)$ |
|---|---|---|---|
| 1 | $\partial_1$ | $\partial_x n$ | 1 |
| 2 | $\partial_2$ | $\partial_y n$ | 1 |
| 3 | $\partial_3$ | $\partial_{xx} n$ | 2 |
| 4 | $\partial_4$ | $\partial_{xy} n$ | 2 |
| 5 | $\partial_5$ | $\partial_{yy} n$ | 2 |

Table 7. An example of set $\Theta$ in (30) with $R = 5$

### 4.1.3 Likelihood models for analysis

Out of the various likelihood models introduced in the literature of image restoration, we consider two recent approaches in Levin et al. (2007) and, Shan et al. (2008) for our analysis.

In Levin et al. (2007), the single image likelihood conforms to (23) and is explicitly given by

$$p(b|g) \propto e^{-\frac{1}{2\sigma^2}\|\mathcal{K}g-b\|^2}, \tag{28}$$

where $\|\cdot\|$ stands for the Frobenius norm.

In Shan et al. (2008), the likelihood is defined with different orders of partial derivatives, denoted by operator $\partial_r$, of a single degraded image. For ease of understanding, we represent their model in the form

$$p(b|g) = \prod_{\partial_r \in \Theta} \prod_{\ell_1=1}^{L_1} \prod_{\ell_2=1}^{L_2} N(n(\ell_1,\ell_2)|0,\sigma)\, N(\partial_r n(\ell_1,\ell_2)|0,\sigma_{\omega(\partial_r)}), \quad r = 1,2,3,\ldots,R \tag{29}$$

where $\Theta$ is a set of partial derivative operators given by

$$\Theta \triangleq \{\partial_1, \partial_2, \partial_3, \ldots, \partial_R\}. \tag{30}$$

For example, in Shan et al. (2008), the set $\Theta$ has the elements $\{\partial_x, \partial_y, \partial_{xx}, \partial_{xy}, \partial_{yy}\}$, in which, $\partial_x$ is the first order derivative in $x$ direction and $\partial_y$ is the first order derivative in $y$ direction and similar interpretations hold for higher order derivatives.

Further, Shan et al. (2008) shows that the partial derivatives of $n$ also follow Normal distributions with standard deviation values based on the order of the partial derivative operator. The standard deviations of the partial derivatives are specified in the form

$$\sigma_{\omega(\partial_r)} = (\sqrt{2})^{\omega(\partial_r)}\sigma, \tag{31}$$

where $\omega(\partial_r)$ represents the order of the partial derivative operator $\partial_r$. Few example elements of the set $\Theta$ in (30) with the respective standard deviation values are given in Table 7.

As there was no analysis presented behind using the higher order partial derivatives of noise in Shan et al. (2008) leading to (29), we provide an interpretation of formula, based on our new general likelihood model for a group of degraded images of a common ground truth $g$ in (27).

Guided by the likelihood expression (27), we can define a virtual group of images for the likelihood model in (29) as

$$b_r = \partial_r b, \quad r = 1,2,3,\ldots,R \tag{32}$$

and in order to align with model (25), define

$$\mathcal{K}_r g \triangleq \partial_r(g * k), \quad r = 1,2,3,\ldots,R \tag{33}$$

$$n_r \triangleq \partial_r n, \quad r = 1,2,3,\ldots,R \tag{34}$$

where $*$ stands for the convolution operator and $k$ is the blur kernel.

From this, we infer that the likelihood (29) implicitly assumes $\partial_p n$ is independent of $\partial_q n$ for all $p \neq q$. Since all virtual images are derived from a single degraded image, we can infer this is a strong assumption made to simplify the likelihood expression. In principle, it should be possible to formulate a model without recourse to the derivative images which add limited new information. We corroborate this claim in section 4.3 with experiments.

### 4.2 Frequency domain deconvolution

In this section we approach image deconvolution with FOPDO regularization and with different likelihood models discussed above. For our analysis, we consider the likelihood models of (23) and (29) using terminology "normal likelihood" and "derivative likelihood" with the notation using subscripts "$n$" and "$d$", respectively. With our experiments, we limit the set $\Theta$ in (30), going up to second order partial derivative operators in (29) and we take elements of $\Theta$ from the following values

$$\Theta = \{\partial_x, \partial_y, \partial_{xx}, \partial_{xy}, \partial_{yy}\}. \tag{35}$$

#### 4.2.1 Normal likelihood deconvolution

Under FOPDO regularization as detailed in section 2.2, the stabilizing functional $\Phi(g)$ takes the form

$$\Phi(g) \triangleq \|\partial_x g\|^2 + \|\partial_y g\|^2. \tag{36}$$

Applying this stabilizing functional to the MAP framework detailed in section 4, the energy functional under "normal likelihood", can be derived as

$$E_n(g) = \|g * k - b\|^2 + \lambda\, \Phi(g). \tag{37}$$

According to the convolution theorem, the convolution operation in the spatial domain becomes an element-wise product in the frequency domain making $\mathcal{F}(g * k) = G \star K$ where $\mathcal{F}(\cdot)$ stands for discrete Fourier transform, $G$ for $\mathcal{F}(g)$, $K$ for $\mathcal{F}(k)$ and "$\star$" denotes element-wise product. Based on the above property, transforming (37) into frequency domain and applying Plancherels theorem, Bracewell & Kahn (1966), we derive the energy in the frequency domain for (37) as follows.

$$\mathcal{F}(E_n(g)) = \|G \star K - B\|^2 + \lambda\, \mathcal{F}(\Phi(g)), \tag{38}$$

where

$$\mathcal{F}(\Phi(g)) = \|\mathcal{F}(\partial_x) \star G\|^2 + \|\mathcal{F}(\partial_y) \star G\|^2,$$

$B$ stands for $\mathcal{F}(b)$ and given $\partial_x$ takes the form of a (convolution) matrix, then $\mathcal{F}(\partial_x)$ denotes its Fourier transform.

Minimizing the energy in (38) and solving for estimated $G$ denoted as $\widehat{G}$ results in

$$\widehat{G_n} = \frac{B \star \overline{K}}{K \star \overline{K} + \lambda \Psi}, \tag{39}$$

where

$$\Psi = \mathcal{F}(\partial_x) \star \overline{\mathcal{F}(\partial_x)} + \mathcal{F}(\partial_y) \star \overline{\mathcal{F}(\partial_y)},$$

$\widehat{G_n}$ is the Fourier transform of the estimated GTI under "normal likelihood", $\overline{(\cdot)}$ stands for the complex conjugate and the division is performed element-wise. The estimated ground truth image $\widehat{g_n}$ can be derived by taking the inverse Fourier transform of $\widehat{G_n}$.

With the above derivations, it is evident that Fourier domain expression used to estimate the GTI is:

1. simple and leads to a closed form solution and
2. amenable to Fast Fourier Techniques leading to a highly efficient solution.

### 4.2.2 Derivative likelihood deconvolution

We now give an analogous derivation for the "derivative likelihood".

The energy functional in this case is derived similar to (37),

$$E_d(g) = \sum_{\partial_r \in \Theta} \frac{1}{2^{\omega(\partial_r)}} \|\partial_r(g * k) - \partial_r b\|^2 + \lambda\, \Phi(g). \tag{40}$$

Transforming (40) into the frequency domain results in

$$\mathcal{F}(E_d(g)) = \sum_{\partial_r \in \Theta} \frac{1}{2^{\omega(\partial_r)}} (\|\mathcal{F}(\partial_r) \star G \star K - \mathcal{F}(\partial_r) \star B\|^2) + \lambda\, \mathcal{F}(\Phi(g)), \tag{41}$$

where, $\partial_r$ is a matrix convolution operator representing a partial order derivative operator and $\mathcal{F}(\partial_r)$ denotes its Fourier transformation.

By minimizing the energy (41), we compute the estimated $G$,

$$\widehat{G_d} = \frac{B \star \overline{K} \star \Omega}{K \star \overline{K} \star \Omega + \lambda \Psi}, \tag{42}$$

where

$$\Omega \triangleq \sum_{\partial_r \in \Theta} \frac{1}{2^{\omega(\partial_r)}} \mathcal{F}(\partial_r) \star \overline{\mathcal{F}(\partial_r)}.$$

By taking the inverse Fourier transforms of (42), we could get the estimated GTI, $\widehat{g_d}$, under "derivative likelihood" model similar to "normal likelihood" model.

| $\lambda$ $\times 10^{-5}$ | MSE Normal likelihood $\times 10^{-4}$ | MSE Derivative likelihood $\times 10^{-4}$ |
|---|---|---|
| 100 | 2.8448 | 4.4371 |
| 5 | 2.4148 | **4.0862** |
| 0.25 | **2.2292** | 4.1852 |

Table 8. Comparison of likelihood models

### 4.3 Likelihood model analysis

In order to come up with the most effective and efficient restoration algorithm, we investigate the contribution of each of the likelihood models for estimating the GTI: (39) corresponding to "normal likelihood" and (42) corresponding to "derivative likelihood", respectively.

We used the same "Picasso" image which was used in Shan et al. (2008) for experiments using the likelihood model in (29). The ground truth images are estimated using the Fourier domain techniques, specifically applying (39) and (42) for the "Normal" and "Derivative" likelihood models respectively. The experiment results are given in Table 8. In order to eliminate the "Model" and "Process" artifacts as discussed in section 3.3.2, in all our simulations, the blurring was carried out under the assumption that the images are periodic.

The MSE values in the table are given as multiples of $10^{-4}$, while the value of $\lambda$ is given in multiples of $10^{-5}$. The values in bold in Table 8 refer to the optimal MSE values the respective likelihood model could reach for varying $\lambda$. As the results show clearly, the "normal likelihood" model has a better estimate for the GTI than the "derivative likelihood" model, we claim that applying "normal likelihood" in the image restoration algorithm results in a better restoration.

Our investigation was further extended to analyze whether higher order derivatives of noise contribute to the spatial randomness of noise as claimed in Shan et al. (2008). The noise maps given in Fig. 11 are computed for different values of $\lambda$ in (39) and (42).

As per the results Fig. 11(c) and Fig. 11(d), when the effect of the prior becomes smaller (i.e., the weight on the data fitting term or the likelihood becomes larger), the noise estimate is more spatially random, but with the increase in the weight of the prior, the noise estimate becomes structured (signal dependant), see Fig. 11(e) and Fig. 11(f). We experienced these results regardless of the likelihood model we used. Based on the above results, we claim that using higher order partial derivatives in the likelihood model for non-blind deconvolution does not result in a better noise map estimation while the same noise map estimation can be achieved through the normal likelihood model with the appropriate Lagrange multiplier.

Hence, through the likelihood model analysis based on benchmark image, we conclude that higher order derivatives in the likelihood model are not required for better performance whereas applying single image likelihood model with appropriate regularization results in a more effective non-blind image restoration.

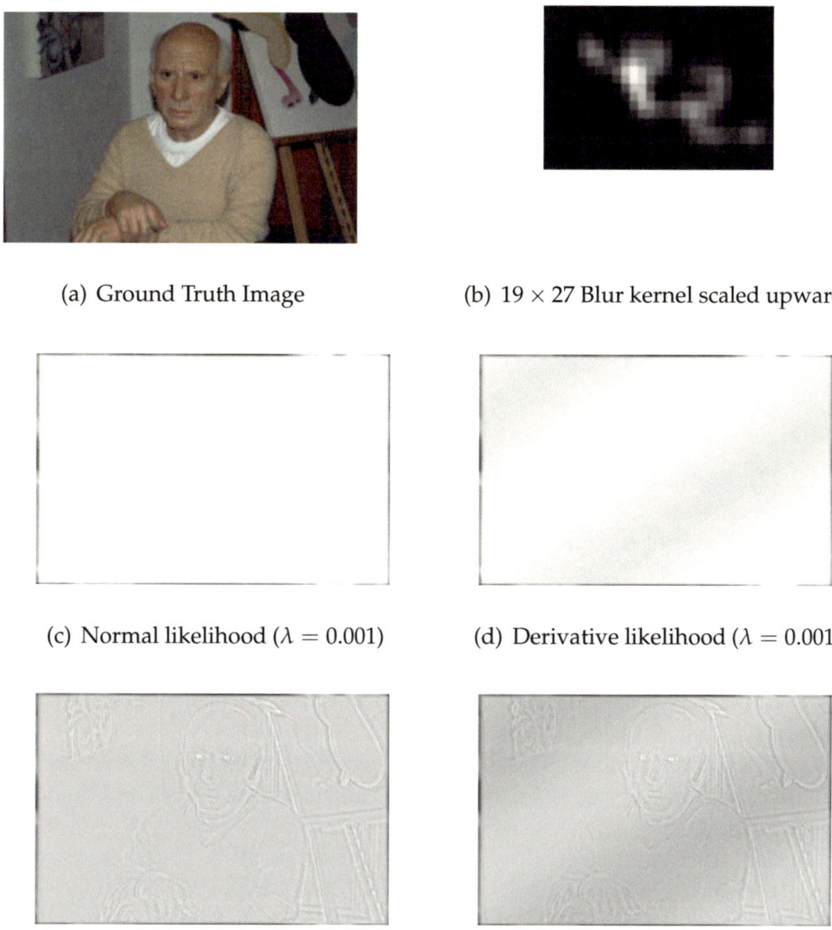

(a) Ground Truth Image

(b) 19 × 27 Blur kernel scaled upwards

(c) Normal likelihood ($\lambda = 0.001$)

(d) Derivative likelihood ($\lambda = 0.001$)

(e) Normal likelihood ($\lambda = 0.8$)

(f) Derivative likelihood ($\lambda = 0.8$)

Fig. 11. Noise maps for Likelihood models

## 5. Contributions

In this chapter, we have contributed to regularization based image restoration techniques in the following:

1. We have developed a general class of quadratic regularization models based on partial derivative operators (PDO), section 2.2. Out of those models, we have shown that the Second Order Partial Derivative Operator (SOPDO) model performs better than First Order Partial Derivative Operator (FOPDO) model for images susceptible to noise, while the novel First and Second Order Partial Derivative Operator (FSOPDO) model performs better than both FOPDO and SOPDO models.

2. We have used the Structured Similarity index (SSIM) map, Mean SSIM (MSSIM) value and histograms of SSIM maps as novel visual metrics for comparison and evaluation of regularization models in image restoration, section 3.3.2.
3. We have critically evaluated Sparse and Laplacian prior models against Quadratic regularization models using the novel visual metrics discussed in section 3.5. By eliminating the effects of processing and modeling artifacts, not present when capturing actual blurred natural images, we have shown that Sparse and Laplacian derivative prior models, which are claimed to be consistent with natural images, do not significantly contribute in restoring natural image features and have significantly slower relative restoration performance.
4. Finally, we have analyzed and evaluated multiple derivative operator based restoration methods under MAP/ML framework with a novel model to represent the likelihood based on multiple images, section 4.1.2. By using this novel model, we demonstrate that complex higher order derivative likelihood models are not required for better performance in image restoration.

## 6. References


Albert, A. E. (1972). *Regression and the Moore-Penrose Pseudoinverse*, Mathematics in science and engineering, New York : Academic Press.

Banham, M. R. & Katsaggelos, A. K. (1997). Digital image restoration, *IEEE Signal Processing Magazine* 14(2): 24–41.

Barrett, R., Berry, M., Chan, T. F., Demmel, J., Donato, J. M., Dongarra, J., Eijkhout, V., Romine, R. P. C. & Vorst, H. V. D. (1994). *Templates for the Solution of Linear Systems: Building Blocks for Iterative Methods*, Society for Industrial Mathematics.

Bracewell, R. & Kahn, P. B. (1966). The Fourier transform and its applications, *American Journal of Physics* .

Demoment, G. (1989). Image reconstruction and restoration: overview of common estimation structures and problems, *IEEE Transactions on Acoustics, Speech and Signal Processing* 37(12): 2024–2036.

Fergus, R., Singh, B., Hertzmann, A., Roweis, S. T. & Freeman, W. T. (2006). Removing camera shake from a single photograph, *ACM Trans. Graph.* 25(3): 787–794.

Geman, S. & Geman, D. (1984). Stochastic relaxation, gibbs distributions and the bayesian restoration of images, *IEEE Transactions on Pattern Analysis and Machine Intelligence* 6(6): 721–741.
URL: *http://dx.doi.org/10.1080/02664769300000058*

Greig, D. M., Porteous, B. T. & Seheult, A. H. (1989). Exact maximum a posteriori estimation for binary images, *Journal of the Royal Statistical Society. Series B (Methodological)* 51(2): 271–279.

Hadamard, J. (1952). *Lectures on Cauchy's problem in linear partial differential equations*, New Haven, CT: Yale University Press.

Hansen, P. C. (1998). *Rank-deficient and discrete ill-posed problems: numerical aspects of linear inversion*, Society for Industrial and Applied Mathematics, Philadelphia, PA, USA.

Haykin, S. (1994). *Blind Deconvolution*, Prentice-Hall: Englewood Cliffs, NJ.

Hunt, B. R. (1971). Biased estimation for nonparametric identification of linear systems, *Mathematical Biosciences* 10(3-4): 215–237.

Hunt, B. R. (1973). The application of constrained least squares estimation to image restoration by digital computer, *IEEE Transactions on Computers* 22(9): 805–812.

Hunt, B. R. (1977). Bayesian methods in nonlinear digital image restoration, *IEEE Transactions on Computers* 26: 219–229.

Hunt, B. R. & Andrews, H. C. (1977). *Digital Image Restoration*, Prentice Hall Professional Technical Reference.

Joshi, N., Szeliski, R. & Kriegman, D. J. (2008). PSF estimation using sharp edge prediction, *IEEE Conference on Computer Vision and Pattern Recognition, CVPR 2008*, pp. 1–8.

Kim, S. J., Koh, K., Lustig, M. & Boyd, S. (2007). An efficient method for compressed sensing, *International Conference on Image Processing, ICIP 2007*, Vol. 3, pp. 117–120.

Krahmer, F., Lin, Y., McAdoo, B., Ott, K., Wang, J. & Widemann, D. (2006). Blind image deconvolution: motion blur estimation, *University of Minnesota, URL: http://www. ima. umn. edu* .

Kundur, D. & Hatzinakos, D. (1996). Blind image deconvolution, *IEEE Signal Processing Magazine* 13(3): 43–64.

Leung, C. M. & Lu, W. S. (1995). On the use of discrete Laplacian operators in image restoration, *IEEE Pacific Rim Conference on Communications, Computers, and Signal Processing*, pp. 411–415.

Levin, A. (2007). Blind motion deblurring using image statistics, *Advances in Neural Information Processing Systems* 19: 841–848.
URL: *http://citeseerx.ist.psu.edu/viewdoc/summary?doi=10.1.1.110.2995*

Levin, A., Fergus, R., Durand, F. & Freeman, W. T. (2007). Image and depth from a conventional camera with a coded aperture, *ACM Transactions on Graphics (Proceedings of SIGGRAPH)* 26(3): 70–79.

Levin, A. & Weiss, Y. (2007). User assisted separation of reflections from a single image using a sparsity prior, *IEEE Transactions on Pattern Analysis and Machine Intelligence* 29(9): 1647–1654.

Levin, A., Weiss, Y., Durand, F. & Freeman, W. T. (2009). Understanding and evaluating blind deconvolution algorithms, *IEEE Conference on Computer Vision and Pattern Recognition, CVPR 2009*, pp. 1964–1971.

Liu, R. & Jia, J. Y. (2008). Reducing boundary artifacts in image deconvolution, *IEEE International Conference on Image Processing, ICIP'08*, Vol. 1-5, pp. 505–508.

Meer, P. (2004). Robust techniques for computer vision, *Emerging topics in computer vision* pp. 107–190.

Mignotte, M. (2006). A segmentation-based regularization term for image deconvolution, *IEEE Transactions on Image Processing* 15(7): 1973–1984.

Miller, K. (1970). Least squares methods for ill-posed problems with a prescribed bound, *SIAM Journal on Mathematical Analysis* 1(1): 52–74.
URL: *http://link.aip.org/link/?SJM/1/52/1*

Nayar, S. K. & Ben-Ezra, M. (2004). Motion-based motion deblurring, *IEEE Transactions on Pattern Analysis and Machine Intelligence* 26(6): 689–698.

Oliveira, J. P., Figueiredo, M. A. & Bioucas-Dias, J. M. (2007). Blind estimation of motion blur parameters for image deconvolution, *IbPRIA '07: Proceedings of the 3rd Iberian conference on Pattern Recognition and Image Analysis, Part II*, Springer-Verlag, Berlin, Heidelberg, pp. 604–611.

Olshausen, B. A. et al. (1996). Emergence of simple-cell receptive field properties by learning a sparse code for natural images, *Nature* 381(6583): 607–609.

Phillips, D. L. (1962). A technique for the numerical solution of certain integral equations of the first kind, *Journal of the ACM (JACM)* 9(1): 84–97.

Portilla, J., Strela, V., Wainwright, M. J. & Simoncelli, E. P. (2003). Image denoising using scale mixtures of Gaussians in the wavelet domain, *IEEE Transactions on Image processing* 12(11): 1338–1351.

Roth, S. & Black, M. (2005). Fields of experts: A framework for learning image priors, *Proceedings of the 2005 IEEE Computer Society Conference on Computer Vision and Pattern Recognition (CVPR'05) - Volume 2*, IEEE Computer Society, Washington, DC, USA, pp. 860–867.

Shan, Q., Jia, J. & Agarwala, A. (2008). High-quality motion deblurring from a single image, *International Conference on Computer Graphics and Interactive Techniques SIGGRAPH 2008*, Vol. 27, ACM, New York, NY, USA, pp. 1–10.

Simoncelli, E. P. (1997). Statistical models for images: compression, restoration and synthesis, *Conference Record of the Thirty-First Asilomar Conference on Signals, Systems and Computers*, Vol. 1, pp. 673–678.

Simoncelli, E. P. (1999). Bayesian denoising of visual images in the wavelet domain, *Lecture Notes in Statistics* 141: 291–308.

Tikhonov, A. N. & Arsenin, V. Y. (1977). *Solutions of ill-posed problems*, John Wiley, New York.

Wang, Z. & Bovik, A. C. (2009). Mean squared error: love it or leave it? - A new look at signal fidelity measures, *IEEE Signal Processing Magazine* 26(1): 98–117.

Wang, Z., Bovik, A. C., Sheikh, H. R. & Simoncelli, E. P. (2004). Image quality assessment: From error visibility to structural similarity, *IEEE Transactions on Image Processing* 13(4): 600–612.

Weiss, Y. (2001). Deriving intrinsic images from image sequences, *9th International Conference on Computer Vision, ICCV*, IEEE Computer Society, pp. 68–75.

Wiener, N. (1942). Extrapolation, Interpolation, and Smoothing of Stationary Time Series.

Zhu, S. C. & Mumford, D. (1997). Prior learning and Gibbs reaction-diffusion, *IEEE Transactions on Pattern Analysis and Machine Intelligence* 19(11): 1236–1250.

# 7

# Iterative Restoration Methods to Loose Estimations Dependency of Regularized Solutions

Miguel A. Santiago[1], Guillermo Cisneros[1] and Emiliano Bernués[2]
[1]*Polythecnic University of Madrid, Department of Signals, Systems and Radiocommunications*
[2]*University of Zaragoza, Department of Electronic Engineering and Communications*
*Spain*

## 1. Introduction

Image restoration is a classical area of digital image processing, appearing in many applications such as remote sensing, medical imaging, astronomy or computerized tomography (González & Woods, 2007). Simply put, the aim is to recover an original image which has been degraded due to the imperfections in the acquisition system: blurring and noise. Restoring this degradation leads to an ill-posed problem since the simple inverse using least-squares yields highly noise-sensitive solutions. A large number of techniques have been developed to cope with this issue, most of them under the regularization or the Bayesian frameworks (a complete review can found in Banham & Katsaggelos, 1997; Bovik, 2005; Chan & Shen, 2005).

Mathematical regularization is used to include prior knowledge about the original image in the restoration process which allows stabilizing the solution in the face of noise. However, two main problems arise for such a regularization approach. First, the non-local property of the underlying convolution implies that part of the blurred image near the boundary integrates information of the original scenery outside the field of view. However, this information is not available in the deconvolution process and may cause strong ringing artifacts on the restored image, i.e., the well-known boundary problem (Woods et al., 1985). Typical methods to counteract the boundary effect is to make assumptions about the behavior of the original image outside the field of view such as Dirichlet, Neuman, periodic or other recent conditions in Calvetti & Somersalo, 2005; Martinelli et al., 2006; Liu & Jia, 2008. Secondly, restoration methods depend on a wide set of parameters which can be roughly grouped into three categories: parameters with respect to the degradation process, the noise and the original image. All parameters require an accurate prior estimation because small errors in their values lead to important deviations in the restoration results. In fact, classical restoration methods tend to improve the estimation of those parameters without prior knowledge about the real scenery, which is known as blind deconvolution (Campisi & Egiazarian, 2007; Molina et al., 2006). The boundary problem and the sensitivity to estimations are the issues to solve in this chapter by means of two iterative algorithms.

The first algorithm copes with the boundary problem taking a blurred image defined in the field of view, but with neither any image information nor prior assumption on the boundary conditions. Furthermore, the objective is not only to reduce the ringing artifacts on the whole image, but also reconstruct the missed boundaries of the original image which becomes a significant step of the research. Neural networks are very well suited to combine both processes in the same restoration algorithm and thus we provide a solution based on a Multilayer Perceptron (MLP) in line with a backpropagation strategy. Other neural-net-based restoration techniques (Paik & Katsaggelos, 1992; Sun, 2000; Han & Wu, 2004) have been proposed in the literature with the Hopfield's model, but they are typically time-consuming and large scaled. In the light of the good results of the total variation (TV) regularizer in recent deconvolution (Wang et al., 2005; Wu et al., 2007; Bioucas-Dias et al., 2006; Oliveira et al., 2009; Molina et al., 2006), we have used it to set the minimization mechanism of the net. The proposed scheme is then an iterative method which performs repeatedly a cycle of two steps: forward and backward, simulating respectively restoration and degradation processes at each iteration.

Following the same iterative concept of restoration-degradation, we present a second algorithm in the frequency domain to reduce the dependency on the estimation of parameters. Hence, a novel desensitized restoration filter is designed by applying an iterative algorithm over the original filter. Analyzing the sensitivity properties of this filter and setting a criterion to choose the number of iterations, we come up with an expression for the desensitized algorithm for traditional filters such as Wiener and Tikhonov (González & Woods, 2007). The results of this algorithm pretend to increase the robustness of the restoration methods when estimating parameters such as the noise variance or degradation related parameters.

The chapter is organized as follows. In the next section, we provide a detailed formulation of the two restoration problems of the chapter, establishing naming conventions and the mathematical basis of the respective algorithms. In Sec. 3, we present the architecture of the iterative methods under analysis: MLP and desensitized filter, going into details about the adjustment of the synaptic weights of the net in every layer and the computation of the number of iterations for the desensitized scheme respectively. We present some experimental results in Sec. 4 and, finally, concluding remarks are given in Sec. 5.

## 2. Problem formulation

To start with image restoration a better understanding of the acquisition system is required. Because of physical limitations or human errors in operating imaging systems, the observed image is actually a degraded version of the original scene. For instance, deterministic degradations such as motion blurs, out of focus lens or effects of atmospheric turbulence in remote sensing cause a bandwidth reduction of the original image. In a linear acquisition scenario this distortion is mathematically described as a point spread function (PSF) denoted by $h(i,j)$, which represents a two dimensional filter mask of size $M_1 \times M_2$. For sake of simplicity we consider spatially invariant functions such that the degradation is independent of the position. In addition to blurring, noise is always present in the observed image due to stochastic variations in the process of image formation, the transmission medium or the recording system. We assume a common additive zero-mean Gaussian white noise $n(i,j)$ of variance $\sigma_n^2$, which also represents the quantization error coming from digitalizing images. The statistical descriptors of the noise are likewise assumed to not vary spatially.

Let $x(i,j)$ be the unknown gray-scaled original image of size $L_1 \times L_2$, degraded by a PSF $h(i,j)$ and corrupted by a noise sample $n(i,j)$. Therefore, we can express the observed image $y(i,j)$ as

$$y(i,j) = h(i,j) ** x(i,j) + n(i,j) \tag{1}$$

where $**$ represents the two dimensional convolution operator. In order to simplify expressions, we shall use lexicographic notation by stacking the columns of a matrix in a vector. Then, the equation (1) is rewritten as

$$\mathbf{y} = \mathbf{Hx} + \mathbf{n} \tag{2}$$

defined by the original image $\mathbf{x}$ of length $L = L_1 \times L_2$, whereas the degraded image $\mathbf{y}$ is a $\tilde{L}$ sized vector bigger than the original image as result of the non-local property of the convolution operation (see 2.1). In terms of blurring, $\mathbf{H}$ is known as the convolution matrix of size $\tilde{L} \times L$ built from the PSF and using the so-called boundary conditions that we will discuss later.

Another way to represent the equation (1) is through its spectral equivalence. By applying discrete Fourier transform (González & Woods, 2007) to that expression, we obtain

$$Y(\varpi_i,\varpi_j) = H(\varpi_i,\varpi_j)X(\varpi_i,\varpi_j) + N(\varpi_i,\varpi_j) \tag{3}$$

where $(\varpi_i,\varpi_j)$ are the spatial frequency coordinates, and the capital letters represent Fourier transforms. In the frequency domain it is assumed that the observed image is a circular period that wraps around the edges, what it is not physically true but typically used for computational convenience.

In view of the above equations, image restoration is defined as an inverse problem that tries to estimate the original image $\hat{\mathbf{x}}$ from the observed image $\mathbf{y}$ using the blurring model $\mathbf{H}$. However, a simple least-squares solution is not possible since the presence of noise or the singularity of the matrix $\mathbf{H}$ make it an ill-conditioned problem. Thus, a regularization method is needed to control the high sensitivity to noise as explained in Banham & Katsaggelos, 1997. Quite a few examples have been presented in the literature by means of the classical Tikhonov regularization which establishes

$$\hat{\mathbf{x}} = \arg\min_{\mathbf{x}} \left\{ \frac{1}{2}\|\mathbf{y} - \mathbf{Hx}\|_2^2 + \frac{\lambda}{2}\|\mathbf{Dx}\|_2^2 \right\} \tag{4}$$

where $\|\mathbf{z}\|_2^2 = \sum_i z_i^2$ denotes the $\ell_2$ norm, $\hat{\mathbf{x}}$ is the restored image and $\mathbf{D}$ is the regularization operator, built on the basis of a high pass filter mask $\mathbf{d}$ of size $N = N_1 \times N_2$. The first term in (4) is the $\ell_2$ residual norm appearing in the least-squares approach and ensures fidelity to data. The second term is the so-called *regularizer* which captures prior knowledge about $\mathbf{x}$ through an additional $\ell_2$ penalty term involving the image. The hyper-parameter (or regularization parameter) $\lambda$ is a critical value which measures the trade-off between a good fit and a regularized solution.

Alternatively, the total variation (TV) regularization proposed by Rudin et al., 1992, has become very popular in recent research as it achieves to preserve edges in the restored image. A discrete version of the TV deblurring problem is given by

$$\hat{\mathbf{x}} = \arg \min_{\mathbf{x}} \left\{ \frac{1}{2} \|\mathbf{y} - \mathbf{H}\mathbf{x}\|_2^2 + \lambda \|\nabla \mathbf{x}\|_1 \right\} \tag{5}$$

where $\|\mathbf{z}\|_1$ denotes the $\ell_1$ norm (i.e., the sum of the absolute value of the elements) and $\nabla$ stands for the discrete gradient operator. The $\nabla$ operator is defined by the matrices $\mathbf{D}^{\xi}$ and $\mathbf{D}^{\mu}$ as

$$\nabla \mathbf{x} = \left|\mathbf{D}^{\xi}\mathbf{x}\right| + \left|\mathbf{D}^{\mu}\mathbf{x}\right| \tag{6}$$

built on the basis of the respective masks $\mathbf{d}^{\xi}$ and $\mathbf{d}^{\mu}$ of size $N = N_1 \times N_2$, which turn out the horizontal and vertical first order differences of the image. Compared to the expression (4), the TV regularization provides a $\ell_1$ penalty term which can be thought as a measure of signal variability. Once again, $\lambda$ is the critical regularization parameter to control the weight assigned to the regularizer with respect to the data misfit term.

Significant amount of work has been addressed to solve any of the above regularizations and mainly the TV deblurring in recent times (Chan & Shen, 2005). However, there are two important issues in those algorithms which require making assumptions and constraining the regularized solution: boundary conditions and parameters estimations. This chapter provides two novel iterative methods aimed to loose this dependency and achieve a more robust solution in terms of estimations. Let us analyze each problem separately.

### 2.1 Boundary conditions

As defined in González & Woods, 2007, the convolution operator of equation (1) integrates a portion of the original scenery $\mathbf{x}$ into a single point by weighting the nearby pixels by a 180 degrees rotated mask $\mathbf{h}$. When computing the pixels near the boundary and depending on the size of the PSF, many pixels of $\mathbf{y}$ contain information coming from the original scenery outside the field of view (FOV) which is indeterminate. We refer to this phenomenon and to its consequences as *boundary effect*. It is well known that if the boundary effect is not properly taken into account, it may cause strong ringing artifacts on the deconvolved image. For that reason, various methods of the literature try to counteract this effect by selecting appropriate boundaries conditions (BCs). These boundary conditions are included in the model of $\mathbf{H}$ used in deconvolution as

$$\mathbf{H} = \mathbf{T} + \mathbf{B} \tag{7}$$

where $\mathbf{T}$ has a Toeplitz structure and $\mathbf{B}$ is often structured, sparse and low rank, and specifically defined for every BC. Common cases are the *Zero* (Bertero & Bocacci, 1998), *Periodic* (Bertero & Bocacci, 1998), *Reflective* (Ng et al., 1999) or *Anti-reflective* (Martinelly et al., 2006) boundary conditions.

As a result of the convolution, it can be easily demonstrated (see Fig. 1) that the degraded image $\mathbf{y}$ increases its size with respect to the original image $\mathbf{x}$ from $L$ to $\tilde{L}$ as

$$\tilde{L} = (L_1 + 2B_1) \times (L_2 + 2B_2) \tag{8}$$

where $B_1$ and $B_2$ are the respective horizontal and vertical bandwidths of the PSF, then the length of $\mathbf{h}$ is $M = M_1 \times M_2 = (2B_1 + 1) \times (2B_2 + 1)$. We have gray colored the pixels affected by the boundary conditions which are not actually present in a real observation. Therefore, a real observed image $\mathbf{y}_{\text{real}}$ is a truncated version of the convolution process to the region called field of view

$$\text{FOV} = \left[ (L_1 - 2B_1) \times (L_2 - 2B_2) \right] \subset \tilde{L} \tag{9}$$

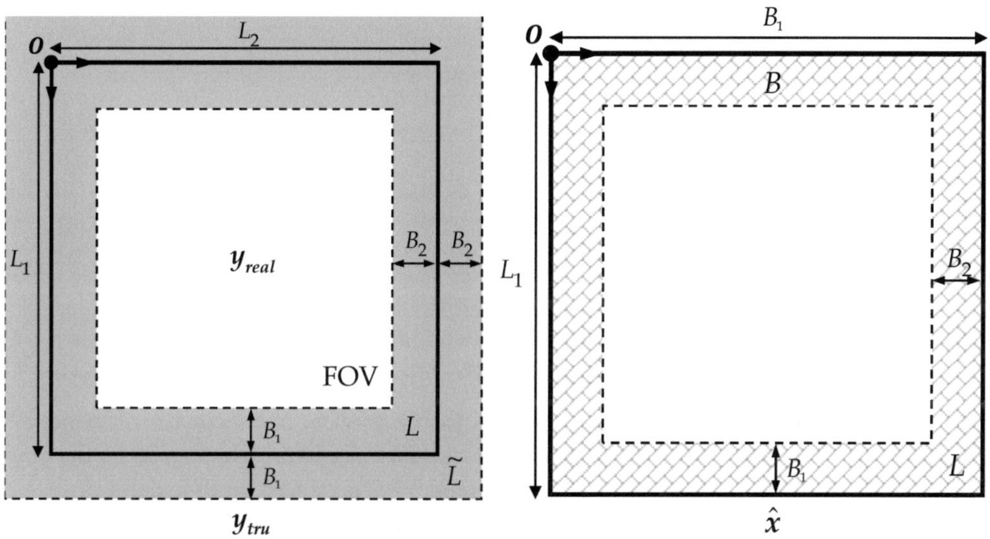


Fig. 1. Real observed image defined in the field of view (left). Restored image which indicates the boundary reconstruction area (right).

Common deblurring methods deal with this real image $\mathbf{y}_{\text{real}}$ and try to restore it minimizing the boundary ringing as much as possible using BCs on the model $\mathbf{H}$ like (7). However, the restored image is only obtained within the FOV domain, that is smaller than the original image size $L$. Our goal is to not only improve the restoration on the whole image but also reconstruct the boundaries that are missed in the observation, without neither any image information nor prior assumption on the boundary conditions.

Let us define an image $\mathbf{y}_{\text{tru}}$ which represents this observed image $\mathbf{y}_{\text{real}}$ using a $\text{trunc}\{\cdot\}$ operator that removes (zero-fixes) the pixels of the boundary region, that is to say

$$y_{tru}(i,j) = \text{trunc}\left\{\mathbf{H_a x} + \mathbf{n}\big|_{(i,j)}\right\} = \begin{cases} \mathbf{y_{real}} = \mathbf{H_a x} + \mathbf{n}\big|_{(i,j)} & \forall (i,j) \in \text{FOV} \\ 0 & \textit{otherwise} \end{cases} \quad (10)$$

where $\mathbf{H_a}$ denotes the Toeplitz matrix when not using boundary conditions (aperiodic model). Therefore, we aim to restore this truncated image $\mathbf{y_{tru}}$ in spite of the discontinuity at the boundaries and reconstruct the region $B$ depicted in Fig. 1

$$B = L - FOV \quad (11)$$

whose area is calculated by $B = (L_1 - B_1) \times 4B_1$, if we consider square dimensions such that $B_1 = B_2$ and $L_1 = L_2$.

Particulary, we intend to study an iterative algorithm using the TV regularizer which loose the dependency on the boundary conditions. So we redefine the restoration problem (5) including the $\text{trunc}\{\cdot\}$ operator as

$$\hat{\mathbf{x}} = \arg\min_{\mathbf{x}} \left\{ \frac{1}{2} \left\| \mathbf{y} - \text{trunc}\{\mathbf{H_a x}\} \right\|_2^2 + \lambda \left\| \text{trunc}\left\{ \left| \mathbf{D_a^{\xi} x} \right| + \left| \mathbf{D_a^{\mu} x} \right| \right\} \right\|_1 \right\} \quad (12)$$

where the subscript **a** denotes the aperiodic formulation of every matrix operator. An equivalent analysis for the Tikhonov regularizer can be found in Santiago et al., 2010.

### 2.2 Estimations dependency

If we have a look to any restoration method of the literature, we come up with their dependency on a wide set of parameters which must be estimated a priori. We can group them basically into three classes

- Parameters with respect to the blurring process.
- Parameters with respect to the noise.
- Parameters with respect to the original image.

In terms of blurring, the convolution matrix $\mathbf{H}$ is not always available in the restoration process and thus it is required to make assumptions about its parameters, such as the length of motion or the radius of out-of-focus among others. We can find a lot of articles devoted to estimate the PSF which are normally referred to as blind deconvolution. Regarding noise we have assumed a Gaussian white noise from the very beginning, so the concrete parameter is just the variance $\sigma_n^2$. Finally, the parameters related to the original image have to do with the regularization term of the equations (4) or (5) and, in turn, with the regularization parameter $\lambda$.

Blind deconvolution methods try to obtain the more accurate parameters but deal with a problem known as sensitivity to estimations, that is to say, relatively small deviations from the real (unknown) values have a severe impact on the restoration quality. Therefore, we aim to define an algorithm that improves the results of a restoration scheme when having wrong estimates of the said parameters, namely, a desensitization process.

We shall work in the frequency domain for this issue so we take for granted the circular boundary conditions of the previous section. In particular, our goal is to desensitize two common algorithms of the literature defined in the Fourier space: Wiener and Tikhonov (Bovik, 2005). Both methods are completely linear so described by a restoration filter as

$$\hat{X}(\varpi_i,\varpi_j) = G(\varpi_i,\varpi_j)Y(\varpi_i,\varpi_j) \tag{13}$$

where $G(\varpi_i,\varpi_j)$ denotes the Fourier transform of the restoration filter. In order to simplify notation, the reference to the element $(\varpi_i,\varpi_j)$ of the matrices in the frequency domain will be removed from all formulae throughout the remainder of the chapter. They are differentiated from the variables of the boundary problem because those are in bold. Besides, it must be taken into account that all mathematical expressions involving matrices in the Fourier Transform domain are scalar computations for each frequency component $(\varpi_i,\varpi_j)$.

From González & Woods, 2007, it is demonstrated that

- Wiener Filter

$$G = \frac{H^*}{|H|^2 + \frac{S_{nn}}{S_{xx}}} \tag{14}$$

where $H^*$ represents the complex conjugate of $H$, $S_{xx}$ and $S_{nn}$ are the respective spectral densities of the original image $\mathbf{x}$ and the noise $\mathbf{n}$.

- Tikhonov Filter

$$G = \frac{H^*}{|H|^2 + \lambda|D|^2} \tag{15}$$

where $D$ is the Fourier transform of the regularization operator $\mathbf{D}$ in (4).

Let us symbolize the restoration filter as $\hat{G}$ when calculated by estimations (not real values) as well as the rest of variables involved in (14) and (15) such as $\hat{H}$, $\hat{S}_{xx}$, $\hat{S}_{yy}$ and $\hat{\lambda}$. Therefore, we shall define an iterative method which achieves a filter $G'$ based on the original $\hat{G}$ with less sensitivity to wrong estimations.

## 3. Iterative methods

In this section we propose two algorithms to cope with the aforementioned constraints of a restoration problem: boundary conditions and estimation dependency. Both methods are iterative and lead to various restoration-degradation processes repeated a certain number of times. A detailed analysis is devoted to each algorithm in the following sections.

### 3.1 MLP approach

The main issues addressed by this algorithm are

- Restore a real observed image $\mathbf{y}_{\mathbf{real}}$ without neither any image information nor prior assumption on the boundary conditions.

- Remove boundary ringing in spite of the discontinuity at the boundaries.
- Reconstruct the boundary region $B$ so that the restored image has the same size $L$ as the original image.
- Make use of the TV regularizer.

To go around this problem we know that neural networks are particularly well-suited as their ability to nonlinear mapping and self-adaptiveness. In fact, the Hopfield network has been used in the literature to solve the optimization problem (4) and recently some neural network solutions as in Wang, 2005 and Wu, 2007 deal with the TV regularization (5).

Our proposal is a MLP (Multiplayer Perceptron) with back-propagation as illustrated inFig. 2. The input layer of the net consists of $\tilde{L}$ neurons with inputs $y_1, y_2, ..., y_{\tilde{L}}$ being respectively the $\tilde{L}$ pixels of the truncated image $\mathbf{y_{tru}}$. At any generic iteration $m$, the output layer is defined by $L$ neurons whose outputs $\hat{x}_1(m), \hat{x}_2(m), ..., \hat{x}_L(m)$ are respectively the $L$ pixels of an approach $\hat{\mathbf{x}}(m)$ to the restored image. After $\overline{m}$ iterations, the neural net outcomes the actual restored image $\hat{\mathbf{x}} = \hat{\mathbf{x}}(\overline{m})$. On the other hand, the hidden layer consists of only two neurons, although being enough to achieve good restoration results while keeping low complexity of the network.

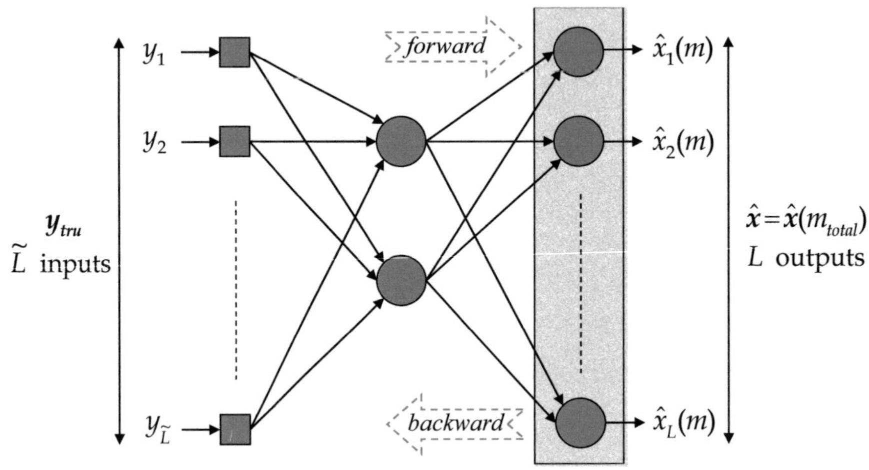


Fig. 2. MLP scheme adopted for image restoration.

The neural network undertakes two processes iteratively: forward and backward. The former is the result of applying from left to right the equations of every layer. It is actually the restoration step. The latter is the back-propagation process where the network must minimize a regularized error function which we will set to the expression (12). It means to adjust the synaptic coefficients of every single neuron from right to left and can be thought as a reblurring step. Since the $\mathrm{trunc}\{\cdot\}$ operator is involved in all those expressions, the truncation of the boundaries is performed at every iteration but also their reconstruction as indicated by the $L$ size at the output. What deserves attention is that no a priori knowledge, assumption or estimation concerning the unknown borders is needed to perform the regeneration. Generally speaking it could be explained by the neural net nature which is able to learn about the degradation model.

A restored image is therefore obtained in real conditions on the basis of a global energy minimization strategy, with reconstructed borders while adapting the center of the image to the optimum solution and thus making the ringing artifact negligible. Finally, we recall that the input to the net is always the image $\mathbf{y}_{tru}$ as no net training is required.

### 3.1.1 Adjustment of the neural net

Let us define each layer of Fig. 2 as an input vector $\mathbf{p}$ of size $R\times 1$, a synaptic weight matrix $\mathbf{W}$ of $S\times R$ in size, and a $S\times 1$ output vector $\mathbf{z}$ of the layer. We utilize a log-sigmoid expression for the transfer function $\varphi\{\cdot\}$ and a null bias vector. A superscript is used to denote the number of layer, but it will be removed when deduced by context. So we can redraw our MLP as depicted in Fig. 3 where we have symbolized the variation of the synaptic matrixes of every layer.

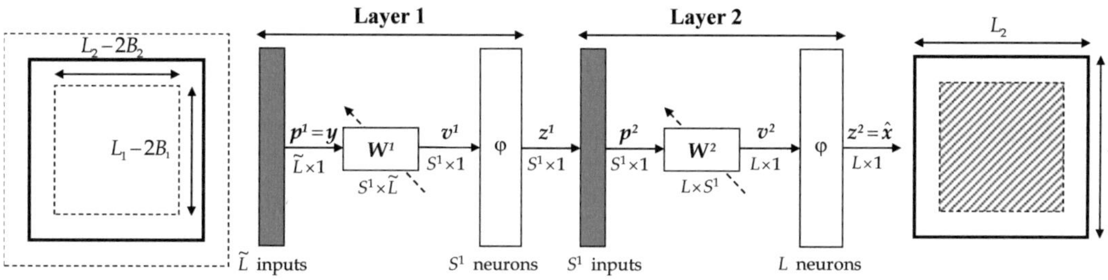


Fig. 3. MLP algorithm with matrix-vector notation.

A variant of the well-known algorithm of back-propagation is used to adjust those matrixes with the truncated cost function of (12). Let $\Delta\mathbf{W}^i(m+1)$ be the correction applied to the weight matrix $\mathbf{W}^i$ of the layer $i$ at the $(m+1)^{th}$ iteration. Then,

$$\Delta\mathbf{W}^i(m+1) = -\eta\frac{\partial E(m)}{\partial\mathbf{W}^i(m)} \tag{16}$$

where $E(m)$ stands for the cost error function after $m$ iterations at the output of the net and the constant $\eta$ indicates the learning speed. Defining the vectors $\mathbf{e}(m)$ and $\mathbf{r}(m)$ for the respective error and regularization terms at the output layer after $m$ iterations

$$\mathbf{e}(m) = \mathbf{y} - \operatorname{trunc}\{\mathbf{H_a}\hat{\mathbf{x}}(m)\} \tag{17}$$

$$\mathbf{r}(m) = \operatorname{trunc}\left\{\left|\mathbf{D}_\mathbf{a}^\xi\hat{\mathbf{x}}(m)\right| + \left|\mathbf{D}_\mathbf{a}^\mu\hat{\mathbf{x}}(m)\right|\right\} \tag{18}$$

we can rewrite the restoration error from (12)

$$E(m) = \frac{1}{2}\|\mathbf{e}(m)\|_2^2 + \lambda\|\mathbf{r}(m)\|_1 \tag{19}$$

Now we aim to compute the so-called gradient matrix $\frac{\partial E(m)}{\partial \mathbf{W}^i(m)}$ in the layers of the MLP. A high detailed analysis can be found in Santiago et al., 2010 based on the algorithm of majorization-minimization developed by Bioucas-Dias et al., 2006 when facing a TV regularization problem like (5). Let us summarize the main results below:

$$\Delta \mathbf{W}^i(m+1) = -\eta \boldsymbol{\delta}^i(m)\left(\mathbf{z}^{i-1}(m)\right)^T \quad (20)$$

where $\boldsymbol{\delta}(m)$ stands for the local gradient vector and is defined for a MLP of $J$ layers as:

- Output layer ($i = J$)

$$\boldsymbol{\delta}(m) = \varphi\{\mathbf{v}(m)\} \circ \left(-\mathbf{H}_\mathbf{a}^T \mathbf{e}(m) + \lambda \mathbf{D}_\mathbf{a}^T \boldsymbol{\Omega}(m)\mathbf{r}(m)\right) \quad (21)$$

where $\circ$ denotes the Hadamard (elementwise) product, $\mathbf{D_a}$ is a composition of the matrices $\mathbf{D}_\mathbf{a}^{\xi}$ and $\mathbf{D}_\mathbf{a}^{\mu}$ as $\mathbf{D_a} = \left[\left(\mathbf{D}_\mathbf{a}^{\xi}\right)^T \left(\mathbf{D}_\mathbf{a}^{\mu}\right)^T\right]^T$ and $\boldsymbol{\Omega}(m)$ represents a weigh matrix which controls the influence of regions with high intensity variation

$$\boldsymbol{\Omega}(m) = \begin{bmatrix} \boldsymbol{\Lambda}(m) & 0 \\ 0 & \boldsymbol{\Lambda}(m) \end{bmatrix}$$
$$\text{with } \boldsymbol{\Lambda}(m) = \text{diag}\left(\frac{1}{2\sqrt{\left(\mathbf{D}_\mathbf{a}^{\xi}\hat{\mathbf{x}}(m)\right)^2 + \left(\mathbf{D}_\mathbf{a}^{\mu}\hat{\mathbf{x}}(m)\right)^2 + \varepsilon}}\right) \quad (22)$$

- Any hidden layer ($i < J$)

$$\boldsymbol{\delta}^i(m) = \text{diag}\left(\varphi\left\{\mathbf{v}^i(m)\right\}\right)\left(\mathbf{W}^{i+1}(m)\right)^T \boldsymbol{\delta}^{i+1}(m) \quad (23)$$

### 3.1.2 Algorithm parameters

Due to the iterative nature of the algorithm the first parameter to establish has to do with the stop rule. It is a condition such that either the number of iterations is more than a maximum; or the error $E(m)$ converges and, thus, the error change $\Delta E(m)$ is less than a threshold; or, even, this error $E(m)$ starts to increase. If one of these conditions comes true, the algorithm concludes and the final outgoing image is the restored image $\hat{\mathbf{x}} = \hat{\mathbf{x}}(\overline{m})$.

In the image restoration field it is remarked the importance of the parameter $\lambda$. Low values of $\lambda$ yield oscillatory solutions because of the presence of noise or discontinuities; high values of $\lambda$ yield over smoothed results though. For that reason, the literature has given significant attention to it with popular approaches such as the unbiased predictive risk estimator (UPRE), the generalized cross validation (GCV), or the L-curve method; see Vogel, 2002 for an overview and references. Most of them were particularized for a Tikhonov regularizer, but lately researches aim to provide solutions for the TV regularization. Specifically, the Bayesian framework leads to successful approaches in this respect.

In Santiago et al., 2010 we adjusted $\lambda$ with solutions coming from the Bayesian state-of-art. However, we still need to investigate a particular algorithm for the MLP since those Bayesian approaches work only for circulant degradation models, but not for the truncated image of this chapter. So we shall compute yet a hand-tuned $\lambda$ which optimizes the results.

As for learning speed it was already demonstrated that $\eta$ shows lower sensitivity compared to $\lambda$. In fact, its main purpose is to speed up or slow down the convergence of the algorithm. Then, for the sake of simplicity, we shall assume $\eta = 2$ for the images of $256 \times 256$ in size.

### 3.2 Desensitization approach

The second of our methods go around the following issues

- Desensitize the restoration filter (assumed linear) with respect to wrong parameter estimations.
- Counteract the effects of mistaking parameters in order to achieve a better restoration quality compared to that without desensitization.
- Alternative to classic restoration approaches which focus on obtaining accurate estimations.
- Particularization to Wiener and Tikhonov filters

Let us define an expression for the desensitized filter $G'$ based on the original $\hat{G}$ in the frequency domain. Again our approach is an iterative algorithm as illustrated in Fig. 4.

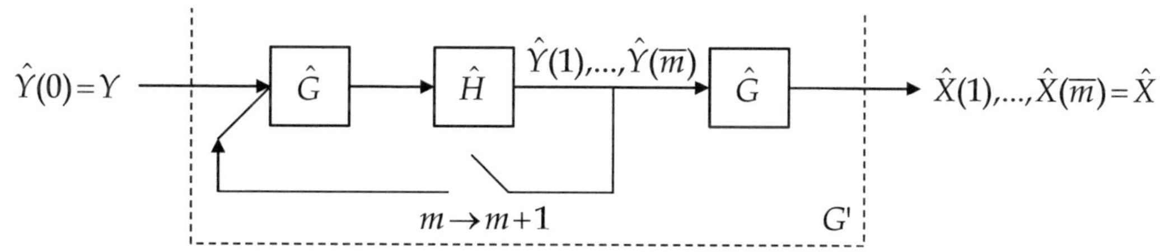


Fig. 4. Desensitized restoration scheme.

The input at any iteration $m$ ($m = 1,2,...,\overline{m}$) is an image $\hat{Y}(m)$ computed by its previous iteration $\hat{Y}(m-1)$ after going through the restoration filter $\hat{G}$ and the estimated transfer function $\hat{H}$. In a first step the image $\hat{Y}(0)$ is equal to the degraded image $Y$ and, after the total number of iterations, the image $\hat{Y}(\overline{m})$ is restored again by the filter $\hat{G}$ leading to the the output image $\hat{X} = \hat{X}(\overline{m})$. This algorithm is somehow based on the same iterative concept of restoration-degradation processes of the MLP but applied to the Fourier domain. Let us recall that the mathematical expressions for this algorithm are particular for each frequency component $(\varpi_i, \varpi_j)$ and, in fact, we put forward that the number of iterations is also a function of these elements, i.e., $\overline{m}(\varpi_i, \varpi_j)$.

It can be easily demonstrated that the filter $G'$ of Fig. 4 is expressed as

$$G' = \hat{G}\left(\hat{G}\hat{H}\right)^{m} \tag{24}$$

where $\hat{G}\hat{H}$ is known as the regularization product. In Santiago et al., 2007 we verified that the higher the regularization is, the lower the product $\hat{G}\hat{H}$ becomes with a dynamic range $0 < \hat{G}\hat{H} < 1$.

### 3.2.1 Sensitivity criteria

So far we have referred to sensitivity as a concept, but now we put it on mathematical expressions. Let us consider that the restoration filter $G$ depends on a set of parameters $P_1, P_2, \ldots, P_r$ which can be grouped into the three groups of Section 2.2: blurring, noise and original image. Then we can define the sensitivity $S_G$ regarding the filter $G$ as

$$S_G = \frac{\partial G}{\partial P_1} dP_1 + \frac{\partial G}{\partial P_2} dP_2 + \ldots + \frac{\partial G}{\partial P_r} dP_r \tag{25}$$

Analogously, the sensitivity concerning the proposed filter $G'$ can be expressed as follows

$$S_{G'} = \frac{\partial G'}{\partial P_1} dP_1 + \frac{\partial G'}{\partial P_2} dP_2 + \ldots + \frac{\partial G'}{\partial P_r} dP_r \tag{26}$$

To compare the sensitivity of both filters we make use of a relative function $Z = S_{G'}/S_G$ which sets the desensitization criteria as $Z < 1$. After differentiating the filter $G'$ of (24) with respect to $G$ we come up with an expression for the relative sensitivity function (see Santiago et al., 2007 for further details)

$$Z(m) = \frac{S_{G'}}{S_G} = (m+1)(\hat{G}\hat{H})^m < 1 \tag{27}$$

As $0 < \left(\hat{G}\hat{H}\right)^m < \hat{G}\hat{H} < 1$ we can foresee that the function $Z(m)$ of (27) is neither monotonically increasing nor decreasing with the number of iterations $m$, but it may show a relative maximum extreme depending on the value of the term $\hat{G}\hat{H}$ for a particular pair $(\varpi_i, \varpi_j)$. This is illustrated in Fig. 5 for several regularization values

Looking into this plot we can observe that the expected maximum extremes of $Z(m)$ depend on the value of $\hat{G}\hat{H}$. The lower the product $\hat{G}\hat{H}$ is, the less iterations $m$ are required to reach the maximum; even high regularization conditions make $Z(m)$ strictly decreasing monotonic. In any case, the main conclusion has to do with the sensitivity condition (27) illustrated by the straight line of the figure. Regardless of the value of the product $\hat{G}\hat{H}$, $G'$ is less sensitive than $G$ if the number of iterations $m$ is high enough. We might therefore increase the value of $m$ as needed to prevent poor restoration results of wrong estimates. However, that is not possible as the restoration error is significantly affected as demonstrated in Santiago et al., 2007.

In González & Woods, 2007 the restoration error is divided into the ringing (or image-dependent) component and the noise-dependent component. What we found out in our previous analysis is that the trend of both errors is contrary for the desensitized filter $G'$. Whereas the noise-dependent error is lower as the number of iterations increases, the ringing component gets higher. Consequently, we need to look for a trade-off between the error components while keeping the desensitization criteria true.

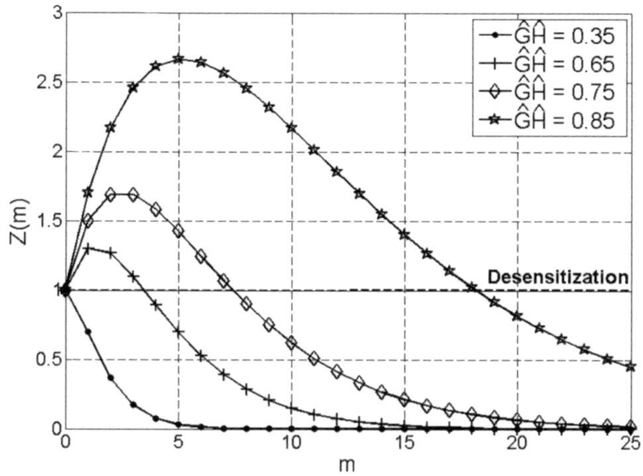


Fig. 5. Relative sensitivity function $Z(m)$.

### 3.2.2 Number of iterations

Since the relative sensitivity function $Z(m)$ does not have a local minimum as viewed in Fig. 5, let us optimize another $Z(m)$ property which also fulfills the desensitization criteria. In particular, we shall look for a maximum of efficiency for the complexity introduced in the restoration process by increasing the number of iterations from $m$ to $m+1$. In other words, let us seek a value of $m$ from that on the improvement on desensitization is lower than the incremental complexity. In mathematical terms we can express this efficiency change as the second derivative of $Z(m)$ denoted by $R(m) = Z''(m)$. It can be easily derived from (27) that

$$R(m) = (\hat{G}\hat{H})^m \ln(\hat{G}\hat{H})\left[2 + (m+1)\ln(\hat{G}\hat{H})\right] \tag{28}$$

The purpose is to maximize this function as well as constrain it to the desensitization condition of $Z(m) < 1$. In Santiago et al., 2007 we came up to a number of iterations as follows

$$\overline{m} = round\left\{-\left[1 + \frac{3}{\ln(\hat{G}\hat{H})}\right]\right\} \tag{29}$$

subject to a constraint on the regularization term $0.14 < \hat{G}\hat{H} < 0.84$.

Finally, let us compute some numeric results of the main variables of the desensitization algorithm for different regularization products $\hat{G}\hat{H}$ : $\overline{m}$, $Z(m)$, $\delta_r(m)$ and $\delta_n(m)$, where these delta functions are respectively the relative error components (ringing and noise) expressed in dB.

| $\hat{G}\hat{H}$ | $\overline{m}$ | $Z(\overline{m})$ | $\delta_r(\overline{m})$ | $\delta_n(\overline{m})$ |
|---|---|---|---|---|
| 0.20 | 1 | 0.40 | 9.15 | -13.98 |
| 0.30 | 1 | 0.60 | 8.41 | -10.46 |
| 0.40 | 2 | 0.48 | 9.43 | -15.92 |
| 0.50 | 3 | 0.50 | 9.66 | -18.06 |
| 0.60 | 5 | 0.47 | 9.97 | -22.18 |
| 0.70 | 7 | 0.66 | 9.94 | -21.69 |
| 0.80 | 12 | 0.89 | 10.03 | -23.26 |

Table 1. Numeric results for the main functions of the desensitized filter.

Looking at the figures of Table 1 we can see that the improvements achieved for $\delta_n(m)$ are greater than the impairments obtained from $\delta_r(m)$, always satisfying the desensitization condition $Z(m) < 1$. For that reason, we may expect to have good restoration results with a rough estimation of noise in a very wide range, much better than other kind of wrong parameters.

## 4. Experimental results

In this section we aim to validate the properties of the previous algorithms using a variety of experiments with very well-known $256 \times 256$ sized images such as Lena, Barbara or Cameraman, or PSFs widely used in the field as the motion, Gaussian or uniforms blurs. Furthermore, we shall compare the results with classic approaches of image restoration to ensure the good performance of our iterative methods.

### 4.1 MLP experiments

Let us see our problem formulation by means of an example. Fig. 6 depicts the original Barbara image blurred by a motion blur of 15 pixels and 45° of inclination, which turns out a PSF mask of $11 \times 11$ in size ($B_1 = B_2 = 5$). We have represented the truncated image $\mathbf{y}_{tru}$ on the right which reflects the zeros at the boundaries and the size of $\tilde{L} = 266 \times 266$. A real model would consist of the $\mathrm{FOV} = 246 \times 246$ region of this image which we named as $\mathbf{y}_{real}$ so far. Most recent algorithms deal with this real image but making assumptions about the boundaries and yielding a restored image of $246 \times 246$. Consequently, the boundaries marked with the white broken line on the left are never restored. In contrast, our MLP outcomes a $256 \times 256$ sized image $\hat{\mathbf{x}}$ reconstructing the boundary area $B = 251 \times 20$.

To resolve this sort of problems we have implemented the MLP according to the following parameters. In the light of the expression (18) we have used the horizontal and vertical Sobel masks ($N = 3 \times 3$) of Bovik, 2005 for the filters $\mathbf{d}^{\xi}$ and $\mathbf{d}^{\mu}$. We already commented that the learning speed of the net is set to $\eta = 2$ and the regularization parameter $\lambda$ relies on a hand tuning basis. Regarding the interconnection weights, they do not require any network training so the weigh matrices are all initialized to zero. Finally, we set the stopping criteria as a maximum number of 500 iterations (though never reached) or when the relative difference of the restoration error $E(m)$ falls below a threshold of $10^{-3}$ in a temporal window of 10 iterations.

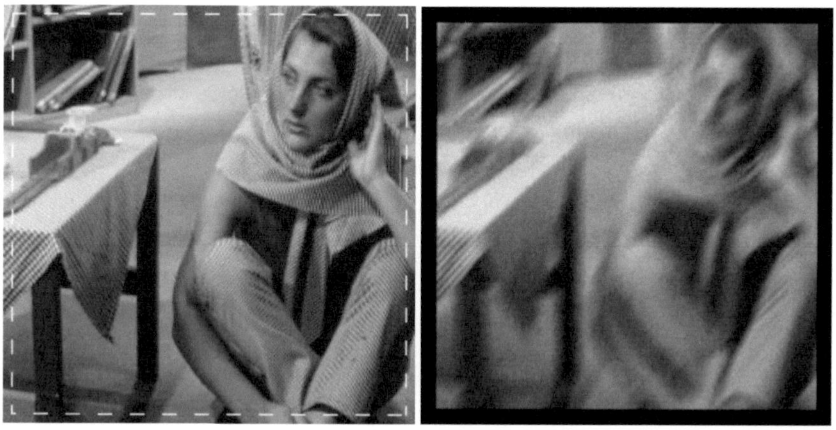

Fig. 6. Degraded and truncated image by diagonal motion blur (right) and the expected boundary region to be reconstructed (left).

In order to measure the performance of our algorithm, we compute the standard deviation $\sigma_e$ of the error image $\mathbf{e} = \hat{\mathbf{x}} - \mathbf{x}$ since it does not depend on the blurred image $\mathbf{y}$ as in the ISNR (Banham and Katsaggelos, 1997). Regarding the boundary reconstruction process we particularize the standard deviation to the pixels of the boundary region $B$.

### 4.1.1 Experiment 1

Our first experiment takes the Lena image degraded by several motion and uniform blurs. Regarding the motion blur, we establish 45° of inclination and the length of pixels is varied between 5 and 15. We have used the approximation of Matlab to construct the filter of motion which leads to masks between $5 \times 5$ and $11 \times 11$ in size. Analogously, the uniform blur is defined with odd sizes between $5 \times 5$ and $11 \times 11$. In terms of Gaussian noise we set a ratio of $\mathrm{BSNR} = 20$ dB.

The results of the MLP are shown in Table 2. As presumable, the quality of restoration is getting worse as the size of the blur increases, but let us remark that the boundary reconstruction area is also expanding. If we compare the results between blurs we can observe that the uniform mask achieves better values at the boundaries, but lower in the center for the same size. It can be thought of a spatial varying restoration process of the MLP in the center with respect to the boundaries.

To visually assess the performance of the MLP we select some of the results indicated in the previous table. On the left of Fig. 7 we depict the Lena restored image for a diagonal motion blur of 10 pixels. The restored boundary area is $252 \times 16$ in size marked by a white broken line and reveals how the borders are successfully regenerated without neither any image information nor prior assumption on the boundary conditions. Likewise, we illustrate the restored image with a uniform blur of $7 \times 7$ on the right and a boundary region of $253 \times 12$.

| Motion | | | |
|---|---|---|---|
| *Length* | *Size* | $\sigma_e$ | $B\sigma_e$ |
| 5 | $5 \times 5$ | 8.70 | 24.59 |
| 6 | $5 \times 5$ | 8.70 | 20.58 |
| 7 | $7 \times 7$ | 10.35 | 27.23 |
| 8 | $7 \times 7$ | 10.25 | 24.05 |
| 9 | $7 \times 7$ | 10.26 | 20.96 |
| 10 | $9 \times 9$ | 11.62 | 26.04 |
| 11 | $9 \times 9$ | 11.50 | 23.36 |
| 12 | $9 \times 9$ | 11.51 | 20.85 |
| 13 | $11 \times 11$ | 12.78 | 25.85 |
| 14 | $11 \times 11$ | 12.61 | 23.15 |
| 15 | $11 \times 11$ | 12.63 | 21.10 |

| Uniform | | |
|---|---|---|
| *Size* | $\sigma_e$ | $B\sigma_e$ |
| $5 \times 5$ | 8.90 | 17.29 |
| $7 \times 7$ | 11.32 | 19.64 |
| $9 \times 9$ | 13.20 | 20.64 |
| $11 \times 11$ | 14.69 | 22.27 |

Table 2. Numeric values of $\sigma_e$ and $B\sigma_e$ for different sizes of degradation.

Fig. 7. Restored images of the MLP when using motion (left) and uniform (right) blurs.

### 4.1.2 Experiment 2

This experiment aims to compare the performance of the MLP with other restoration algorithms which need BCs to deal with a realistic capture model: zero, periodic, reflective and anti-reflective as commented in Section 2.1. We have used the RestoreTools, 2007 library patched with the anti-reflective modification which implements the matrix-vector operations for every boundary condition. In particular, we have selected an algorithm of this library named as HyBR (hybrid bidiagonalization regularization) that is a modified version of the Tikhonov regularization.

Let us consider the Barbara image degraded by a $7 \times 7$ Gaussian blur and the same additive white noise of the previous experiments with $\text{BSNR} = 20 \text{ dB}$. Fig. 8 shows the restored images of the HyBR method from a real acquisition of $\text{FOV} = 250 \times 250$ in size (field of view). We can observe that the restored images for each boundary condition are all $250 \times 250$ sized images which miss the information of the boundaries up to $256 \times 256$. Furthermore, a remarkable boundary ringing can be appreciated for the periodic BCs as result of the discontinuity of the image in the boundaries. As demonstrated in Martinelli et al., 2006 the reflexive and the anti-reflexive conditions perform considerably better removing that boundary effect.

The restored image of our MLP algorithm is shown on the bottom-right of Fig. 8 and makes obvious the good performance of the neural net. First, the boundary ringing is negligible without prior assumption on the boundary condition. Moreover, the visual aspect is better compared to the others which recalls the good properties of the TV regularizer. To numerically contrast the results, the parameter $\sigma_e$ of the MLP is measured only in the FOV region. It leads to $F\sigma_e = 12.47$ which is notably lower to the values of the HyBR algorithm (e.g. $F\sigma_e = 12.99$ for the reflexive BCs). Finally, the MLP is able to reconstruct the $253 \times 12$ sized boundary region and outcomes the original image size of $256 \times 256$.

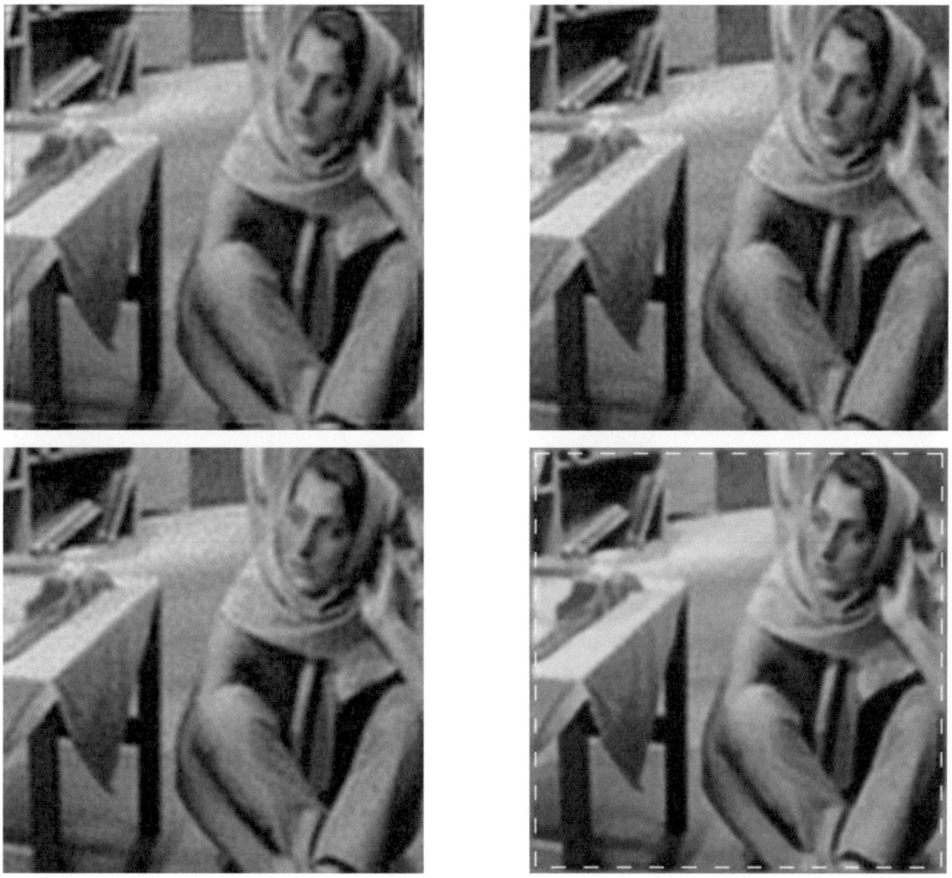

Fig. 8. Restored images with HyBR under periodic (upper-left), reflective (upper-right) and anti-reflective (bottom-left) BCs. Restored image with our MLP (bottom-right).

### 4.1.3 Experiment 3

Finally, let us compare with other algorithms of the literature which deal with the boundary problem in a different sense from the typical BCs and that reconstruct the area $B$ bordering the field of view. In recent research Bishop, 2008 proposed a method based on the Bayesian model and treated the truncation effect as modeling error. To make a better comparison we have updated the MLP to leverage the concept of extended image of this method by removing the operator $\text{trunc}\{\cdot\}$ from all formulae of Section 3.1 and setting the observed image $\mathbf{y}_{\text{real}}$ at the input of the MLP instead of the truncated image $\mathbf{y}_{\text{tru}}$.

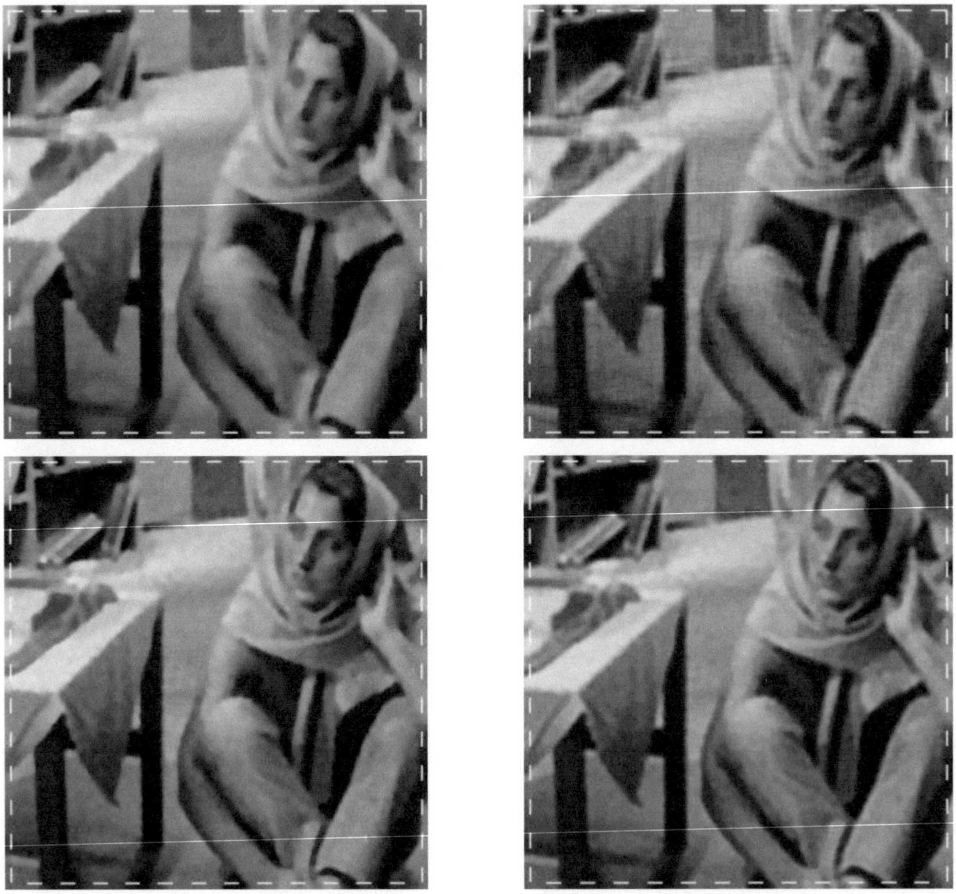

Fig. 9. Restored images with Bishop's method: uniform (upper-left) and Gaussian (bottom-left) blurs. Likewise for MLP: uniform (upper-right) and Gaussian (bottom-right).

Looking at Table 3 we find out that the values of $\sigma_e$ are quite similar for both methods, being the MLP which outperforms in the Gaussian and motion blurs. But what really deserves attention are the results in the boundary region $B$. The MLP is considerably better reconstructing the missed boundaries as indicated by the lower values of $B\sigma_e$. Then, it reveals the outstanding properties of the neural net in terms of learning about the unknown image.

| | Bishop | | | MLP | | |
|---|---|---|---|---|---|---|
| **Blur** | $\sigma_e$ | $B\sigma_e$ | $F\sigma_e$ | $\sigma_e$ | $B\sigma_e$ | $F\sigma_e$ |
| *Uniform* | 13.23 | 17.43 | 12.99 | 13.53 | 15.05 | 13.45 |
| *Gaussian* | 12.49 | 17.79 | 12.18 | 12.33 | 14.13 | 12.24 |
| *Motion* | 11.37 | 17.63 | 10.97 | 11.33 | 12.58 | 11.27 |

Table 3. Comparison between Bishop's method and MLP for various PSFs

Let us visually assess the performance of both methods for some experiments of Table 3. In particular, we have used two $250 \times 250$ sized images degraded by uniform and Gaussian blurs of $7 \times 7$. The restored images appear in Fig. 9 with $256 \times 256$ in size and thus reconstructing the boundary area $B = 253 \times 12$. Despite the fact that the value of $\sigma_e$ is lower for the Bishop's method in the uniform blur, we can observe that the subjective quality of the MLP output is better. As for the Gaussian blur the restored images look similar although the value of $\sigma_e$ is in favor of the neural net.

### 4.2 Desensitization experiments

In this case our experiments aim to compare the performance of the desensitization filter $G'$ with respect to the classical filters $G$ Wiener and Tikhonov when having errors on the estimations. So let us define a way to measure the deviations from the real value of the parameters. Let $\varepsilon_P$ be the relative error of a generic parameter $P$ defined as follows

$$\varepsilon_P = \frac{P_{real} - P_{estimated}}{P_{real}} \cdot 100 \tag{30}$$

where $P_{real}$ and $P_{estimated}$ stand for the respective real and estimated values of the parameter $P$. Provided that these parameters are real variables, the relative error $\varepsilon_P$ is also extended along the range $-\infty < \varepsilon_P < +\infty$, even though we only consider the significant values ranged between $-100$ and 100 %.

The types of parameters for these experiments have to do with the noise and blurs of previous experiments. As for the noise we shall deal with the variance $\sigma_n^2$ of a Gaussian additive sample ($\varepsilon_\sigma$). On the other hand, we shall focus on the motion blur so that we can observe the effects of mistaking the angle $\phi$ ($\varepsilon_\phi$).

In terms of implementation let us recall that the proposed desensitization algorithm yields a different number of iterations $\overline{m}$ for every pair $(\varpi_i, \varpi_j)$ due to its dependence on the product $\hat{G}\hat{H}$. By using the expression (29) we obtain a value of $\overline{m}$ for those pairs whose regularization term $\hat{G}\hat{H}$ is within the range $0.14 < \hat{G}\hat{H} < 0.84$. Thus, a criterion will be adopted for choosing a number of iterations for the rest of frequencies. Owing to the increasing trend of $\overline{m}$ with respect to $\hat{G}\hat{H}$ (see Table 1), all pairs whose corresponding regularization value exceeds 0.84 are associated to the upper bound of iterations and likewise the minimum value (cero) if $\hat{G}\hat{H}$ is below 0.14.

In view of the expressions (14) and (15) let us do some remarks. First, the spectral density of the Gaussian white noise is just its variance $S_{nn} = \sigma_n^2$. As for the spectral density $S_{xx}$ it is commonly estimated by means of the spectral density of the observed image $S_{yy}$, which in turn is estimated by the periodogram approximation (Marple, 1987)

$$S_{yy} = \frac{1}{L^2}|Y|^2 \tag{31}$$

Finally, the parameter $\lambda$ of (15) is typically computed by the discrepancy principle (Bonesky, 2009) which establishes that

$$\|\mathbf{y} - \mathbf{H}\hat{\mathbf{x}}\|_2^2 = \|\mathbf{n}\|_2^2 = L\sigma_n^2 \tag{32}$$

In these experiments we do use the common ISNR (improvements on the signal-to-noise ratio) as the objective metric.

#### 4.2.1 Experiment 1

In a first simulation we shall execute the desensitization filter for the whole range $-100 < \varepsilon_P < +100$ of the relative error of the parameters $\sigma_n^2$ and $\phi$. The original motion blur is described by a length of 15 pixels and an angle of 45 degrees in a counter-clockwise direction. And the Gaussian noise is added according to a specific BSNR of $20\text{ dB}$. This experiment is computed for the two original filters Wiener and Tikhonov when facing a degraded image Cameraman.

In Fig. 10 we can observe the regions of desensitization for the Wiener filter. As for the noise estimation the desensitization filter outperforms from a specific value $\varepsilon_\sigma$ on. Regarding the angle estimation $\varepsilon_\phi$ our method achieves better results outside a bandwidth. In Santiago, 2007 it is demonstrated that the desensitization method may completely outperform in case of high enough noise conditions.

If we look into the results of the Tikhonov filter in Fig. 11 we come up with better results as it is required a lower value of $\varepsilon_\sigma$ to be in the desensitization region (with less than 10%). This situation may be typical in a method of estimation of the noise variance and therefore our iterative scheme means a successful solution. With regard to the blur estimation $\varepsilon_\varphi$ the region of desensitization is practically the same as in the Wiener example, so it reveals the better behavior of our algorithm in case of the noise.

#### 4.2.2 Experiment 2

Finally, we devote this section to visually analyze the results of the desensitization filter for the optimum case: noise estimation and Tikhonov filter. We shall use the Barbara and Lena images degraded by a Gaussian blur of size $10 \times 10$, and we keep the same noise level as in previous experiments with $\text{BSNR} = 20\text{ dB}$. The estimation error $\varepsilon_\sigma$ is fixed to 10%.

We have printed in Fig. 12 the restored images obtained by the Tikhonov and the desensitization filter in each case. It is remarkable how the Tikhonov algorithm is highly affected by the small error in noise estimation with a significant noise-dependent error on the textures of Barbara and Lena. However, our algorithm is able to counteract this effect and provide a restored image with a better visual aspect. The numeric figures of ISNR also make evidence of this situation. In Barbara we obtain a value of $\text{ISNR} = -2.46\ \text{dB}$ for the Tikhnov filter whereas the desensitization clearly improves it with $\text{ISNR} = 2.38\ \text{dB}$. Analogously, we end up with $\text{ISNR} = -3.53\ \text{dB}$ and $\text{ISNR} = 2.45\ \text{dB}$ in the Lena example.

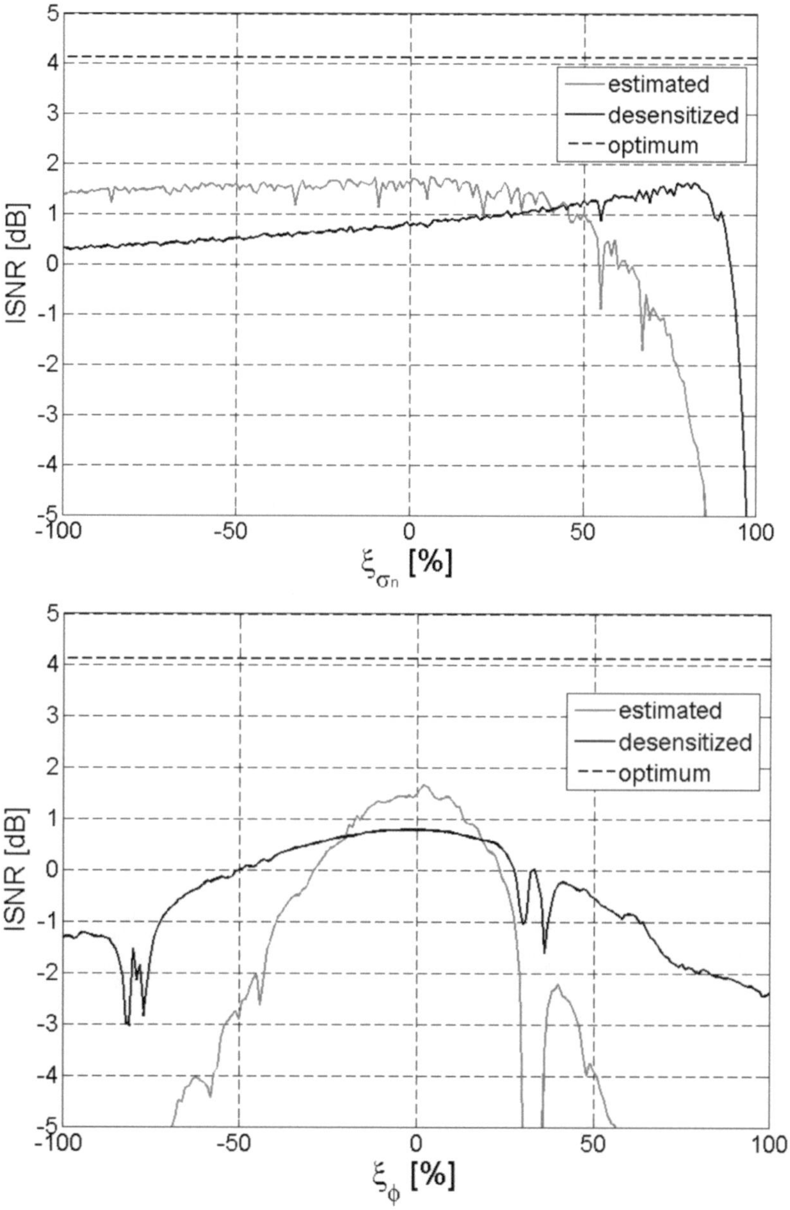


Fig. 10. ISNR for errors on estimations $\sigma_n^2$ and $\phi$ of Wiener filter.

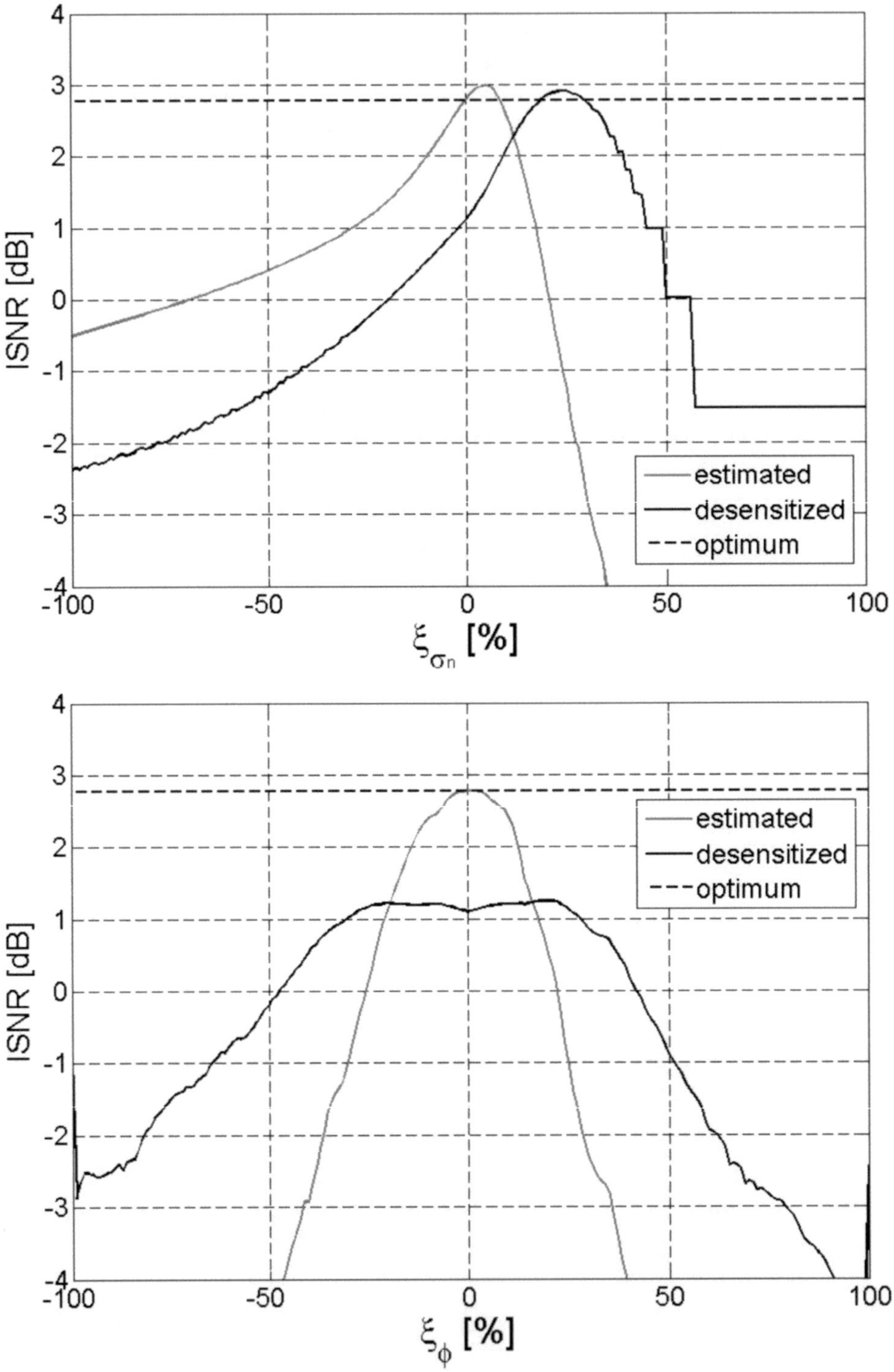


Fig. 11. ISNR for errors on estimations $\sigma_n^2$ and $\phi$ of Tikhonov filter.

Fig. 12. Restored images with Tikhonov filter (upper-left and bottom-left) compared to the restored images of the desensitization filter (upper-right and bottom-right).

## 5. Conclusion

This chapter has addressed two well-known problems of the regularization solutions in image restoration: dependency of boundary conditions and sensitivity to parameters estimations. Following a similar iterative concept of restoration-degradation we have provided two algorithms in the spatial and frequency domain respectively.

On the one hand, we have presented a neural network which aims to restore a real observed image where the borders outside the field of view (FOV) have been truncated. The idea is to apply a TV-based regularization function in an iterative minimization of a MLP (Multilayer perceptron) according to a backpropagation strategy. It achieves to not only restore the center of the image following the optimum linear solution (the ringing artifact thus being negligible), but also reconstruct the boundary area without any prior.

The proposed restoration scheme has been validated by means of several tests. As a result, we can conclude the ability of our neural net to deal with the non-linearity of border truncation and its learning properties about the degradation model so as to regenerate the missed boundaries. In fact, it clearly outperforms when comparing with other methods of the state-of-the-art which also try to inpaint the boundary area.

The second algorithm of this chapter outcomes a frequency-based restoration filter which desensitizes an original method when having errors on its parameters. By means of an iterative sequence of restoration-degradation processes for each frequency pair we come up with a trade-off between desensitization and restoration error. In particular, the noise-dependent error is more robust to estimations than the ringing error which gets higher as the iterations increase.

Various tests demonstrate that the region of desensitization is located from a low value of parameters errors, being more evident in the noise variance and using the Tikhonov filter. We observed the undesirable effects on the original filter in spite of the low error, while our desensitized filter counteract this noise error with successful results.

## 6. References


Banham, M. R. & Katsaggelos, A. K. (1997). Digital Image Restoration. *IEEE Signal Processing Magazine*, Vol. 14, No. 2, pp. 24–41, ISSN 1053-5888

Bertero, M. & Bocacci, P. (1998). *Introduction to Inverse Problems in Imaging*, Institute of Physics Publishing, ISBN 0750304359

Bishop, T. E. (2008). *Bayesian image deblurring and boundary effects*, PhD Thesis, University of Edimburg, UK

Bioucas-Dias, J.; Figueiredo, M. & Oliveira, J. P. (2006). Total variation-based image deconvolution: a majorization–minimization approach, *Proceedings of International Conference on Acoustics, Speech and Signal Processing*, Vol. 2, pp. 861–864, ISBN 1-4244-0469-X, Tolouse, France

Bonesky, T. (2009). Morozov's discrepancy principle and Tikhonov-type functionals. *Inverse Problems*, Vol. 25, No. 1, Article ID 015015, 11 pages, ISSN 0266-5611

Bovik, A. (2005). *Handbook of Image & Video Processing* (2nd edition), Elsevier, ISBN 0-12-119792-1, Burlington, USA

Calvetti, D. & Somersalo, E. (2005). Statistical elimination of boundary artifacts in image deblurring. *Inverse Problems*, Vol. 21, No. 5, pp. 1697–1714, ISSN 0266-5611

Campisi, P. & Egiazarian, K. (2007). *Blind image deconvolution: theory and applications*, CRC Press, ISBN 0-8493-7367-0, New York, USA

Chan, T.F. & Shen, J. (2005). *Image Processing and Analysis Variational, PDE, Wavelet and Stochastic Methods*, SIAM, ISBN 0-89871-589-X, Philadelphia, USA

González, R. C. & Woods, R. E. (2007). *Digital Image Processing* (3rd edition), Prentice Hall, ISBN 0-13-168728-X

Han, Y. B. & Wu, L. N. (2004). Image restoration using a modified hopfield neural network of continuous state change. *Signal Processing*, Vol. 12, No. 3, pp.431–435, ISSN 1003-0530

Liu, R. & Jia, J. (2008). Reducing boundary artifacts in image deconvolution, *Proceedings of International Conference on Image Processing*, pp. 505–508, ISBN 978-1-4244-1765-0, San Diego, USA

Marple, S. L. (1987). *Digital Spectra Analysis: With Applications*, Prentice-Hall, ISBN 0-132-14149-3, Upper Saddle River, USA.

Martinelli, A.; Donatelli, M.; Estatico, C. & Serra-Capizzano, S. (2006). Improved image deblurring with anti-reflective boundary conditions and re-blurring. *Inverse Problems*, Vol. 22, No. 6, pp. 2035–2053, ISSN 0266-5611

Molina, R.; Mateos, J. & Katsaggelos, A. K. (1999). Bayesian and regularization methods for hyperparameter estimation in image restoration. *IEEE Transactions on Image Processing*, Vol. 8, No. 2, pp. 231-246

Molina, R.; Mateos, J. & Katsaggelos, A. K. (2006). Blind deconvolution using a variational approach to parameter, image and blur estimation. *IEEE Transactions on Image Processing*, Vol. 15, No. 12, pp. 3715–3727, ISSN 1057-7149

Ng, M. K.; Chan, R. H. & Wun-Cheung, T. (1999). A fast algorithm for deblurring models with Neumann boundary conditions. *SIAM Journal on Scientific Computing*, Vol. 21, No. 3, pp. 851-866, ISSN 1064-8275

Oliveira, J.; Bioucas-Dias, J. & Figueiredo, M. (2009). Adaptive total variation image deblurring: a majorization-minimization approach. *Signal Processing*, Vol. 89, No. 9, pp. 2479–2493, ISSN 0165-1684

Osher, S.; Rudin, L. & Fatemi, E. (1992). Nonlinear total variation based noise removal algorithms. *Physica D: Nonlinear Phenomena*, Vol. 60, pp. 259-268, ISSN 0167-2789

Paik, J. K. & Katsaggelos, A. K. (1992). Image restoration using a modified hopfield network. *IEEE Transactions on Image Processing*, Vol. 1, No. 1, pp. 49–63, ISSN 1057-7149

Restore Tools (2007). In: *Emory University*, 14.10.2011, Available from http://www.mathcs.emory.edu/~nagy/RestoreTools/

Santiago, M. A.; Cisneros, G. & Bernués, E. (2007). Iterative Desensitisation of Image Restoration Filters under Wrong PSF and Noise Estimates. *EURASIP Journal on Advances in Signal Processing*, Vol. 2007, Article ID 72658, 18 pages, ISSN 1687-6172

Santiago, M. A.; Cisneros, G. & Bernués, E. (2010). An MLP Neural Net with L1 and L2 Regularizers for Real Conditions of Deblurring. *EURASIP Journal on Advances in Signal Processing*, Vol. 2010, Article ID 394615, 18 pages, ISSN 1687-6172

Sun, Y. (2000). Hopfield neural network based algorithms for image restoration and reconstruction - Part I: algorithms and simulations. *IEEE Transactions on Signal Processing*, Vol. 48, No. 7, pp. 2119–2131, ISSN 1053-587X

Vogel, C. R. (2002). *Computational methods for inverse problems*, SIAM, ISBN 0-89871-550-4, Philadelphia, USA

Wang, J.; Liao, X. & Yi, Z. (2005). Image restoration using hopfield neural network based on total variational model, *Proceedings of the Second international conference on Advances in neural networks*, Vol. 2, pp. 735–740, ISBN 3-540-25913-9, Chongqing, China

Woods, J.; Biemond, J. & Tekalp, A. (1985). Boundary Value Problem in Image Restoration, *Proceedings of International Conference on Acoustics, Speech and Signal Processing*, Vol. 10, pp. 692–695, ISBN 1-4244-0469-X, Tampa, Florida

Wu, Y. D.; Sun, Y.; Zhang, H. Y. & Sun, S. X. (2007). Variational PDE based image restoration using neural network. *IET Image Processing*, Vol. 1, No. 1, pp. 85–93, ISSN 1751-9659

8

# Defocused Image Restoration with Local Polynomial Regression and IWF

Liyun Su
*School of Mathematics and Statistics, Chongqing University of Technology*
*China*

## 1. Introduction

Shooting a real world image with a camera through an optical device gives a 2-D image where at least some parts are affected by a blur and noise. Images can be blurred by atmospheric turbulence, relative motion between sensors and objects, longer exposures, and so on, but the exact cause of blurring may be unknown. Restoration of blurred noisy images (Spiros et al., 2009; 2010; Su et al., 2007) is one of the main topics in many processing. The literatures Alonso et al. (2008; 2005); Bar et al. (2006) have given good methods to improve image qualities. The purpose of image restoration is to reconstruct an unobservable true image from a degraded observation. An observed image can be written, ignoring additive noise, as the two-dimensional (2-D) convolution of the true image with a linear space-invariant ($LSI$) blur, known as the $PSF$. Restoration in the case of known blur, assuming the linear degradation model, is called linear image restoration and it has been presented extensively in the last three decades giving rise to a variety of solutions Chen et al. (2000); Suyash et al. (2006); Gu et al. (2009); Lu et al. (2009) . In many practical situations, however, the blur is unknown. Hence, both blur identification and image restoration must be performed from the degraded image. Restoration in the case of unknown blur is called blind image restoration Filip et al. (2003); Mario et al. (2003); Liao et al. (2005) . Existing blind restoration methods can be categorized into two main groups: (i) those which estimate the $PSF$ a priori independent of the true image so as to use it later with one of the linear image restoration methods, such as zero sheet separation, generalized cross validation, and maximum likelihood and expectation maximization based on the $ARMA$ image model Chang et al., (1991); Reeves et al. (1992); Lagendijk et al. (1990) , and (ii) those which estimate the $PSF$ and the true image simultaneously, such as nonnegative sand support constraints recursive inverse filtering, maximum likelihood and conjugate gradient minimization, and simulated annealing Kundur et al. (1998); Katsaggelos et al. (1991) . Algorithms belonging to the first class are computationally simple, but they are limited to situations in which the $PSF$ has a special form, and the true image has certain features. Algorithms belonging to the second class, which are computationally more complex, must be used for more general situations. In this paper, a kind of semi-blind image restoration algorithm is proposed in case of known the blur type (defocused blurring).

In general, discrete model for a linear degradation caused by blurring can be given by the following equation

$$y(i,j) = h(i,j) * f(i,j) + n(i,j) \tag{1}$$

where * indicates two-dimensional convolution, $f(i,j)$ represents on original image, $y(i,j)$ is the degraded image, $h(i,j)$ represents the two-dimensional $PSF$, and $n(i,j)$ is the additive noise. In this article, we deal only with additive Gaussian noise, as it effectively models the noise in many different imaging scenarios. The difficulty in solving the restoration problem with a spatially varying blur commonly motivates the use of a stationary model for the blur. This leads to the following expression for the degradation system,

$$y(i,j) = h(i,j) * f(i,j) + n(i,j) = \sum_{k=1}^{M}\sum_{l=1}^{N} h(i-k, j-l) f(k,l) + n(i,j) \tag{2}$$

The use of linear techniques for solving the restoration problem is facilitated by using space-invariant model. Models that utilize space-variant degradations are also common, but lead to more complex solutions. As for defocused blur, $PSF$ is modeled as a uniform intensity distribution within a circular disk,

$$h(i,j) = \begin{cases} \frac{1}{\pi R^2} & \text{if } \sqrt{i^2+j^2} \leq R \\ 0 & \text{otherwise} \end{cases} \tag{3}$$

where disk radius $R$ is the only unknown parameter for this type of blur.

Many existing image restoration algorithms assume that the $PSF$ is known, but in practical it is not always the case. The restoration without knowing of the $PSF$ is called blind image restoration. Fourier methods can be used to estimate the defocused parameter $R$ through calculating a ratio of power of high frequencies portion to that of low frequencies portion. However, a main drawback of the method is its bad noise immunity. To solve this problem, a novel algorithm is proposed to overcome this shortcoming based on $RBF$ neural network and iterative Wiener filtering. The $RBF$ neural network is applied to fit $R$. This scheme has good fitting, but bad prediction. To avoid the weak generalization ability, a more efficient method for estimating parameter $R$ is also proposed. The prediction ability of these two methods is compared with the trained five images. The steps of the presented algorithm in this chapter is as follows: Firstly we construct feature vectors of several blurred images with known defocused radius $R$ in wavelet domain, then a $RBF$ neural network or a multivariate local polynomial estimation model is trained using the vectors as inputs and defocused parameters as outputs. After the model is trained, the new defocused images are applied to the trained model for predicting the parameter $R$. For a semi-blind defocused image, $R$ can be estimated through calculating the feature vectors and using it as input of the trained model. With known radius $R$, many traditional algorithm could be applied to restore the degraded image. In this chapter, iterative Wiener filtering($IWF$) is adopted to image restoration.

## 2. Relationship between wavelet coefficients and $R$

The wavelet transform provides a powerful and versatile framework for image processing. It is widely used in the fields of image de-noising, compression, fusion, image restoration Patrick et al. (2004); Zhou et al. (2007); Guo et al. (2007), etc.

The two-dimensional discrete wavelet transform ($DWT$) Li et al. (2009; 2010) hierarchically decompose an input image into a series of successively lower resolution images and their associated detail images. $DWT$ is implemented by a set of filters, which are convolved with the image rows and columns. An image is convolved with low-pass and high-pass filters and the odd samples of the filtered outputs are discarded resulting in down sampling the image by a factor of 2. The $l$ level wavelet decomposition of an image $I$ results in an approximation image $X_l$ and three detail images $H_l$, $V_l$, and $D_l$ in horizontal, vertical, and diagonal directions respectively. Decomposition into $l$ levels of an original image results in a down sampled image of resolution $2^l$ with respect to the image as well as detail images.

When an image is defocused, edged in it are smoothed and widened. The amount of high frequency band decreased, and that corresponding to low frequency band increases.

In order to denote the relationship between wavelet coefficients and defocused radius $R$, we define five variables named $v_1, v_2, v_3, v_4$, and $v_5$ as:

$$\begin{cases} v_1 = |V_2|_s / |H_2|_s \\ v_2 = |H_2|_s / |X_2|_s \\ v_3 = |H_1|_s / num\{H_1\} \\ v_4 = |H_2|_s / num\{H_2\} \\ v_5 = |D_1|_s / num\{D_1\} \end{cases} \tag{4}$$

where $|\cdot|_s$ represents the summation of all coefficients' absolute value, $num\{\cdot\}$ is total number of coefficients.

An original image is blurred artificially by a uniform defocus $PSF$ with $R$ whose value ranging from 1 to 20. The relationship between $v_1, v_2, v_3, v_4, v_5$ and $R$ are shown in Fig.1, where the curves are normalized in [0,1] interval. When $R$ increases, $v_2, v_3, v_4$ and $v_5$ decrease monotonously.

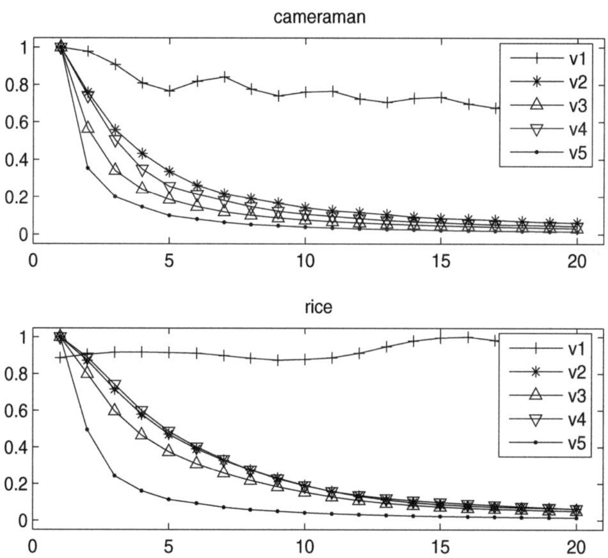


Fig. 1. Relationship Between $v_{1-5}$ and $R$

In order to estimate defocus parameter $R$, only known the roughly similar relationship is not enough. As shown in Fig. 2, every image has monotonous curve between $v_2, v_5$ and $R$, but they are not superposition. For a degraded unknown $PSF$ image, $R$ can not be calculated

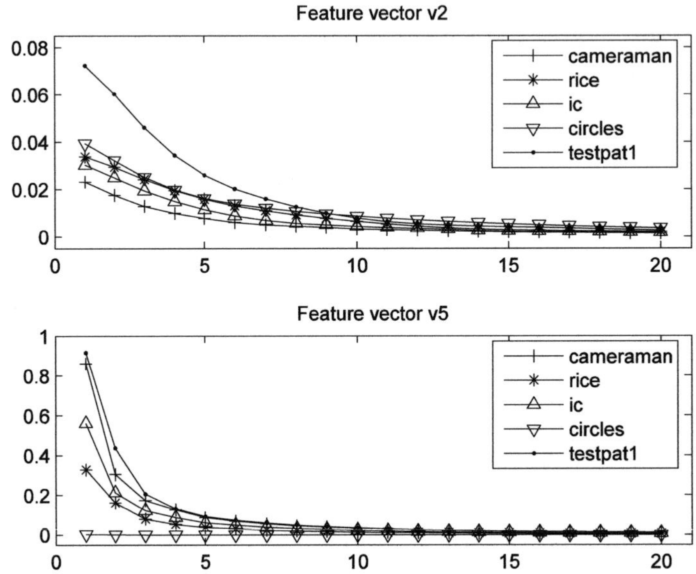


Fig. 2. Curve $v_2$, and $v_5$ of Different Images

because the curve of the given image is not known. For example, if $v_2$ of image "rice" has been calculated, and then we estimate $R$ according curve if "ic" in Fig. 2, wrong results are obtained obviously. To solve this problem, one of the methods is to choose neural networks. Computational artificial neural networks are known to have the capability for performing complex mappings between input and output data, but neural network method has bad generalization ability. Here we also propose another multivariate local polynomial regression model to estimate $R$. The variables $v_{1-5}$ are chosen to train the $RBF$ neural network and multivariate local polynomial estimation model. Prediction Comparisons are made to verify the advantages of multivariate local polynomial fitting.

## 3. Training $RBF$ neural network and multivariate local polynomial estimation model

### 3.1 $RBF$ neural network for defocused parameter

We propose and implement a parameter estimation technique in this section. Fig. 3 shows the description of this technique. In the first phase a $RBF$ neural network is designed and trained. In the second phase $R$ can be estimated using the trained neural network. A brief description of this technique is given in the following paragraphs.

RBF neural network is a most commonly-used feed-forward network. It usually has one hidden layer, and the basis function is radial symmetry. The output of the network looks like:

$$y_k(\chi) = \sum_{j=1}^{\alpha} w_{kj}\varphi_j(\chi) + w_{k0} \Leftrightarrow y(\chi) = W\varphi(\chi) \tag{5}$$

where $\chi$ is a put vector, $w_{k0}$ is a set of bias constants, $\varphi_0(\| \chi - \mu_j \|) \equiv 1$, $\alpha$ is the number of $RBF$ hidden neurons and $W$ holds both weights and bias. In the experiments, the radial basis

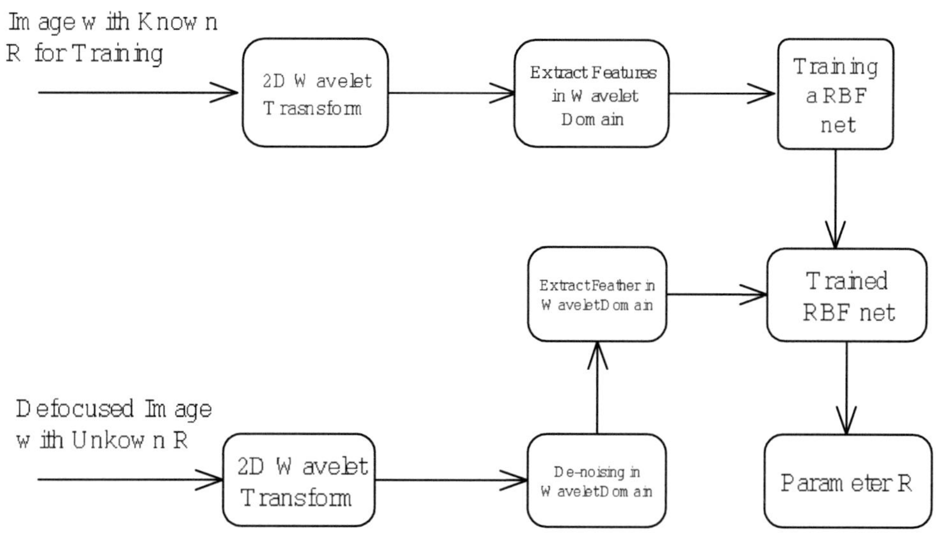


Fig. 3. Defocus Parameter Estimation Process

functions are chosen as of Gaussian type:

$$\varphi_j(\| \chi - \mu_j \|) = exp[-\frac{1}{2\gamma_j^2} \| \chi - \mu_j \|^2] \tag{6}$$

where $\mu_j$ is the center and $\gamma_j$ is the standard deviation of the Gaussian function, respectively.

Sixteen original images are chosen to train the *RBF* net. The images are defocused artificially with *R* whose value ranging from 2 to 7. So the total number of training samples are 96. Then feature vectors are constructed using variables $p_{1-5}$ of each image:

$$\chi = (p_1, p_2, p_3, p_4, p_5) \tag{7}$$

For the network output vector, we use one-of-*k* encoding method, that is, for $R$ =2, $t = (0,0,0,0,0,1)^T$; for $R = 3, t = (0,0,0,0,1,0)^T$, and so on.

When training samples $\{\chi_i, t_i\}_{i=1}^{96}$ are given, the weights matrix $W$ can be obtained as $W = \overline{T}\Phi^{\dagger}, \Phi^{\dagger}$ is pseudo-inverse of $\Phi$, where $\Phi$ is a matrix:

$$\Phi = \begin{pmatrix} 1 & \cdots & 1 \\ \varphi(||\chi_1 - \mu_1||) & \cdots & \varphi(||\chi_{96} - \mu_1||) \\ \vdots & \vdots & \vdots \\ \varphi(||\chi_1 - \mu_\alpha||) & \cdots & \varphi(||\chi_{96} - \mu_\alpha||) \end{pmatrix} \tag{8}$$

and $\overline{T} = (t_1, t_2, \cdots, t_{96})$.

After obtaining weights matrix $W$, the defocused parameter $R$ can be calculated using the trained *RBF* network.

### 3.2 Multivariate local polynomial regression for defocused parameter

Multivariate local polynomial fitting is an attractive method both from theoretical and practical point of view. Multivariate local polynomial method has a small mean squared error compared with the $Nadaraya - Watson$ estimator which leads to an undesirable form of the bias and the $Gasser - Muller$ estimator which has to pay a price in variance when dealing with a random design model. Multivariate local polynomial fitting also has other advantages. The method adapts to various types of designs such as random and fixed designs, highly clustered and nearly uniform designs. Furthermore, there is an absence of boundary effects: the bias at the boundary stays automatically of the same order as the interior, without use of specific boundary kernels. The local polynomial approximation approach is appealing on general scientific grounds: the least squares principle to be applied opens the way to a wealth of statistical knowledge and thus easy generalizations. In this Section, we briefly outline and review the idea of the extension of multivariate local polynomial fitting Kantz et al. (1997); Fan et al. (1996); Su (2010) to the parameter $R$ of defoused $PSF$.

#### 3.2.1 Multivariate kernel function

To localize data in the $m$-dimension, we need a multi kernel function. Generally speaking, a multivariate kernel function refers to a $m$-variate function satisfying

$$\int_{-\infty}^{+\infty} \cdots \int_{-\infty}^{+\infty} K(\underline{x})d\underline{x} = 1 \tag{9}$$

Here and hereafter, we use $\int$ to indicate multivariate integration over the $m$-dimensional Euclidean space.

There are two common methods for constructing multivariate kernel functions. For a univariate kernel $k(x)$, the product kernel is given by

$$K(\underline{x}) = \prod_{i=1}^{m} k(x_i), \tag{10}$$

and the spherically symmetric kernel is defined as

$$K(\underline{x}) = c_{K,m}K(\|\underline{x}\|). \tag{11}$$

where $c_{K,m} = \{\int K(\|\underline{x}\|)d\underline{x}\}^{-1}$ is a normalization constant and $\|\underline{x}\| = (x_1^2 + x_2^2 + \cdots + x_m^2)^{-1/2}$. Popular choices of $K(\underline{x})$ include the standard $d$-variate normal density

$$K(\underline{x}) = (2\pi)^{-m/2}exp(-\|\underline{x}\|^2/2) \tag{12}$$

and the spherical $Epanechnikov$ kernel

$$K(\underline{x}) = \{d(d+2)\Gamma(m/2)/(4\pi^{m/2})\}(1 - \|\underline{x}\|^2)_+ \tag{13}$$

The latter is the optimal kernel, according to Fan et al Fan et al. (1996); Su (2010).

The localization in multivariate nonparametric regression is frequently carried out by the kernel weighting. Let $\underline{H}$ be a symmetric positive-definite matrix called a bandwidth matrix.

The localization scheme at a point $\underline{x}$ assigns the weight

$$K_{\underline{H}}(\underline{X_i} - \underline{x}), \quad with \quad K_{\underline{H}}(\underline{x}) = |\underline{H}|^{-1} K(\underline{H}^{-1}\underline{x}), \tag{14}$$

where $|\underline{H}|$ is the determinant of the matrix $\underline{H}$. The bandwidth matrix is introduced to accommodate the dependent structure in the independent variables. For practical problems, the bandwidth matrix $\underline{H}$ is taken to be a diagonal matrix. The different independent variables will be accommodated into different scales. For simplification, the bandwidth matrix is designed into $\underline{H} = h\underline{I_m}$ ($\underline{I_m}$ denoting the identity matrix of order $m$).

### 3.2.2 Multivariate predictor with local polynomial fitting

Suppose that the input vector is $\underline{V} = (v_1, v_2, v_3, v_4, v_5)$. The model is fitted by the function

$$R = f(\underline{V}). \tag{15}$$

Our purpose is to obtain the estimation $\hat{R} = \hat{f}(\underline{V})$ of function $f$. This paper, we use the $d$th order multivariate local polynomial $f(\underline{V})$ to predict the defocused parameter $R_T$ value based on the point $\underline{V_T}$ of the test image. The polynomial function can be described as

$$f(\underline{V}) \approx \sum_{0 \le |\underline{j}| \le d} \frac{1}{\underline{j}!} D^{(\underline{j})} f_i(\underline{V_T})(\underline{V} - \underline{V_T})^{\underline{j}} = \sum_{0 \le |\underline{j}| \le d} \underline{b_j}(\underline{V_T})(\underline{V} - \underline{V_T})^{\underline{j}} \tag{16}$$

where

$$m = 5, \quad \underline{j} = (j_1, j_2, \cdots, j_m), \quad \underline{j}! = j_1! j_2! \cdots j_m!, \quad |\underline{j}| = \sum_{l=1}^{m} j_l, \tag{17}$$

$$\sum_{0 \le |\underline{j}| \le d} = \sum_{|\underline{j}|=0}^{d} \Big( \underset{|\underline{j}| = j_1 + j_2 + \cdots + j_m}{\sum_{j_1=0}^{|\underline{j}|} \sum_{j_2=0}^{|\underline{j}|} \cdots \sum_{j_m=0}^{|\underline{j}|}} \Big), \quad \underline{V}^{\underline{j}} = v_1^{j_1} v_2^{j_2} \cdots v_m^{j_m}, \tag{18}$$

$$D^{(\underline{j})} f_i(\underline{V_T}) = \frac{\partial^{|\underline{j}|} f_i(\underline{V})}{\partial v_1^{j_1} \partial v_2^{j_2} \cdots \partial v_m^{j_m}} \Big|_{\underline{V}=\underline{V_T}}, \quad \underline{b_j}(\underline{V_T}) = \frac{1}{\underline{j}!} D^{(\underline{j})} f_i(\underline{V_T}). \tag{19}$$

In the multivariate prediction method, $\underline{V_{T_a}}(a = 1, 2, \cdots, A)$ denoting the trained image feature vectors. Using $A$ pairs of $(\underline{V_{T_a}}, R_a)$, for which the values are already known, the coefficients of $f_i$ is determined by minimizing

$$\sum_{a=1}^{A} [R_a - \sum_{0 \le |\underline{j}| \le d} \underline{b_j}(\underline{V_T})(\underline{V_{T_a}} - \underline{V_T})^{\underline{j}}]^2 \cdot K_{\underline{H}}(\underline{V_{T_a}} - \underline{V_T}) \tag{20}$$

For the weighted least squared problem, a matrix form can be described by

$$\underline{W}^{1/2} \cdot \underline{Y} = \underline{W}^{1/2} \cdot \underline{X} \cdot \underline{B} + \underline{\varepsilon} \tag{21}$$

where

$$\underline{Y} = (y_1, y_2, \cdots, y_A)^T, \quad y_a = R_a, \tag{22}$$

$$\underline{B} = (\underline{b_0}(\underline{V_T}), \underline{b_1}(\underline{V_T}), \cdots, \underline{b_d}(\underline{V_T}))^T, \tag{23}$$

$$\underline{W} = diag\{K_{\underline{H}}(\underline{V_{T_1}} - \underline{V_T}), K_{\underline{H}}(\underline{V_{T_2}} - \underline{V_T}), \cdots, K_{\underline{H}}(\underline{V_{T_A}} - \underline{V_T})\} \tag{24}$$

and $\underline{X}$ is the $A \times S$ $\quad (S = \sum\limits_{0 \le |\underline{j}| \le d} \frac{|\underline{j}|}{\underline{j}!})$

$$\underline{X} = \begin{pmatrix} 1 & (\underline{V_{T_1}} - \underline{V_T})^1 & \cdots & (\underline{V_{T_1}} - \underline{V_T})^d \\ 1 & (\underline{V_{T_2}} - \underline{V_T})^1 & \cdots & (\underline{V_{T_2}} - \underline{V_T})^d \\ \vdots & \vdots & \ddots & \vdots \\ 1 & (\underline{V_{T_A}} - \underline{V_T})^1 & \cdots & (\underline{V_{T_A}} - \underline{V_T})^d \end{pmatrix} \tag{25}$$

We then have the least squared solution with multivariate local polynomial fitting.

$$\hat{\underline{B}} = (\underline{W}^{1/2}\underline{X})^{+}\underline{Y} \tag{26}$$

or, when $\underline{X}^T\underline{WX}$ is inverse, the estimation can be written by

$$\hat{\underline{B}} = (\underline{X}^T\underline{WX})^{-1}\underline{X}^T\underline{WY} \tag{27}$$

then, we can get the estimation $\hat{R}_T = \hat{f}(\underline{V_T})$

$$\hat{R}_T = \hat{f}(\underline{V_T}) = \underline{E_1}(\underline{X}^T\underline{WX})^{-1}\underline{X}^T\underline{WY} \tag{28}$$

where $\underline{E_1} = (1, 0, 0, \cdots, 0)_{1\times S}$.

Computing the $\hat{\underline{B}}$ will suffer from large computational cost. we can use the recursive least squared method to reduce the computation complexity, and it is very powerful especially in the real time prediction problems. There are several important issues about the bandwidth, the order of multivariate local polynomial function and the kernel function which have to be discussed. The three problems will be presented in Section 3.2.3.

### 3.2.3 Parameters selections

For the multivariate local polynomial predictor, there are three important problems which have significant influence to the prediction accuracy and computational complexity. First of all, there is the choice of the bandwidth matrix, which plays a rather crucial role. The bandwidth matrix $\underline{H}$ is taken to be a diagonal matrix. For simplification, the bandwidth matrix is designed into $\underline{H} = h\underline{I_m}$. So the most important thing is to find the bandwidth $h$. A too big bandwidth under-parameterizes the regression function, causing a large modeling bias, while a too small bandwidth over-parameterizes the unknown function and results in noisy estimates. In theory, there exists a optimal bandwidth $h_{opt}$ in the meaning of mean squared error, such that

$$h_{opt} = arg \quad \min_h \int (f(\underline{x}) - \hat{f}(\underline{x}))^2 d\underline{x} \tag{29}$$

But the optimal bandwidth can not be solved directly. So we discuss how to get the asymptotically optimal bandwidth. There are quite a few important techniques for selecting the bandwidth. such as cross-validation and plug-in bandwidth selectors. a conceptually simple technique, with theoretical justification and good empirical performance , is the plug-in technique.

Another issue in multivariate local polynomial fitting is the choice of the order of the polynomial. Since the modeling bias is primarily controlled by the bandwidth, this issue is less crucial however. For a given bandwidth $h$, a large value of $d$ would expectedly reduce the modeling bias, but would cause a large variance and a considerable computational cost. Since the bandwidth is used to control the modeling complexity, and due to the sparsity of local data in multi-dimensional space, a higher-order polynomial is rarely used. We use the local quadratic regression to indicate the flavor of the multivariate local polynomial fitting, that is to say, $d = 2$.

The third issue is the selection of the kernel function. In this paper, of course, we choose the optimal spherical *Epanechnikov* kernel function, which minimizes the asymptotic $MSE$ of the resulting multivariate local polynomial estimators, as our kernel function.

### 3.2.4 Estimating the defocused parameter

Twenty original images are chosen to train the model. The images are defocused artificially with $R$ whose value ranging from 2 to 7. So the total number of training samples are 120. Then feature vectors are constructed using variables $v_{1-5}$ of each image:

$$\underline{V} = (v_1, v_2, v_3, v_4, v_5) \tag{30}$$

The defocused parameters $R$ is the model output.

When training samples $\{\underline{V_{T_a}}, R_a\}_{a=1}^{120}$ are given, obtaining weights matrix $B$, according to the relationship between the $\overline{V}$ and $R$, then the defocused parameter $R$ can be calculated using the trained model.

## 4. Iterative Wiener filter

Wiener filtering (minimizing mean square error ) is commonly used to restore linearly-degraded images. To obtain optimal results,there must be accurate knowledge of the covariance of the ideal image. In this section, the so-called iterative Wiener filter Su et al. (2008); Allen et al. (1990)is used to restore the original image.

The imaging system H is assumed to be linear shift invariant with additive, independent, white noise processes of known variance. the model for the observed image y is given in matrix notation by

$$y = Hf + n \tag{31}$$

where f is the ideal image. The optimal linear minimum mean-squared error, or Wiener restoration filter given by

$$\hat{f} = By \tag{32}$$

where $B = R_{ff}H^T[HR_{ff}H^T + R_{nn}]^{-1}$, requires accurate knowledge of $R_{ff}$, the autocorrelation of ideal image $f$. However, in practical situations $f$ is usually not available and only a single copy of the blurred image to be restored, $y$, is provided. In the absence of a more accurate knowledge of the ideal image $f$, the blurred image $y$ is often used in its place simply because there is no other information about $f$ readily available. The signal $y$ is subsequently used to compute an estimate of $R_{ff}$ and this estimate is used in place of $R_{ff}$ in Equation (32).

The following summarizes the iterative Wiener filtering procedure.

step 1 Initialization: Use $y$ to compute an initial (i=0) estimate of $R_{ff}$ by

$$R_{ff}(0) = R_{yy} = E\{yy^T\} \tag{33}$$

Step 2 Filter construction: Use $R_{ff}(i)$, the i$^{th}$ estimate of $R_{ff}$ to construct the $(i+1)^{th}$ restoration filter $B(i+1)$ given by

$$B_{i+1} = R_{ff}H^T[HR_{ff}H^T + R_{nn}]^{-1} \tag{34}$$

Step 3 Restoration: Restore $y$ by the $B(i+1)$ filter to obtain $\hat{f}(i+1)$, the $(i+1)^{th}$ estimate of $f$

$$\hat{f}(i+1) = B(i+1)y \tag{35}$$

Step 4 Update: Use $\hat{f}(i+1)$ to compute an improved estimate of $R_{ff}$, given by

$$R_{ff}(i+1) = E\{\hat{f}(i+1)\hat{f}^T(i+1)\} \tag{36}$$

Step 5 Iteration: Increment $i$ and repeat steps 2,3,4, and 5.

## 5. Experimental results and analysis

The experiments are carried out by using the Matlab image processing toolbox. The performance of the proposed image restoration algorithm has been evaluated using the classical gray-scale *Moon* image, *Coins* image, *Saturn* image, and *Tire* image in Matlab toolbox. To verify the good ability of restoration of the proposed algorithm, one real blurred image is used for the deconvolution procedure. The results show our method is very successful for this kind of blurred image.

In image restoration studies, the degradation modelled by blurring and additive noise is referred to in terms of the metric blurred signal-to-noise ratio ($BSNR$). This metric for a zero-mean $M \times N$ image is given by

$$BSNR = 10log_{10}\{\frac{\frac{1}{MN}\sum_{m=1}^{M}\sum_{n=1}^{N} z^2(m,n)}{\sigma_v^2}\} \tag{37}$$

where $z(m,n)$ is the noise free blurred image and $\sigma_v^2$ is the additive noise variance.

For the purpose of objectively testing the performance of linear image restoration algorithms, the improvement in signal-to-noise ratio ($ISNR$) is often used. $ISNR$ is defined as

$$ISNR = 10log_{10}\{\frac{\sum_{m=1}^{M}\sum_{n=1}^{N}[f(m,n) - y(m,n)]^2}{\sum_{m=1}^{M}\sum_{n=1}^{N}[f(m,n) - \hat{f}(m,n)]^2}\} \tag{38}$$

where $f(m,n)$ and $y(m,n)$ are the original and degraded image pixel intensity values and $\hat{f}(m,n)$ is the restored true image pixel intensity value. $ISNR$ cannot be used when the true image is unknown, but it can be used to compare different methods in simulations when the true image is known.

In order to find the good performance of the proposed multivariate local polynomial Regression method (MLPR) compared with the RBF neural network algorithm (RBFNN) Su et al. (2008), the same defocused blurred images are used for the experiments. Mean squared prediction errors are shown in Table1. From Table 1, we can conclude that the prediction results of *MLPR* predictor are significantly better than the RBF neural network method in the same simulated data.

| training image | different methods | $e_{MSE}$ |
|---|---|---|
| Moon | RBFNN | $4.81 \times 10^{-6}$ |
| Moon | MLPR | $4.13 \times 10^{-8}$ |
| Coins | RBFNN | $5.06 \times 10^{-6}$ |
| Coins | MLPR | $3.97 \times 10^{-8}$ |
| Saturn | RBFNN | $6.62 \times 10^{-6}$ |
| Saturn | MLPR | $5.65 \times 10^{-9}$ |
| Tire | RBFNN | $8.04 \times 10^{-6}$ |
| Tire | MLPR | $7.19 \times 10^{-8}$ |

Table 1. MSE using both methods

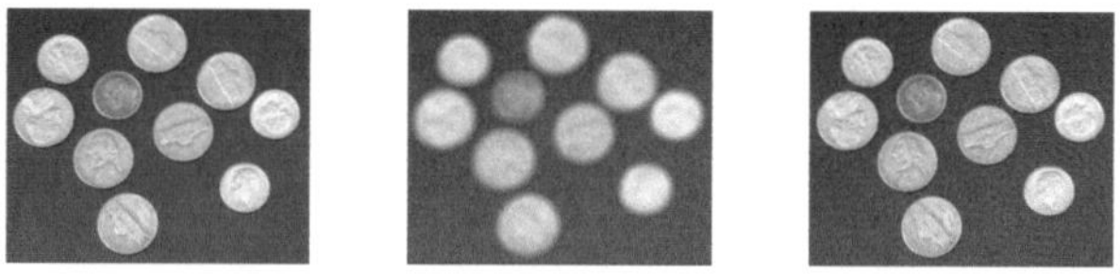

Fig. 4. RBFNN method result of *Coins*. True image(left); blurred image(middle); estimated image(right), BSNR=12.35, ISNR=22.56

Fig. 5. RBFNN method result for *Tire*. True image(left); blurred image (middle); restored image(right), BSNR=11.22, ISNR=23.14

Figures 4 and 5, in which the true images, blurred images and estimated true images are depicted in the left, middle and right column, respectively, illustrate how the method behaves in *Coins* and *Tire* images. It is clear from Figs. 4 and 5 that performance of the RBFNN method is effective in different images. Figures 6, 7, 8 and 9, in which the true images,

Fig. 6. Result of *Moon*. True image(left); blurred image(middle); estimated image(right), BSNR=12.35, ISNR=22.56

blurred images and estimated true images are depicted in the left, middle and right column,

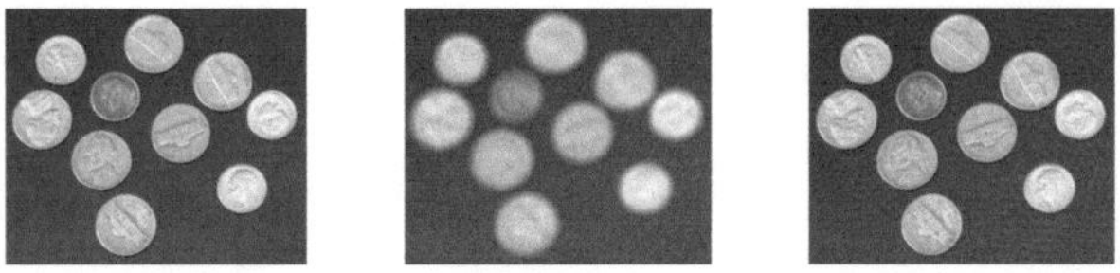

Fig. 7. Result for *Coins*. True image(left); blurred image (middle); restored image(right), BSNR=11.22, ISNR=23.14

Fig. 8. Result for *Saturn*. True image(left); blurred image (middle); restored image(right), BSNR=13.17, ISNR=24.31

Fig. 9. Result for *Tire*. True image(left); blurred image (middle); restored image(right), BSNR=11.56, ISNR=22.09

Fig. 10. Result for real blurred image. blurred image (left); restored image(right)

respectively, illustrate how the method behaves in *Moon*, *Coins*, *Saturn* and *Tire* images. It is clear from Figs.6-9 that performance of the new method is effective in different images. Figure 10 also shows that the presented MLPR algorithm is good for real blurred image. And from the BSNR and ISNR in Figures 4, 5, 7, 9 we can see that the MLPR defocused image restoration method is better than RBFNN algorithm.

## 6. Conclusions

Two new methods that are based on RBF neural network, multivariate local polynomial regression model and iterative Wiener filtering for semi-blind restoration of blurred noisy images were proposed in this chapter. Defocused parameter was estimated by a RBF neural network or multivariate local polynomial regression model trained in wavelet domain. The main advantages of the proposed techniques are that they are not only robust to noise because wavelet transform have an excellent de-noising ability, but also effective to artificially and practically defocused blurred image. Restoration is successfully realized by the iterative Wiener filter, resulting in improved the image quality. The algorithm was justified via simulation and real image. Defocused image parameter can be successfully estimated by using trained model. Experimental results show the proposed schemes are reliable and robust for defocused blurred image restoration. Comparisons are made to verify the advantages of multivariate local polynomial regression based method.

## 7. Acknowledgment

This work was supported by Chongqing CSTC foundation of China (CSTC2010BB2310, CSTC2011jjA40033), Chongqing CMEC foundation of China (KJ080614,KJ100810,KJ100818), CQUT foundation of China (2007ZD16).

## 8. References

Spiros C., Vasilios N. K., and Dimitrios P. (2009). Applications of the Moore-Penrose Inverse in Digital Image Restoration. *Mathematical Problems in Engineering*, 2009:1-12.

Spiros C., Vasilios N. K., and Dimitrios P. Digital Image Reconstruction in the Spectral Domain Utilizing the Moore-Penrose Inverse. *Mathematical Problems in Engineering*, 2010, Article ID 750352, 14 pages.

Su L., Ma H., Li Z., and Ju S. Blind image restoration based on constant modulus with averaging and ANFIS. *in Proceedings of Fourth International Conference on Image and Graphics (ICIG'07)*, pp.143-148, Chengdu, China.

Alonso M., and Adjouadi M., Digital image inverse filtering for improving visual acuity for computer users with visual aberrations. *Inverse Problems in Science and Engineering*, 16(8): 957-966.

Alonso M., Cremades J. G., Jacko J., and Adjouadi M., Image Pre-compensation to facilitate computer access for users with refractive errors. *Behaviour & Information Technology*, 24(3):161-173.

Bar L., Sochen N., and Kiryati N., Semi-blind image restoration via Mumford-Shah regularization. *IEEE Trans. Image Process*, 15(2):483-493.

Chen W., Chen M., and Zhou J., Adaptively Regularized Constrained Total Least-Squares Image Restoration. *IEEE Trans. on Image Processing*, 9(4):588-596.

Suyash P. A. and Ross T. W., Unsupersived, Information-Theoretic, Adaptive Image Filtering for Image Restoration. *IEEE Trans. on Pattern Analysis and Machine Intellgence*, 28(3):364-375.

Gu X. and Li G., A new method for parameter estimation of edge-preserving regularization in image restoration. *Journal of Computational and Applied Mathematics*, 225(2):478-486.

Lu L., Michael K. N., and Lin F., Approximation BFGS methods for nonlinear image restoration. *Journal of Computational and Applied Mathematics*, 226(1):84-91.

Filip S. and Jan F., Multichannel Blind Iterative Image Restoration. *IEEE Trans. on Image Processing*, 12(9):1094-1106.

Mario A. T. F., Robert D. N., An EM Algorithm for Wavelet-Based Image Restoration. *IEEE Trans. on Image Processing*, 12(8):906-916.

Yehong Liao and Xueyin Lin, "Blind Image Restoration with Eigen-Face Subspace," *IEEE Trans. on Image Processing*, vol. 14, no. 11, pp. 1766-1772, 2005.

M. M. Chang, A. M. Tekalp, and A. T. Erdem, "Blur Identification using the Bi-Spectrum," *IEEE Trans. on Image Processing*, vol. 39, no. 10, pp.2323-2325, 1991.

Reeves S. J. and Mersereau R. M. , Blur Identification by the Method of Generalized Cross-Validation. *IEEE trans. on Image Processing*, 1(7):301-311.

Lagendijk R. L., J. Biemond, and B. E. Boekee, Identification and Restoration of Noisy Blurred Images using the Expectation-Maximization Algorithm. *IEEE Trans. on Acoustics, Speech, Signal Processing*, 38(7):1180-1191.

D. Kundur and D. Hatzinakos, A Novel Blind Deconvolution Scheme for Image Restoration using Recurisive Filtering. *IEEE Trans. on Signal Processing*, 46(2):375-390.

A. K. Katsaggelos and K. T. Lay, Maximum Likelihood Blur Identification and Image Restoration using the EM Algorithm," *IEEE Trans. on Signal Processing*, 39(3):729-733.

Su L., Li F., Xu F., and Liu Y., Defocused Image Restoration Using RBF Network and Iterative Wiener Filter in Wavelet Domain. *in Proceedings of 2008 International congress on image and signal processing(CISP'08)*čňpp. 311-315, Sanya, Hainan, China, 2008.

Kantz H and Schreiber T, *Nonlinear Time Series Analysis*, Cambridge University Press, Cambridge, UK, 1997.

Fan J and I. Gijbels, *Local polynomial modelling and its applications*, Chapman and Hall, London, UK, 1996.

Su L., Prediction of multivariate chaotic time series with local polynomial fitting. *Computers & Mathematics with Applications*, 59(2):737-744.

Allen D. Hillery and Roland T. Chin, Iterative Wiener Filters for Image Restoration. *in Proceedings of The international conference on Acoustics, Speech, and Signal Processing*, pp. 1901-1904, Albuquerque, NM , USA, 1990.

Patrick L. Combettes and Jean-Christophe Pesquet, Wavelet-constrained image restoration. *International Journal of Wavelets, Multiresolution and Information Processing*, 2(4):371-389.

Zhou Huiyu, Liu Tangwei, Lin Faquan, Pang Yusheng, and Wu Ji, Image restoration and detail preservation by Bayesian estimation. *International Journal of Image and Graphics*, 7(2):497-514.

Guo P., Li H., and Michael T. L., Blind Image restoration by combining wavelet transform and RBF neural network. *International Journal of Wavelets, Multiresolution and Information Processing*, 5(1):371-389.

Li M. and Wu Y., Qiang ZhangSAR image segmentation based on mixture context and wavelet hidden-class-label Markov random field. *Computers & Mathematics with Applications*, 57(6):961-969.

Li P. and Fang Y., A Wavelet Interpolation Galerkin Method for the Simulation of MEMS Devices under the Effect of Squeeze Film Damping. *Mathematical Problems in Engineering*, vol. 2010, Article ID 586718, 25 pages, 2010.

Su L., Liu R. (2011). Blind Image Restoration with Modified CMA. *International Journal of Image and Graphics*, 11(3): 403-413.

Su L., Li F., Li J., Chen B. (2011). A Novel Digital Image Covert Communication Scheme based on Generalized FCM in DCT Domain. *Fuzzy Information and Engineering*, 3(2):127-136.

Su L. (2011). Multivariate local polynomial regression with application to Shenzhen component index. *Discrete Dynamics in Nature and Society*, 2011:1-11.

Liu, R., Su, L., Li, F. (2011). Image reconstruction based on the TV and Mumford-Shah-Euler model. *Advanced Materials Research*, 186:198-202.

Su L. and Li F. (2010). Deconvolution of Defocused Image with Multivariate Local Polynomial Regression and Iterative Wiener Filtering in DWT domain. *Mathematical Problems in Engineering*, 2010:1-14.

# 9

# Image Restoration Using Two-Dimensional Variations

Olga Milukova[1], Vitaly Kober[1,2] and Victor Karnaukhov[1]
[1]*Institute for Information Transmission Problems of RAS,*
[2]*Computer Science Department, CICESE,*
[1]*Russia*
[2]*Mexico*

## 1. Introduction

In many applications (consumer and commercial imaging, medical imaging, robotics, space research, and etc.) observed images are often degraded due to atmospheric turbulence, relative motion between a scene and a camera, nonuniform illumination, wrong focus, etc. Image restoration refers to the problem of estimating the ideal image from its observed degraded one. Numerous restoration techniques (linear, nonlinear, deterministic, stochastic, etc.) optimized with respect to different were introduced (Banham & Katsaggelos, 1997 ; Jain, 1989; Sezan & Tekalp, 1990; Bovik, 2005; Gonzalez & Woods 2008). The amount of *a priori* information about degradation such as the size and shape of blurs, noise level determines how mathematically ill-posed the problem is. *A priori* information can be used in a variety of ways in modeling and algorithm development. The information about the nature of blur (e.g., linear or nonlinear and space-variant or space-invariant) and noise (additive or multiplicative) is used in modeling the input-output relation of imaging systems. In blur modeling, when the type of blur is known (e.g., out of focus, motion, turbulence), the blurring operator can be parameterized using only a few parameters. In image modeling, the ideal image can be modeled, for instance, on the basis of *a priori* Markovian assumption. In algorithm development, *a priori* information is used in defining constraints on the solution and in defining a criterion or a quantitative description of the solution. The blind and non-blind deconvolutions were extensively studied, and many techniques were proposed for their solution (Kundur & Hatzinakos, 1996; Bertero & Boccacci, 1998; Biemond et al., 1990; Sroubek & Flusser, 2003). They usually involve some regularization which assures various statistical properties of the image or constrains on the estimated image and restoration filter according to some assumptions. This regularization is required to guarantee a unique solution and stability against noise and some model discrepancies. One of the most popular fundamental techniques is a linear minimum mean square error method. It finds the linear estimate of the ideal image for which the mean square error between the estimate and the ideal image is minimal. This linear operator acting on the observed image to determine the estimate on the base of *a priori* second-order statistical information about the image and noise processes. For images with sharp changes of intensity, the appropriate regularization is based on variational integrals (Rudin, et al.,

1992; Perona & Malik, 1990; Chan & Wong, 1998). Minimization of the variational integrals preserves edges and fine details in the image. It is obvious that quality of the restored image depends on accuracy of mathematical model of image formation process. In particular, a good estimation of distortion parameters such as speed of camera movement, transparency of atmosphere or water, etc. is very important for restoration (Biemond et al., 1990).

Recently, restoration methods based on image variations were proposed (Milukova et al., 2010a, 2010b, 2011). In this chapter, image restoration with two-dimensional variations is presented. The restored image minimizes two-dimensional variations defined by Kronrod (Kronrod, 1950). We also consider the identification of distortion operator and estimation of its parameters. It is assumed that a monochrome stationary image distorted by homogeneous integrated transformation. Various physical problems can be modeled by such transformation. The spectral method of identification of distortion parameters uses only degraded image. Computer simulation results illustrate the performance of the proposed method for restoration of blurred images.

## 2. Restoration of linear degraded images with variation methods

### 2.1 Variation concept for image restoration

Image restoration problem is usually formulated as follows. Undistorted (original) image $z$ is recovered from the given equation:

$$v = Az + n \ , \tag{1}$$

where $A: \mathrm{Z} \to \mathrm{Q}$ ( $\mathrm{Z},\mathrm{Q}$ are metric spaces) is linear or nonlinear operator, $z \in \mathrm{Z}$ , $n$ is noise, $v$ is observed distorted image. A general approach for image restoration can be formulated using statistical estimation methods and the theory of solving of ill-posed problems (Tikhonov & Arsenin, 1977). The restoration problem is a typical inverse problem of mathematical physics, and, therefore, it can be correctly solved on the base of mathematical methods. The restored image can be obtained by minimization of the following functional:

$$z^* = \inf_{z \in \mathrm{Z}} \rho_Q(Az, v) \ , \tag{2}$$

where $\rho_Q$ is a metric in $Q$. Note that various definitions of a distance $\rho_Q$ between two images may be used. It is easy to show that the solution of the optimization problem in Eq. (2) is not unique even when the operator $A$ and the distorted image $v$ are exactly known, and no additive noise. *A priori* information about the original image should be used to obtain a unique and stable solution from the set of solutions. The simplest way to guarantee uniqueness and stability of the solution is to describe the image model with a functional $\Omega(z)$ that possesses stabilizing properties. In this case the image restoration problem can be reduced to conditional or unconditional optimization problem, in particular to the Tikhonov's minimization (Tikhonov & Arsenin, 1977),

$$z^* = \inf_{z \in \mathrm{Z}} \{\rho_Q(Az, v) + \alpha\Omega(z)\} \ , \tag{3}$$

where $\alpha$ is a parameter of regularization. Note that the statistical methods used in image restoration lead to optimization problems, which are similar to that of Eq. (3). For instance, using Bayes' strategy (Kay, 1993) we can obtain the optimal estimation in the following form:

$$z^* = \inf_{z \in Z}\{-\ln p_2(Az - v) - \ln p_1(z)\}, \tag{4}$$

where $p_1(\xi)$ and $p_2(\xi)$ are *a priori* probability densities of the original image $z$ and additive noise $n = Az - v$. The main difference between the regularization method of image restoration in Eq. (3) and the statistical method in Eq. (4) is the regularization parameter $\alpha$. This leads to a family of solutions as a function of the parameter $\alpha$. The best restored image can be chosen from the set of solutions using, for instance, a subjective criterion. If the space Q in Eq. (3) is the Euclidian space with the norm $(v, Bv)$, where B is a positive defined operator, we obtain,

$$z^* = \inf_{z \in Z}\{\|Az - v\|_B^2 + \alpha\Omega(z)\}. \tag{5}$$

It is commonly assumed that the original image is a smooth function with respect to the Sobolev space (Adams, 1975), and the stabilization functional in Eq. (5) is $\Omega(z) = \|z\|_{W_q^p}^q$. Quadratic forms can be used in order to avoid nonlinear restoration algorithms. Note that a Gaussian image model leads to minimization of a quadratic form. In discrete case it corresponds to the Sobolev norm for $p = 2$ in Eq. (5). On the other hand, the use of quadratic forms in image restoration often yields undesirable results because of real images are not Gaussian. Now suppose that an image to be restored is a function of bounded variations. Therefore, it may be written as

$$z^* = \inf_{z \in Z}\{\rho_Q(Az, v) + \alpha Var(z)\}. \tag{6}$$

The variation of a 1D function $f(x)$, $x \in [a,b]$ is defined as follows:

$$\overset{b}{\underset{a}{V}}(f) = \sup_{x_1, \dots, x_n} \sum_{k=2}^{n} |f(x_k) - f(x_{k-1})|. \tag{7}$$

It can be shown, that if the image $z(x,y)$, $(x,y) \in D$ consists of 1D functions of bounded variation along its rows and columns then the image is also a 2D function of bounded variation. Different multidimensional variations were proposed such as variations of Arzela, Vitali, Tonelly, etc. (Vitushkin, 1955). A different approach was suggested by Kronrod, who introduced two functionals in order to describe an image as a function of two variables (Kronrod, 1950). The functionals are given as follows:

$$d_1(z) = \int_{-\infty}^{\infty} m_0(e_t)dt, \text{ and } d_2(z) = \int_{-\infty}^{\infty} m_1(e_t)dt, \tag{8}$$

where $e_t$ is $t$ - level set of the function $z(x,y)$, i.e. a set of points $(x,y)$ with function values equal to $t$, $m_0(e_t)$ is the number of components of $e_t$, and $m_1(e_t)$ is the length of the set $e_t$.

The class of functions of bounded variations given in Eq. (8) is very extensive. These functions possess the following attractive properties: they are differentiable almost everywhere and their Fourier series are convergent almost everywhere. Note that numerous attempts to create a mathematical image model with the help of one functional were unsatisfactory. It can be done on the base of two (independent in a certain way) functionals. It is interesting to point out, that the first variation $d_1$ in Eq. (8) is a topological characteristic of the image. If the original image is a continuous differentiable function, then the second variation can be represented as

$$d_2(z) = \int_a^b \int_c^g \left| grad\, z(x,y) \right| dx\, dy \,. \tag{9}$$

If only the second variation is used, the image restoration can be carried out as follows (Perona & Malik,1990):

$$z^* = \inf_{z \in Z} \{ \left| Az - v \right|_B^2 + \alpha \int_a^b \int_c^g \left| grad\left( z(x,y) \right) \right| dx\, dy \} \,, \tag{10}$$

where *grad(.)* is a gradient operator.

It is of interest to note that this nonlinear method of image restoration minimizes the functional that is identical to the Kronrod's second variation. We propose to minimize the functional in Eq. (10) subject to constraint on the first Kronrod's variation of the image. This approach is referred to as conditional variation approach (Milukova et al., 2010). Next with the help of computer simulation we illustrate the difference in the performance of two variation methods: minimization of the functional in Eq. (10) and conditional minimization of the same functional. Additionally, the performance of minimum norm image restoration from Eq. (10) without considering variations is also provided.

### 2.2 Restoration of uniformly blurred image with spatial variations

The impulse response of the 1D uniform blur can be expressed as follows:

$$h_L(x) = \begin{cases} 1/L, & \text{if } 0 \le x \le L-1 \\ 0, & \text{otherwise} \end{cases} \,, \tag{11}$$

where $L$ determines a blur extension. It is known that point spread functions for such blurs do have zeros in the frequency domain, and they can be uniquely identified by the location of these zero crossings (Cannon, 1976; Gennery, 1973). If the original image is blurred and noiseless then the blur matrix $A$ in Eq. (1) is given as

$$A = 1/L \left\| \begin{array}{cccc|ccccc} 1 & 1 & \ldots & & 1 & & & & \\ & 1 & 1 & & \ldots & 1 & & D_2 & \\ & & & 1 & 1 & \ldots & 1 & & \\ & & & & 1 & 1 & \ldots & 1 & \\ & D_1 & & & . & . & . & . & . \\ & & & & & 1 & 1 & \ldots & 1 \end{array} \right\|_{MxN} \,, \tag{12}$$

and the linear system of equations in Eq. (1) is rewritten as

$$Az = D_1 z_L + D_2 z_R = v\,, \tag{13}$$

where $z_L = \{z_1,...,z_{L-1}\}$ , $z_R = \{z_L,...,z_N\}$ , $M=N-L+1$. A general solution of Eq. (13) can be written as

$$z^* = z^p + \sum_{m=1}^{B} \beta_m \mathbf{e}_m\,, \tag{14}$$

where $\mathbf{e}_m$ is a basis of kernel $A$, $\{\beta_m\}$ are real variables, $z^p = \{z_L, D_2^{-1}(v - D_1 z_L)\}$ is a particular solution of linear system of equations in Eq. (13). Suppose that $z_L = 0$, the particular solution can be expressed as

$$z^p = \{0, D_2^{-1} v\}\,. \tag{15}$$

The basis $\mathbf{e}_m$ can be found from Eq. (13) as

$$\mathbf{e}_m = \{e_L^m, -D_2^{-1} D_1 e_L^m\}\,, \tag{16}$$

where $e_L^m = \{\delta_{1m}, \delta_{2m}, ..., \delta_{L-1m}\}$ , $\delta_{ij}$ is the Kronecker delta function. The basis of kernel $A$ has the following form:

$$\begin{Vmatrix} 1 & & -11 & & -1 & 1 & & -1 \\ & 1 & -1 & 1 & -1 & & 1 & -1 \\ & . & . & . & . \;\cdots & & . & . \\ & & 1-1 & & 1-1 & & & 1-1 \end{Vmatrix}.$$

It is of interest to note that the basis of kernel $A$ contains vertical columns of unities; therefore, a general solution of Eq. (13) could contain a periodic structure with the period of blurring (Buades et al., 2006). In our computer simulation we compared three methods: 1) first, substituting Eq. (15) into Eq. (10) and minimizing the functional with respect to $\{\beta_m\}$; 2) the second method minimizes the same functional subject to the first Kronrod's variation given in Eq. (8), which is taken close to that of the original image; 3) minimum norm image restoration from Eq. (10) without considering variations. Actually, if the inverse of the blur operator exists, it can be applied to the observed image to obtain an estimate. This is called inverse filtering. The estimate differs from the actual image by the additional error of amplified noise, and depending on the nature of the blur operator and the noise, it may drastically obscure the desired image information. Hence, inverse filtering is extremely noise sensitive. If the inverse operator does not exist, a solution can be found on the basis of a least squares criterion. A least squares solution minimizes the norm of the residual signal $Az$-v. The least squares solution with minimum norm (energy) is called also the pseudoinverse filtering (Jain, 1989). The first tested method is referred to as Grad method, the second one is called Grad-conditional method, and the last method is named Min-norm method. Fig. 1(a) shows a test input image used in experiments. The size of the image is

256×256 pixels, $N$=256. The signal range is [0-255]. The test input scene is homogeneously blurred with $L$=7. The blurred image is shown in Fig. 1(b).

(a)

(b)

Fig. 1. (a) Test image, (b) test image uniformly blurred in horizontal direction with L=7.

The original image has the following values of the Kronrod variations: $d_1$=2105, $d_2$=12210. The results of image restoration with the variation methods are shown in Figs. 2(a) and 2(b), respectively. The restoration result with the Min-norm algorithm is shown in Fig. 2(c). Subjective visual criterion is defined as an enhanced difference between original and restored images. A pixel is displayed as gray if there is no error between the original image and the restored image. For maximum error, the pixel is displayed either black or white (with intensity values of 0 and 255, respectively).

(a)

(b)

(c)

Fig. 2. Image restoration with (a) Grad method, (b) Grad-conditional method, and (c) Min-norm method.

Figs. 3(a), 3(b), and 3(c) show differences between the original image and that of restored with the Grad algorithm, the Grad-conditional algorithm, and the Min-norm algorithm, respectively. We see that the second algorithm, which takes into account two Kronrod's variations yields the best recognition performance. A quantitative comparison is given by the peak signal-to-noise ratio (PSNR),

$$PSNR(z,z^*) = 20\log_{10}\left(\frac{255}{\left\| z - z^* \right\|}\right). \tag{17}$$

(a)

(b)

(c)

Fig. 3. Differences between the original image and restored with (a) Grad method, (b) Grad-conditional method, and (c) Min-norm method.

The image restored with the Grad method has d1=2050, d2=12015, the image restored with Grad-conditional method has d1=2103, d2=12120, and finally, the image restored by the Min-norm method possesses d1=2218, d2=12343. Table 1 shows the restoration performance of the tested methods in terms of the PSNR versus the blur extension.

| L | Min-norm | Grad | Grad-conditional |
|---|---|---|---|
| 3 | 28.3 | 34.5 | 35.2 |
| 5 | 25.1 | 30.2 | 31.3 |
| 7 | 22.2 | 28.5 | 29.4 |
| 9 | 18.4 | 26.2 | 27.3 |

Table 1. PSNR (dB) results for the tested methods.

So, in order to achieve a good restoration, it is important take into account topological characteristics of the image to be restored. These characteristics can be described by the first Kronrod's variation.

## 3. Identification of degradation operators and estimation parameters in the Fourier domain

In this section, identification of operator degradation type and estimation of distortion parameters is discussed. Monochrome stationary image distorted by homogeneous linear transformation is considered. Various physical problems can be modeled by such degradations (Bertero & Boccacci, 1998). Identification of the distortion operator is carried out using the Fourier spectrum of the distorted image. Automatic image restoration is performed in three steps, that is, i) identification of distortion operator, ii) estimation of distortion parameters, and iii) image restoration with estimated parameters. Certain types of distortion operators are completely characterized by attributes such as the location of frequency-domain zeros. The techniques (Cannon, 1976; Gennery, 1973) make the following two assumptions: (i) the blurring produces zero crossings in the frequency domain and it can be completely characterized by the location of these zero crossings, and (ii) the location of zero crossings can be determined from the Fourier transform or power cepstrum (the logarithm of the power spectrum) of the observed image. These methods are very simple to use and they can successfully applied in many real-life situations. It is indeed true that the models for motion and focus blurs do have zeros in the frequency domain, and they can be uniquely identified by the location of these zero crossings. On the other hand, blurring models that do not have zero crossings in the frequency domain (e.g., Gaussian modeling atmospheric turbulence) cannot be identified by these techniques. Furthermore, the identification of the zero crossings from the observed image may be quite difficult due to the presence of strong observation noise. Almost all practical implementations of the restoration algorithms assume that the observation noise is a zero-mean, white Gaussian process that is uncorrelated to the image signal. In this case, the noise field is completely characterized by its variance, which is commonly estimated by the sample variance computed over a low-contrast local region of the observed image (Yaroslavsky & Eden, 1996).

Let us consider an observed image degraded with a linear spatially invariant system and additive sensor noise, that is,

$$v = Az + n = \int_{-\infty}^{\infty}\int_{-\infty}^{\infty} h(x-\xi, y-\eta) z(\xi,\eta) d\xi d\eta + n(x,y), \tag{18}$$

where $h(x,y)$ is the impulse response of the system. The Fourier spectrum of the observed image is given by

$$V(\omega_1,\omega_2) = H(\omega_1,\omega_2)Z(\omega_1,\omega_2) + N(\omega_1,\omega_2), \tag{19}$$

where $H(\omega_1,\omega_2)$ is the frequency response of the liner degradation filter, $V(\omega_1,\omega_2)$, $Z(\omega_1,\omega_2)$, and $N(\omega_1,\omega_2)$ are spectra of the observed image, original image, and noise realization, respectively. Several typical examples of linear degradations are provided (Jain,

1989). Motion blur occurs when there is relative motion between the object and camera during exposure. In this case the impulse response and the frequency response of the linear system of horizontal motion blur are given, respectively, as

$$h(x,y) = \frac{1}{L} rect\left(\frac{x}{L} - \frac{1}{2}\right)\delta(y), \tag{20}$$

$$H(\omega_1,\omega_2) = e^{-i\pi w_1 L}\text{sinc}(w_1 L), \tag{21}$$

where $L$ is the motion path, $rect(x) = 1,\ if\ x \in [0,1],\ else\ 0,\ \delta(y)$ is the Dirac delta function.

Atmospheric turbulence is a common blur in remote sensing and aerial imaging. For long term exposure through the atmosphere Gaussian model is used. So, the impulse response and the frequency response of the linear system of turbulence blur are given, respectively, as

$$h(x,y) = e^{-\pi a^2 \left(x^2 + y^2\right)}, \tag{22}$$

$$H(\omega_1,\omega_2) = \frac{1}{a^2} e^{\frac{-\pi\left(\omega_1^2 + \omega_2^2\right)}{a^2}}, \tag{23}$$

where $a$ is the parameter that determines the severity of blur.

Defocusing is another common type of blurring owing to the finite size of the camera aperture. When the defocusing blur is large, the following uniform model is used. The impulse response and the frequency response of the linear system can be expressed, respectively, as

$$h(x,y) = \begin{cases} \frac{1}{\pi r^2}, x^2 + y^2 \le r^2 \\ 0, \text{elsewhere} \end{cases}, \tag{24}$$

$$H(\omega_1,\omega_2) = \frac{J_1(rp)}{rp},\ p = \omega_1^2 + \omega_2^2, \tag{25}$$

where $J_1$ is the first-order Bessel function.

Image blurring also occurs in image acquisition by scanners in which the image pixels are integrated over the scanning aperture. Example of such degradations can be found in image capturing by radar, beam-forming arrays, and display systems using television raster. The impulse response and the frequency response of the linear system can be written, respectively, as

$$h(x,y) = rect\left(\frac{x}{a}, \frac{y}{b}\right), \tag{26}$$

$$H(\omega_1,\omega_2) = ab\text{sinc}(a\omega_1)\text{sinc}(b\omega_2), \tag{27}$$

where *axb* is the rectangular aperture.

It is of interest to compare the spectra of the original and degraded images. From numerous experiments it is known, that the spectral magnitude of a realistic image is not very informative. It contains information about distribution of the signal energy in the frequency domain. For instance, if we exchange the spectral magnitudes of two similar images belonging to the same class and perform the inverse Fourier transform, then the difference in visual appearance of the original and obtained images will be negligible (Yaroslavsky & Eden, 1996). However, the difference between the spectral magnitudes of the original and degraded images may be significant due to the spectral magnitude of the frequency response of the linear system. Figs. 4(a) and 4(b) show a test original image and its spectral magnitude.

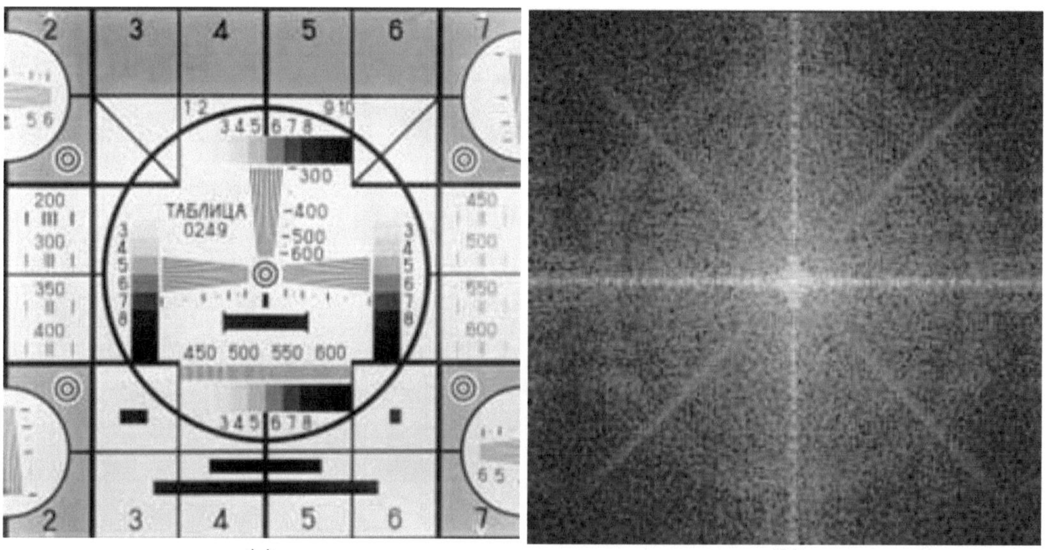


(a) (b)

Fig. 4. (a)Test original image, (b) spectral magnitude of the original image.

In order to identify the distortion operator a database containing various images of spectral magnitudes was created. Training elements of database were obtained on the base of mathematical modeling or computer simulation. In practice, the number of degradation operators is not very large. Next, the spectral magnitude of a degraded image is matched to those of the database. This simple recognition system works well to identify the type of degradation operator for common blurs. Figs. 5 illustrate spectral magnitudes for different common blurring operators. One can observe that spectral magnitudes of distorted images contain mainly the information about distortion operators such as zero crossings on the plane $(\omega_1, \omega_2)$.

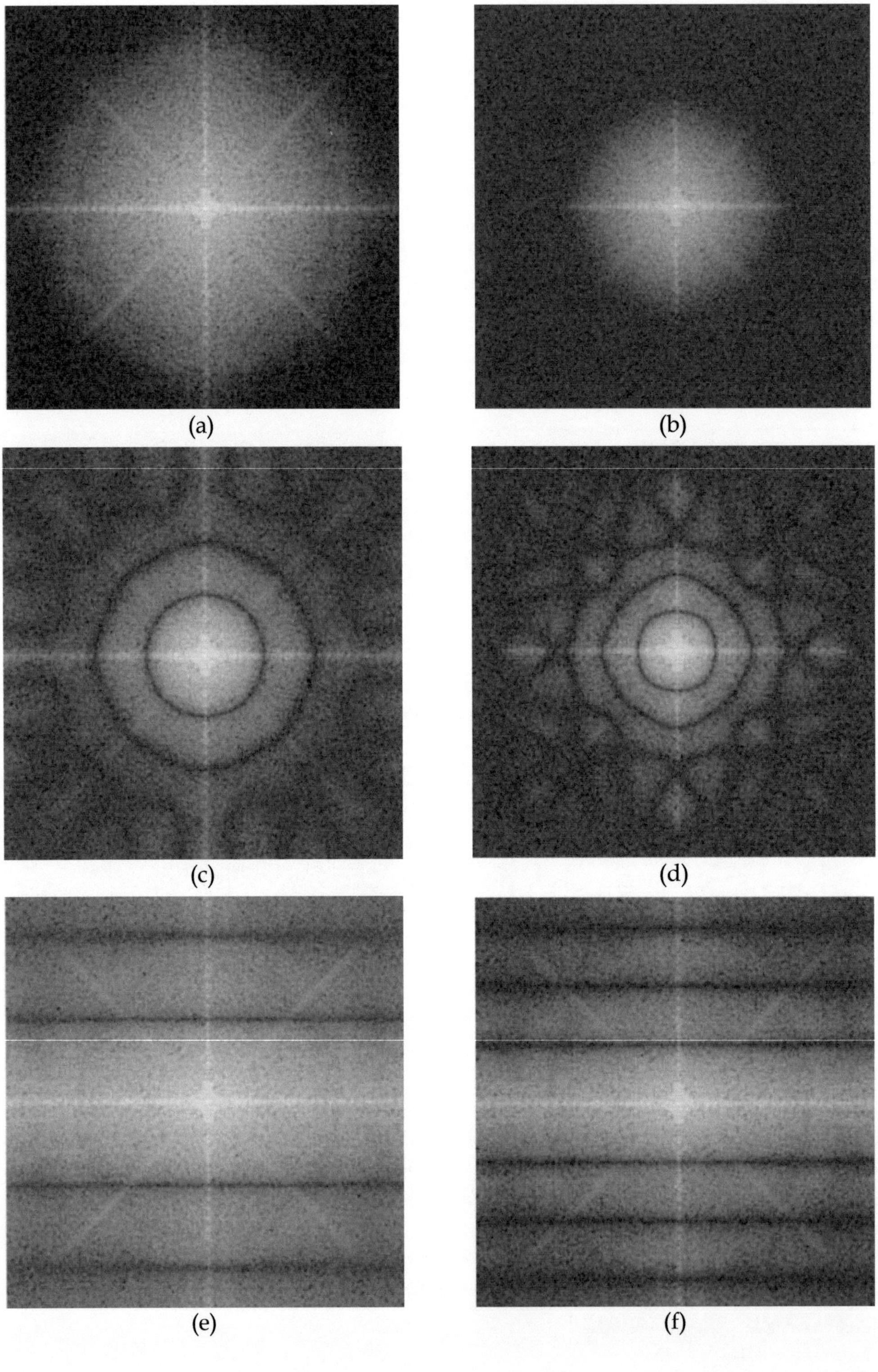

(a) (b) (c) (d) (e) (f)

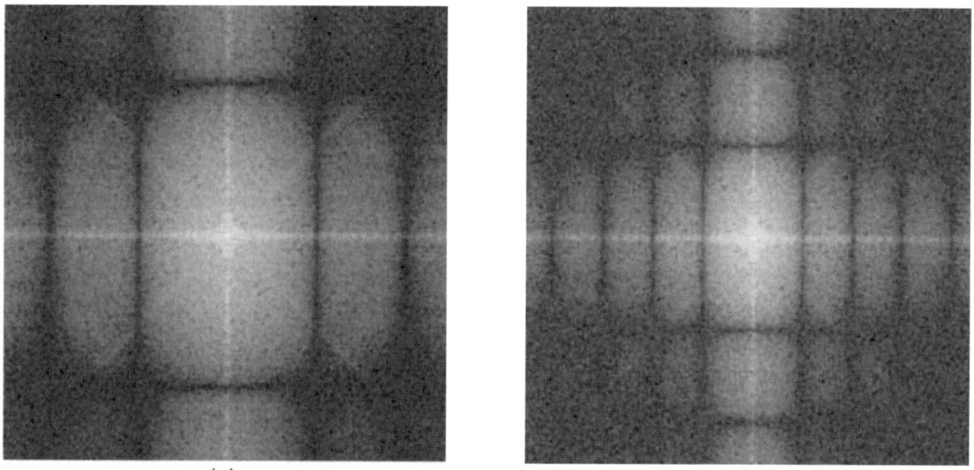

(g) (h)

Fig. 5. Spectral magnitudes of the test original image shown in Fig. 4(a) degraded by: (a) atmosphere turbulence defocusing (Eq. 23) with $a = 2$, (b) atmosphere turbulence defocusing (Eq. (23) with $a = 4$, (c) isotropic defocusing (Eq. 25) with $r = 4$, (d) isotropic defocusing (Eq. 25) with $r = 6$, (e) 1D motion blur (Eq. 21) with $L = 4$, (f) 1D motion blur (Eq. 21) with $L= 6$, (g) convolution with rectangular aperture (Eq. 27) with $a$=4, $b$=2, and (h) convolution with rectangular aperture (Eq. 27) with $a$=8, $b$=4.

Actually, composite degradations can be considered as a combination of the basic distortion operators. In this case, the Fourier spectrum of a new composite operator is the product of the spectra of used basic operators. Figs. 6(a) and 6(b) show the spectral magnitudes of the test original image degraded with isotropic blur and horizontal motion.

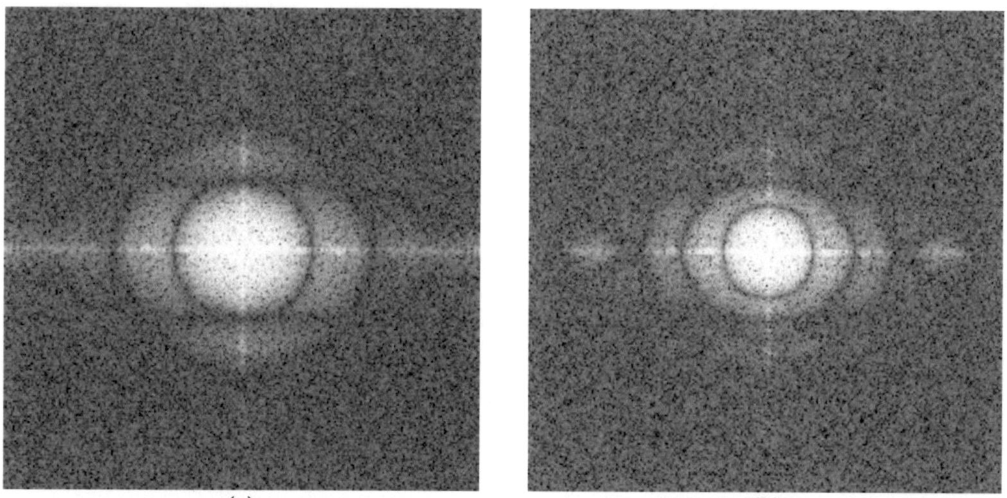

(a) (b)

Fig. 6. Spectral magnitudes of the test original image shown in Fig. 4(a) with composite degradations: (a) isotropic defocusing (Eq. 25) with $r = 6$ and 1D motion blur (Eq. 21) with $L = 4$, (b) isotropic defocusing (Eq.25) with $r = 6$ and 1D motion blur (Eq. 21) with $L = 6$.

One can observe that since one of the distortion operators dominates, the spectral magnitudes of composite degradations cannot be synthesized by a simple combination of those of the basic degradation operators. This means that the number of training elements of a matching system should be drastically increased.

In the Fourier representation of images, spectral magnitude and phase tend to play different roles (Oppenheim & Lim, 1981). For instance, in some situations many of the important features of an image are preserved if only the phase is retained. Furthermore, under a variety of conditions, phase information alone is sufficient to completely reconstruct an image to within a scale factor.

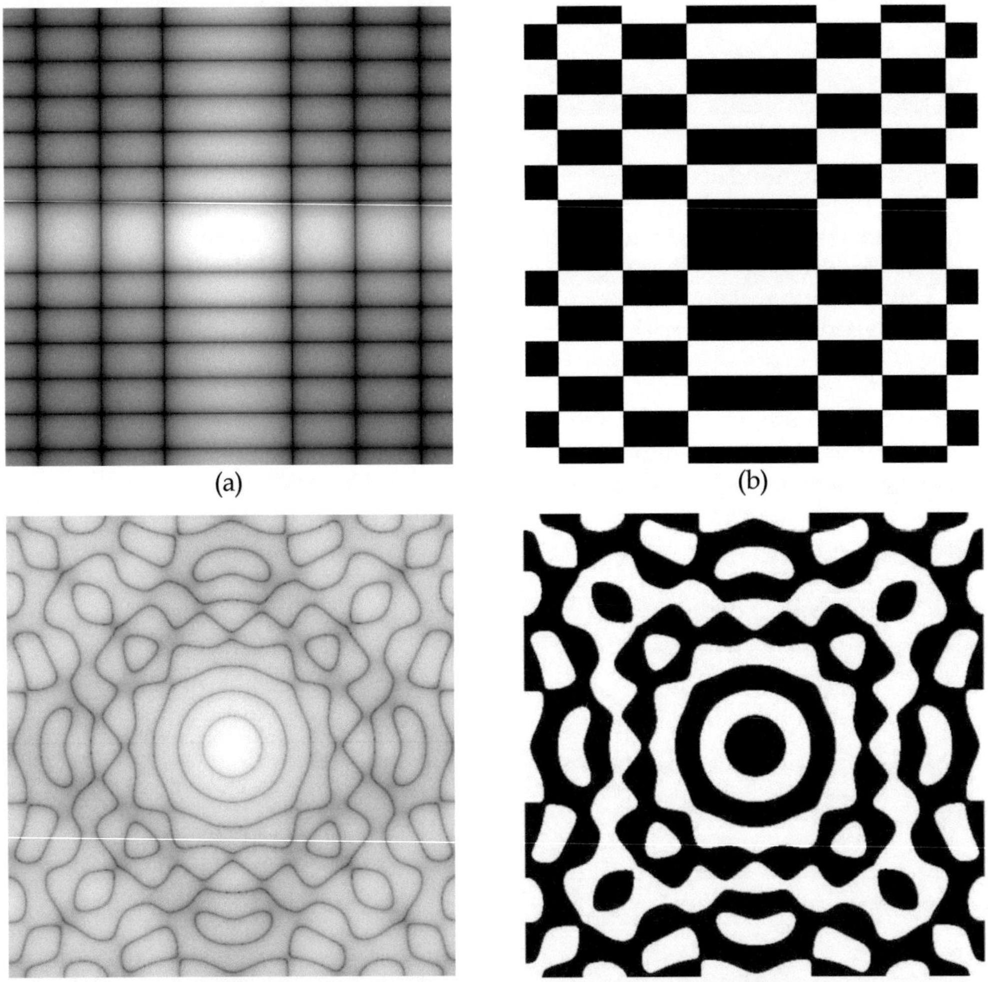

(a) (b) (c) (d)

Fig. 7. (a) Cepstrum of the original image degraded by convolution with rectangular aperture (Eq. 27) with $a$=2, $b$=4, (b) the difference of phases of the original and distorted (Fig. 7(a)) images, (c) cepstrum of the original image degraded by convolution with circular aperture with radius of 4, and (d) the difference of phases of the original and distorted (Fig. 7(c)) images.

If noise fluctuation in Eq. (19) is small, the phase of the distortion operator is equal to the difference between the phases of the degraded and original images. If the distortion operator is Gaussian, its phase is zero, and the phases of the distorted and original images coincide If the distortion operator is a finite function, e.g. $(x,y) \in W$ , then the phase of the distorted image may differ from the phase of the original image by $\pm\pi$, and points at which the phase jumps by $\pm\pi$ coincide with the location of zeros of the spectral magnitude of the degraded image. These zeros, for even functions are all located on the real axis. So, the phase of the original image either coincides with that of the distorted image or differs from that of the distorted image by $\pm\pi$. Fig. 7 shows the differences between the phases of the distorted and original images for rectangular and circular aperture blurs. Therefore, under certain conditions, we can identify the type of the distortion operator and estimate its spectral phase from the observed degraded image.

## 4. Conclusion

In this chapter we treated the problem of restoring linearly degraded image using two-dimensional image variations. The restored image minimizes the objective functional subject to the Kronrod's variations. In order to achieve a good restoration, it is important take into account topological characteristics of the original image, which are well described by the first Kronrod's variation. The first step in restoring a degraded image is the identification of the type of degradation operator. It can be done by matching of the spectral magnitude of the degraded image with those of created database. Under certain conditions, the phase of the distortion operator may be also estimated from the distorted image. Extensive testing it was shown that the original image can be automatically restored by proper choice of the parameters of the proposed method.

## 5. Acknowledgment

This work was supported by the Russian Foundation for Basic Research, project no. 11_07_00361.

## 6. References

Adams, R. A. (1975). *Sobolev Spaces*, Academic Press, ISBN 978-0-12-044150-1, Boston, USA

Banham, M., & Katsaggelos, A. (1997). Digital image restoration. *IEEE Signal Processing Magazine*, Vol. 14, No.2, (March 1997), pp. 24-41, ISSN 1053-5888

Buades, A., Coll, B. & Morel, J.M. (2006). The staircasing effect in neighborhood filters and its solution. *IEEE Trans. Image Process.*, Vol. 15, No. 6, (June 2006), pp 1499-1505, ISSN 1057-7149

Bertero, M. & Boccacci, P. (1998). *Introduction to inverse problems in imaging*, Institute of Physics Publishing, ISBN 0-7503-0435-9, Bristol, UK

Biemond, J., Lagendijk, R.L. & Mersereau, R.M. (1990). Iterative methods for image deblurring. *Proc. IEEE. Vol. 78*, No. 5, (May 1990), pp. 856-883, ISSN 0018-9219

Bovik, A. (2005). *Handbook of image and video processing* (2nd ed.), Academic Press, ISBN 0-12-119792-1, NJ, USA

Cannon, M. (1976). Blind deconvolution of spatially invariant image blurs with phase. *IEEE Trans. Acoust. Speech Sig. Proc.*, Vol. ASSP-24, No. 1, (Fenruary 1976), pp. 58–63 (1976), ISSN: 0096-3518

Chan, T. & Wong, C. (1998). Total variation blind deconvolution. *IEEE Trans. Image Process.*, Vol. 7, No. 3, (March 1998), pp 370–375, ISSN 1057-7149

Gennery, D.B. (1973). Determination of optical transfer function by inspection of frequency-domain plot. *J. Opt. Soc. Am.*, Vol. 63, No. 12, (December 1973), pp. 1571–1577, ISSN 1084-7529

González, R. & Woods, R. (2008). Digital image processing (3rd ed.), Prentice Hall, ISBN 0-13-1687288, NJ, USA

Jain, A.K. (1989). *Fundamentals of digital image processing*, Prentice Hall, ISBN 0-13-332578-4, NY, USA

Kay, S. (1993). *Fundamentals of statistical signal processing: estimation theory*, Prentice Hall, ISBN 0-13-345711-7, NJ, USA

Kundur, D., & Hatzinakos, D. (1996). Blind image deconvolution. *IEEE Signal Processing Magazine*, Vol. 13, No. 3, (May 1996), pp. 73-76, ISSN 1053-5888

Kronrod, A. S. (1950). On functions of two variables. *Uspekhi Mat. Nauk*, Vol. 5, No. 1, (January 1950), pp. 24–134, ISSN 0042-1316

Milukova, O., Kober, V., Karnaukhov, V. & Ovseevich, I.A. (2010). Restoration of blurred images with conditional total variation method. *Pattern Recognition and Image Analysis* Vol. 20, No. 2, (May 2010), pp. 179-184, ISSN 1054-6618

Milukova, O., Kober, V., Karnaukhov, V. & Ovseevich, I.A. (2010). Spectral analysis of distorted images in restoration problems. *Pattern Recognition and Image Analysis* Vol. 20, No. 3, (September 2010), pp. 335-340, ISSN 1054-6618

Milukova, O., Kober, V., Karnaukhov, V. & Ovseevich, I.A. (2011). Iterative global and local methods of image restoration. *Pattern Recognition and Image Analysis* Vol. 21, No. 2, (May 2011), pp. 309-311, ISSN 1054-6618

Oppenheim, A.V. & Lim, J.S. (1981). The importance of phase in signals. *Proceedings of the IEEE*, Vol. 69, No. 5, (May 1981), pp. 529 - 541, ISSN 0018-9219

Perona, P. & Malik, J. (1990). Scale-space and edge detection using anisotropic diffusion. *IEEE Transaction on Pattern Analysis and Machine Intelligence*, Vol. 12, No. 7, (July 1990), pp. 629-639, ISSN 0162-8828

Rudin, L., Osher, S. & Fatemi, E. (1992). Nonlinear total variation based noise removal algorithms. *Phys. D*, Vol. 60, pp. 259–268, ISSN 0167-278

Sezan, M.I. & Tekalp, A.M. (1990). Survey of recent developments in digital image restoration. *Optical Engineering*, Vol. 29, No. 5, (May 1990), pp. 393-404, ISSN 0091-3286

Sroubek, F. & Flusser, J. (2003). Multichannel blind iterative image restoration. *IEEE Trans. Image Process.*, Vol. 12, No. 9, (September 2003), pp. 1094–1106, ISSN 1057-7149

Tikhonov, A.N. & Arsenin, V.Y. (1977). *Solution of ill-posed problems*, Winston & Sons, ISBN 0-470-99124-0, Washington, USA

Vitushkin, A.G. (1955). *On multidimensional variations*, GITTL, Moscow, Russia (in Russian)

Yaroslavsky, L. P. & Eden, M. (1996). *Fundamentals of digital optics*, Birkhauser, ISBN 3-7643-3833-9, Boston, USA

10

# Harnessing the Potentials of Image Extrema for Blind Restoration

Rachel Mabanag Chong and Toshihisa Tanaka
*Tokyo University of Agriculture and Technology*
*Japan*

## 1. Introduction

Images contain a wealth of information. The advances in modern technology makes it easier to deal with different kinds of images. As a result, its applications have been increasing and spreading out to different fields of research. Despite these, degradations are unavoidable owing to the fact that the acquisition systems are imperfect and the environment can highly vary. One of the most studied type of degradation is the blur. The process of removing this from an image is known as image deconvolution, restoration or reconstruction. We illustrate its importance in the field of image processing with an example in Fig. 1. In Fig. 1(a), an image is acquired but degradations make it difficult for further processing. Reconstruction is applied and the resulting image in Fig. 1(b) can now be used in order to obtain an accurate representation of the original bar code as shown in Fig. 1(c). In essence, reconstruction is necessary as a preprocessing step for degraded images in order to extract more information from it. As a result, this has been studied in various fields of applications such as bar code interpretation (Choksi & van Gennip, 2010; Esedoglu, 2004; Yahyanejad & Strom, 2010), fingerprint identification (Cappelli et al., 2007), iris recognition (Kang & Park, 2007), face identification (Chu, Yang & Chen, 2010; Nishiyama et al., 2010; Xin et al., 2003), among others.

In the two-dimensional domain, degradation is mathematically modelled as (Lagendijk & Biemond, 2005):

$$g(x,y) = f(x,y) * h(x,y) + n(x,y) \tag{1}$$

where the symbol $*$ is the two-dimensional convolution process. On the other hand, the variables $g(x,y)$, $f(x,y)$, $h(x,y)$, and $n(x,y)$ represent the degraded image, original image,

(a) degraded image (b) reconstructed image (c) reconstructed code

Fig. 1. Reconstruction of 2D bar code images in (Chu, Yang, Pan & Chen, 2010).

blur point spread function (PSF), and noise, respectively. In most cases, it is assumed that noise is negligible and the model is simplified to a purely convolutional process. Thus, the vector-matrix form of the model in the image domain is:

$$g = Hf \tag{2}$$

and

$$g = Fh \tag{3}$$

in the blur domain. The small letters are vectors that represent their respective quantities, which are lexicographically ordered. On the other hand, the capital letters are Toeplitz matrices constructed from their corresponding quantities. We adapt the terms image and blur domain as used in (He et al., 2009) to indicate the quantity being estimated and the direction to which the reconstruction cost function is being projected. In this way, derivations can be more succinct. Based on these equations, the unblurred image can be easily computed if the models for the degraded image and PSF are known. However, this is not the case in actual applications. Images cannot be modelled in a straightforward manner thus, their features and properties are usually utilized. For some applications, probability models are created based on the imaging conditions and type of scenes (Simoncelli, 2005). On the other hand, blurring functions can be mathematically modelled (Lagendijk & Biemond, 2005). Exploiting the characteristics of these models can decrease the complexity of determining the unblurred image.

The reconstruction of a degraded image undergoes the following major steps: blur detection and identification; reference PSF (RPSF) determination; deconvolution; and image quality assessment. In this chapter, we will explore the various characteristics of image extrema that make it useful in each step. These are tested on numerous natural color images wherein synthetic and actual blurs are also considered. Experimental data will illustrate the effectiveness of the methods.

## 2. Blur detection and identification

Reconstruction algorithms assume that blurs are always present. However, subjecting an unblurred image to this will only waste resources. To avoid this, preprocessing the image with a blur detection method is a must. Some methods are based on edge information (Chung et al., 2004; Marziliano et al., 2002; Rooms et al., 2002; Tong et al., 2004) or frequency domain characteristics (Aizenberg et al., 2002; n.d.; 2006; 2008). A downside to these is its restrictiveness towards image size and orientation. Aside from this, most edge-based methods are only limited to detection and are not capable of identifying the type of degradation. Transform-based methods have promising results but are mostly applicable to non-Gaussian types since these exploit the null patterns. These limitations can be overcome by using the characteristics of image extrema (Chong & Tanaka, 2008; 2009). This method can be applied to images with different sizes and orientations. Additional parameters or settings are not necessary and different types of degradations can be included.

### 2.1 Images and their extrema

The presence of blurs will lessen the perception of details in an image. The method herein will show that the loss of details is not only obvious in edges but also in the extrema. For this reason, we can generally call this as image extrema analysis (IEXA)(Chong & Tanaka, 2009).

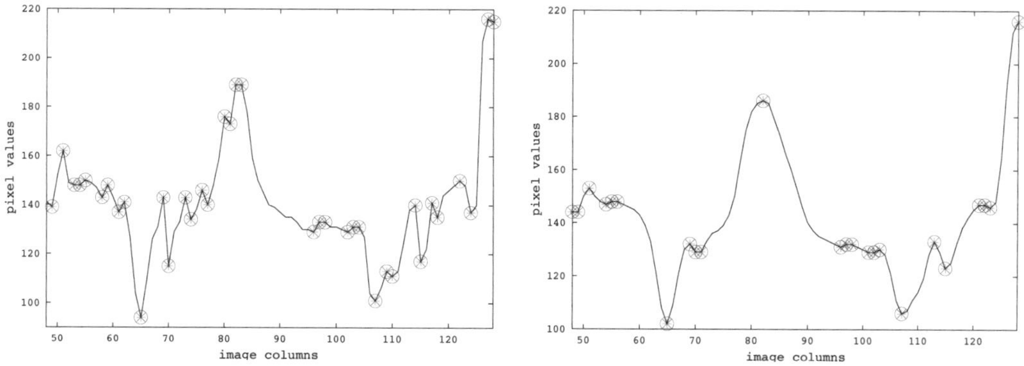


(a) Unblurred (b) Gaussian blurred

Fig. 2. Sample plots of extrema values in a row.

The plots in Fig. 2 show a row of pixel values where the extrema are marked. Fig.2(a) is from the unblurred image while its Gaussian blurred version is shown in Fig. 2(b). These illustrate that there are more extrema values in an unblurred image than its blurred version. Thus, the presence of blur makes some extrema disappear resulting to a decrease in its number. Aside from this, the unblurred images have pixel values that are highly separated from each other. In other words, the extrema are non-neighbouring pixels with distances that are only small.

On the other hand, the blurred images have more neighbouring extrema because the presence of blur flattened the image pixels. This results to extrema values that are more clustered with greater separation from each other. This is illustrated in Fig. 3. It can be seen that the minima and maxima values have the same behaviour in the presence of blur. Similarly, these characteristics can also be observed not only in the image's rows but also in its columns.

### 2.2 Detection and identification technique

Taking into account the above-mentioned observations, blur detection and identification can be accomplished by extracting the features and using a classifier. Consider a blur classification problem with $K$ categories consisting of unblurred images and $K-1$ types of blurs. For each extrema in an image, the distances and plateaus are counted by rows then by columns. In the context of this work, we define distance as the number of pixels between extrema while plateau as the number of consecutive extrema values. Let $h_S(i)$ be an extrema histogram of $S$ with $S \in \{\text{dn}, \text{dx}, \text{pn}, \text{px}\}$ and the letters $i$, d, p, n, and x stand for histogram index, distance, plateau, minima, and maxima, respectively. Since there are two possible directions in populating the histogram, $S$ is appended with _c or _r to indicate column-wise or row-wise, respectively. For each extrema histogram, the feature values are defined as follows:

1. dispersion, $disp_S$

   This reflects the closeness between extrema for distances. On the other hand, it also quantifies the number of standalone extrema or those that do not have neighbours for plateaus.

$$disp_S = \hat{h}_S(1) = \frac{h_S(1)}{\sum_{i=1}^{m_S} h_S(i)} \tag{4}$$

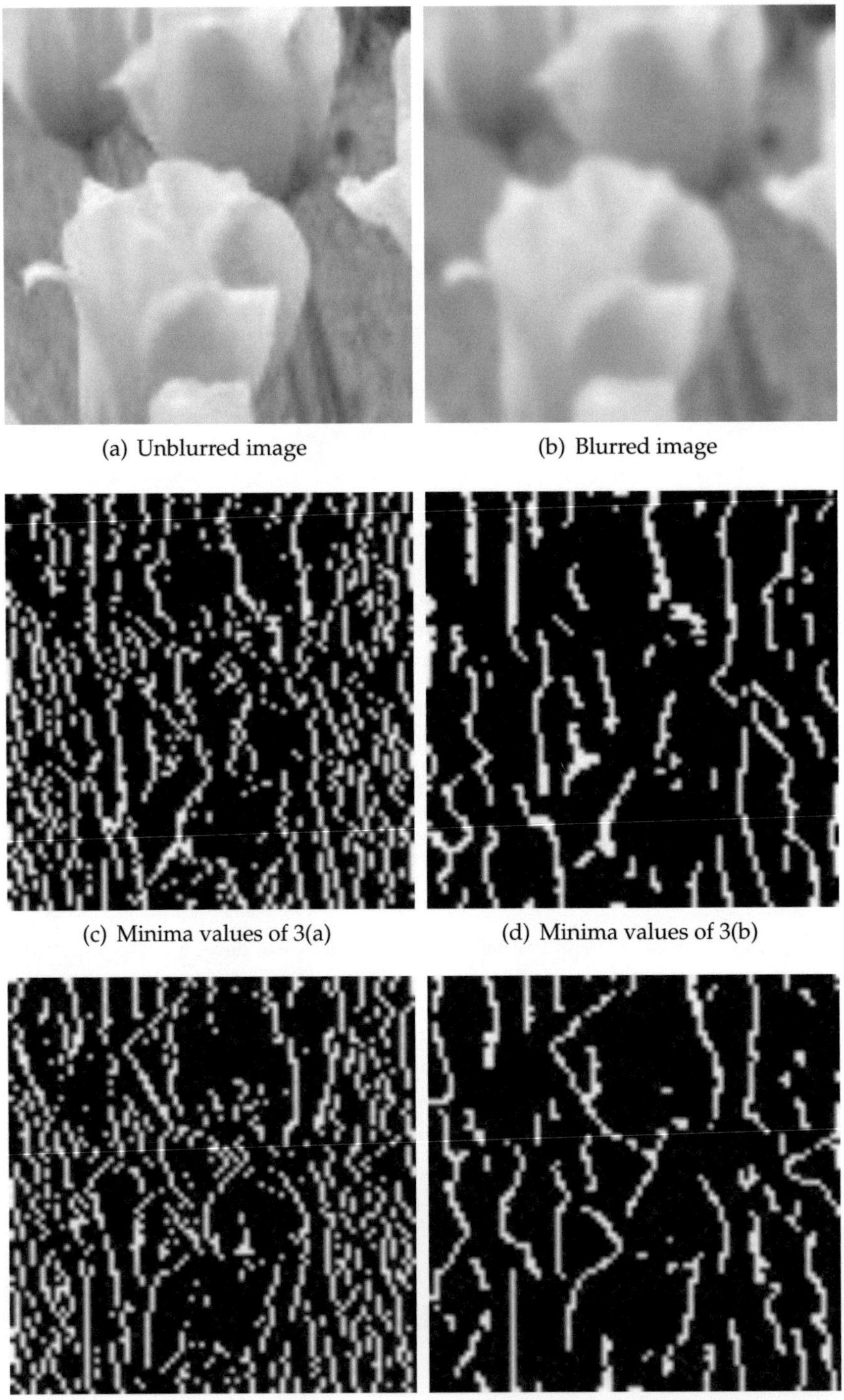

(a) Unblurred image (b) Blurred image

(c) Minima values of 3(a) (d) Minima values of 3(b)

(e) Maxima values of 3(a) (f) Maxima values of 3(b)

Fig. 3. Example of an unblurred image with its Gaussian blurred version.

where $m_S$ is the maximum histogram index in $S$.

2. concentration, $ctn_S$
This is the density of the highest count with respect to the total count either for distances or plateaus.
$$ctn_S = \max\{\hat{h}_S(i) : 1 \leq i \leq m_S\} \tag{5}$$

3. arithmetic mean of the counts, $\bar{h}_S$
This is the average distance or plateau count for a given histogram.
$$\bar{h}_S = \frac{1}{m_S} \sum_{i=1}^{m_S} \hat{h}_S(i). \tag{6}$$

4. histogram width, $hw_S$
This measures the range of distances or plateaus where its counts are considered significant. The histogram indices with significant counts are determined by:
$$i_w \in \{i : \hat{h}_S(i) \geq \bar{h}_S\}$$
thus, $hw_S$ can be computed as follows:
$$hw_S = \max\{i_w\} - \min\{i_w\} \tag{7}$$

5. variance of the counts, $\sigma_S^2$
This is the measure of count dispersion of a histogram.
$$\sigma_S^2 = \frac{1}{m_S} \sum_{i=1}^{m_S} \left(\hat{h}_S(i) - \bar{h}_S\right)^2 \tag{8}$$

In summary, there are 5 feature values for each $S$ where the directions for counting the distances (or plateaus) are row- and column-wise in order to completely account the extrema behaviour. Thus, each image must have a total of 40 features. Finally, all quantities are normalized with their respective maximum feature values for the training and testing sets.

The blur classification is accomplished by using nearest neighbour (Cover & Hart, 1967).It is noteworthy to mention that other more sophisticated classifiers are also applicable that may yield better performance. In this section, the discriminative power of the proposed features will be demonstrated despite the simplicity of the classifier. Through the experimental data, it will be shown that high values of accuracy are attainable.

### 2.3 Experimental results

#### 2.3.1 Experiment descriptions

The images in the experiments were coloured however, we prefer to use the green channel. This is based on the fact that cameras have twice as much green sensors than the red or blue and that computations will be lesser as opposed to using the three channels. As a result, the experiment starts with the extraction of green component for each image. A database of different coloured natural images is used. This is composed of 300 unblurred images with sizes that randomly varies between $640 \times 480$ and $480 \times 640$. These images are then synthetically blurred using (1). We consider the following models for the synthetic blurs (Banham & Katsaggelos, 1997; Lagendijk & Biemond, 2005):

1. Gaussian or atmospheric turbulence blur:

$$h(x,y) = K\exp\left(-\frac{x^2+y^2}{2\sigma^2}\right) \tag{9}$$

   where $K$ is a normalizing constant and $\sigma$ is the variance. This is generally used to model a variety of imaging devices as well as long-term atmospheric exposure.
2. Horizontal motion (HM) blur:

$$h(b,d) = \begin{cases} \frac{1}{L}, & b = 0, |d| \leq \frac{L-1}{2} \\ 0, & \text{otherwise} \end{cases} \tag{10}$$

   where $L$ is the length of motion. The variables $b$ and $d$ represent the PSF coordinates. This models the effect on the acquired image when the camera or object is horizontally moving faster than the camera's exposure period.
3. uniform out-of-focus (OOF) blur:

$$h(b,d) = \begin{cases} \frac{1}{\pi R^2}, & \sqrt{b^2+d^2} \leq R^2 \\ 0, & otherwise \end{cases} \tag{11}$$

   where $R$ is the blur radius. This blur is observable as defocus in images and is caused by the finite size of camera aperture.

The Gaussian blurs have standard deviations of $\sigma \in \{1, 1.33, 1.66, 2, 2.33, 2.66, 3\}$ with a spread determined by $6\sigma$. The uniform HM are set to have lengths of $L \in \{3, 5, 7, 9, 11, 13\}$. The radii for the OOF blur are $R \in \{1, 2, \ldots, 6\}$.

The synthetically degraded images are subjected to extrema extraction and histogram creation. The required features can then be computed from the histograms. The training set consisted of 2,660 images that is composed of 133 images with their corresponding 20 variations. The testing set also has 20 variations for 167 images for a total of 3,340 images. In the classification process, the Euclidean distances from the test image to all of the training images are first calculated. The training image with the minimum distance from the test image is considered as the nearest neighbour. The unknown object's class is then identified by the class of this neighbour.

There are two IEXA experiments being compared. The first (IEXA1) used the complete 40 features while IEXA2 had only 20. The reduction in number is achieved by applying forward selection (Theodoridis & Koutroumbas, 2006). Since this is computationally expensive and time consuming, a naive method is first applied in order to determine the order of features to be added. The resulting required features are:

1. $d_S$ : $S$ ∈{dx_c, dn_r, dx_r, pn_r, px_r}
2. $c_S$ : $S$ ∈{dx_c, px_c, dn_r, dx_r, pn_r, px_r}
3. $\hat{h}_S$ : $S$ ∈{dx_c, dn_r, dx_r}
4. $hw_S$ : $S$ ∈{dx_c, dn_r, dx_r}
5. $\sigma_S^2$ : $S$ ∈{dn_r, dx_r, pn_r}

It is important to note that features from dn_c and pn_c are not included so these need not be determined.

| Input | No. of Images | Accuracy ( % ) | | |
|---|---|---|---|---|
| | | IEXA1 | IEXA2 | BDHWT |
| Unblurred | 167 | 99.40 | 99.40 | 98.80 |
| Gaussian | 1,169 | 100.00 | 100.00 | NA |
| HM | 1,002 | 100.00 | 100.00 | 13.17 |
| OOF | 1,002 | 99.90 | 100.00 | 98.80 |
| TOTAL | 3,340 | **99.94** | **99.97** | 59.28 |

Table 1. Comparison of blur detection accuracy.

| Input | No. of Images | Accuracy ( % ) | |
|---|---|---|---|
| | | IEXA1 | IEXA2 |
| Unblurred | 167 | **99.40** | **99.40** |
| Gaussian | 1,169 | 90.16 | **95.21** |
| HM | 1,002 | **99.40** | 98.90 |
| OOF | 1,002 | 93.61 | **96.01** |
| TOTAL | 3,340 | 94.43 | **96.77** |

Table 2. Comparison of blur classification accuracy.

### 2.3.2 Data and results

The blur detection performance in this section is compared with the work in (Tong et al., 2004), which detects blur with Haar wavelet transform (BDHWT). This involves the creation of an edge map based on a three-level decomposition of an image. The different edge types are then identified and counted by using a threshold and comparative conditions. The resulting ratio between the counts is used to detect the blur by comparing it with another threshold.

The accuracy of the detection algorithms are shown in Table 1. The NA in the table indicates not applicable since the method in (Tong et al., 2004) is only for unblurred, motion, and OOF blurs. It can be observed that accuracies are consistently higher when extrema analysis is used. Furthermore, the result after feature selection yielded a better performance than using all the features.

The classification accuracies for IEXA1 and IEXA2 are in Table 2. Only the accuracy for the unblurred images did not change after feature selection. Motion classification performance slightly decreased however, Gaussian and OOF have higher values. As a result, the decrease became negligible and the overall accuracy improved.

This section shows the effectiveness of using extrema features for blur detection and identification. Furthermore, the accuracy is further improved by feature selection. In the next section, maxima and RPSF will be presented.

## 3. RPSF: Characteristics and extraction methods

The previous section shows that maxima and minima can be exploited to determine and identify the blur in an image. In contrast, this section will only use maxima in order to determine a quantity that closely resembles the PSF that is present in an image. We call this quantity as reference PSF (RPSF) (Chong & Tanaka, 2010a). Its purpose is to yield a rough idea regarding the blurring function by exploiting the effect of blurs on the maxima values and locations. Additional uses of RPSF will be discussed in the next section. In comparison with the previous section, this does not require a classifier or image features. It is extracted from the given image assuming only a PSF size.

### 3.1 Motion blurs and maxima

The presence of blur has the effect of flattening the pixel values. As a result, the locations of the maxima values are influenced by the blurring function. In (Chong & Tanaka, 2010a; 2011b) the extraction of RPSF has been tested on motion and OOF blurred images. However, the most commonly encountered type of blur is motion. Thus, more focus will be given to this type. In this case we will consider the general model of the motion blur given by:

$$h(b,d;L,\theta) = \begin{cases} \frac{1}{L}, & \sqrt{b^2+d^2} \leq \frac{L}{2} \text{ and } \frac{b}{d} = -\tan\theta \\ 0, & \text{otherwise} \end{cases} \tag{12}$$

where the parameter $\theta$ represents motion angle in degrees.

Figure 4 shows images blurred by motion in different directions. Each degraded image consists of two maxima images based on the direction of scanning. These are shown as binary images in Figs. 4(c)-4(f) where the white pixels indicate the maxima. It can be observed that the locations are influenced by the direction of motion that is present. As a result, the maxima locations tend to be arranged in the direction of motion. Considering a small window in the image where the maxima are present, it is obvious that this will give us an idea regarding the direction of motion. This is indicated by the larger pixel values located at the direction of motion. To detect the direction Hough transform has been utilized in (Chong & Tanaka, 2010b; 2011a). In image processing, this is commonly used to detect lines and circles in binary images. For a straight line, all of its points will intersect in the parameter space [(Gonzales & Woods, 2008)]. The parameters ($\zeta$ and $\theta$) are specified from the representation of a line in the PSF space domain:

$$b\cos\theta + d\sin\theta = \zeta \tag{13}$$

where parameter $\theta$ can be interpreted as the direction of motion. Since the PSFs are discrete and have sizes smaller than the image, the parameter space can be easily subdivided. For practical purposes, we set $\theta = \{0°, 45°, 90°, 135°\}$. The accumulator for a certain combination of $\zeta$ and $\theta$ is incremented based on the point located at $(b,d)$. The detection of the motion direction is accomplished by selecting the accumulator with the maximum number of points.

### 3.2 RPSF extraction

The RPSF can be extracted from motion blurred images by the following steps:

1. Scan the green channel of the image for local maxima locations in the horizontal and vertical directions.
2. Determine the number of locations for each scanning direction and let Z be the total count.
3. If $z$ is the index of the maxima locations and assuming a blur support size of $s \times s$, create a set of windows $\{w_z\}_{z=1}^{Z}$ of the same size whose elements are the pixel values with the maxima value at the center.
4. Compute the sum of these windows by

$$w = \omega \sum_{z=1}^{Z} w_z. \tag{14}$$

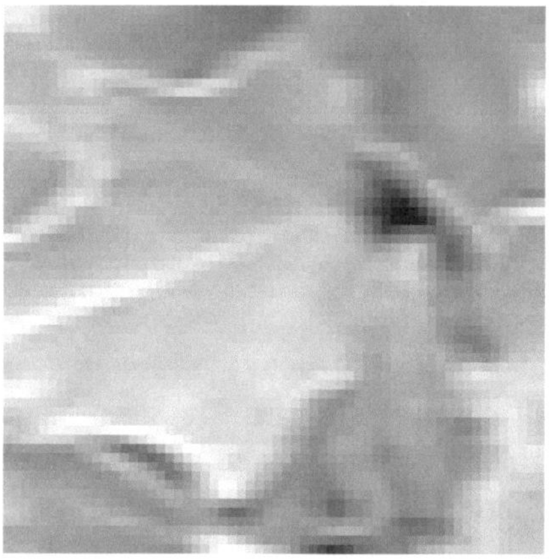

(a) Blurred with $L = 5$ and $\theta = 0°$

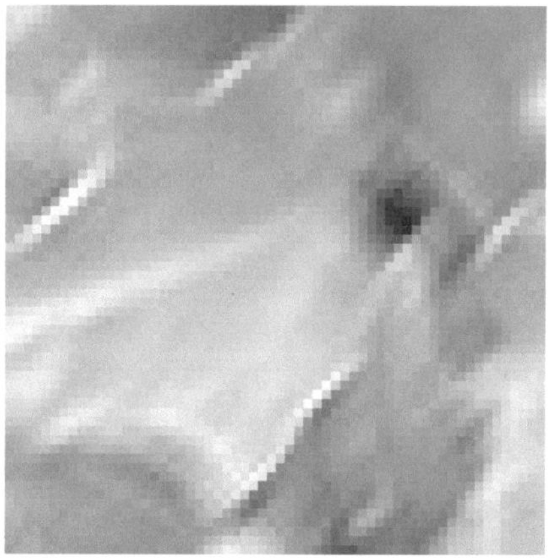

(b) Blurred with $L = 5$ and $\theta = 45°$

(c) Horizontal scanning of 4(a)

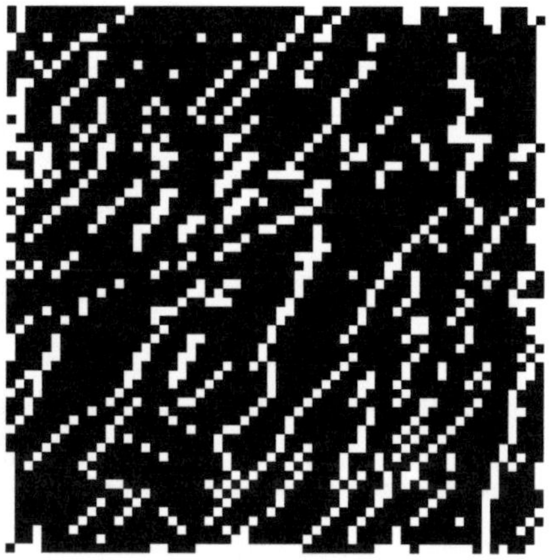

(d) Horizontal scanning of 4(b)

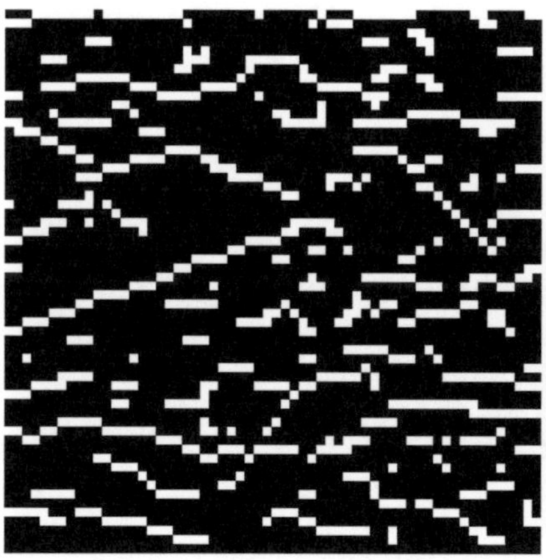

(e) Vertical scanning of 4(a)

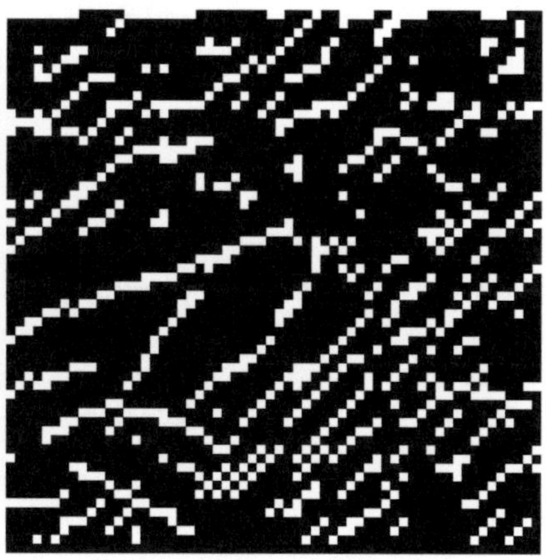

(f) Vertical scanning of 4(b)

Fig. 4. Blurry images and their maxima locations.

Determine the value of the constant $\omega$ that will normalize $w$ such that:

$$\sum_{\forall(b,d)} w(b,d) = 1 \tag{15}$$

where $(b,d) \in \{0,1,\ldots,s-1\}$.

5. Create a binary matrix ($o$) that will mask out unnecessary values

$$o(b,d) = \begin{cases} 1, w(b,d) \geq t \\ 0, \text{otherwise} \end{cases} \tag{16}$$

where $t$ is the threshold that can be determined by the mean of the central and outermost elements of $w$.

6. Non-zero elements of $o$ must satisfy the symmetry condition:

$$o(b,d) = o(-b,-d). \tag{17}$$

7. Apply Hough transform on binary matrix $o$ using $\theta = \{0^o, 45^o, 90^o, 135^o\}$. When there are $\eta$ accumulators with maximum number of points:
   (a) Create $\eta$ binary masks, $o_{\eta,\theta}$, that correspond with $\theta$ represented by the accumulator.
   (b) For each $\eta$, compute:

$$a_{\eta,\theta} = w \cdot o_{\eta,\theta}.$$

   (c) The direction is selected by:

$$\theta = \arg\max_{\theta}\{a_{\eta,\theta}\}$$

8. Determine the matrix form of the RPSF ($r$) by

$$r(b,d) = w(b,d)o(b,d) \tag{18}$$

where the matrix must satisfy the conditions in equations (15) and (17).

### 3.3 Experimental results

#### 3.3.1 Experiment descriptions

The experiment herein uses 300 unblurred images with sizes that may be $640 \times 480$ or $480 \times 640$. These are then motion blurred with $L \in \{3,5,7,9,11,13\}$ and $\theta \in \{0°, 45°, 90°, 135°\}$. The detection process was also applied only to the green channels to minimize computational time.

#### 3.3.2 Data and results

The data in Table 3 shows the accuracy of the method in detecting the direction of motion. It can be seen that horizontal and vertical motions have consistently high values for different PSF sizes. On the other hand, slanting directions (45° and 135°) yielded lower values, which are fluctuating as the PSF size increases. These are attributed by the direction in scanning for the maxima. When the motion has the same direction as the scanning, the chances of preserving the blur's effects are higher.

These results show that RPSF is capable of giving us an idea of the PSF's characteristics using only the maxima of the degraded image. Although only one colour channel was processed, a high accuracy in detecting the motion direction was manifested in the experiment with various natural images. Due to these we can also use it for image deconvolution, which will be discussed in the next section.

| angle (°) | no. of images | Accuracy (%) | | | | | |
|---|---|---|---|---|---|---|---|
| | | 3 | 5 | 7 | 9 | 11 | 13 |
| 0 | 300 | **100.0** | **100.0** | **100.0** | **100.0** | **100.0** | **100.0** |
| 45 | 300 | 97.0 | 87.0 | 94.3 | 96.7 | 94.0 | 96.3 |
| 90 | 300 | **99.7** | **99.7** | **99.7** | **99.7** | **100.0** | **100.0** |
| 135 | 300 | 97.7 | 86.7 | 96.0 | 97.0 | 95.0 | 96.3 |

Table 3. Accuracy (%) in determining the motion direction with different PSF sizes.

## 4. Image deconvolution

In this section, we consider the deconvolution of a degraded image. This involves the estimation of $f$ and $h$ given only $g$. Since it is highly ill-posed, we use the alternating minimization (AM) technique. This enables the incorporation of information about $f$ and $h$ so that the solution is more stable. AM is a technique that is used in the minimization of a cost function involving two variables. In each cycle, one variable is set constant while the other is being solved. The roles are then reversed and the cycle repeats until a criterion is achieved.

### 4.1 Cost function

The estimation process involves the minimization of a cost function generally defined by:

$$J = \frac{1}{2}\left((g - \hat{H}\hat{f})^T(g - \hat{H}\hat{f}) + J_{\hat{f}} + J_{\hat{h}}\right) \tag{19}$$

where $J_{\hat{f}}$ is the image smoothness term and $J_{\hat{h}}$ is the PSF characterization term. The symbol $\hat{\cdot}$ represents an estimated quantity. The first term is known as the fidelity term and is a basic term in most reconstruction cost functions. This was proposed in (Yang et al., 1994) wherein minimization was accomplished by projection-based blind deconvolution. The results showed good convergence properties and high flexibility for incorporation of prior knowledge. The image smoothness term is based on the concept of total variation (TV) proposed in (Rudin et al., 1992), which can be modelled by:

$$J_{TV} = \int_{\Omega} |\nabla f|. \tag{20}$$

The work of (Chan et al., 1999) added a variable to avoid its non-differentiability. Thus, the equation becomes

$$J_{\gamma} = \int_{\Omega} \sqrt{|\nabla f|^2 + \gamma^2}. \tag{21}$$

TV in vector-matrix form was derived in (He et al., 2009) to make the minimization process simpler. We will be employing here the TV norm in equation (20) instead of the commonly used $L_2$ norm. This can be reformulated as

$$\int |\nabla f| = \int \frac{|\nabla f|^2}{\varepsilon} \tag{22}$$

where $\varepsilon$ is an auxiliary variable, $\varepsilon = |\nabla f|$. By following the fixed point scheme in (Chan & Wong, 1998), $\varepsilon$ can be computed using the value from the previous iteration of the AM loop. For simplicity, consider the gradients of the image in the $x$ direction

$$\sum_{\forall(x,y)} (f(x+1,y) - f(x,y))^2 = ||Vf||_2^2 = f^T V^T V f \tag{23}$$

where

$$V = \begin{bmatrix} 1 & -1 & 0 & \cdots & 0 \\ 0 & 1 & -1 & \cdots & \vdots \\ \vdots & \vdots & \vdots & \ddots & -1 \\ 0 & 0 & 0 & \vdots & 1 \end{bmatrix}.$$

Applying the concept of equation (22) to equation (23)

$$\begin{aligned} \sum_{\forall(x,y)} (f(x+1,y) - f(x,y))^2 &= \sum_{\forall(x,y)} \frac{1}{\varepsilon(\vec{x})} (f(x+1,y) - f(x,y))^2 \\ &= f^T V^T W V f \end{aligned} \quad (24)$$

where

$$W = \text{diag}\left\{ \frac{1}{\varepsilon(\vec{x})} \right\}.$$

For practical purposes, we also implement the following conditions:

$$\frac{1}{\varepsilon(\vec{x})} = \begin{cases} \frac{1}{\varepsilon(\vec{x})} & , \varepsilon(\vec{x}) \neq 0 \\ 0 & , \text{otherwise} \end{cases}.$$

From equation (24), let $T_x(\varepsilon) = V^T W V$. The same derivation will follow for the $y$ direction. The result of using the two directions will be $T(\varepsilon) = T_x(\varepsilon) + T_y(\varepsilon)$ and equation (24) can be rewritten as

$$\sum_{\forall(x,y)} (f(x+1,y) - f(x,y))^2 = f^T T(\varepsilon) f. \quad (25)$$

Thus, the image smoothness term will be

$$J(\hat{f}) = \lambda \hat{f}^T T_{\hat{f}}(\varepsilon) \hat{f} \quad (26)$$

where $\lambda$ is the image regularization parameter. On the other hand, the PSF characterization term in (He et al., 2008; 2009) uses a reinforcement blur estimation (RBE) framework. This assumes that real-life blurs satisfy a certain degree of parametric structure. Mathematically, this can be modelled by

$$J_{\hat{h}\_RBE} = \left(\hat{h} - t\right)^T \left(\hat{h} - t\right) \quad (27)$$

where $t$ is the best-fit parametric PSF selected from a training set. This is highly dependent on the current estimate as well as the contents of the training set. As a result, failure of reinforced learning is possible when the estimate changes as the iteration progresses. In some cases, learning can also be erroneous when the selected model does not match the actual PSF. Furthermore, the learning set must be exhaustive to ensure an accurate model selection. To overcome these problems, RPSF can be used in its place. Thus,

$$J(\hat{h}) = \alpha \hat{h}^T T_{\hat{h}}(\varepsilon) \hat{h} + \beta(\hat{h} - r)^T (\hat{h} - r) \quad (28)$$

where $\alpha$ and $\beta$ are the regularization parameters and $r$ is RPSF. The first term is the PSF smoothness term while the second is PSF learning term. The image and PSF smoothness terms have the same derivations. These are employed for the reason that the TV norm is known for edge preservation and robustness in the presence of noise. The use of RPSF will yield a rough idea on the blurring function using only the degraded image. As a result, the need for a training set is eliminated, the learning model is determined only once and it is independent from other estimated values.

The cost function that will be minimized is defined in equation 19 where $J_{\hat{f}}$ is in equation 26 and $J_{\hat{h}}$ is in equation 28. As a whole, this is not convex however, iterative projection into $\hat{f}$ and $\hat{h}$ will result in convex functions. Thus, we use the AM technique to solve the two unknowns. The first step is the partial differentiation of the cost function with respect to $\hat{f}$ where $\hat{h}$ is set as constant:

$$\frac{\partial J(\hat{f},\hat{h})}{\partial \hat{f}} = \left(\hat{H}^T\hat{H} + \lambda T_{\hat{f}}(\varepsilon)\right)\hat{f} - \hat{H}^T g. \tag{29}$$

Equating this with zero will yield $\hat{f}$ at $(n+1)$-th iteration:

$$\hat{f}_{n+1} = \left(\hat{H}_n^T\hat{H}_n + \lambda T_{\hat{f}_n}(\varepsilon)\right)^{-1}\hat{H}_n^T g. \tag{30}$$

Reversing the roles will yield:

$$\frac{\partial J(\hat{f},\hat{h})}{\partial \hat{h}} = \left(\hat{F}^T\hat{F} + \alpha T_{\hat{h}}(\varepsilon) + \beta I\right)\hat{h} - \left(\hat{F}^T g + \beta r\right) \tag{31}$$

where $I$ is an identity matrix. Thus,

$$\hat{h}_{n+1} = \left(\hat{F}_{n+1}^T\hat{F}_{n+1} + \alpha T_{\hat{h}_n}(\varepsilon) + \beta I\right)^{-1}\left(\hat{F}_{n+1}^T g + \beta r\right). \tag{32}$$

To summarize, the AM technique involves solving equations 30 and 32 alternately until convergence or when the desired number of iterations is reached.

### 4.2 Regularization parameters

The computations of $\hat{f}$ and $\hat{h}$ involve $\lambda$, $\alpha$, and $\beta$, which are collectively called as regularization parameters. These are positive values that measure the trade off between a good fit and the regularity of the solutions. These can be accurately determined using many methods. However, these are usually computationally expensive and time consuming. To make the selection process less complicated, we will follow the concept used in (Sroubek & Flusser, 2003; You & Kaveh, 1996). The idea is based on the fact that the partial derivatives of the cost function are zero assuming that we are given the correct values of $f$ and $h$. Thus equations 29 and 31 will become:

$$H^T Hf - H^T g + \lambda T_f(\varepsilon) f = 0 \tag{33}$$

and

$$F^T Fh - F^T g + \alpha T_h(\varepsilon) h + \beta(h - r) = 0, \tag{34}$$

respectively. The resulting equations are overdetermined system of linear equations (OSLE). In general, an OSLE with $E$ linear equations and $N$ unknowns can be expressed as:

$$c = A\chi \tag{35}$$

where $c$ is a vector of given values with $c \in \Re^{E\times 1}$ , $A$ is a matrix of coefficients with $A \in \Re^{E\times N}$, and $\chi$ is a vector of unknown variables with $\chi \in \Re^{N\times 1}$. Using minimum sum of squared error approximation (Cadzow, 2002), the solution can be determined by:

$$\chi = (A^T A)^{-1} A^T c. \tag{36}$$

Based on equation 33, $\lambda$ can then be computed by:

$$\lambda = (A_f^T A_f)^{-1} A_f^T c_f \tag{37}$$

where $A_f = -T_f(\varepsilon) f$ and $c_f = H^T H f - H^T g$. Similarly, $\alpha$ and $\beta$ can be solved from equation 34:

$$[\alpha \ \beta]^T = (A_h^T A_h)^{-1} A_h^T c_h \tag{38}$$

where $A_h = -[T_h(\varepsilon) h \ (h - r)]$ and $c_h = F^T F h - F^T g$.

In practical applications, the correct values of $f$ and $h$ are unknown. The estimated values, $\hat{f}$ and $\hat{h}$, may be utilized in lieu of the unknown correct values then equations 37 and 38 can be used to compute approximate values of the regularization parameters. In this case, parameter tuning is done iteratively with a stopping criterion that may be based on the maximum PSNR; a fixed iteration count; or the minimum cost function, among others.

### 4.3 Experimental results

#### 4.3.1 Experiment descriptions

The experiment in this section will investigate the effects of integrating the RPSF during the deconvolution of synthetically blurred images. An unblurred image shown in Fig. 5(c) has a size of 60 × 60 pixels. This is synthetically blurred with a PSF defined by equation 10 with the following parameters: $L \in \{3, 5, 7\}$ and $\theta \in \{0°, 45°, 90°, 135°\}$. The unblurred image and PSF are known thus, the results can be easily monitored and verified. In this way, a reference can be established for cases when both the unblurred image and PSF are unknown.

The regularization parameters are computed for 50 iterations. The selection is based on the maximum peak signal-to-noise ratio (PSNR) in dB, which can be computed as follows:

$$\text{PSNR}_{\text{dB}} = 10 \log_{10} \frac{\left(2^b - 1\right)^2}{\text{MSE}} \tag{39}$$

where MSE is defined by

$$\text{MSE} = \frac{1}{XY} \sum_{\forall(x,y)} \left(f(x,y) - \hat{f}(x,y)\right)^2 \tag{40}$$

and $b$ is the number of bits used to represent a pixel value. The selected parameters are shown in Table 4. Using these values, $\hat{f}$ and $\hat{h}$ are computed for 20 iterations. The initial estimated image is equated to the given degraded image while the PSF is composed of positive real random numbers.

The quality of the estimated image is quantitatively evaluated by computing its PSNR. On the other hand, the estimated PSF is compared with the actual PSF by mean squared error

| Motion Direction | Regularization Parameters | | |
|---|---|---|---|
| | $\lambda$ | $\alpha$ | $\beta$ |
| $(s = 3)$ | | | |
| 0° | 0.47 | $3.35 \times 10^3$ | $9.06 \times 10^4$ |
| 45° | 1.21 | $2.59 \times 10^4$ | $7.26 \times 10^5$ |
| 90° | 1.13 | $1.09 \times 10^4$ | $2.13 \times 10^5$ |
| 135° | 1.05 | $1.85 \times 10^4$ | $4.34 \times 10^5$ |
| $(s = 5)$ | | | |
| 0° | 0.79 | $1.06 \times 10^4$ | $2.45 \times 10^5$ |
| 45° | 1.83 | $3.25 \times 10^3$ | $1.64 \times 10^6$ |
| 90° | 1.16 | $1.69 \times 10^4$ | $3.68 \times 10^5$ |
| 135° | 2.03 | $2.62 \times 10^3$ | $1.77 \times 10^6$ |
| $(s = 7)$ | | | |
| 0° | 1.55 | $1.61 \times 10^4$ | $6.56 \times 10^5$ |
| 45° | 1.68 | $3.63 \times 10^3$ | $1.79 \times 10^6$ |
| 90° | 2.44 | $1.91 \times 10^3$ | $3.58 \times 10^6$ |
| 135° | 1.84 | $1.84 \times 10^3$ | $3.08 \times 10^6$ |

Table 4. Selected regularization parameters.

(MSE). To demonstrate the effectiveness of using the cost function in equation 26, three techniques are compared. These have cost functions wherein the image term uses TV while the PSF term is varied. The first technique uses TV on PSF as proposed in (Chan & Wong, 1998). The second uses reinforced blur estimation (RBE) as in (He et al., 2009) with a training set containing the same number of parameters as previously mentioned. The third, maxima-based deconvolution (MXB), uses the cost function in equation 28.

#### 4.3.2 Data and results

The PSNRs of the estimated images with various motion directions and PSF sizes are shown in Table 5. It can be observed that MXB values are mostly higher in contrast with the other methods. Furthermore, the horizontal and vertical directions tend to have higher PSNRs than the diagonal motions. This is attributed by the fact that the gradients used in the TV prior are also in the same directions. The PSF estimation errors for the three methods can be compared in Table 6. The lower values demonstrate the method's effectiveness in estimating the PSF in different conditions. Notice that when the error is low in Table 6, a high PSNR in Table 5 can be observed. A sample image reconstructed by MXB is shown in Fig. 5. It shows the method's capability in recovering the details of the image.

This section shows the effects of integrating the RPSF during image deconvolution. The PSF smoothness and learning terms resulted to a lesser PSF estimation error with a larger PSNR value. Furthermore, we can see the importance of monitoring the image quality. This is very useful in selecting the regularization parameters as well as the estimated image. In the next section, we consider the case wherein the unblurred image is unknown making it impossible for the computation of the PSNR.

| Motion Direction | PSNR (dB) | | |
|---|---|---|---|
| | TV | RBE | MXB |
| $(s = 3)$ | | | |
| 0° | 28.82 | 28.22 | **31.63** |
| 45° | 25.32 | 24.85 | **26.65** |
| 90° | 28.76 | 28.64 | **29.51** |
| 135° | 25.47 | 24.75 | **26.76** |
| $(s = 5)$ | | | |
| 0° | 22.99 | 19.22 | **26.43** |
| 45° | 22.29 | 21.45 | **23.65** |
| 90° | 21.96 | 20.64 | **25.06** |
| 135° | 22.57 | 23.66 | **23.68** |
| $(s = 7)$ | | | |
| 0° | 19.30 | 17.19 | **23.97** |
| 45° | 20.74 | 20.47 | **21.81** |
| 90° | 21.56 | **23.34** | 23.32 |
| 135° | 19.60 | 18.15 | **21.83** |

Table 5. Comparison of the image PSNR (dB)for different methods.

| Motion Direction | Method | | |
|---|---|---|---|
| | TV | RBE | MXB |
| $(s = 3)$ | | | |
| 0° | $1.8 \times 10^{-2}$ | $2.0 \times 10^{-2}$ | $\mathbf{9.9 \times 10^{-4}}$ |
| 45° | $7.0 \times 10^{-2}$ | $4.1 \times 10^{-2}$ | $\mathbf{7.3 \times 10^{-3}}$ |
| 90° | $1.9 \times 10^{-2}$ | $1.0 \times 10^{-2}$ | $\mathbf{4.2 \times 10^{-3}}$ |
| 135° | $7.1 \times 10^{-2}$ | $4.1 \times 10^{-2}$ | $\mathbf{4.2 \times 10^{-3}}$ |
| $(s = 5)$ | | | |
| 0° | $5.9 \times 10^{-3}$ | $8.4 \times 10^{-3}$ | $\mathbf{4.4 \times 10^{-4}}$ |
| 45° | $5.4 \times 10^{-3}$ | $7.2 \times 10^{-3}$ | $\mathbf{2.2 \times 10^{-4}}$ |
| 90° | $1.1 \times 10^{-2}$ | $1.0 \times 10^{-2}$ | $\mathbf{9.2 \times 10^{-4}}$ |
| 135° | $7.6 \times 10^{-3}$ | $\mathbf{1.9 \times 10^{-4}}$ | $2.0 \times 10^{-4}$ |
| $(s = 7)$ | | | |
| 0° | $4.8 \times 10^{-3}$ | $4.2 \times 10^{-3}$ | $\mathbf{1.5 \times 10^{-4}}$ |
| 45° | $2.1 \times 10^{-3}$ | $3.1 \times 10^{-3}$ | $\mathbf{1.3 \times 10^{-4}}$ |
| 90° | $3.9 \times 10^{-3}$ | $\mathbf{3.9 \times 10^{-5}}$ | $\mathbf{3.9 \times 10^{-5}}$ |
| 135° | $3.3 \times 10^{-3}$ | $4.4 \times 10^{-3}$ | $\mathbf{2.4 \times 10^{-5}}$ |

Table 6. Comparison of the PSF estimation error.

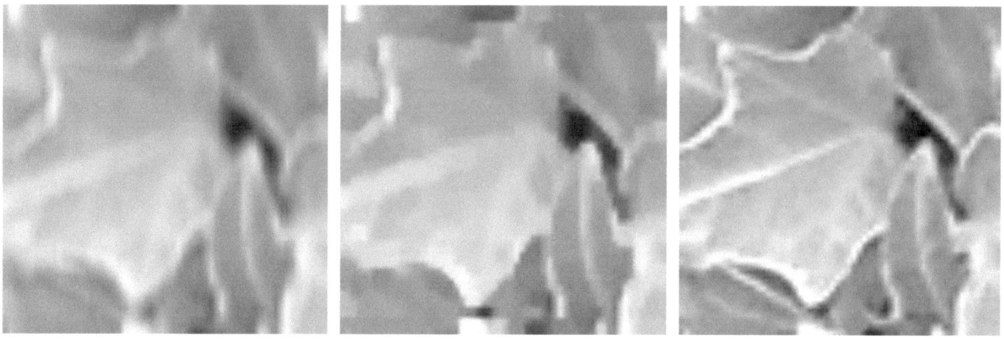

(a) degraded (b) estimated (c) unblurred

Fig. 5. An image degraded with $L = 5$ and $\theta = 90°$.

## 5. Quality assessment

As mentioned in the previous section, image reconstruction is highly ill-posed. This results to the solution being solved through an iterative method wherein several images and PSFs will be produced. In most cases, the image quality is given more priority. Comparison between them can be easily achieved if the unblurred image is known or given. However, this is not the case in practical applications. It is, therefore, crucial to establish a method of evaluating an image that is independent of its unblurred version.

The most common approach of evaluating an image is through a measure based on the edges. An image is composed of different types of edges whose number is affected by the type of blur that is present. Haar Wavelet Transforms (HWT) can discriminate these edges and can be used for blur extent measurement as proposed in (Tong et al., 2004). Another technique is to employ edge active measure on $8 \times 8$ blocks of the wavelet coefficients as proposed in (Xin et al., 2003). A downside to these is that it requires a transformation with at least three levels of decompositions. Thus, it greatly increases the computational cost when considering an iterative reconstruction method. A technique that does not require a transform has been proposed in (Marziliano et al., 2002; 2004) where the blur metric is computed using the edge points and their local extrema. The metric's accuracy is dependent on the edges that can be detected. However, when blur increases edge points will decrease and in turn result to inaccurate values.

In (Li et al., 2005) selection of the best deblurred image with Wiener filter is achieved by kurtosis minimization. It has been shown that the results are similar to those of PSNR maximization. However, it can be empirically shown that this is not consistent in natural images (Chong & Tanaka, 2011c). A different objective criterion using variance and kurtosis will be discussed next.

### 5.1 Maxima and image quality

The variance and kurtosis will be considered for the characterization of images. The variance can be computed by

$$v = \frac{1}{N} \sum_{\forall(x,y)} \left(f(x,y) - \bar{f}\right)^2 \tag{41}$$

| Name | Conditions |
|---|---|
| Cond A | $v_{p,z\neq 4} < v_{p,z=4}$ |
| Cond B | $k_{m,z\neq 4} < k_{m,z=4}$ |
| Cond C | $v_{p,z} < v_{p,z+1}$ |
| Cond D | $k_{m,z} < k_{m,z+1}$ |

Table 7. Conditions for experiment 1.

where $\bar{f}$ is the mean of the image and $N$ represents the total number of pixels. On the other hand, kurtosis can be represented by

$$k = \frac{\frac{1}{N}\sum_{\forall(x,y)}\left(f(x,y)-\bar{f}\right)^4}{v^2} - 3. \tag{42}$$

These quantities can be used to describe the distribution of the values for a given image. To demonstrate this, the unblurred image shown in Fig. 6 is synthetically blurred with OOF. The PSF sizes are $\{7\times 7, 5\times 5, 3\times 3\}$ and these are indexed by an integer number where the smallest index represents the largest size. Thus, a large index number indicates a smaller PSF size and an image with better quality. For each image, the maxima values are scanned from left to right and from top to bottom. The variance and kurtosis are computed using the pixel and maxima values. This means that every degraded image will have four quantities. Fig. 7 shows that the variance of the pixel values monotonically increases as the size becomes smaller or as the index becomes larger. This trend is also the same for the kurtosis of the maxima values. Although kurtosis of the pixel values decreased, this trend is not monotonic. Therefore, the decrease in blur can be described by the increase of pixel variance ($v_{\text{p}}$) and maxima kurtosis ($k_{\text{m}}$). The subscripts are used to indicate the values that are used i.e., p for pixel values and m for maxima values. These characteristics are empirically proven to be consistent in many images as will be shown by the data. Due to this, the trends of $v_{\text{p}}$ and $k_{\text{m}}$ can be used for the selection of the regularization parameters and the deblurred image. For a method with $n$ iterations, $v_{\text{p}}$ and $k_{\text{m}}$ will be composed of a set with $n$ values. Each set is first scaled such that the minimum value is zero and the maximum is one. The average ($q$) for each iteration is then computed as

$$q = \frac{v_{\text{p}} + k_{\text{m}}}{2}. \tag{43}$$

Thus, the criterion for selection is the maximum $q$ among the $n$ values.

### 5.2 Experimental results

#### 5.2.1 Experiment descriptions

There are three experiments that are being considered here. The first will investigate the effect of the different PSF sizes to the distribution of the pixel and maxima values. The latter are extracted by scanning the green channel from left to right and from top to bottom. The variances and kurtoses are compared for different conditions (Cond) as shown in Table 7. The subscript $z \in \{1, 2, ..., 4\}$ is the index of the PSF support size where $z = 4$ indicates an unblurred image. The support sizes are $\{7\times 7, 5\times 5, 3\times 3\}$. There are 300 unblurred images with natural scenes that may be $640\times 480$ or $480\times 640$ pixels in size. Synthetic blurs include horizontal motion (HM), vertical motion (VM), and OOF.

Fig. 6. An unblurred image.

The second experiment is the evaluation of the parameter selection and the resulting reconstructed images. For practical purposes, the image size is $60 \times 60$ and degradations are the same with the previous experiment but the support sizes are $\{3 \times 3, 5 \times 5\}$. The regularization parameters are computed for 100 iterations using the PSF sizes $\{3 \times 3, 5 \times 5, 7 \times 7\}$. RGB images are used so that subtle changes in the images can be seen easily. As a result, the modified cost function in (Chong & Tanaka, 2010b) is used. The final PSF size and parameters are selected using the maximum value of $q$. These values are then used for the reconstruction of the degraded image computed for 50 iterations. Although this experiment deals with RGB, the images are evaluated using only the green channel.

The third experiment involves the selection of the motion blur parameters, $L$ and $\theta$, through image deconvolution with Wiener filter. We follow the procedure in (Li et al., 2005) where deconvolution is computed over a set of parameters. In this experiment, the values are $L = \{3, 5, 7, 9, 11, 13, 15\}$ and $\theta = \{0°, 45°, 90°, 135°\}$. The selection is based on a criterion specifically, maximum PSNR, minimum $k_p$, and maximum $q$.

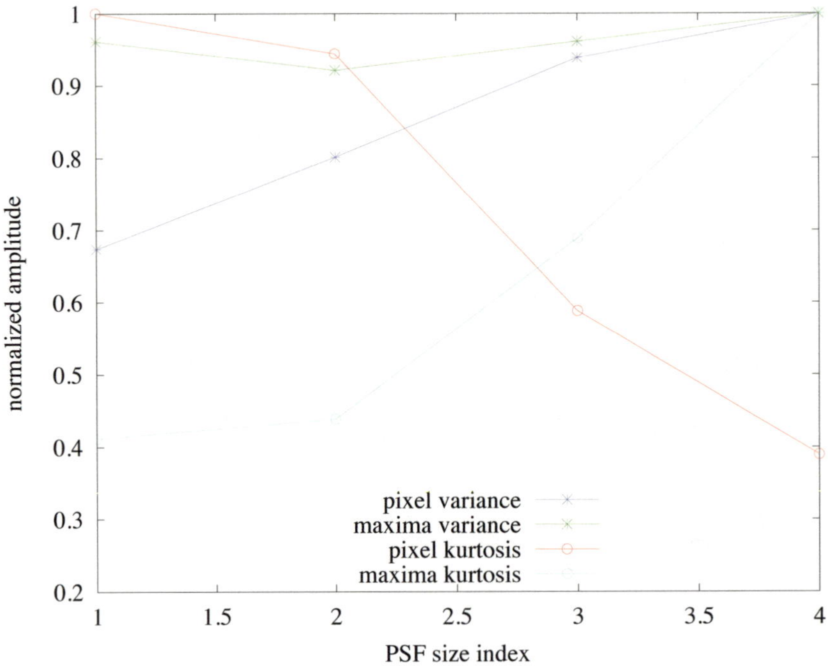


Fig. 7. Variances and kurtoses for OOF degraded versions of Fig. 6.

| Setting | Number of Images | Accuracy (%) | | | Total |
|---|---|---|---|---|---|
| | | HM | VM | OOF | |
| Cond A | 900 | 100.0 | 100.0 | 100.0 | 100.0 |
| Cond B | 900 | 100.0 | 100.0 | 100.0 | 100.0 |
| Cond C | 300s | 100.0 | 100.0 | 100.0 | 100.0 |
| Cond D | 300s | 98.7 | 98.3 | 95.3 | 97.4 |

Table 8. Condition consistency with $v_p$ and $k_m$ (%).

#### 5.2.2 Data and results

Table 8 shows the consistency of specific conditions using image pixels and maxima values. The consistency here refers to the trueness of a condition when tested to a number of images. The letter s indicates sets where each set consists of four images with increasing PSF size. Cond A shows that all $v_p$ of the degraded images are lower than the unblurred image. This means that a high $v_p$ is expected in the absence of blur. The same is observable for $k_m$ as shown by the data for Cond B. The monotonicity of the increase in $v_p$ is evaluated by Cond C. The percentage indicates that this is true for all the tested images. This shows that the $v_p$ value consistently increases as the PSF size decreases. On the other hand, monotonicity of $k_m$ is not true for all the tested images. However, these only affect a few images as manifested by the high consistency values in row Cond D. With reference to the conditions in Table 7, it can be observed that these indicate that both $v_p$ and $k_p$ will increase as blur decreases. Since their behaviour are similar, integration will be easier in order to produce a single quantity that can reflect an image's quality.

| PSF | maximum $q$ | | | Regularization Parameters | | |
|---|---|---|---|---|---|---|
| Type | $3 \times 3$ | $5 \times 5$ | $7 \times 7$ | $\lambda$ | $\alpha$ | $\beta$ |
| $(s = 3)$ | | | | | | |
| HM | 0.56 | 0.69 | **0.84** | 0.60 | $3.68 \times 10^5$ | $5.17 \times 10^6$ |
| VM | **0.87** | 0.74 | 0.64 | 0.22 | $3.09 \times 10^2$ | $4.51 \times 10^5$ |
| OOF | **0.94** | 0.89 | 0.75 | 0.51 | $2.46 \times 10^4$ | $1.32 \times 10^6$ |
| $(s = 5)$ | | | | | | |
| HM | 0.72 | **0.73** | 0.72 | 0.50 | $9.40 \times 10^4$ | $3.42 \times 10^6$ |
| VM | **0.89** | 0.73 | 0.68 | 0.13 | $4.51 \times 10^2$ | $2.33 \times 10^5$ |
| OOF | **0.72** | 0.70 | 0.66 | 0.41 | $2.26 \times 10^4$ | $7.38 \times 10^5$ |

Table 9. Selection of the PSF size and regularization parameters using maximum $q$.

For the second experiment, the PSF size and regularization parameters are chosen by the maximum value of $q$. This is shown in Table 9 for each PSF size. The emphasized number is the maximum considering a certain degraded image. The underlined number indicates correct identification of the PSF size. Based on the emphasized values, the resulting regularization parameters are also shown in Table 9. It can be observed that when $s = 3$, the correct size is selected for those blurred with VM and OOF. For HM, the selected size is larger than the actual. In contrast, this reverses when $s = 5$. Only HM is correct while VM and OOF have smaller sizes than the actual. The parameters are employed during reconstruction and the image quality measures are computed and shown in Table 10. The PSNR and $q$ values are compared when one of these is the maximum. The rows with emphasized values are those with correct PSF sizes. It can be seen that when the size is incorrect the PSNRs are approximately the same. These are consistent despite the fact that when $s = 3$ the selected size is larger and when $s = 5$ the size is smaller. The same can be observed with the values of $q$ except for VM when $s = 5$. On the other hand, when the size is correct both values (PSNR and $q$) are different. If we consider maximum PSNR then $q$ is smaller and vice versa. To illustrate the difference in values, the corresponding images, when $s = 3$, are shown in Fig. 8. It can be observed, from the first row in Fig. 8, that reconstruction with an incorrect PSF size will yield images with a higher contrast. The second and third rows used correct PSF sizes. The reconstructed images show more details than the degraded versions. The difference is with the perceptible focus of the image. When PSNR is maximum the image appears smoother. However, when $q$ is maximum the image appears sharper. The same observations are true even if the blur types are different. Thus, a $q$ with higher value indicates a sharper image and low indicates a smoother image. This is due to the fact that the statistical distributions of the pixels and maxima are taken into consideration.

The data in Table 11 show the selected parameters using different criteria. It can be observed that only the angle, $\theta = 0°$, are correctly identified by the maximum PSNR criterion. In contrast, $\theta = 90°$ and $L = 3$ are selected by minimum $k_p$. Finally, for maximum $q$ all parameters are correct for small PSFs while only $\theta$ are correct for larger PSFs.

This section shows the effects of blur on the pixel variance and maxima kurtosis. The values are highest when the image is unblurred and these decrease as the PSF size increases. A new criterion for comparing images is also discussed. This does not require the unblurred image, which makes it useful for the reconstruction of images. By exploiting the pixel variance and maxima kurtosis, perceptible focus can be quantized. Higher values have sharper images while lower ones have smoother images.

(a) degraded by HM (b) PSNR=18.58, $q = 0.92$ (c) PSNR=18.56, $q = 0.93$

(d) degraded by VM (e) PSNR=22.95, $q = 0.53$ (f) PSNR=20.55, $q = 0.84$

(g) degraded by OOF (h) PSNR=27.54, $q = 0.17$ (i) PSNR=22.88, $q = 1.00$

Fig. 8. Degraded images and their reconstructed versions based on Table 10 when $s = 3$.

| PSF Type | maximum PSNR | | maximum $q$ | |
|---|---|---|---|---|
| | PSNR | $q$ | PSNR | $q$ |
| $(s = 3)$ | | | | |
| HM | 18.58 | 0.92 | 18.56 | 0.93 |
| VM | **22.95** | **0.53** | **20.55** | **0.84** |
| OOF | **27.54** | **0.17** | **22.88** | **1.00** |
| $(s = 5)$ | | | | |
| HM | **20.05** | **0.64** | **19.53** | **0.86** |
| VM | 18.26 | 0.54 | 17.59 | 0.80 |
| OOF | 21.87 | 0.99 | 21.87 | 1.00 |

Table 10. Comparison between PSNR and $q$ (dB).

| Type of Motion | Criterion | | |
|---|---|---|---|
| | $\text{PSNR}_{\text{max}}$ | $k_{\text{p\_min}}$ | $q_{\text{max}}$ |
| $L = 3$ $\theta = 0°$ | $L = 15$ $\theta = \mathbf{0}°$ | $L = 3$ $\theta = 90°$ | $L = \mathbf{3}$ $\theta = \mathbf{0}°$ |
| $L = 3$ $\theta = 90°$ | $L = 15$ $\theta = 0°$ | $L = \mathbf{3}$ $\theta = \mathbf{90}°$ | $L = \mathbf{3}$ $\theta = \mathbf{90}°$ |
| $L = 5$ $\theta = 0°$ | $L = 15$ $\theta = \mathbf{0}°$ | $L = 15$ $\theta = 135°$ | $L = 3$ $\theta = \mathbf{0}°$ |
| $L = 5$ $\theta = 90°$ | $L = 15$ $\theta = 0°$ | $L = 3$ $\theta = \mathbf{90}°$ | $L = 3$ $\theta = \mathbf{90}°$ |

Table 11. Motion parameter selection with a Wiener filter.

## 6. Summary

This chapter explores the different aspects of image deconvolution and the uses of extrema. For an efficient usage of resources, the whole deconvolution process is divided into several tasks. This begins with the detection and identification of blurs followed by the determination of RPSF. The resulting quantity is integrated into the cost function that is used to estimate the unblurred image. Since the method is iterative, several images will result and these must be compared to determine the best one.

Section 1 introduces image deconvolution and its importance in different fields of applications. Some variations of its mathematical model are also mentioned as a backgrounder. The next section discusses image extrema and its exploitation for blur detection and identification. The concept is based on how blur changes the extrema locations and distributions. A histogram is first created and from which, specific features are computed. By using a classifier, the presence of the blur can be detected. Aside from this, it is also possible to identify its type. This has been tested to have high accuracy for Gaussian, motion and OOF blurs.

Degraded images must be processed further in order for them to yield more information. An initial step is to extract some details regarding its blurring function. This is accomplished by exploiting the maxima and computing for the RPSF as shown in section 3. This is especially applicable for motion blurs because the maxima locations also align with the motion direction. By employing the Hough transform, a single direction is detected and the resulting RPSF will be more similar to the actual PSF. Testing the accuracy of detecting the direction involved various natural images that are blurred synthetically with different PSF sizes. High values indicate the efficacy of the method. An advantage of this is that it can reveal the nature of the embedded PSF using only the degraded image. It does not require a training set to determine the direction of motion.

RPSF can also be used during the estimation of the unblurred image. In section 4 the classical cost function for deconvolution is reformulated. It contains the terms for fidelity, image smoothness , and PSF characterization, which consists of the PSF smoothness and learning terms. The smoothness terms are included due to the fact that images as well as piecewise PSFs have edges. The PSF learning term integrates the RPSF during deconvolution. In this way, RPSF provides a way of reinforcement without the need for a training set. During the estimation process, RPSF also eliminates the dependence of learning on the current computed PSF. The cost function requires three regularization parameters that can be solved using the OSLEs. All equations have been expressed in the vector-matrix form to facilitate easier derivations. The resulting data show consistently high PSNRs for different motion directions and PSF sizes. This means that the image quality are improved. Furthermore, the MSEs of the PSFs are also very low, which indicates a high accuracy in estimating the PSF.

Lastly, a method to compare images is discussed in section 5. Iterative methods for deconvolution will naturally result in several estimated images and PSFs. When image quality is given more importance, an assessment technique is needed to choose the best one. Classical methods require the unblurred version however, this is not applicable in practical applications. Thus, the pixel variance and maxima kurtosis have been exploited to overcome this problem. It has been shown that both quantities are low when the blur is high and these monotonically increase as the blur decreases. Their combination resulted to a single value that can be used to compare several images. Experimental results have shown that this is high when an image is sharp. In contrast, when the value is low the image is smooth.

The extrema considered in this chapter are extracted by horizontal and vertical scanning. The effects of using other scanning directions are still unknown. Additionally, the degraded images are all invariantly blurred. This means that the PSF is assumed to be uniform all throughout the image. In practical applications, the variant case is also possible. The results for this case remain an open problem at this time. Finally, the image comparison technique is capable of differentiating images based on the sharpness of the details without the unblurred image. However, it cannot indicate the presence of distortions such as ringing and color artefacts. Quantizing these is not only important in image deconvolution but also in other applications of image processing.

## 7. References


Aizenberg, I., Butakoff, C., Karnaukhov, V., Merzlyakov, N. & Milukova, O. (2002). Type of blur and blur parameters identification using neural network and its application to image restoration, *Proceedings of the International Conference on Artificial Neural Networks (ICANN2002)*, Madrid, Spain, pp. 1231–1236.

Aizenberg, I., Butakoff, C., Karnaukhov, V., Merzlyakov, N. & Milukova, O. (n.d.). Blurred image restoration using the type of blur and blur parameters identification on the neural network, *Proceedings of the SPIE*, Vol. 4667.

Aizenberg, I., Paliy, D., Moraga, C. & Astola, J. (2006). Blur identification using neural network for image restoration, *Proceedings of the International Conference 9th Fuzzy Days*, Dortmund, Germany, pp. 441–455.

Aizenberg, I., Paliy, D. V., Zurada, J. M. & Astola, J. T. (2008). Blur identification by multilayer neural network based on multivalued neurons, *IEEE Trans. on Neural Networks* 19(5): 883–898.

Banham, M. R. & Katsaggelos, A. K. (1997). Digital image restoration, *IEEE Signal Processing Magazine* 14(2): 24–41.

Cadzow, J. A. (2002). Minimum $\ell_1$, $\ell_2$, and $\ell_\infty$ norm approximate solutions to an overdetermined system of linear equations, *Digital Signal Processing* 12(4): 524–560.

Cappelli, R., Lumini, A., Maio, D. & Maltoni, D. (2007). Fingerprint image reconstruction from standard templates, *IEEE Transactions on Pattern Analysis and Machine Intelligence* 29(9): 1489–11503.

Chan, T. F., Golub, G. H. & Mulet, P. (1999). A nonlinear primal-dual method for total variation-based image restoration, *SIAM Journal on Scientific Computing* 20(6): 1964–1977.

Chan, T. F. & Wong, C. K. (1998). Total variation blind deconvolution, *IEEE Transactions on Image Processing* 7(3): 370–375.

Choksi, R. & van Gennip, Y. (2010). Deblurring of one dimensional bar codes via total variation energy minimisation, *SIAM J. on Imaging Sciences* 3-4: 735–764.

Chong, R. M. & Tanaka, T. (2008). Image extrema analysis and blur detection with identification, *Proceedings of the International Conference on Signal Image Technology and Internet Based System (SITIS2008)*, Vol. 1, Bali, Indonesia, pp. 320–326.

Chong, R. M. & Tanaka, T. (2009). Detection and classification of invariant blurs, *IEICE Transactions on Fundamentals* E92-A(12): 3313–3320.

Chong, R. M. & Tanaka, T. (2010a). Blur identification based on maxima locations for color image restoration, *Proceedings of the International Conference on Multimedia and Ubiquitous Engineering (MUE2010)*, Cebu, Philippines.

Chong, R. M. & Tanaka, T. (2010b). Motion blur identification using maxima locations for blind color image restoration, *Journal of Convergence* 1(1): 49–56.

Chong, R. M. & Tanaka, T. (2011a). Detection of motion blur direction based on maxima locations for blind deconvolution, *Proceedings of the IS&T/SPIE Electronic Imaging*. to be published.

Chong, R. M. & Tanaka, T. (2011b). Maxima exploitation for reference blurring function in motion deconvolution, *IEICE Transactions on Fundamentals* E94-A(3): 921–928.

Chong, R. M. & Tanaka, T. (2011c). An objective criterion for the comparison of reconstructed images, *Proceedings of the International Conference on Information, Communications and Signal Processing (ICICS2011)*, Singapore. to be published.

Chu, C. H., Yang, D. N. & Chen, M. S. (2010). Single image deblurring for a real-time face recognition system, *Proceedings of the 36th Annual Conference on IEEE Industrial Electronics Society (IECON 2010)*, Glendale, AZ, pp. 1185–1192.

Chu, C. H., Yang, D. N., Pan, Y. L. & Chen, M. S. (2010). Stabilization and extraction of 2D barcodes for camera phones, *Multimedia Systems* pp. 1–21.

Chung, Y. C., Wang, J. M., Bailey, R. R., Chen, S. W. & Chang, S. L. (2004). A non-parametric blur measure based on edge analysis for image processing applications, *Proceedings of the IEEE International Conference on Cybernetics and Intelligent Systems (CIS2004)*, Vol. 1, Singapore, pp. 356–360.

Cover, T. M. & Hart, P. E. (1967). Nearest neighbor pattern classification, *IEEE Transactions on Information Theory* 13(1): 21–27.

Esedoglu, S. (2004). Blind deconvolution of bar code signals, *Inverse Problems* 20(1): 121–135.

Gonzales, R. C. & Woods, R. E. (2008). *Digital Image Processing*, third edn, Pearson Education, USA.

He, Y., Yap, K. H., Chen, L. & Chau, L. P. (2008). A novel hybrid model framework to blind color image deconvolution, *IEEE Transactions on Systems, Man, and Cybernetics–Part A: Systems and Humans* 38(4): 867–880.

He, Y., Yap, K. H., Chen, L. & Chau, L. P. (2009). A soft MAP framework for blind super-resolution image reconstruction, *Image and Vision Computing* 27(4): 364–373.

Kang, B. J. & Park, K. R. (2007). Real-time image restoration for iris recognition systems, *IEEE Transactions on Systems, Man, and Cybernetics-Part B: Cybernetics* 37(6): 1555–1566.

Lagendijk, R. L. & Biemond, J. (2005). Basic methods for image restoration and identification, *in* A. Bovik (ed.), *Handbook of Image & Video Processing*, second edn, Elsevier Academic Press, Orlando, FL, chapter 3.5, pp. 167–181.

Li, D., Mersereau, R. M. & Simske, S. (2005). Blur identification based on kurtosis minimization, *Proceedings of the IEEE International Conference on Image Processing (ICIP2005)*, Genoa, Italy, pp. I–905–8.

Marziliano, P., Dufaux, F., Winkler, S. & Ebrahimi, T. (2002). A no-reference perceptual blur metric, *Proceedings of the IEEE International Conference on Image Processing (ICIP2002)*, Vol. 3, Rochester, NY, pp. 57–60.

Marziliano, P., Dufaux, F., Winkler, S. & Ebrahimi, T. (2004). Perceptual blur and ringing metrics: application to JPEG2000, *Signal Processing: Image Communication* 19: 163–172.

Nishiyama, M., Hadid, A., Takeshima, H., Shotton, J., Kozakaya, T. & Yamaguchi, O. (2010). Facial deblur inference using subspace analysis for recognition of blurred faces, *IEEE Transactions on Pattern Analysis and Machine Intelligence* PP(99): 1–1.

Rooms, F., Pizurica, A. & Philips, W. (2002). Estimating image blur in the wavelet domain, *Proceedings of the IEEE International Conference on Acoustics, Speech, and Signal Processing (ICASSP2002)*, Vol. 4, Orlando, FL, pp. IV–4190.

Rudin, L. I., Osher, S. & Fatemi, E. (1992). Nonlinear total variation based noise removal algorithms, *Physica D* 60: 259–268.

Simoncelli, E. P. (2005). Statistical modeling of photographic images, *in* A. Bovik (ed.), *Handbook of Image & Video Processing*, second edn, Elsevier Academic Press, Orlando, FL, chapter 4.7, pp. 431–441.

Sroubek, F. & Flusser, J. (2003). Multichannel blind iterative image restoration, *IEEE Transactions on Image Processing* 12(9): 1094–1106.

Theodoridis, S. & Koutroumbas, K. (2006). *Pattern Recognition*, third edn, Elsevier Academic Press, USA.

Tong, H., Li, M., Zhang, H. & Zhang, C. (2004). Blur detection for digital images using wavelet transform, *Proceedings of the IEEE International Conference on Multimedia and Expo (ICME2004)*, Vol. 1, Taipei, Taiwan, pp. 17–20.

Xin, F., Qi, Z., Dequn, L. & Ling, Z. (2003). Face image restoration based on statistical prior and image blur measure, *Proceedings of the IEEE International Conference on Multimedia and Expo (ICME 2003)*, Vol. 3, pp. III–297–300.

Yahyanejad, S. & Strom, J. (2010). Removing motion blur from barcode images, *IEEE Computer Society Conference on Computer Vision and Pattern Recognition Workshops (CVPRW) 2010*, San Francisco, CA, pp. 41–46.

Yang, Y., Galatsanos, N. P. & Stark, H. (1994). Projection-based blind deconvolution, *J. Opt. Soc. Am. A* 11(9): 2401–2409.

You, Y. & Kaveh, M. (1996). A regularization approach to joint blur identification and image restoration, *IEEE Transactions on Image Processing* 5(3): 416–428.

# Part 2

## Applications

# 11

# Image Restoration for Long-Wavelength Imaging Systems

Min-Cheng Pan
*Department of Electronic Engineering, Tungnan University*
*New Taipei City*
*Taiwan*

## 1. Introduction

### 1.1 Overview

Basically, the quality of an image can be evaluated on its spatial and spatial-frequency resolutions, image interpolation and superresolution are perhaps the way to respectively produce high spatial and spatial-frequency resolutions of images especially for a single down-sampled image. For convenience, the term "hyper-resolution" used here represents the approach to enhancing both the spatial and the spatial-frequency resolutions of an image.

As known, the process of decimation or down-sampling is an effective way often used to reduce image sizes, thus, reducing the amount of information transmitted through the communication channels and the local storage requirements, while trying to preserve as much as possible the image quality. Conversely, the reverse procedure of this, referred to as interpolation or up-sampling, is useful in restoring the original high resolution image from its decimated version or for resizing or zooming a digital image. Decimation and interpolation are used for several purposes in many practical applications, such as progressive image transmission systems, multimedia applications, and so forth. A number of conventional interpolation techniques [Hou & Andrews, 1978; Jain, 1989; Keys, 1981] have been proposed to increase the spatial resolution of an image. Undoubtedly, these techniques degrade the quality of the magnified image.

Furthermore, images may be corrupted by degradation such as blurring distortion, noise, and blocking artifacts. These sources of degradation may arise during image capture or processing and have a direct bearing on visual quality. Various methods of restoration have been described in the literature; this diversity reveals the importance of the problem and its great difficulty. The purpose of image deconvolution or restoration is to recover degraded images by removing noise, highlighting image contrast, and preserving edge features of image.

Image superresolution was developed in 1950s to improve image quality and pilot research of this field is derived from the early work (Toraldo di Francia, 1952, 1955) where the term "superresolution" was used in the paper. Following that, clear definition, description and some of the obvious contribution to this field can be found in the work (Gerchberg, 1974; Hunt & Sementilli, 1992) in which their work, superresolution, was meant to seek to recover object information from above the spatial-frequency limit of diffraction. Originally, superresolution referred to a technique of one-frame-to-one-frame and its interest was in the spatial-frequency domain, neither for multi-frames-to-one-frame nor for interpolation. Since then, signal/image restoration/superresolution has been concerned for the spatial-frequency domain from one low-resolution frame to one high-resolution frame; basically, the distinct nature of those algorithms is iterative and nonlinear. A process of interpolation along with restoration/superresolution was used with one frame to enhance the spatial and spatial-frequency resolution of the frame (Pan, 2006). Else, the processing of multi-frame-to-one-frame has been quite concerned (Gillette et al., 1995; Ng et al., 2003; Segal et al., 2003), where a single high-resolution frame was reconstructed from multiple low-resolution frames.

### 1.2 Long-wavelength imaging system

Image restoration is able to be applied to the long-wavelength imaging systems, millimeter-wave (mm-wave) and near-infrared diffuse optical tomography (NIR DOT) imaging systems, shown as Fig. 1.1.. The advantage of long-wavelength imaging systems is to provide special information with no radioactive characteristics but the physical property of long wavelength with diffraction or scattering results in lower spatial-frequency resolution images, however, which can be improved using image restoration to enhance its applicability.

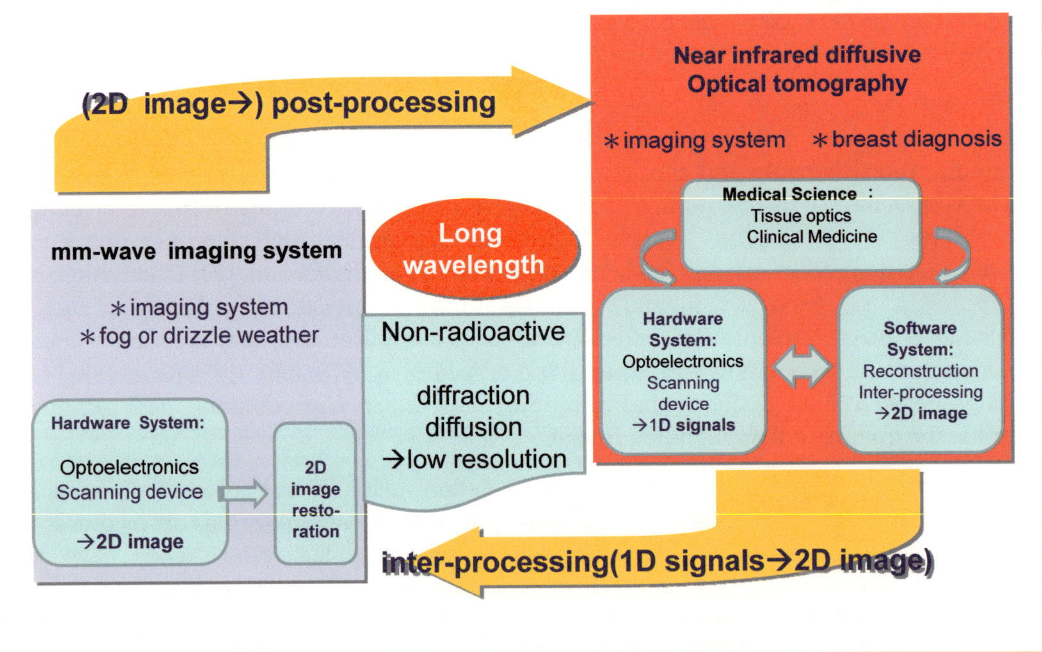


Fig. 1.1. Long Wavelength Imaging Systems v.s. Image Restoration

Images acquired from millimeter-wave imaging system for the fog or rain weather can be applied to navigation; its image resolution of 2D image can be improved with the technology of image restoration. NIR DOT imaging system provides computed tomography (CT) images of the human body or biological tissue/organ, used in medical diagnosis;

image processing techniques can improve the image quality of tomographic images between iterations of image reconstruction.

The technique using image restoration gradually becomes popular for an mm-wave or an NIR DOT imaging system; the difference of both imaging systems is that the former is post-processing and the latter is inter-processing.

### 1.3 Varied algorithms of Image restoration

There are two categories of restoration methods for improving image quality: (i) noniterative restoration such as the inverse filter, the Wiener filter (Wiener, 1942) and (ii) nonlinear iterative restoration/superresolution techniques such as Lorentzian restoration method (Lettington & Hong, 1995), maximum *a posteriori* (MAP) (Hunt & Sementilli, 1992), Richardson-Lucy (RL) deconvolution method (Richardson, 1972; Lucy, 1974), maximum entropy (Frieden, 1972), projection onto convex sets (Sezan & Tekalp, 1988), Gerchberg error energy reduction process (Gerchberg, 1974), and edge-preserving regularization (Teboul et al., 1998). In these methods, it is essential to use the adequate blurring function (a low-pass filter) to restore a degraded image.

### 1.4 Remark

In this section, we have described a number of terms such as spatial resolution, spatial-frequency resolution, interpolation, restoration, superresolution, hyper-resolution, inter-processing, and post-processing. In addition, advantages and drawbacks of long wavelength imaging systems were addressed and general description of restoration algorithms was made. It is worth emphasizing that long wavelength imaging systems have the same problem to be dealt with so image restoration can be used to improve such an imaging system.

Following this introduction, this chapter is organized as follows. Section 2 describes mathematical model of image formation; image restoration algorithms and further consideration on image restoration are explained in Sec. 3 and Sec. 4, respectively. Subsequently, Sec. 5 demonstrates related applications of image restoration. Finally, conclusion is drawn in Sec. 6.

## 2. Mathematical model of Image formation

In this section, imaging systems, image formation model, and forward problem and inverse problem are described in the following.

### 2.1 Imaging systems

#### 2.1.1 Common imaging system

Usually, the imaging process of a common imaging system is formed as follows. Suppose we have a scene of interest that is going to pass through a common imaging system where it has been corrupted by a linear blurring function and some additive noise. The blurring function $h$ accounts for the imperfectness of the imaging system including optical lens or the human factors in shooting the images. Some typical examples are a diffraction-limited or defocused lens and camera motion or shaking during the exposure. The noise arises from the inherent characteristics of the recording media, e.g., electronic noise and quantization noise when the images are digitized (or discretized).

In practice, the available blurred image not only follows exactly the above description but also is constrained with the film size, in most cases the images have to be truncated at the boundaries. Instead, what is available now becomes a windowed blurred image where a rectangular window is usually accounting for the film aperture shape and size. One inherent problem with this is that many ringing artifacts are introduced into the restored image when the linear or nonlinear filter is applied directly to the truncated blurred image.

### 2.1.2 Medical imaging system

Here, we use NIR DOT imaging system as an example. Basically, an NIR DOT imaging system is composed of a measuring instrument associated with image reconstruction scheme for the purpose of reconstructing the NIR optical-property tomographic images of phantoms/tissue of interest. The reconstructed images reveal the NIR optical properties of tissue computed by using measured radiances emitted from the circumference of the object. A schematic diagram of the NIR DOT measuring system in the frequency domain is shown in Fig. 2.1.

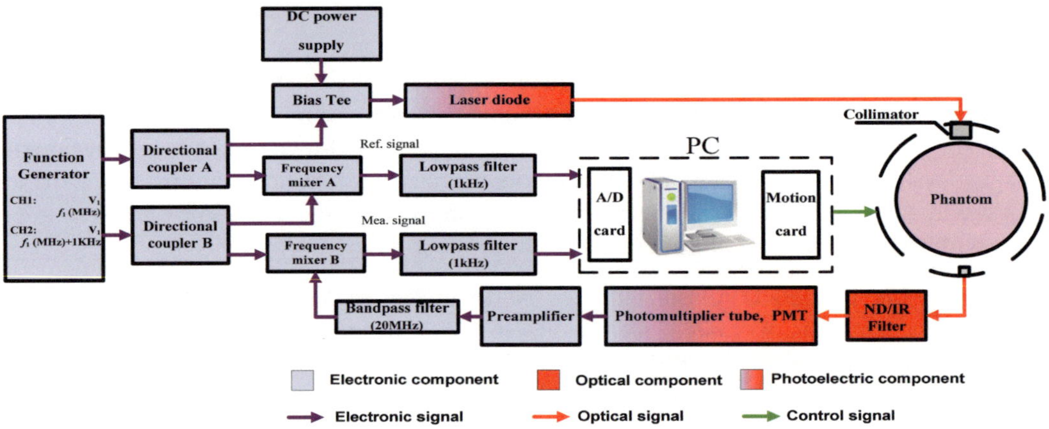


Fig. 2.1. Schematic diagram of NIR DOT measuring system in the frequency domain.

### 2.2 Image formation model

The image formation is modelled as

$$g = f \otimes h + n \tag{2.1}$$

where $f$ is the original scene, $h$ is the point-spread function (p.s.f.) of the imaging system, $\otimes$ is the convolution operator, $n$ is the noise, and $g$ is the corrupted image. Subsequently, the corrupted image is windowed due to the film size/support area and sampled for digitization.

Aliasing is arising, which causes different signals to become indistinguishable when sampled. It also refers to the distortion or artifact that results when the signal reconstructed from samples is different from the original continuous signal.

### 2.3 Forward problem & inverse problem

In a common imaging system, the image is formed as the above description in which finding an estimated original signal/image (f) is an inverse problem for a given corrupted signal/image (g) while the reverse process is a forward problem. In tomographic imaging, the reconstruction of optical-property images is done iteratively using a Newton method, requiring inversion of a highly ill-posed and ill-conditioned matrix. The goal of DOT is to estimate the distribution of the optical properties in tissue from non-invasive boundary measurements. For the purpose of determining the optical properties (the absorption coefficient and the diffusion/scattering coefficient) from measurement data, which is an inverse problem in DOT, a forward model is needed to describe the physical relation between the boundary measurements of tissue and the optical properties that characterize the tissue.

#### 2.3.1 Forward problem in DOT

In general, such a forward model of NIR DOT that gives the description of this physical relation is the diffusion equation,

$$\nabla \cdot \kappa(\mathbf{r})\nabla\Phi(\mathbf{r},\omega) - \left[\mu_a(\mathbf{r}) - \frac{i\omega}{c}\right]\Phi(\mathbf{r},\omega) = -S(\mathbf{r},\omega) \tag{2.2}$$

where $\Phi(\mathbf{r},\omega)$ is the photon density at position $\mathbf{r}$ and $\omega$ is the light modulation frequency. $S(\mathbf{r},\omega)$ is the isotropic source term and $c$ is the speed of light in tissue. $\mu_a$ and $\kappa$ denote the optical absorption and diffusion coefficients, respectively. In addition, the finite element method (FEM) and a Robin (type-III) [Brendel & Nielsen, 2009; Holboke et al., 2000] boundary condition are applied on Eq. (2.2) to solve this forward problem, i.e., calculating the photon density for a given set of optical property within the tissue.

#### 2.3.2 Inverse problem in DOT

Owing to the non-linearity with respect to the optical properties, an analytic solution to the inverse problem in DOT is absent. Instead, the numerical way of obtaining the inverse solution is to iteratively minimize the difference between the measured diffusion photon density data, $\mathbf{\Phi}^M$, around the tissue and the calculated model data, $\mathbf{\Phi}^C$, from solving the forward problem with the current estimated optical properties. This data-model misfit difference is typically defined as follows,

$$\chi^2 = \sum_{i=1}^{N_M}\left[\Phi_i^C - \Phi_i^M\right]^2 \tag{2.3}$$

where $N_M$ is the number of measurements.

By means of the first order Taylor series to expand $\mathbf{\Phi}$, one can get Eq. (2.4),

$$\left(\mathbf{\Phi}^M\right) \approx \left(\mathbf{\Phi}^C\right) + \left[\frac{\partial\mathbf{\Phi}^C}{\partial\boldsymbol{\mu}_a}\right]\left(\Delta\boldsymbol{\mu}_a\right) + \left[\frac{\partial\mathbf{\Phi}^C}{\partial\boldsymbol{\kappa}}\right]\left(\Delta\boldsymbol{\kappa}\right), \tag{2.4}$$

since the goal is to reach $\mathbf{\Phi}^M$ from the current $\mathbf{\Phi}^C$, and, thus, $\mathbf{\Phi}^M$ and $\mathbf{\Phi}^C$ have been used in the left and right parts of Eq. (2.4), respectively. As well, the vector $(\Delta\boldsymbol{\mu}_a)$ and $(\Delta\boldsymbol{\kappa})$ denote the updates respectively for $\mu_a$ and $\kappa$ with dimension $N_N$, the number of total nodes in the finite element mesh, and the dimension of the matrices $\left[\partial\mathbf{\Phi}^C/\partial\boldsymbol{\mu}_a\right]$ or $\left[\partial\mathbf{\Phi}^C/\partial\boldsymbol{\kappa}\right]$ is $N_M \times N_N$. From Eq. (2.4), the inverse problem in DOT can be formulated as

$$\begin{bmatrix} \dfrac{\partial\mathbf{\Phi}^C}{\partial\boldsymbol{\mu}_a} & \dfrac{\partial\mathbf{\Phi}^C}{\partial\boldsymbol{\kappa}} \end{bmatrix} \begin{pmatrix} \Delta\boldsymbol{\mu}_a \\ \Delta\boldsymbol{\kappa} \end{pmatrix} = \left(\mathbf{\Phi}^M - \mathbf{\Phi}^C\right), \tag{2.5}$$

or simply denoted as $\mathbf{J}\Delta\boldsymbol{\chi} = \Delta\mathbf{\Phi}$, where $\mathbf{J} = \left[\partial\mathbf{\Phi}^C/\partial\boldsymbol{\mu}_a \quad \partial\mathbf{\Phi}^C/\partial\boldsymbol{\kappa}\right]$ is the Jacobian matrix, the rate of change of model data with respect to optical parameters.

However, solving this linearized inverse problem from Eq. (2.5) usually runs into difficulty with an ill-conditioned problem which typically happens as the number of model parameters increases, so as to solve the inverse problem by means of regularization to remedy such a drawback.

### 2.4 Remark

In this section, we have explained a common imaging system which includes the operation of convolution, support area, sampling, and noise as well as a medical imaging system of which the optical-property images are formed with the reconstruction algorithm from 1D signals.

## 3. Image restoration algorithms

This section will discuss non-iterative, iterative and statistical methods; in addition, regularization is also used frequently in image restoration algorithms. More descriptions are explained in the following.

As known, the image degradation is basically modelled as

$$g = f \otimes h + n \tag{3.1}$$

where $f$ is the original scene, $h$ is the point-spread function (p.s.f.) of the imaging system, $\otimes$ is the convolution operator, $n$ is the noise, and $g$ is the corrupted image.

Generally, the non-linear iterative restoration algorithms (Archer & Titterington, 1995; Hunt, 1994; Meinel, 1986; Singh et al., 1986; Stewart & Durrani, 1986) to enhance image quality by restoring the high frequency spectrum of the corrupted images can be simply modelled as the following form:

$$f_n \sim f_{n-1} + \Delta f_n \tag{3.2}$$

$$\Delta f_n = \Psi(f_{n-1}, g, h, \alpha) \tag{3.3}$$

where the subscript n is the n-th iteration, Eqs. (3.2) and (3.3) represent that a new update ($f_n$) is equal to a previous one ($f_{n-1}$) plus an updating increment ( $\Delta f_n$ ). Furthermore, the update ( $\Delta f_n$ ) is related to the function ($\Psi$) of the previous update, the corrupted image, p.s.f., and a user-defined weight ($\alpha$). $\Psi$ can have various forms derived from the different algorithms. As known, there are several approaches to enhancing image quality including non-iterative restoration algorithms such as a Gaussian filter and non-linear iterative algorithms such as Poisson maximum *a posteriori* superresolution algorithm.

### 3.1 Non-iterative methods

Non-iterative restoration algorithms are described in this sub-section such as the inverse and Wiener filters usually recovering the spatial-frequencies below the diffraction limit. Filters in the Fourier domain are respectively given by the following expressions:

$$\text{Inverse Filter} = \frac{1}{H} \tag{3.4}$$

However, Eq. (3.4) is not able to be directly implemented; usually, one uses a so called pseudo-inverse filter with a small constant $\varepsilon$ as below.

$$\text{Pseudo-inverse Filter} = \frac{1}{H+\varepsilon} \tag{3.5}$$

Wiener filter is described as Eq. (3.6) in the following.

$$\text{Wiener Filter} = \frac{H^*}{|H|^2 + [\phi_n / \phi_f]} \tag{3.6}$$

where $H$ is the modulation transfer function (MTF) of p.s.f.; the superscript asterisk (*) denotes the complex conjugate; $[\phi_n/\phi_f]$, the ratio of noise-to-signal. $\phi_n$ and $\phi_f$ represent the power spectral densities for noise and the true images, respectively. Apparently, applying the Wiener filter to the restoration problem has to know the power spectral densities for the noise and the original image (or more precisely, their ratio). Unfortunately, this *a priori* knowledge is not available in most cases. Nevertheless, the noise-to-signal ratio (NSR), $[\phi_n/\phi_f]$, is usually approximated by a small constant $\varepsilon$. In such a case, the Wiener filter becomes

$$\frac{H^*}{|H|^2 + \varepsilon} \tag{3.7}$$

Wiener filtering achieves a compromise between the improvement obtained by boosting the amplitude of spatial-frequency coefficients up to the diffraction limit and the degradation that occurs because of the noise amplification of the inverse filtering. Noise propagation tends to be reduced by the convolution with p.s.f.; this has a smoothing effect in the result. This fact reveals that Wiener filtering is more immune to noise than inverse filtering.

### 3.2 Iterative methods

#### 3.2.1 Recursive wiener filter

This technique is briefly described here; further, a more detailed description of the implementation of this algorithm can be found in the literature [Kundur & Hatzinakos, 1998].

Briefly, such a recursive Wiener-like filtering operation in the Fourier domain can be expressed as Eqs. (3.8) and (3.9).

$$\hat{H}_n = \frac{G.\times \hat{F}^*_{n-1}}{\left|\hat{F}_{n-1}\right|^2 + \alpha / \left|\hat{H}_{n-1}\right|^2} \tag{3.8}$$

$$\hat{F}_n = \frac{G.\times \hat{H}^*_{n-1}}{\left|\hat{H}_{n-1}\right|^2 + \alpha / \left|\hat{F}_{n-1}\right|^2} \tag{3.9}$$

The real constant α represents the energy of the additive noise and is determined by prior knowledge of the noise contamination level, if available. The algorithm is run for a specified number of iterations or until the estimates begin to converge. The method is popular for its low computational complexity. The major drawback of the method is its lack of reliability. The uniqueness and convergence properties are, as yet, uncertain.

### 3.2.2 Lucy-Richardson method

The Richardson–Lucy algorithm, also known as Lucy–Richardson deconvolution, is an iterative procedure for recovering a latent image that has been blurred by a known point spread function.

The Richardson-Lucy (RL) algorithm has been widely used for the data from astronomical imaging. The RL algorithm (Richardson, 1972; Lucy, 1974) generates a restored image through an iterative method, which is derived using a Bayesian statistical approach to guess the original image ($f$), to convolute it ($f_{n-1}$) with the p.s.f. ($h$) and to compare the result with the real image ($g$). Usually the guessed image for the first iteration is the blurred image. It uses such an iterative approach:

$$f_n = f_{n-1}\left[\frac{g}{f_{n-1} \otimes h} \otimes h^*\right] \tag{3.10}$$

## 3.3 Statistical methods

### 3.3.1 Poisson MAP algorithm

The Poisson MAP superresolution algorithm begins with Bayes' law associated with Poisson models for the statistics of image and object to estimate the object by finding the maximum probability on the object ($f$) given the image (g). Mathematically, the Poisson MAP (Hunt & Sementilli, 1992) is given by

$$f_n = f_{n-1} exp\left[\left(\frac{g}{f_{n-1} \otimes h} - 1\right) * h\right] \equiv f_{n-1}C \tag{3.11}$$

where ⊗ represents a convolution; *, a correlation; $f_n$ , the restored signal/image; g is the blurred signal/image; $h$, p.s.f.; $f_0$ , the initial guess signal/image; subscript $n$, the iteration number. Here,

$$C = exp\left[\left(\frac{g}{f_{n-1} \otimes h} - 1\right) * h\right] \tag{3.12}$$

C can be regard as the correction term during the iterative restoration process. In terms of the operation of the Poisson MAP, it is an iterative algorithm where successive estimate of the restored image is obtained by multiplication of the current estimate by a quantity close to one. The quantity close to one is a function of the detected image divided by a convolution of the current estimate with p.s.f.. Indeed, one can replace the exponential in Eq. (3.12) by the first order approximation $e^x \sim 1+x$ because of low contrast in a blurred signal/image to achieve Eq. (3.13).

$$C \sim 1 + \left[\left(\frac{g}{f_{n-1} \otimes h} - 1\right) * h\right] \tag{3.13}$$

Thus, Eq. (3.11) can approach to Eq. (3.14).

$$f_n \sim f_{n-1} + f_{n-1}\left[\left(\frac{g}{f_{n-1} \otimes h} - 1\right) * h\right] \equiv f_{n-1} + \Delta f_n \tag{3.14}$$

Equation (3.14) shows that the Poisson MAP superresolution is consistent with Eq. (3.2). Experience reveals that when implemented for simple point objects, the Poisson MAP algorithm is able to expand the bandwidth much more than done for more complex objects and the Poisson MAP superresolution algorithm requires hundreds of iterations for a final solution.

### 3.3.2 Improved P-MAP

Following that, the Poisson MAP can be improved by itself by operating upon the edge map with a re-blurring technique; that is, the $g$ and $f_{n-1}$ of the Poisson MAP are replaced by the corresponding gradients of the $g \otimes h$ and $f_{n-1}$ along with the integrated p.s.f. ($h \otimes h$). Mathematically, it is shown that

$$(f_n)' = (f_{n-1})' exp\left[\left(\frac{(g \otimes h)'}{(f_{n-1})' \otimes (h \otimes h)} - 1\right) * (h \otimes h)\right] \tag{3.15}$$

Thus, the final hyper-resolved image $f$ can be obtained by integrating $(f_n)'$. The whole process of this improved Poisson MAP includes re-blurring, differentiation, restoration, integration, and then correction for a DC offset. More details concerning this algorithm can be found in the author's previous work [Pan, 2003].

## 3.4 Regularization

Regularization presents a very general methodology for image restoration. The main technique of a regularization procedure is to transform this ill-posed problem into a well-posed one. Roughly speaking, restoration problem with regularization comes down to the minimization problem [Chen et al., 2000; Landi, 2007].

In our real life, one cannot get the whole blurred and noisy images but only can get part of blurred and noisy images because of the limited support size. According to the part of blurred and noisy image, ones want to reconstruct an approximate true image by deconvolving the part of blurred and noisy image. Thus, noise ($n$) in general meaning should include both additive noise ($n_{add}$) and the effect of the limited support size ($n_{limited}$) at least.

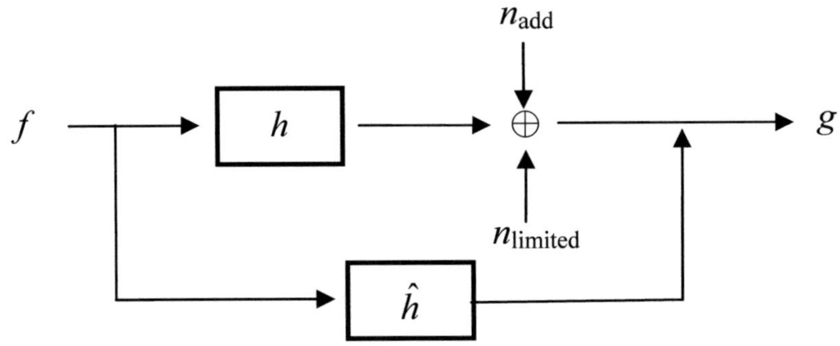


Fig. 3.1. A schematic diagram of forming a real image and proposing our algorithm.

To develop the novel algorithm with regularization, we plot a schematic diagram, Fig. 3.1, to show the mechanism of the concept proposed here and thus define the following functions, Equation (3.16).

$$Q_1 = \|g - f_{n-1} \otimes h\|^2 \leq n^2 \text{ and } Q_2 = \|g - f_{n-1} \otimes \hat{h}\|^2 \tag{3.16}$$

Normally, $Q_1$ is usually used with a true $h$ which is, however, not known and optimal, whereas $Q_2$ is expected to be used with an $\hat{h}$, which is supposed to be optimal in practice. Here, $Q_2$ is proposed for the purpose of reducing the error energy coming from noise and ringing artifacts while only $Q_1$ is considered. Thus, a new objective function combines $Q_1$ with $Q_2$, and its regularization term is $\|\Delta f_n\|^2$; it is approaching to null when iteration is increasing. Finally, we define an objective function as Eq. (3.17)

$$Q \equiv Q_1 - Q_2 + \lambda\|\Delta f_n\|^2 \tag{3.17}$$

where $\lambda$ is the regularization parameter and then minimize Eq. (3.17) with respect to $f_{n-1}$; i. e. ,

$$\min_{f_{n-1}}\{Q\} = 0 \tag{3.18}$$

thus,

$$\min_{f_{n-1}}\{Q_1 - Q_2 + \lambda\|\Delta f_n\|^2\} = 0 \tag{3.19}$$

Then, we can find Eq. (3.20)

$$2(\hat{h})^* \otimes (g - f_{n-1} \otimes \hat{h}) - 2h^* \otimes (g - f_{n-1} \otimes h) - 2\lambda(\Delta f_n) = 0 \tag{3.20}$$

Following that, an approximate equation is obtained as Eq. (3.21)

$$\Delta f_n \sim \alpha\, h_{\mathrm{hp}} \otimes \Delta f_n \tag{3.21}$$

where $\Delta f_n \approx g - f_{n-1} \otimes \hat{h}$ *or* $g - f_{n-1} \otimes h$ , $a \sim 1/\lambda$ and $h_{\mathrm{hp}} = \hat{h} - h$ ($\hat{h} = \hat{h}^*$ and $h = h^*$ because of the symmetry of p.s.f.) have been introduced. Furthermore, $h_{\mathrm{hp}}$ can be designed as a high-pass filter such as $h_{\mathrm{lp1}} - h_{\mathrm{lp2}}$ in general or $\delta$- $h_{\mathrm{lp}}$ in the extreme case where $h_{\mathrm{lp1,2}}$ are low-pass filters.

Subsequently, we substitute

$$\Delta f_n = f_n - f_{n-1} \tag{3.22}$$

into the left part of Eq. (3.21) and use the projection of the right pat in Eq. (3.21) on $\Delta f_n$ for the purpose of true value invariance. Consequently, the new relation function, Eq. (3.23), can be achieved for our novel method and expressed as

$$f_n = f_{n-1} + \Delta \hat{f}_n \tag{3.23}$$

where

$$\Delta \hat{f}_n = \alpha \frac{\Delta f_n ( h_{hp} \otimes \Delta f_n )}{\left\| \Delta f_n \right\|} \tag{3.24}$$

$$\Delta f_n = g - f_{n-1} \otimes \tilde{h} \tag{3.25}$$

Note that $\tilde{h}$ in Eq. (3.25), normally, is equal to $h$ but it is chosen as a user-guess p.s.f. when h is unknown. Here, $h_{\mathrm{hp}}$ is chosen as $\delta - \tilde{h}$ , where a delta function and a Gaussian function adopted for $h_{\mathrm{lp1}}$ and $h_{\mathrm{lp2}}$ in numerical simulation, respectively. Equations (3.23)-(3.25) show that the restored signal/image can be obtained from the increment iteratively updated using the projection of the high frequency spectra of the increment. As discussed, $h_{\mathrm{hp}}$ is defined as the difference of a delta function and a Gaussian function; in addition, an edge operator like a Laplacian operator defined as Eq. (3.26) is adopted for $h_{\mathrm{hp}}$ in the following experimental verification.

$$\text{operator} = \begin{bmatrix} 0 & -\frac{1}{4} & 0 \\ -\frac{1}{4} & 1 & -\frac{1}{4} \\ 0 & -\frac{1}{4} & 0 \end{bmatrix} \tag{3.26}$$

### 3.5 Remark

In this section, we have established a framework of image restoration/superresolution including (pseudo) inverse filter, Wiener filter, recursive Wiener filter, Lucy-Richardson method, Poisson MAP algorithm, and improved P-MAP algorithm. Of restoring image quality and reducing ringing artifacts, the error-energy-reduction-based regularization algorithm has been proposed here for long-wavelength imaging systems as well.

## 4. Further consideration on image restoration

In this section, the topics of improvement of spatial resolution, rapid convergence, and inverse pitfall for image restoration are described.

### 4.1 Improvement of spatial resolution

Usually, hyper-resolution of a noisy image is considered as an interpolation followed with restoration/superresolution; generally, the procedure for processing noisy images is shown in Fig. 4.1(a), that is, noise removal, interpolation, and then superresolution, whereas the proposed scheme is dealing with interpolation and noise removal simultaneously, as shown in Fig. 4.1(b).

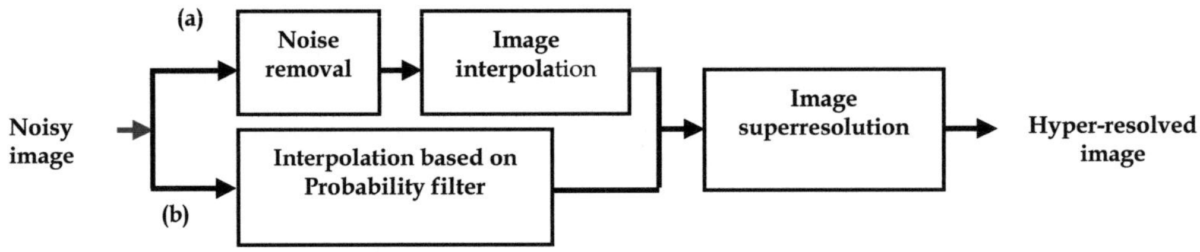


Fig. 4.1. The block diagram of hyper-resolution for a noisy image. (a) Conventional approach and (b) proposed approach.

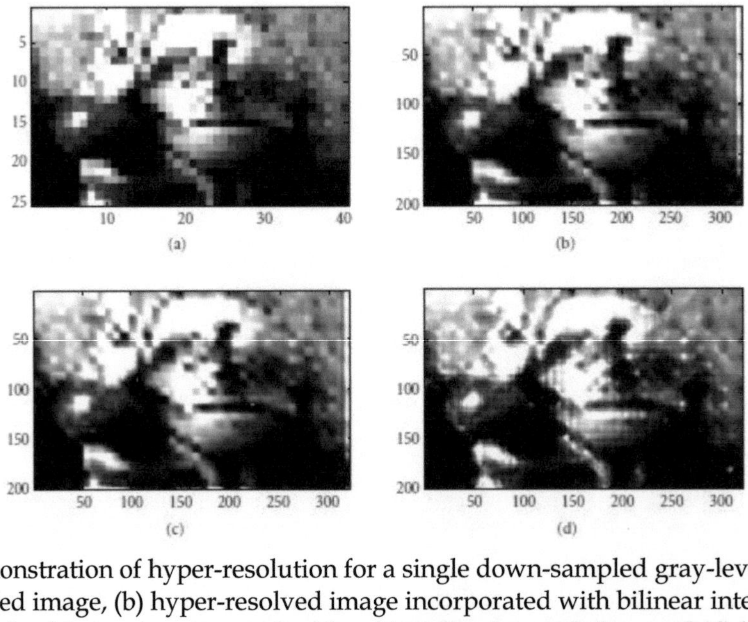


Fig. 4.2. Demonstration of hyper-resolution for a single down-sampled gray-level image. (a) Down-sampled image, (b) hyper-resolved image incorporated with bilinear interpolation, (c) hyper-resolved image incorporated with cubic spline interpolation, and (d) hyper-resolved image incorporated with probability-filtering-based interpolation.

In this section, we address an approach to simultaneous image interpolation and smoothing by exploiting the probability filter [Pan & Lettington, 1998] coupled with a pyramidal decomposition, thereby extending the conventional applications of the probability filter originally designed for noise removal. Then, the improved Poisson maximum *a posteriori* (MAP) superresolution [Pan & Lettington, 1999; Pan, 2002] is performed to reconstruct the high spatial-frequency spectrum of the interpolated image. Thus, the hybrid scheme shown in Fig. 4.1(b) is proposed for enhancing the spatial and the spatial-frequency resolutions of a down-sampled image. For more detailed description and examples, readers can refer to the previous work [Pan, 2006]. To illustrate the performance of this proposed scheme, comparisons are shown among the superresolution coupled with different interpolators as the following examples, Fig. 4.2 and Fig. 4.3.

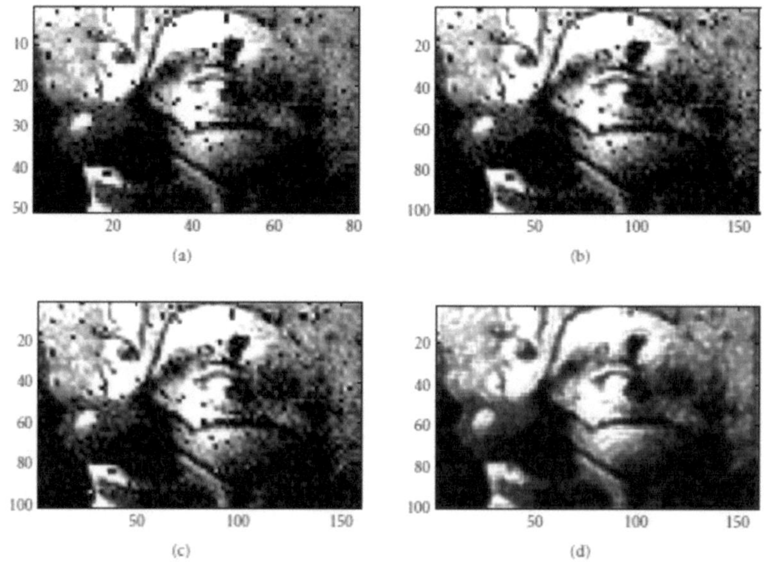


Fig. 4.3. Demonstration of hyper-resolution for a single down-sampled noisy gray-level image. (a) Down-sampled image, (b) hyperresolved image incorporated with bilinear interpolation, (c) hyper-resolved image incorporated with cubic spline interpolation, and (d) hyper-resolved image incorporated with probability-filtering-based interpolation.

### 4.2 Rapid convergence

As known, restoration/superresolution or the reconstruction of optical-property images with an iteration procedure is usually computed off-line and computationally expensive. Most of studies, however, focused mainly on improving the spatial and spatial-frequency resolutions. If a real-time resolution processing is required, dedicated reconstruction hardwares or specialized computers are mandatory. Moreover, fast reconstruction algorithms should also be considered to reduce the computation load. It is worth emphasizing that our proposed method can reduce computation time with the regularization term which is designed on the viewpoint of the update characteristics in the iteration procedure but not utilizing any spatial/spectral *a priori* knowledge or constraints; some results can be found in the author's work [M.-Cheng & M.-Chun Pan, 2010]. Here, we show how to speed up the computation to find an inverse solution for reconstructing optical-property images by using regularization with an iteration domain technique; similarly, this proposed method is capable of being applied to image restoration/superresolution for other imaging systems.

### 4.2.1 Algorithm of rapid convergence

Image reconstruction tasks contain forward modeling and inverse problem. The forward computation consists in obtaining the intensity out of a subject under investigation for a given source, and the initial-guess (or iterated result) on scattering and absorption coefficients. The inverse computation is to compute the scattering and absorption coefficients for a known light source and measured intensities in an iterative manner.

Since we utilize cw light illumination or DC data, the physical process of NIR light illuminating through a highly-scattering medium can be approximated by the steady-state diffusion equation

$$\nabla \cdot D(\mathbf{r})\nabla\Phi(\mathbf{r}) - \mu_a(\mathbf{r})\Phi(\mathbf{r}) = -S(\mathbf{r}), \tag{4.1}$$

where $S(\mathbf{r})$ and $\Phi(\mathbf{r})$ denote the source and the intensity, respectively, as well as $\mu_a(\mathbf{r})$, $c$ and $D(\mathbf{r})$ are the absorption coefficient and the diffusion coefficient, respectively. For solving Eq. (4.1), the boundary condition, $-D\nabla\Phi \bullet \hat{n} = Flux = \alpha\Phi$, and finite element method are employed. Thus, the following discrete equations can be obtained [Paulsen and Jiang, 1995]

$$A\Phi = C, \tag{4.2}$$

where $A$ and $C$ are matrices dependent on the optical properties and the source-detection locations, respectively. The forward solution, $\Phi$, can be explicitly evaluated by Eq. (4.2). Partially differentiating Eq. (4.2) with $\frac{\partial}{\partial D}$ and $\frac{\partial}{\partial \mu}$, respectively, yields

$$\Phi' = -A^{-1}A'\Phi + A^{-1}C'. \tag{4.3}$$

With an approximation to applying the Newton-Raphson method and ignoring higher order terms, we obtain

$$J\Delta\chi = \Delta\Phi \tag{4.4}$$

where the Jacobian matrix $J$ denotes the matrix consisting of $\frac{\partial \Phi_b}{\partial D_k}$ and $\frac{\partial \Phi_b}{\partial \mu_l}$, $\Delta\chi$ is the vector composed of $\Delta D_k$ and $\Delta\mu_l$, and $\Delta\Phi$ is the vector with differences between calculated intensities ($\Phi^{cal.}$) and measured intensities ($\Phi^{meas.}$). Also, $D_k$ for $k$ = 1, 2, …, K and $\mu_l$ for $l$ = 1, 2, …, L are the reconstruction parameters for the optical-property profile. The optical-property image reconstruction is actually a process of successively updating the distribution of optical coefficients so as to minimize the difference between measured intensities and computed ones from the forward process. More details can be found in [Paulsen and Jiang, 1995] where the Levenberg-Marquardt procedure was adopted to update the diffusion and absorption coefficients iteratively.

It is known that to solve Eq. (4.4) is an ill-posed problem. Tikhonov regularization is a method stabilizing the inverse problem through incorporating *a priori* assumptions to constraint the desired solution. It is able to convert an ill-posed problem into a well-posed one, and further to improve an ill-conditioned problem. The regularization term (penalty term) introduced in the process regularizes the problem and makes the update stable. It also strengthens the robustness of algorithm to noisy data with the adequate design of the regularization term. Generally, Tikhonov regularization is to optimize this ill-conditioned problem as

$$\min_{\Delta\chi} \| J\Delta\chi - \Delta\Phi \|^2 \text{ subject to } \Psi(\Delta\chi) \leq E \tag{4.5}$$

where $\Psi(\Delta\chi)$ is a constraint on the estimate $\Delta\chi$, and $E$ is a quantity confining the constraint to be an energy bound. Applying Lagrange optimization technique, we seek a solution to the constrained objective function

$$\mathrm{O} = \| J\Delta\chi - \Delta\Phi \|^2 - \lambda\Psi \tag{4.6}$$

with the condition

$$\min_{\Delta\chi}\{\mathrm{O}\} = \min_{\Delta\chi}\left\{ \| J\Delta\chi - \Delta\Phi \|^2 - \lambda\Psi \right\}, \tag{4.7}$$

where λ is referred to as the regularization parameter. A solution to Eq. (4.7) is given by

$$2J^T(J\Delta\chi - \Delta\Phi) - \lambda\frac{\partial\Psi}{\partial\Delta\chi} = 0, \tag{4.8}$$

and equivalently

$$(J^T J\Delta\chi - \frac{\lambda}{2}\frac{\partial\Psi}{\partial\Delta\chi}) = J^T\Delta\Phi \tag{4.9}$$

where Eq. (4.9) is a constrained estimate of $\Delta\chi$, but becomes an unconstrained one when λ equals to zero. It is noted that the minus sign in Eq. (4.6), the objective function, corresponds to the regularization term proposed here as the term is constrained to an energy bound.

### 4.2.2 Constraints on the spatial domain

A constraint on the spatial domain can generally be expressed as

$$\Psi(\Delta\chi) = \|L\Delta\chi\|^2 \tag{4.10}$$

where $L$ can be the identity matrix ($I$) or the discrete Laplacian matrix [Pogue et al., 1999; Davis et al., 2007].

If $L$ is the identity matrix ($I$), a solution to Eq. (4.9) is given by

$$\Delta\chi = (J^T J - \lambda I)^{-1} J^T \Delta\Phi . \tag{4.11}$$

On the other hand, if $L$ is the discrete Laplacian matrix, substituting Eq. (4.10) into Eq. (4.9), the corresponding solution is

$$\Delta\chi = (J^T J - \lambda L^T L)^{-1} J^T \Delta\Phi . \tag{4.12}$$

Equation (4.11) is usually a primary inverse solution to optical-property image reconstruction, which is also Levenberg's contribution to the inverse problem; and Eq. (4.12) is a constrained inverse solution implemented to improve the quality of the reconstructed NIR DOT images, which is identical to Marquardt's work.

### 4.2.3 Constraints on the iteration domain

In NIR DOT, it is also crucial to accelerate the computation. But, up to now, speeding up the computation in the iteration domain has not been explored yet. Here we consider this issue through the use of a Lorentzian distributed function taking a natural logarithm computation as a constraint, i.e.

$$\Psi(\Delta\chi) = \sum_{p=1}^{K+L} \ell n \frac{\gamma / \pi}{(\Delta\chi)_p^{\ 2} + \gamma^2} , \tag{4.13}$$

where $p$ is the calculated nodes in the subject under investigation and $\gamma$ is a user defined positive parameter. As can be seen, $\Psi(\Delta\chi) \le \sum_p \ln(\frac{1}{\pi\gamma})$, $\forall \Delta\chi$, meets the requirement of Eq. (4.5). Performing the differentiation indicated in Eq. (4.9), we can obtain the solution in an iterative formality

$$(\Delta\chi)_n = \left( J^T J + \frac{\lambda I}{(\Delta\chi)_{n-1}^2 + \gamma_n^2 I} \right)^{-1} J^T \Delta\Phi . \tag{4.14}$$

For further inspection in Eqs. (4.13) and (4.14), as known, $\mu_a$ and $D$ are generally searched in a range of $[10^{-3}:10^{-1}]$ $mm^{-1}$and mm, respectively; and thus $\Delta\chi$ is much smaller than a unit. It can be proven that even the use of the natural logarithm in the constraint $\Psi(\Delta\chi)$ still makes it a positive and finite value. The other reason to use *ln* is because the regularization term in Eq. (4.14) still remains in a form of the Lorentzian distributed function derived from the constraint associated with the Lorentzian distributed function in Eq. (4.13).

The Lorentzian distributed function, as depicted in Fig. 4.4, is employed here owing to its following two characteristics:

a. Lorentzian distributed function has a sharp peak with a long tail, describing the histogram distribution of $\Delta\chi$, many of $\Delta\chi$ (~0) at its peak and a small rest of $\Delta\chi$ distributing along its long tail, and
b. its histogram distribution can be further tuned with the parameter ($\gamma$) as iteration increasing. Related to the consideration in convergence, the updated quantity, $\Delta\chi$, decreases, ranging from the peak to the tail, as the iteration increases whereas it has a smooth distribution in the beginning stage of iteration.

In addition, as the shape of the histogram would be affected, it is smooth with a big value of $\gamma$ and sharp with a small value of $\gamma$. Thus, Lorentzian distributed function can characterize the nature of $\Delta\chi$ in the iterative process as the distribution from a smooth to a sharp distribution to be used as a constraint for the purpose of speeding up computation.

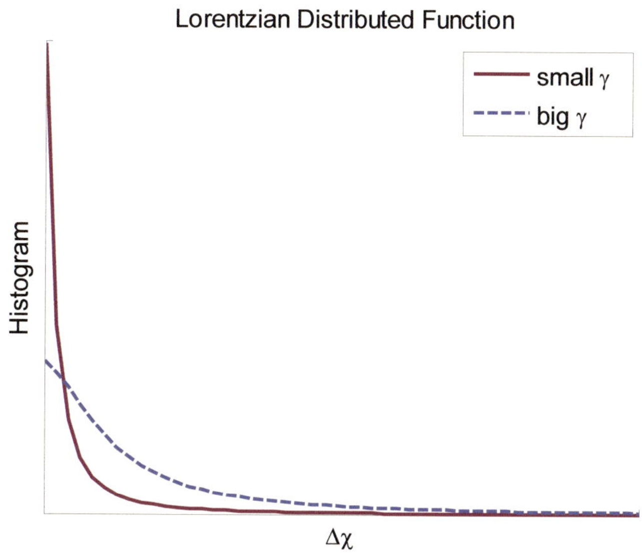


Fig. 4.4. Charts of the Lorentzian distributed functions ($\frac{\gamma/\pi}{(\Delta\chi)^2+\gamma^2}$) at various $\gamma$. As can be seen, it has a smooth distribution for a big $\gamma$ and a sharp distribution as $\gamma$ is small.

### 4.3 Inverse pitfall

The ill-posed nature of inverse problems means that any restoration or reconstruction algorithm will have limitations on what images it can accurately reconstruct and that the images degrade with noise in the data. When developing a restoration or reconstruction algorithm it is usual to test it initially on simulated data. Moreover, the restoration or reconstruction algorithm typically incorporates a forward solver. A natural first test is to use the same forward model to generate simulated data with no simulated noise and to then find that the simulated data can be recovered fairly well. If one is fortunate enough to have a good data collection system and phantom, and someone skilled enough to make some accurate measurements with the system, one could then progress to attempting to reconstruct images from experimental data. However, more often the next stage is to test further with simulated data and it at this stage that one must take care not to cheat and commit a so-called inverse pitfall or inverse crime. Simply to say, inverse pitfall or inverse crime arises from the reason of 'limited for infinite', e.g., limited support area for infinite scenery, finite elements for continuous zone, or given noise for unknown noise. The best practice is to use a forward model independent of an inverse model. For example, in the case of a finite element forward model one would use a much finer mesh while a coarse mesh is used in the inverse model.

### 4.4 Remark

In this section, we have proposed some extra points about image restoration. Interpolator with noise removal, design of regularization term for reducing computational burden, and inverse pitfall/crime have been illustrated and discussed.

## 5. Related application

In this section, application to a mm-wave imaging system or near infrared diffuse optical tomography using image restoration is demonstrated for post-processing or inter-processing. To verify the proposed method in the previous section (Sec. 3.4), a computer-generated signal/image and an image of real scene were tested.

### 5.1 Post-processing: Application to a millimeter-wave imaging system [Pan, 2010]

A 1-D noiseless signal and a 2-D noisy image were used, originally blurred with a p.s.f. of Gaussian function plus additive white Gaussian noise. White Gaussian noise is defined with a zero mean and variance, $\sigma^2$, specified by a blurred signal-to-noise ratio (BSNR). Recall that

$$BSNR = 10\log_{10}\left( \frac{\sum_{i,j=1}^{M,N} \frac{\left( (f \otimes h)_{i,j} - \overline{f \otimes h} \right)^2}{\sigma^2}}{MN} \right) \quad \text{(in dB)} \tag{5.1}$$

where $M$, $N$ are the dimension of the processed image and i, j are the indexes of a pixel and $\overline{X}$ means the average value of $X$. In many practical situations, the blur is often unknown and little information is available about the true image; therefore, several $\sigma_{\tilde{h}}$ of the Gaussian blur around the true $\sigma_h$ were tested in the following examples; $f_o$ and $\alpha$ are chosen to g and $\sqrt{g}$, respectively. In this work, the stopping criterion is $\frac{\|\Delta f_n\|}{\|\Delta f_0\|} \leq 0.01\%$ (for 1-D signal) or 1% (for 2-D image). The mean square error (MSE) of the restored signal/image relative to the original signal/image is provided here for the evaluation of image quality, thus supporting the visual assessment.

The proposed algorithm was applied to a 1-D signal as well as both simulated and real atmospherically degraded images, one of a simulated blur and one of a real blur. The purpose of the simulation was to enable a comparative evaluation of the results given the original signal/image and to explain the algorithm characteristics. In the real-blur example shown here, a 256 × 400 pixel millimeter-wave image was tested and the image was captured at 94 GHz by the Defence Evaluation and Research Agency, Malvern, UK.

For a comparison purpose, non-iterative Gaussian filtering was used in the case of 1-D signal and the common Richardson–Lucy (RL) deconvolution method was implemented using a built-in MATLAB function deconvlucy in the cases of both 1-D signal and 2-D images. This RL method employs an iterative procedure to estimates the original signal/image, and therefore requires an initial guess of it as well.

### 5.1.1 Results for synthetically blurred signal and image

Figure 5.1(a) and (c) present an original signal containing 256 pixels and a blurred version of this signal, obtained by convolving it with a Gaussian function with $\sigma_h$ equal to 1.5, Fig. 5.1(b), which approximates an atmospheric blur. Figure 5.1(d)-(f) show a comparison between the results obtained from the implementation of Gaussian filtering, the RL deconvolution method and our proposed algorithm, the MSEs of which are 188.29, 210.23, and 184.50, respectively. The resulting Wiener-filtered restored signal (with $\varepsilon$ = 0.001) is shown in Fig. 5.1(d). It is clear that this restored signal is considerably better than the blurred signal shown in Fig. 5.1(c) whereas the restored signal using the RL method reveals lots of ringing artifacts. Figure 5.1(f) shows that the result using the proposed algorithm with $h_{\text{hp}}$ equal to $\delta - \tilde{h}$ ($\sigma_{\tilde{h}}$ =1.5) presents higher contrast and less ringing artifact than other two methods.

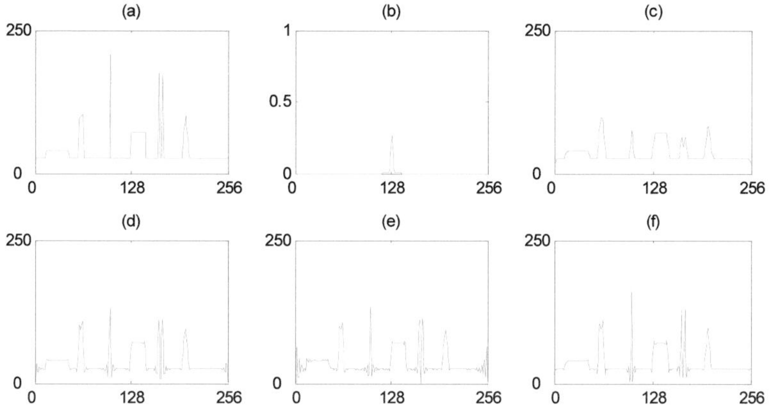


Fig. 5.1. Comparison among the deconvolution for 1-D signal. (a) Original signal, (b) p.s.f. ( $\sigma_h$ = 1.5), (c) blurred signal, and restored signals by using (d) Gaussian filter, (e) the RL algorithm and $\sigma_h$ = 1.5, and (f) our proposed algorithm with $\delta - \tilde{h}$ and $\sigma_{\tilde{h}}$ =1.5.

Following the above discussion, Fig. 5.2 shows the iterations used by the RL method and the proposed algorithm satisfying with the stopping criterion. In the case of 1-D signal, our algorithm usually converges within fewer iterations than the RL method, the former using 34 iterations and the latter using 187 iterations.

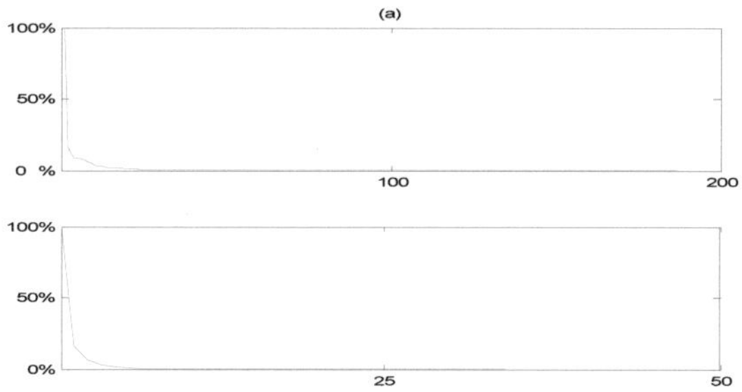


Fig. 5.2. Convergence rate vs. iteration no. of Fig. 5.1 for (a) the RL algorithm, and (b) our proposed algorithm.

Figure 5.3 shows that the nature of our proposed method possesses the ability to reconstructing frequency spectrum beyond the diffraction limit, where a 1-D noiseless signal was used. Figure 5.3(a)-(c) shows the original signal, p.s.f. and its modulation transfer function (MTF); the degraded ($\sigma_h$ = 1.5) and the restored signals are shown in Fig. 5.3(d)-(f) with $\sigma_{\tilde{h}}$ equal to 1.2, 1.5, and 1.8, respectively; and the MTFs of the original and the restored signals are depicted in Fig. 5.3(g)-(i). The restored signals in Fig. 5.3(e) and (f) display the performance of high resolution and the two peaks are separated in Fig. 5.3(d) even with a small $\sigma_{\tilde{h}}$. Compared with that of the original signal, high-frequency information of the restored signals was definitely generated beyond the diffraction limit as shown between the two dashed lines in Fig. 5.3(g)-(i), explaining that the proposed method possesses the high-resolution ability.

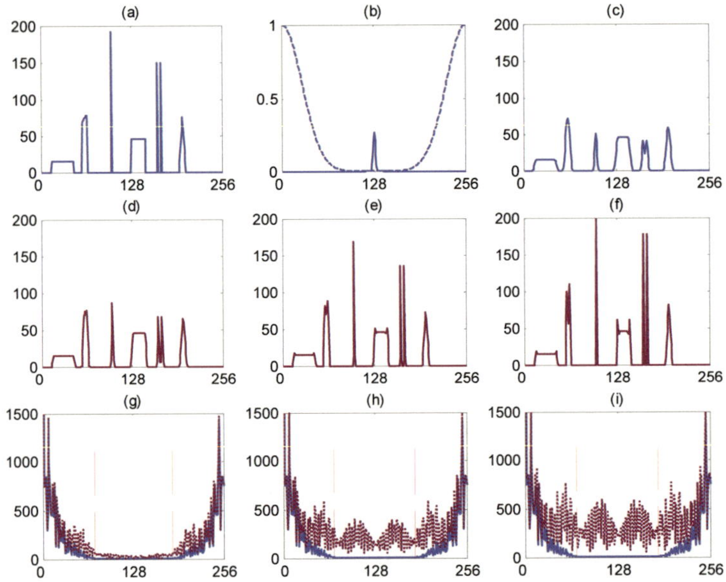


Fig. 5.3. Demonstration of the high resolution of the proposed algorithm. (a) Original signal, (b) Gaussian form (solid line) and MTF (dotted line) of the blurring function ($\sigma_h$ = 1.5), (c) blurred signal, (d)-(f) restored signals with $\delta - \tilde{h}$ and $\sigma_{\tilde{h}}$ =1.2, 1.5, and 1.8, respectively, and (g)-(i) MTFs of the blurred (solid line) and the restored (dotted line) signals. Note that the region between two dashed lines is the high frequency beyond the diffraction limit.

Figure 5.4 represents an image (256 × 256) of clown which is a built-in image in MatLab. Figure 5.4 displays a comparison between the results obtained from the implementation of the RL deconvolution method and our proposed algorithm. Figure 5.4(a) shows the original image, convolving it with a 2-D Gaussian function with $\sigma_h$ equal to 2.5 to obtain a blurred image shown in Fig. 5.4(b). Figure 5.4(c)-(e) show the images restored with the RL deconvolution method and our proposed algorithm with δ-$\tilde{h}$ and the Laplacian filter where $\sigma_{h,\tilde{h}}$ =2.5 was used; the MSEs of these three results are 181.17, 49.45, and 52.61, respectively. These three restored images demonstrate high quality but Fig. 5.4(c) still shows ringing artifact especially in the boundary of the image. In Fig. 5.4(d), simultaneously, the image quality can also be improved by reducing most of the ringing artifact and preserving more edge information. Also, it can be seen that our method with a Laplacian filter still works well, shown in Fig. 5.4(e).

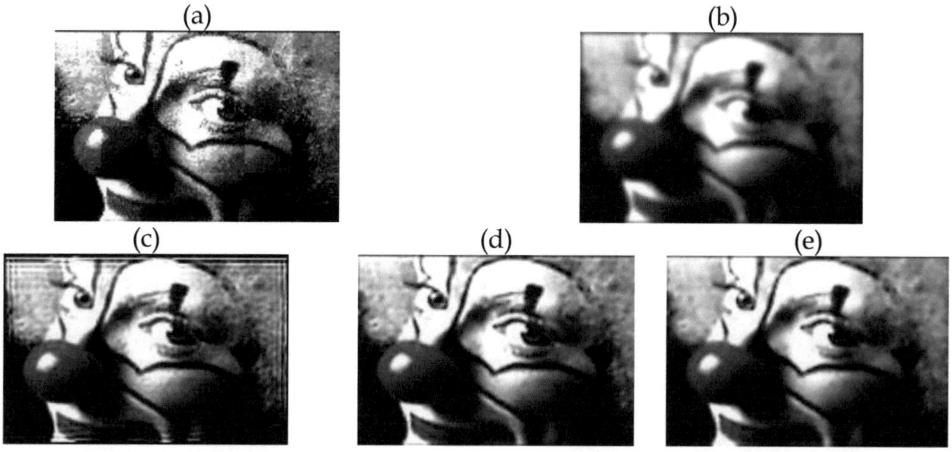


Fig. 5.4. Comparison among the deconvolution for 2-D image. (a) Original image, (b) blurred image ($\sigma_h = 2.5$), and restored images by using (c) the RL algorithm and $\sigma_h = 2.5$, and our proposed algorithm with (d) $\delta - \tilde{h}$ and $\sigma_{\tilde{h}}$ =2.5 and (f) 2-D Laplacian filter and $\sigma_{\tilde{h}}$ =2.5, respectively.

Corresponding to Fig. 5.4(c)-(e), Fig. 5.5 shows the iterations used by the RL method and the proposed algorithm where fewer iterations was used in the RL method than our algorithm, the former using 46 iterations and the latter two using about 200 iterations. It should be noted that the proposed algorithm is considerably more computationally expensive than the RL method. However, in our experiments we did not find any significant improvement but even more ringing artifacts when the RL method was employed for a further iteration number.

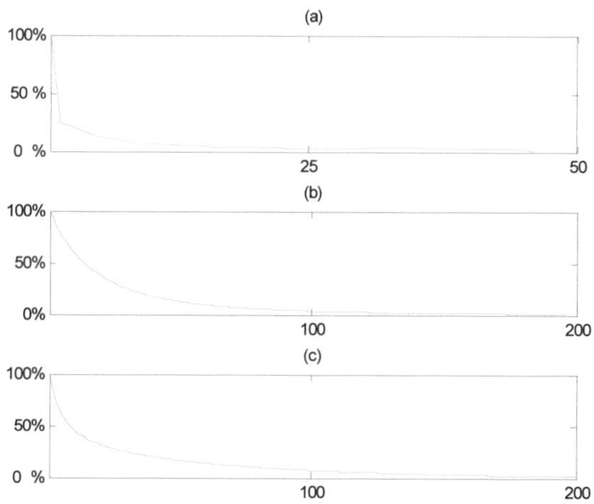


Fig. 5.5. Convergence rate vs. iteration no. of Fig. 5.4 for (a) the RL algorithm, and our proposed algorithm with (b) $\delta - \tilde{h}$ and (c) 2-D Laplacian filter, respectively.

For further inspection into our proposed algorithm, we investigated the effect of this algorithm using the high pass filter, $\delta$-$\tilde{h}$ , with varied $\sigma_{\tilde{h}}$. Figure 5.6 demonstrates this case where the original and the noisy ($\sigma_h$ = 2.5 and BSNR=30 dB) images are displayed in Fig. 5.6(a), (b), and the restored images are shown in Fig. 5.6(c)–(e) obtained with the use of $\sigma_{\tilde{h}}$ equal to 2, 2.5, and 3, respectively. The MSEs of these results are 163.77, 76.82, and 97.97, respectively. Of all the restored images, Fig. 5.6(c) shows a worse image quality than the others, in which noise was intensively produced and hard to be removed although the contrast of the restored image was enhanced. Figure 5.6(d) and (e) show the promising results where high contrast was generated and noise was suppressed. As a result, it is recommended that a small $\sigma_{\tilde{h}}$ , together with adequate iterations, should be avoided to use in the restoration process of the proposed algorithm.

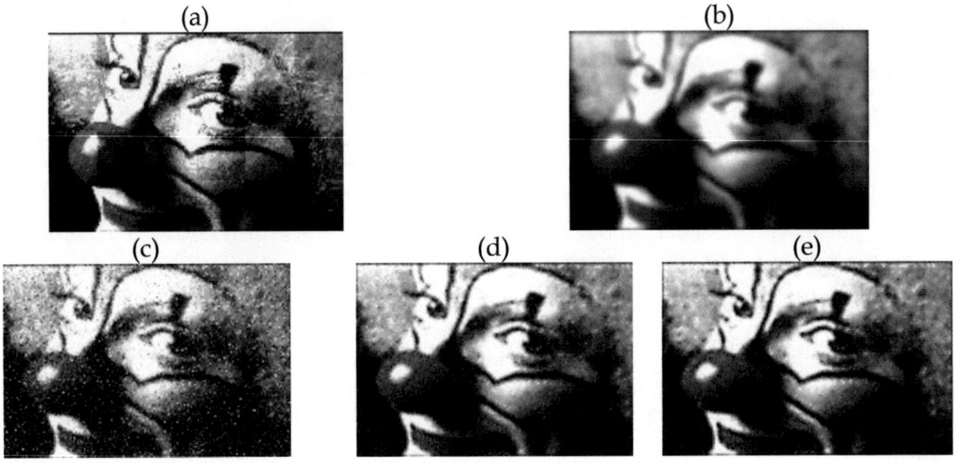


Fig. 5.6. Demonstration of the deconvolution for a 2-D image using the proposed algorithm. (a) Original image, (b) noisy image ($\sigma_h$ = 2.5 and BSNR=30 dB), and restored images by using our proposed algorithm incorporating $\delta - \tilde{h}$ with (c) $\sigma_{\tilde{h}} = 2$, (d) $\sigma_{\tilde{h}} = 2.5$ and (f) $\sigma_{\tilde{h}} = 3$, respectively.

### 5.1.2 Results for a real degraded image

It is always expected that a novel algorithm can be implemented on a real image; Fig. 5.7(a) presents a real degraded image captured by an mm-wave imaging system. Figure 5.7(b) was restored using the RL method and Fig. 5.7(c), (d) were obtained by using our proposed method where Fig. 5.7(b)-(d) were obtained with $\sigma_{h,\tilde{h}}$ equal to 3. It is obvious that the restored images, Fig. 5.7(c) reveals sharp edges, high contrast and much more details like a number 2, two cars, and three lamps of the floodlight, etc., but Fig. 5.7(b) has shown ringing artifact spreading through the whole image. Furthermore, it is worth mentioning that Fig. 5.7(d) also shows a good image quality which was achieved with the use of a 3 × 3 Laplacian operator.

Corresponding to Fig. 5.7(c)-(e), Fig. 5.8 shows the iterations used by the RL method and the proposed algorithm satisfying with the stopping criterion. In the case of 2-D image, the RL method used less iteration than our algorithm, the former using 35 iterations and the latter two using about 150 iterations.

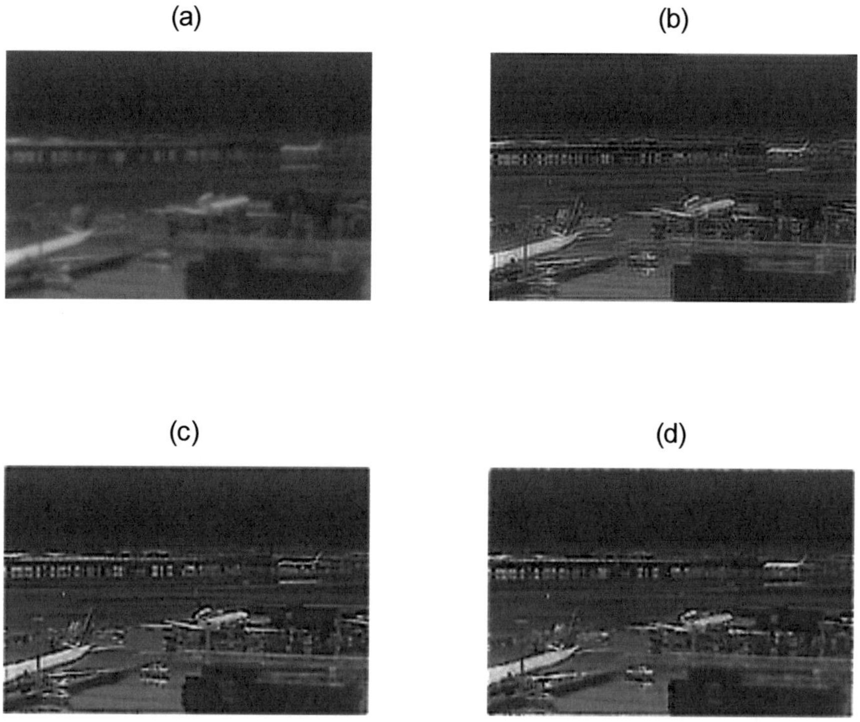


Fig. 5.7. Comparison among image deconvolution for a 94 GHz millimeter-wave image. (a) Real degraded image, and restored images by using (b) the RL algorithm and $\sigma_h$ =3, and our proposed algorithm with (c) $\delta - \tilde{h}$ and $\sigma_{\tilde{h}}$ =3 and (d) 2-D Laplacian filter and $\sigma_{\tilde{h}}$ =3, respectively.

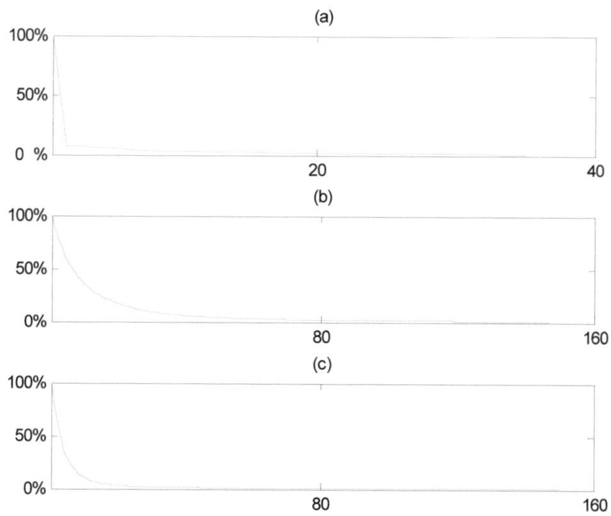


Fig. 5.8. Convergence rate vs. iteration no. of Fig. 5.7 for (a) the RL algorithm, and our proposed algorithm with (b) $\delta - \tilde{h}$ and (c) 2-D Laplacian filter, respectively.

## 5.2 Inter-processing: Application to near infrared diffuse optical tomography

### 5.2.1 Rapid convergence algorithm applied to NIR DOT

Corresponding to Eq. (4.14), some parameters are chosen as

$$\lambda = 0.75\max\{J^T J\}\,,\ (\Delta\chi)_0^2 = I\,,\ \gamma_n = \lambda\ \ or\ \ 2.5e^{-2n}\,, \tag{5.2}$$

where the subscript $n$ is the $n$-th iteration, "max" means the maximum value, and the superscript $T$ denotes a transposition operation. One way to improve the convergence rate is using $\gamma_n = \lambda$ as the Type-1 soft prior and using $\gamma_n = 2.5e^{-2n}$, an exponentially decreasing form, as the Type-2 soft prior, where Type-1 is a parameter related to the system function (Jacobian matrix) and Type-2 is a user-defined parameter. Both values of $\gamma_n$ have been respectively employed to seek an inverse solution for comparison.

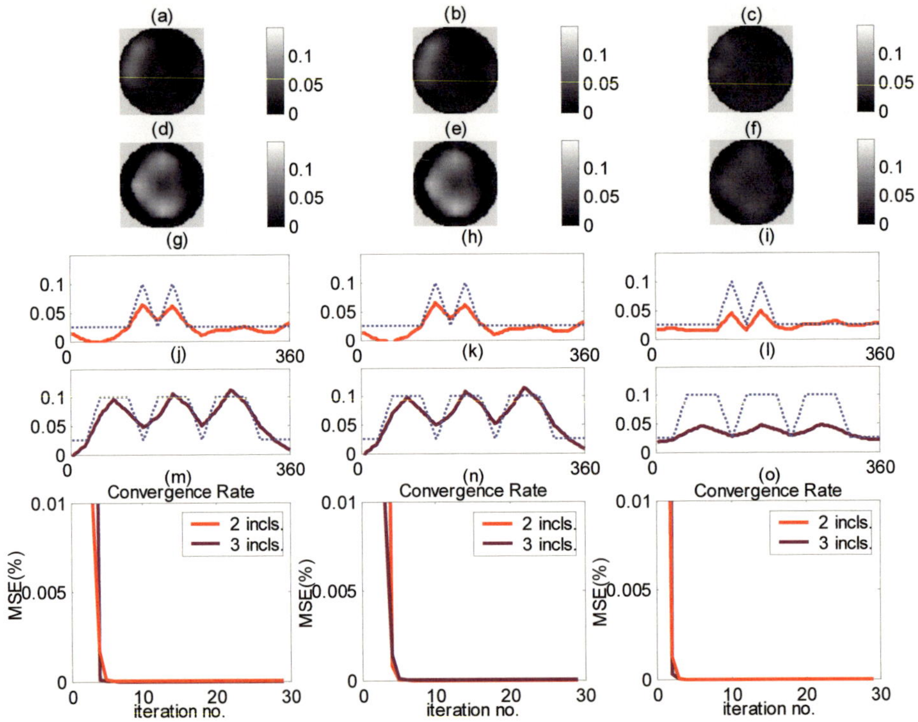


Fig. 5.9. Reconstruction data through various priors with intensity signals corrupted by Gaussian white noise (SNR=20 dB). Left column: constrained inverse solution with soft prior 1; middle column: constrained inverse solution with soft prior 2; right column: constrained inverse solution with hard prior.

Figure 5.9 illustrates the comparisons between constrained solutions using soft priors (Type 1 and 2) and a hard prior, where the left, middle and right columns are the constrained inverse solutions with soft prior 1, soft prior 2, and hard prior [M.-Cheng & M.-Chun Pan, 2010], respectively. Figure 5.9 (a-f) shows the 2D reconstructions of phantoms with two and three inclusions, where slight discrepancy can be observed. Figure 5.9 (g-l) depicts their corresponding 1D circular transection profiles to reveal noticeable differences. Basically, there is a better separation resolution but a lower intensity owing to a highly suppressed signal by a hard prior rather than a soft prior. Additionally, Fig. 5.9 (m-o) exhibits good convergences obtained by using both soft and hard priors.

### 5.2.2 Image restoration applied to NIR DOT

The phantoms employed for justifying our proposed technique (Sec. 3.4) incorporate two or three inclusions with various sizes, locations and separations, illustrated in Fig. 5.10, where $R$ denotes radius in the unit of *mm*. Of the phantom, the background absorption ($\mu_a$) and reduced scattering ($\mu'_s$) values are about 0.0025 mm$^{-1}$ and 0.25 mm$^{-1}$, respectively, while the maximum absorption and reduced scattering for the inclusion are 0.025 mm$^{-1}$ and 2.5 mm$^{-1}$, thereby assuming the contrast ratio of the inclusion to background 10:1, because high contrast results in much more overlapping effects than low contrast although a contrast of 2~10 were used throughout other published works.

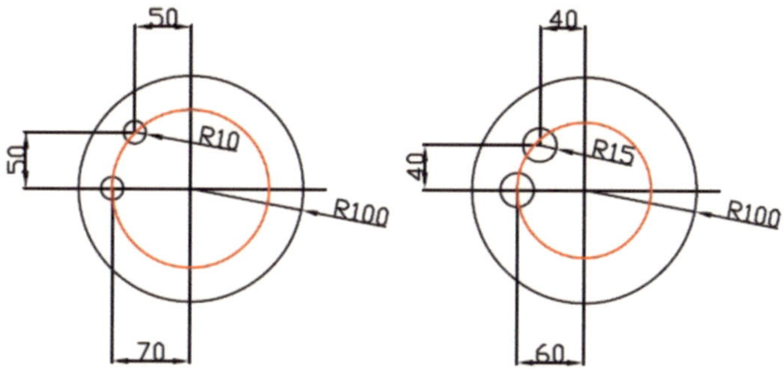


(a) (b)

Fig. 5.10. Schematic diagram for the dimensions of two different test cases in simulation. (a) and (b) are Case 1, 2, respectively, where R is radius in the unit of mm.

As depicted in Fig. 5.10, Case 1, 2, respectively, have two inclusions separated with a similar distance but different sizes. As the separation resolution of inclusions is examined, several (two or three) embedded inclusions are necessary, and different inclusion sizes are considered as well. For the convenience in discussion latter, we denote M0-4 as the reconstructions with the schemes using non-filtering, δ-g2 ($\sigma_2$=1.5), g1-g2($\sigma_1$=0.75, $\sigma_2$=1.5), wavelet (a dilated factor $a$=0.5), and Laplacian high-pass filter (HPF) in their 2D form, respectively. Currently, absorption-coefficient images are presented for our continuous wave image reconstruction algorithm.

In FEM-based image reconstruction, the homogeneous background ($\mu_a$ = 0.0025mm$^{-1}$, $\mu'_s$ = 0.25mm$^{-1}$) was adopted as an initial guess. Thirty-iteration assignment was employed for each case as the normalized increasing rate, i.e. mean value of $\left|\frac{\Phi_{n+1}-\Phi_n}{\Phi_n}\right|^2$, reaches smaller than $10^{-2}$.

### 5.2.3 Examples illustration

#### 5.2.3.1 Case 1

This case was designed as a phantom with three smaller inclusions. Several improved images were obtained by using appropriate filtering, as shown in Fig. 5.11(b-e) of 1D circular profiles passing through the centers of inclusions. Likewise, M2 resulted in worse resolved image than others with HP filtering. Negative artifacts occurred in each reconstructed image, as depicted in Fig. 5.11(g-j). It is well noted that M4 overestimated the inclusion amplitudes, which yields a higher inclusion-to-background contrast.

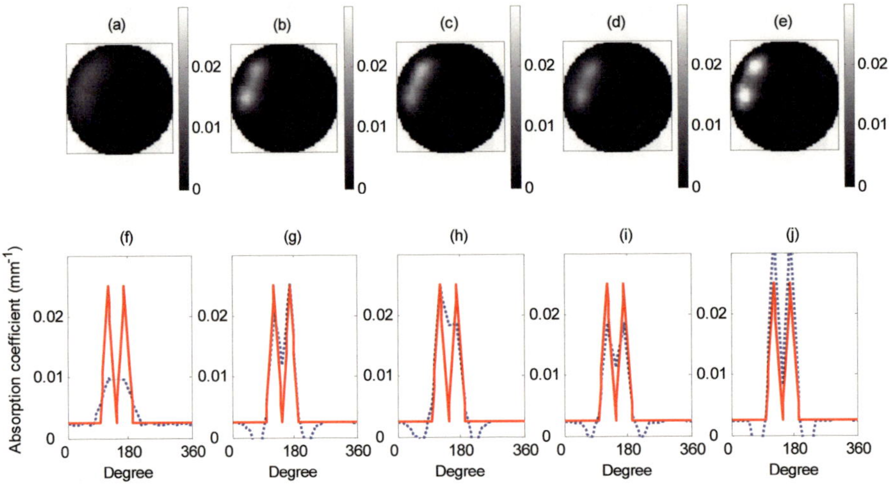


Fig. 5.11. Case 1- 2D reconstructed absorption images (a) without HPF (M0) and (b)-(e) with M1, M2, M3, M4 filtering, respectively; (f)-(j) are 1D circular profiles corresponding to (a)-(e), where solid lines are the designed, and dotted lines represent the reconstructed.

#### 5.2.3.2 Case 2

In this highly challenging case, a phantom with two closest-separation inclusions was designed. As shown in Fig. 5.12(a-e), all reconstructed images underestimated inclusions, and offered relatively bad resolution for two separate inclusions. It is rather competitive for these employed filters. Based upon a quantitative comparison, as depicted in Fig. 5.12(i) and (j), M3 and M4 schemes demonstrate better resolution discrimination to separate bigger and closer inclusions in comparison of Case 1.

From the results of Case 1 and 2 for a phantom with inclusions of both small size and close separation, it can be concluded that the wavelet-like HP filtering (M3) demonstrates the best spatial-frequency resolution capability to the inclusions.

It evidently shows that the enhancement of reconstruction through the incorporation of our proposed HPF approach can effectively improve computed images. As illustrated above, the wavelet-like HP filtering schemes (M3, M4) further yields better results than the LPF-combined HP filtering schemes (M1, M2). In the aspects of sensitivity and stability of evaluation, M3 yielded results closest to the true absorption property than other schemes. However, M4 visually characterizes the inclusion-to-background contrast best.

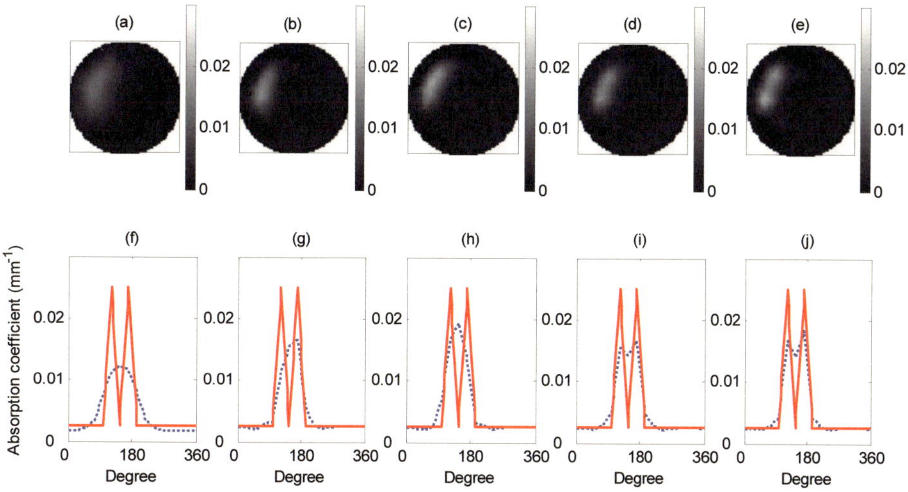


Fig. 5.12. Case 2- 2D reconstructed absorption images (a) without HPF (M0) and (b)-(e) with M1, M2, M3, M4 filtering, respectively; (f)-(j) are 1D circular profiles corresponding to (a)-(e), where solid lines are the designed, and dotted lines represent the reconstructed.

### 5.2.4 Performance investigation

In terms of the optical properties within the inclusion and background, it is worth noted that the image reconstruction is not only pursuing qualitative correctness but also obtaining favorably quantitative information about the optical properties of either the inclusions or background. Parameters of interest such as size, contrast and location variations associated image quantification measures are most frequently investigated and discussed. Readers can refer to the research work [Pan et al., 2008].

### 5.3 Remark

In this section, we have demonstrated the performance of our proposed image restoration algorithms exactly applied in the imaging process for 'inter-processing' and to corrupted images for 'post-processing.'

## 6. Conclusions

### 6.1 Concluding remark

In this chapter, we have explained the background and the mathematical model of image formation and image restoration for long-wavelength imaging systems; as well, image restoration algorithms, further consideration on image restoration, and their related application have been described and demonstrated. In the meanwhile, a promising method to restore images has been proposed. As discussed in this chapter, the proposed algorithm was applied to both simulated and real atmospherically degraded images. Restoration results show significantly improved images. Especially, the restored millimeter-wave image highlights the superior performance of the proposed method in reality. The main novelty here is that error energy resulting from noise and ringing artifact is highly suppressed with the algorithm proposed in this chapter. Also, we have used such a resolution-enhancing technique with HP filtering incorporated with the FEM-based inverse computation to obtain highly resolved tomographic images of optical-property.

In addition, we have developed and realized the schemes for expediting NIR DOT image reconstruction through the inverse solution regularized with the constraint of a Lorentzian distributed function. Substantial improvements in reconstruction have been achieved without incurring additional hardware cost. With the introduction of constraints having a form of the Lorentzian distributed function, rapid convergence can be achieved owing to the fact that decreasing $\Delta\chi$ results in the increase of $\lambda$ as the iteration process proceeds, and vice versa. It behaves like a criterion in the sense of a rapid convergence that the optimal iteration number is founded as seeking an inverse solution regularized with the Lorentzian distributed function.

### 6.2 Future work

It is anticipated that of regularizing mean square error (residual term) with error energy reduction and rapid convergence (*a priori* terms) an algorithm is explored to restore images effectively and efficiently. In addition, it is no doubt that image restoration for inter-discipline application is the focus in the future research.

## 7. Acknowledgements

In collaboration with the DASD laboratory at the Department of Mechanical Engineering of National Central University, the author wish to thank group leader and members to develop the software (NIR.FD_PC) and validate the instrumentation for NIR DOT imaging system. Also, the author would like to acknowledge the funding support from the grants by the National Science Council (NSC 93-2213-E-236-002, NSC 95-2221-E-236-002, NSC 98-2221-E-236-013, NSC 99-2221-E-236-014, NSC 100-2221-E-236-012) in Taiwan (ROC).

## 8. References

[1] Archer, G. & Titterington, D. M. (1995). On Some Bayesian/Regularization Methods for Image Restoration. *IEEE Trans. on Image Process*ing, Vol. 4, pp. 307-310

[2] Brendel, B. & Nielsen, T. (2009). Selection of Optimal Wavelengths for Spectral Reconstruction in Diffuse Optical Tomography. *Journal of Biomedical Optics*, Vol. 14, 034041

[3] Chen, W.; Chen, M. & Zhou, J. (2000). Adaptively Regularized Constrained Total Least-Squares Image Restoration. *IEEE Trans. on Image Processing*, Vol. 9, pp. 588-596

[4] Davis, S. C.; Dehghani, H.; Wang, J.; Jiang, S.; Pogue, B. W. & Paulsen, K. D. (2007). Image-guided Diffuse Optical Fluorescence Tomography Implemented with Laplacian-type Regularization. *Opt. Exp.* , Vol. 15, pp. 4066-4082

[5] Frieden, B. R. (1972). Restoring with Maximum Likelihood and Maximum Entropy, *J. Opt. Soc. Am.*, Vol. 62, pp. 511-518

[6] Gerchberg, R. W. (1974). Super-Resolution through Error Energy Reduction. *Opt. Acta*, Vol. 21, pp. 709-720

[7] Gillette, J. C.; Stadtmiller, T. M. & Hardie, R. C. (1995). Aliasing Reduction in Staring Infrared Imagers Utilizing Subpixel Techniques. *Opt. Eng.*, Vol. 34, pp. 3130-3137

[8] Holboke, M. J.; Tromberg, B. J.; Li, X.; Shah, N.; Fishkin, J.; Kidney, D.; Butler, J.; Chance, B. & Yodh, A. G. (2000). Three-dimensional Diffuse Optical Mammography with Ultrasound Localization in a Human Subject. *Journal of Biomedical Optics*, Vol. 5, pp. 237-247

[9] Hou, H. & Andrews, H. (1978). Cubic Splines for Image Interpolation and Digital Filtering. *IEEE Transactions on Acoustics, Speech, and Signal Processing*, Vol. 26, No. 6, pp. 508–517

[10] Hunt, B. R. & Sementilli, P. J. (1992). Description of a Poisson Imagery Superresolution Algorithm, *Astronomical Data Analysis Software and System I., A.S.P. Conf. Ser.* , Vol. 25, pp. 196-199

[11] Hunt, B. R. (1994). Prospects for Image Restoration, *Int. J. Mod. Phys.*, C 5, pp. 151-178

[12] Jain, A. K. (1989).*Fundamentals of Digital image Processing*, Prentice- Hall, Englewood Cliffs, NJ, USA

[13] Keys, R. (1981). Cubic Convolution Interpolation for Digital Image Processing. *IEEE Transactions on Acoustics, Speech, and Signal Processing*, Vol. 29, No. 6, pp. 1153–1160

[14] Kundur, D. & Hatzinakos, D. A (1998). Novel Blind Deconvolution Scheme for Image Restoration Using Recursive Filtering. *IEEE Transactions on Signal Processing*, Vol. 46, No. 2, pp375-390

[15] Landi, G. (2007). A Fast Truncated Lagrange Method for Large-Scale Image Restoration Problems, Applied Mathematics and Computation, Vol. 186, pp. 1075–1082.

[16] Lettington, A. H. & Hong, Q. H. (1995). Image Restoration Using a Lorentzian Probability Model. *J. Mod. Opt.* , Vol. 42, pp. 1367-1376

[17] Lucy, L. B. (1974). An Iterative Technique for the Rectification of Observed Distributions. *The Astron. J.*, Vol. 79, pp. 745-765

[18] Meinel, E. S. (1986). Origins of Linear and Nonlinear Recursive Restoration Algorithms. *J. Opt. Soc. Am.*, A 3, pp. 787-799

[19] Ng, M. K.; Molina, R. & Bose, N. K. (2003). Mathematical Analysis of Super-Resolution Methodology, *IEEE Signal Processing Mag.* , Vol. 20, pp. 62-74

[20] Pan, M. C. & Lettington, A. H. (1998). Smoothing Images by a Probability Filter. *Proc. IEEE International Joint Symposia on Intelligence and Systems*, pp.343-346.

[21] Pan, M. C. & Lettington, A. H. (1999). Efficient Method for Improving Poisson MAP Super-resolution. *Electronics Letters*, Vol. 35, No. 10, pp. 803-805

[22] Pan, M. C. (2003). A Novel Blind Super-resolution Algorithm for Restoring Gaussian Blurred Images. *The International Journal of Imaging Systems & Technology*, Vol. 12, pp. 239-246

[23] Pan, M. C. (2006). Improving a Single Down-sampled Image Using Probability - filtering-based Interpolation and Improved Poisson Maximum *a posteriori* Super-resolution. *EURASIP Journal on Applied Signal Processing*, Vol. 2006, Article ID 97492 (1-9)

[24] Pan, M.-Cheng; Chen, C. H.; Chen, L.Y.; Pan, M.-Chun & Shyr, Y. M. (2008). Highly-resolved Diffuse Optical Tomography: A Systematical Approach Using High-pass Filtering for Value-preserved Images. *Journal of Biomedical Optics*, Vol. 13, No. 02, pp. Article ID 024022 (1-14)

[25] Pan, M.-Cheng & Pan, M.-Chun (2010). Rapid Convergence to the Inverse Solution Regularized with the Lorentzian Distributed Function for Near-infrared Continuous Wave Diffuse Optical Tomography," *Journal of Biomedical Optics*, Vol. 15, 016014(1-11)

[26] Pan, M. C. (2010). Image Restoration Through Regularization Based on Error Energy Minimization. *International Journal of Imaging Systems & Technology*, Vol. 20, No. 4, pp. 308-315

[27] Paulsen, K. D. & Jiang, H. (1995). Spatially Varying Optical Property Reconstruction Using a Finite Element Diffusion Equation Approximation. *Med. Phys.*, Vol. 22, pp. 691-701

[28] Pogue, B. W.; McBride, T. O.; Prewitt, J.; Österberg, U. L. & Paulsen, K. D. (1999). Spatially Variant Regularization Improves Diffuse Optical Tomography. *Appl. Opt.*, Vol. 38, pp. 2950-2961

[29] Richardson, W. H. (1972). Bayesian-based Iterative Method of Image Restoration. *J. Opt. Soc. Am.*, Vol. 62, pp. 55-59

[30] Segal, C.; Molina, R. & Katsaggelos, K. (2003). High-resolution Images from Low-Resolution Compressed Video. *IEEE Signal Processing Mag.* , Vol. 20, pp. 37-48

[31] Sezan, M. I. & Tekalp, A. M. (1988). Iterative Image Restoration with Ringing Suppression Using POCS. *Proceedings of IEEE Int. Conf. Acoust., Speech, Signals Processing*, pp. 1300-1303

[32] Singh, S.; Tandon, S. N. & Gupta, H. M. (1986). An Iterative Restoration Technique. *Signal Processing*, Vol. 11, pp. 1-11

[33] Stewart, K. & Durrani, T. S. (1986). Constrained Signal Reconstruction--A Unified Approach. *EURASIP Signal Processing* III, pp. 1423-1426

[34] Teboul, S.; Blanc-Feraud, L.; Aubert, G. & Barlaud, M. (1998). Variational Approach for Edge-Preserving Regularization Using Coupled PDE's. *IEEE Transactions on Image Processing*, Vol. 7, pp. 387-397

[35] Toraldo di Francia, G. (1952). Supergain Antennas and Optical Resolving Power. *Nuovo Cimento Suppl*, Vol. 9, pp. 426-435

[36] Toraldo di Francia, G. (1955). Resolving Power and Information. *J. Opt. Soc. Am.* , Vol. 45, pp. 497-501

[37] Wiener, N. (1942). *Extrapolation, Interpolation, and Smoothing of Stationary Time Series*, MIT Press, USA

# 12

# Super–Resolution Restoration and Image Reconstruction for Passive Millimeter Wave Imaging

Liangchao Li, Jianyu Yang and Chengyue Li
*University of Electronic Science and Technology of China*
*China*

## 1. Introduction

According to blackbody radiation theory [1], all substances at a finite absolute temperature will radiate electromagnetic energy. Passive millimeter-wave (PMMW) imaging system forms images by detecting the millimeter-wave radiation energy from the scene and utilizing the differences of the radiation intensity[2,3]. Although such imaging has been performed for decades (or more, if one includes microwave radiometric imaging), new sensor technology in the millimeter-wave regime has enabled the generation of PMMW imaging at video rates and has renewed interest in this area. Clouds and fog are effectively transparent to millimeter-wave and the cold sky is reflected by metallic objects on the ground making PMMW images similar to infrared (IR) and visible images. Due to being able to perform well under adverse weather conditions, PMMW imaging offers advantages over IR and visible imaging. It is widely used in airport security, scene monitoring, plane blind landing, medical diagnosis and environmental detection, et al [4-8].

However, the obtained images usually have the inherent problem of poor resolution, which is caused by limited aperture dimensions and the consequent diffraction limit. Images acquired from practical sensing operations usually suffer from poor resolution due to the finite size limitations of the antenna, or the lens, and the consequent imposition of diffraction limits. The fundamental operation underlying the sensing operation is the "low-pass" filtering effect due to the finite size of the antenna lens. The image at the output of the imaging system is a low-pass filtered version of the original scene. There is no useful signal beyond the cut-off frequency in the measured data, and the information lost by the imaging system are the fine details, i.e. high-frequency spectral components. In order to restore the details and improve the resolution of the image, some methods of image restoration will be needed. As is well-known that the problem of image restoration is a inverse problem and inverse problem is always singular or ill-posed. Traditional image restoration methods based on de-convolution approaches principally try to restore the information of the pass band and eliminate the effect of additive noise components. Therefore, these methods have merely limited resolution enhancement capabilities. Greater resolution improvements can only be achieved through a class of more sophisticated algorithms, called super-resolution algorithmsor image reconstruction algorithms, before the PMMW imaging can be employed.Some studies have indicated that the cost of an imager increases as (1/Resolution) raised to the power 2.5. Hence, a possible two-fold improvement in resolution by super resolution processing, roughly translates into a cost reduction of an imager by more than 5 times.

Super-resolution algorithms can be classified into iterative and non-iterative algorithms. Iterative algorithms are generally the preferred approach due to their numerous advantages and also since the iteration can be terminated once a solution of a reasonable quality is achieved. Non-iterative algorithms nvolves convolution operations in the spatial domain, direct inverse methods, regularizedpseudo inverse techniques [9].The existing iterative super-resolution methods include Lucy-Richardson method [10-11], MAP method [12], steepest descent, conjugate gradients[13] and projection on convex set (POCS) method[14].

This chapter considers the general problem of super-resolution restoration and image reconstruction. While our focus will be on application to PMMW imaging. This chapter is based on work presented in [15], portions of which appeared in [13,15-19]. To solve the inherent problem of poor resolution which is caused by limited aperture dimensions and the consequent diffraction limit, this chapter presents system model, analyses the theoretical research results and design specifically for PMMW imaging. Firstly, we estimate the PSF of the PMMW imaging system by a variational Bayesian blind restoration algorithm. Secondly, we focus on mainly four algorithms, including Conjugate-Gradient algorithm (CG), Adaptive Projected Landweber super-resolution algorithm(APL), and Undedicated Steerable Pyramid Transform Projected Landweber algorithm (USPTPL), and Two-step Projection Iteration Thresholding (tw-PIT) supper resolution using compressed sensing architecture. Finally, we have verified the system model and super-resolution algorithms by experiment in different plane using differentsystem.

## 2. PMMW image formulation model

Passive millimeter-wave (PMMW) imaging is a method of forming images through the passive detection ofnaturally occurring millimeter-wave radiation from a scene.According toblackbody radiation theory[1], all substances with a finite absolute temperature will radiate electromagnetic energy. The radiated energy spectral intensitycan be described as a Brightness Temperature $B_f$

$$B_f = \frac{2hf^3}{c}\left(\frac{1}{e^{hf/KT}-1}\right) \tag{1}$$

where $h = 6.63\times10^{-34}$ (J) is the Plank's Constant; $f$ (Hz) is the frequency; $K = 1.38\times10^{-23}$ (J.K-1) is Boltzmann's Constant; $c$ is velocity of light and the $T$ represents the absolute temperature. The brightness temperature can be assigned a gray level to generate a millimeter wave image. For the convenience of analyzing, we introduce a simplified focal plane model to calculate the imaging process, as illustrated in Fig.1 and Fig.2. The noise power can be received by sensor in the data Plane or in the image plane. Thus the millimeter wave image can be formed in the data plane or in the image plane.

Fig.1 shows the imaging process of PMMW Focal Plane Array (FPA) imaging. The process is Space-variant by the non-uniformity of the antenna beam and inconsistencies of channels. Fig.2 shows the principle of imaging in different planes. System will obtain the higher resolution and rate near to video when lens or reflectors are used in focal plane real-time imaging.

In Fig.2, the propagation process from object-plane to data-plane is two-dimensional (2D) spatial Fourier transformation (FT), while the propagation process from data-plane to focal-plane is 2D spatial inverse Fourier transformation (IFT). FPA system forms images in the image-plane by receiving object-radiation energy, without 2D FT and IFT in post-data processing. Thus, the system is high real-time.

According to Fresnel and Fraunhofer diffraction theory [20], the incoherent image is given by

$$g(u,v) = S[\iint f(x,y)h_1(u,v;x,y)dxdy] + n(u,v) \tag{2}$$

where $f(x,y)$ denotes the object's intensity function on the region $(x,y)$, $g(x,y)$ denotes the gray level function on the region $(u,v)$, $h_1(u,v,x,y)$ denotes the PSF (Point Spread function) of the imaging sensor, and $n(u,v)$ is the noise of image plane, $S[\bullet]$ denotes the non-uniformity of the antenna beams and inconsistencies of channels.

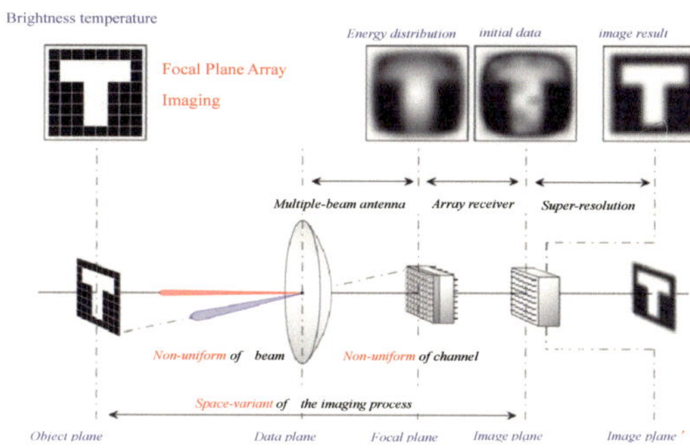


Fig. 1. Space-variant-model of Focal Plane Array imaging

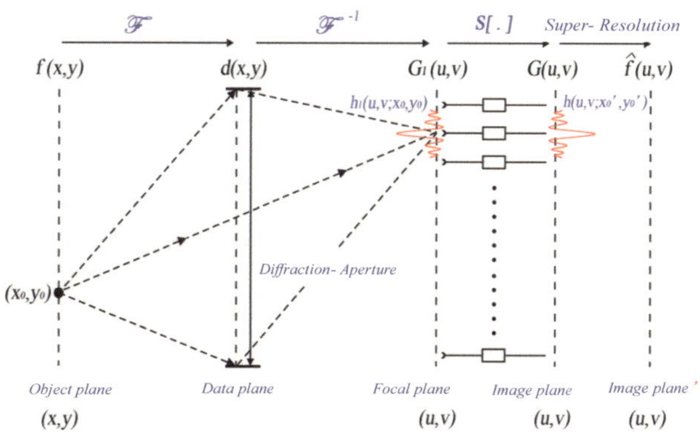


Fig. 2. Principle of FPA imaging

Practically, the system model above can be improved appropriately according to certain conditions. For example, if the gain consistency of the channels is well, the model can be expressed space-variant model

$$g(u,v) = S_0 \iint f(x,y)h(u,v;x,y)dxdy + n(u,v) \tag{3}$$

Where $S_0$ is the gain consistency of the receiver-channels. This model only considers the non-uniform effects of array antenna beams.

The imaging system is linear space-invariant when the non-uniformity of antenna beams and the inconsistencies of channels can be ignored together. Fig.2 can be shown as a simplified convolution model

$$g(u,v) = f(u,v) \otimes h(u,v) + n(u,v) \tag{4}$$

Where the function $h(u,v)$ is the PSF of the imaging, which determines the radiant energy distribution in the image plane from a point source of radiant energy located in the object plane.

In matrix and vector form, we can write the problem as

$$g = Hf + n \tag{5}$$

Where $g$ , $f$ , $n$ are lexicographically ordered vectors created from the observed image, original image, noise image respectively and $H$ is the matrix resulting from the PSF. If the original image is represented by a $N \times N$ matrix, these vectors represent image of $N^2 \times 1$ and the size of $H$ is $N^2 \times N^2$ .

The corresponding imaging model in frequency domain is

$$\hat{G}(u,v) = \hat{H}(u,v)\hat{F}(u,v) + \hat{N}(u,v) \tag{6}$$

Where $u$ , $v$ are the discrete frequency variables, $\hat{G}(u,v)$ , $\hat{F}(u,v)$ , $\hat{N}(u,v)$ signify the FFT transform of $G(x,y)$ , $F(x,y)$ , $N(x,y)$ respectively.

The so-called image restoration problem is solving for $f(x,y)$ based on the above mathematic model, namely the inverse problem of equation (5). And the inverse problem is usually bizarre or morbid. According to equation (6), there is:

$$\hat{F}(u,v) = \hat{G}(u,v) / \hat{H}(u,v) + \hat{N}(u,v) / \hat{H}(u,v) \tag{7}$$

From the equation (6) we know, when using the wrong or inaccurate PSF, the solution of $\hat{F}(u,v)$ would be wrong. And under the effect of system noise, using the inaccurate PSF can seriously influence the imaging quality. So on condition that it's unable to accurately determine the PSF of the imaging system, the way which according to the obtained blurred image, using blind processing method to estimate more accurate PSF, and then utilizing the classic image restoration algorithm to recover the image, can improve the passive millimeter wave imaging quality.

As the $\hat{H}(u,v)$ is zero outside the cut-off frequency of the imaging system. Only from the frequency domain point of view, to restore high-frequency components outside the cutoff frequency appears to be impossible.

The analytical continuation theory is the theoretical basis for to achieve super-resolution. Analytic continuation theory includes two aspects, 1) The Fourier transform of any airspace bounded function is analytic functions. 2) For any analytic function, as long as we can accurately know the part information in a limited range , we can uniquely determine the entire function. Given the values of analytic function in a range, the overall reconstruction of the function is called analytic continuation [21].

## 3. Variational bayesian estimate the PSF of the imaging system

In passive millimeter wave imaging signal processing, using accurate point spread function (PSF) is important for getting high quality restored image. In the process of imaging, the PSF is decided by antenna beam, atmospheric transmission, system noise etc. So the real PSF can not be substituted by a simple model. We can't use a simple model to replace the real PSF. And the PSF will change due to the specific imaging environment so that it is difficult to acquire the exact PSF. The common methods to obtain the PSF include direct measurement and model parameter estimation. In order to improve the quality of image restoration, a variational Bayesian blind restoration algorithm for PMMW imaging is proposed in this section, which combines the posterior probability model of the PMMW imaging to obtain accurate point spread function by variational Bayesian estimation

The variational Bayesian estimation algorithm is based on Bayesian framework [22]. The idea of this algorithm is according to the known priori information and assumptions establish a posteriori distribution model of the imaging system first. And then under a certain criterion, use the variational [23,24] method to obtain a optimal distribution which approximates with the posteriori distribution, so that reducing the complexity of the model and make the problem more analytic. Finally work out the estimation under the restriction of the cost function.

According to the Bayesian theorem, the posteriori distribution of passive millimeter wave imaging system is decided by the prior distribution of original image, the prior distribution of PSF, noise probability distribution and likelihood probability distribution. Because of the prior distribution of original image is established on its gradient value of the statistical distribution, according to the linear relationship of the above imaging model we can get

$$\nabla G(x,y) = H(x,y) \otimes \nabla F(x,y) + \nabla N(x,y) \tag{8}$$

The $\nabla$ is the gradient operator. Assuming that every point value of original image is independent, $f_{i,j} = \nabla F(i,j)$ is the gradient value of each point. The prior distribution of original image can be expressed by c-th order zero mean mixture gaussian distribution, the mathematical expressed as

$$P(\nabla F) = \prod_{i,j} P(f_{ij}) = \prod_{i,j} \sum_{c=1}^{C} \pi_c G(f_{ij} \mid 0, v_c) \tag{9}$$

Where $v_c$ is the variance of the c-th Gaussian distribution, $\pi_c$ is the weight of the c-th Gaussian distribution.

Also, assuming that every point value of PSF is independent $h_{m,n} = H(m,n)$ is the point value of the PSF. In passive millimeter wave imaging, the receive antenna's power pattern is nonnegative, its side lobe attenuate quickly, and can be treated as limited support domain. So The prior distribution of the PSF can be expressed by modified Gaussian distribution, the mathematical expressed as

$$P(H)=\prod_{m,n\in S}P(h_{mn})=\prod_{m,n\in S}G^{(R)}(h_{mn}\,|\,0,v_R)=\begin{cases}\prod_{m,n\in S}\sqrt{\frac{2v_R}{\pi}}\exp(-\frac{v_R}{2}h_{mn}{}^2) & h_{mn}\ge 0\\ 0 & h_{mn}<0\end{cases} \quad (10)$$

Where $v_R$ is the variance of the Gaussian distribution, $S$ is the support domain of the PSF.

The probability distribution of the system noise's gradient can be expressed as a Gaussian distribution the mean is zero and the variance is $\sigma^2$. Due to the different scene, the variance of the noise distribution is different, so the Gamma distribution is used to simulate the variance's distribution of different scene, the mathematical expressed as

$$P(\sigma^{-2}\,|\,\alpha,\beta)=Gamma(\sigma^{-2}\,|\,\alpha,\beta) \quad (11)$$

$\alpha$ , $\beta$ is the parameters of Gamma distribution. The likelihood distribution of the system can be obtained through the formulation $\nabla G=\nabla F\otimes H+\nabla N$ , assumption that $g_{i,j}=\nabla G(i,j)$ is the gradient of the blurred image, so the likelihood distribution is

$$P(\nabla G\,|\,H,\nabla F)=\prod_{i,j}G(b_{ij}\,|\,(\nabla F\otimes H)_{ij},\sigma^2) \quad (12)$$

Combine the equation (5), (6), (7), (8), the posteriori distribution of the passive millimeter wave imaging system is

$$\begin{aligned}P(H,\nabla F\,|\,\nabla G)&\propto P(\nabla G\,|\,H,\nabla F)P(\nabla F)P(H)P(\sigma^{-2})\\&=\prod_{i,j}G(b_{ij}\,|\,(\nabla F\otimes H)_{ij},\sigma^2)\prod_{i,j}\sum_{c=1}^{C}\pi_c G(f_{ij}\,|\,0,v_c)\\&\prod_{m,n}G^{(R)}(h_{mn}\,|\,0,v_R)Gamma(\sigma^{-2}\,|\,\alpha,\beta)\end{aligned} \quad (13)$$

After getting the posteriori distribution of the system, use the variational method to find an optical distribution $Q_{opt}=(H,\nabla F,\sigma^{-2})$ that minimizes the Kullback-Leibler (K-L) distance $D_{KL}$ (K-L distance is the value that describes the difference between two probability distributions, $D_{KL}$ is nonnegative, and $D_{KL}(Q\,||\,P)=0$ if and only if $P=Q$ )between $Q(H,\nabla F,\sigma^{-2})$ and $P(H,\nabla F,\nabla G)$. $Q(H,\nabla F,\sigma^{-2})$ is the approximation of the real posteriori distribution $P(H,\nabla F|\nabla G)$. Assumption that $H,\nabla F,\sigma^{-2}$ is independent of each other, namely:

$$P(H,\nabla F\,|\,\nabla G)=P(H\,|\,\nabla G)P(\nabla F\,|\,\nabla G) \quad (14)$$

$$Q(H,\nabla F,\sigma^{-2})=Q(H)Q(\nabla F)Q(\sigma^{-2}) \quad (15)$$

The K-L distance between $Q(H,\nabla F,\sigma^{-2})$ and $P(H,\nabla F|\nabla G)$ can be deserved by the definition of $D_{KL}$ :

$$D_{KL}(Q||P)=\left\langle \log\left[\frac{Q(H,\nabla F,\sigma^{-2})}{P(H,\nabla F|\nabla G)}\right]\right\rangle_Q$$
$$=\iiint Q(H,\nabla F,\sigma^{-2})\log\left[\frac{Q(H,\nabla F,\sigma^{-2})}{P(H,\nabla F|\nabla G)}\right]dHd\nabla Fd\sigma^{-2} \tag{16}$$
$$=\iiint Q(H,\nabla F,\sigma^{-2})\log\left[\frac{Q(H,\nabla F,\sigma^{-2})P(\nabla G)}{P(\nabla G|H,\nabla F)P(H,\nabla F)}\right]dHd\nabla Fd\sigma^{-2}$$

Due to it is uncorrelated between $P(\nabla G)$ and $H,\nabla F,\sigma^{-2}$, so the new definition of K-L distance is:

$$D_{KL}(Q||P)=\left\langle \log\left[\frac{Q(H,\nabla F,\sigma^{-2})}{P(\nabla G|H,\nabla F)P(H,\nabla F)}\right]\right\rangle_Q$$
$$=\left\langle \log\left[\frac{Q(H)}{P(H)}\right]+\log\left[\frac{Q(\nabla F)}{P(\nabla F)}\right]+\log\left[\frac{Q(\sigma^{-2})}{P(\nabla G|H,\nabla F)}\right]\right\rangle_Q \tag{17}$$

In order to minimize $D_{KL}$, the minimum value can be deserved by partial derivate the equation (13), so that we can get the $Q_{opt}(H)$, the expression is:

$$Q_{opt}(H)=\frac{1}{Z_H}P(H)\exp(\langle\log[P(\nabla G|H,\nabla F)]\rangle_{Q(\nabla F,\sigma^{-2}|H)}) \tag{18}$$

Where $Z_H$ is a normalized variable. And then the optimum estimation of PSF can be obtained by $E\left[Q_{opt}(H)\right]$.

The estimation $Q_{opt}(H)$ is not analytical, it has the form of $P(x)\propto\exp(\sum_i a_i f_i(x))$, so we can use the iteration method to get the $Q_{opt}(H)$. The solution procedure is as follows:

Obtain the parametric expression of $Q(H)$ from the form of the known $P(H)$. Factor $Q(H)$ into $D_{KL}$, and get the update equations.Use the gradient descent method to get the $Q_{opt}(H)$.Get the expected value of $Q_{opt}(H)$ so that get the estimation of the PSF.

For PMMW imaging, the power pattern of the antenna is similar to gaussian function, so at the beginning of the iteration we could use the gaussian function as its initial value, and then through variational bayesian estimation to get more accurate PSF. That can reduce the iteration times, and estimate the PSF faster.

According to the above analysis and derivation, the process of variational bayesian blind restoration algorithm as shown in figure 3. First input blurred image and compute its gradient value. Second set the initial value of variational bayesian iteration algorithm. Then begin the variational bayesian estimation through the known priori information, when the K-L distance less than the threshold, stop the iteration and output the estimated PSF. At last use the Lucy-Richardson algorithm to restore the image, get the millimeter image of the scene.

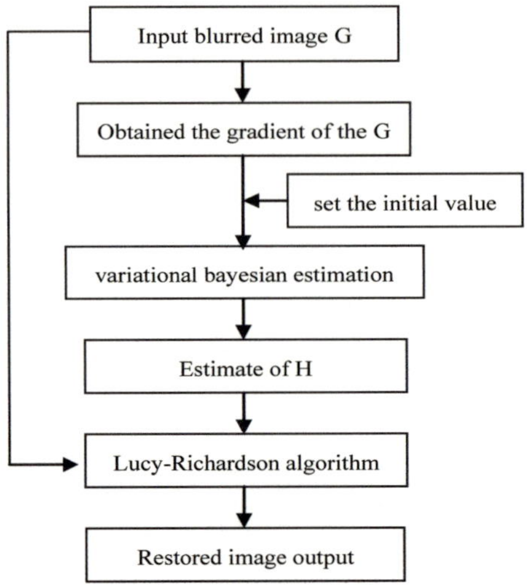


Fig. 3. Variational Bayesian Blind Restoration

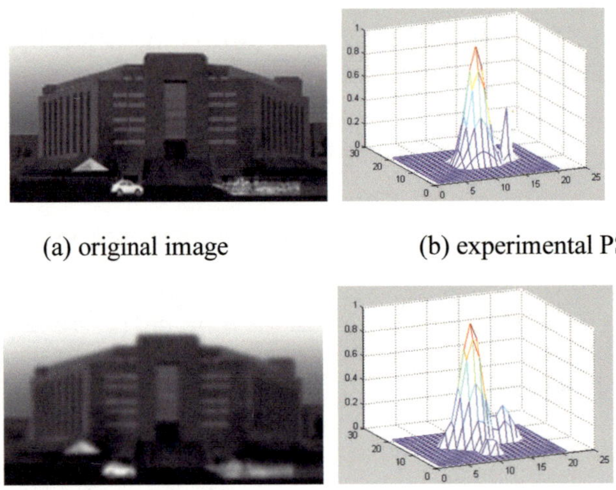

(a) original image (b) experimental PSF

(c) blurred image (d) estimated PSF

Fig. 4. Experiment 1 verify the accurate

In order to testify the effect of variational bayesian algorithm, we hold three experimentsto verify the accurate of the variational bayesian blind restoration algorithm. Fig4-a is stimulated original image, the pixel size is $110 \times 231$. Fig4-b is the experimental PSF, the pixel size is $21 \times 21$. Let the experimental PSF convolute with the original image to get the blurred image which is showed in fig4-c. Utilize the variational bayesian estimate algorithm to get the PSF, the result is showed in fig4-d. Compare the estimated PSF with experimental one, we can find that the shapes are roughly same, only a few details are different.

In order to illustrate the correct of the variational bayesian estimation, we restore the image through the Lucy-Richardson algorithm using experimental PSF and estimated PSF separately. Each restoration process iterates 20 times, the recovery results are showed in fig5.

The image restoration effect is assessed by sum of squared differences (SSD) between recovery image and original scene, the formula is as follows:

$$SSD(M,N)=\sum_{i=1}^{n}\sum_{j=1}^{n}(M(i,j)-N(i,j))^2 \tag{19}$$

M, N are two images. The SSD error is smaller the recovery image is more approximate to the original one, namely the restoration effect is better. The SSD error of fig3-a is 179, the SSD error of fig3-b is 184. We can find that the SSD errors of the images which restored by two kind of PSF are proximate, so verifying the correct of the estimated PSF.

(a) experimental PSF recovery (b) estimated PSF recovery

Fig. 5. The cooperation of two PSF recovery effect

The second experiment is the variational bayesian blind restoration of the simulated passive millimeter wave image. Assumption that the view field is $30^\circ \times 50^\circ$, the $3dB$ power beam angle of the scan antenna $\theta_{3dB}$ is 0.57 degree. Due to diffraction cut-off characteristics of the system, the sample interval is $\theta_{3dB}/2$. Considering the follow-up image processing, we set pixel interval $\theta_{3dB}/4$, so the original image of the scene is $210\times 350$ pixels, showed in fig6-a. The blurred image obtained through simulation is also $210\times 350$ pixels, showed in fig6-b.

(a) original image (b) blurred image

Fig. 6. Blurred image through simulated passive millimeter

The PSF that deserved through variational bayesian estimation, showed in fig7-a, and then use the Lucy-Richardson algorithm through 20 iteration to get the recovery image, showed in fig7-b. And for PMMW image processing, we can also get the estimated PSF through the parameter model method that according to the diffractiFon cut-off characteristics of the image system, utilizing the spectrum of the blurred image to get the parameters of the gaussian-form PSF. The result showed in fig7-c. Then uses the same restoration algorithm to get the recovery image.

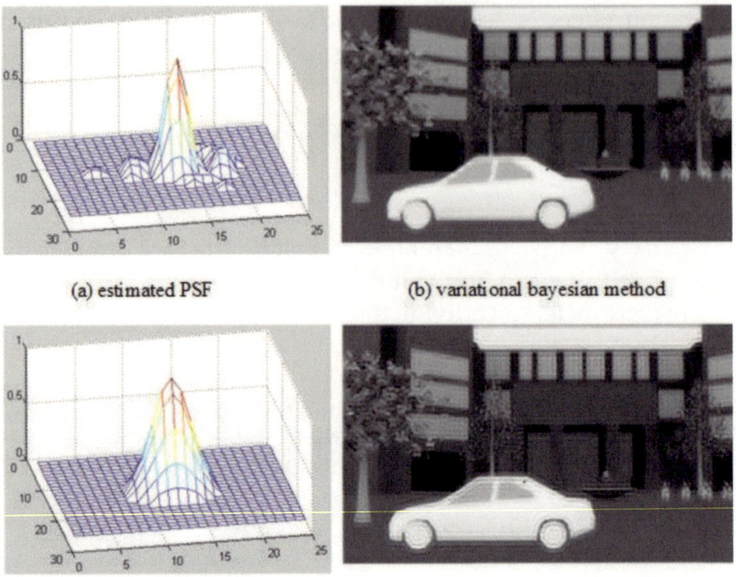

(a) estimated PSF (b) variational bayesian method

(c) gaussian-form PSF (d) parameter model method

Fig. 7. The restoration of two methods

According to the results of the above experiment, the PSF estimated by variational bayesian method is more approximate to the antenna power pattern, the recovery image is more clearer. Also compute the SSD error between recovery image and original image. For fig7-b the SSD error is 878, and for fig7-d the SSD error is 1088. We can find that the SSD error is smaller and the recovery image is more approximate to the original scene when using the variational bayesian blind restoration algorithm rather than the parameter model method.

The third experiment uses the measured data that from PMMW imaging system to verify the algorithms availability. We use a single-channel scanning radiometer for imaging. Due to the limitation of scanning angle in pitch direction, the PMMW image isstitched together.Fig8-a is the optical image of the scene, fig8-b is the obtained millimeter wave image which is blurred, fig8-c is the estimated PSF, and fig8-d is the recovery image from variational bayesian blind restoration algorithm. We can find that the recovery image's contour and details are clearer, the imaging quality is improved effectively.

## 4. Super-resolution restoration and image reconstruction

In order to improve the resolution of the image, some methods of image restoration will be needed. The image restoration is an inverse problem in general, which is always ill posed. Traditional de-convolution approaches restore the information of the pass band and eliminate the effect of additive noise components. Therefore, these methods have only limited resolution enhancement capabilities. Greater resolution improvements can only be achieved through a class of more sophisticated algorithms, called super-resolution algorithms, including Lucy-Richardson algorithm, Conjugate-gradient (CG) algorithm,Adaptive Projected Landweber (APL) super-resolution algorithm, Undecimated Steerable Pyramid Transform Projected Landweber (USPTPL) algorithm and Two-step

Projection Iteration Thresholding (*tw*-PIT) supper resolution using compressed sensing architecture algorithm. In this section,wepresentthe image restoration algorithms.

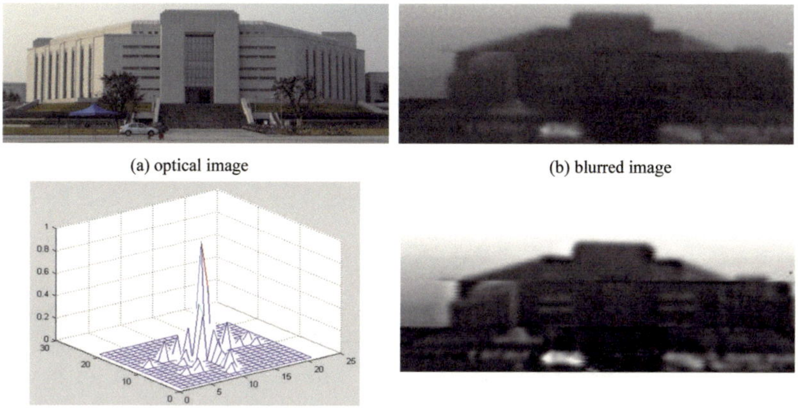


(a) optical image (b) blurred image

(c) estimated PSF (d) recovery image

Fig. 8. Measured data restoration

Stochastic super-resolution image restoration, typically a Bayesian approach, provides a flexible and convenient way to model a priori knowledge concerning the solution. Bayesian estimation methods are used when the a posteriori probability density function (PDF) of the original image can be established. Using maximum-a-posteriori estimation, we can obtain an exact solution of the formula.

### 4.1 Conjugate-gradient algorithm

The Conjugate-gradient (CG) algorithm is an effective Krylov subspace method of solving an unconstrained large-scale optimization problem, which is equivalent to solve the quadratic minimization problem[25, 26].

$$\min J = \frac{1}{2}\|Hf - g\|_2, \quad f > 0 \tag{20}$$

$\|\bullet\|_2$ The target function can be denoted as

$$J(f) = \frac{1}{2} f^T H^T H f - g^T H f + \frac{1}{2} H^T H \tag{21}$$

And the gradient function is

$$grad(J(f)) = H^T H f - H^T g \tag{22}$$

The $f_k$ is the k-th iteration estimate of the original scene, it generates a descent direction $d_k$, n~ is conjugate to all previous search directions: $d_1, d_2 ...... d_n$ with respect to matrix $H^T H$; that is $d_n^T H^T H d_k$, k.=0,1,…n-1. In other words, conjugate gradient algorithm deals with problem of 1D searching:

$$f_{k+1} = f_k + \lambda_k d_k \tag{23}$$

where $\lambda_k$ denotes optimal size at searching directions, which is decided by $\min J(f_k + \lambda_k d_k); d_k = -\nabla J(f_k)$.

Because the standard conjugate gradient algorithm is a linear restoration method, it has only limited capability of super-resolution, that is, spectral extrapolation. Furthermore, during each iteration, we can not guarantee the nonnegative constraint of estimated images. An interesting feature of the CG method is that it can be modified in order to take into account the additional priori-information about the solution. The information can be expressed as a number of closed convex sets.

An example of a constraint which is rather natural in many problems of image restoration is the positivity of the solution. The constraint can also be projected as a closed convex set. Thus we can impose the constraint that the image is nonnegative on the iteration. Because the projection operation is non-linear operations, it introduces frequencies beyond the pass-band. Thus, the modified CG algorithm has the capacity of spectrum extrapolation. It can be shown as

$$f_P^{k+1} = P_C[f_{k+1} = f_k + \lambda_k d_k] \tag{24}$$

where $P_c$ denotes the projection operator on the constraint set $C$. Then the projection operator is given by

$$P_C f = \begin{cases} f & if\ f > 0 \\ 0 & if\ f \le 0 \end{cases} \tag{25}$$

Other convex and closed sets include finite support constraint, band limited constraint, and spatial limited constraint[27]. The super-resolution performance of the modified CG algorithm can be verified from subsequent experiments.

Along with the increase of image size($n \times n$), the dimensions of matrix $H$ is larger($n^2 \times n^2$), it is bad for calculating and storage. However, $H$ is Toeplitz matrix, a circulant convolution matrix $B_h$ can be produced by $H$, it has features as follow[26]:

$$B_h = W\Lambda_h W^{-1},\ B_h^T = W\Lambda_h^* W^{-1} \tag{26}$$

where

$$W(m,n) = \frac{1}{L^2}\exp(-\frac{j \times 2\pi mn}{L}), m,n \in 0,1,...L-1,\ \Lambda_h = diag(DFT(h)) \tag{27}$$

The relationship between W, $W^{-1}$and Discrete Fourier Transform (DFT) is as follows:

$$Wp = IDFT(p(n)),\ W^{-1}p = DFT(p(n)) \tag{28}$$

In image processing, n is selected in the 2-power, such as 28-2128, etc. The amount of calculation of image direct iteration restoring is very great at this time. However, $H$ is Toeplitz matrix(BTTB), so the matrix $H$ (BTTB) can be continued to circulant matrix structure (BCCB) by the above mentioned matrix-vector computing and Fast Fourier Transform (FFT). Thus, the CG algorithm has quick convergence.

### 4.1.1 Simulation and experiments

To verify the super-resolution capability of the CG algorithm, representative results of restoring blurred images is shown in Figs. 10a-c. The simulation image is a $256 \times 256$ synthetic image composed of a series of concentric disks with the background (dark) at intensity value zero and the disks (bright) at intensity value one.

The simulation image and its spectrum are shown in Fig.10a and Fig.11a, respectively. To simulate the blurring caused by a diffraction limited imaging sensor, we blur the ideal image by the PSF of a circular aperture antenna which is equivalent to a low-pass filter. Zero-mean Gaussian noise is added to the blurred image to get the noisy blurred image. The blurred image and its spectrum are shown in Fig.4b and Fig.5b, respectively. The simulation results of the CG algorithms are shown Fig.4c, and its spectrum are shown in Fig.5c.

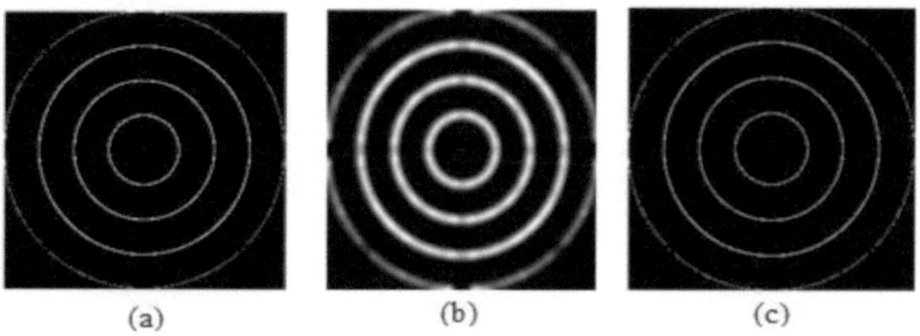

Fig. 9. (a) Original Image, (b) Blurred Image (c) Conjugate gradient after 50 iterations

From Fig.9 and Fig.10, we can see that the super resolution capability (spectral-extrapolation) of the CG algorithm is improvement remarkable. Furthermore, the CG algorithm can effectively reduce rings effects.

To evaluate the capacity of the recovery algorithm, the simplest common assessment criteria is to calculate the $L_2$ norms of the deviation between the original image and restore image, that is the Mean Square Error (MSE), which is expressed as

$$MSE = \frac{1}{N^2} \sum \left| f - \tilde{f}^k \right|^2 \tag{29}$$

where $f$ denotes the ideal image, $\tilde{f}^k$ represents the k-th restoration result, $\|\bullet\|_2$ is $L_2$ norms. Fig. 11 plots the MSE of the CG algorithms versus iteration numbers. Obviously, the CG algorithm has a fast convergence of the MSE. Generally, the MSE will be below 0.065 when the iterations number is 6. Clearly, the CG algorithm has the good convergence performance.

In the second experiment, a small number of 32x32 gun images are collected by 91.5GHz mechanically scanned mono-channel radiometer with horn antenna in the lab and around surroundings, as shown in Fig.12. The captured PMMW image is shown in Fig.12b. The restored image is shown in Fig.12c. From Fig.12, we can see that the super-resolution performance and spatial resolution are enhanced by the algorithm.

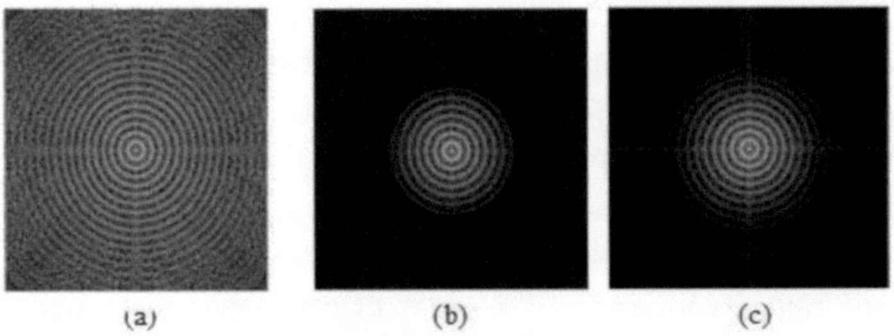


Fig. 10. Spectrum of Fig. 10 (a) Original Image, (b) Blurred Image (c) Result after CG

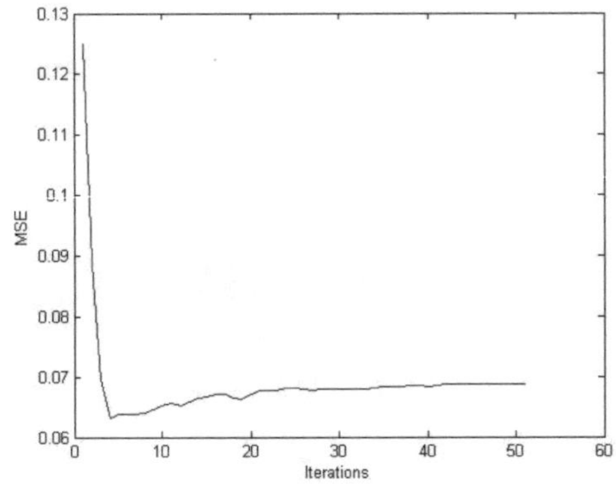


Fig. 11. MSE of the CG

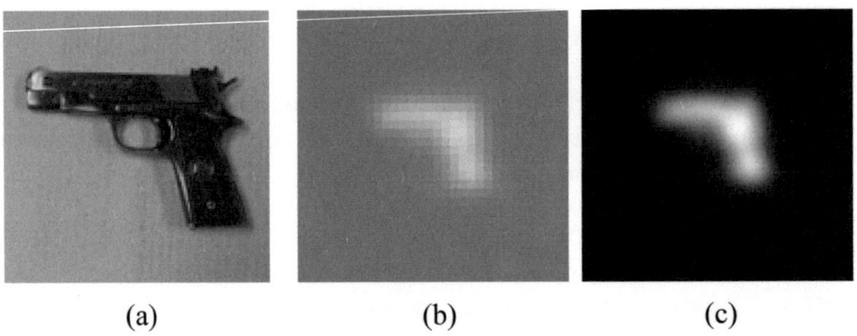


Fig. 12. (a) Visible Image (b) Captured Image (c) Result of CG after 50 iterations

Experiment results demonstrate that the CG super-resolution algorithm has fast convergent rate and the good spectral-extrapolation capacity. The CG algorithm improves the spatial resolution and reduce the ringing effects which are caused by regularizing the image restoration. Thus, the CG algorithm can be used in image restoration and PMMWI to enhance the super-resolution performance and eliminate most of the effects of blurring.

### 4.2 Adaptive projected Landweber super-resolution algorithm

It is well-known that the problem of image restoration is the computation of $f$, given the image data $g$ and the PSF $h$. Some iterative methods have been introduced to solve equation (5) [28]. Thebasic feature is that the number of iterations plays the role of a regularization parameter because semi-convergence holds true in the case of noisy images. Iterative methods of image restoration have an advantage over one-step methods in that the partial solution may be examined at each step of the iteration and any constraints on the solution can be enforced at that time.

#### 4.2.1 Landweber algorithm

The Landweber method (successive-approximation method) [29] is the simplest iterative regularizing algorithm to solve linear ill-posed problems. Because standard Landweber algorithm is a linear restoration method, it has only limited capability of super-resolution (spectral extrapolation). Furthermore, during each iteration, we cannot guarantee the nonnegative constraint of estimated image. Other disadvantages of the Standard Landweber method are slow convergence and the difficulty of choosing proper update parameter.

Landweber algorithm is the simplest iterative method for approximating the least-square solutions of equation (5). It is characterized by the equation

$$f^{k+1} = f^k + \tau H^T(g - Hf^k) \tag{30}$$

Where $H^T$ is the transpose of the blurring operator $H$; superscript $k$ denotes the $k$th iteration; $\tau$ is a relaxation parameter controlling the convergence, in order to guarantee the convergence of $f^k$, the value of $\tau$ are given by

$$0 < \tau < \frac{2}{\sigma_1^2} \tag{31}$$

Where $\sigma_1$ is the largest singular value of matrix H [30]. The initial guess $f^0$ is usually set to 0.

#### 4.2.2 Projected Landweber super-resolution algorithm

Because standard Landweber algorithm is a linear restoration method, it has only limited capability of super-resolution, that is, spectral extrapolation. Furthermore, during each iteration, we cannot guarantee the nonnegative constraint of estimated image.

An interesting feature of the Landweber method is that it can be modified in order to take into account additional priori information about the solution. Fundamental of reliable estimation of high frequencies is the utilization of a priori known information during the processing iteration. In fact, since image restoration is inherently an ill-posed problem, the quality of restoration and the extent for achievable super-resolution depend on the accuracy and the amount of a priori information. As shown there, many physical constraints on the unknown object can be expressed by requiring that it belong to some given closed and convex sets. While efforts at the modeling of constraint sets and the use of these in projection-based set theoretic image recovery constitutes a popular direction for current research, it seems that the idea of combining the strong point of Landweber schemes and that of the projection-based methods has not been paid much attention to. The modified Landweber method, also called the Projected Landweber Algorithm[31] is as follows

$$f^{k+1} = P_C\left[f^k + \tau H^*(g - Hf^k)\right] \tag{32}$$

Where $P_C$ denotes the projection operator onto the constraint set $C$.

An example of a constraint which is rather natural in many problems of image restoration is the positivity of the solution. We can impose the constraint that the image is nonnegative on the iteration. Because this constraint is non-linear operation, it introduces frequencies beyond the passband. The super-resolution performance of the Projected Landweber algorithm can be verified from subsequent experiments. Then the projection operator is given by

$$P_C f = \begin{cases} f & if\ f > 0 \\ 0 & if\ f \le 0 \end{cases} \tag{33}$$

Other convex and closed set $C$ include finite support constraint, band limited constraint and spatial limited constraint[27].

### 4.2.3 Adaptive projected Landweber Super-resolution alogithm

One disadvantage of the Landweber method is slow convergence and the difficulty to choose proper update parameter. If $\tau$ is too large, the iterative process may diverge. If $\tau$ is too small, the iterative process would be slow. Therefore, it is necessary to determine a suitable $\tau$ for the iterative algorithm. Lie Liang and Yuanchang Xu proposed modification of this method, Adaptive Landweber method [32], in which constant $\tau$ is calculated adaptively in each iteration. The Adaptive Landweber algorithm has a better result and faster convergence than standard Landweber algorithm. Instead of using a constant update parameter, the Adaptive Landweber method computes the update parameter at each iteration and chooses the maximum of the computed parameter and the preset constantparameter to use in the next iteration.

Then we proposed a hybrid algorithm that attempt to combine the strong points of both Projected Landweber scheme (simplicity of execution, Super-resolution, etc.) and the Adaptive adjustments relax parameter $\tau$ (faster convergence rate, lower mean square error, etc.). For a brief description, each cycle of this "Adaptive Projected Landweber algorithm" consists of executing the three steps:

**Step 1.** Implement standard Landweber algorithm with initial relax parameter $\tau_0$ and $f^0 = 0$

$$f^{k+1} = f^k + \tau_k H^T (g - Hf^k) \tag{34}$$

**Step 2.** Implement projection onto the convex set $C$

$$f^{k+1} = P_C f^{k+1} \tag{35}$$

**Step 3.** Implement relax parameter $\tau_{k+1}$ updating algorithm

$$\tau_{k+1} = \max(\tau_0, \frac{\left\|\nabla f^{k+1}\right\|_2}{\left\|\nabla f^k\right\|_2}) \tag{36}$$

Where $\nabla f^k$ denotes the first order derivative of $f^k$. The algorithm hence adaptively updates the relax parameter $\tau$ to speed up convergence and obtain improved object estimation after each cycle of implementation. A flow-chart depicting the various step is shown in Fig. 13.

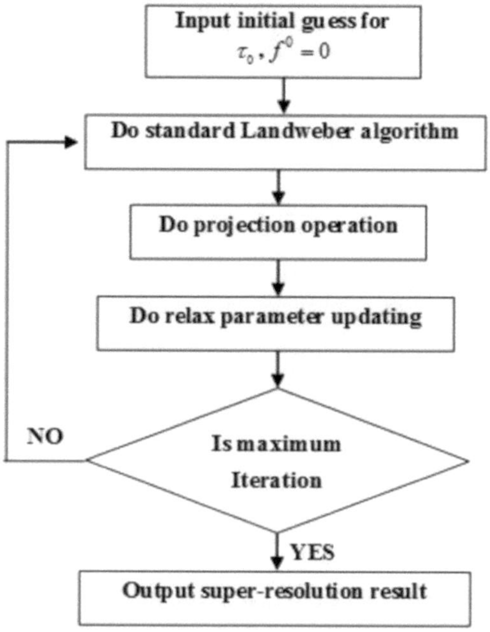


Fig. 13. Flow-chart for implementation of Adaptive Projected Landweber algorithm

### 4.2.4 Simulation and experiments

In order to verify the super-resolution capability of this algorithm mentioned above, two images have been adopted in simulation experiments, one is a 256x256 synthetic image composed of a series of concentric disks, and the other is an 32x32 gun image captured by 91.5 GHz mechanically scanned mono channel radiometer.

In the first experiment, the ideal image and its spectrum are shown in Fig.14a and Fig.16a, respectively. For simulating the blurring caused by a diffraction limited imaging sensor, we blur the ideal image by the PSF of a low-pass filter that simulates a sensor with a circular aperture of diameter 8 pixels. The blurred image and its spectrum are shown in Fig.14b and Fig.15b respectively. the simulation results of these algorithms are shown Fig.14c-14e, and their spectrum are shown in Fig.15c-15e, respectively. It is clear that from Fig.14 and Fig.15 the results obtained by the Adaptive Porjected Landweber algorithm are better than the results obtained by the Porjected Landweber algorithm and the standard Landweber algorithm. The super-resolution capabilities (spectrum extrapolation) of these projection-based methods are obvious. However, the convergence of the standard Landweber method is slow compared to the Adaptive Porjected Landweber algorithm and the Porjected Landweber algorithm, mainly because the standard Landweber algorithm is a linear method, and it has hardly super-resolution capability.

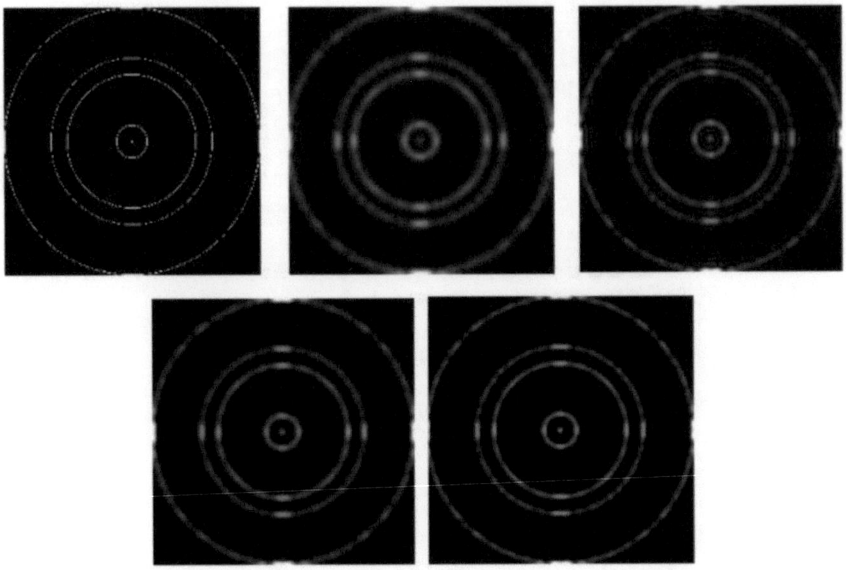

Fig. 14. (a) Original Image (b) Blurred (c) Standard Landweber after 100 iterations (d)Projected Landweber (e) Adaptive Projected Landweber

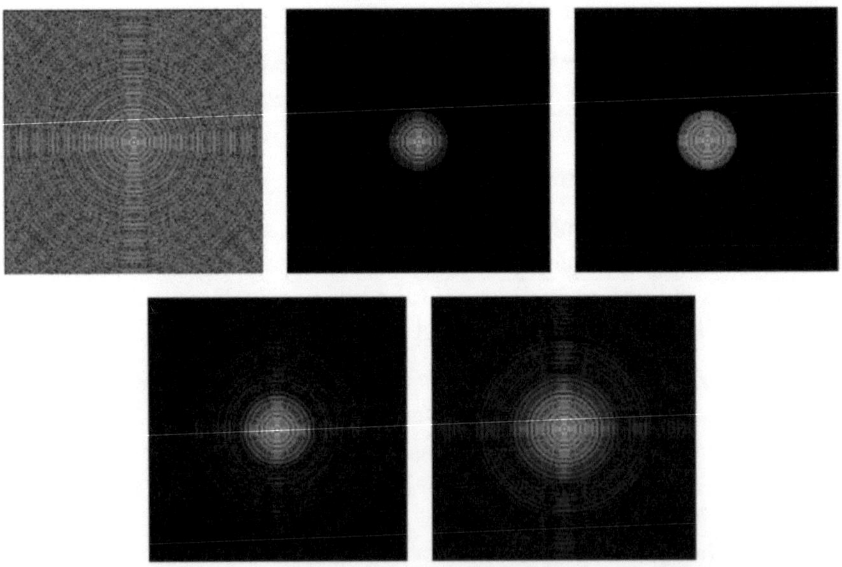

Fig. 15. Spectrum of Fig. 1 (a) Original Image, (b) Blurred (c) Standard Landweber after 100 iterations (d) Projected Landweber (e) Adaptive Projected Landweber

Fig. 16 plots the MSE of the three algorithms. It can be observed that the Adaptive Porjected Landweber algorithm has a faster decrease of the MSE than the other two algorithms. Also, the MSE of the Adaptive Porjected Landweber algorithm is lower than that of the other two algorithms.

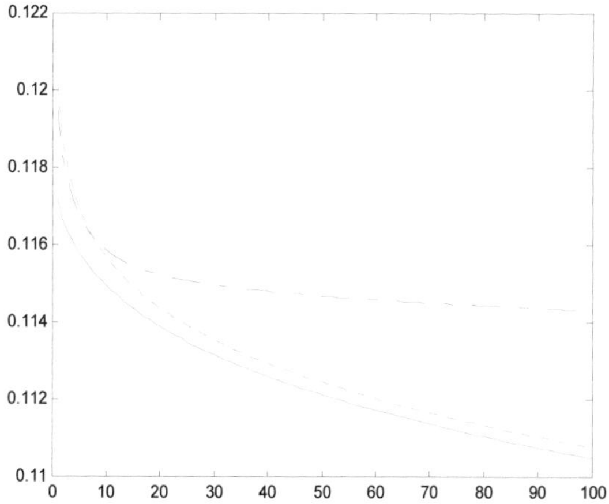


Fig. 16. MSE of the Adaptive Projected Landweber(solid line). MSE of the Projected Landweber(dash-dot line). MSE of the Standard Landweber(dash line).

In the second experiment, the visual image is shown in Fig.17a. The blurred image is shown in Fig.17b acquired by the PMMW radiometer. The restored images are shown in Fig.17c-17e respectively. The Adaptive Projected Landweber algorithm gives better result than standard Landweber algorithm. The results obtained by the Adaptive Projected Landweber algorithm are very similar to (slightly better than) the results obtained by the Projected Landweber algorithm. Furthermore, Gibbs rings of standard Landweber algorithm aggravate as the iteration increases.

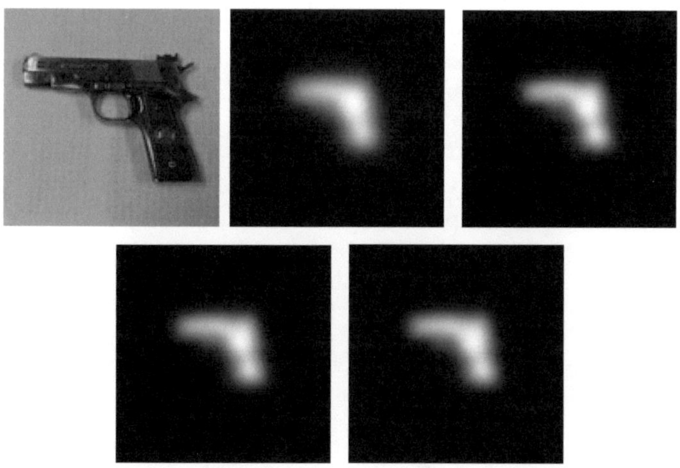

Fig. 17. (a) Visible Image (b) Captured Image (c) Standard Landweber (d) Projected Landweber (e) Adaptive Projected Landweber

The APL algorithm, which iteratively applies a cycle of Projected Landweber algorithm followed by a relax parameter adaptive adjustment, combines the strong points of the two approaches and hence possesses a number of implementation benefits. The adaptive update parameter aims to emphasize speed and stability. Experiment results demonstrate that the results of Adaptive Projected Landweber algorithm are better than those of standard Landweber algorithm and Projected Landweber algorithm. The Adaptive Projected Landweber Super-resolution algorithm has lower MSE and produces sharper images. These constraints and adaptive character speed up the convergence of the Landweber estimation process. The superior restoration of the object features observed in the image domain and the significant extrapolation of spatial frequencies observed in the spectral domain lead to the conclusion that the Adaptive Prejected Landweber super-resolution algorithm can be used for restoration and super-resolution processing for PMMW imaging.

### 4.3 Undecimated steerable pyramid transform projected Landweber algorithm

Super resolution algorithms have two tasks: restoring the spectrum components within the passband (by reversing the effects of convolution with the point spread function of imaging system) and re-create the lost frequencies due to the imposition of sensor diffraction limits by spectral extrapolation. Recently, a more sophisticated spectrum decomposition technique is adopted. Using multi-scale technique, an image is decomposed into a hierarchical manner where each level corresponds to a reduced-resolution approximation of the image. It is equivalent to a filter bank that decomposes an image into different frequency components. By such decomposition, one can restore the passband firstly and then extrapolate high frequency components stage by stage. The most commonly used multi-scale methods are based on the Pyramid transform (such as Laplacian Pyramid, steerable Pyramid), the wavelets transform, the contourlets transform and so on [33-36]. The multi-scale transforms mentioned above belong to linear transform, but they are not shift invariant due to the down sampling. The lack of shift-invariance is a problem for many applications such as image restoration and image denoising because it causes pseudo-Gibbs phenomena around singularities [33]. Undecimated multi-scale methods can avoid such problem thus it has been introduced in several studies [34-36].

#### 4.3.1 Undecimated pyramid transform

The Undecimated Pyramid transform (UPT) uses filter bank ($H_{10}$, $H_{11}$) in the analysis part and ($G_{10}$, $G_{11}$) in the synthesis part. The ideal frequency response of the building block of the UPT is shown in Fig. 18(a). The perfect reconstruction condition is given as

$$H_{10}G_{10} + H_{11}G_{11} = 1 \tag{37}$$

Filters of the UPT do not need to be orthogonal or bi-orthogonal and this lack of the need for orthogonality or bi-orthogonality is beneficial for design freedom.

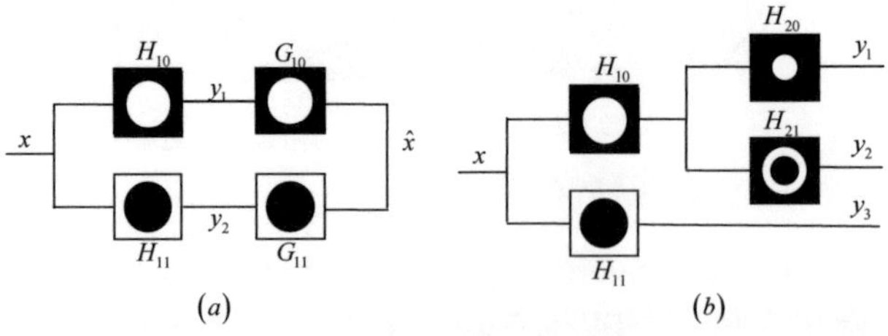


Fig. 18. Undecimated Pyramid transform. (a) The structure of the two-channel undecimated filter bank (b) Two stage Pyramid decomposition.

To perform the multi-scale decomposition, we construct non-subsampled pyramids by iterated non-subsampled filter banks. For the next level, we upsample all filters by 2 in both dimensions. Therefore, they also satisfy the perfect reconstruction condition. The cascading of the analysis part is shown in Fig. 18(b).

Seen from frequency domain, the UPT decomposes an image into different frequency bands. Suppose $N$ is the order of the cascading decomposition, $H_{N0}$ is a low frequency band and $H_{n1}$ $(1 \le n \le N)$ corresponds to high frequency component of the $n^{th}$ stage. Let $\Psi_n$ be the passband of $H_{n0}$, we have $\Psi_1 \supset \Psi_2 \supset \Psi_3 ...$. If the UTP is designed to acquire low frequency component contained in $\Psi$, we can easily determine $N$ by the inclusion relation in frequency domain: $\Psi_N \supseteq \Psi \supset \Psi_{N+1}$.

In above mentionProjection Landweber algorithm, essentially the property of semi-convergence indicates that the Landweber algorithm is a regularization method. Suppose a perturbed linear equation is given as below

$$Ax = b^{\delta} \tag{38}$$

Where $A$ is an $m \times n$ system matrix, which describes the system geometry, $x$ is an $n \times 1$ vector of the image pixels and $b^{\delta}$ is an $m \times 1$ vector of the measured data with perturbation $\delta$. Let $x_k^{\delta}$ be the solution of equation (35) acquired by the Landweber after the $k^{th}$ iteration, $x_k$ be the solution of $Ax = b$. If $b^{\delta} \notin D(A^{+})$, the Landweber algorithm has [37]

$$|| x_k^{\delta} - x_k || \le \sqrt{k\tau}\delta \tag{39}$$

Where $A^{+}$ is the Moore-Penrose inverse of $A$. For a given $\delta$, the data error $|| x_k^{\delta} - x_k ||$ is amplified with the increase of iterative steps $k$. The algorithm stops at the semi-convergence point when the data error reaches the magnitude of approaching error $|| x^{+} - x_k ||$, where $x^{+} = A^{+}b$.

Known from equation (36), the Landweber stops more quickly if it is used to restore an image with a bigger $\delta$. In the restoration of a badly contaminated image, the Landweber may have not plenty iterative steps to restore or re-create the frequency components that we need. Unfortunately, signal-to-noise ratio of PMMW image is quite low due to limited integral time and bandwidth. Because of this, the PL algorithms can not provide a satisfied resolution improvement in most practical applications. The practical performance of the PL algorithm is shown in Fig. 23(c).

The denoising technique can avoid the fast termination of the Landweber algorithm. Because PSF of a PMMW imaging system is approximately band-limited, a low passband filter can perform the function. By such pre-procession, the high-frequency component of $\delta$ is attenuated thus the Landweber algorithm avoid the adverse effect of the amplification of high-frequency noise.

### 4.3.2 Undecimated Pyramid Projected Landweber (UPPL) super-resolution algorithm

The basic strategy of image super-resolution based on the UPT is to use a band-limit frequency selection rule to construct a multilevel Pyramid-like restoration model from the

Pyramid representations of the original data. The UPT of an image can be described as collection of low- or band-pass copies of an original image. For a band-limited image, the decomposition of UPT can implement the function of image denoising.

The framework of the UPPL algorithm is shown in Fig. 19. First the UPPL algorithm decomposes a PMMW images by the UPT. Sub images $(y_1, y_2, \cdots, y_{j+1})$ acquired by the decomposition correspond to the frequency bands shown in Fig. 18(b). Then the UPPL restores these frequency components from the lowest frequency band to the highest. Because the UPT has the capability to attenuate noise in higher frequency bands, the UPPL is able to improve the restoration of lower frequency bands by providing the PL algorithm plenty iterate steps. In each stage the initial guess of the current PL iterations is the restored result of the last stage. So the restoration of current frequency band is always based on a sufficient restoration of lower frequency components.

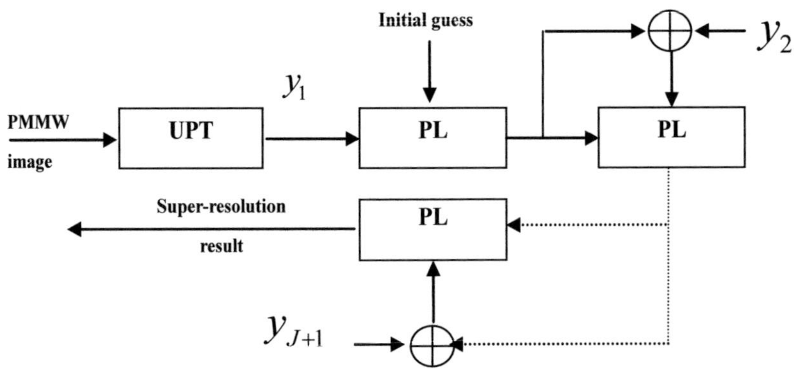


Fig. 19. The UPPL algorithm framework

The UPPL algorithm is summarized as below:

**Step 1.** Compute the UPT of the input image for $J$ levels $(y_1, y_2, \cdots, y_{J+1})$.

**Step 2.** Implement $K_1$ PL iterations with initial update parameter $\tau_1$ , $f_1^0 = 0$ and $g_1 = y_1$ .

**Step 3.** Implement $K_j$ PL iterations with initial update parameter $\tau_j$ , $f_j^0 = f_{j-1}^{K_{j-1}}$ and $g_j = y_j + g_{j-1}$, where $f_{j-1}^{K_{j-1}}$ denotes the restored image of the $(j-1)^{th}$ scale, $j \in (1, 2, \cdots, J)$ .

**Step 4.** Repeat step 3 to the highest scale of $J + 1$ .

In each stage, the UPPL restores a frequency band by an independent PL algorithm, which has its own update parameter. Known from equation (36), a big update parameter accelerates the amplification of the data error $||x_k^\delta - x_k||$ thus it decreases the number of iterative steps. Because of this, the UPPL enjoys the flexibility of controlling the convergence speed of different frequency bands. The principle for choosing a suitable $\tau_j$ is that the number of iterative steps should be sufficient but not excessive. Commonly the concrete value of $\tau_j$ is acquired by a number of experiments.

#### 4.3.3 Simulation and experiments

In comparison with PL algorithm, two images have been adopted in simulation experiments, one is a 256x256 synthetic image composed of a series of disks, and the other is an 32x32 gun image captured by 91.5 GHz mechanically scanned mono channel radiometer.

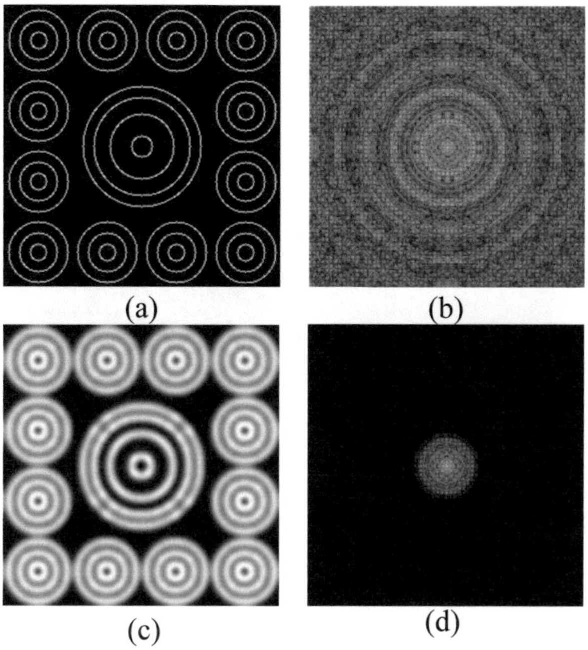

Fig. 20. (a) Original Image, (b) Original Image Spectrum, (c) Blurred Image, (d) Blurred Image Spectrum

In the first experiment, the ideal image and its spectrum are shown in Fig. 20(a) and Fig. 20(b), respectively. For simulating the blurring caused by a diffraction limited imaging sensor, we blur the ideal image by the PSF of a low-pass filter that simulates a sensor with a circular aperture of diameter 16 pixels. Zero-mean Gaussian noise was added to the blurred image to get the observed noisy blurred image at 30 dB Blurred Signal-to-Noise Ratio (BSNR). The blurred image and its spectrum are shown in Fig. 20(c) and Fig. 20(d), respectively.

In the experiment, scale number of UPT is 3. The update parameters are $\tau_1 = 1.5$, $\tau_2 = 1.2$, $\tau_3 = 1.0$ and $\tau_4 = 0.4$ respectively. The simulation results of the PL algorithm and UPPL algorithm are shown in Fig. 21(a) and 21(c) after 200 iterations, and their spectrum are shown in Fig. 21(b) and 21(d), respectively. It is clear that the results obtained by the UPPL algorithm are better than the results of the PL algorithm. The super-resolution capability (spectrum extrapolation) of the UPPL algorithm is more obvious.

Fig. 22 plots the MSE of the two algorithms. It is clear that the UPPL algorithm has a faster decrease of the MSE than the PL algorithm. The MSE of UPPL algorithm is lower than that of the PL algorithm.

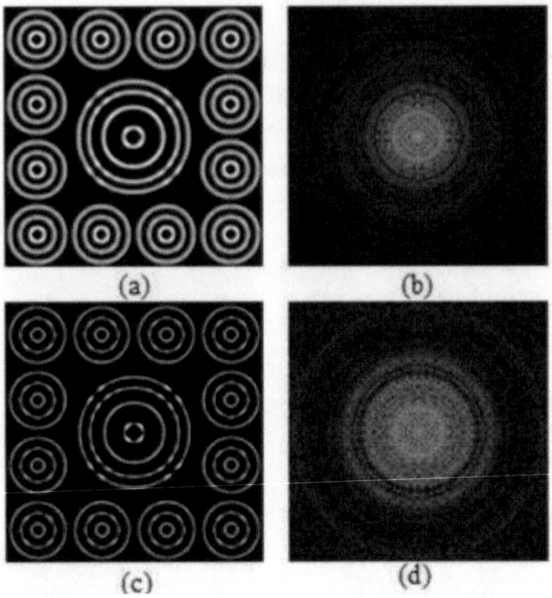


Fig. 21. (a) Result of PL, (b) Spectrum of PL, (c) Result of UPPL, (d) Spectrum of UPPL

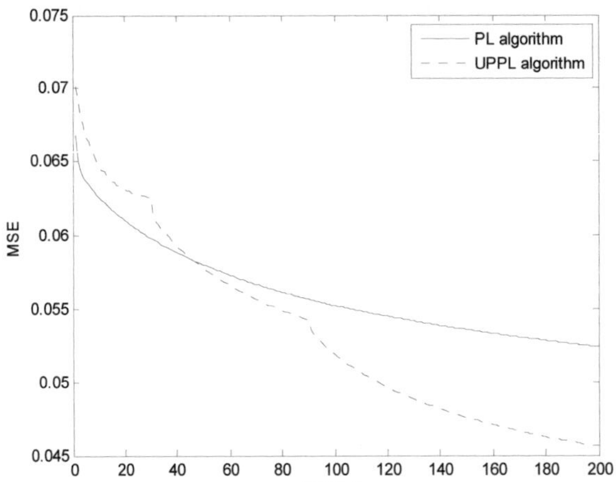


Fig. 22. MSE vs Iterations

In the second experiment, the visual image is shown in Fig. 23(a). The blurred image is shown in Fig. 23(b) acquired by a 91.5 GHz mechanically scanned radiometer. We use the same experimental parameter as the first experiment. The restored images are shown in Fig. 23(c) and 23(d) respectively. It is clear that a significant resolution improvement is achieved by the UPPL algorithm.

A reasonable frequency decomposition scheme, the UPT is also presented. Experiment results demonstrate that the result of UPPL is better than that of the PL algorithm. The UPPL algorithm has lower MSE and produces sharper images. The effectiveness of the UPPL algorithm for practical PMMW images is also validated.

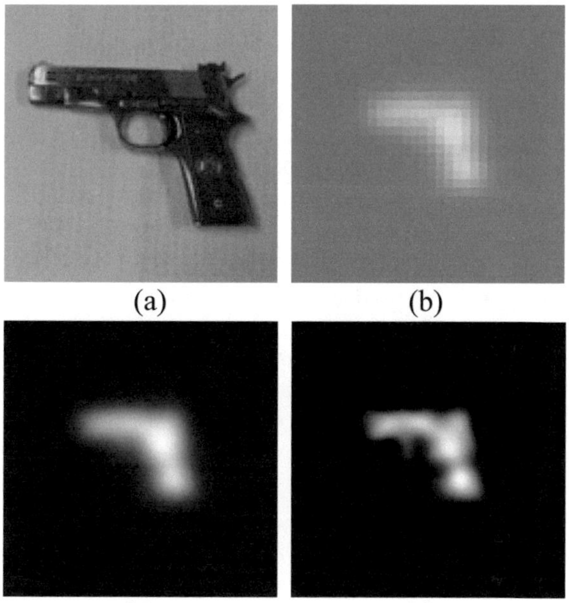

(a) (b) (c) (d)

Fig. 23. (a) Visible Image, (b) Captured Image, (c) Result of PL, (d) Result of UPPL.

Undecimated steerable pyramid decomposition of the image generates a number of different sub-band frequency images. As these details and the differences between the useful signals and noise in the approximate sub-band images, we can use different relaxation parameters and iterations in order to suppress the noise. The UPPL algorithm combines the advantages of the PL algorithms and multi-level pyramid recovery methods. The acquired image are first decomposed by non-sampling pyramid transform into some sub-images. Then we operate the super-resolution process to each grade low-pass image using the PL algorithm. Since each sub-image contains different frequency content, we select different relaxation parameters and iterations in the super-resolution processing. The algorithm improves the ability of spectral extrapolation, and makes the restored image more sharpen.

### 4.4 Two-step projection iteration thresholding supper-resolution using compressed sensing architecture

For passive millimeter wave image, it has certain structure, which can be sparse decomposed in a particular base. Therefore, we can use the sparse prior information of PMMW images for the image reconstruction process. Because the noise is not sparse, the supper-resolution based on sparse prior information can suppress noise. The low-pass effect of the PMMW imaging system make the space resolution very poor. The *tw*-PIT algorithm uses the sparse prior information and the non-negative finite value information of PMMW images, which can separate the noise from the signals in the iteration process. The algorithm is very effective when the image noise is existed which can also has good super-resolution performance.

### 4.4.1 Projection Iteration Threshold (PIT) supper-resolution

In the compressed sensing(CS) theory, we use sparsity to describe a signal's feature or structure. Passive millimeter wave(PMMW) images have a certain structure so that they can have sparse representation on some basis. Therefore, during the processing of super-resolution, we can use the prior that the PMMW images can be sparse represented to reconstruct them. And in image restoration, the introduction of l1-norm optimization can proform a more effective way to recover a original image.

In the CS theory, we take advantage of the signal's sparsity by bringing p-norm restrict condition in solving the objective function. So far, using iterative way to solve nonlinear reconstruct problem has achieved remarkable results in the field of CS. So in the field of image restoration, we can also bring in p-norm restriction to obtain images' sparse prior information. The process of image degradation as shown in section 2, for the model of PMMW imaging system which is supposed space-invariable, the operator K is simplified a convolution process. And the solution of this problem requires minimizing the difference between the optimal solution and the real one:

$$\Delta f = \|Kf - g\|^2 \tag{40}$$

Unlike classical regularization way, we add regularization to the sparse prior information of image, where the constraint is not quadric, but the lp-norm( $1 \le p \le 2$ ) of signal f. It is here that the introduction of p-norm make the solution of objective function have sparsity.

The objective function to be optimized is:

$$\begin{aligned}\Phi_{w,p}(f) &= \Delta(f) + \sum_{\lambda \in \Gamma} w_\gamma \left|\langle f, \varphi_\gamma \rangle\right|^p \\ &= \|Kf - g\|^2 + \sum_{\lambda \in \Gamma} w_\gamma \left|\langle f, \varphi_\gamma \rangle\right|^p\end{aligned} \tag{41}$$

Where $\varphi_\gamma$ is the orthogonal basis which f could be sparse represented with, and $w = (w_\gamma)_{\gamma \in \Gamma}$ is the weight of the coefficients in transform-domain. When K is a identitymatrix, and $\varphi_\gamma$ is a wavelet basii function, the objective function mentioned above turns to denoising via wavelet transform based on Besov priori information .

Then, the corresponding variational equation is:

$$\forall \gamma \in \Gamma: \quad \langle K^H K f, \varphi_\gamma \rangle - \langle K^H g, \varphi_\gamma \rangle + \frac{w_\gamma p}{2} \left|\langle f, \varphi_\gamma \rangle\right|^{p-1} sign(\langle f, \varphi_\gamma \rangle) = 0 \tag{42}$$

The nonlinear equation shown above which involved symbolic function is a tricky one in practice. Define constant C satisfies:

$$\left\|K^H K\right\| < C \tag{43}$$

And the function as follow:

$$sur(f;a) = C\|f - a\|^2 - \|Kf - Ka\|^2 \tag{44}$$

According the definition of C, $CI - K^H K$ is a strictly positive definite matrix. So function $sur(f;a)$ is a strictly convex function for any value a. For image degradation, we can always have $\|K\| < 1$. So let C equal to value 1, and we can replace objective function by:

$$\begin{aligned}\Phi_{w,p}^{sur} &= \Phi_{w,p}(f;a) - \|Kf - Ka\|^2 + \|f - a\|^2 \\ &= \sum_{\gamma} [f_\gamma^2 - 2f_\gamma (a + K^H g - K^H Ka)_\gamma + w_\gamma |f_\gamma|^p] \\ &+ \|g\|^2 + \|a\|^2 + \|Ka\|^2\end{aligned} \tag{45}$$

To acquire the solution of the equation above, the process of iteration is shown as follows. For any initial point $f^0$,

$$f^n = \arg-\min(\Phi_{w,p}^{sur}(f;f^{n-1}) \quad n = 1,2,... \tag{46}$$

In equation (43), when $\mathbf{w} = \mathbf{0}$, it means the objective function doesn't include any sparse priori information. Therefore, the algorithm is degraded to a process of landweber iteration algorithm.

When p=1, the variational equation of the objective function is expressed as:

$$2f_\gamma + w_\gamma sign(f_\gamma) = 2(a_\gamma + [K^H (g - Ka]_\gamma) \tag{47}$$

For the process of symbolic function, when $f_\gamma$ >0, the solution is:

$$f_\gamma = a_\gamma + [K^H (g - Ka)]_\gamma - w_\gamma / 2 \tag{48}$$

Under the condition of $a_\gamma + [K^H (g - Ka)]_\gamma > w_\gamma / 2$, when $f_\gamma$ <0, the solution turns to:

$$f_\gamma = a_\gamma + [K^H (g - Ka)]_\gamma + w_\gamma / 2 \tag{49}$$

otherwise, when the equation do not satisfy the two conditions mentioned above, which is

$$f_\gamma = 0 \tag{50}$$

In conclusion, the iterating thresholding algorithm based on sparse prior is described as follow

$$f_\gamma = S_{w_\gamma,1}(a_\gamma + [K^H (g - Ka)]_\gamma) \tag{51}$$

Where $S_{w_\gamma,1}$ is defined as follow:

$$S_{w_\gamma,1}(x) = \begin{cases} x + \mu / 2 & if \ x_i < -w / 2 \\ 0 & if \ |x_i| \le w / 2 \\ x - \mu / 2 & if \ x_i > w / 2 \end{cases} \tag{52}$$

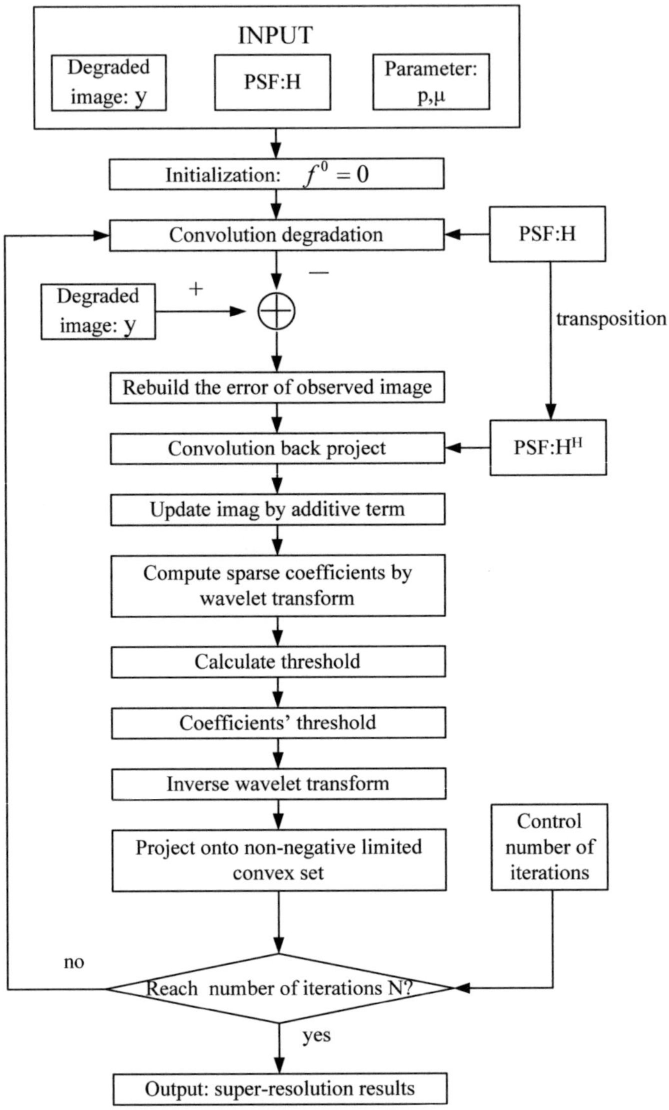


Fig. 24. Flow-chart for PIT super-resolution algorithm

The sparse prior iterating thresholding algorithm will achieve a better effect in image restoration, which is introducted $l_1$-norm restricted condition and the sparse priori information. And in the PMMW imaging system, the non-negative limitation of the image can be used as a prior in image super-resolution process. So we add that in our algorithm, and we have the sparse prior super-resolution algorithm restricted by $l_1$-norm - projected iterating thresholding(PIT) algorithm. The iterative formula is shown as follows:

1. Updating sparse coefficients of image by a additive term

$$\theta^{k+1} = \theta^k + (H\Psi)^T(g - H\Psi\theta^k) \tag{53}$$

2. Computing soft threshold by the coefficients acquired above

$$\theta^{k+1} = S_u(\theta^{k+1}, \mu) == \begin{cases} \theta^{k+1} + \mu / 2 & \theta^{k+1} < -\mu / 2 \\ 0 & \left|\theta^{k+1}\right| \leq \mu / 2 \\ \theta^{k+1} - \mu / 2 & \theta^{k+1} > \mu / 2 \end{cases} \tag{54}$$

3. Projecting onto a non-negative limited convex set

$$f^{k+1} = P_C(\Psi\theta^{k+1}) \tag{55}$$

Where the definition of operator $S_u$ is soft threshold operation, and $\theta$ is the coefficient of the image's sparse representation on a certain orthogonal basis function.

Passive millimeter wave images can be sparsely represented. Assuming the orthogonal basis is $\Psi = [\Psi_1, \Psi_2, ..., \Psi_N]$, the sparsity of image is expressed as follows:

$$f = \Psi\theta \tag{56}$$

Where, $f$ is the scene signal, $\theta$ is the sparse coefficient in orthogonal basis.

A flow chart depicting the various steps of Projected Iterating Thresh-holding (PIT) super-resolution algorithm is shown as Fig. 24.

Fig. 25. (a) Original Image, (b) BlurredImage, (c) After Projected Landweber , (d) After *tw*PIT

After the above steps, one iteration is finished. Depending on the specific situation, the algorithm can perform multiple iterations until reaching design requirement. The PIT algorithm taking advantage of the sparse prior of the image, can have a better recovery performance. Because of the isotropy, the noise has no sparsity in transform-domain. Since we keep projecting to the l1-ball in every iteration, the algorithm can effectively eliminate the impact of the noise's amplification. We will verify it in the later simulation.

In one iteration, there are two convolutions of images, two wavelet transform operations, two plus-minus operation and thresholding operation. The convolutions of images can perform in frequency-domain, which could reduce calculations by using FFT, and wavelet transform could achieve quickly by using Mallat algorithm.

#### 4.4.2 tw-PIT supper-resolution

To improve the above algorithm, we can modify equation (52) by updating algorithm two-step projection iteration [38-41]. Thus we can get two-step Projected Iterating Threshholding, which is *tw-PIT* supper-resolution.

For a brief description, each cycle of this "*tw-PIT* supper-resolution algorithm" consists of executing the four steps:

**Step 1.** The iterative principal process

$$\theta^{k+1} = \theta^k + (H\Psi)^T (g - H\Psi\theta^k) \tag{57}$$

Where $H$ is the PSF of system, $g$ is the Captured PMMW image, $\theta$ is the sparse coefficient in orthogonal basis $\Psi$ .

**Step 2.** Soft threshold procedure:

$$\theta_i^{k+1} = \begin{cases} \theta_i^k + \mu/2 & \theta_i^k < -\mu/2 \\ 0 & \left|\theta_i^k\right| \le \mu/2 \\ \theta_i^k - \mu/2 & \theta_i^k > \mu/2 \end{cases} \tag{58}$$

$\mu$ is the given parameters.

**Step 3.** Updating algorithm two-step projection iteration

$$f^{k+1} = (1-\alpha) f^{k-1} + (\alpha - \beta) f^k + \beta\Psi\theta^{k+1} \tag{59}$$

The designation "two-step" stems from the fact that depends on both $f^k$ and $f^{k-1}$, rather than only on $f^k$ .

**Step 4.** Projection process

$$f^{k+1} = P_C(f^{k+1}) \tag{60}$$

Where $\alpha = \dfrac{2}{1+\sqrt{1-\rho^2}}$, $\beta = \dfrac{2\alpha}{\lambda_1 + \lambda_N}$, $\rho = \dfrac{\lambda_N - \lambda_1}{\lambda_N + \lambda_1}$, $\lambda_N = 1$, $\lambda_1$ can be 0.1,0.01,0.001,0.0001, *et al.*

*Tw-PIT* supper-resolution algorithm can finish one iteration though the above four steps. The algorithm converges very fast. The convergence is much faster with $\lambda_1$ is much smaller. But it does not guarantee optimal performance of the reconstruction algorithm.

### 4.4.3 Simulation and experiments

In order to verify the super-resolution capability of the*tw-PIT*algorithm mentioned above, two images have been adopted in simulation and experiments, one is a lena image, and the other is an 210×96 University of ElectronicScience and Technology of China (UESTC) library's image captured by 94 GHz mechanically scanned mono channel radiometer.

In the first experiment, the optical lena image and the blurred image are shown in Fig.25a and Fig.25b respectively. The blurred image is from the lena image via a 5×5 Gaussian templates convolution. Zero-mean Gaussian white noise is added to the blurred image. The noise variance is 10. The Blurred Signal-to-Noise Ratio (BSNR) is 30 dB of the noisy blurred image. The experimental parameters $\lambda_1$ is 0.1. The results obtained by the Projected Landweber and *tw*PIT are shown in Fig.25c and Fig.25d. This metric is given by[42]

$$BSNR = 10\log_{10}\left(\frac{\frac{1}{MN}\sum_{i,j}[y(i,j)-\overline{y}(i,j)]^2}{\sigma^2}\right) \tag{61}$$

Where, $y(i,j)=g(i,j)-n(i,j)$ is the noise free blurred image, $\overline{y}(m,n)=E\{y\}$ , $\sigma^2$ is the additive noise variance.

It is clear from Fig.25 that the results obtained by the *tw*PIT algorithm are better than the results obtained by the PL algorithm.

When the ideal image is available for comparison, various distance metrics can be readily postulated to compare the images and their spectra. Straightforward measure is the Mean Square Error (MSE), which given by

$$MSE = \frac{1}{N^2}\sum\left|f-\tilde{f}^k\right|^2 \tag{62}$$

Where $f$ denotes the ideal image, $\tilde{f}^k$ represents the $k$th restoration result, $\|\bullet\|_2$ is $L_2$ norms. Fig. 26 plots the MSE of the three algorithms.

It can be observed that the *tw*PIT algorithm has a faster decrease of the MSE than the PL algorithm and PIT algorithm from Fig.27. Also, the MSE of the *tw*PIT algorithm is lower than that of the other two algorithms. Clearly, the *tw*PIT algorithm has the best convergence performance and lowest MSE. This is because the *tw*PIT algorithm suppress the noise in an iterative process. The experiments show that the *tw*PIT algorithm convergence faster, which is suitable for the required real-time applications, such as airport security and Concealed Weapons Detection.

In the second experiment, the visual image is shown in Fig.28a. The PMMW image is shown in Fig.28b, which is captured by a 3mm Passive millimeter wave focal plane linear array scanning imaging system. The restored images are shown in Fig.28c-28e, respectively. Fig.27

is the PSF which is estimated by variational bayesian. In captured image, the image are assembled together by three times mechanically scanned mono-channel radiometer, as a single mechanical scan pitch direction field limit.

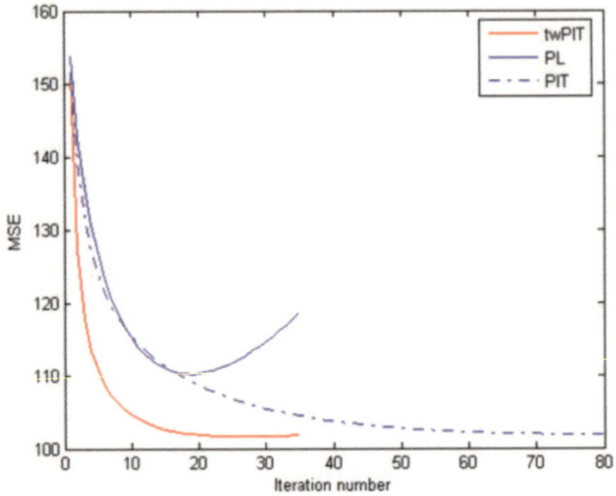


Fig. 26. Mean square error of the reconstructed image

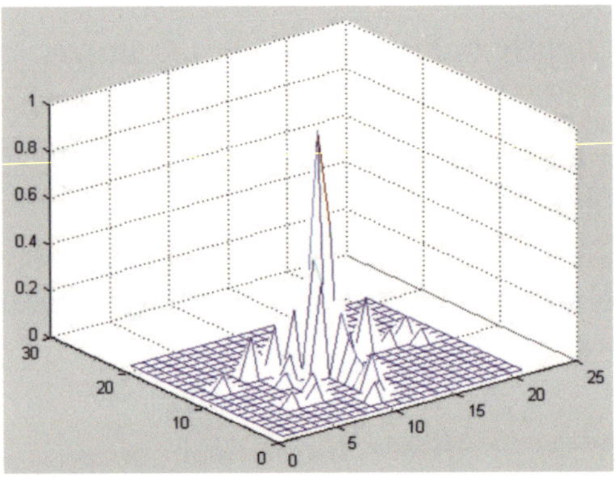

Fig. 27. Variational bayesian estimated PSF

The MSE is a global evaluation criterion for super-resolution algorithm. We can use the local image variance method to estimate the image noise level. This approach is based on the assumption, which the image is a large number of small pieces of uniform composition, and image noise to additive noise based. The captured passive millimeter wave images meet this requirement, which there are many flat background and noise is mainly additive noise, basically meet the above assumptions. Local variance calculated as follows [43]:

1. The image is divided into many small block, such as 4×4, 5×5. Then, we calculated the local mean and local variance of each block. The local variance is defined as:

$$\sigma_y^2(i,j) = \frac{1}{(2P+1)(2Q+1)} \sum_{k=-P}^{P} \sum_{l=-Q}^{Q} [y(i+k,j+l) - \mu_y(i,j)]^2 \tag{63}$$

The $\mu_y$ is the local mean, which is defined as:

$$\mu_y = \frac{1}{(2P+1)(2Q+1)} \sum_{k=-P}^{P} \sum_{l=-Q}^{Q} y(i+k, j+l) \tag{64}$$

Where, $(i, j)$ indicates the location of the image. $P, Q$ is the local variance calculation window size.

2. The equally spaced intervals are created between the maximum local variance and minimum local variance. The each local variance is enclosed into the appropriate interval. The local variance average of which contains the largest number of extents is used as the image noise variance. For the simulation image and the actual millimeter wave image, we set the block number is 100.

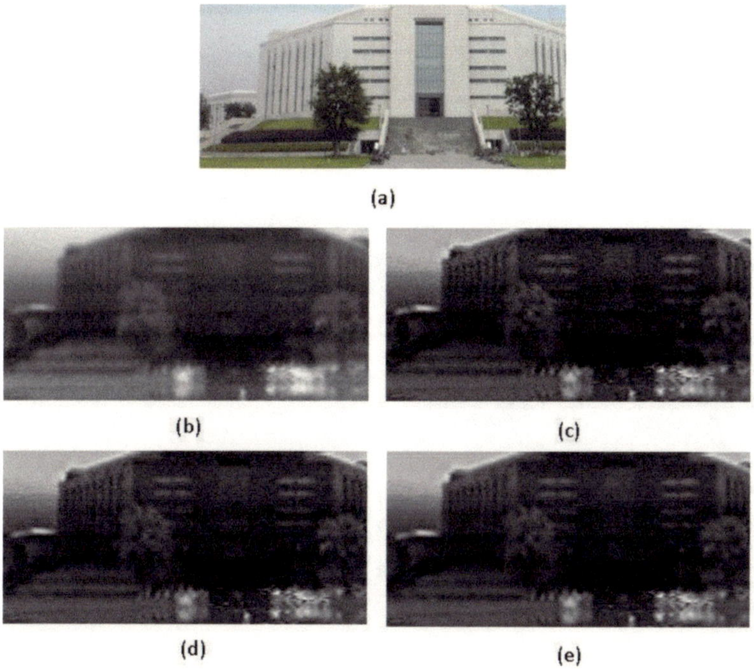

Fig. 28. (a) Visible Image, (b) Captured PMMW image, (c) Result of Projected Landweber, (d) Result of PIT, (e) Result of *tw*PIT

In our experiments, the three kinds of super-resolution algorithm including PL, PIT and *tw*PIT are executed for low resolution PMMW images.The symmetric extension technology is adopted in the image boundaries convolution for eliminating shock ringing. The restored result of PL, PIT and *tw*PIT are shown in Fig.28c-28e after 20 iterations, respectively.

The calculated local noise variance is 55.3552, 24.2451 and 34.6997 by PL, PIT and *tw*PIT algorithm, while the $P = Q = 2$ and the window size of the local variance is 5×5.

From above the results, we can see that PL algorithm can effectively perform super-resolution processing, but the noise is magnified in the recovery process. PIT and *tw*PIT algorithm can effectively suppress high frequency noise and make the flat region of original image maintain its flatness in the iterative process and maintain high-resolution of the images.

In the second experiment, the scene is relatively simple millimeter-wave imaging image processing. The Point Spread Function of the imaging system is estimated by the variational Bayesian method. For the PIT algorithm, the parameter $\mu$ is chosen as 1. For *tw*-PIT algorithm, the parameter $\mu$ is settled to 2, the parameter $p$ is set to 0.5. All the algorithms are iterative 100 times, the experimental results as shown below: the covered the car visual image is shown in Fig. 29(a),the unobstructed visual image is shown in Fig. 29(b). The obtainedPMMW image is shown in Fig. 29(c), which is acquired by a W band mechanically scanned radiometer. The spectrum of the PMMW image is shown in Fig. 29(d). The result and its spectrum after100 iterations PL algorithm are shown in Fig. 29(e) and Fig. 29(f). The result and its spectrum after100 iterations PIT are shown in Fig. 29(g) and Fig.29 h). The result and its spectrum after100 iterations *tw*-PIT are shown in Fig. 29(i) and Fig. 29(j).

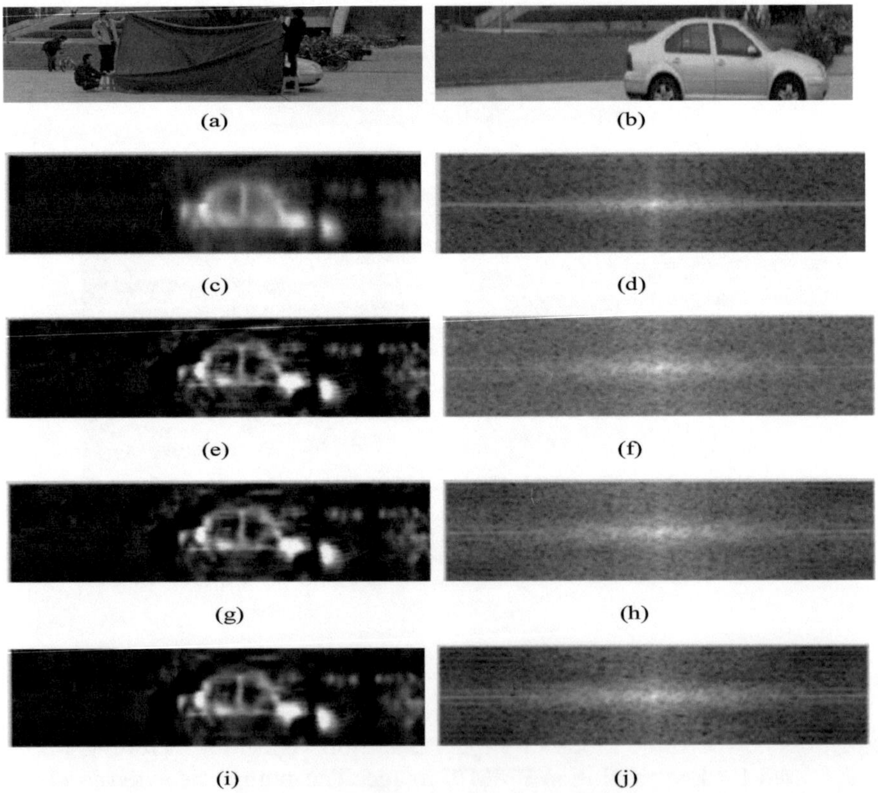

Fig. 29. (a) Visible Image the covered the car, (b) The unobstructed visual image, (c) (d) Captured PMMW image and its spectrum, (e) (f)Result of Projected Landweber and its spectrum, (g) (h) Result of PIT and its spectrum , (i) (j)Result of twPIT and its spectrum

In the third experiment, we process the obtained PMMW image is the UESTC Qingshuihe campus's Classroom Building, as shown in Fig.30a-30e. The Point Spread Function of the system is estimated by the variational Bayesian method. For the PIT algorithm, the parameter $\mu$ is chosen as 1. For *tw*-PIT algorithm, the parameter $\mu$ is settled to 2, the parameter $p$ is set to 0.5. All the algorithms are iterative 100 times, the experimental results as shown below:

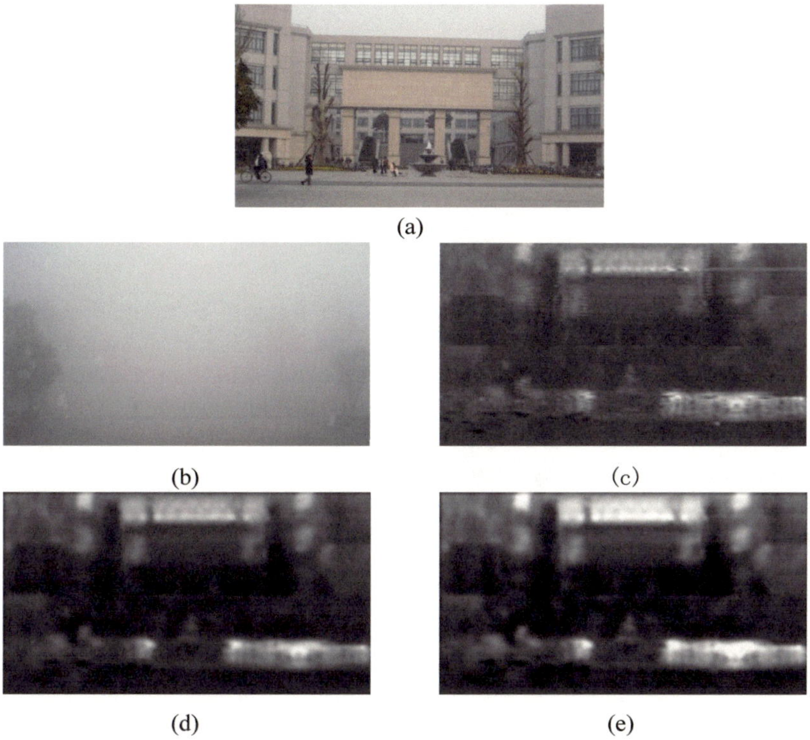

Fig. 30. (a) Visible Image, (b) The visual image under the fog, (c) Captured PMMW image, (d) The denoised image (e) After tw-PIT super-resolution

The *tw*PIT algorithm is introduced for the PMMW supper resolution process. The update equation depends on the two previous estimates (thus, the term two-step), rather than only on the previous one. This class contains and extends the iterative thresholding methods recently introduced. This algorithm uses the sparse prior information and the non-negative finite value information of PMMW images, which can separate the noise from the signals in the iteration process. Our algorithm is very effective when the image noise is existed, which can also has good super-resolution performance. The experimental results have shown that PL, PIT and *tw*PIT algorithm can effectively be super-resolution processing, but the noise is magnified in the PL algorithm recovery process. The PIT and *tw*PIT algorithm can effectively suppress high frequency noise smooth the region and maintain its flatness in an iterative process, while maintaining a high-resolution images.

And the *tw*PIT algorithm can in fact be tuned to converge much faster than PL and PIT algorithm, specially in severely ill-conditioned problems. The *tw*PIT algorithm has minimum MSE, which restore original signal more accurate. The reason is that noise is restrained in the iteration process. Sparse prior super-resolution algorithm has good MSE performance is mainly due to which can separate the noise in the iterative process and minimize the impact of noise for image restoration. Thus, the *tw*PIT algorithm can be used in the occasion which requires PMMW imaging quality and real-time such as airports and Concealed Weapons Detection (CWD).

In the second experiment, due to the limited field of view, the single-channel scanning process has introduced a certain artifacts. So eliminate and abate the artifacts is the problem that need to be researched and solved in our follow-up work.

## 5. Acknowledgment

This work is supported by the National Natural Science Foundation of China.

## 6. References

F.T Ulaby, R.K. Moore,A.K. Fung(1981).Microwave Remote Sensing: Fundamentals and Radiometry.*Artech House* I:402-403, Norwood.

Larry Yujiri, Merit Shoucri, and Philip Moffa.Passive Millimeter Wave Imaging.*IEEE Microwave magazine*, 1527-3342/02,September,39-50(2003).

Richard J. Lang, Laurence F. Ward, John W. Cunningham. Close-range high-resolution W band radiometric imaging system for security screening applications.*Proceedings of SPIE, Passive Millimeter-Wave Imaging Technology IV*, 4032:34-39(2000).

Evelyn J. Boettcher, Keith Krapels, Ron Driggers, et al.Modeling passive millimeter wave imaging sensor Modeling passive millimeter wave imaging sensor.*APPLIED OPTICS*, 49(19) :E58-E66( 2010).

Thomas Lüthi, Christian Mätzler.Stereoscopic Passive Millimeter-Wave Imaging and Ranging.*IEEE Transaction on Microwave Theory and Techniques*,53(8):2594-2599(2005).

Stuart E. Clark, John A. Lovberg, and Christopher A. Martin. Passive Millimeter-Wave Imaging for Airborne and Security Applications.*Proc. of SPIE*, 5077:16-21(2003).

P. Moffa, L.Yujiri,H.H.Agravante,et al, "Large-aperture passive millimeter wave push broom camera", Passive Millimeter-wave Imaging Technology V, Proc.of SPIE , 4373:1-6(2001).

Chritopher A. Martin, Will Manning, and Vladimir G. Koliano, "Flight Test of a Passive Millimeter-Wave Imaging System", Proc. of SPIE, 5789:24-34(2005).

G.Gleed, A.H.Lettington.High-speed super-resolution techniques for passive millimeter-wave imaging systems. SPIE Conference on Image and Video Processing II, Vol. 2182:255-265 (1994)

L. B. Lucy. "An iteration technique for the rectification of observed distributions," Astronomical Journal, vol. 79, no.6, pp.745–754, 1974.

W. H. Richardson. "Bayesian-based iterative method of image restoration," Journal of the Optical Society of America, vol.62, pp55–59, 1972.

B. R. Hunt, P. Sementilli, "Description of a poisson imagery super resolution algorithm," Astronomical Data Analysis Software and Systems 1, Ch123, pp.196-199, 1992.

L. C. Li, J. Y. Yang, J. T. Xiong, et al.,Super-resolution Processing of passive millimeter wave image based on conjugate-gradient algorithm, Journal of Systems Engineering and Electronics, Vol. 20, No. 4, 2009, pp.762–767.

Zelong Xiao, Jianzhong Xu, Shusheng Peng, et al. "Super resolution image restoration of a PMMW sensor based on POCS algorithm. Systems and Control in Aerospace and Astronautics, " 2006. ISSCAA 2006, 2006, 680-683

L. C. Li, Research on Passive Millimeter Wave Imaging Theory and Super-resolution Signal Processing Technology, Ph.D. dissertation, Dept. of Electronic Engineering, University of Electronic Science and Technology of China, 2009.

L. C. Li, J. Y. Yang, J. T. Xiong, et al., "W Band Dicke-Radiometer For Imaging," Int J Infrared Milli Waves, 29:879–888(2008).

L. C. Li, J. Y. Yang, et al., "Method of passive mmW image detection and identification for close target," Int. J. Infrared Milli. Waves, (2011) 32: 102-115.

L. C. Li, J. Y. Yang, et al., Research on 3mm radiometric imaging, Journal of infrared and millimeter waves, Vol.28(1):11-15, 2009.

L. C. Li, J. Y. Yang, et al., An Focal Plane Array Space Variant Model For PMMW Imaging, IET International Radar Conference 2009.

Goodman, J.W. Introduction to Fourier Optics 2nd.(McGraw-Hill Book Co, New York, 1996)

Su Bing-hua, Jin Wei-qi, Niu Li-hong, NIU Li-hong, LIU Guang-rong. Super-resolution image restoration and progress. Optical Technique, 2001, 27(1):6-9.

Steven M. Kay.Fundamentals of Statistical Signal Processing, Volume I: Estimation Theory and Volume :Detection Theory [M]. Beijing: Publishing House of Electronics Industry, 2003.

Sina Farsiu, M. Dirk Robinson,and et al. "Fast and Robust Multiframe Super Resolution", IEEE Trans. On Image Process, 2004, 13(10), pp. 1327–1344.

A. Chambolle. "Total variation minimization and a class of binary MRF models", Proc. Int. Workshop on Energy Minimization Methods in Computer Vision and Pattern Recognition, 2005,Vol 3757,pp.136-152.

Kyung Sub Joo, Tamal Bose, and Guo Fang Xu. Image restoration using a conjugate gradient based adaptive filtering algorithm. Circuits system signal processing, 1997,16 (2) :197-206.

Zou Mouyan. Deconvolution and Signal Recovery [M. Beijing: National Defence Industry Press, 2001

Stark H. "Image recovery: theory and application," New York:Academic Press, 1987.

J. Biemond, R. L. Lagendijk, R.M.Mersereau, "Iterative methods for image deblurring," Proc.of IEEE, Vol.78, pp.856-883, 1990.

L. Landweber. "An iteration formula for Fredholm integral equations of the first kind," American Journal of Mathematics, vol 73, pp 615–624, 1951.

R. W. Schafer, R. M. Mersereau, and M. A. Richards, "Constrained iterative restoration algorithms," Proc. IEEE, vol. 69, pp. 432-450, 1981.

Piana M, Bertero M. "Projected Landweber method and preconditioning," Inverse Problems, Volume 13, Issue 2, pp. 441-463,1997.

Lei Liang and Yuanchang Xu, " Adaptive Landweber method to deblur images," IEEE Signal Processing Letters, Vol. 10, No. 5, 2003.

Marta Peracaula, Joan Martí, Jordi Freixenet, etc. Multi-Scale Image Analysis Applied to Radioastronomical Interferometric Data, Pattern Recognition and Image Analysis, Vol. 5524, 2009, pp. 192-199.

Eslami R, Radha H. Translation-invariant contourlet transform and its application to image denoising. IEEE Transactions on image processing, Vol. 15, No. 11, 2006, pp. 3362 - 3374.

A. L. Cunha, J. Zhou, and M. N. Do, The non-subsampled contourlet transform: Theory, design, and applications, IEEE Transactions on Image Processing, Vol. 15, No. 10, 2006, pp. 3089-3101.

J.-L. Starck, J. Fadili, and F. Murtagh, The undecimated wavelet decomposition and its reconstruction, IEEE Trans. Image Processing, Vol. 16, No. 2, 2007, pp. 297-308.

Wang Yanfei, Computational methods for inverse problems and their applications. Higher education press of China, 2005.

I Daubechies, M Defrise, C De Mol.An iterative thresholding algorithm for linear inverse problems with a sparsity constraint[J]. Comm.Pure Appl.Math., 2004, 57(11):1413-1457.

Emmanuel Candes and Terence Tao. "Near optimal signal recovery from random projections Universal encoding strategies", IEEE Trans. on Information Theory, 2006, 52(12), pp. 1-39.

J. Bioucas-Dias and M. Figueiredo, "A new TwIST: Two-step iterative shrinkage/thresholding algorithms for image restoration", IEEE Trans. Image Process, 2007, 16(12), pp. 2992-3004.

A. Beck and M. Teboulle. "A fast iterative shrinkage-thresholding algorithm for linear inverse problems". SIAM Journal on Imaging Sciences, Mar 2009, 2(1):183-202.

Bahnam M A , Katsaggelos A K. Digital image restoration[J]. IEEE Signal Process. 1997, 14(2): 24–41.

Gao B C. An OperationalMethod for Estimating Signal to Noise Ratios from Data Acquired with Imaging Spectrometers. Remote Sensing of Environment, 1993, 43 (1):23—33.

# 13

# Blind Image Restoration for a Microscanning Imaging System

José Luis López-Martínez[1] and Vitaly Kober[2]
[1]*Mathematics School, UADY, Mérida, Yucatán,*
[2]*Computer Science Department, CICESE,*
*México*

## 1. Introduction

Image restoration is an important topic in the area of image processing because its techniques are useful to recover images degraded during a capturing process (Bovik, 2005). There are a wide range of degradations in real world, such as blurring (i.e. camera motion capture process), nonuniform illumination, cloud environments (fog, clouds, smoke), noise (white noise, impulse noise, etc.), and damaged elements in imaging array sensors (Gonzalez & Woods, 2008; Hautiere & Aubert, 2005; Jain, 1989; Narasimhan & Nayar, 2002).

Common restoration methods are based on *a priori* knowledge of the degradation process. They usually use the degradation model and a single observed scene to carry out restoration (Banham & Katsaggelos, 1997; Kundur & Hatzinakos, 1996). There are also methods of restoration based on unknown functions of degradation referred to as blind methods (Jain,1989). Although there are numerous algorithms, the process of restoration is still open problem.

Image restoration methods described in this chapter belong to the class of blind adaptive methods. The techniques use camera microscanning (Shi et al., 2006) for the restoration of images degraded with nonuniform additive, nonuniform multiplicative interferences, and sensor noise.

The spatial nonuniform additive interference is present in infrared focal-plane array sensors (IFPA), because each photodetector has a variation in its photoresponse as intrinsic result of the IFPA's fabrication stage (Hayat et al., 1999; Ratliff et al., 2002). On the other hand, the nonuniform illumination may be characterized as multiplicative interference. Nonuniform illumination limits the performance of others algorithms of image processing such as pattern recognition (Lee & Kim, 2009).

Microscanning is a technique to acquire time-sequential images of the same scene with a slight shifting between the scene and camera. Recently, restoration methods for different models of observed scenes using three images anisotropically captured with a microscanning imaging system were investigated (López-Martínez & Kober, 2008, 2010; López-Martínez et al., 2010). In order to carry out restoration, we consider three degraded images captured with a microscanning imaging system. Next, an explicit system of equations is derived and solved.

The proposed method is analyzed in terms of restoration accuracy, execution time, and computational complexity. Experimental results are also provided.

## 2. Image restoration methods for a microscanning system

Microscanning acquires multiple images of the same scene by slight shifting image acquisition system (Shi et al., 2006). Microscanning can be implemented either with a controlled movement of a sensor array that captures images or with a controlled motion of a light source, for example in the case of nonuniform illumination.

Microscanning is usually used for supper-resolution (Milanfar, 2011). However, controlled camera microscanning can be also used for image restoration, if the original image and interferences are spatially displaced relatively each other during the microscanning process. At least three observed images should be captured. The first image is taken without any displacement, the second one is captured with shift of one pixel down, and finally the third one is obtained with shift of one pixel to the right. In practice, microscanning may be implemented using a piezoelectric actuator to precision positioning of a sensor array. In the case of nonuniform illumination, controlled motion performs a light source.

Let us introduce some useful notation and definitions. Let $\{s_t(i,j), t = 1,2,..,T\}$ be a set of observed images, where $t$ is the index of time-sequential images captured during microscanning, $T$ is the number of observed images captured around the origin with a small displacement of a camera, and (i, j) are the pixel coordinates. Without loss of generality, suppose that each image has the size of $M \times N$ pixels. Let $\{f(i,j)\}$, $\{a(i,j)\}$ and $\{b(i,j)\}$ denote an original image, an additive interference, and a multiplicative interference, respectively. Assume that these images are time-invariant during the capture process. Let $\{n_t(i,j)\}$ be a time-varying zero-mean white Gaussian noise.

### 2.1 Additive degradation model

An example of spatially nonuniform additive interference is IFPA with a low gain variation (Hayat et al., 1999; Ratliff et al., 2002). IFPA sensor is a mosaic of photodetectors placed at the focal plane of an imaging system. It is known that the performance of IFPA sensors is affected by the presence of fixed-pattern noise (spatially nonuniform noise). The nonuniform noise occurs because each detector has the photoresponse slightly different from that of its neighbors.

When image degradation is caused by additive nonuniform interference and additive noise, the observed scene can be described as

$$s_1(i,j) = a(i,j) + f(i,j) + n_1(i,j), \quad 1 \le i \le M, 1 \le j \le N. \tag{1}$$

With a help of the technique of microscanning, two frames with vertical and horizontal displacements of one pixel can be obtained as follows:

$$s_2(i,j) = a(i+1,j) + f(i,j) + n_2(i,j), \quad 1 \le i < M, 1 \le j \le N, \tag{2}$$

and

$$s_3(i,j) = a(i,j+1) + f(i,j) + n_3(i,j), \quad 1 \le i \le M, 1 \le j < N. \tag{3}$$

The additive interference and the original image are spatially displaced by the microscanning. Let us compute gradient matrices as follows:

$$r(i,j) = s_2(i,j) - s_1(i+1,j) = f(i,j) - f(i+1,j) + n_2(i,j) - n_1(i+1,j), \quad 1 \le i \le M-1, 1 \le j \le N, \tag{4}$$

and

$$c(i,j) = s_3(i,j) - s_1(i,j+1) = f(i,j) - f(i,j+1) + n_3(i,j) - n_1(i,j+1), \quad 1 \le i \le M, 1 \le j \le N-1. \tag{5}$$

Hence

$$r(i,j) = \begin{bmatrix} s_2(1,1) - s_1(2,1) & s_2(1,2) - s_1(2,2) & \cdots & s_2(1,N) - s_1(2,N) \\ s_2(2,1) - s_1(3,1) & s_2(2,2) - s_1(3,2) & \cdots & s_2(2,N) - s_1(3,N) \\ \vdots & \vdots & \vdots & \vdots \\ s_2(M-1,1) - s_1(M,1) & s_2(M-1,2) - s_1(M,2) & \cdots & s_2(M-1,N) - s_1(M,N) \\ 0 & 0 & \cdots & 0 \end{bmatrix}, \tag{6}$$

and

$$c(i,j) = \begin{bmatrix} s_3(1,1) - s_1(1,2) & s_3(1,2) - s_1(1,3) & \cdots & s_3(1,N-1) - s_1(1,N) & 0 \\ s_3(2,1) - s_1(2,2) & s_3(2,2) - s_1(2,3) & \cdots & s_3(2,N-1) - s_1(2,N) & 0 \\ \vdots & \vdots & \vdots & \vdots & \vdots \\ s_3(M,1) - s_1(M,2) & s_3(M,2) - s_1(M,3) & \cdots & s_3(M,N-1) - s_1(M,N) & 0 \end{bmatrix}. \tag{7}$$

We want to minimize the additive noise variance contained in these matrices. So, the objective function to be minimized using the least-squares approach (Kay, 1993), is given as

$$\begin{aligned} \tilde{F} = &\left\{ \sum_{i=1}^{M-1} \sum_{j=1}^{N-1} \left[ r(i,j) - f(i,j) + f(i+1,j) \right]^2 + \left[ c(i,j) - f(i,j) + f(i,j+1) \right]^2 \right\} \\ &+ \sum_{j=1}^{N-1} \left[ c(M,j) - f(M,j) + f(M,j+1) \right]^2 + \sum_{i=1}^{M-1} \left[ r(i,N) - f(i,N) + f(i+N,j) \right]^2, \end{aligned} \tag{8}$$

where the first terms takes into account the noise information present in the most part of the image, and the last two terms are inserted to the objective function in order to take into account the noise information in the bottom row and the right column of the image, respectively. To solve the minimization problem, we differentiate the objective function with respect to elements of the image $\{f(i,j)\}$ and set derivatives equal to zero. The minimization of the objective function leads to a linear system of equations. In matrix-vector notation the linear system is given by

$$\mathbf{A}\mathbf{x} = \mathbf{u}, \tag{9}$$

where matrix $\mathbf{A}$ has the size $MN \times MN$, $\mathbf{x}$ is a vector version of $\{f(i,j)\}$ of size $MN \times 1$, and vector $\mathbf{u} = \mathbf{u}_r + \mathbf{u}_c$ has the size $MN \times 1$. The vectors $\mathbf{u}_r$ and $\mathbf{u}_c$ are computed as follows

$$\mathbf{u}_r(j) = r(1,j), \quad 1 \le j \le M, \tag{10}$$

$$\mathbf{u}_r(iN + j) = r(i+1,j) - r(i,j), 1 \le i \le M-2, 1 \le j \le N, \tag{11}$$

$$\mathbf{u}_r(NM - j) = -r(M-1, N-j), \quad 0 \le j \le N-1, \tag{12}$$

$$\mathbf{u}_c(iM + 1) = c(i+1,1), \quad 0 \le i \le M-1, \tag{13}$$

$$\mathbf{u}_c(iN + j) = c(i+1,j) - c(i+1,j-1), 2 \le j \le N-1, 0 \le i \le M-1, \tag{14}$$

$$\mathbf{u}_c(iN) = -c(i, N-1), \quad 1 \le i \le M. \tag{15}$$

The matrix A is sparse, and it is calculated as

$$\mathbf{A} = \begin{bmatrix} \mathbf{A}_1 & \mathbf{A}_3 & 0 & 0 & 0 & 0 \\ \mathbf{A}_3 & \mathbf{A}_2 & \mathbf{A}_3 & 0 & 0 & 0 \\ 0 & \mathbf{A}_3 & \mathbf{A}_2 & \mathbf{A}_3 & 0 & 0 \\ 0 & 0 & \ddots & \ddots & \ddots & 0 \\ 0 & 0 & 0 & \mathbf{A}_3 & \mathbf{A}_2 & \mathbf{A}_3 \\ 0 & 0 & 0 & 0 & \mathbf{A}_3 & \mathbf{A}_1 \end{bmatrix}, \tag{16}$$

where the matrices $\mathbf{A}_1$, $\mathbf{A}_2$, and $\mathbf{A}_3$, of the size $N \times N$, are given by

$$\mathbf{A}_1 = \begin{bmatrix} 4 & -2 & 0 & 0 & 0 & 0 \\ -2 & 6 & -2 & 0 & 0 & 0 \\ 0 & -2 & 6 & -2 & 0 & 0 \\ 0 & 0 & \ddots & \ddots & \ddots & 0 \\ 0 & 0 & 0 & -2 & 6 & -2 \\ 0 & 0 & 0 & 0 & -2 & 4 \end{bmatrix}, \tag{17}$$

$$\mathbf{A}_2 = \begin{bmatrix} 6 & -2 & 0 & 0 & 0 & 0 \\ -2 & 8 & -2 & 0 & 0 & 0 \\ 0 & -2 & 8 & -2 & 0 & 0 \\ 0 & 0 & \ddots & \ddots & \ddots & 0 \\ 0 & 0 & 0 & -2 & 8 & -2 \\ 0 & 0 & 0 & 0 & -2 & 6 \end{bmatrix}, \tag{18}$$

and

$$\mathbf{A}_3 = diag\left[-2, -2, \ldots, -2\right]. \tag{19}$$

The rank of the matrix **A** is $MN-1$, therefore the original image can be restored if one pixel of the image is *a priori* assigned to a constant, for instance the last pixel of the image is set to zero. So, the matrix **A** associated to the lineal system has the size $MN-1 \times MN-1$, and it becomes symmetric and positive-definite. In this case there exists a unique solution. After solving the linear system, the obtained image is point-wise processed to have the same mean value (assumed to be known) with original image. To solve the linear system, iterative conjugate gradient method is used (Golub & Van Loan, 1996).

The computational complexity of the algorithm is given by the execution order of conjugate gradient and the size of an image to be restored. It is estimated as $O(kp)$ operations, where $p$ is the number of nonzero entries in the matrix associated to lineal system, and $k$ is the number of iterations required for solving the system of equations. Without loss of generality, we assume that $M = N$. Therefore, $p = O(5M^2)$ and $k = qM$ where $q$ depends on precision of the solution. The computational complexity of the method can be estimated as $O(5qM^3)$.

Impulse noise is caused by sensor failures in a camera or transmission through a noisy channel. The proposed method is able to interpolate implicitly the pixel values corrupted with impulsive noise based on the information contained in neighboring pixels. This is because, during the microscanning the information of each pixel of the original image is captured in three different observed images. If one of sensors is damaged, partial information about the pixel intensity of the original image could be available in the other observed images.

### 2.2 Multiplicative degradation model

A typical example of multiplicative interference is nonuniform illumination. When an input image degraded by a multiplicative nonuniform interference and additive noise, the observed scene can be described as

$$s_1(i,j) = b(i,j)f(i,j) + n_1(i,j), \quad 1 \le i \le M, 1 \le j \le N \tag{20}$$

Suppose that microscanning is able to separate the original image and the interference, and then the shifted frames are obtained as follows:

$$s_2(i,j) = b(i+1,j)f(i,j) + n_2(i,j), \quad 1 \le i < M, 1 \le j \le N, \tag{21}$$

$$s_3(i,j) = b(i,j+1)f(i,j) + n_3(i,j), \quad 1 \le i \le M, 1 \le j < N. \tag{22}$$

Now we define two quotient matrices using spatial information between rows and columns of the images,

$$h(i,j) = \frac{s_2(i,j)}{s_1(i+1,j)}, \quad 1 \le i < M, \quad 1 \le j \le N, \quad s_1(i+1,j) \ne 0, \tag{23}$$

$$v(i,j) = \frac{s_3(i,j)}{s_1(i,j+1)}, \quad 1 \le i \le M, \quad 1 \le j < N, \quad s_1(i,j+1) \ne 0. \tag{24}$$

Hence, the matrices $\{h(i,j)\}$ and $\{v(i,j)\}$ as defined as

$$h(i,j)=\begin{bmatrix} \left(\frac{s_2(1,1)}{s_1(2,1)}\right) & \left(\frac{s_2(1,2)}{s_1(2,2)}\right) & \cdots & \left(\frac{s_2(1,N)}{s_1(2,N)}\right) \\ \left(\frac{s_2(2,1)}{s_1(3,1)}\right) & \left(\frac{s_2(2,2)}{s_1(3,2)}\right) & \cdots & \left(\frac{s_2(2,N)}{s_1(3,N)}\right) \\ \vdots & \vdots & \vdots & \vdots \\ \left(\frac{s_2(M-1,1)}{s_1(M,1)}\right) & \left(\frac{s_2(M-1,2)}{s_1(M,2)}\right) & \cdots & \left(\frac{s_2(M-1,N)}{s_1(M,N)}\right) \\ 0 & 0 & \cdots & 0 \end{bmatrix}, \tag{25}$$

and

$$v(i,j)=\begin{bmatrix} \left(\frac{s_3(1,1)}{s_1(1,2)}\right) & \left(\frac{s_3(1,2)}{s_1(1,3)}\right) & \cdots & \left(\frac{s_3(1,N-1)}{s_1(1,N)}\right) & 0 \\ \left(\frac{s_3(2,1)}{s_1(2,2)}\right) & \left(\frac{s_3(2,2)}{s_1(2,3)}\right) & \cdots & \left(\frac{s_3(2,N-1)}{s_1(2,N)}\right) & 0 \\ \vdots & \vdots & \vdots & \vdots & \vdots \\ \left(\frac{s_3(M,1)}{s_1(M,2)}\right) & \left(\frac{s_3(M,2)}{s_1(M,3)}\right) & \cdots & \left(\frac{s_3(M,N-1)}{s_1(M,N)}\right) & 0 \end{bmatrix}. \tag{26}$$

The multiplicative interference in the matrices $\{h(i,j)\}$ and $\{v(i,j)\}$ is eliminated when the observed images have no additive noise. However, for small standard deviation of noise the matrices are close to the correspondent quotient matrices constructed with the original image and its shifted versions. In a similar manner, the objective function can be written as

$$\begin{aligned} \tilde{F} &= \left\{ \sum_{i=1}^{M-1}\sum_{j=1}^{N-1} \left[ h(i,j) - \left( \frac{f(i,j)}{f(i+1,j)} \right) \right]^2 + \left[ v(i,j) - \left( \frac{f(i,j)}{f(i,j+1)} \right) \right]^2 \right\} \\ &+ \sum_{j=1}^{N-1} \left[ v(M,j) - \left( \frac{f(M,j)}{f(M,j+1)} \right) \right]^2 + \sum_{i=1}^{M-1} \left[ h(i,N) - \left( \frac{f(i,N)}{f(i+N,j)} \right) \right]^2. \end{aligned} \tag{27}$$

Since it is difficult to solve the system of nonlinear equation then a logarithm transformation to the system of nonlinear equations is applied. In this way the system can be converted to the linear system as follows:

$$\begin{aligned} \log(\tilde{F}) &= \left\{ \begin{aligned} &\sum_{i=1}^{M-1}\sum_{j=1}^{N-1} \left[ \log(h(i,j)) - \log(f(i,j) - f(i+1,j)) \right]^2 \\ &+ \left[ \log(v(i,j)) - \log(f(i,j) - f(i,j+1)) \right]^2 \end{aligned} \right\} \\ &+ \sum_{j=1}^{N-1} \left[ \log(v(M,j)) - \log(f(M,j) - f(M,j+1)) \right]^2 \\ &+ \sum_{i=1}^{M-1} \left[ \log(h(i,N)) - \log(f(i,N) - f(i+N,j)) \right]^2. \end{aligned} \tag{28}$$

In a similar manner, the iterative conjugate gradient method can be used for solving this linear system. Finally, the restored image is obtained by applying the exponential function to the solution of the linear system. Since this method is based on the conjugate gradient method, its computational complexity is close to that of for the additive degradation. Additional expenses are required for logarithm and exponential transformations.

## 3. Computer simulation results

In this section computer simulation results for restoration of images degraded by additive and multiplicative interferences are presented. The root mean square error (RMSE) criterion is used for comparison of quality of restoration. Additionally, a subjective visual criterion is used. The RMSE is given by

$$RMSE\left(f,\tilde{f}\right)=\sqrt{\frac{\sum_{i}^{M}\sum_{j}^{N}\left(f(i,j)-\tilde{f}(i,j)\right)^{2}}{MN}}, \tag{29}$$

where $\{f(i,j)\}$ is the original image and $\left\{\tilde{f}(i,j)\right\}$ is the restored image. The size of images used in our experiments is $256\times256$ pixels. The intensity values are in the range of [0,255]. The experiments were performed using a laptop computer (Intel Core 2 Duo 2.26 GHz with 2GB of RAM). To guarantee statistically correct results, 30 statistical trials of each experiment for different realizations of the random noise process were performed. The conjugate gradient method is used to solve the linear system. The convergence criterion is when the residual value drops below $10^{-10}$. The subjective visual criterion is defined as an enhanced difference between original and restored images. This enhanced difference (Kober, 2001) is defined as follows:

$$EDF(i,j)=\omega_1(f(i,j)-\tilde{f}(i,j))+\omega_2, \tag{30}$$

where $\omega_1$ and $\omega_2$ are predetermined constants. In our experiments we set $\omega_1=4$ and $\omega_1=1$ for additive and multiplicative models, respectively, and $\omega_2=128$. A pixel is displayed as gray if there is no error between the original image and the restored image. For maximum error, the pixel is displayed either black or white (with intensity values of 0 and 255, respectively).

The linear minimum mean square error method is a popular technique in image restoration. In the case of stationary processes and in the absence of any blur, the method takes a simplified form of the Wiener smoothing filtering (Jain, 1989). The frequency response of the empirical Wiener filter is

$$H_{Wiener}(u,v)=\frac{P_S(u,v)-P_{Noise}(u,v)}{P_S(u,v)}, \tag{31}$$

where $P_s(u,v)$ is the power spectral density of the observed degraded input scene and $P_{Noise}(u,v)$ is the power spectral density of additive interference. It is assumed that all degradation parameters for the Wiener filter are exactly known. Note that the proposed method does not need any information about the degradation function. When observed images are degraded by multiplicative interference, first we apply a logarithm function to the degraded images to convert the multiplicative interference to additive one (ignoring the sensor noise). Then the empiric Wiener filtering with known parameters is utilized. Finally, the exponential function is applied to the Wiener restored image to obtain the output image.

### 3.1 Restoration of noisy image degraded with additive interference

Figs. 1(a), 1(b), and 1(c) show a test original image, a nonuniform additive interference, and the original image degraded with the interference and a zero-mean white Gaussian noise with a standard deviation of 2, respectively. The mean value and standard deviation of the interference are 118.8 and 59.7, respectively. Fig. 2(a) shows restored images with the proposed method. Fig. 2(b) shows enhanced difference between the original image and the restored image.

(a) (b)

(c)

Fig. 1. (a) Original image, (b) additive interference, (c) observed image degraded with additive interference and white noise with standard deviation of 2.

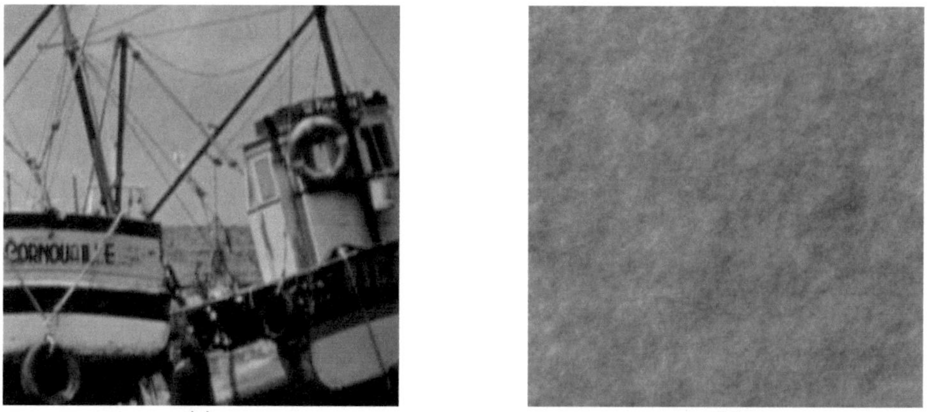

(a) (b)

Fig. 2. Performance of the proposed method for additive degradation and additive noise with standard deviation of 2: (a) restored image, (b) enhanced difference between the original image and the restored image.

Fig. 3 shows the performance in terms of the RMSE of the proposed methods using three images (Am3), and the Wiener filter versus the standard deviation of additive noise. It can be seen that the performance of the proposed method is much better than that of the Wiener filtering with known parameters. It happens because the additive interference is spatially inhomogeneous, and therefore, it cannot be considered as a realization of a stationary process and correctly used in the filtering. The time required to restore the image with the proposed method is approximately 46 sec. The iterative conjugate gradient algorithm requires about 1070 iterations.

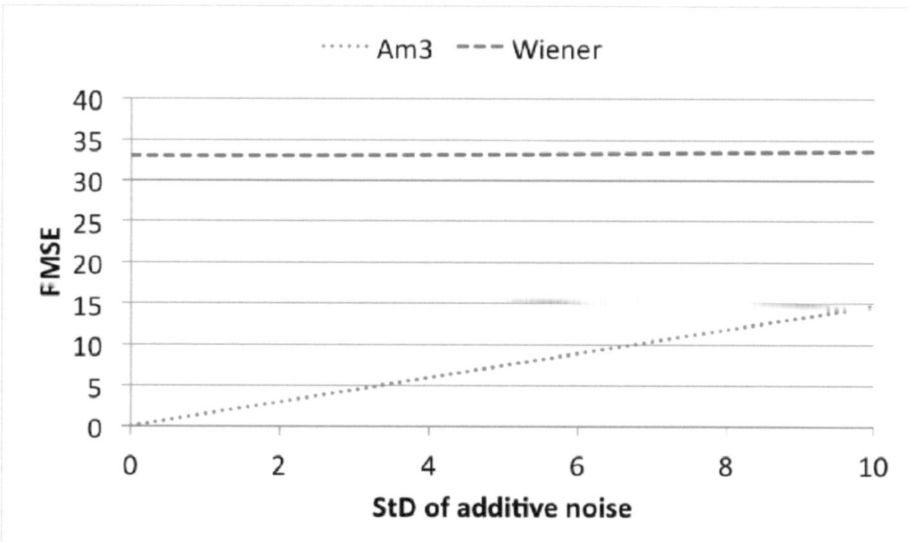


Fig. 3. Performance of the proposed method for additive degradation: RMSE versus a standard deviation of additive noise.

Fig. 4(a) shows the observed scene degraded by nonuniform additive interference, zero-mean white Gaussian noise with a standard deviation of 2, and impulse noise with the occurrence probability of 0.03. The value of impulse noise is zero (physical meaning is defective sensor element). Figs. 4(b) and 4(c) show the restored image and the enhanced difference between the original and restored images, respectively.

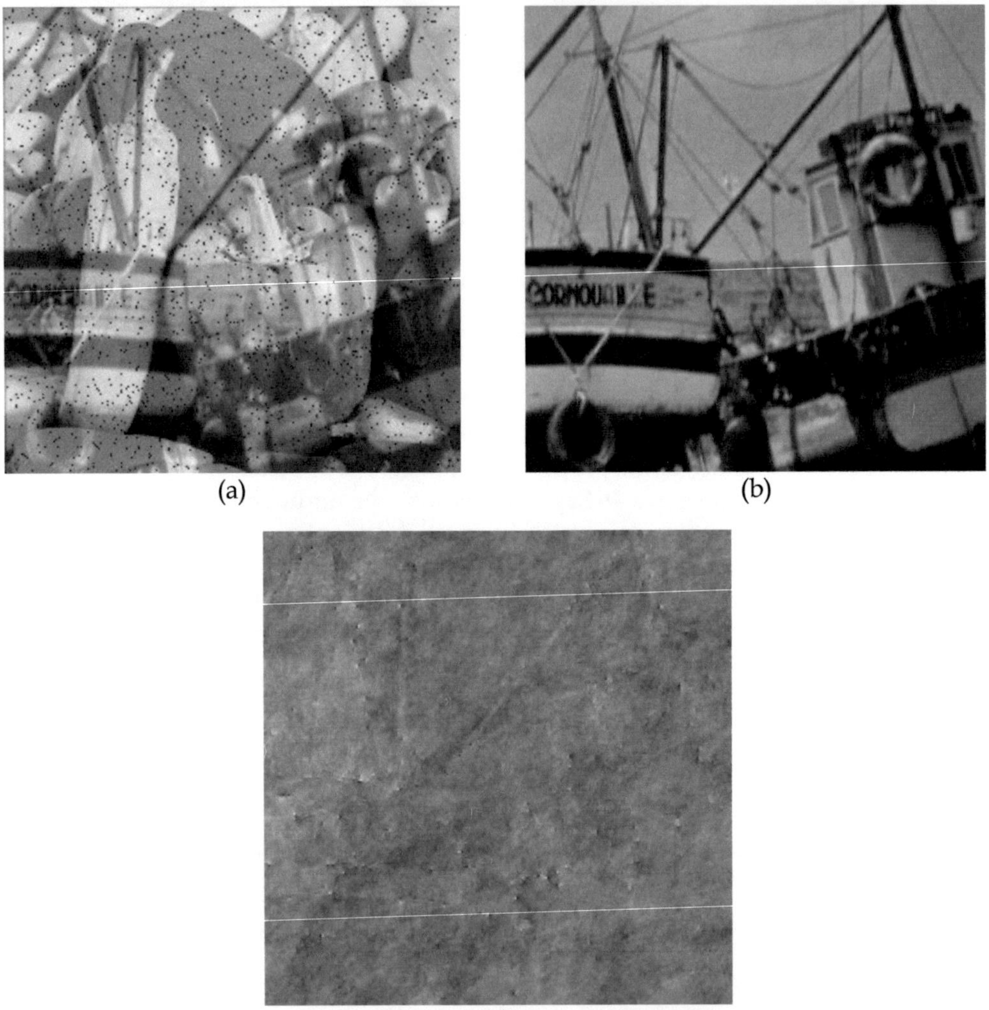

(a) (b)

(c)

Fig. 4. (a) Observed image degraded with additive interference, white noise with standard deviation of 2, and impulse noise with probability of 0.03, (b) restored image, and (c) enhanced difference between the original image and restored image.

Finally, we show computer simulation results when the original image additional degraded by impulse noise cluster of size 15x15 elements. Figs. 5(a), 5(b), and 5(c) show the observed image, the restored image, and enhanced difference between the original and restored images, respectively.

(a)

(b)

(c)

Fig. 5. (a) Observed image degraded with additive interference, white noise with standard deviation of 2, and impulse noise cluster (15x15 pixels), (b) restored image, and (c) enhanced difference between the original image and restored image.

Note that outside of damaged elements the restoration performance of the proposed method is good. At the location of the damaged elements the method carries out a smooth interpolation using information containing in neighboring pixels.

### 3.2 Restoration of noisy image degraded with nonuniform illumination

Nonuniform illumination is an example of multiplicative interference. In our experiments we use the Lambertian model of illumination, which reflects light equally in all directions. Its reflectance map (Diaz-Ramirez & Kober, 2009) can be expressed as

$$I(p_0,q_0)=\cos\left\{\frac{\pi}{2}-\arctan\left[\frac{r}{\cos(\tau)\left[(r\tan(\tau)\cos(\alpha)-p_0)^2+(r\tan(\tau)\sin(\alpha)-q_0)^2\right]^{1/2}}\right]\right\}, \quad (32)$$

where $\tau$ is the slant angle, $\alpha$ is the tilt angle, and r is the magnitude of the vector from point-light source to surface. These parameters define the position of the light source with respect to the surface origin. In our simulations, we set $\tau = 5^{\circ}$, $\alpha = 245^{\circ}$, and $r = \{1.1, 1.5, 2\}$. Table 1 shows the values taken by the illumination function in our experiments.

| $r$ | Range of values taken by the illumination function | Mean value | Standard deviation | Shading |
|---|---|---|---|---|
| 1.1 | 0.35-1 | 0.60 | 0.14 | 65% |
| 1.5 | 0.45-1 | 0.70 | 0.12 | 55% |
| 2 | 0.55-1 | 0.79 | 0.10 | 45% |

Table 1. Values of the illumination function.

The mean value and standard deviation of the original image are 112.3 and 50, respectively, with maximum and minimum values of 237 and 17, respectively. Fig. 6 shows a test original image.

Fig. 6. Test original image.

Figs. 7(a), 9(a), and 11(a) show degraded images with different illuminations functions shown in Figs. 7(b), 9(b), and 11(b) ($r = \{1.1, 1.5, 2\}$). The degraded image also contains a zero-mean Gaussian noise with a standard deviation of 1. Figs. 7(c), 9(c), and 11(c) show the restored images using the proposed method. Figs. 7(d), 9(d), and 11(d) show enhanced difference between the original image and the restored images.

Figs. 8, 10, and 12 show the performance in terms of the RMSE of the proposed methods using three images (Mm3) and the Wiener filter versus the standard deviation of additive noise with different parameters of illumination. One can observe that the proposed method is useful when the standard deviation of additive noise is low. Note that the performance of the proposed method is essentially better than that of the Wiener filter, which is designed with known parameters. Time required to restore the image using the Mm3 is approximately 51 sec. In this case, the iterative conjugate gradient algorithm requires about 1070 iterations.

Fig. 7. Nonuniform illumination correction with the proposed method: (a) observed image degraded with multiplicative interference and white noise with a standard deviation of 1, (b) multiplicative interference with $r = 1.1$, (c) restored image, (d) enhanced difference between the original image and the restored image.

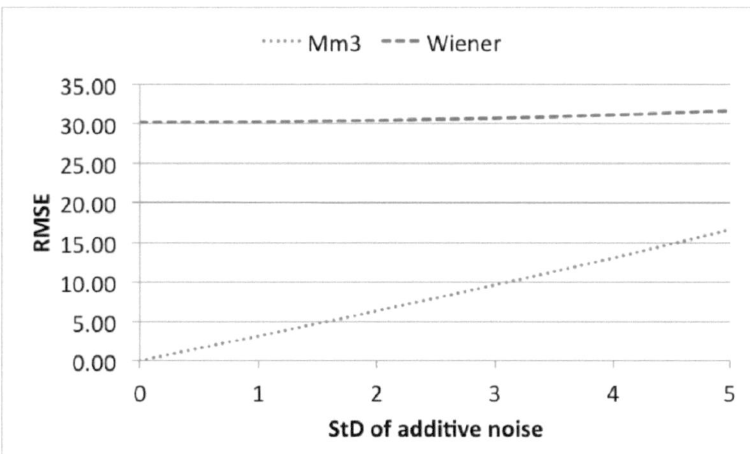


Fig. 8. Performance of the proposed method when $\tau = 5^\circ$, $\alpha = 245^\circ$, and $r = 1.1$: RMSE versus a standard deviation of additive noise.

Fig. 9. Nonuniform illumination correction with the proposed method: (a) observed image degraded with multiplicative interference and white noise with a standard deviation of 1, (b) multiplicative interference with $r = 1.5$, (c) restored image, (d) enhanced difference between the original image and the restored image.

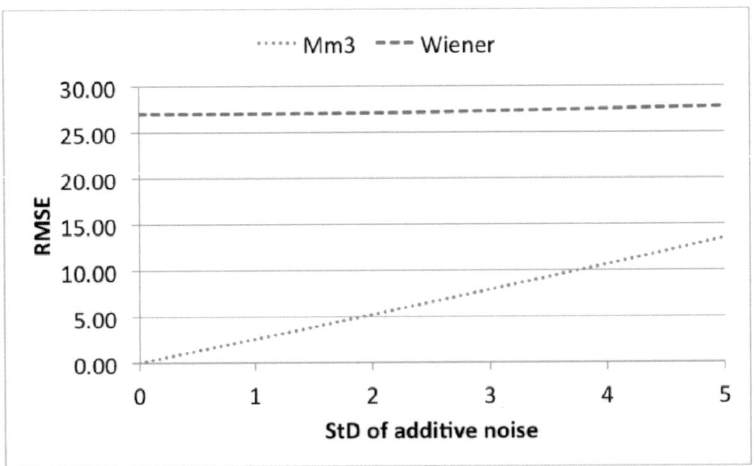


Fig. 10. Performance of the proposed method when $\tau = 5^{\circ}$, $\alpha = 245^{\circ}$, and $r = 1.5$ : RMSE versus a standard deviation of additive noise.

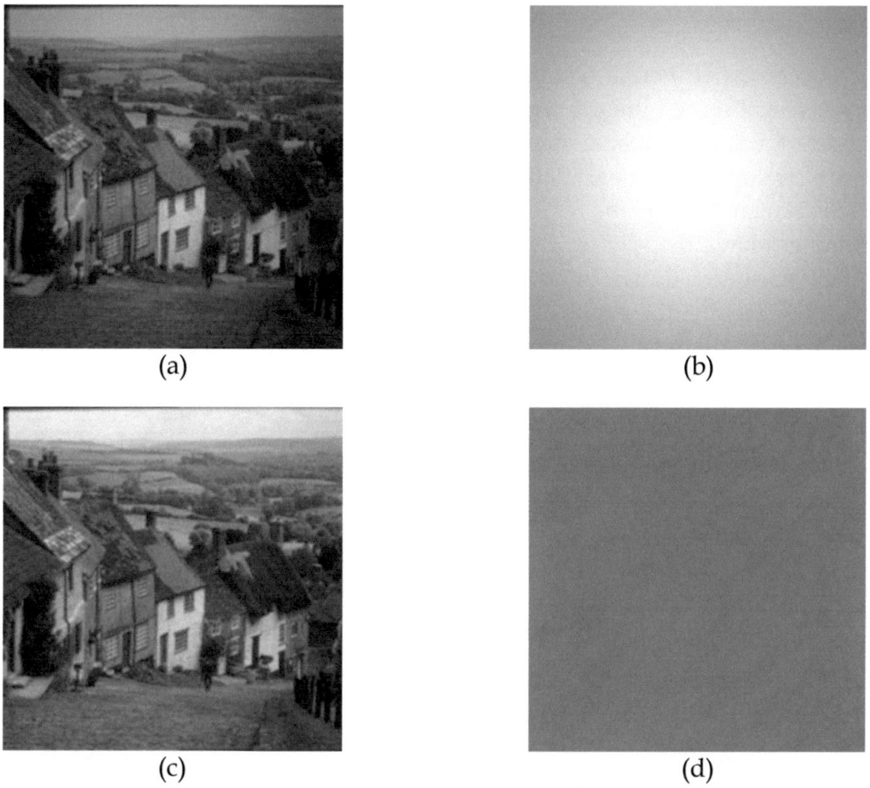


Fig. 11. Nonuniform illumination correction with proposed method: (a) observed image degraded with multiplicative interference and white noise with a standard deviation of 1, (b) multiplicative interference with $r = 2.0$, (c) restored image, (d) enhanced difference between the original image and the restored image.

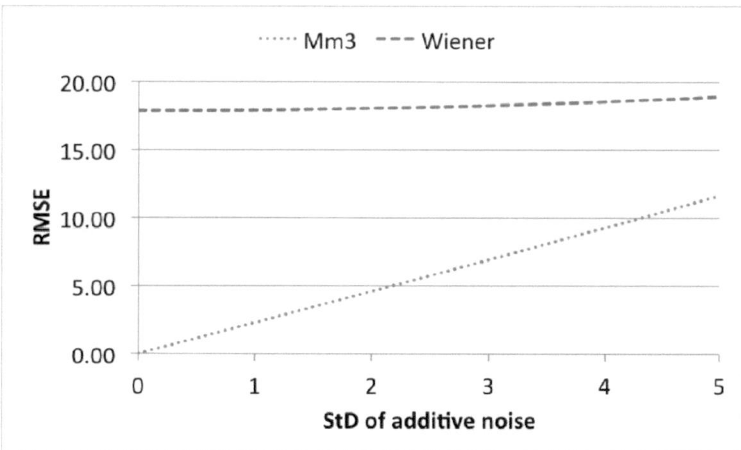


Fig. 12. Performance of the proposed method for multiplicative degradation with parameters of illumination of $\tau = 5^\circ$, $\alpha = 245^\circ$, and $r = 2.0$ : RMSE versus a standard deviation of additive noise.

## 4. Experimental results

Here we present experimental results with a real-life image degraded by a multiplicative interference. The observed images were obtained as follows. A test image was displayed on a LCD screen. A printed transparency was placed between a camera and the screen in order to simulate a multiplicative degradation. Microscanning was performed by shifting the test image on the screen. Finally, the three observed images were captured with the camera. The observed images have the size of 256 × 256 pixels. First, the observed images were passed through the logarithmic transformation. Next, the proposed method was utilized to obtain a resulting image. Finally, the exponential transformation was applied to the resulting image to restore the original image. The original image, multiplicative degradation, and one of the observed images taken by a camera are shown in Figs. 13(a), 13(b), and 13(c), respectively. The restored image is presented in Fig. 13(d).

Since in the experiment the level of additive noise is low, the quality of the restoration with the proposed method is very good.

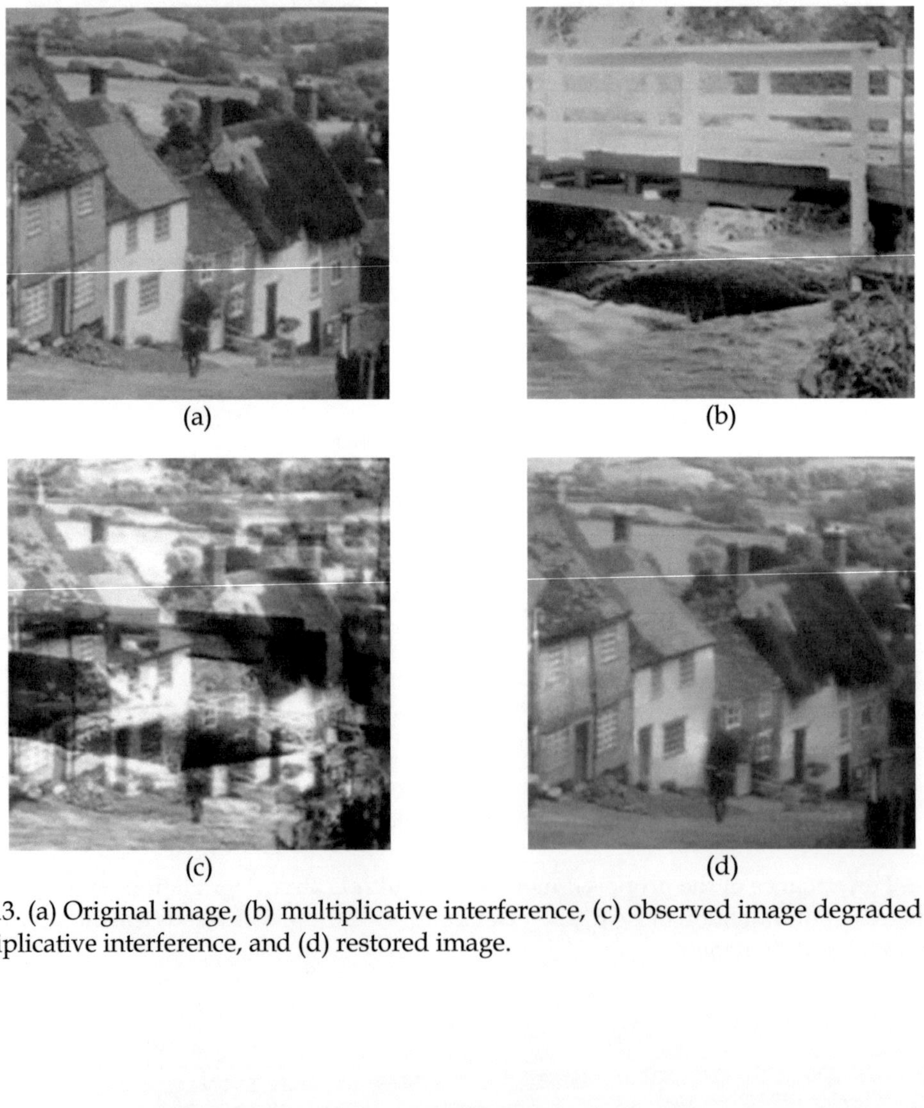

Fig. 13. (a) Original image, (b) multiplicative interference, (c) observed image degraded with multiplicative interference, and (d) restored image.

## 5. Conclusion

In this chapter we presented methods for restoration of images degraded with additive and multiplicative interferences, and corrupted by sensor noise. Using three observed images taken with a microscanning imaging system, an explicit system of equations for additive and multiplicative signal models was derived. The restored image is a solution of the system. With the help of computer simulations we demonstrated the performance of the proposed method in terms of restoration accuracy and execution time. The performance of the proposed method is essentially better than that of the Wiener filter, which is designed with known parameters

## 6. References


Banham, M. & Katsaggelos, A. (1997) Digital image restoration. *IEEE Signal Processing Magazine,* Vol. 14, No.2, (March 1997), pp. 24-41, ISSN 1053-5888

Bovik, A. (2005). *Handbook of image and video processing* (2nd ed.), Academic Press, ISBN 0-12-119792-1, NJ, USA

Diaz-Ramirez, V. & Kober, V. (2009) Target recognition under nonuniform illumination conditions. *Applied Optics,* Vol. 48, No. 7, (March 2009), pp.1408–1418, ISSN 1559-128X

Golub, G. & Van Loan, C. (1996). *Matrix computations,* (3rd ed.), The Johns Hopkins University Press, ISBN 0-8018-5414-8, Baltimore, Maryland, USA

González, R. & Woods, R. (2008). *Digital image processing* (3rd ed.), Prentice Hall, ISBN 0-13-1687288, NJ, USA

Hautiere, N. & Aubert, D. (2005). Contrast restoration of foggy images through use of an onboard camera, *Proceedings of IEEE Conference Intelligent Transportation System,* pp. 1090-1095, ISBN 0-7803-9215-9, Versailles, France, September 13-15, 2005

Hayat, M., Torres, S., Armstrong, E., Cain, S. & Yasuda, B. (1999). Statistical algorithm for nonuniformity correction in focal-plane arrays. *Applied Optics,* Vol. 38, No. 8, (March 1999), pp. 772-780, ISSN 1559-128X

Jain, A. (1989). *Fundamentals of Digital Image Processing.* Prentice Hall, ISBN 0-13-336165-9, Englewood Cliffs, NJ, USA

Kay, S. (1993). *Fundamentals of statistical signal processing : estimation theory,* Prentice Hall, ISBN 0-13-345711-7, NJ, USA

Kober, V., Mozero, M. & Alvarez-Borrego, J.(2001). Nonlinear filters with spatially connected neighborhoods. *Optical Engineering,* Vol. 40, No. 6, (June 2001), pp. 971-983, ISSN 0091-3286

Kundur, D. & Hatzinakos, D. (1996). Blind image deconvolution. *IEEE Signal Processing Magazine,* Vol. 13, No. 3, (May 1996), pp. 73-76, ISSN 1053-5888

Lee, H. & Kim, J. (2009). Retrospective correction of nonuniform illumination on bi-level images. *Optics Express,* Vol. 17, No. 26, (December 2009), pp. 23880-23893, eISSN 1094-4087

López-Martínez, J. & Kober, V. (2008). Image restoration based on camera microscanning, *Proceedings of Applications of Digital Image Processing XXXI* , ISBN 9780819472939, San Diego, CA, USA, August 10-14, 2008.

López-Martínez, J. & Kober, V. (2010). Image restoration of nonuniformly illuminated images with camera microscanning, *Proceedings of Applications of Digital Image Processing XXXIII*, ISBN 9780819482945 , San Diego, CA, USA, August 2-4 , 2010

López-Martínez, J., Kober, V. & Ovseyevich, I. (2010). *Image restoration based on camera microscanning*. Pattern Recognition and Image Analysis, Vol. 20, No. 3,(September 2010), pp.370–375, ISSN 1054-6618

Milanfar, P. (2011). *Super-resolution imaging*, CRC Press, ISBN 13-978-1-4398-1931-9, NJ, USA

Narasimhan, S. & Nayar, S. (2002). Vision and the atmosphere. *International Journal of Computer Vision*, Vol. 48, No.3, (July-August 2002), pp. 233–254, ISSN 0920-5691

Ratliff, B., Hayat, M. & Hardie, R. (2002). An algebraic algorithm for nonuniformity correction in focal-plane arrays. *Journal Optical Society of America A*, Vol. 19, No. 9, (September 2002), pp. 1737–1747, ISSN 1084-7529

Shi, J., Reichenbach, S. & Howe, J. (2006) Small-kernel superresolution methods for microscanning imaging systems. *Applied Optics*, Vol. 45, No. 6,(February 2006), pp. 1203–1214, ISSN 1559-128X

# 14

# 2D Iterative Detection Network Based Image Restoration: Principles, Applications and Performance Analysis

Daniel Kekrt and Miloš Klíma
*Dept. of Radio Engineering, Czech Technical University in Prague*
*Czech Republic*

## 1. Introduction

Image capturing is corrupted by numerous perturbing influences. These influences are divisible to time-invariant and temporal. The typical time-invariant influence is an image blurring, rising from various causes, that can be mathematically understood as deterministic 2D ISI channel or FSM (Finite state machine). Among temporal influences pertain especially noises on the other hand. There are four significant noise sources in the case of a camera with CCD (CMOS) sensor: photon noise (signal dependent additive Poisson stochastic process), thermal noise (additive Poisson stochastic process), readout noise (additive Gaussian stochastic process) and quantization noise (J. van Vliet L. et al., 1998). The photon noise is caused by the time inhomogeneous photon emission, incident to the lens in individual par-axial light rays, with the mean value and squared standard deviation $\mu_P$ equal to the averaged intensity of these rays. The photon noise cannot be compensated because its origin is located front of the lens. Therefore we will not take it into account. The thermal noise, readout noise and quantization noise together create one composite noise of the CCD/CMOS sensor that affects on the captured blurred image as the random IECS-ML channel. Such channel is biased by three parameters $\mu_R$, $\sigma_R$ (mean value and standard deviation of the readout noise), depending on the sensor readout rate, and $\mu_T$ (mean value and squared standard deviation of the thermal noise), exponentially raising according to the sensor temperature $T_s$. All mentioned influences can be eliminated by iterative detection network (IDN). Such system solves effectively the 2D MAP criterion through feedback process based on the exchange and precision of certain probability density functions (PDFs). Similar networks (simpler one-dimensional alternatives) have found utilization in the sphere of Turbo code detection (Chugg et al., 2001; Vucetic & Juan, 2003; 2000). There will be discussed de facto theirs generalization to the two-dimensional form. The explanation begins by decomposition of the 2D MAP criterion that elucidates the essential principle of IDNs functioning. The necessary conditions for this decomposition will be defined too. Consequently, we focus closer to the IDNs dedicated for restoration of dichromatic images and using PDFs marginalization at the symbol level and symbol block level.

## 2. System model

We assume the model of image capturing system in Fig. 1 including three major sections. The first and second section are emulating all perturbing influences affecting the captured image. The first section presents the hypothetical model of the time-invariant image blurring (2D ISI channel). The second one is image capturing section (IECS-ML channel) modeling all significant noises incident this kind of capturing systems. Such noises rise especially in the camera sensor with on-chip electronics, but no only there. The last section is the MAP criterion based iterative detector (restorative circuits) containing IDN with its front-end, so-called soft output demodulator (SODEM).

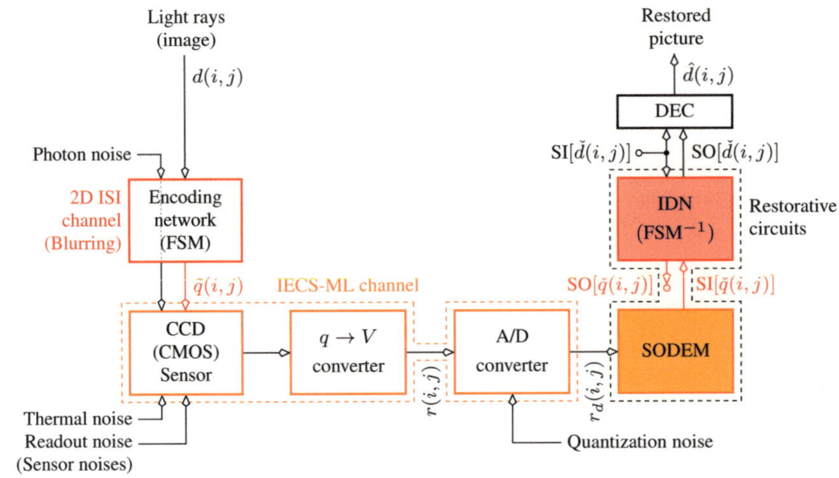


Fig. 1. Block diagram of a CCD/CMOS camera with dichromatic image restorative section.

## 3. Deterministic 2D ISI channel (blurring model)

A time-invariant image blurring can be emulated by the signal transmission through the 2D ISI channel defined via convolution

$$\begin{aligned}\tilde{q}(i,j) &= f(\mathbf{A}, \mathcal{N}_d(i,j) \subset \mathbf{D}) \\ &= \sum_{0 \le i',j' \le H_{\mathbf{A}},W_{\mathbf{A}}} a(i',j')d(i+i',j+j'),\end{aligned} \tag{1}$$

where $\mathcal{N}_d(i,j) = \{d(i+i',j+j')\}_{0\le i',j'\le H_{\mathbf{A}},W_{\mathbf{A}}}$ denotes the convolution region and $\mathbf{D} = [d(i,j)]_{i,j}$ the page of black and white pixels $d(i,j) \in \{d^{(\ell)}\}_{\ell=1}^{M_d} = \{0,1\}$ (relative photon quantity impacting at the lens in several par-axial rays). The discrete 2D finite impulse response $\mathbf{A} = [a(i',j')]_{0\le i',j'\le H_{\mathbf{A}},W_{\mathbf{A}}}$ with the high $H_{\mathbf{A}}$ and width $W_{\mathbf{A}}$ model time-invariant image blurring. There we focus closer to the two basic time-invariant distortion — defocusing in the imperfectly adjusted lens and blurring due to object moving.

### 3.1 Defocusing in the inperfectly adjusted lens

The image blurring in a defocused lens can be mathematically imitated as the Gaussian blurring channel (GBC). It is defined by the point spread function $PSF(x,y) = \frac{\Delta}{\pi}e^{-\Delta(x^2+y^2)}$, where $\Delta$ is the spread parameter. Two examples of $PSF(x,y)$ with different $\Delta$ shows Fig. 2.

If we want transform such PSF to the 2D ISI channel, we have to assume approximation, that the distribution of light is uniform on the flats with the size and shape congruous to the sensor cells. Thereafter, the discrete convolution kernel can be got by the integration $a(i,j) = \int_{i-1/2}^{i+1/2}\int_{j-1/2}^{j+1/2} PSF(x,y)dxdy = \frac{\Delta}{4}(\mathrm{erf}(i-1/2)-\mathrm{erf}(i+1/2))(\mathrm{erf}(j-1/2)-\mathrm{erf}(j+1/2))$ of the $PSF(x,y)$ over the individual sensor cells. They are marked in Fig. 2 by the carnation lines and adjusted, without detriment to generality, as the unit size areas. Concretely, the results of the mentioned integration in our examples are two kernels

$$\mathbf{A}_{\mathrm{GBC},3/10} = \begin{bmatrix} 0.0458 & 0.1172 & 0.0458 \\ 0.1172 & 0.3000 & 0.1172 \\ 0.0458 & 0.1172 & 0.0458 \end{bmatrix}, \quad \mathbf{A}_{\mathrm{SGBC},6/10} = \begin{bmatrix} 0 & 0.0872 & 0 \\ 0.0872 & 0.6000 & 0.0872 \\ 0 & 0.0872 & 0 \end{bmatrix}, \tag{2}$$

marked in the given figure by red stem graphs. The first is 9-ray kernel and the second one is 5-ray kernel with suppressed insignificant rays.

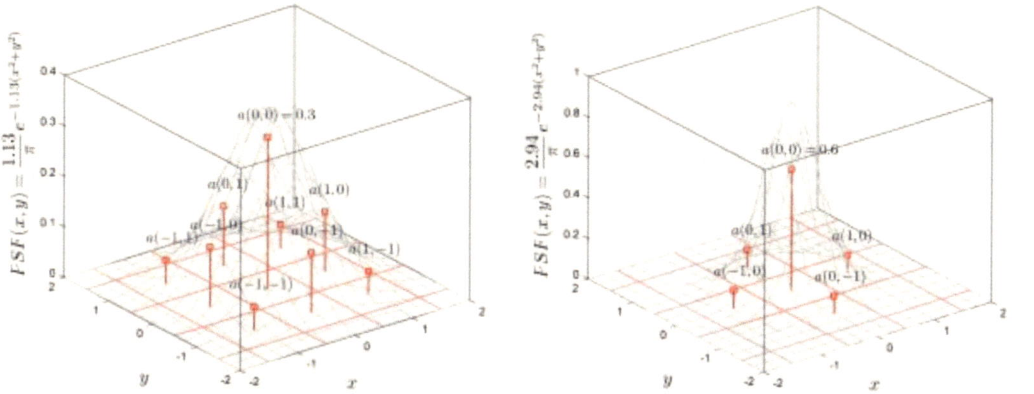


(a) $\mathbf{A}_{\mathrm{GBC},3/10}$. (b) $\mathbf{A}_{\mathrm{SGBC},6/10}$.

Fig. 2. The two examples of GBCs with corresponding convolutional kernels.

$a(0,0) = 0.2$ $a(0,0) = 0.3$ $a(0,0) = 0.4$ $a(0,0) = 0.5$ $a(0,0) = 0.7$ $a(0,0) = 1$

Fig. 3. Examples of the defocusing by GBC on the QR code snapshot.

### 3.2 Blurring due to object moving

We have an object moving on the certain known trajectory as well as in Fig. 4. Each point of this object pass the curve $\mathbf{s}(t') = [s_x(t')\ s_y(t')]$ with the starting $\mathbf{s}_s = \mathbf{s}(t)$ and ending $\mathbf{s}_e = \mathbf{s}(t+T_e)$ point. These points are projected through the lens (it is not included to Fig. 4 for simplicity) to the plane $\{\mathbf{b}_x, \mathbf{b}_y\}$ of the CCD/CMOS sensor, where $T_e$ is the exposure time. We denote impulse response of the channel emulating blurring due to object moving as $\mathbf{A}_{\mathrm{BOM},\alpha}$ and with respect to discrete character of this response let us approximate the realization of par-axial intensity on the plane $\{\mathbf{b}_x, \mathbf{b}_y\}$, in the time $t$, as the mosaic $D(x,y) = \sum_{i,j} d(i,j) f_P(i,j,x,y)$ of pixels $d(i,j) \in \{d^{(\ell)}\}_{\ell=1}^{M_d}$ shaped by square function

$$f_P(i,j,x,y) = \begin{cases} 1 \text{ iff } |x - iL_p| \leq \frac{L_p}{2} \wedge |y - jL_p| \leq \frac{L_p}{2} \\ 0 \qquad\qquad \text{otherwise} \end{cases}, \tag{3}$$

where $L_p$ establish their size, that is equal or less then size $L_c$ of the sensor cell (potential well).

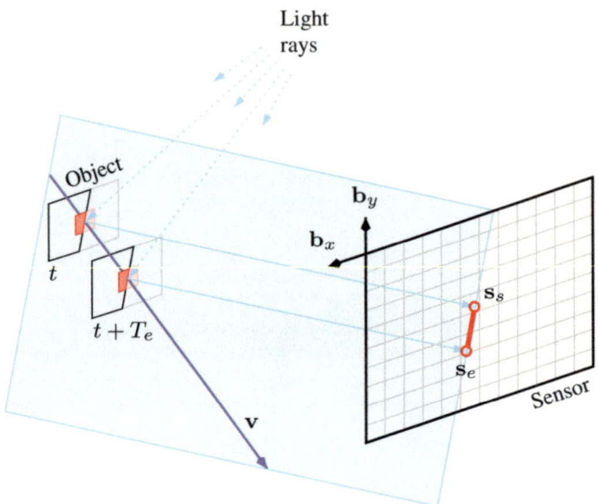


Fig. 4. The projection of the moving object point to the CCD/CMOS sensor plane.

On the basis of declared definitions and approximations, we can subsequently express useful signal impacting the sensor by the convolution Eq. 1 emulating the situation, when the snapshot $\mathbf{D}$, gained in the time $t$, is slided on the sensor surface and stepwise trapped to the its cells. The said fact can be also conceived from the opposite side, when potential well sliding on the immovable pattern $\mathbf{D}$. If the velocity radial component is insignificant in the comparison with axial component (expansion of the object is negligible between times $t$ and $t + T_e$) and starting time $t$ is equated to zero, we can obtain the impulse response coefficients by the integration

$$a(i',j') \propto \int_0^{T_e} \int_{s_y(t')-\frac{1}{2}L_p}^{s_y(t')+\frac{1}{2}L_p} \int_{s_x(t')-\frac{1}{2}L_p}^{s_x(t')+\frac{1}{2}L_p} f_P(i(\mathbf{s}_s) + i', j(\mathbf{s}_s) + j', x', y') dx' dy' dt'. \tag{4}$$

This situation illustrate Fig. 5a or Fig. 5b. The responses

$$\mathbf{A}_{\mathrm{BOM},0} = [\, \tfrac{1}{12} \ \tfrac{1}{6} \ \tfrac{1}{6} \ \tfrac{1}{6} \ \tfrac{1}{6} \ \tfrac{1}{6} \ \tfrac{1}{12} \,]^T, \ \mathbf{A}_{\mathrm{BOM},\pi/4} = \begin{bmatrix} \frac{1}{6} & \frac{1}{12} & 0 \\ \frac{1}{12} & \frac{1}{3} & \frac{1}{12} \\ 0 & \frac{1}{12} & \frac{1}{6} \end{bmatrix} \tag{5}$$

can be stated as the examples of such distortion channels that come from Eq. 4 biased by angles $\varphi = 0$, $\varphi = \frac{\pi}{4}$ and with confinement only to equable movement, when $\mathbf{s}(t')$ is linear function of time $t'$.

If the object expansion on the plane $\{\mathbf{b}_x, \mathbf{b}_y\}$, between the times $t$ and $t+T_e$, is not insignificant the situation in Fig. 5c occurs. Computation of the constants

$$a(i',j') \propto \int_0^{T_e} \int_{s_y(t')-\frac{1}{2}L_c(t')}^{s_y(t')+\frac{1}{2}L_c(t')} \int_{s_x(t')-\frac{1}{2}L_c(t')}^{s_x(t')+\frac{1}{2}L_c(t')} f_p(i(\mathbf{s}_s)+i',j(\mathbf{s}_s)+j',x',y')dx'dy'dt' \qquad (6)$$

is analogical to Eq. 4, only with the difference that size of sliding sensor cell will not be equal to pixel size $L_p$ anymore, but it will present the function $L_c(t')$ linearly (Fig. 5c) or non-linearly dependent on the time $t'$ in compliance with the movement of scanning object.

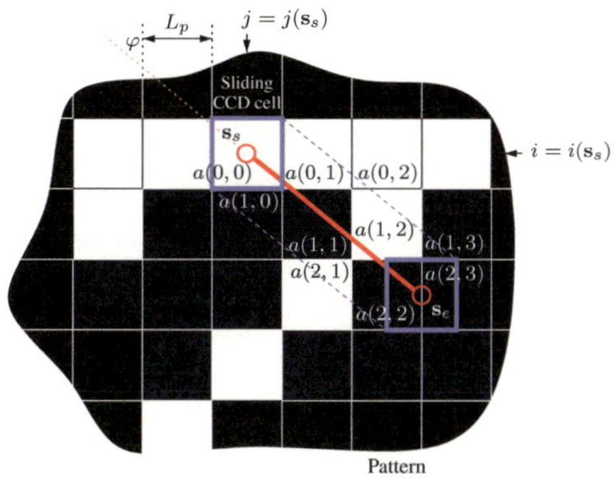


(a) The example with $\mathbf{s}_s$ situated inside of the pixel $(i(\mathbf{s}_s), j(\mathbf{s}_s))$. Negligible radial component of the velocity.

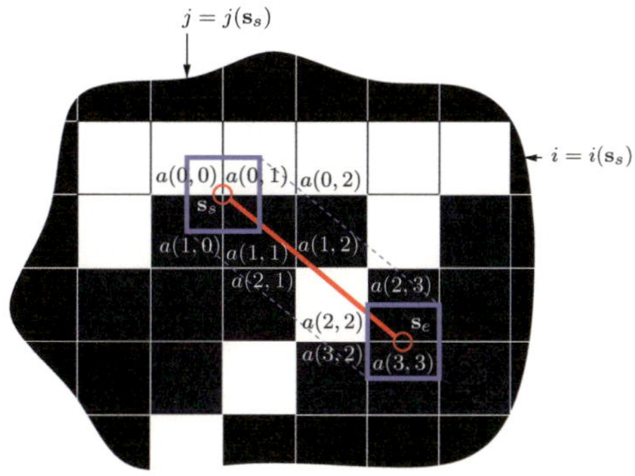


(b) The example with $\mathbf{s}_s$ situated on the edge of the pixel $(i(\mathbf{s}_s), j(\mathbf{s}_s))$. Negligible radial component of the velocity.

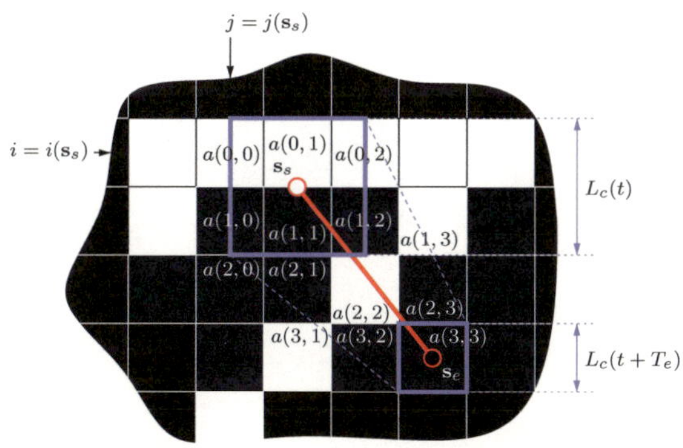


(c) The example with $\mathbf{s}_s$ situated on the edge of the pixel $(i(\mathbf{s}_s), j(\mathbf{s}_s))$. Indispensable radial component of the velocity.

Fig. 5. The equivalent movement trajectory of the sensor sensing cell sliding on the pattern **D** (snapshot of the straight-line moving object with negligible and indispensable radial component of the velocity **v**).

### 3.3 Hypothetical cellular model of a 2D ISI channel — Encoding network (EN)

The convolution Eq. 1 can be emulated by certain 2D hypothetical encoding network (EN). The assembly of this EN is variable and contains specific, relatively simple, functional blocks $f_G()$. We denote these functional blocks as general processing elements (GPEs) and one such elements is illustrated in Fig. 6a.

In principle, a GPE presents a simple FSM whose inputs as well as outputs are variables $\mathcal{S}(k)$ discrete in values, that are derivable from alphabets $\{\mathcal{S}^{(\ell)}(k)\}_\ell$. The inputs together with the outputs consequently create the set $\mathcal{N} = \bigcup_k \mathcal{S}(k)$ flowing from the alphabet $\{\mathcal{N}^{(\ell)}\}_\ell$.

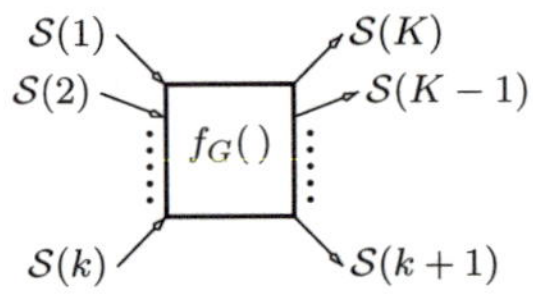


(a) A GPE.

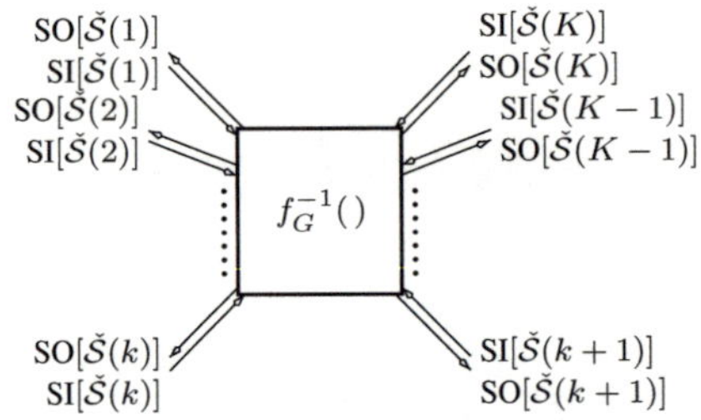


(b) A SISO module.

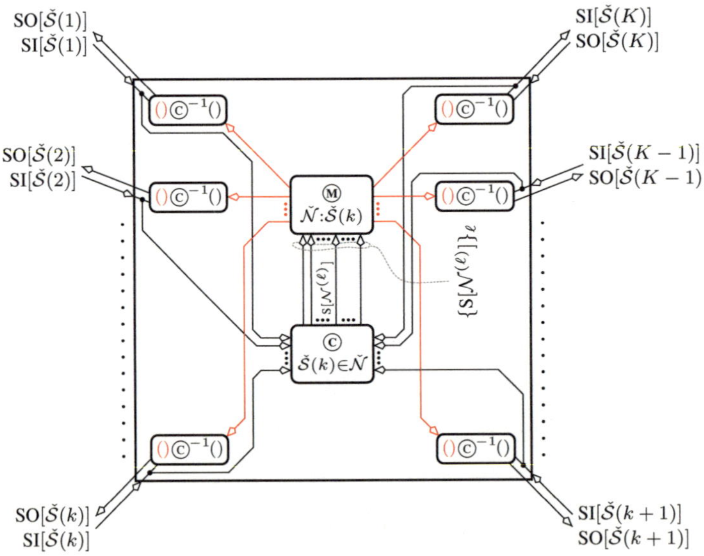


(c) Structure of a SISO module.

Fig. 6. A general processing element (GPE) and its soft inversion (SISO module).

## 4. Random IECS-ML channel (noise model)

### 4.1 Composite noise of the CCD/CMOS sensor

The presence of the signal independent composite CCD/CMOS sensor noise in mutually correlated rays $0 \leq \tilde{q}(i,j) \leq 1$ can be expressed as the blurred image transmission through the random IECS-ML channel with I/O equation $r(i,j) = C\tilde{q}(i,j) + w_T(i,j) + w_R(i,j)$, where $r(i,j)$ is the channel output, $w_T(i,j)$ is the total thermal noise accumulated with the useful signal $q(i,j) = C\tilde{q}(i,j)$ as a charge in the CCD sensor cell at the position $(i,j)$ and $w_R(i,j)$ is the readout noise. The constant $C$ (above limited by a full well capacity FWC of the CCD sensor) defines a quantity of generated charge and it is directly proportional to the exposure time $T_e$.

### 4.2 Quantization noise of the A/D converter

The output $r(i,j)$ (IECS-ML channel output also registrable in the matrix form $\mathbf{R} = \mathbf{Q} + \mathbf{W}_T + \mathbf{W}_R$ for entire sensor) is further quantized in the $N_b$-bit A/D converter that can be approximated by the random channel $r_d(i,j) = r(i,j) + w_Q(i,j)$ with uniformly distributed noise $w_Q(i,j)$ in light of probability theory. We denote the output of this converter as $r_d(i,j) = Q(r(i,j))$, where $Q(\xi) = \sum_{1\leq\ell\leq 2^{N_b}} H(\xi - t_Q(\ell))$ and $H(\xi) = \{^{0 \text{ iff } \xi<0}_{1 \text{ otherwise}}$ is a Heaviside step function. For simplicity we will assume the linear quantization only with threshold values

$$t_Q(\ell) = \begin{cases} 0 & \text{iff} \quad \ell = 1 \\ (\ell-1)\Delta_Q + 1/2 & \text{iff} \ 1 < \ell \leq 2^{N_b} \end{cases} \tag{7}$$

and quantization step $\Delta_Q$, where for the highest quantization level $t_Q(2^{N_b}) \leq FWC$ is applied.

## 5. Image restoration — Symbol and page 2D MAP detection

### 5.1 Optimal MAP detection

The channel has independent eliminated states (IECS), if noise sources in CCD sensor cells are mutually independent. It makes joint probability density function (PDF) $p_{\mathbf{W}}(\Xi) = \prod_{i,j} p_w(\xi)$ as the product of marginal densities. The channel is memory-less (ML), if the current $x(i,j)$ depends only on the corresponding $q(i,j)$. The fulfillment of both conditions creates the likeli-hood function

$$\begin{aligned} p_{\mathbf{R}}(\Xi|\check{\mathbf{Q}}) &= \int_{\mathbf{W}} p_{\mathbf{R}|\mathbf{Q},\mathbf{W}}(\Xi|\check{\mathbf{Q}},\Xi')p_{\mathbf{W}}(\Xi')d\Xi' \\ &= \prod_{i,j} \underbrace{\int_{w(i,j)} p_{r|q,w}(\xi|\check{q}(i,j),\xi')p_w(\xi')d\xi'}_{p_r(\xi|\check{q}(i,j))} \end{aligned} \tag{8}$$

factorizable that is necessary to transition from a single-stage detector to an IDN.

The optimal 2D MAP detector is based on the criterion

$$\hat{d}(i,j) = \arg \underset{\check{d}(i,j)}{Ⓜ} \left[ \underset{\check{\mathbf{D}}:\check{d}(i,j)}{Ⓜ} \mathrm{S}[\mathbf{R}_d, \check{\mathbf{D}}] \right], \tag{9}$$

where $\hat{d}(i,j)$ denotes the wanted estimation, $\check{d}(i,j)$ denotes a testing estimator (takes individual values from data alphabet), $\check{\mathbf{D}} : \check{d}(i,j)$ denotes the set of possible image realizations containing the estimator $\check{d}(i,j)$ and Ⓜ with Ⓜ denote certain types of marginalization operators.

The quantity $\mathrm{S}[\mathbf{R}_d, \check{\mathbf{D}}]$ is to be understood as some kind of the joint soft measure and due to IECS-ML condition fulfillment

$$\begin{aligned}\mathrm{S}[\mathbf{R}_d|\check{\mathbf{D}}] &= \mathop{\copyright}_{i,j} \mathrm{S}[r_d(i,j)|\check{\mathbf{D}}] \\ &= \mathop{\copyright}_{i,j} \mathrm{S}[r_d(i,j)|\check{\mathcal{N}}_d(i,j) \subset \check{\mathbf{D}}] \end{aligned} \tag{10}$$

with assumption of a statistically independent data $\mathrm{S}[\check{\mathbf{D}}] = \mathop{\copyright}_{i,j} \mathrm{S}[\check{d}(i,j)]$ can be decomposed to the form

$$\begin{aligned}\mathrm{S}[\mathbf{R}_d, \check{\mathbf{D}}] &= \mathrm{S}[\mathbf{R}_d|\check{\mathbf{D}}] \copyright \mathrm{S}[\check{\mathbf{D}}] \\ &= \left( \mathop{\copyright}_{i,j} \mathrm{S}[r_d(i,j)|\check{\mathcal{N}}_d(i,j) \subset \check{\mathbf{D}}] \right) \copyright \left( \mathop{\copyright}_{i,j} \mathrm{S}[\check{d}(i,j)] \right) \end{aligned} \tag{11}$$

that is joined by certain types of combination operators (©, ©). On the basis of marginalization and combination operators, we can split detectors into four groups in light of detection technique (symbol or page) and implementing domain (probability P[] or equivalent logarithmic metric $\mathrm{M}[\,] = -\ln(\mathrm{P}[\,])$). All possibilities are summarized in Table 1.

The symbol technique (SyD) seeks to minimize of the actual symbol detection error only. The page detection (PgD) has tendency to minimization the entire page detection error. The most numerically effective is the Md-PgD alternative, because it contains the simple combination operator as well as the simple marginalization operator. Close to the Md-PgD, the Md-SyD conjunction with the relatively simple marginalization operator $\min^*(x,y) = \min(x,y) - \ln(1+e^{-|x-y|})$.

| Domain | S[] | Detection | Ⓜ | Ⓜ | © | © | $©^{-1}$ |
|---|---|---|---|---|---|---|---|
| Probability (Pd) | P[] | Page (PgD) | max | max | $\Pi$ | $\times$ | $\div$ |
| Probability (Pd) | P[] | Symbol (SyD) | max | $\Sigma$ | $\Pi$ | $\times$ | $\div$ |
| Metric (Md) | M[] | Page (PgD) | min | min | $\Sigma$ | $+$ | $-$ |
| Metric (Md) | M[] | Symbol (SyD) | min | $\min^*$ | $\Sigma$ | $+$ | $-$ |

Table 1. Summary of combination and marginalization operators.

### 5.2 Suboptimal MAP detection

The direct evaluation of the $\hat{\mathbf{D}}$ from the criterion (9) (single-stage detection) is impossible, because it requires a sequent substitution of all potential image realizations $\check{\mathbf{D}}$. But Eq. 10 (IECS-ML condition) makes possible decomposition of the detection problem from the entire page $\mathbf{D}$ to the level of individual (mutually overlapping) convolution regions $\mathcal{N}_d(i,j)$, corresponding to individual captured pixels. Therefore, we can substitute the single-stage MAP detector by the sub-optimal iterative detection network (IDN).

Such network is formed from a definite number of functional blocks, so-called soft inversions (SISO modules), that exchange the soft measures with each other. The SISO modules present statistical devices complementary to the GPEs in the appropriately designed hypothetical EN emulating the image blurring. The fulfillment of the condition IECS-ML enables a usage of such GPEs that compose the hypothetical realization $\check{\mathbf{D}}$ of a sensing image even by smallest parts (by individual pixels $\check{d}(i,j)$) if this yields a implementation benefits in light of concrete modeled distortion.

The IDN output can be regarded as a optimal (identical with the output of single-stage detector) after the execution of infinite number of iterations (information interchange between inversions). It is not practicable. Therefore, the IDN with the finite number of iterations is sub-optimal detector, that generally provides an inferior estimation to the single-stage detector. Roughly speaking the IDN contains simpler SISO modules, the IDN is more numerically effective and more sub-optimal (it includes more iteratively refining variables).

In the course of each iteration $I$ of the IDN, from count $N_I$, is every SISO module once activated at the least. The activation rests in the reading of soft measures (whole probability or metric densities $\{\mathrm{SI}[\mathcal{S}^{(\ell)}(k)]\}_\ell$, corresponding to certain random variable $\mathcal{S}(k)$ in the hypothetical model) on inputs of a SISO module, followed by the enumeration of output soft measures (whole densities $\{\mathrm{SO}[\mathcal{S}^{(\ell)}(k)]\}_\ell$). The current iteration concludes the exchange of soft measures

$$\begin{aligned} \{\mathrm{SO}[\mathcal{S}^{(\ell)}(k)]\}_\ell &\rightarrow \{\mathrm{SI}[\mathcal{S}^{(\ell)}(k)]\}_\ell \\ \{\mathrm{SI}[\mathcal{S}^{(\ell)}(k)]\}_\ell &\leftarrow \{\mathrm{SO}[\mathcal{S}^{(\ell)}(k)]\}_\ell \end{aligned} \tag{12}$$

among the neighboring modules. After execution of all iteration $N_I$, the estimations of all wanted (output) random variables are performed from the formula

$$\hat{\mathcal{S}}(k) = \arg \underset{\check{\mathcal{S}}(k)}{Ⓜ} [\mathrm{SI}[\check{\mathcal{S}}(k)] © \mathrm{SO}[\check{\mathcal{S}}(k)]]. \tag{13}$$

We express this operation as a hard decision provided by a decision block (DEC).

## 6. Iterative detection networks

### 6.1 IDN topology and soft inversion $f_G^{-1}()$ (SISO module) of general processing element $f_G()$ (FSM)

An IDN presents a soft inversion of an arbitrary EN formed from certain mutually concatenated GPEs that jointly execute an arbitrary processing with input signal. In the our case, as was said in the paragraph 3.3, such EN executes the convolution Eq. 1 and due to fulfillment of the IECS-ML condition can contain the simplest GPEs working on the level of individual pixels. The IDN topology exactly agrees to the EN topology only with the difference, that each of GPE is substituted by its SISO module, just like in Fig. 6a, 6b. The signal processing in the soft inversion is implied in Fig. 6c and takes place in two steps. Firstly, the inputs $\{\mathrm{SI}[\mathcal{S}^{(\ell)}(k)]\}_{\ell,k}$ are combined to particular joint soft measures

$$\mathrm{S}[\check{\mathcal{N}}] = \underset{\check{\mathcal{S}}(k)\in\check{\mathcal{N}}}{©} \mathrm{SI}[\check{\mathcal{S}}(k)] \ \text{ for } \forall\check{\mathcal{N}}. \tag{14}$$

Consequently, all joint measures $\{\mathrm{S}[\mathcal{N}^{(\ell)}]\}_\ell$, corresponding to the set $\forall\check{\mathcal{N}}$ of possible realizations $\mathcal{N}^{(\ell)}$, are marginalized to outputs $\{\mathrm{SO}[\mathcal{S}^{(\ell)}(k)]\}_{\ell,k}$

$$\mathrm{SO}[\check{\mathcal{S}}(k)] = \left(\underset{\check{\mathcal{N}}:\check{\mathcal{S}}(k)}{Ⓜ} \mathrm{S}[\check{\mathcal{N}}]\right) ©^{-1} \mathrm{SI}[\check{\mathcal{S}}(k)] \ \text{ for } \forall\check{\mathcal{S}}(k) \tag{15}$$

that are connected to the inputs $\{\mathrm{SI}[\mathcal{S}^{(\ell)}(k)]\}_{\ell,k}$ of neighboring soft inversions. This update of soft information is known as a soft inversion activation. The activation accomplishment of all soft inversions in the IDN afterwards makes one iteration of the IDN.

### 6.2 Soft-output demodulator

The IDN closely cooperates with the SODEM (Soft output demodulator) providing fundamental hypothesis about captured signal $\mathbf{R}_d$. This functional block presents a gateway between the domain of a real realizations (realizations of certain random variables), where are operated with scalars (factual realizations), and the probability (metric) domain of the IDN, where are operated with whole densities. The SODEM includes the likeli-hood function (or transfer function) of the IECS-ML channel emulating all noises incident in the image capturing system chain (in the our case it is CCD/CMOS camera). The SODEM input forms realization $r_d(i,j)$ that is inside transformed to the discrete a posteriori density $\{\mathrm{SI}[q^{(\ell)}(i,j)]\}_\ell$ presenting the input (sufficient statistic) of the IDN.

Before the sufficient statistic derivation as such, it should be noted that the derivation is purely theoretical and does not correspond to any particular type of CCD / CMOS sensor. We start the SODEM derivation with the definition of discrete cut off Gaussian PDF

$$\begin{aligned} p_{\mathcal{N}_0^{\mathrm{FWC}}}(\xi,\mu,\sigma) \approx{} & \frac{1}{\sqrt{2\pi}\sigma}\sum_{\ell=0}^{\mathrm{FWC}}\delta(\xi-\ell)\exp\left(-\frac{(\ell-\mu)^2}{2\sigma^2}\right) \\ & +\frac{1}{2}\delta(\xi-\mathrm{FWC})\mathrm{erfc}\left(\frac{2\mathrm{FWC}+1-2\mu}{\sqrt{8}\sigma}\right) \\ & +\delta(\xi)\left(1-\frac{1}{2}\mathrm{erfc}\left(-\frac{1+2\mu}{\sqrt{8}\sigma}\right)\right). \end{aligned} \tag{16}$$

All parameters FWC, $\xi$, $\mu$, $\sigma$, etc. in all densities, we will assume in terms of number of electrons [-] either directly or as equivalent quantities related to number of electrons (for example: the quantization noise occurring in the A/D converter, we will consider as if the equivalent electron noise source deteriorative in the sensor, etc.). On the basis of the mentioned definition can be formed thermal and readout noise PDFs as

$$p_{w_T}(\xi) \approx \begin{cases} 0 & \text{iff } {\mu_T<40 \atop \xi\geq 70} \\ e^{-\mu_T}\sum_{\ell\in\mathbb{N}_0}\frac{\mu_T^\ell}{\ell!}\delta(\xi-\ell) & \text{iff } {\mu_T<40 \atop \xi<70} \\ p_{\mathcal{N}_0^{\mathrm{FWC}}}(\xi,\mu_T,\sqrt{\mu_T}) & \text{iff } \mu_T\geq 40 \end{cases} \tag{17}$$

and

$$p_{w_R}(\xi) = p_{\mathcal{N}_0^{\mathrm{FWC}}}(\xi,\mu_R,\sigma_R). \tag{18}$$

Both noises together then create the composite noise $w(i,j) = w_T(i,j) + w_R(i,j)$ and examples of theirs densities, for certain parameters $\mu_T$, $\mu_R$ and $\sigma_R$, is shown in Fig. 7.

The mentioned PDFs are biased by three parameters $\mu_R$, $\sigma_R$ and $\mu_T$. First two parameters are known, because depend on the sensor readout rate that is also known. The last one is the nuisance unknown parameter consisting in the unknown CCD/CMOS sensor temperature and has to be estimated by a suitable way. A ML estimation $\hat{\mu} = N^{-1}\sum_{k=1}^{K} w(k)$ can be used

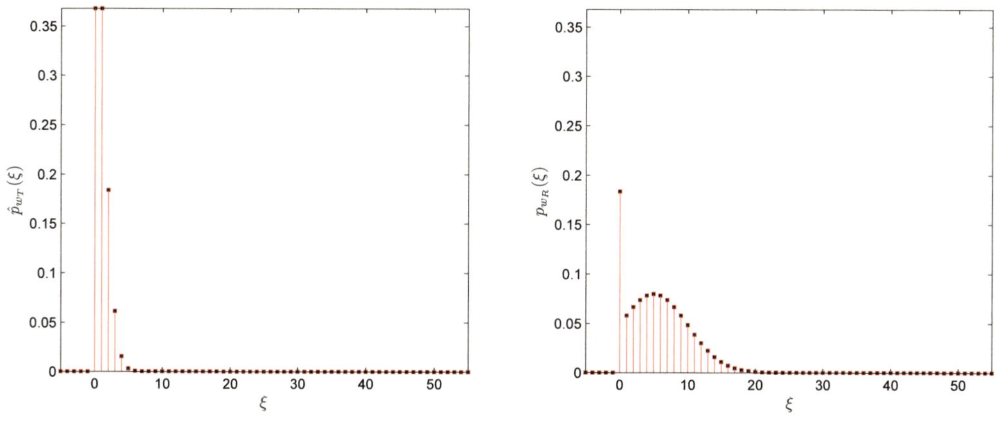


Fig. 7. The example of the thermal and readout noise PDF for $\mu_T = 1$, $\mu_R = 5$, $\sigma_R = 5$ and FWC $= 50$.

for such purpose, which represents the solution of the equation

$$\frac{d}{d\mu}\sum_{k=1}^{K} \ln\left(e^{-\mu}\frac{\mu^{w(k)}}{w(k)!}\right)\Bigg|_{\mu=\hat{\mu}} = 0 \tag{19}$$

derived from the ML criterion. The set of values $\{w(1), w(2), \ldots, w(k), \ldots, w(K)\}$ is the realization of the composite noise on the blacked out CCD sensor strip. The average value of the composite noise $\hat{\mu}$, obtained by the measurement from the blacked out area is used for the computation of $\hat{\mu}_T = \hat{\mu} - \mu_R$. That, substituted back to the density $p_{w_T}(\xi)$, produces its estimation $\hat{p}_{w_T}(\xi)$.

Statistical properties of the composite noise $w(i,j)$ presents the wanted noise model, that controls the IECS-ML channel (channel with additive noise) behavior and results from the

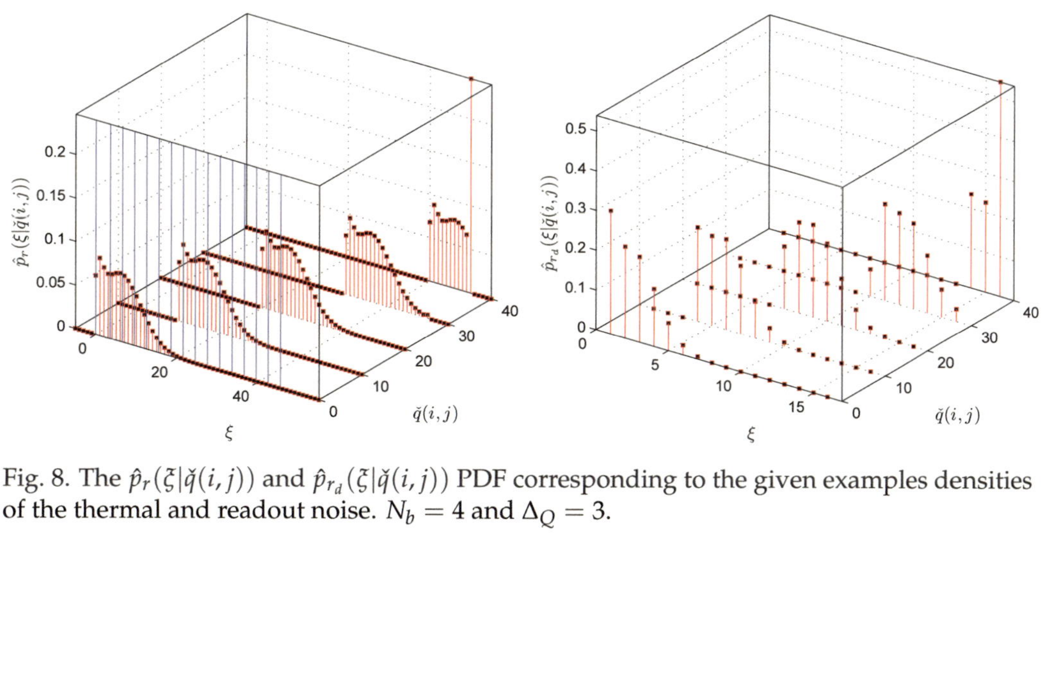


Fig. 8. The $\hat{p}_r(\xi|\check{q}(i,j))$ and $\hat{p}_{r_d}(\xi|\check{q}(i,j))$ PDF corresponding to the given examples densities of the thermal and readout noise. $N_b = 4$ and $\Delta_Q = 3$.

cut off PDF

$$\hat{p}_w(\xi) \approx \hat{p}'_w(\xi) + \delta(\xi - \text{FWC})\left(1 - \int_{-\frac{1}{2}}^{\text{FWC}+\frac{1}{2}} \hat{p}'_w(\xi')d\xi'\right), \tag{20}$$

based on the convolution

$$\hat{p}'_w(\xi) = \sum_{\ell=0}^{\text{FWC}} \delta(\xi - \ell) \int_{-\frac{1}{2}}^{\xi+\frac{1}{2}} \hat{p}_{w_T}(\ell - \xi') p_{w_R}(\xi')d\xi' \tag{21}$$

of densities $\hat{p}_{w_T}(\xi)$ and $p_{w_T}(\xi)$.

The procedure obtaining the metric $\text{SI}[\check{q}(i,j)]$ from the derived noise model begins with the elimination Eq. 10 of the noise density $\hat{p}_w(\xi)$ out of the likeli-hood function of a channel with additive noise $p_{\mathbf{R}|\mathbf{Q},\mathbf{W}}(\Xi|\check{\mathbf{Q}},\Xi') = \delta(\Xi - (\check{\mathbf{Q}} + \Xi'))$ or $p_{r|q,w}(\xi|\check{q}(i,j),\xi') = \delta(\xi - (\check{q}(i,j) + \xi'))$, assuming perfect knowledge of the noise realization $\mathbf{W}$. The result of this elimination is the density $\hat{p}_r(\xi|\check{q}(i,j)) = \hat{p}_w(\check{q}(i,j) - \xi)$. Along with the thermal noise, another source of noise is found in the chain. It is the quantization noise with the uniform PDF $p_{w_Q}$ which is added to the signal in the A/D converter. It can be eliminated out of the density $\hat{p}_r$ by the integrating

$$\hat{p}_{r_d}(\xi|\check{q}(i,j)) = \delta(\xi - 2^{N_b}) \lim_{\epsilon\to 0^+} \int_{t_Q(2^{N_b})-\epsilon}^{\text{FWC}+\frac{1}{2}} \hat{p}_r(\xi'|\check{q}(i,j))d\xi'$$

$$+ \sum_{\ell=1}^{2^{N_b}-1} \delta(\xi - \ell) \lim_{\epsilon\to 0^+} \int_{t_Q(\ell)-\epsilon}^{t_Q(\ell+1)-\epsilon} \hat{p}_r(\xi'|\check{q}(i,j))d\xi' \tag{22}$$

over individual quantization steps (by averaging with the density $p_{w_Q}$) of the size $\Delta_Q$ expressed in the number of electrons and defined, in our case, by Eq. 7. In Fig. 8 you can see the examples of the densities $\hat{p}_r(\xi|\check{q}(i,j))$ and $\hat{p}_{r_d}(\xi|\check{q}(i,j))$ coming out of the given demonstrations in Fig. 7 if and only if $\check{q}(i,j) \in \{q^{(\ell)}\}_{\ell=1}^{M_q} = \{0, 10, 20, 30, 40\}$. We would like to emphasize that it is just a simple example and actually the cardinality of set $\{q^{(\ell)}\}_{\ell=1}^{M_q} = f(\mathbf{A}, \{\mathcal{N}_d(i,j)\}_{\ell=1}^{M_{N_d}})$ is much larger then 5. Blue lines on Fig. 8 represent boundaries of the individual quantization steps.

The SODEM output can be obtained from the derived density by the integration

$$\text{PI}[\check{q}(i,j)] = \int_{r_d(i,j)-\frac{1}{2}}^{r_d(i,j)+\frac{1}{2}} \hat{p}_{r_d}(\xi'|\check{q}(i,j))d\xi'. \tag{23}$$

On the following Fig. 9a, 9c, 9e, 9g are introduced four examples of the SODEM transfer function constituting the derived composite CCD/CMOS noise model for the blurring channel $\mathbf{A}_{\text{GBC},3/10}$ (Eq. 2) and $\mathbf{A}_{\text{BOM},\pi/4}$ (Eq. 5). For the purpose of higher lucidity was chosen continuous plotting, although the transfer functions have a discrete domain of definition. The individual demonstrations of transfer functions afterwards construe with samples (realizations) of captured images on Fig. 9b, 9d, 9f, 9h.

## 7. Distributed iterative detection networks

### 7.1 Distributed IDN marginalizing at the symbol block level

Firstly we focus on the IDNs marginalizing at the symbol block level with horizontal and vertical state variable. These IDNs result from the EN [1] in Fig. 10a where each node (GPE), shown in Fig. 11b, creates a one functional block with the fixed system of inputs and outputs $\mathcal{N}_f(i,j) = \{\mathcal{R}(i,j), \mathcal{C}(i,j), d(i+H_{\mathbf{A}}, j+W_{\mathbf{A}}), \mathcal{R}(i,j+1), \mathcal{C}(i+1,j), q(i,j)\}$, where $\mathcal{R}(i,j)$ and $\mathcal{C}(i,j)$ present auxiliary state variables containing more symbols together. Shapes of these variables are established by the condition

$$\begin{aligned}\mathcal{N}_d(i,j) &\subseteqq \mathcal{R}(i,j) \cup \mathcal{C}(i,j) \cup d(i+H_{\mathbf{A}}, j+W_{\mathbf{A}}) \\ &\supset \mathcal{R}(i,j+1), \mathcal{C}(i+1,j).\end{aligned} \tag{24}$$

The optimal decomposition of the convolution region is $\mathcal{N}_d(i,j) = \mathcal{R}(i,j) \cup \mathcal{C}(i,j) \cup d(i+H_{\mathbf{A}}, j+W_{\mathbf{A}})$ and it is possible when $a(H_{\mathbf{A}}, W_{\mathbf{A}}) \neq 0$.

In the case of a channel $\mathbf{A}_{\mathrm{GBC},a(0,0)}$, with regard to the condition Eq. 24, the variables are $\mathcal{R}(i,j) = \{d(i,j), d(i,j+1), d(i+1,j), d(i+1,j+1), d(i+2,j), d(i+2,j+1)\}$ and $\mathcal{C}(i,j) = \{d(i,j), d(i,j+1), d(i,j+2), d(i+1,j), d(i+1,j+1), d(i+1,j+2)\}$. Their shapes you can see in Fig. 12a. In a similar way we can get decomposition of the $\mathcal{N}_d(i,j)$ for a channel $\mathbf{A}_{\mathrm{GBC},a(0,0)}$. One of possible results is shown in Fig. 12b.

The IDN has same topology as the EN and each its node forms SISO module, illustrated in Fig. 11b, performing the combination

$$\begin{aligned}\mathrm{S}[\check{\mathcal{N}}_f(i,j)] = \mathrm{SI}[\check{\mathcal{R}}(i,j)] \copyright \mathrm{SI}[\check{\mathcal{C}}(i,j)] \copyright \mathrm{SI}[\check{d}(i+H_{\mathbf{A}}, j+W_{\mathbf{A}})] \copyright \mathrm{SI}[\check{\mathcal{R}}(i,j+1)] \\ \copyright \mathrm{SI}[\check{\mathcal{C}}(i+1,j)] \copyright \mathrm{SI}[\check{q}(i,j)]\end{aligned} \tag{25}$$

with marginalizations

$$\mathrm{SO}[\check{\mathcal{R}}(i,j+j')] = \left( \underset{\check{\mathcal{N}}_f(i,j):\check{\mathcal{R}}(i,j+j')}{Ⓜ} \mathrm{S}[\check{\mathcal{N}}_{f()}(i,j)] \right) \copyright^{-1} \mathrm{SI}[\check{\mathcal{R}}(i,j+j')] \ \text{ for } j' \in \{0,1\}, \tag{26}$$

$$\mathrm{SO}[\check{\mathcal{C}}(i+i',j)] = \left( \underset{\check{\mathcal{N}}_f(i,j):\check{\mathcal{C}}(i+i',j)}{Ⓜ} \mathrm{S}[\check{\mathcal{N}}_{f()}(i,j)] \right) \copyright^{-1} \mathrm{SI}[\check{\mathcal{C}}(i+i',j)] \ \text{ for } i' \in \{0,1\}, \tag{27}$$

$$\mathrm{SO}[\check{d}(i+H_{\mathbf{A}}, j+W_{\mathbf{A}})] = \left( \underset{\check{\mathcal{N}}_f(i,j):\check{d}(i+H_{\mathbf{A}}, j+W_{\mathbf{A}})}{Ⓜ} \mathrm{S}[\check{\mathcal{N}}_{f()}(i,j)] \right) \copyright^{-1} \mathrm{SI}[\check{d}(i+H_{\mathbf{A}}, j+W_{\mathbf{A}})], \tag{28}$$

and

$$\mathrm{SO}[\check{q}(i,j)] = \left( \underset{\check{\mathcal{N}}_f(i,j):\check{q}(i,j)}{Ⓜ} \mathrm{S}[\check{\mathcal{N}}_{f()}(i,j)] \right) \copyright^{-1} \mathrm{SI}[\check{q}(i,j)]. \tag{29}$$

One iteration of such IDN rests in the serial activation of each SISO module from the upper left corner to the lower right corner in the IDN as is marked by the light blue curve in Fig. 10a. After finishing all iterations, of the chosen count $N_I$, the IDN makes hard decisions $\hat{d}(i,j)$ per Eq. 13.

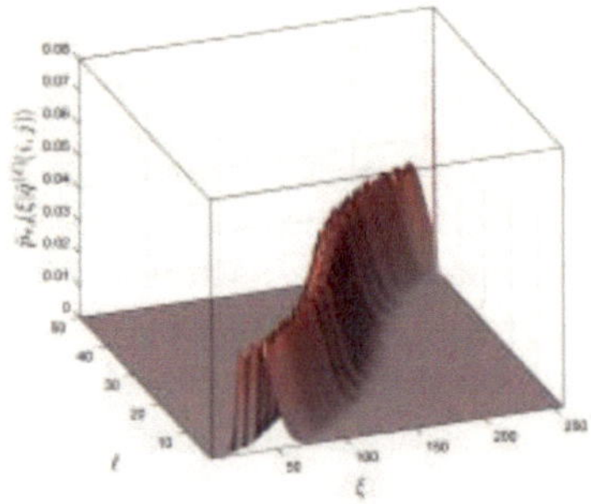

(a) The PDF for the blurring channel $\mathbf{A}_{\text{GBC},3/10}$: $C = 612$, $\mu_T = 60$, $\mu_R = 40$, $\sigma_R = 35$.

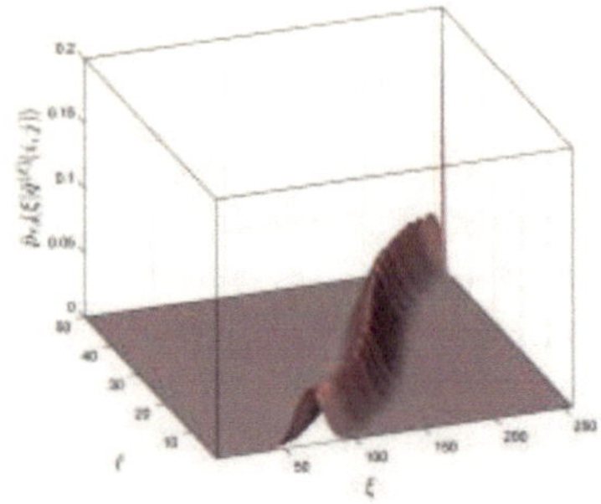

(b) The PDF for the blurring channel $\mathbf{A}_{\text{GBC},3/10}$: $C = 542$, $\mu_T = 150$, $\mu_R = 50$, $\sigma_R = 25$.

(c)

(d)

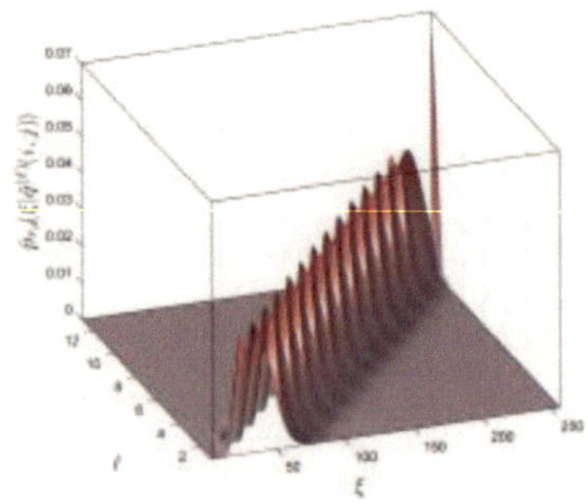

(e) The PDF for the blurring channel $\mathbf{A}_{\text{BOM},\pi/4}$: $C = 612$, $\mu_T = 60$, $\mu_R = 40$, $\sigma_R = 35$.

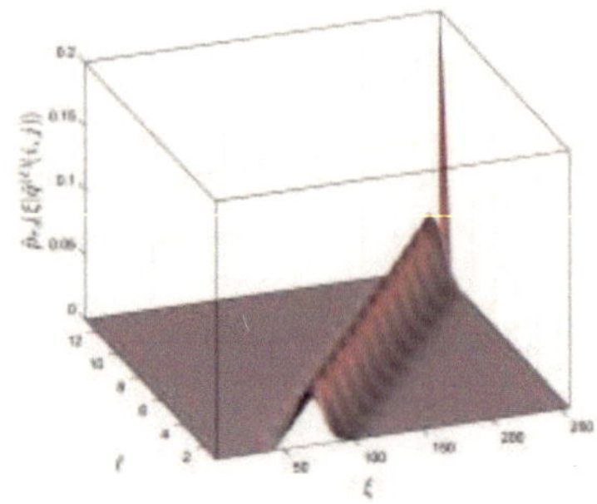

(f) The PDF for the blurring channel $\mathbf{A}_{\text{BOM},\pi/4}$: $C = 542$, $\mu_T = 150$, $\mu_R = 50$, $\sigma_R = 25$.

(g)

(h)

Fig. 9. The examples of SODEM transfer (likeli-hood) functions with the corresponding realization $\mathbf{R}_d$ of the A/D converter output: $N_b = 8$, $\Delta_Q = 3$. All alphabets $\{q^{(\ell)}\}_{\ell=1}^{M_q}$ are sorted according to the size ($q^{(1)}$ is the least element and $q^{(M_q)}$ is the greatest element).

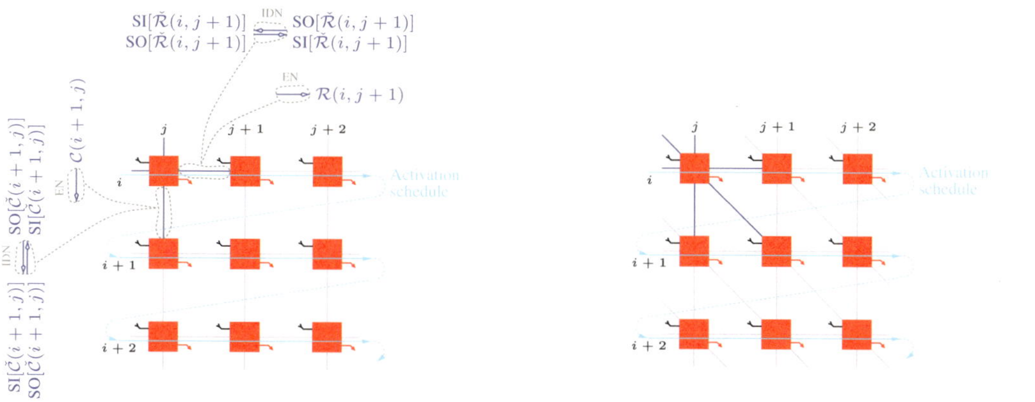


(a) The EN and IDN marginalizing at the symbol block level.

(b) The EN and IDN marginalizing at the symbol block level with bias state variables.

Fig. 10. The topology of the EN and IDN with denotation of the IDN activation schedule.

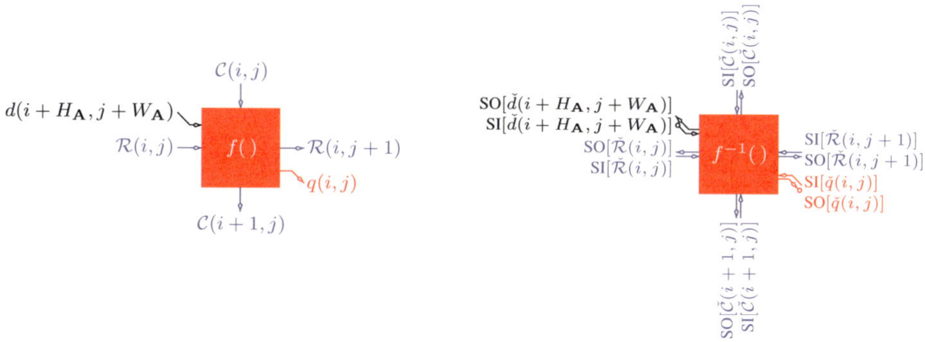


(a) The EN cell.

(b) The IDN cell (SISO module).

Fig. 11. The cells in the node $(i,j)$ of the EN and IDN marginalizing at the symbol block level.

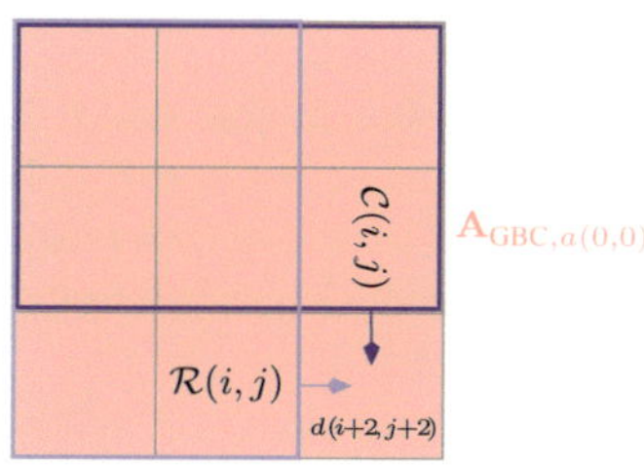


Fig. 12. The primary layout of auxiliary state variables $\mathcal{R}(i,j)$ and $\mathcal{C}(i,j)$ for the ISI channel $\mathbf{A}_{\mathrm{GBC},a(0,0)}$ .

The quantities

$$\mathrm{SI}[\check{\mathcal{R}}(i,j)] = \underset{\check{d}(i,j)\in\check{\mathcal{R}}(i,j)}{\copyright} \mathrm{SI}[\check{d}(i,j)] \tag{30}$$

and

$$\mathrm{SI}[\check{\mathcal{C}}(i,j)] = \underset{\check{d}(i,j)\in\check{\mathcal{C}}(i,j)}{©} \mathrm{SI}[\check{d}(i,j)], \tag{31}$$

before the first iteration of the IDN, are adjusted via combination of the a priori measures $\mathrm{SI}[\check{d}(i,j)]$ corresponding to testing estimators $\check{d}(i,j)$, that form block estimators $\check{\mathcal{R}}(i,j)$ and $\check{\mathcal{C}}(i,j)$.

### 7.2 Distributed IDN marginalizing at the symbol block level with bias state variables

The fundamental disadvantage of IDNs described in the previous paragraph rests in cardinality of state variables. For example decomposition in Fig. 12a has cardinality for dichromatic pictures $2^6$ per variable and therefore both bidirectional concatenations of all SISO modules have to transfer $2 \times 2^6 = 128$ soft measures in the each direction. However, this is not only one disadvantage. The another rests in potential absence of the optimal decomposition for irregular kernels which can extremely gross up computational exigencies of the algorithm.

Impacts of both mentioned disadvantages can be reduced by the suggestion of EN structure in Fig. 10b that is expanded by the bias state variable $\mathcal{B}(i,j)$. All inputs and outputs of each node, shown in Fig. 13a, forms the set $\mathcal{N}_f(i,j) = \{\mathcal{R}(i,j), \mathcal{C}(i,j), \mathcal{B}(i,j), d(i+H_{\mathbf{A}}, j+W_{\mathbf{A}}), \mathcal{R}(i,j+1), \mathcal{C}(i+1,j), \mathcal{B}(i,j), q(i,j)\}$, where state variables are shaped by more liberal condition

$$\begin{aligned}\mathcal{N}_d(i,j) &\subseteqq \mathcal{R}(i,j) \cup \mathcal{C}(i,j) \cup \mathcal{B}(i,j) \cup d(i+H_{\mathbf{A}}, j+W_{\mathbf{A}}) \\ &\supset \mathcal{R}(i,j+1), \mathcal{C}(i+1,j), \mathcal{B}(i+1,j+1).\end{aligned} \tag{32}$$

In Fig. 12 are expressed three examples of decompositions for two different cores. Concretely, in the case of 1st version of kernel $\mathbf{A}_{\mathrm{GBC},a(0,0)}$ partitioning, where state variables are $\mathcal{R}(i,j) = \{d(i+1,j), d(i+1,j+1), d(i+2,j), d(i+2,j+1)\}$, $\mathcal{C}(i,j) = \{d(i,j+1), d(i,j+2), d(i+1,j+1), d(i+1,j+2)\}$ and $\mathcal{B}(i,j) = \{d(i,j), d(i+1,j), d(i,j+1), d(i+1,j+1)\}$, is necessary to transfer and store only $3 \times 2^4 = 48$ soft measures in the each direction. In the 2nd version for same kernel this number is smaller, namely $2 \times 2^3 + 2^2 = 20$.

The IDN topology copies the EN topology as in the previous case and activation schedule is identical too. A SISO module used in this IDN is approached in Fig. 13b.

### 7.3 Distributed IDN marginalizing at the symbol level

The topology of the IDN marginalizing at the symbol level is dependent on the shape of the response $\mathbf{A}$. It is the basic difference from the IDN marginalizing at the symbol block level, whose topology is invariable. There are two possible kinds of the topology. Either the topology centered on the response central coefficient or the shifted topology, that is fixed on the coefficient other than the central coefficient.

Firstly, we focus on the IDN example with the centered topology for the ISI channel $\mathbf{A}_{\mathrm{GBC},a(0,0)}$ with order $L = H_{\mathbf{A}} + 1 = W_{\mathbf{A}} + 1 = 3$. Let us suppose the source EN in Fig. 15a emulating the convolution

$$\begin{aligned}q(i,j) &= Cf(\mathbf{A}_{\mathrm{GBC},a(0,0)}, \mathcal{N}_d(i-1,j-1) \subset \mathbf{D}) \\ &= C \sum_{|i'|,|j'|\leq 1} a(i',j')d(i+i',j+j')\end{aligned} \tag{33}$$

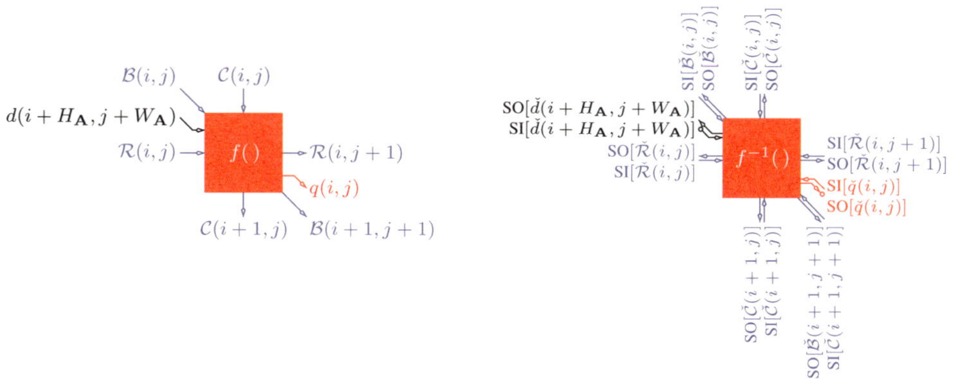


(a) The EN cell. (b) The IDN cell (SISO module).

Fig. 13. The cells in the node $(i, j)$ of the EN and IDN marginalizing at the symbol block level with bias state variables.

Fig. 14. The two possible layouts of auxiliary state variables $\mathcal{R}(i,j)$, $\mathcal{C}(i,j)$ and $\mathcal{B}(i,j)$ for the ISI channel $\mathbf{A}_{\mathrm{GBC},a(0,0)}$.

centered on the central (dominant) coefficient $a(0,0)$. Each node (GPE) in this EN contains two functional blocks (broadcaster and combining element) with the generally variable system of inputs and outputs. In the our current example, each node has the framework shown in Fig. 15b and it is connected to the eight nearest neighbors. All these cells together creating the convolutional region $\mathcal{N}_d(i-1, j-1)$. An input and outputs of each broadcaster make the set

$$\mathcal{N}_B(i,j) = \{d(i,j), c(i,j,k) = d(i,j)\}_{1 \le k \le 9}. \tag{34}$$

The outputs of nine neighboring broadcasters create inputs for one combining element. These inputs with the output

$$q(i,j) = C \sum_{0 \le k \le 7} a(\lfloor 1/2 + \sin(\pi k/4) \rfloor, \lfloor 1/2 - \cos(\pi k/4) \rfloor) c(i + \lfloor 1/2 + \sin(\pi k/4) \rfloor, \\ j + \lfloor 1/2 - \cos(\pi k/4) \rfloor, k+1) + Ca(0,0)c(i,j,9) \tag{35}$$

make the set

$$\mathcal{N}_f(i,j) = \{c(i + \lfloor 1/2 + \sin(\pi k/4) \rfloor, j + \lfloor 1/2 - \cos(\pi k/4) \rfloor, k+1), c(i,j,9), q(i,j)\}_{0 \le k \le 7}. \tag{36}$$

As is known, the IDN has topology corresponding with the EN topology. One of the composite SISO modules creating the present IDN is illustrated in Fig. 15c, where the SISO module $B^{-1}$ performing the combination

$$\mathrm{SO}[\check{d}(i,j)] = \underset{k}{\copyright}\mathrm{SI}[\check{c}(i,j,k) = \check{d}(i,j)] \tag{37}$$

with the marginalization

$$\mathrm{SO}[\check{c}(i,j,k)] = \left(\underset{k' \neq k}{\copyright}\mathrm{SI}[\check{c}(i,j,k') = \check{c}(i,j,k)]\right) \copyright \mathrm{SI}[\check{d}(i,j) = \check{c}(i,j,k)] \tag{38}$$

and the SISO module $f^{-1}()$ performing combination

$$\mathrm{S}[\check{\mathcal{N}}_f(i,j)] = \left(\underset{\check{c}(i',j',k) \in \check{\mathcal{N}}_f(i,j)}{\copyright}\mathrm{SI}[\check{c}(i',j',k)]\right) \copyright \mathrm{SI}[\check{q}(i,j)] \tag{39}$$

with the marginalizations

$$\mathrm{SO}[\check{c}(i',j',k)] = \left(\underset{\check{\mathcal{N}}_f(i,j):\check{c}(i',j',k)}{\circledM}\mathrm{S}[\check{\mathcal{N}}_f(i,j)]\right) \copyright^{-1}\mathrm{SI}[\check{c}(i',j',k)] \tag{40}$$

and $\mathrm{SO}[\check{q}(i,j)]$ acquisitionable from Eq. 29.

A soft measure processing in the composite SISO modules is mirrored to the signal processing in the EN nodes (from $d(i,j)$ to $q(i,j)$) and begins with activation all SISO modules $f^{-1}()$. Consequently, the activations of the SISO modules $B^{-1}$ take place. Both activations, intimated by activation loops in Fig. 15a, form one iteration of the entire IDN. After finishing of all required iterations, the IDN makes hard decisions $\hat{d}(i,j)$ in accordance with Eq. 13.

The quantities $\mathrm{SI}[\check{c}(i,j,k)]$, before the first iteration of the IDN, are adjusted pursuant to the a priori measures $\mathrm{SI}[\check{d}(i,j)]$, because the $c(i,j,k)$ constitute copies of the $d(i,j)$. Henceforth, we come up to the IDN example again for the $\mathbf{A}_{\mathrm{GBC},3/10}$, but now it will be the IDN with the shifted topology. In this case, the source EN in Fig. 16a implements the convolution Eq. 1 centered on the upper left coefficient. One of the EN cells is shown in Fig. 16b. In comparison with the previous example, there is a difference only in the combining element. It has the I/O set

$$\mathcal{N}_f(i,j) = \{c(i - \lceil k/3 \rceil + 3, j + 3\lceil k/3 \rceil - k, k), q(i,j)\}_{1 \leq k \leq 9} \tag{41}$$

where

$$q(i,j) = C \sum_{1 \leq k \leq 9} a(i - \lceil k/3 \rceil + 3, j + 3\lceil k/3 \rceil - k)c(i - \lceil k/3 \rceil + 3, j + 3\lceil k/3 \rceil - k, k). \tag{42}$$

The soft inversion of the mentioned EN cell is represented by Fig. 16c and along with other cooperative SISO modules forming the resulting IDN. A similar IDN can be synthesized by the analogical way for any other ISI channel.

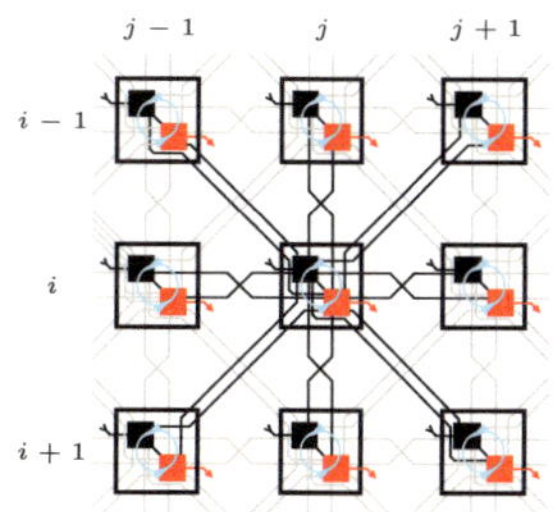

(a) The topology of the EN and IDN with denotation of the IDN activation schedule.

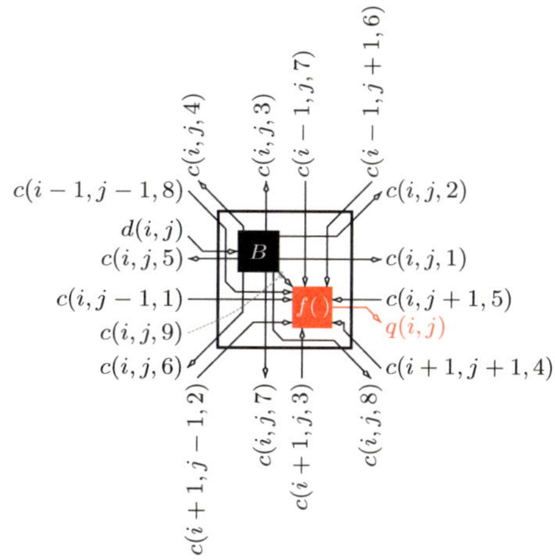


(b) The EN cell in the node $(i,j)$. The connection of the broadcaster (■) and combining element (■).

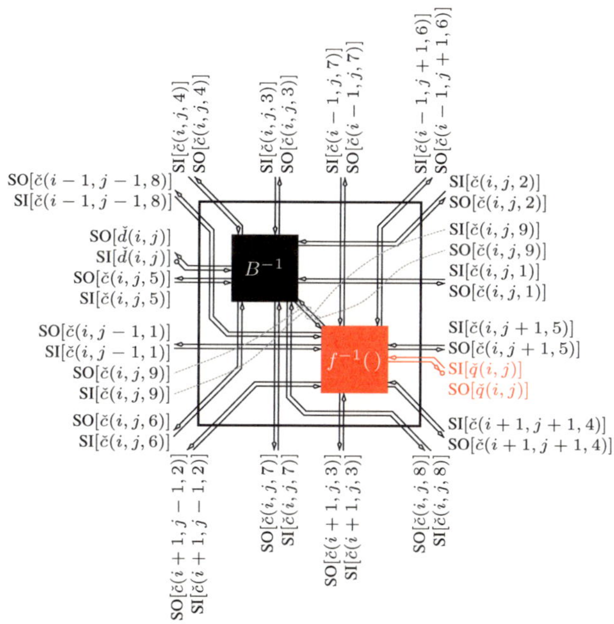


(c) The IDN cell (SISO module) in the node $(i,j)$.

Fig. 15. The EN and IDN marginalizing at the symbol level with the centered topology for the ISI channel$\mathbf{A}_{\text{GBC},a(0,0)}$.

### 7.4 Simplified distributed IDN marginalizing at the symbol level

If the response $\mathbf{A}$ has a dominant coefficient and the IDN topology is centered on this coefficient, then such IDN can be further numerically simplified by the approximation $\text{SO}[\check{d}(i,j)] \approx \text{SO}[\check{c}(i,j,\max(k))]$ (Chugg et al., 2001). It reduces a number of marginalizations

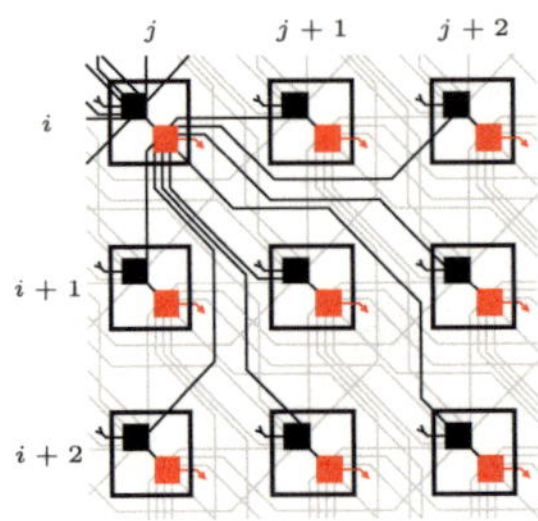


(a) The topology of the EN and IDN.

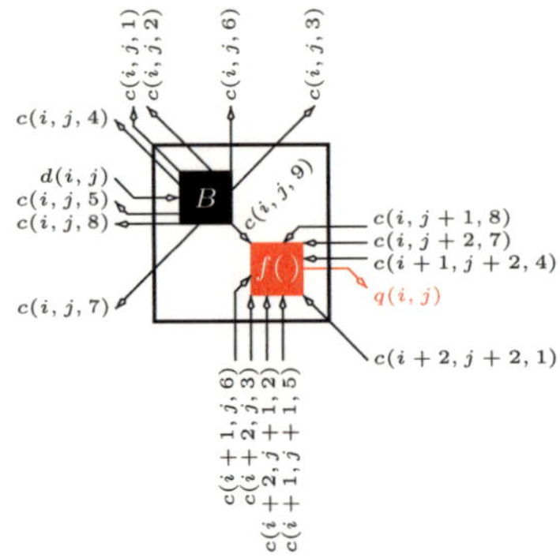


(b) The EN cell in the node $(i,j)$.

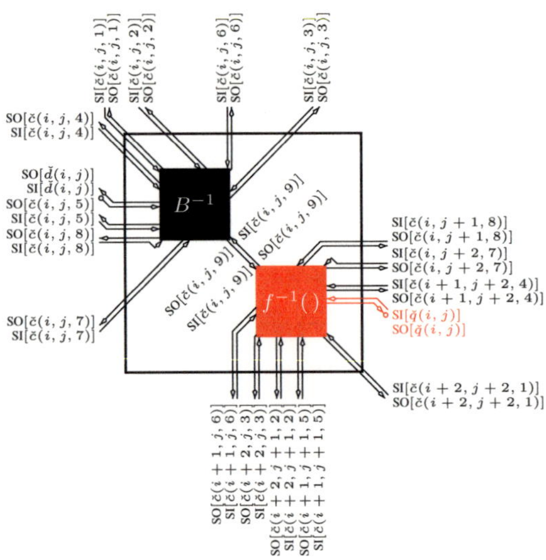


(c) The IDN cell in the node $(i,j)$.

Fig. 16. The EN and IDN marginalizing at the symbol level with the shifted topology for ISI channel $\mathbf{A}_{\mathrm{GBC},a(0,0)}$.

in the SISO modules $f^{-1}()$ only to the variable $\check{c}(i,j,\max(k))$ and enables removing of all SISO modules $B^{-1}$.

Let us approach the principle of this approximation at the first IDN example in the paragraph 7.3. There had $\mathbf{A}$ the dominant coefficient $a(0,0)$. Therefore, the $\mathrm{SO}[\check{d}(i,j)]$ can be approximated by the $\mathrm{SO}[\check{c}(i,j,9)]$ and inputs $\{\mathrm{SI}[\check{c}(i+\lfloor 1/2+\sin(\pi k/4)\rfloor,\ j+\lfloor 1/2-\cos(\pi k/4)\rfloor, k+1)]\}_{0\leq k\leq 7}$ of associated SISO modules will be directly equal to $\mathrm{SO}[\check{c}(i,j,9)]$, as is shown in Fig. 17.

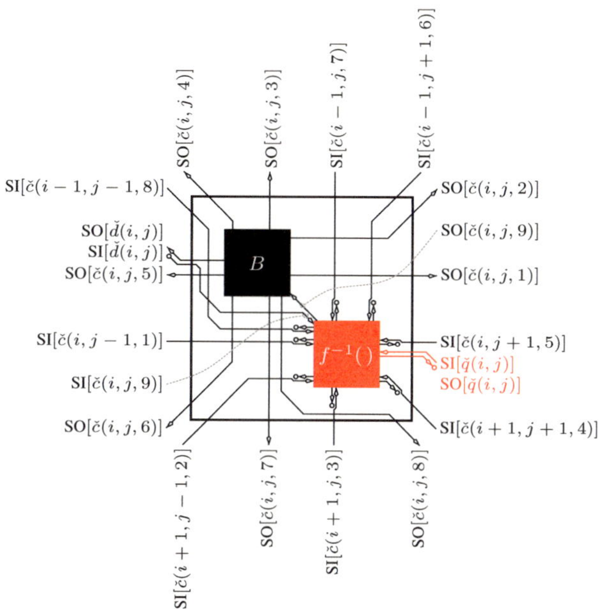


Fig. 17. The cell in the node $(i,j)$ of the simplified IDN marginalizing at the symbol level with centered topology for the ISI channel $\mathbf{A}_{\mathrm{GBC},a(0,0)}$.

### 7.5 Layered IDN for an ISI channel with a decomposition-able impulse response

Finally, we focus on the Layered IDN for ISI channels with a decomposition-able impulse response to the horizontal $\mathbf{h} = [\,h'\ h\ h'\,]$ and vertical $\mathbf{g} = [\,g'\ g\ g'\,]$ direction. For example, the GBC has this property and therefore we assume, without detriment to generality, the GBC

$$\mathbf{A}_{\mathrm{GBC},gh} = \mathbf{h}\mathbf{g}^T = \begin{bmatrix} h'g' & hg' & h'g' \\ h'g & hg & h'g \\ h'g' & hg' & h'g' \end{bmatrix} \tag{43}$$

with size $L \times L = 3 \times 3$ that will be used for exemplary construction of the layered EN, shown in Fig. 18a, and mutually corresponding IDN, shown in Fig. 18b.

The signal processing (two-step convolution) starts on the EN bottom layer $c(i,j) = f_R(\mathbf{h}, \{d(i,j-2), d(i,j-1), d(i,j)\}) = h'd(i,j-2) + hd(i,j-1) + h'd(i,j)$ and continues on the EN top layer $\tilde{q}(i,j) = f_C(\mathbf{g}, \{c(i-2,j), c(i-1,j), c(i,j)\}) = g'c(i-2,j) + gc(i-1,j) + g'c(i,j))$. Each row-wise or column-wise concatenated node (GPE) creates a one functional block with the fixed system of inputs and outputs $\mathcal{N}_{f_R}(i,j) = \{\mathcal{R}(i,j), d(i,j), \mathcal{R}(i,j+1), c(i,j)\}$ or $\mathcal{N}_{f_C}(i,j) = \{\mathcal{C}(i,j), c(i,j), \mathcal{C}(i,j+1), q(i,j)\}$, where $\mathcal{R}(i,j) = \{d(i,j-2), d(i,j-1)\}$ and $\mathcal{C}(i,j) = \{c(i-2,j), c(i-1,j)\}$ present auxiliary state variables containing two symbols together, as in the case of the distributed IDN marginalizing at the symbol block level.

This specific case of the 2D ISI channel makes 2D detection, through the chosen EN topology, decomposition-able into double 1D detection, when in separate rows and columns can be used the well known Fixed interval forward-backward algorithm (FI FBA) Chugg et al. (2001). Let us elucidate the FI FBA principle on the IDN top layer. Its current recursion, in the node

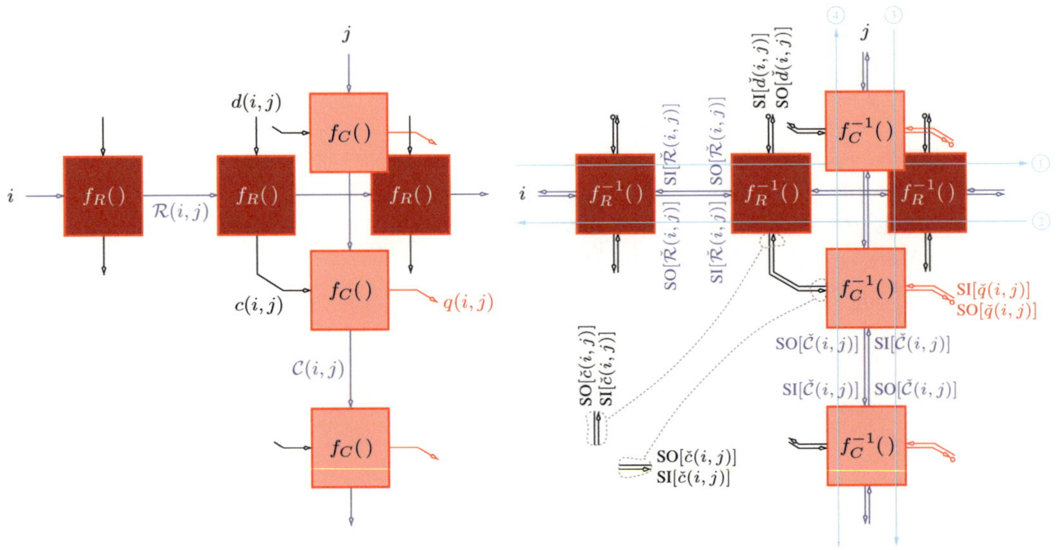


(a) The topology of the layered EN with illustration of individual EN cells.

(b) The topology of the layered IDN with illustration of individual IDN cells (SISO modules) and denotation of activation schedule.

Fig. 18. The layered EN and IDN for an ISI channel with a decomposition-able impulse response.

$(i, j)$, is performed by following the sequence of operations: the combination (preprocessing — enumeration of auxiliary variables

$$\mathrm{S}[\check{\mathcal{N}}_{f_C}(i,j) \setminus \{\check{\mathcal{C}}(i,j), \check{\mathcal{C}}(i+1,j)\}] = \mathrm{S}[\check{c}(i,j)] \copyright \mathrm{SI}[\check{q}(i,j)] \tag{44}$$

and

$$\mathrm{S}[\check{\mathcal{N}}_{f_C}(i,j) \setminus \{\check{c}(i,j), \check{q}(i,j)\}] = \mathrm{S}[\check{\mathcal{C}}(i,j)] \copyright \mathrm{S}[\check{\mathcal{C}}(i+1,j)] \tag{45}$$

with their storage), the forward recursion ③ (top-down)

$$\mathrm{SO}[\check{\mathcal{C}}(i+1,j)] = \mathop{\textcircled{M}}_{\check{\mathcal{N}}_{f_C}(i,j):\check{\mathcal{C}}(i+1,j)} \mathrm{S}[\check{\mathcal{N}}_{f_C}(i,j) \setminus \{\check{\mathcal{C}}(i,j), \check{\mathcal{C}}(i+1,j)\}] \copyright \mathrm{SI}[\check{\mathcal{C}}(i,j)], \tag{46}$$

the backward recursion ④ (bottom-up)

$$\mathrm{SO}[\check{\mathcal{C}}(i,j)] = \mathop{\textcircled{M}}_{\check{\mathcal{N}}_{f_C}(i,j):\check{\mathcal{C}}(i,j)} \mathrm{S}[\check{\mathcal{N}}_{f_C}(i,j) \setminus \{\check{\mathcal{C}}(i,j), \check{\mathcal{C}}(i+1,j)\}] \copyright \mathrm{SI}[\check{\mathcal{C}}(i+1,j)] \tag{47}$$

and the completion operation (postprocessing — enumeration of output variables

$$\mathrm{SO}[\check{c}(i,j)] = \mathop{\textcircled{M}}_{\check{\mathcal{N}}_{f_C}(i,j):\check{c}(i,j)} \mathrm{S}[\check{\mathcal{N}}_{f_C}(i,j) \setminus \{\check{c}(i,j), \check{q}(i,j)\}] \copyright \mathrm{SI}[\check{q}(i,j)] \tag{48}$$

and

$$\mathrm{SO}[\check{q}(i,j)] = \mathop{\textcircled{M}}_{\check{\mathcal{N}}_{f_C}(i,j):\check{q}(i,j)} \mathrm{S}[\check{\mathcal{N}}_{f_C}(i,j) \setminus \{\check{c}(i,j), \check{q}(i,j)\}] \copyright \mathrm{SI}[\check{c}(i,j)] \text{ (optional)} \tag{49}$$

with their distribution to cooperative SISO modules). On the bottom layer is done identical process, directed by the rotated activation schedule merging the forward recursion ① and the backward recursion ②. The several iteration of the entire layered IDN creates firstly the FBA initiation on the top layer, terminated by the inter-marginalization $\{\mathrm{SO}[\check{c}(i,j)]\}_{i,j}$, and subsequently the same procedure on the bottom layer.

The hard decision $\hat{d}(i,j)$ and primary adjustment of the input soft measures $\mathrm{SI}[\check{\mathcal{R}}(i,j)]$ and $\mathrm{SI}[\check{\mathcal{C}}(i,j)]$ (before first iteration of the IDN) is similar as in the previous cases and they are directed by Eq. 13, Eq. 30 and Eq. 31.

### 7.6 Summary of IDNs properties

The introduced IDNs can be evaluated in four angles: computation exigences, implementation complexity, application flexibility and performance.

A distributed IDN marginalizing at the symbol level in comparison with the distributed IDN marginalizing at the symbol block level has less computation exigences and it is effectively applicable at whatever kind of the impulse response **A**. However it has plenty of jumpers on the other hand and its structure changes in accordance with the shape of the **A**. Each jumper presents one inside (auxiliary) variable, thus this IDN is highly suboptimal and with respect to marginalizations at the level of individual symbols (pixels) it fails on lower signal to noise ratios.

The structure of the distributed IDN marginalizing at the symbol block level is invariable for all responses **A**. Each SISO module always has the same inputs and outputs. Only shapes of the estimators $\check{\mathcal{R}}(i,j)$, $\check{\mathcal{C}}(i,j)$ and $\mathcal{B}(i,j)$ are various and for certain special responses **A** don't have to exist in the optimal form that leads to the computationally simplest IDN. Therefore this IDN can have considerably more exacting computational complexity than IDN marginalizing at the symbol level, but due to marginalizations at the level of symbol (pixel) blocks it offers a quality output, even as the signal to noise ratio is very low.

The advantage of the layered IDN for an ISI channels with a decomposition-able impulse responses rests in the inter-marginalization between both layers, that makes its computational complexity $\propto M_d^L + (M_d(2M_d-1)^{\frac{L-1}{2}})^L$ lower than complexity $\propto M_d^{L^2}$ of the both distributed IDNs. The worst properties has in the angle of application flexibility, because it can be applied only to some few ISI channels. In term of implementation complexity it is a structure relatively simple.

## 8. Implementation and complexity reduction issue

### 8.1 Tree-structured enumeration of combinations and marginalizations

We should use the tree-structured enumeration everywhere it is possible. It represents de facto a pipeline signal processing based upon an intermediate data usage. Fig. 19 shows this principle.

As the example using tree-structured implementation, let us expose the simple SISO module $f^{-1}()$ in Fig. 20, where $\check{\mathcal{N}}_f(i,j) = \{\check{c}(i,j-1,1), \check{c}(i,j,3), \check{c}(i,j+1,2), \check{q}(i,j)\}$. Such soft inversion is a component of the IDN marginalizing at the symbol level in Fig. 21.

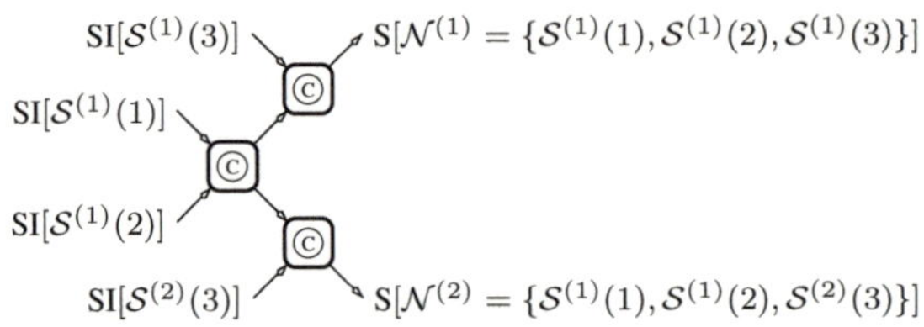


o[h]

(a) Combinations.

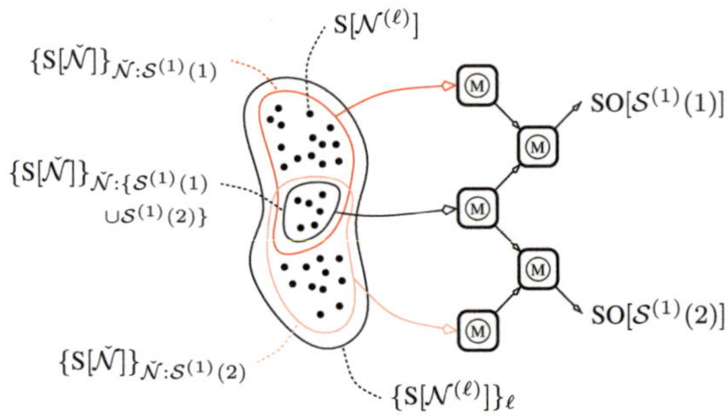


(b) Marginalizations.

Fig. 19. The tree-structured enumeration of combinations and marginalizations.

### 8.2 Fixation of the arithmetics

The most sensitive arithmetics have the IDNs implemented in the Pd. A large number of quantities less than 1 are multiplied in the SISO modules of such IDNs and the underflow of the arithmetics can happen. Therefore the Pd requires the regular scaling of the output measures

$$\mathrm{PO}[\mathcal{S}^{(\ell)}(k)] = \frac{\mathrm{PO}[\mathcal{S}^{(\ell)}(k)]}{\sum_\ell \mathrm{PO}[\mathcal{S}^{(\ell)}(k)]} \tag{50}$$

and so, the Md is preferable to a real implementation of the IDN. The arithmetics of the Md is relatively stable and can be protected from the incidental overflow by the scaling

$$\mathrm{MO}[\mathcal{S}^{(\ell)}(k)] = \mathrm{MO}[\mathcal{S}^{(\ell)}(k)] - \min_\ell \mathrm{MO}[\mathcal{S}^{(\ell)}(k)]. \tag{51}$$

But since the overflow is rare as the better scaling is $\mathrm{MO}[\mathcal{S}^{(\ell)}(k)] = \mathrm{MO}[\mathcal{S}^{(\ell)}(k)] - \mathrm{MO}[\mathcal{S}^{(1)}(k)]$ that allows discount the number of swapped measures by the fixed measure $\mathrm{MO}[\mathcal{S}^{(1)}(k)] = 0$.

### 8.3 Additional sub-optimality embedding complexity reduction

The distributed IDNs can be simplified in addition by the approximation neglecting least significant rays in the original response of the blurring channel. For example, the

$$\mathbf{A}_{\mathrm{GBC},0.2574} = \begin{bmatrix} 0.0607 & 0.1250 & 0.0607 \\ 0.1250 & 0.2574 & 0.1250 \\ 0.0607 & 0.1250 & 0.0607 \end{bmatrix}. \tag{52}$$

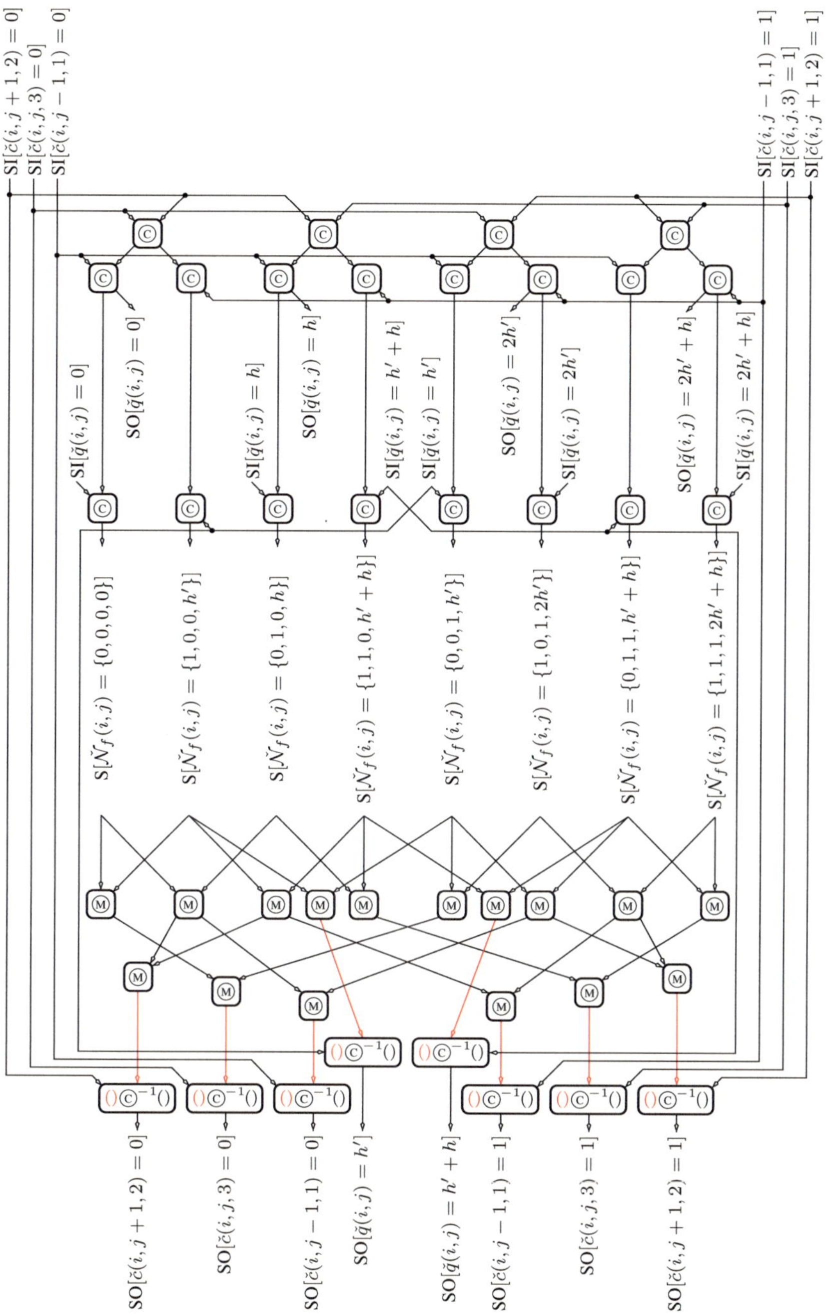


Fig. 20. The implementation of the SISO module $f^{-1}()$ using tree-structured enumeration of combinations and marginalizations, where $f()$: $q(i,j) = h'c(i,j-1,1) + hc(i,j,3)$ $+h'c(i,j+1,2)$

can be simplified to the form

$$\mathbf{A}_{\mathrm{SGBC},0.3399} = \begin{bmatrix} 0 & 0.1650 & 0 \\ 0.1650 & 0.3399 & 0.1650 \\ 0 & 0.1650 & 0 \end{bmatrix}. \tag{53}$$

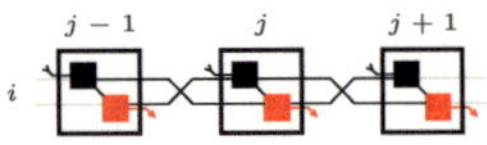


(a) The topology of the EN and IDN.

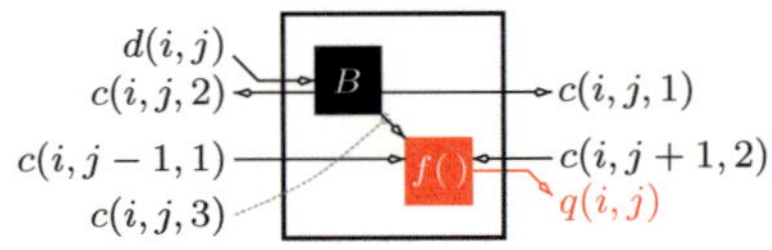


(b) The EN cell in the node $(i, j)$.

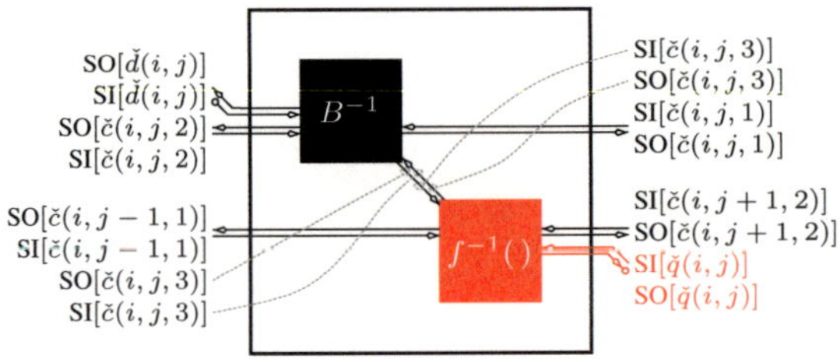


(c) The IDN cell in the node $(i, j)$.

Fig. 21. The EN and IDN marginalizing at the symbol level with the centered topology for the horizontal ISI channel $\mathbf{A} = [\, h' \ h \ h' \,]$.

by the truncation of last four insignificant rays. The consequences of such approximation are illustrated in Fig. 23 and Fig. 22. In the both cases it reduces computational complexity to $\frac{1}{16}$. Moreover, it lowers the number of jumpers to one half in the case of the IDN marginalizing at the symbol level. The price paid for this rapid simplification rests in a quality degradation of the reconstructed picture.

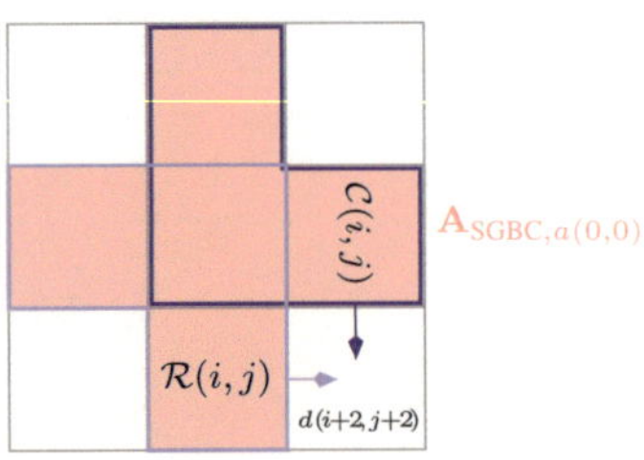


(a) Layouts for the IDN without bias state variable.

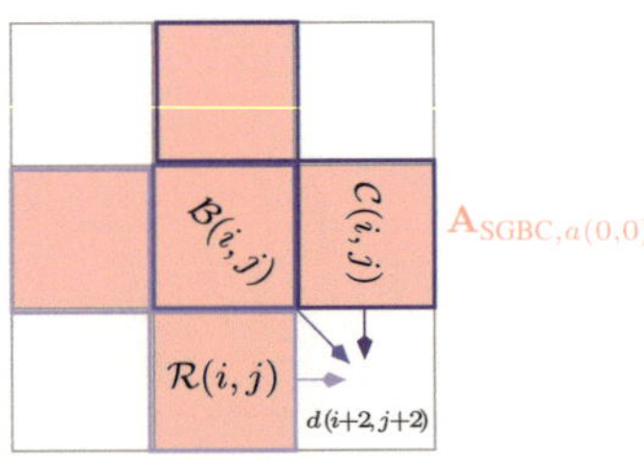


(b) Layouts for the IDN with bias state variable.

Fig. 22. The layouts of auxiliary state variables $\mathcal{R}(i,j)$, $\mathcal{C}(i,j)$ and $\mathcal{B}(i,j)$ in the IDN marginalizing at the symbol block level for the ISI channel $\mathbf{A}_{\mathrm{SGBC},a(0,0)}$.

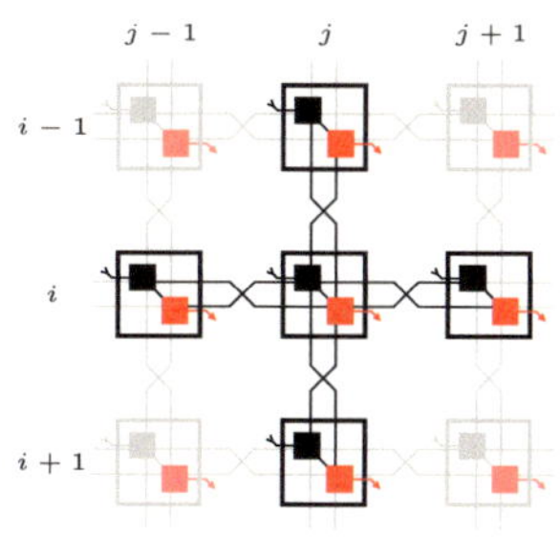


(a) The topology of the EN and IDN.

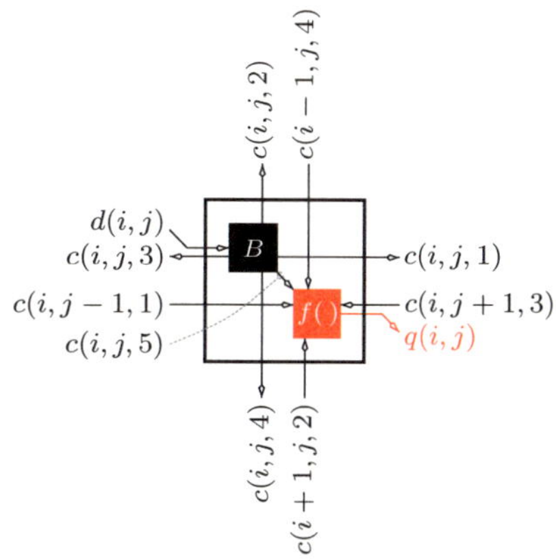


(b) The EN cell in the node $(i, j)$.

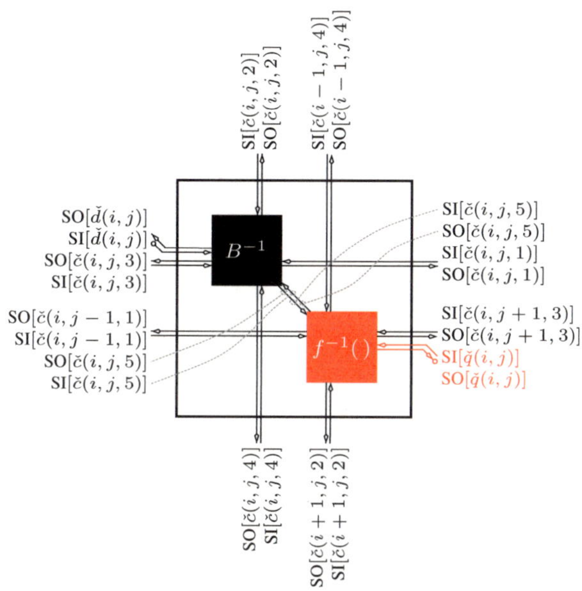


(c) The IDN cell in the node $(i, j)$.

Fig. 23. The EN and IDN marginalizing at the symbol level with the centered topology for the ISI channel $\mathbf{A}_{\mathrm{SGBC},a(0,0)}$.

Can happen the situation, when the channel truncation causes the original 2D ISI channel atypical. Therefore, such kind of approximation is suitable especially for the IDN marginalizing at the symbol level, because it is a very flexible structure, applicable to the absolutely arbitrary 2D ISI channel. In case of the IDN marginalizing at the symbol block level can occur the problem with fulfillment of the condition $\mathcal{N}_d(i,j) = \mathcal{R}(i,j) \cup \mathcal{C}(i,j) \cup d(i + H_{\mathbf{A}}, j + W_{\mathbf{A}})$ and the estimators $\check{\mathcal{R}}(i,j)$ and $\check{\mathcal{C}}(i,j)$ don't have to exist in the optimal shapes that lead to the computationally simplest IDN.

# 9. Examples of dichromaric picture restoration, performance analyses and conclusions

## 9.1 Suppression of the defocusing in the imperfectly adjusted lens (GBC) with BER performance analyses

We will demonstrate the IDNs functionality on QR code snapshot restorations by the IDNs marginalizing at the symbol block level that were described in paragraphs 7.1 and 7.2. In Fig. 24 and Fig. 25 are shown example restorations of two different QR codes by the 1st and 2nd version of IDNs with bias state variables. Additionally, all versions of these IDNs has been tested with the Monte Carlo method for performance and compared with simple threshold detector, based on the relation $\hat{d}_{TD}(i,j) = \arg\min_{\check{d}(i,j)\in\{0,1\}} |\frac{x_d(i,j)-\hat{\mu}_T}{C} - \check{d}(i,j)|$. The result of this analysis is the set of BER curves shown in Fig. 26 and Fig. 27. As we can see in the BER curves, all tested IDNs have almost same performance and especially in the area of higher defocusing the usage is expedient. However, the performance slightly falls down in the focusation rising and at the beginning of iterative process. It is caused by diminishing corelation among individual neighboring pixels when iteratively precised state variables do not carry so fundamental and strong information worth to the current node of the network.

$\mathbf{R}_d$ | $\hat{\mathbf{D}}, I=1$, BER $=0.208$ | $\hat{\mathbf{D}}, I=3$, BER $=0.033$ | $\hat{\mathbf{D}}, I=5$, BER $=0.022$ | $\hat{\mathbf{D}}, I=7$, BER $=0.018$ | $\hat{\mathbf{D}}_{TD}$, BER $=0.141$

Fig. 24. The example of the QR code restoration by the distributed IDN marginalizing at the symbol block level with bias state variables (Pd-SyD, 1st version): Kernel $\mathbf{A}_{\mathrm{GBC},2/10}$, $N_b = 8$, $\Delta_Q = 3, C = 612, \mu_T = 50, \mu_R = 25, \sigma_R = 10$.

$\mathbf{R}_d$ | $\hat{\mathbf{D}}, I=1$, BER $=0.168$ | $\hat{\mathbf{D}}, I=3$, BER $=0.021$ | $\hat{\mathbf{D}}, I=5$, BER $=0.006$ | $\hat{\mathbf{D}}, I=7$, BER $=0.004$ | $\hat{\mathbf{D}}_{TD}$, BER $=0.085$

Fig. 25. The example of the QR code restoration by the distributed IDN marginalizing at the symbol block level with bias state variables (Pd-SyD, 2nd version): Kernel $\mathbf{A}_{\mathrm{GBC},2/10}$, $N_b = 8$, $\Delta_Q = 3, C = 612, \mu_T = 50, \mu_R = 25, \sigma_R = 10$.

In other words, the output $\{\mathrm{SI}[d^{(\ell)}(i+H_{\mathbf{A}}, j+W_{\mathbf{A}})]\}_\ell$ of current node strongly depends only on the input $\{\mathrm{SI}[q^{(\ell)}(i,j)]\}_\ell$ (product of the SODEM) and not so much on the state information $\{\mathrm{SI}[\mathcal{R}^{(\ell)}(i,j)]\}_\ell$, $\{\mathrm{SI}[\mathcal{R}^{(\ell)}(i,j+1)]\}_\ell$, $\{\mathrm{SI}[\mathcal{C}^{(\ell)}(i,j)]\}_\ell$, $\{\mathrm{SI}[\mathcal{C}^{(\ell)}(i+1,j)]\}_\ell$, $\{\mathrm{SI}[\mathcal{B}^{(\ell)}(i,j)]\}_\ell$ and $\{\mathrm{SI}[\mathcal{B}^{(\ell)}(i+1,j+1)]\}_\ell$ from other nodes as in the case of high defocusing.

Mentioned BER curves leads to conclusion, that the application of IDNs with bias state variables is better than standard IDNs marginalizing at the symbol block level, because bring evident implementation advantages beside performance preservation. In the case of 1st version it is consensus in the output state variables $\mathcal{R}(i,j+1) = \mathcal{C}(i+1,j) = \mathcal{B}(i+1,j+1)$, that warrants equation $\mathrm{SI}[\check{\mathcal{R}}(i,j+1)] © \mathrm{SI}[\check{\mathcal{R}}(i,j+1)] = \mathrm{SI}[\check{\mathcal{C}}(i+1,j)] © \mathrm{SI}[\check{\mathcal{C}}(i+1,j)] = \mathrm{SI}[\check{\mathcal{B}}(i+1,j+1)] © \mathrm{SI}[\check{\mathcal{B}}(i+1,j+1)]$ and allows only one and same marginalization for whole triplet of the state variables. On the other hand, the 2nd version is visible significant reduction of state variable cardinalities.

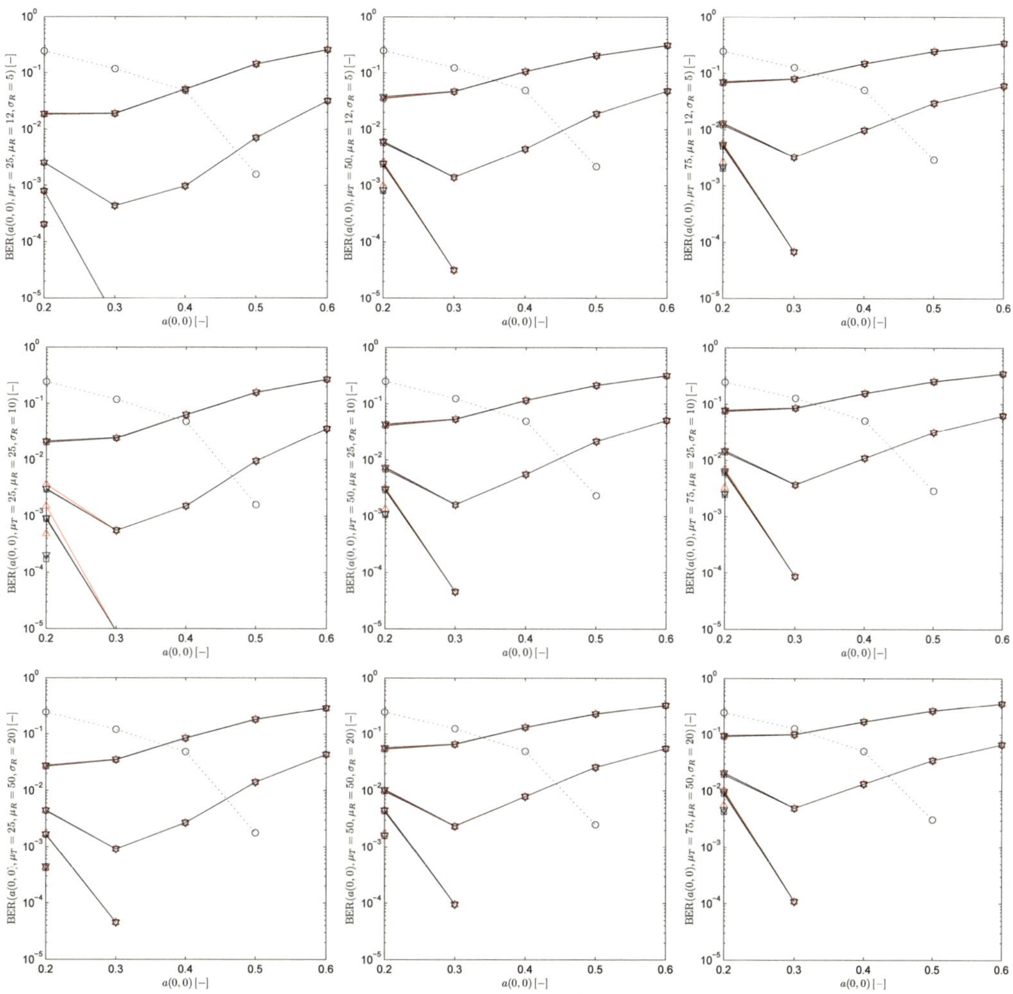


Fig. 26. The BER curves (1st, 2nd, 3th and 7th iteration) of the distributed IDN marginalizing at the symbol block level (Pd-SyD, black line with squares) and distributed IDN marginalizing at the symbol block level with bias state variables (Pd-SyD, 1st version — red line with triangles, 2nd version — black line with triangles): Kernel $\mathbf{A}_{\mathrm{GBC},a(0,0)}$, $N_b = 8$, $\Delta_Q = 3$, $C = 612$. The comparison with BER curves (dot line with circles) of the threshold detector.

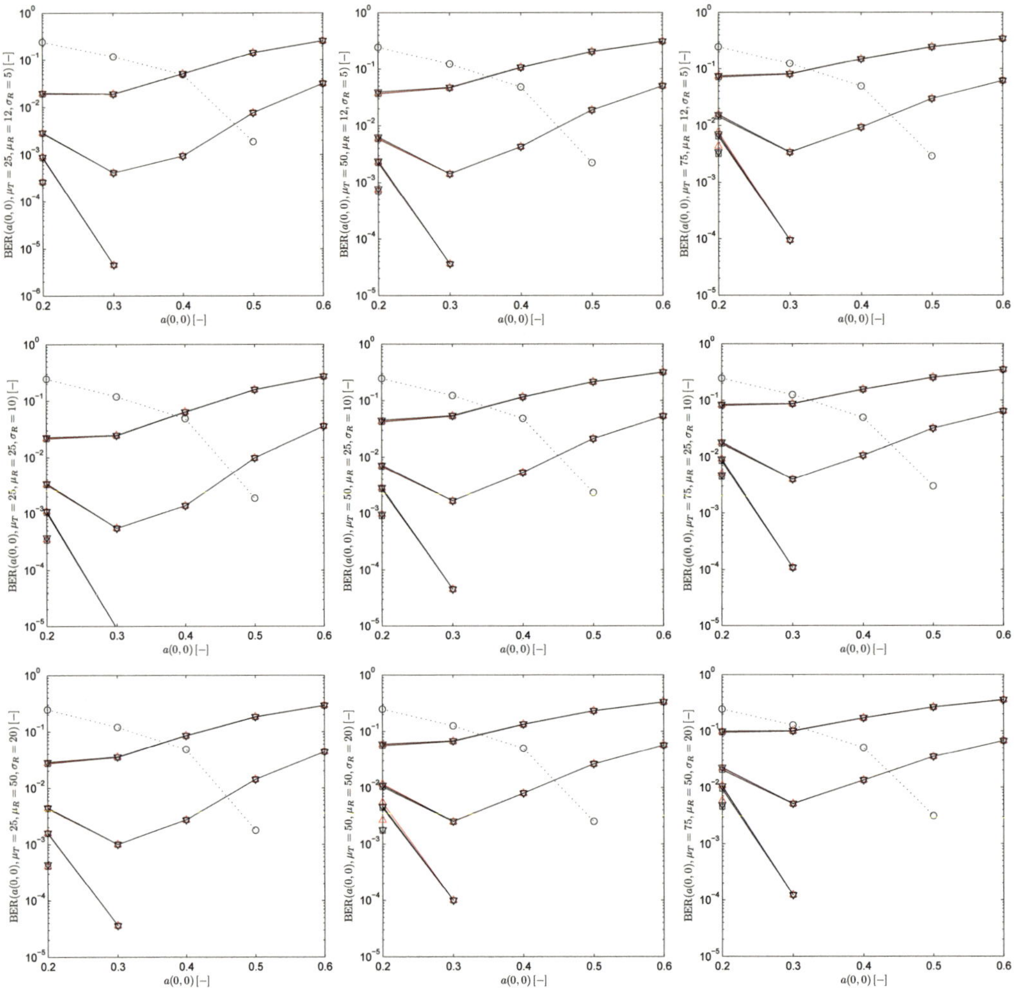


Fig. 27. The BER curves (1st, 2nd, 3th and 7th iteration) of the distributed IDN marginalizing at the symbol block level (Pd-PgD, black line with squares) and distributed IDN marginalizing at the symbol block level with bias state variables (Pd-PgD, 1st version — red line with triangles, 2nd version — black line with triangles): Kernel $\mathbf{A}_{GBC,a(0,0)}$, $N_b = 8$, $\Delta_Q = 3$, $C = 612$. The comparison with BER curves (dot line with circles) of the threshold detector.

### 9.2 Suppression of the blurring due to object moving (BOM)

In this case we use for functionality demonstration the IDNs marginalizing at the symbol level. The following Fig. 31 shows the sample pictures restored by these IDNs for two different combination of the BOM. Used IDNs (theirs topologies) are represented in Fig 29 and Fig 30. Of course the IDNs marginalizing at the symbol block level can be used for this issue too. Theirs state variables are shown in Fig. 28.

The usage without whatever other supporting aids (external synchronization) demands the perfect knowledge about the scanned moving object ($\mathbf{s}_S$ and velocity vector). But, if all mentioned conditions are fulfilled, the IDN produces a high quality output (estimation $\hat{\mathbf{D}}$) on the other hand.

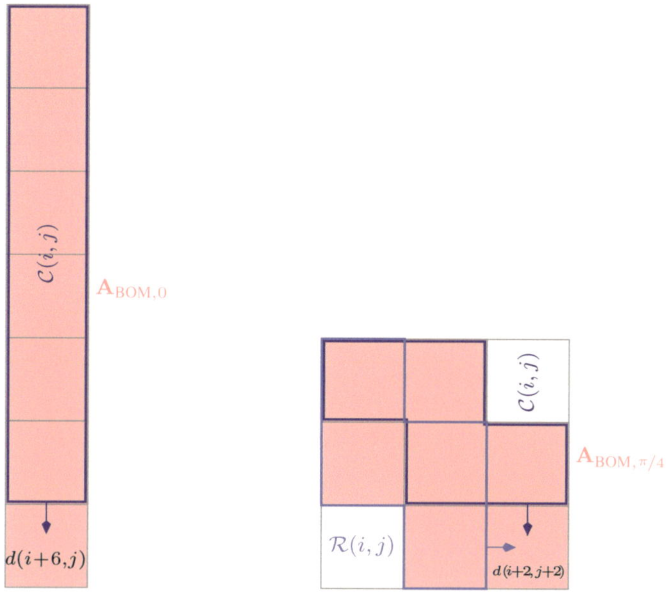


(a) $\mathbf{A}_{\mathrm{BOM},0}$.  (b) $\mathbf{A}_{\mathrm{BOM},\pi/4}$.

Fig. 28. The shapes of auxiliary state variables $\mathcal{R}(i,j)$ and $\mathcal{C}(i,j)$ in the IDN marginalizing at the symbol block level for the ISI channel $\mathbf{A}_{\mathrm{BOM},\varphi}$.

The example of the IDN malfunction, caused by the wrong movement parameters adjustment, is demonstrated in Fig. 32. Suppose that the true starting point is $\mathbf{s}'_s$ and corresponds with the correct impulse response

$$\mathbf{A}'_{\mathrm{BOM},0} = \begin{bmatrix} \frac{1}{24} & \frac{1}{12} & \frac{1}{12} & \frac{1}{12} & \frac{1}{12} & \frac{1}{24} \\ \\ \frac{1}{24} & \frac{1}{12} & \frac{1}{12} & \frac{1}{12} & \frac{1}{12} & \frac{1}{24} \end{bmatrix}^T, \tag{54}$$

This response makes the blurring in Fig. 32b. If the IDN is consequently fed by the wrong impulse response $\mathbf{A}_0$ coming from the shifted point $\mathbf{s}_s$ , then its failure, shown in Fig. 32c, is going to happen. It presents a serious problem, because we mostly have not available so accurate information about the movement of the scanned object. Thus, in the overwhelming majority of real applications, the IDN will have been supplemented by the auxiliary synchronizer performing the reliable estimation $\hat{\mathbf{s}}'_s$ of the $\mathbf{s}'_s$ placement inside the blue square in Fig. 32a.

The section vehicle speed measurement appears to be the most suitable application of the described method, because it is based on the signplate detection at the beginning and at the end of the monitored section, where the scanned vehicles have the same direction of the movement. So, the synchronization of the IDN will not represent a serious issue in this application.

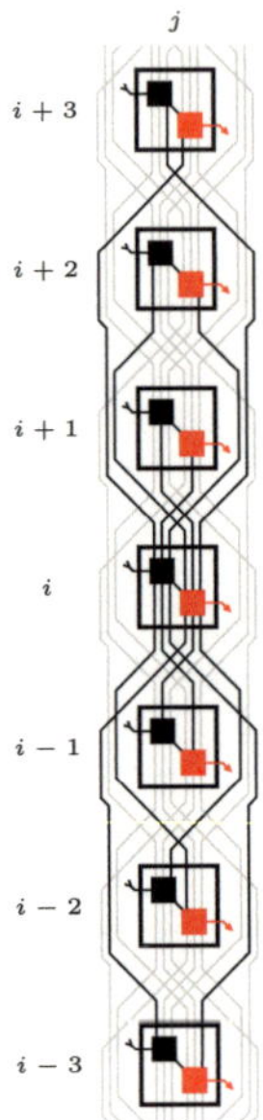


(a) The topology of the EN and IDN.

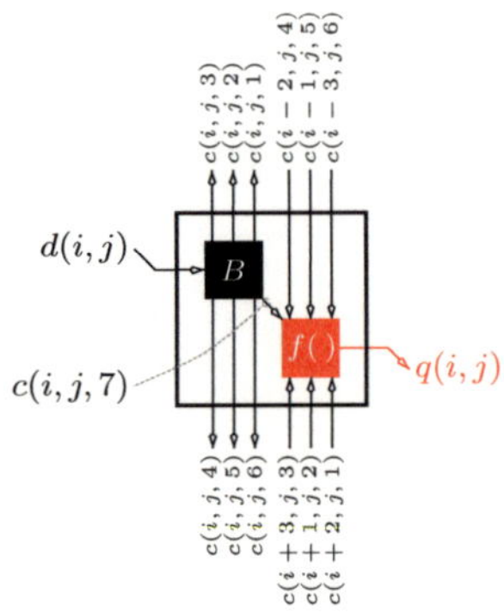


(b) The EN cell in the node $(i, j)$.

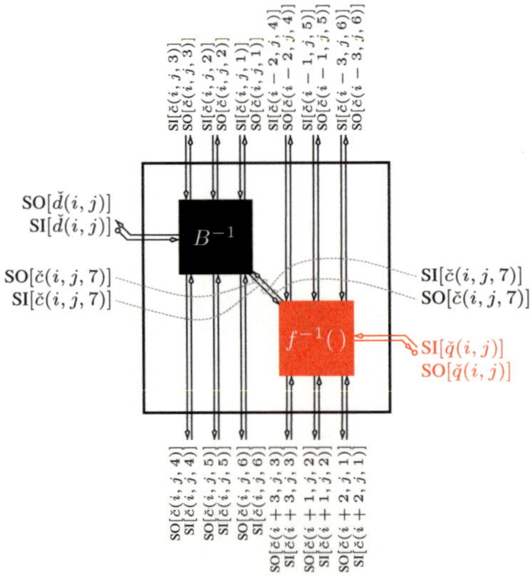


(c) The IDN cell in the node $(i, j)$.

Fig. 29. The EN and IDN marginalizing at the symbol level with the centered topology for the ISI channel $\mathbf{A}_{\text{BOM},0}$.

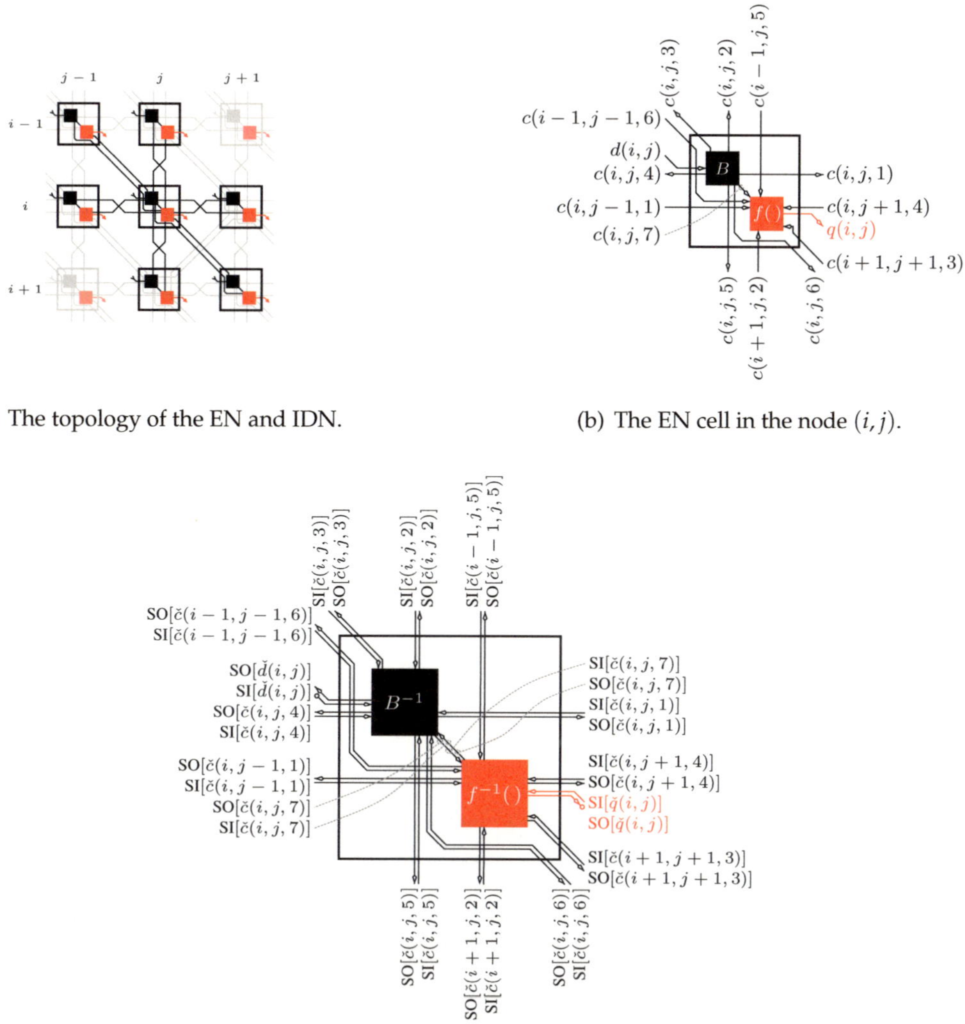


(a) The topology of the EN and IDN.

(b) The EN cell in the node $(i, j)$.

(c) The IDN cell in the node $(i, j)$.

Fig. 30. The EN and IDN marginalizing at the symbol level with the centered topology for the ISI channel $\mathbf{A}_{\text{BOM},\pi/4}$.

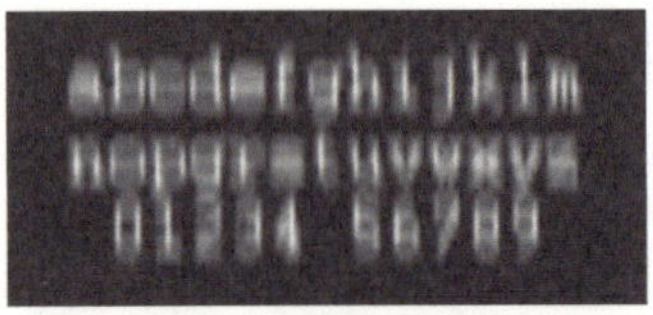

(a.1) The realization $\mathbf{R}_d$ of the A/D converter output.

(a.2) The hard decision $\hat{\mathbf{D}}$ after $3^{\text{th}}$ iteration of the IDN.

(a.3) The hard decision $\hat{\mathbf{D}}$ after $7^{\text{th}}$ iteration of the IDN.

(b.1) The realization $\mathbf{R}_d$ of the A/D converter output.

(b.2) The hard decision $\hat{\mathbf{D}}$ after $3^{\text{th}}$ iteration of the IDN.

(b.3) The hard decision $\hat{\mathbf{D}}$ after $7^{\text{th}}$ iteration of the IDN.

Fig. 31. The examples of image restorations by the distributed IDN marginalizing at the symbol level (Pd-PgD) for the channels $\mathbf{A}_{\mathrm{BOM},0}$(a) and $\mathbf{A}_{\mathrm{BOM},\pi/4}$(b) merged with the simple noise model including the thermal noise and the quantization noise: $N_b = 8$, $\Delta_Q = 3$, $C = 768$, $\mu_T = 200$.

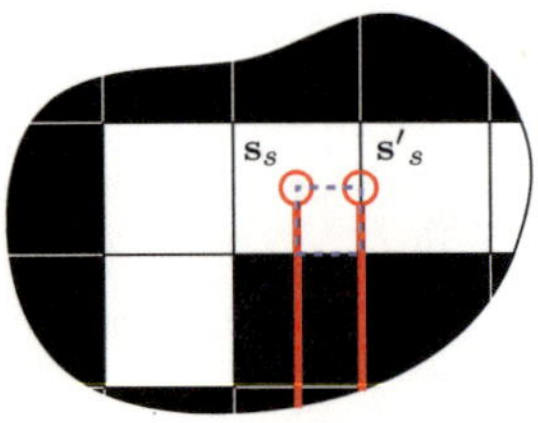


(a) The trajectory starting point displacement.

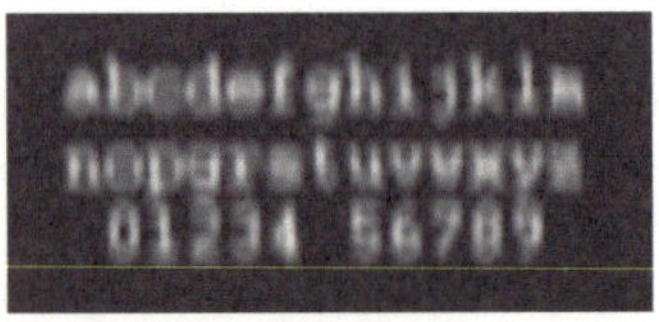

(b) The realization $\mathbf{R}_d$ of the A/D converter output.

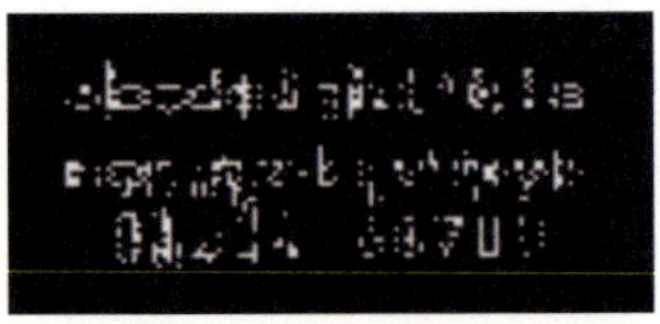

(c) The hard decision $\hat{\mathbf{D}}$ after $7^{\text{th}}$ iteration of the wrong adjusted IDN.

Fig. 32. The example of the wrong image restoration by the distributed IDN marginalizing at the symbol level (Pd-PgD), that was incorrectly set by the $\mathbf{A}_{\mathrm{BOM},0}$ at the true blurring $\mathbf{A}'_{\mathrm{BOM},0}$ merged with the simple noise model including the thermal noise and the quantization noise: $C = 768$, $N_b = 8$, $\Delta_d = 3$, $\mu_T = 200$.

### 9.3 Conclusions and open problems

The IDNs are based on the optimal (the best) MAP detector and so they are mostly able to obtain the optimal estimation. The IDN, analogous to the optimal detector, forms all possible variants of the input image and compares them with the corrupted image by the decision metric perfectly matched to the noise distribution. There is the difference only in fact, that the IDN solves this issue smartly by the suitable image segmentation and with minimal computational exigencies. This can be considered as the greatest advantage of the IDNs.

The important disadvantage rests in the application limitations, because the contemporary IDNs are able to restore a dichromatic (or black and white) patterns only (texts, car sign plates, QR codes, etc.). For restoration of grayscale or color image restorations and larger 2D ISI channels, where the number of all possible realizations of current convolution region $\{\mathcal{N}^{(\ell)}\}_{\ell}$ extremely grows, the IDN will require the another sub-optimality embedding simplification (generalization). Although the IDNs perform the segmental image processing, the numerical complexity is extreme. Individual SISO modules in the IDN can not be implemented directly as was shown on the simple example in Fig. 20, but must be realized also as the certain iterative system. This would establish an iterative detection network where each inner cell presents iterative subnet. The question remains how a single-shot SISO can be approximated to the iterative subnet. If it is possible and what level of sub-optimality this establish and whether this sub-optimality allows the good and fast convergence of the entire system to the correct solution. At present it is only surmise without concrete and functional results. But it is clear, that such network will be more suboptimal and its performace will not be so good as in the case of black & white images, where SISO module can be implemented as a single-shot (optimal) system. The next problem rests in fact, that is not possible analytically predicate the behaviour of such network due to extreme quantity of functional blocks and interconnections. Therefore the computer simulation and debuging will be very difficult and based on the labour principle. However, this method has very good application in the case of black & white images and it is completely different from classical methods like adaptive filtration, minimum mean square errors, etc. Because it is perfectly matched to the noise distribution and reconstruct image from all possible images by the intelligent way. Thanks to this ability the IDN is very powerful and can find good use in the area of image halftoning (Chugg et al., 2001), text detection, QR code detection, number plate detection of cars (traffic monitoring system), etc.

The last problem rests in the iterative detection network synchronization. In all cases it was considered that the IDN has perfect knowledge about kernel of the 2D ISI channel. This information, however, in reality it is not known and must be estimated. A Soft decision directed (SDD) Channel state estimator (CSE) can be used for this purposes. One of the most suitable CSEs for an IDN synchronization is the Expectation-Maximization (EM) algorithm. Its greatest benefit rests in the implementation simplicity and additional information about the algorithm can be found in (Noels et al., 2003).

## 10. References

Chugg, K.; Anastasopoulos, A. & Chen, X. (2001). *Iterative detection : Adaptivity, Complexity reduction and Applications*, Kluwer Academic Publishers, ISBN 0-470-84757-3.

Vucetic, B. & Juan, J. (2003). *Space-Time coding,* Kluwer Academic Publishers, ISBN 0-470-84757-3.

Vucetic, B. & Juan, J. (2000). *Turbo codes : Principles and Applications,* Kluwer Academic Publishers, ISBN 0-792-37868-7.

Kekrt, D. & Klíma, M. (2008). A black & white picture reconstruction by iterative detection network in the image capturing system with CCD (CMOS) sensor, *50th International Symposium ELMAR-2008,* Vol. 1, pp. 125-128, ISBN 978-953-7044-06-0, Zadar, Croatia, September 2008.

Kekrt, D. & Klíma, M. (2008). The iterative detection network based recovery of black & white pictures shot by camera — implementation and complexity reduction issue, *In Proceedings of the 18th International Conference Radioelektronika 2008,* pp. 219-222, ISBN 978-1-4244-2087-2, Prague, Czech Republic, April 2008.

Kekrt, D. & Klíma, M. (2008). Layered Iterative detection network based text recognition in the snapshot gained by camera with CCD (CMOS) sensor, *In Proceedings of the 12th International Student Conference on Electrical Engineering POSTER 2008* [CD-ROM], Prague, Czech Republic, May 2008.

Kekrt, D.; Klíma, M. & Podgorny, R. (2008). The iterative detection network suppression of defocusing and thermal noise in black and white pictures shot by a camera with CCD/CMOS sensor, *6th International Conference on Photonics, Devices and Systems,* Vol. 7138, pp. 71381Z-1-71381Z-7, ISBN 978-0-8194-7379-0, Prague, Czech Republic, August 2008.

Kekrt, D.; Klíma, M. & Fliegel, K. (2008). The iterative detection network based suppression of the thermal noise and blurring due to object moving in black and white pictures shot by a camera with CCD/CMOS sensor, *In Proceedings of SPIE Optics + Photonics,* Vol. 7076, pp. 70760M-1-70760M-9, ISBN 978-0-8194-7296-0, San Diego, USA, August 2008.

Kekrt, D.; Klíma, M. & Podgorny, R. (2008). Aspects of Image Quality Enhancement in Security Technology, *IEEE International Carnahan Conference on Security Technology 2008,* pp. 142-149, ISBN 978-1-4244-1816-9, Prague - Czech Republic, October 2008.

Kekrt, D. & Klíma, M. (2008). The advanced noise model for an IDN based restoration of black and white pictures captured by a camera with CCD/CMOS sensor, *IEEE International Carnahan Conference on Security Technology 2008,* pp. 126-130, ISBN 978-1-4244-1816-9, Prague, Czech Republic, October 2008.

J. van Vliet L.; Boddeke F. R.; Sudar D. & Young I.T. (1998). Image detectors for digital image microscopy. *M.H.F. Wilkinson, F. Schut (eds.), Digital Image Analysis of Microbes; Imaging, Morphometry, Fluorometry and Motility Techniques and Applications, Modern Microbiological Methods,* pp. 37-64, John Wiley & Sons, Chichester, The United Kingdom, 1998.

Anastasopoulos, A. & Chugg, K. (2000). Adaptive soft-input soft-output algorithms for iterative detection with parametric uncertainty. *IEEE Trans. Commun.,* Vol. 48, pp. 1638-1649, Oct. 2000.

Noels, N.; Herzet, C.; Dejonghe, A.; Lottici, V. ; Steendam, H.; Moeneclaey, M.; Luise, M.; Vandendorpe, L. (2003). Turbo synchronization : an EM algorithm interpretation, *IEEE International Conference on Communications - ICC,* 2003.

# Part 3

## Interdisciplinarity

15

# An Application of Digital Image Restoration Techniques to Error Control Coding

Pål Ellingsen
*Department of Computer Science*
*University College of Bergen*
*Norway*

## 1. Introduction

Digital image restoration has been a field of very active research for many years, and digital image restoration techniques has been put to use in a lot of different contexts including astronomy, medicine, intelligence work and many others (Banham & Katsaggelos (1997)). Common to these fields of application is that the restoration techniques are applied to image data of some kind true to the original intentions of the algorithms. In this text we present an application of principles from digital image restoration to the field of coding theory, and the objects of application are not images but rather general information data.

Information can be represented in many different ways. A typical approach in information theory is to represent information as binary vectors, but there are many situations where information can rather be represented as a matrix or grid containing the information symbols giving rise to the concept of two-dimensional channels. Good examples of this can be found in the fields of magnetic and optical storage, bar codes and others.

When transmitting information of any kind, a central problem is how to deal with errors that result from the transmission process, and a solution to this problem is to add redundancy to the information in such a way that it is possible to detect and eventually also correct the errors that occur. Adding this redundancy is called error control coding, and the techniques for doing so is called error correcting or detecting codes. There exists a huge variety of error control coding techniques for channels with different characteristics and for fulfilling different sets of requirements. However, most of the channel coding techniques assumes the information that is to be encoded, are one-dimensional vectors or a stream of information symbols. Channel coding for two-dimensional channels on the other hand, is a part of coding theory that has only recently attracted attention from the coding theory community.

There are different models for describing how errors occur in a two-dimensional communication channel.

- The errors can be modeled as independent and identically distributed over the information symbols. In this case the problem of error control coding is reduced to the case of error control coding for a one-dimensional channel with an equal information rate.
- The errors can be modeled by considering two-dimensional intersymbol interference, which is the effect of the information symbols interfering with their neighboring information symbols. This error model applies to many practical communication channels, most notably magnetic and optical storage media (which can be seen as

communication channels). This error model has been studied extensively, see for example Singla & O'Sullivan (2005) and Kurkoski (2008).

- The errors can be modeled as spatially contagious areas bounding a cluster of errors. The underlying channel model assumes that the information symbols are affected by some physical process that affects a limited part of the information. Error that result from such processes would form error bursts that may take the form of clusters or be concentrated to a limited area. Such error clusters are defined differently in the literature, but a very common approach is to define an error cluster as a rectangular area of a given size $n_1 \times n_2$. Code constructions for this type of cluster errors can be found in Farrell (1982) Schwartz & Etzion (2005) and Breitbach et al. (1998). More recently, error clusters of arbitrary form has been considered in several works, and most of these use interleaving strategies to correct cluster errors. This approach is used in Blaum et al. (1998), Schwartz & Etzion (2003) and Xu & Golomb (2007).

In the following we take the latter perspective on the nature of errors on a two-dimensional channel, and we apply techniques from digital image restoration to support the decoding process since these methods can exploit the information inherent in the two-dimensional cluster error model. The core element in this application of digital image restoration is looking at the encoded information as "noise" and the areas affected by burst errors as the "original image" that we want to restore. The strategy is to first encode the information at the source using ordinary error control coding. At the receiver, ordinary decoding and detection of the error clusters are combined in an iterative system where the decoding process produces an estimate of the probability of error in each information symbol, and this estimate is then used as input to a component that produces an estimate of the size and shape of the error burst based on image restoration techniques. The information that is extracted from this process is then used to support the decoding process as a priori information about the error clusters.

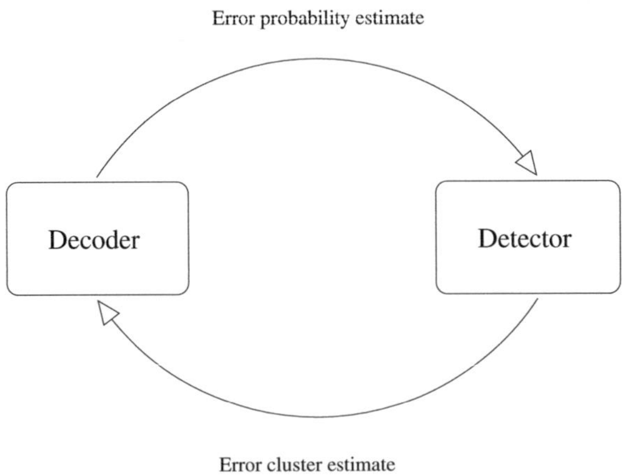


Fig. 1. Basic principle of iterative process

## 2. General overview over relevant image restoration techniques

In our application we are concerned with describing the statistical properties of context dependent entities such as neighboring bits in a two-dimensional representation of digital information. One technique for describing such properties is the use of Markov random field theory which uses conditional probabilities to describe spatial dependencies in an n-dimensional system. This approach is based on the results of Shridhar, Ahmadi and

El-Gabali who developed the applied techniques in Shridhar et al. (1989), El-Gabali et al. (1987), El-Gabali et al. (1988) and El-Gabali et al. (1990) but similar techniques are also presented in Geman & Geman (1993), Zhang (1993), Jeng & Woods (1991) and Chalmond (1988). The basis for all of these image restoration techniques is that simulated annealing is used to produce an estimate of the maximum a posteriori probability of the original image and the techniques has been extensively used for different purposes within the field of image processing, including image restoration, image segmentation, object identification and texture analysis. Using a system model based on Markov random field theory, one wants to find the joint distribution of the variables representing the image (e.g. pixels) and then use this distribution as basis for detecting the original scene and eliminate or reduce noise in the image. However, finding the joint distribution directly from a Markov random field model is mathematically intractable, so one needs to compute the distribution by aid of the so-called Hammersley-Clifford theorem which states the equivalence between the joint distribution of the variables in a Markov random field and Gibbs distribution which can be treated mathematically in an efficient way. Given this distribution one common method for performing the actual detection of the original image is to find the maximum a priori probability for the image given the observed output.

## 3. General overview of the iterative decoding and detection process

two-dimensional channels are subjected to different kinds of errors, but in this setting we are interested in sources of errors that will affect spatially limited parts of a two-dimensional codeword. This is called an error cluster or equivalently a burst error. Burst error correction is a well known and much studied problem, but none of the classical techniques in this field are able to take into account the fact that such spatially correlated error clusters gives rise to a statistical correlation on the error probability for neighboring positions in the codeword. Using the above mentioned techniques from digital image restoration is one way one can exploit this extra information given in the error model.

Several different approaches are possible when trying to use the information gleaned from the image restoration to enhance the decoding process. However, our approach is based on the use of so-called soft input - soft output (SISO) decoding. The principle behind this decoding strategy is that the decoder should accept input values in the form of conditional probabilities as a measure of the reliability of the corresponding channel value, and as output produce a new measure of reliability for the corresponding channel value. Such a decoder can take advantage of the information produced by the restoration process in a very natural way by supplying conditional probabilities resulting from the estimation process described below.

Based on results from our papers Ellingsen et al. (2004) Ellingsen & Kvamme (2010) we show how this principle can be used to implement an actual decoding system based on the techniques described above. We study two different channel models, the two-dimensional binary asymmetric channel and the two-dimensional binary symmetric channel, and use LDPC-codes for error correction. Then we show how the redundant information of the code can be used to provide prior information to an image restoration process, while the results from the image restoration process is used to assist the decoding process by providing a priori information to the decoder. Thus we construct an iterative decoding process where estimates in the form of conditional probabilities for each bit in the codeword is exchanged back and forth between the LDPC-decoder and the image restoration module. The results from this process are compared to the results when using the LDPC decoder alone and we see that there is a significant gain in performance.

## 4. Details of restoration technique

### 4.1 Modelling a two-dimensional channel using Markov Random Fields

A channel with memory is characterized by the existence of dependencies in the noise generating process. Such dependencies can e.g. be described by a Markov chain in the case of one-dimensional channels as is the case for the Gilbert-Elliott channel Gilbert et al. (1960). This implies that the channel will have characteristics that are varying with time. We want to extend this line of thinking to the case of two-dimensional channels and look at spatial dependencies in the noise generating process rather than temporal dependencies as in the one-dimensional case. Such spatial dependencies can be modeled using a Markov Random Field (MRF).

An MRF can be seen as a generalization of Markov chains, but while a Markov chain is often defined over a domain of time as a sequence of random variables, an MRF can be defined in space to describe dependencies between variables on a grid of dimension 2 or higher.

### 4.2 Markov Random Fields

Consider a set of random variables $A = \{A_i | i \in I\}$ for some index set $I$, where the variables are organized in a two dimensional grid. Let the variables correspond to the vertices and the statistical dependencies between the variables correspond to edges in an undirected graph $G$. We shall use this setup to model both codewords and errors in our system. Two connected vertices in $G$ are said to be *neighbors*, and a *neighborhood* $\mathcal{N}_i$ of a vertex $a_i$ can be defined as the set of vertices that are connected to $a_i$ in $G$. Different sizes of neighborhoods can be defined for an MRF. By convention, a node is not a neighbor of itself. On a regular lattice we define the first order neighborhood to be the four closest neighbors of a node as seen below, the second order neighborhood as the eight closest neighbors and so on. The collection of all neighborhoods $\mathcal{N} = \{\mathcal{N}_i \mid \forall i \in I\}$ in a graph, is called a *neighborhood system*.

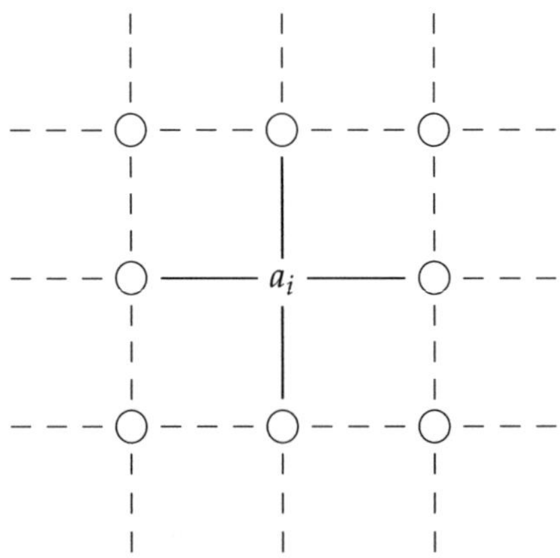


Within the neighborhood of a vertex $a_i$, we define a *clique* to be any collection of vertices that contains $a_i$ and forms a fully connected subgraph of $G$, i. e. that the vertices are mutual neighbors relative to the neighborhood system $\mathcal{N}$. In the case of a first order neighborhood, all nodes within distance 1 of the center are said to be neighbors, and the cliques become the center node $a_i$ and all pairs of $(a_i, a_j)$ where $a_j$ is a neighbor of $a_i$. In a second order neighborhood, all nodes within distance $\sqrt{2}$ are defined as neighbors:

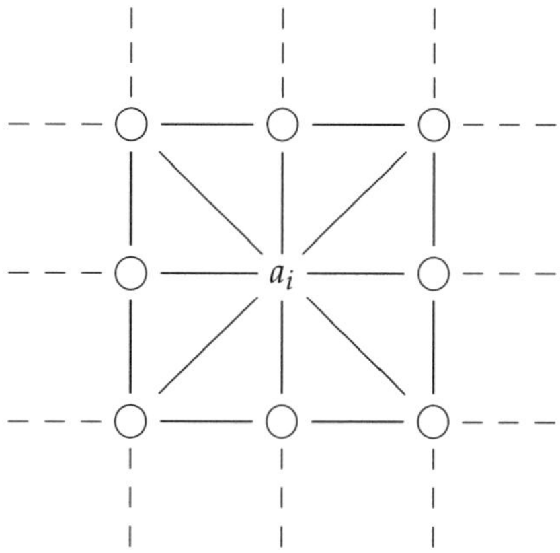


and in this case the cliques becomes any configuration of

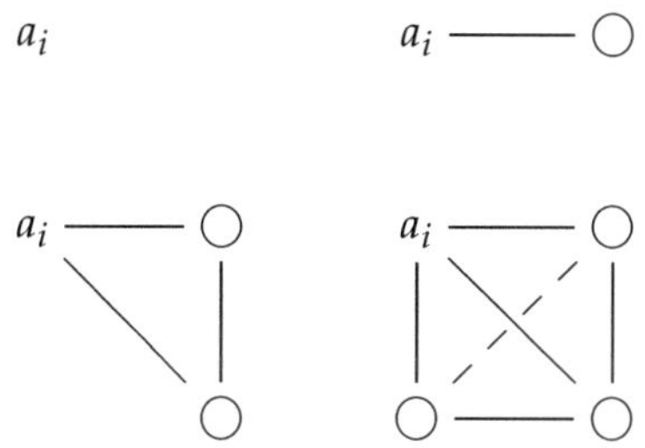


The collection of all cliques of size $i$ in a neighborhood system $\mathcal{N}$ is called $C_i$. The set $C$ of all cliques in a graph can then be partitioned into the subsets $C_i$ for $1 \leq i \leq n$

Now, based on the concept of neighborhoods we can then proceed to define a Markov Random Field. Just as a Markov chain $\{\ldots, a_k, a_{k-1}, a_{k-2}, \ldots\}$ satisfies

$$P(a_i | a_{i-1}, a_{i-2}, \ldots) = P(a_i | a_{i-1}, a_{i-2}, \ldots, a_{i-n})$$

for some $n$, a Markov Random Field should satisfy

$$P(a_i | a_{I-\{i\}}) = P(a_i \mid \mathcal{N}_i)$$

where $I$ is the set of indices of $a$ and $\mathcal{N}_i$ is the neighborhood of $a_i$ as defined above.

#### 4.3 Probability distribution

The fact that the errors of our channel can be represented by an MRF does not immediately enable us to analyze the error patterns statistically. By assuming that the dependencies in a collection of random variables can be represented by an MRF, the joint probability of the variables is given by the so called *Gibbs distribution*.

**Definition 1** (Gibbs distribution). *A set of random variables is said to be a* Gibbs random field *(GRF) if the joint distribution of the variables takes the following form:*

$$P(X = x) = \frac{1}{Z} \exp\left[-\frac{1}{T}U(X)\right] \tag{1}$$

*This distribution is called a* Gibbs distribution.

- $Z$ is a constant called *the partition function* and can be expressed as $Z = \sum_{x \in \mathbb{X}} e^{-\frac{1}{T}U(x)}$, so that $Z^{-1}$ becomes a normalizing constant in the expression.
- $U(x)$ is called *the energy function* and is a function of the values of the variables forming cliques in the field. It can be written as

$$U(x) = \sum_{c \in C} V_c(x) \tag{2}$$

  We can expand (2) further by summing over the cliques of the same degree separately

$$\sum_{c \in C} V_c(x) = \sum_{a \in C_1} V_1(a) + \sum_{a,b \in C_2} V_2(a,b) + \sum_{a,b,c \in C_3} V_3(a,b,c) + \ldots \tag{3}$$

  where $C_i$ is the collection of all cliques of degree $i$, so that $V_i$ is a function of $i$ variables forming a clique, and $\sum_{C_i} V_i$ mean that we sum over all possible cliques in the field of degree $i$.
- $T$ is called the *temperature* (this is a legacy from the distribution's origin in statistical physics). The parameter $T$ influences the degree of cohesion between the variables on a grid, so that a higher temperature corresponds to a lower degree of cohesion in the sense that the values of the variables becomes more and more independent, while a lower temperature gives a higher probability of the formation of large clusters of variables with the same value. We shall assume that the temperature is 1 in our simulations, even if the parameter will be used in the theoretical treatment of the decoding algorithm.

The Clifford-Hammersley theorem states that for a set of variables $\mathcal{F}$ with a neighborhood system $\mathcal{N}$, $\mathcal{F}$ is an MRF with respect to $\mathcal{N}$ if and only if $\mathcal{F}$ is a GRF with respect to $\mathcal{N}$. See Kindermann & Snell (1980).

Unfortunately, $Z$ is very hard to compute. Since we have to consider all possible of values of $x$ in order to find $Z$, the computational complexity of the task is a formidable $O(2^n)$, effectively preventing us from computing the absolute probabilities for the configurations of $X$. It is nevertheless possible to use the Gibbs distribution to find an estimate of the error patterns generated by the channel.

### 4.4 MAP estimation

We want to find an estimate of the error pattern that was added to the codeword, based on the assumptions about the dependence between errors given in the previous sections. In order to avoid computing the constant $Z$ in the Gibbs distribution, we will do a MAP estimation of the errors. That is, given a received word $Y$, we want to find an estimate of the most likely error pattern $X$ that was added to $C$. Some terminology is needed in order to develop this.

Let $A$ be a set of random variables defined on the set $\mathcal{L}$, and let the elements of $A$ be indexed by $1 \leq i \leq n$. If $A_i = a_i$ for each variable $A_i$, where $a_i \in \mathcal{L}$, we call $\{a_1, \ldots, a_n\} = a$ a *configuration* of $A$

MAP estimation of the error pattern $X$ based on the received word $Y$ can be formulated as the optimization of the *a posteriori* probability $P(X = x|Y = y)$ with respect to $x$. That is, we want to find a configuration $x$ that makes the probability $P(X = x|Y = y)$ as high as possible.

Bayes rule gives us

$$P(X = x|Y = y) = \frac{P(X = x)P(Y = y|X = x)}{P(Y = y)}$$

Since $P(Y = y)$ does not depend on $P(X = x)$, we can maximize over

$$P(X = x)P(Y = y|X = x) \tag{4}$$

To find the probabilities $P(Y = y|X = x)$, we must take care to remember that the error pattern $X$ is now considered as the original information that we want to estimate, and the codeword $C$ is to be considered as errors obscuring the information. In the following, we shall make some assumptions about $X$ and $C$.

- The variables are bipolar, with 1 corresponding to 0 and $-1$ corresponding to 1 in the channel model.
- The codeword $C$, when treated as errors, can be seen as random bipolar variables so that

$$P(C = c) = \prod_i P(c_i) = (\frac{1}{2})^n$$

The conditional probabilities must then be expressed by by using the characteristics of the channel and this expression must then be optimized with respect to the input configuration. In chapter 5.3 and 6.3 we show two examples of how this optimization can be done for a given channel. In both of our cases, finding a global maximum of the conditional probabilities with respect to $x$ would become computationally infeasible as the size of $x$ increases. Instead, we use the local dependencies between bits to do a local optimization along the lines of the PDFE in Neifeld & King (1998); Neifield et al. (1996) or the partial binary segmentation algorithm of Shridhar et al. (1989).

### 4.5 Error generation

Generation of two dimensional burst errors for simulation purposes is done by the use of a Monte Carlo Markov chain technique called the Metropolis algorithm. We do not have very strict requirements for the generated sample configurations, other than that they should be "somewhat likely" to occur given the condition that the variables' distribution is given by the Gibbs distribution.

The Metropolis algorithm is a general method for generating samples from a joint distribution of two or more variables, and can be applied to distributions that are either continuous or discrete as long as it is possible to compute the difference of the likelihoods for two configurations of the variables.

We would like to sample the joint distribution $A = \{A_1, \ldots, A_n\}$. This is achieved by generating random changes to the components $A_i$ of $A$, and accepting or rejecting these changes based on how they affect the likelihood of the configuration. In our case, the natural change to a component of a configuration would be to flip the bit value.

Given an initial configuration $A$, a new configuration $A^*$ is obtained as explained above by flipping a bit. Then, the difference of the likelihood of the new configuration and the old configuration is calculated by

$$\Delta U = U(A^*) - U(A) = \sum_{a^* \in C_1} V_1(a^*) + \sum_{a^*,b^* \in C_2} V_2(a^*,b^*) + \sum_{a^*,b^*,c^* \in C_3} V_3(a^*,b^*,c^*) + \dots$$
$$- \sum_{a \in C_1} V_1(a) + \sum_{a,b \in C_2} V_2(a,b) + \sum_{a,b,c \in C_3} V_3(a,b,c) + \dots$$

and the new configuration is accepted with probability 1 if the new likelihood is higher than the old one. Otherwise, the new configuration is accepted with probability $e^{-\Delta U/T}$, so the probability of accepting the new configuration becomes:

$$P(A \to A^*) = \begin{cases} 1 & \Delta U \geq 0 \\ e^{-\Delta U/T} & \Delta U < 0 \end{cases}$$

A pass through all the components in $A$ in this way is called a *sweep* over the variables in $A$. In our case, we generate a sample from the distribution by doing 4 sweeps over $A$, resulting in the evaluation of a total of $4n$ new configurations. This should result in a sample that has high enough probability to be detected by the estimation algorithm described above.

## 5. Application to the two-dimensional binary asymmetric channel

### 5.1 Channel model

In this section, we will apply this general method for cluster error detection and correction to the binary asymmetric channel As the name of the channel implies, we will assume that errors are asymmetric so that only the transition $-1 \to 1$ occurs in a received codeword.

**Definition 2** (Matrix OR). *Assume $A$ and $B$ are matrices with dimensions $d_1 \times d_2$ where $d_1 \cdot d_2 = n$, and with coordinates $a_i$ and $b_i$ respectively. Then the OR of these matrices is defined as*

$$A \vee B \triangleq a_i \vee b_i, \qquad 1 \leq i \leq n$$

The received word $Y$ can then be defined as the combination of

$$Y = C \vee X$$

$Y$ - received word
$C$ - original codeword
$X$ - error pattern
$\vee$ - OR operator on matrices as defined above

### 5.2 System model

Information $I$ is encoded, producing a codeword $C$. For each generated codeword $C$, the channel induces two-dimensionally correlated noise $X$ and the resulting word $Y$ is passed to the decoder. Information is converted to likelihood ratios and sent to the SISO. The output likelihood values $L$ from the SISO are then sent to the detector. Based on these values, the detector produces an estimate of the error pattern that was multiplied with the codeword. This information is subsequently fed back into the SISO in the next iteration. The decoding process continues until either the SISO finds a valid codeword, or a set of stopping criteria is reached. The final estimate of the codeword is produced by the SISO. See figure 2.

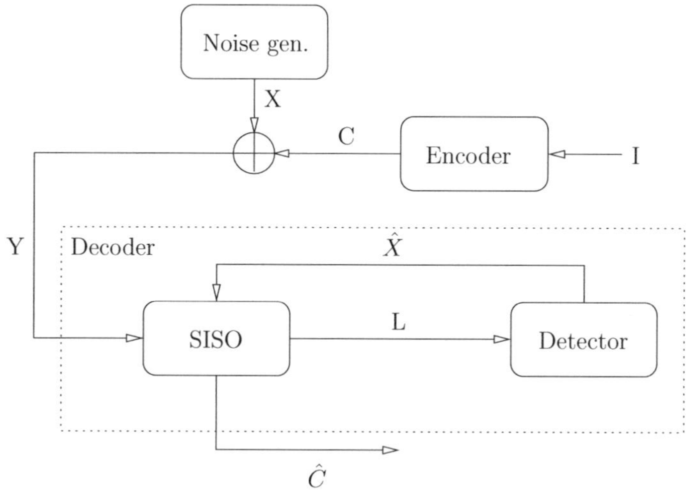


Fig. 2. System model

### 5.3 MAP estimation

To optimize the maximum a priori probability, we need to find some expression for the conditional probability $P(Y = y|X = x)$ as noted in chapter 4.4. Based on the assumptions in chapter 4.4, the conditional probabilities $P(Y_i = y_i|X_i = x_i)$ for each information symbol is given in Table 1.

| $x$ \ $y$ | 1 | −1 |
|---|---|---|
| 1 | $\frac{1}{2}$ | $\frac{1}{2}$ |
| −1 | 0 | 1 |

Table 1. Transition probabilities

The conditional probabilities in the table can be expressed as an exponential function by

$$P(Y_i = y_i|X_i = x_i) = \lim_{\epsilon \to 0} \frac{1}{2} \exp\left[\frac{-y_i(1-x_i)\ln 2}{1-y_i+\epsilon}\right]$$

We can then express the probability of a given $y$ conditioned on a configuration $x$ by

$$P(Y = y|X = x) = \prod_i \lim_{\epsilon \to 0} \frac{1}{2} \exp\left[\frac{-y_i(1-x_i)\ln 2}{1-y_i+\epsilon}\right] \tag{5}$$

Substituting (1) and (5) into (4), we can find the joint probability by

$$P(X=x,Y=y)=\left[Z^{-1}e^{-\frac{1}{T}U(x)}\right]\prod_i \lim_{\epsilon\to 0}\frac{1}{2}\exp\left[\frac{-y_i(1-x_i)\ln 2}{1-y_i+\epsilon}\right] \quad (6)$$

Since the natural logarithm is strictly increasing, the following equality holds:

$$\arg\max_X(P(X,Y))=\arg\max_X(\ln(P(X,Y))) \quad (7)$$

In order to avoid computing $Z$ in (6), we take the logarithm of both sides and eliminate constants to get

$$V(x)=U(x)+\sum_i \lim_{\epsilon\to 0}\left[\frac{-y_i(1-x_i)\ln 2}{1-y_i+\epsilon}\right]$$

where $V(x)=\ln\left[P(X=x,Y=y)\right]$.

We define the partial functions $V_i$ of $U(x)$ according to Li (2000); Shridhar et al. (1989)

$$V_1(x_i)=\alpha x_i$$

$$V_2(x_i,x_{i'})=\beta_{i,i'}x_i x_{i'}$$

$$V_3(x_i,x_{i'},x_{i''})=\cdots=0$$

Note that the expression for $V_2$ implies that $V_2(x_i,x_{i'})=\beta_{i,i'}$ for $x_i=x_{i'}$and $V_2(x_i,x_{i'})=-\beta_{i,i'}$for $x_i\neq x_{i'}$.

From this we get a new expression for $V(x)$:

$$V(x)=\sum_i\left[\alpha x_i+\beta_{i,i'}\sum_{i'\in\mathcal{N}_i}x_i x_{i'}+\lim_{\epsilon\to 0}\left[\frac{-y_i(1-x_i)\ln 2}{1-y_i+\epsilon}\right]\right],$$

and splitting the last term into a constant and a non-constant term yields

$$V(x)=\sum_i\left[\alpha x_i+\beta_{i,i'}\sum_{i'\in\mathcal{N}_i}x_i x_{i'}+\lim_{\epsilon\to 0}\left[\frac{x_i y_i\ln 2}{1-y_i+\epsilon}\right]+\lim_{\epsilon\to 0}\left[\frac{-y_i\ln 2}{1-y_i+\epsilon}\right]\right].$$

Since the last term only depends on $y$, we can find the MAP configuration by simplifying the expression to:

$$\begin{aligned}\mathcal{V}(x)&=\sum_i\left[\alpha x_i+\beta\sum_{i'\in\mathcal{N}_i}x_i x_{i'}+\lim_{\epsilon\to 0}\left[\frac{x_i y_i\ln 2}{1-y_i+\epsilon}\right]\right]\\&=\sum_i\left[\alpha+\beta\sum_{i'\in\mathcal{N}_i}x_{i'}+\lim_{\epsilon\to 0}\left[\frac{y_i\ln 2}{1-y_i+\epsilon}\right]\right]x_i\end{aligned} \quad (8)$$

Having obtained an estimate

$$\hat{X}=\{\hat{X}_1,\ldots,\hat{X}_i,\ldots,\hat{X}_n\}$$

of the error pattern, it can be used to find likelihood ratios for input to the decoder. For each bit, we set the likelihood ratio to

$$L_i = \frac{P(C_i = -1|Y_i, \hat{X}_i)}{P(C_i = 1|Y_i, \hat{X}_i)}$$

The resulting probabilities can be seen in Table 2. In the table, $\rho$ is the probability that a bit

| $\hat{X}$ \ $Y$ | $-1$ | $1$ |
|---|---|---|
| $-1$ | $\frac{1-\rho}{\rho}$ | $\frac{\rho}{1-\rho}$ |
| $1$ | $\frac{\rho}{1-\rho}$ | $\frac{1-\rho}{\rho}$ |

Table 2. Input probabilities to the decoder

belonging to the error pattern is incorrectly estimated as a 1-bit. The parameter $\rho$ must be estimated by simulation, but should in general be small, indicating a relatively certain $-1$-bit.

### 5.4 Performance of estimation algorithm

The performance of the estimation algorithm depends heavily on the value of $\beta$, which determines the degree of clustering in the error pattern. A critical performance parameter is the probability $\varepsilon$ that not all bits in the error pattern are detected by the estimation algorithm. A bit that belongs to the error pattern, but is not detected as such, is given a high probability of being correct, and can hence be the source of errors that are hard to correct. Therefore, $\varepsilon$ is an important measure of the reliability of the algorithm. As can be seen in Fig. 3, $P(\varepsilon)$ is high for $\beta < 0.5$, reflecting the fact that small and very irregular error clusters appear in this range. $P(\varepsilon)$ drops sharply initially, but levels out when $\beta > 1$ as a result of the clusters becoming bigger and more coherent. As we shall see later, this is also reflected in the performance of the algorithm.

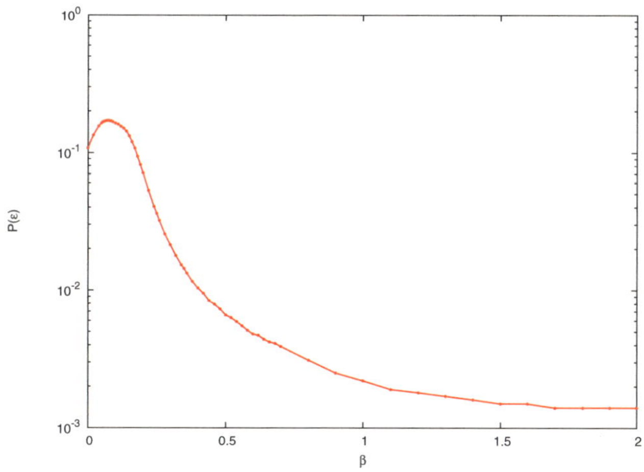


Fig. 3. $P(\varepsilon)$ for fixed $\beta = 0.2$ in the estimation algorithm.

### 5.5 Results

A regular LDPC code was used as the error correcting code component , with different values of $\beta$ in the simulations, and $\alpha = \gamma = \cdots = 0$ in the estimation algorithm. We assumed that the receiver does not know the value of $\beta$ used by the noise generating process. The components of the simulator was then connected as shown in Fig. 6 The simulations show that there is a large performance gain for some choices of parameter using the LDPC-MRF combination described above. The value of $\beta$ has great influence over the relative performance of the two decoding methods. Looking in Fig. 5 at the performance of a code in combination with the MAP error estimate and alone, under varying $\beta$, we can observe that the performance difference between the two decoders increases as $\beta$ increases. This is due to the effect described in Section 5.4: as $\beta$ increases, the reliability of the error estimate also increases. We also notice that the drop in BER levels off at about $\beta = 1$ corresponding to the reliability of the estimate leveling off from the same point. The performance of the decoder could also be measured under varying bit error probabilities, but because the bit error probability depends

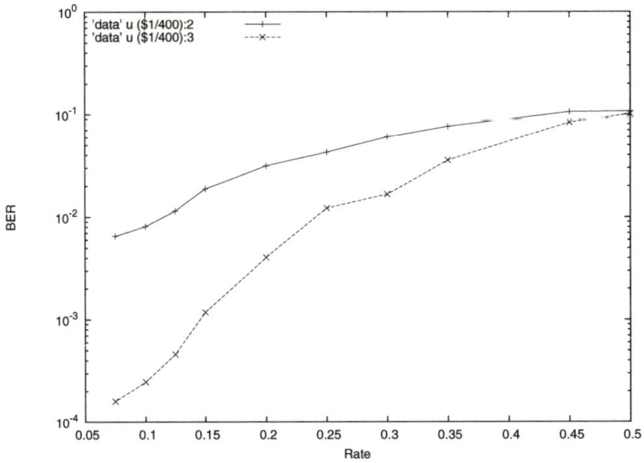


Fig. 4. Performance under varying rate with $\beta = 0.2$ and $\beta = 1.0$

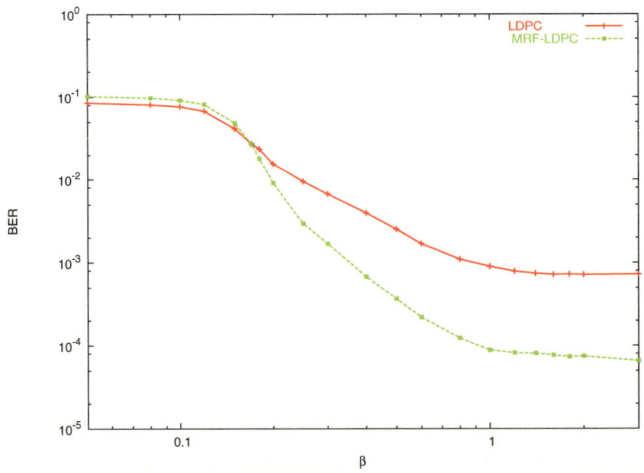


Fig. 5. Performance under varying $\beta$ with rate $\frac{3}{8}$

on the parameter $\beta$ in the Gibbs distribution in a way that makes it hard to predict the average error probability over codewords, we fix the value of $\beta$ to $\beta = 0.2$ and $\beta = 1.0$ which gives an average error rate of about 0.12 and 0.02 respectively, and study the performance of joint LDPC - MRF decoding for different code rates using these parameters. We see in Fig. 4 that the effect of the MRF estimator gives very good results in combination with the LDPC code when the code rate is sufficiently low, while the performance gap between the two decoders gets smaller as the code rate grows. This occurs because the MRF-LDPC decoder needs a certain amount of information from the code itself to determine the value of the bits in the error pattern, even if the MRF estimator provides a perfect estimate of the errors.

## 6. Application to the two-dimensional binary symmetric channel

### 6.1 Channel model

In this section we will see how the outlined cluster detection technique can be applied to the two-dimensional binary symmetric channel. On this channel, both the transition $1 \rightarrow -1$ and $-1 \rightarrow 1$ may take place.

**Definition 3** (Componentwise product). *Assume A and B are matrices with the same dimensions $d_1 \times d_2$ where $d_1 \cdot d_2 = n$, and with coordinates $a_i$ and $b_i$ respectively. Then the componentwise product of these matrices is defined as*

$$A * B = a_i \cdot b_i, \qquad 1 \leq i \leq n$$

Now assuming $X$, $Y$ and $C$ are $d_1 \times d_2$ matrices with bipolar coordinates, the effect of the channel can be described as:

$$Y = C * X$$

where
$Y$ - received word
$C$ - original codeword
$X$ - error pattern
$*$ - multiplicative operator on matrices defined as above

### 6.2 System model

Like in chapter 5.2, information $I$ is encoded, producing a codeword $C$. Two-dimensionally correlated noise $X$ is applied to the codeword and the result $Y$ is passed to the decoder. The decoding process is different in this case, however. The likelihood values $L$ from the SISO are used to find some values $\delta$ that measures the distance between the received input and the output of the SISO, multiplied by the channel value. The $\delta$ value can be seen as an estimate of the value of the corresponding bit in $X$. These values are sent to the cluster detector to be used as basis for producing an estimate of the error cluster which is in turn fed back to the SISO. As in 5.2, the iterative process continues until a valid codeword is found or a set of stopping criteria is met.

### 6.3 MAP estimation

#### 6.3.1 distribution of $\Delta_i$

The values $Y$ received from the channel is used to compute likelihood ratios $L^I = \{L_1^I, L_2^I, \ldots, L_n^I\}$ for the bits. Since we assume that the variables are bipolar, the likelihood

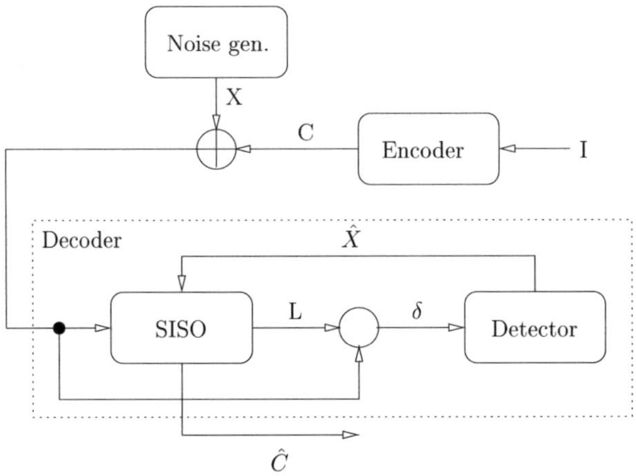


Fig. 6. System model

ratios can be expressed as

$$L_i^I = \frac{P(C_i = -1|Y_i)}{P(C_i = +1|Y_i)}.$$

These values are the channel values used in the SISO. The soft output from the SISO-component in the decoder is $L^O = \{L_1^O, L_2^O, \ldots, L_n^O\}$. The output $L^O$ of the SISO also has the form of likelihood ratios. We now take the logarithm of $L^I$ and $L^O$ giving us the values $\widetilde{L}^I$ and $\widetilde{L}^O$. These variables are now real valued in the range $\langle -\infty, \infty \rangle$, with a negative value indicating a possible $-1$ bit and a positive value indicating a possible $+1$ bit. The difference $\widetilde{L}_i^I - \widetilde{L}_i^O$ measures the distance between the input- and output values, and multiplication by $Y_i$ gives the relative direction $\Delta_i$ of the change.

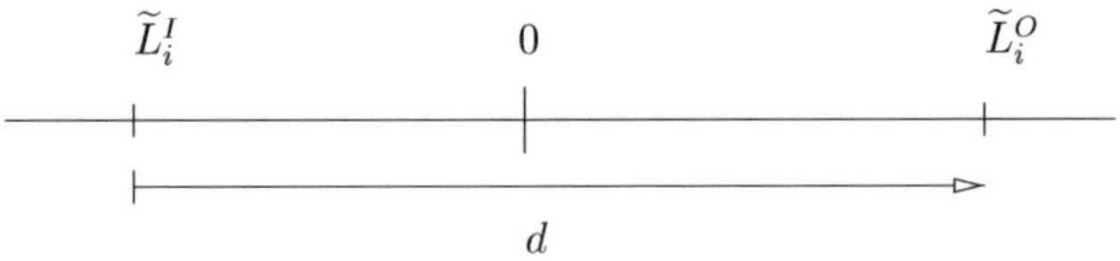


Fig. 7. Negative $\Delta_i$

As an example, in figure 7 the distance between the input and the output $d$ is positive, but $Y_i = -1$, so the relative direction $\Delta_i = -1 \cdot d = -d$ is negative. This corresponds to a higher probability that the bit was flipped by the channel.

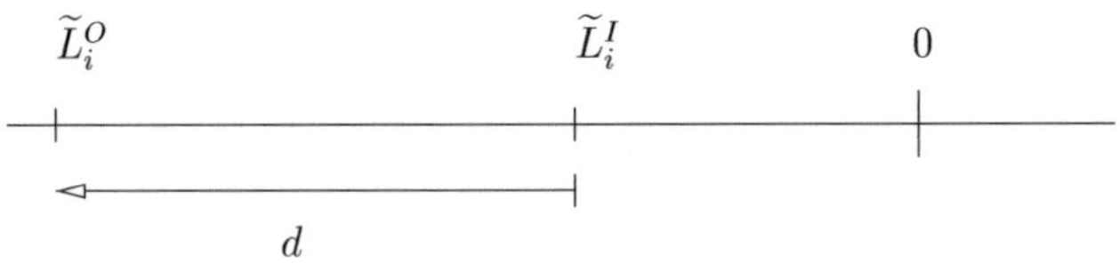


Fig. 8. Positive $\Delta_i$

In figure 8 on the other hand, the distance $d$ is negative and $Y_i = -1$ so the relative distance $\Delta_i = -d$ is positive, indicating a higher probability that the bit is correct.

The values $\Delta_i = Y_i(\widetilde{L}_i^I - \widetilde{L}_i^O)$ are sent to the detector, which computes the MAP estimate of the configuration of $X$, i.e. the most likely $X$ to produce the observed values. As is shown below, knowing the distribution of $P(\Delta_i = \delta_i \mid X_i = x_i)$ is essential to the MAP estimate calculation, so we shall make the assumption that the information from the SISO, $\Delta_i$, conditioned on $X_i$ has a normal distribution with variance $\sigma$ and mean $X_i\mu$. The conditional probabilities can then be expressed as an exponential function by approximating them with the normal distribution with mean $x_i\mu$ so that

$$P(\Delta_i = \delta_i \mid X_i = x_i) = \frac{1}{\sigma\sqrt{2\pi}} e^{-\frac{(\delta_i - x_i\mu)^2}{2\sigma^2}}. \tag{9}$$

As an example of this, we can see in Fig. 9(a) and Fig. 9(b) the distribution of the $\Delta_i$'s for $X_i = -1$ and $X_i = +1$ respectively, compared with the normal distribution with $\mu = \pm 0.55$ and $\sigma = 1.4$. We can see that this approximation is reasonably good. MAP estimation of the

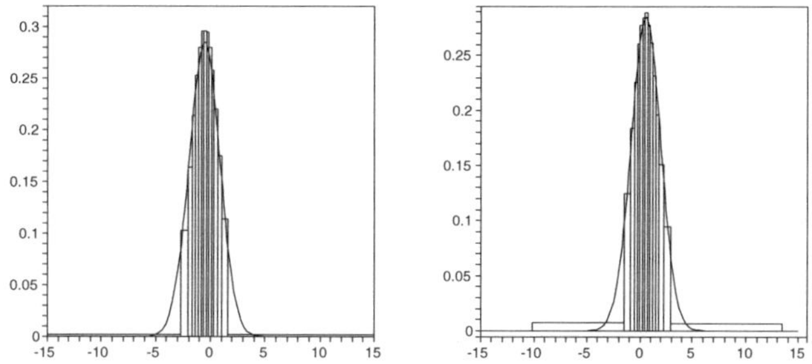

(a) $X_i = +1$ and $\mu = 0.55$ (b) $X_i = -1$ and $\mu = -0.55$

Fig. 9. Distribution of the $\Delta_i$'s

error pattern $X$ based on the values $\Delta$ from the SISO, can be formulated as the maximization of the *a posteriori* probability $P(X = x|\Delta = \delta)$ with respect to $x$. That is, we want to find a configuration $x$ that makes the probability $P(X = x|\Delta = \delta)$ as high as possible for a given $\delta$. Bayes rule gives us

$$P(X = x|\Delta = \delta) = \frac{P(X = x)P(\Delta = \delta|X = x)}{P(\Delta = \delta)} \tag{10}$$

Since we are optimizing the expression for a given value of $\delta$, we can maximize over

$$P(X = x)P(\Delta = \delta|X = x) \tag{11}$$

instead of (10).

Based on the assumption that the distribution of $P(\Delta_i = \delta_i \mid X_i = x_i)$ is given by (9), we can express the probability of a given $\delta$ conditioned on a configuration $x$ by

$$P(\Delta = \delta \mid X = x) = \prod_i P(\delta_i \mid x_i) = \prod_i \frac{1}{\sigma\sqrt{2\pi}} e^{-\frac{(\delta_i - x_i\mu)^2}{2\sigma^2}} \tag{12}$$

Substituting (1) and (12) into (11), and taking $T = 1$, we can express the product of the probabilities as:

$$P(X = x)P(\Delta = \delta \mid X = x) = \left[Z^{-1}e^{-U(x)}\right] \prod_i \frac{1}{\sigma\sqrt{2\pi}} e^{-\frac{(\delta_i - x_i\mu)^2}{2\sigma^2}}$$

In order to avoid computing $Z$ in the above expression, we take the logarithm of both sides and eliminate the constants to get

$$V(x) = U(x) - \sum_i \frac{(\delta_i - x_i\mu)^2}{2\sigma^2}. \tag{13}$$

Since the natural logarithm is strictly increasing, optimizing (13) with respect to $x$ also optimizes (5).

We define the partial functions $V_t$ of $U(x)$ in (3) according to Li (2000) and Shridhar et al. (1989):

$$\sum_{c \in \mathcal{C}_1} V_1(c) = \sum_i \alpha x_i$$

$$\sum_{c \in \mathcal{C}_2} V_2(c) = \sum_i \sum_{x_{i'} \in \mathcal{N}_i} \beta x_i x_{i'} \quad i \neq i'$$

$$V_t(\cdot) = 0 \quad \forall t > 2$$

This implies that we let the total probability depend on the value of each bit represented by $\alpha x_i$ and the value of each neighboring bit represented by $\beta x_i x_{i'}$, while we do not consider more complex dependencies like three-ways dependencies and up. Note that the expression for $V_2$ implies that $V_2(x_i, x_{i'}) = \beta$ for $x_i = x_{i'}$and $V_2(x_i, x_{i'}) = -\beta$ for $x_i \neq x_{i'}$.

From this we get a new expression for $V(x)$:

$$V(x) = \sum_i \left[ \alpha x_i + \beta \sum_{x_{i'} \in \mathcal{N}_i} x_i x_{i'} - \frac{(\delta_i - x_i\mu)^2}{2\sigma^2} \right],$$

and expanding the last term of the sum yields

$$V(x) = \sum_i \left[ \alpha x_i + \beta \sum_{x_{i'} \in \mathcal{N}_i} x_i x_{i'} - \frac{(\delta_i^2 - 2x_i\delta_i\mu + x_i^2\mu^2)}{2\sigma^2} \right].$$

The variables $x_i$ are bipolar so $x_i^2 = 1$ and we can simplify the expression to:

$$\begin{aligned} \mathcal{V}(x) &= \sum_i \left[ \alpha x_i + \beta \sum_{x_{i'} \in \mathcal{N}_i} x_i x_{i'} - \frac{(\delta_i^2 - 2x_i\delta_i\mu + \mu^2)}{2\sigma^2} \right] \\ &= \sum_i \left[ \alpha x_i + \beta \sum_{x_{i'} \in \mathcal{N}_i} x_i x_{i'} - \frac{\delta_i^2}{2\sigma^2} + \frac{2x_i\delta_i\mu}{2\sigma^2} - \frac{\mu^2}{2\sigma^2} \right] \end{aligned}$$

As we are doing a maximization with respect to $x_i$, any term in the sum that does not contain or otherwise depend on $x_i$ will not affect the result, and hence we cancel the terms $-\frac{\delta_i^2}{2\sigma^2}$ and

$-\frac{\mu^2}{2\sigma^2}$, and the expression to maximize over becomes:

$$\mathcal{V}(x) = \sum_i \left[ \alpha x_i + \beta \sum_{x_{i'} \in \mathcal{N}_i} x_i x_{i'} + \frac{2x_i \delta_i \mu}{2\sigma^2} \right]$$
$$= \sum_i \left[ \alpha + \beta \sum_{x_{i'} \in \mathcal{N}_i} x_{i'} + \frac{\mu}{\sigma^2} \delta_i \right] x_i \quad (14)$$

### 6.3.2 Optimization of $\mathcal{V}(x)$

To do a global optimization of the expression above with respect to $x$ would become computationally infeasible as the size of $x$ increases. Instead we can use the local dependencies between bits to do a local optimization along the lines of the PDFE in Neifeld & King (1998); Neifield et al. (1996) or the partial binary segmentation algorithm of Shridhar et al. (1989). It is apparent that when $\mathcal{V}(x)$ is expressed as in (14), we can always choose the value of $x_i$ so that each term in the sum becomes positive, and thus the sum is non-decreasing. For each node we compute the value of

$$\alpha x_i + \beta \sum_{x_{i'} \in \mathcal{N}_i} x_{i'} + \frac{\delta_i \mu}{\sigma^2}$$

and set the value of $x_i$ so that the product is positive. This procedure is iterated until we converge on a solution where all terms in the sum are positive, or a maximum number of iterations is reached. Normally the process arrives at a solution after less than 10 iterations.

Having obtained an estimate

$$\hat{X} = \{\hat{X}_1, \ldots, \hat{X}_i, \ldots, \hat{X}_n\}$$

of the error pattern, it can be used to find likelihood ratios for input to the SISO. For each bit, we set the likelihood ratio to

$$L_i = \frac{P(C_i = -1 | Y_i, \hat{X}_i)}{P(C_i = 1 | Y_i, \hat{X}_i)}$$

The resulting probabilities can be seen in Fig. 10. In the table, $\rho$ is the probability that a bit

| $\hat{X}$ \ $Y$ | $-1$ | $1$ |
|---|---|---|
| $-1$ | $\frac{1-\rho}{\rho}$ | $\frac{\rho}{1-\rho}$ |
| $1$ | $\frac{\rho}{1-\rho}$ | $\frac{1-\rho}{\rho}$ |

Fig. 10. Input probabilities to the decoder

detected as belonging to the error pattern is actually a $-1$-bit, i.e. $\rho = P(X_i = -1 \mid \hat{X}_i = -1)$. For a given channel, the parameter $\rho$ must be found experimentally by sending some known codewords over the channel. When the receiver knows the value of $X$, the value of $\rho$ can be computed based on the value of the estimates $\hat{X}$. $\rho$ should in general be large indicating a relatively certain $-1$-bit.

### 6.4 Results

We have implemented the system with an LDPC decoder as the SISO component, and we assume a priori knowledge of the values $\alpha$, $\beta$ and $\rho$. The error-simulation process allows upper bounding of the overall error rate of the channel, and the performance of the decoder is measured for two different upper bounds on the error rate, denoted $E_h$, to investigate the effect of varying error rates on the performance of the joint decoding and estimation. The parameter $\beta$ in the Gibbs distribution should ideally depend on the the bit error probability of the channel, but in the simulations we have chosen to fix the value of $\beta$ to $\beta = 0.2$ which corresponds to an average error rate of about 0.12, and study the performance of joint LDPC - MRF decoding for different code rates under this assumption. This is a rather "harsh" assumption in the sense that in practice it should be possible to find an estimate of the value of $\beta$ before transmission takes place. The performance of the joint decoding and estimation algorithm is compared to decoding of the same received information using the same LDPC decoder component but under a random error assumption, i.e., the decoder assumes that there are no dependencies in the error generating process. The LDPC codes used in the simulations are generic regular LDPC codes that were not optimized for use on this particluar type of channel. We see in Fig. 11 that the effect of the MRF estimator gives very good results in combination with the LDPC code when the code rate is sufficiently low, while the performance gap between the two decoders gets smaller as the code rate grows. This indicates that even if the MRF estimator provides a perfect estimate of the errors, the MRF-LDPC decoder still needs a certain amount of information from the code itself to determine the value of the bits in the error pattern, and therefore the mutual gain when exchanging information between the LDPC component and the channel detector component decreases as the code rate increases.

Fig. 12 shows that the performance of an LDPC-decoder in combination with the MAP error estimate, relative to an LDPC code alone. We see that the gain is even greater for a higher upper bound on the error rate, mainly because the MRF-estimate makes the most difference in face of a high number of errors.

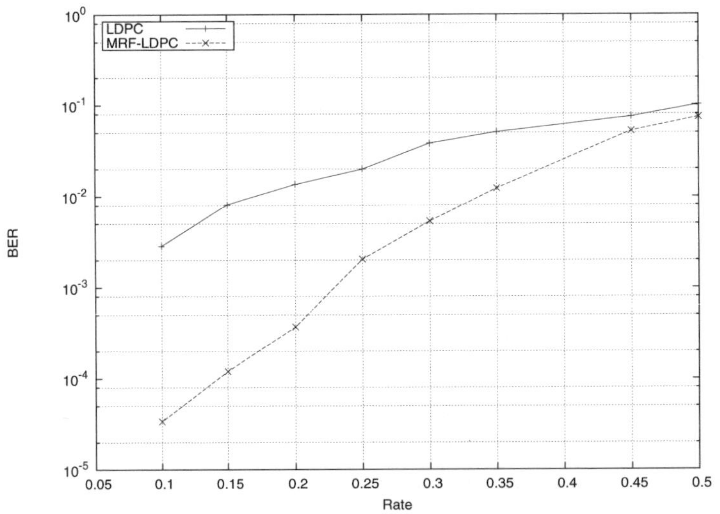


Fig. 11. Performance under varying rate with $E_h = 0.1250$

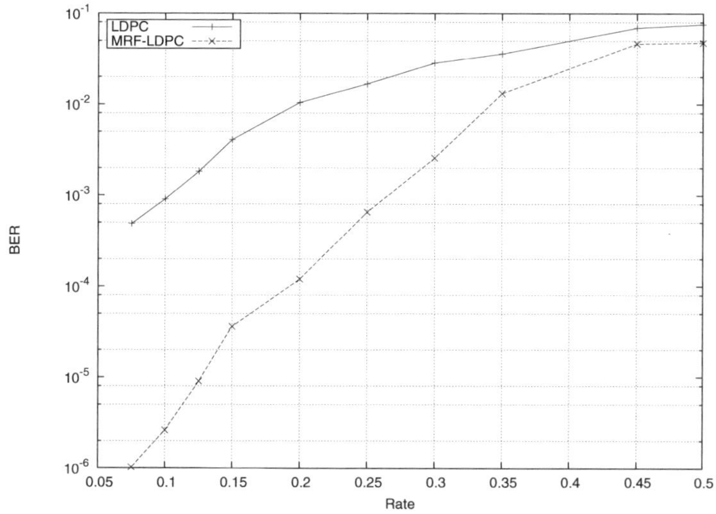


Fig. 12. Performance under varying rate with $E_h = 0.2250$

## 7. Conclusion

By applying principles known form digital image restoration, we have introduced a channel model for two-dimensional channels with memory based on Markov random fields which allows us to describe spatially dependent errors. We have showed that a significant performance gain over an ordinary error correcting code can be achieved , for both the symmetric and the asymmetric binary two-dimensional channel by combining an error-correcting component with an MRF-based burst detection algorithm. We have also demonstrated that this decoding technique gives the most gain for larger clusters and for lower information rates.

## 8. References

Banham, M. & Katsaggelos, A. (1997). Digital image restoration, *Signal Processing Magazine, IEEE* 14(2): 24–41.

Blaum, M., Bruck, J. & Vardy, A. (1998). Interleaving schemes for multidimensional cluster errors, *Information Theory, IEEE Transactions on* 44(2): 730–743.

Breitbach, M., Bossert, M., Zyablov, V. & Sidorenko, V. (1998). Array codes correcting a two-dimensional cluster of errors, *Information Theory, IEEE Transactions on* 44(5): 2025–2031.

Chalmond, B. (1988). Image restoration using an estimated markov model, *Signal Processing* 15(2): 115–129.

El-Gabali, M., Shridhar, M. & Ahmadi, M. (1987). Segmentation of noisy images modelled by markov random fields with gibbs distribution, *Acoustics, Speech, and Signal Processing, IEEE International Conference on ICASSP'87.*, Vol. 12, IEEE, pp. 551–554.

El-Gabali, M., Shridhar, M. & Ahmadi, M. (1988). Restoration of degraded images using markov random fields, *Acoustics, Speech, and Signal Processing, 1988. ICASSP-88., 1988 International Conference on*, IEEE, pp. 1004–1007.

El-Gabali, M., Shridhar, M., Ahmadi, M. & Kekre, J. (n.d.). Restoration of blurred images, *Signals, Systems and Computers, 1990. 1990 Conference Record Twenty-Fourth Asilomar Conference on*, Vol. 2, IEEE, p. 549.

Ellingsen, P. & Kvamme, A. (2010). Iterative decoding and estimation of two-dimensional channels with memory, *2010 Third International Conference on Communication Theory, Reliability, and Quality of Service*, IEEE, pp. 43–48.

Ellingsen, P., Ytrehus, O. & Siegel, P. (n.d.). Enhanced decoding by error detection on a channel with correlated two-dimensional errors, *Information Theory Workshop, 2004. IEEE*, IEEE, pp. 17–21.

Farrell, P. (1982). Array codes for correcting cluster-error patterns, *Proc. IEE Conf. Elect. Signal Processing (York, England)*.

Geman, S. & Geman, D. (1993). Stochastic relaxation, gibbs distributions and the bayesian restoration of images, *Journal of Applied Statistics* 20(5-6): 25–62.

Gilbert, E. et al. (1960). Capacity of a burst-noise channel, *Bell Syst. Tech. J* 39(9): 1253–1265.

Jeng, F. & Woods, J. (1991). Compound gauss-markov random fields for image estimation, *Signal Processing, IEEE Transactions on* 39(3): 683–697.

Kindermann, R. & Snell, J. L. (1980). Markov random fields and their applications.

Kurkoski, B. M. (2008). Towards efficient detection of two-dimensional intersymbol interference channels.

Li, S. Z. (2000). Modeling image analysis problems using markov random fields, Vol. 20, pp. 1–43.

Neifeld, M. . & King, B. M. (1998 ). Parallel detection algorithms for page oriented optical memories. *Applied optics*(37(26) pp. 6275–6298

Neifield, M. A., Chugg, K. M. & King, B. M. (1996). Parallel data detection in page-oriented optical memory, *Optics Letters* 21(18): 1481–1483.

Schwartz, M. & Etzion, T. (2003). Optimal 2-dimensional 3-dispersion lattices, *Applied Algebra, Algebraic Algorithms and Error-Correcting Codes* pp. 606–606.

Schwartz, M. & Etzion, T. (2005). Two-dimensional cluster-correcting codes, *IEEE Trans. Info. Theory* 51: 2121–2132.

Shridhar, M., Ahmadi, M. & El-Gabali, M. (1989). Restoration of noisy images modeled by markov random fields with gibbs distribution, *Circuits and Systems, IEEE Transactions on* 36(6): 884–890.

Singla, N. & O'Sullivan, J. A. (2005). Joint equalization and decoding for nonlinear two-dimensional intersymbol interference channels.

Xu, W. & Golomb, S. (2007). Optimal interleaving schemes for correcting two-dimensional cluster errors, *Discrete applied mathematics* 155(10): 1200–1212.

Zhang, J. (1993). The mean field theory in em procedures for blind markov random field image restoration, *Image Processing, IEEE Transactions on* 2(1): 27–40.